INEQUALITY AND THE CITY IN THE LOW COUNTRIES (1200-2020)

SEUH

STUDIES IN EUROPEAN URBAN HISTORY (1100-1800)

VOLUME 50

Series Editors
Marc Boone
Anne-Laure Van Bruaene
Ghent University

Inequality and the City
in the Low Countries (1200-2020)

Edited by

BRUNO BLONDÉ, SAM GEENS, HILDE GREEFS,
WOUTER RYCKBOSCH, TIM SOENS & PETER STABEL

BREPOLS

© 2020, Brepols Publishers n.v., Turnhout, Belgium.

D/2020/0095/122
ISBN 978-2-503-58868-1
eISBN 978-2-503-58869-8
DOI 10.1484/M.SEUH-EB.5.119604

ISSN 1780-3241
eISSN 2294-8368

Printed on acid-free paper.

In memory of Raymond van Uytven (1933-2018), founder of the Urban History Workshop at the University of Antwerp

Contents

Part V
Cultural and Consumer Dynamics of Inequality

Part VI
Methodological, Theoretical and Contemporary Perspectives

Acknowledgments

In January 2019, the editors of this book launched an open call for contributions. We challenged colleagues specialised in the history of the Low Countries to interrogate their personal research from the perspective of this book: the link between urbanisation, urban society and social inequality. In doing so we invited scholars to reflect upon the connection and interaction of two phenomena that are well studied, but often in isolation: 'urban history' and 'social inequality'. Central to these questions would be what we labelled as the 'Low Countries' paradox'. The Low Countries are marked by the coexistence of apparent low levels of income inequality, the presence of strong middle classes and high levels of (sub)urbanisation. Yet, at the same time the Low Countries are also characterised by enduring difficulties for specific social groups in escaping poverty and accessing upward social mobility.

The Low Countries have a poly-nuclear and decentralised urban system. But it is a well-integrated system nonetheless, with inter-urban competition, complementarity and cooperation. In a way, this holds true for the present-day university landscape as well. In the past decades urban history especially profited from intensive interuniversity collaboration, as is exemplified by numerous joint research projects. More than 20 individual scholars and research teams responded enthusiastically to our call and eventually their work resulted in the present volume. The editors cannot but sincerely thank the scholars who wrote stimulating essays for the priority they have been giving to this enterprise. Several other colleagues were unfortunately unable to contribute, given the time constraints that were imposed at the outset of this enterprise. Yet, this book owes a lot to the intellectual and empirical base to which these specialists have contributed elsewhere.

The editors want explicitly to thank Marc Boone and Anne-Laure Van Bruaene, series editors of the Studies in European Urban History. They generously offered to speed up the external reviewing and editorial supervision process. Likewise, Brepols Publishers need to be credited for giving preferential treatment to the processing of this book project. The articles in this book greatly profited from the critical comments that were formulated by the anonymous reviewers. Kate Elliott, Bachelor of Law from the London School of Economics and Solicitor, proved, once again, to be a first-class language corrector and manuscript editor. Iason Jongepier (University of Antwerp – Centre for Urban History), drew several of the maps in chapters 1 and 3. We are also obliged to the European Association for Urban History which gave this book a platform for international academic exchange. This publication was facilitated by Aipril, the Antwerp Interdisciplinary Platform for Research into Inequality.

The ambition of this book is little more than to provide a stage for discussion about a topic that immediately links up to 'big themes,' even to several sustainable development goals as they are currently defined by the United Nations. Departing from the experience of the

Low Countries, its aim is to become a stepping stone – albeit a modest one – for academic debate on the drivers of social inequality. If ever this goal is achieved the editors hope that it will compensate all parties involved for the efforts that went into the making of this volume.

University of Antwerp (Centre for Urban History) and Vrije Universiteit Brussel (HOST Research Group), 3 March 2020.

PART I

Introduction

BRUNO BLONDÉ, SAM GEENS, HILDE GREEFS, WOUTER RYCKBOSCH,
TIM SOENS AND PETER STABEL

The Low Countries' Paradox

Historical Perspectives on Inequality and the City

Social inequality and the city

The political landscapes of Europe and the United States have been changed dramatically in the course of the 2010s by so-called populist movements. These were often connected to a growing unease and anxiety about various societal trends, such as globalising economies, migration and politics of identity in an increasingly complex and super-diverse society (Carlos de la Torre 2019). What is striking about the twenty-first-century success of populism is that it is generally perceived in connection with clear shifts in social inequality. While worldwide the polarisation between what used to be described as the 'developed' and the 'developing' world seems to be declining, social tensions within countries have been dramatically increasing. The violence-prone manifestations of the *gillets jaunes* in France in 2018 and the destructive and deadly October protests in Chile in 2019 are examples of growing economic frictions and cultural anxieties caused by shifting social inequalities.

Social inequality has indeed become one of the most pressing global challenges at the start of the twenty-first century. The work of economists such as Tony Atkinson, Thomas Piketty, Joseph E. Stiglitz, Branko Milanovic, Emmanuel Saez and many others shows how the awareness of the intellectual community, the general public and some policy makers of the imminent danger of disproportionate social inequality has rapidly gained currency in the last ten years (Piketty 2001; Milanovic 2016; Stiglitz 2013; Piketty 2013). An alarming process of growing inequality in many countries throughout the world is said to disrupt societal stability (Wilkinson & Picket 2010), impact on economic growth (Neves et al. 2016) and threaten the political foundations of democratic societies. Meanwhile urbanisation worldwide is on the rise: more than half of the global population now clusters in urban agglomerations, and urbanisation still continues at a fast pace, particularly in non-European regions confronted with the rapid demographic growth of existing cities and the creation of new urban environments. These two phenomena are by no means unrelated. Cities are often considered to be sites of growing polarisation and rising inequality (United Nations 2020). As a result, some observers have deduced bleak prospects from the combined force of both phenomena. In a world governed by neoliberal markets a rapidly growing surplus labour force without access to education or resources is probably driven towards the informal economies at the fringes of megacities, lumped together in ever sprawling slums (Davis 2006). In Chile, the wealthiest country

Bruno Blondé, Sam Geens, Hilde Greefs, Tim Soens and Peter Stabel • University of Antwerp

Wouter Ryckbosch • Vrije Universiteit Brussel

Inequality and the City in the Low Countries (1200-2020), ed. by Bruno BLONDÉ, Sam GEENS, Hilde GREEFS,
Wouter RYCKBOSCH, Tim SOENS & Peter STABEL, SEUH 50 (Turnhout, 2020), pp. 15-42.

© BREPOLS 🕮 PUBLISHERS   DOI 10.1484/M.SEUH-EB.5.120436

in Latin-America (as measured in GDP per capita), the number of slums has nearly doubled in the last decade. The lack of basic services such as electricity, sanitation and clean drinking water, combined with limited and insecure economic opportunities, bolsters social discontent. Unsurprisingly, the October protests were disproportionally composed of poor urban immigrants living in Santiago's *campamento*. In other parts of the world and in other times, increased urbanisation has likewise gone hand in glove with increased inequality and social tensions, as the rookeries in nineteenth-century London and the *Komboni* in present-day Zambia illustrate.

The question of how urbanisation and inequality are interconnected is therefore an urgent one. It is also a question on which the historical sciences can shed light. In fact, it is foremost the historical relationship between urbanisation and inequality (in a more recent past) that informs many of the sociological and economic models and theories underlying the analysis today. The relationship is often framed in a negative way: cities are often considered to be drivers of inequality. Already in the concept of the 'urban revolution' – the transition from agricultural villages to urban societies in the ancient East – introduced by Vere Gordon Childe in the 1930s the central idea was that the rise of cities brought about socially complex and layered societies (Childe 1950). Today as well as in ancient times, the highest income earners tend to cluster together in major urban settlements, thereby more or less 'automatically' triggering processes of income concentration (Royuela, Veneri & Ramos 2014, 15). At the same time, major cities tend to attract less affluent or less qualified people in search of better living conditions, as is exemplified by present-day Brussels in this volume (Coenen Chapter 6). This idea also plays a role in the central theories traditionally invoked to explain changes of income inequality, foremost among which is the Kuznets curve hypothesis (Kuznets 1955, 7-8). As people moved from the agricultural sector to non-agricultural employment opportunities, often concentrated in cities, higher productivity levels and per capita incomes were achieved, fostering income inequality at the early stages of economic growth and modernisation (levelling off and declining again only at later stages). Although new empirical research by economic historians has gradually nuanced and corrected the Kuznets hypothesis as a universal model for the relationship between growth and inequality, the relationship between urbanisation and inequality still deserves closer scrutiny.

In the wake of the recent re-discovery of social inequality, historians of the pre-industrial era have also taken up the challenge to chart and re-assess pre-industrial social inequalities. This has led to the growing availability of new empirical studies and data, pointing to a sustained period of declining inequality in many parts of late medieval Europe, seemingly triggered by the Black Death of 1347-1351 and following plague epidemics and massive mortality. Yet, starting from around 1450 (with considerable regional variation), a renewed increase of income and wealth inequality can be observed in almost all the European regions for which we have evidence (Alfani & Ryckbosch 2016). These findings have tended to re-establish the presumed relationship between the rise of cities and growing social polarisation: cities in the past tended to be more unequal than rural settlements and bigger cities were *as a rule* more unequal than smaller towns (Milanovic 2018; Alfani & Ammannati 2017, 1084-1085). In his chapter in the current volume, Rogier Van Kooten (Chapter 13) exemplifies this basic mechanism for Antwerp in the post-1585 period. After the conquest of the commercial metropolis by the Habsburg troops, the city lost much of its demographic and economic potential. As a result, the crisis also provoked a social 'compression': emigration was dominated by both the lower ends of the social hierarchy and the urban elites forging a renewed dominance of middle groups in society. In an inverse way, this short episode strongly illustrates the twin relationship between urban growth and social inequality. Urban decline (and de-urbanisation) also had profound consequences for inequality rates.

It needs little emphasis that such findings appear to pose major challenges to present-day urbanisation policies across the world, the more so because very diverse social, economic, political and cultural urban problems are usually associated with social inequality. Inequality is, for example, often reported as a breeding ground for violent crime. Citizens tend to feel more unhappy as inequality grows. Social and cultural identities and even ethical attitudes change because of it (Glaeser, Resseger & Tobio 2009). Yet, urban hierarchies and urbanisation patterns differ greatly across time and space, and so does the legacy of history, the context of place-specific customs and institutions that affect social inequality (Barca, McCann & Rodriguez-Pose 2012; Corfield 2013). Perhaps more importantly, there also exists a counter-narrative about the historical relationship between inequality and the city. A venerable tradition going back to Louis Wirth and his fellow members of the Chicago School of Sociology attributed to the city a great potential for social emancipation and for the erosion of traditional social hierarchies (Wirth 1937; 1938). The influential Belgian historian Henri Pirenne argued that the rise of cities in north-western Europe fundamentally contributed to the breakdown of the feudal order and replaced its hierarchical social structures with more diverse, fluent and horizontal social ties (Pirenne 1927; and the Marxian interpretation of Pirenne's model in Sweezy & Dobb 1950). Some historians attribute to the spread of urban lifestyles and fashion an important role in undermining the social order of the *ancien régime*, thus preparing the way for the French Revolution at the end of the eighteenth century (Sewell 2010). In a similar way, the breakdown of traditional patriarchal social structures and ossified gender roles is often attributed to processes of urbanisation today as well as in the past (Evans 2018).

Given such contrasting interpretations of the relationship between urbanisation and inequality, it is paramount to address the interaction between these two global processes still prominent today by starting from a wide-ranging and thoroughly historical perspective. The aim of this book is therefore not to start from an overarching theoretical framework or from one specific paradigm or variable. Rather we will tackle the subject by looking at the historicity of different aspects of political status, economic organisation, social relations and cultural behaviour, all elements that conglomerate in urban life. This enquiry departs from one specific region, the early and densely urbanised Low Countries, a society where the urban way of life became hegemonic at an early stage.

The Low Countries: urban societies in a river-delta urbanization

This book focuses on the Low Countries. But why does this region provide an important yet challenging case-study for the relationship between inequality and urban development? Ever since the Middle Ages, Italy and the Low Countries (Flanders, Brabant and Holland-Zeeland in particular) have figured among the most densely populated and urbanised

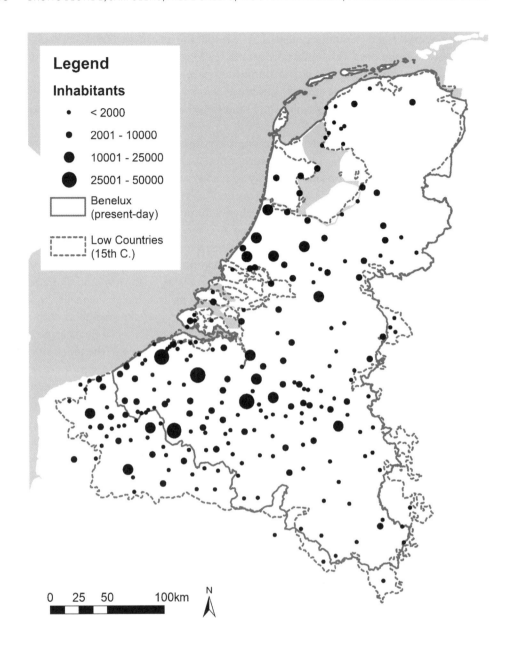

Map 1. Population figures Low Countries, fifteenth century

© Iason Jongepier – GIStorical Antwerp, data: Stabel 2008: 58-63. See also Blondé, Boone & Van Bruaene 2018.

societies of Europe (Map 1) (Crouzet-Pavan & Lecuppre-Desjardin 2008). In fact, Belgium and the Netherlands are still today one of the constituting parts of Europe's so-called 'blue banana' that lights up the sky every night on satellite images. While the Low Countries did not escape from tendencies to urban primacy that marked European urbanisation prior to industrialisation (De Vries 1984; Blondé & Van Uytven 1996; Stabel 1997), they were characterised nonetheless by a surprising absence of metropolitan town development. The establishment of a distinctly multinuclear pattern of urbanisation, with a large number of medium-sized and small towns in a fairly limited space and unequalled urban ratios in Europe, above all resulted in a wide distribution of specialised central places across the region and the urban hierarchy.

This specific pattern of urbanisation was closely linked to easy access to cheap water transport. It provided an important check on the political and economic power balance in the region; between city and state but also within the urban system itself (Blockmans Chapter 7; Blondé, Boone & Van Bruaene 2018). In the decentralised urban system of the Low Countries, most people did not conglomerate in very large cities, but in small and medium-sized cities of a dense urban network that pervaded even the countryside. As a result, the structure of the urban network probably contributed to smoothing the harshest effects of urbanisation on economic inequality. Indeed, the link between urban size, population density and inequality was diffuse: while some towns and villages registered inequality levels as high as in a commercial metropolis like sixteenth-century Antwerp or seventeenth-century Amsterdam, others were significantly less polarised (Alfani & Ryckbosch 2016, Appendix B; Lambrecht & Ryckbosch forthcoming). In the late Middle Ages, there are even indications – although interpreting fiscal data through, for example, Gini must always be done with great care – that typological patterns appear. Industrial cities such as Ghent and Leiden were clearly and substantially more unequal than similarly sized commercial cities such as Bruges. In the fifteenth century, a small industrial centre such as Oudenaarde with 6,000 inhabitants may have been more polarised and more unequal than the much larger commercial city of Bruges with its 45,000 inhabitants (Stabel forthcoming). Hence, economic organisation and the specific typology of the city seem to have been crucial variables, as is also apparent in Van der Meulen's analysis (Chapter 2) where the product specialisation and the specific institutional context of a settlement to a large extent determined the social fabric of the towns investigated. While craft guilds in Armentières were very exclusive, they achieved higher internal levels of social equality compared to the more 'inclusive', but also more polarised textile industry in neighbouring Nieuwkerke. In the latter, the institutional context allowed for the participation of numerous smaller players, yet this inclusiveness came at the cost of a more pronounced degree of social inequality. This trade-off between inclusiveness and equality appears to have been a central paradox characterising the relationship between urbanisation and inequality in the Low Countries.

In eighteenth-century Brabant, to give another example, it was especially the industrial towns, marked by a pronounced proletarianisation process, that proved most unequal. By contrast, the resilience of urban middle classes was especially pronounced in the more important central places where both urban and rural demand were serviced (Blondé 1996). While generally speaking the city size-social inequality rule applies to present-day Belgium as well, Ann Coenen (Chapter 6) unveils myriad inequality indicators that cannot easily be reconciled with urban size alone. In the case of Verviers, for example, a small

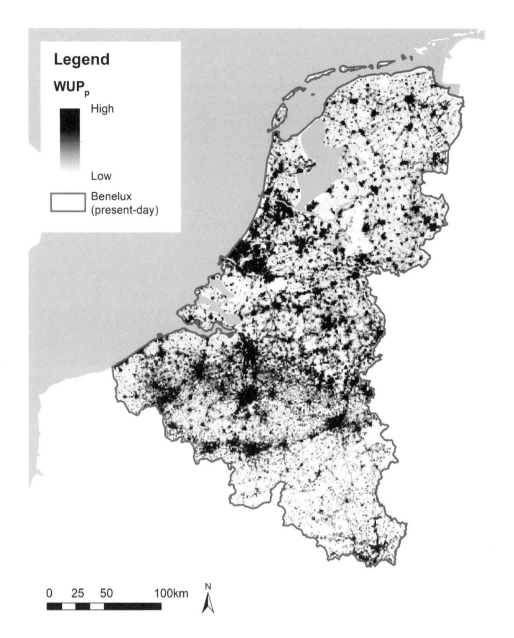

Map 2. Weighted urban proliferation in 2009

© Iason Jongepier, GIStorical Antwerp, Source: European Environmental Agency

town that fell victim to de-industrialisation in recent decades, social deprivation seems to have been historically connected to a specific (and perhaps path-dependent) urban typology. On balance it seems safe to hypothesise that –other things equal- the specific architecture of the Low Countries' polynuclear urban network may have contributed to smoothing inequality tendencies.

This did, however, not prevent the Low Countries from escaping growing inequality as it has been recorded elsewhere in pre-industrial Europe (Van Zanden 1994; Van Bavel 2016, 192-195; Ryckbosch 2015; Alfani & Ryckbosch 2016). Here as well regressive taxation, the long-term relative shift towards capital incomes, a strong process of proletarianisation and the relative decline in the remuneration of labour provoked growing levels of inequality (Lis & Soly 1979; Tilly 1993; Van Zanden 1995; Alfani & Ryckbosch 2016). Remarkably, despite high and rising inequality rates several authors have also stressed how, both in the northern and southern Low Countries, urban middling groups continued to be a strong and resilient factor in urban society (Van der Wee 1971; Blondé & Hanus 2010; Blondé et al. 2018; Stabel, forthcoming). This 'exceptionalism' is sometimes placed in a longer timeframe and linked to the specific social and economic characteristics of Dutch capitalism (Prak & Van Zanden 2013). But the southern Low Countries seem to have been characterised by a similar resilience of the 'middling sort of people' as well. Even today, in sharp contrast to the general trend towards growing economic inequality under the pressure of globalisation, technological change and unstoppable shifts in the functional distribution of income, both Belgium and the Netherlands demonstrate moderate levels of economic inequality (Marx & Verbist 2018; Decoster et al. 2017). There is little reason for optimism though, since, Belgium's apparently low levels of economic inequality not-withstanding, the country also faces severe difficulties in lowering educational inequalities and integrating immigrants, a paradox that probably can be linked to specific forms of urbanisation (Clycq et al. Chapter 21). In her analysis of the Belgian labour market in this volume, Coenen (Chapter 6) also observes that even in cities with excellent labour market performance, some groups are almost structurally left behind. Once again, lower inequality does not equal higher inclusiveness.

Hence the importance of addressing the questions how, why and when cities and the ongoing urbanisation process have historically contributed to the (re)production of social inequality. Unfortunately, in recent debates and major publications on contemporary economic inequality, both the Netherlands and Belgium have been prominent absentees (Coenen 2017). Given the high levels of (early) urbanisation, the exceptionally low levels of income inequality today and the persistent challenges in coping with poverty rates and issues of immigrant integration, the Low Countries offer a major opportunity to fundamentally tackle, verify but also qualify the historical relationship between inequality and urbanisation. Central to this book is the question in what ways specific forms of urbanisation – such as the polycentric river delta urbanisation model of the Low Countries – contributed to different causes and outcomes of social inequality. A crucial player in this specific constellation is 'the' middle class and how its dominant role and its institutions shaped the impact of shocks and crises, the relationship between social inequality and consumption as well as the complex interplay between town and countryside (Van Uytven & Blockmans 1971).

This volume attempts to go beyond a narrow focus on income and wealth inequality. Maïka de Keyzer and Bert de Munck have mapped the methodological, theoretical and epistemological challenges and pitfalls of trying to capture (let alone explain) long-term trends of social and economic inequality (Chapters 20 and 21 respectively). The recent revival of interest in inequality as an important historical subject has produced important new empirical data shedding light on the distribution of income and wealth in cities. However, as is noted critically by De Munck, the new history of inequality tends to use very narrow and even anachronistic definitions of inequality. Prominent scholarship on economic inequality is often concerned almost exclusively, with the 'personal' distribution of income and wealth: the distribution thereof across theoretically homogeneous economic actors in society, be it individuals or households. Meanwhile we are, however, still far removed from an integrated approach of material wellbeing as advocated by De Keyzer in her chapter. Moreover, this book clearly wants to move beyond the dominant quantitative measures of economic inequality by exploring the multiple dimensions and drivers of social inequality and their relationship with urban society as a whole.

In order to approach such a vast topic from different and complementary angles, a team of historians with different backgrounds has joined forces. This book is the outcome of this collaborative effort. However voluminous the book has become, the ambition was never to offer a comprehensive and integrated treatment of the central theme. In fact, the table of contents reflects a pronounced geographical and chronological imbalance, prioritising the history of Flanders and Brabant, the most densely urbanised parts of the southern Low Countries. The contributions place a heavy emphasis on the pre-industrial period. Major aspects of inequality, such as gender inequality, to give but one obvious example, are in an embarrassing way underexplored (Bardyn 2018).

However incomplete from a descriptive point of view, this book nevertheless helps to clarify, exemplify and question several of the key mechanisms that govern the urbanisation of social inequality. The variety of subjects is great and so is the wealth of the insights that can be harvested from them. In what follows we will depart from the major hypotheses that actually reign in the international debate on social inequality and project them upon the history of the Low Countries. We will do so by returning to the point of departure of this venture: the Low Countries' paradox.

The Low Countries' paradox: strong middle classes reproduce social inequality

A long-standing tradition of historical research in the Low Countries with roots in the neo-Smithian work of Henri Pirenne tends to ascribe to the cities of the region an important role in 'the rise of the bourgeoisie' or 'the rise of the middle class'. The particular pattern of urbanisation in the Low Countries, which fostered strong middling groups and led to a fragile balance of power between the state, the aristocracy and the urban elites, is credited not just with a distinct urban lifestyle and culture of respectability. It has been suggested that this social context was also the perfect breeding ground for the seventeenth-century enlightenment in the Dutch Republic (Mijnhardt 2010). Several chapters in the current volume offer tantalising hints of the potential that resides in connecting this old – but rich – social and cultural historiography of the Low Countries with the new empirical studies on income and wealth distribution. They suggest that the process of 'the rise of the middle class' was not necessarily at odds with the evidence on the growing inequality in income and wealth in most cities of the Low Countries from the fifteenth century on. Moreover, middle-class institutions and cultural repertoires often had strong exclusionary effects towards lower social groups – which could, if necessary, be enforced through court, the police or more subtle cultural markers of social distinction (Blockmans & Janse 1999).

Eventually, social (in)equality in the Low Countries was moulded in cultural repertoires and the urban middling sort of people played a crucial role in that process. Stabel and De Meyer (Chapter 15) show how around 1300 the balance of power in the Flemish and Brabantine cities shifted away from the mercantile elites towards the craft guilds and the masters who dominated them. Their analysis of practices of self-identification demonstrates how the social, economic and political power of the craft guilds was cemented into the urban fabric with the help of specific cultural repertoires focusing on reputation. This marks the ascendance of a strong middling groups, who could wrestle some degree of control away from the mercantile and land-owning elites while at the same time also distinguishing themselves clearly from the lower social groups of subordinate status within and outside the craft guilds. At the same time, brotherly values of solidarity among guild members could be judicially enforced. The most tangible example of how these typical middle-class values effectively contained the potential for extreme polarisation can be encountered in this book in the export-oriented draperies of south-west Flanders, highlighted in Jim van der Meulen's contribution (Chapter 2). Although with variable degrees of success, collective action by the 'master' weavers impeded a complete vertical integration of the industries. 'Getting rich had its limits' in the sixteenth-century Low Countries, van der Meulen tentatively concludes. And strikingly enough, in safeguarding or acquiring their social and symbolic positions almost all actors seem to borrow from a dominant urban middle-class ideology (Haemers & Dumolyn 2013). Bert de Munck evidences how corporations, by acknowledging apprenticeship training received elsewhere in the urban network, could even overrule the territory (the city) as the relevant political context, as long as the training was done under the supervision of a guild-based master (Chapter 21). The flipside of this corporate-based middle-class resilience was the constant drive for distinction and protection by the middling sort. This came at the cost of excluding the lower segments in urban society and contemporary rent-seeking behaviour in the redistribution of income via social welfare programmes (Engbersen et al. 2017). Tellingly, many requests for free legal aid in eighteenth-century Antwerp stemmed not from the structurally poor, but from newly impoverished people, formerly belonging to the middling sort. While they were on the verge of losing their economic independence, they often emphasised that their poverty was recent and had arisen unexpectedly (Vermeesch Chapter 11).

The strength of a distinctly middle-class urban culture that focused on ideals of respectability is also the subject of Baatsen's analysis of domestic sociability in sixteenth-century Bruges (Chapter 16). Baatsen shows how, despite a process of economic decline, urban middling groups exerted a strong impulse towards more refined patterns of taste and lifestyle, which they typically associated with the city itself. Hence the term 'boers' (or 'boorish' as in peasant-like) for unrefined behaviour (Freedman 1999). The urban behavioural model was so powerful that even countryside dwellers in the most dense rural settlements, taking part in the vivid cultural life and civil society that marked the countryside in the Low Countries, excluded members for their uncivilised manners, which they strikingly labelled *dorpernie*, hence stressing the villainous nature of the peasant way of life (Van Dijck 2005, 105-107). Thus, the continued cultural and social dominance of such urban middling groups did not preclude the possibility of growing social polarisation nor the use of taste as an active means of distinction between different social groups. In his chapter on the use of violence in Mechelen (Chapter 18), Maarten van Dijck moreover shows how the elites in this court city were still strikingly violent in the early sixteenth century. By the early seventeenth century, however, violent behaviour was stratified, i.e. socially confined to the lower strata of urban society, and as such clearly reflected the divergent behavioural repertoires between the elites and the lower ranks of urban society.

In sum, within the polynuclear urban network of the Low Countries, in both economic and cultural terms the urban middling sort deployed all means possible to safeguard their social position. Yet, in this process, they also constructed thresholds and contributed to the reproduction of social inequality in its cultural, political and social dimensions. Middle-class values and anxieties are also apparent when we look at the social frictions and tensions arising in the nineteenth century. Rapid urbanisation was strongly connected to problems of overcrowding, poverty, vice and death (Greefs & Winter Chapter 4). Social problems were tackled by a profound reorganisation of the urban territory, as is illustrated by the demolition of old city walls, the redesigning of urban space according to bourgeois aspirations and anxieties, and the sanitation of unhealthy and poor city quarters, as well as by regulating and policing urban space. The chapter by De Koster and Vrints (Chapter 19) on the social uses of policing in nineteenth-century Antwerp offers a nuanced perspective on this issue. Based on a careful study of police records the authors conclude that by the end of the nineteenth century the Antwerp police force took up a disciplining role, and thus acted as instruments in the hands of the middle and upper classes. While initially the police concentrated on the richer neighbourhoods and administrative/economic tasks, the cultural values and norms of 'respectability' became an important criterion that affected police behaviour vis-à-vis lower social classes. However, paradoxically, the institutional apparatus could also be put to active use by the more disadvantaged layers of the Antwerp population – a phenomenon also recognised by Griet Vermeesch. The ongoing process of proletarianisation drove the poor segments of society at the end of the early modern period out of civil litigation. Indeed, most civil cases were related to credit cases and it was the urban poor that faced increasing difficulties in forging such durable credit relations. Meanwhile, criminal courts attracted claimants on a larger social scale and people of lesser means actively appropriated these legal instruments for their own social strategies as well (Vermeesch Chapter 11).

Consumption inequalities: the underexplored dimension

The specificity of the urban lifestyle and urban consumption patterns plays an important role in the sociological tradition that attributes an emancipating and socially corrosive role to urbanisation (Simmel 1903; 1904). In this tradition the urban lifestyle and the fashion cycles it generates are no longer regarded merely as a reflection of changes in the social sphere but as a causal factor themselves. The urban (or even metropolitan) consumer culture is then taken as a driving force behind the erosion of traditional status-based social stratifications.

Consumption is a key theme throughout the debates on urbanisation in the Low Countries. It also figures prominently in this volume. Yet, the connection between material culture, consumption and social inequality is one of the least analysed in the economic history of the early modern city. Certainly, economic historians are aware of the key importance played by expenditure patterns in assessing long-term evolutions in 'real inequality'. Social divergences in standards of living and material wellbeing often resulted from relative price developments and differential expenditure patterns across the social spectrum (Hofmann 2002). However, in contrast to wealth and income measurements, historical research into consumer and expenditure patterns is much more limited. As a result, even though consumption is generally considered the ultimate underlying rationale of economics, historical studies of 'consumption inequality' have received far less attention (Attanasio & Pistaferri 2016). Whether or not consumption had a 'smoothing' impact on income and wealth inequality is a key question economic historians should address. Strikingly enough, the house rent taxes that are often used as the best proxy to map income disparities are generally considered to underestimate the actual income inequalities. In the case of sixteenth-century 's-Hertogenbosch five income levies generally yielded a Gini coefficient of between 0.69 and 0.73, while the house rent taxes moved between 0.40 and 0.49 (Hanus 2014, 141). Hence, from a consumer perspective one could argue that the actual distribution of living comfort was a reduced reflection of actual income inequalities. Yet, as Heidi Deneweth convincingly argues, differential pressures on the housing markets also caused differential development of house rents. In the long run the declining degree of house ownership and the process of proletarianisation drove up the price of housing in the lower segments of the market. As a result, house rent taxes at the end of the early modern period contributed to an artificial under-estimation of actual income inequalities, while in reality house rents were actively contributing to the inequality process. In other words: the apparent drop in inequality on the housing market, as revealed by house rent taxes, was hiding a situation in which the gap in material living standards was actually increasing as a result of rising house rents (Deneweth Chapter 14)!

A large literature has developed on the 'birth of a consumer society' in the late early modern period, and on the multiple consequences changing consumer patterns had on social relationships. In his introduction to the seminal 'Birth of the consumer society', Neil McKendrick explicitly hypothesised about the triad of economic growth, political freedom and social equality that would have fostered the coming into being of a new consumption model in the eighteenth century (McKendrick 1982). Ever since, several authors have pointed to the so-called blurring of social boundaries that would have marked the advent of the 'new luxuries' in the eighteenth century (De Vries 2008). In fact, according to De Vries, the advent of a 'new luxury' pattern and consumption morale was closely intertwined with the bourgeois, middle-class society that originated in the seventeenth-century Dutch Republic (De Vries 2003). Recently, the geography and chronology of this claim have been called into question (Blondé & Ryckbosch 2015). In fact, empirical evidence clearly indicates that the cities of the Low Countries, through their comparatively powerful and affluent middle classes, have pioneered consumption innovations geared towards the urban middling sort of people at least since the late Middle Ages (Baatsen et al. 2019). Already in the fifteenth and sixteenth centuries, standardisation and cheaper materials offered the lower middle classes the chance to participate in a more refined material culture, and this happened centuries before the proclaimed 'industrious' and 'consumer' revolution. Yet, while numerous affordable luxuries such as maiolica, for example, entered the market, social status was reflected by high quality ceramics, next to the diversity and quantity of material, as Inneke Baatsen uncovers in an exploration of the material culture in Bruges in the fifteenth and sixteenth centuries (Chapter 16). As such, the 'levelling effect' of the new consumer culture might have gone hand in hand with growing cultural polarisation, as has also been suggested for the cities of the southern Low Countries in the eighteenth century (Soly 1988).

Indeed, in recent years, serious doubts have been cast on the inclusiveness of acclaimed eighteenth-century consumer innovations (Blondé 2009; Ryckbosch 2015). An illuminating micro-story of the way in which consumer models conflicted in this period is offered by Wout Saelens (Chapter 17). Thanks to the use of cheaper coal, thermal comfort in Ghent gradually trickled down the social ladder, contributing to a kind of 'democratisation' of living comforts. Yet, on closer inspection, this new luxury did little to narrow the gap between the poor and the rich in Ghent society. In fact, the richer urban households not only deepened the gap by investing disproportionately more in the 'new luxuries', they also developed a hybrid material culture in which the old (and energy-inefficient) use of the hearth was cherished as a means to elaborate a status-seeking sociability. Many of the new luxuries were indeed accessible even to the poor, as is often noticed for the consumption of hot drinks, for instance (McCants 2008). Yet, while the 'new luxuries' were substituted for 'old luxuries' among the lower middle classes of society, the elites continued to invest heavily in both repertoires. This is also exemplified by Antwerp probate inventory research. The enormous expansion of hot drinks went hand in glove with a minor reduction in the inequality of the material culture related to coffee and tea. Meanwhile the unequal growth in silverware ownership remained considerable and became even more obvious as the age of enlightenment progressed (Blondé & Van Damme 2010). Given the social coverage of probate inventories, excluding the inventories of real paupers, the recorded levels of inequality are very suggestive: it seems safe to hypothesise that the much applauded transformations in material culture were actively deepening social differences rather than smoothing them over. Preliminary data for early eighteenth-century Amsterdam lend additional support to this working hypothesis. In contrast to what one would infer from the historiography, chinaware ownership (the affordable 'new luxuries') was clearly more socially polarised than the ownership of silverware (the 'old luxury') was (Faber 1980). Much more comparative research is needed to test this hypothesis, but the available evidence already warns us not to interpret the social consequences of consumer innovations too hastily. Moreover and rather cynically, at least in the southern Low Countries, the cities that specialised in the production of the 'new luxuries' proved to have a weaker and more polarised social structure, employing especially poorly paid semi-skilled and proto-industrial workers. In this way, on the production side as well, the 'sweatshops of the consumer revolution' were part and parcel of an urban society that was growing more unequal (Blondé 1996).

More research is still needed to determine how the expansion of consumer culture in the nineteenth century interacted with social inequality trends during this turbulent period. Belgium's precocious industrialisation and rural proletarianisation reinforced social polarisation between the middle classes, who could often profit from new economic opportunities, and the lower ranks of unskilled labourers, who were confronted with unstable employment. Studies of consumption have indicated how upper middle classes – such as independent shopkeepers, small businessmen, professionals and white-collar employees – could enjoy new and more luxurious lifestyles and consumption patterns (Scholliers 2008). The widespread ideal of 'domesticity' accompanied the consumerist lifestyle of the urban middling ranks (Denis 2016), and increasingly sophisticated retailing spaces turned shopping into a favourite and polite pastime for the urban bourgeois, yet how people of different social classes partook in the shopping culture and appropriated it still needs research (Arnout 2019, 257). Yet, until deep in the nineteenth century, the consumption levels of many unskilled labourers remained restricted because the major part of the household budget had to be spent on daily needs, such as food and housing. While food consumption, generally speaking, deteriorated in the first half of the nineteenth century, luxurious food consumption expanded, pointing to a pronounced polarisation process across different cities in the urban hierarchy (Lis & Soly 1977; Segers 2001). The living and working conditions of the poor remained critical until the last quarter of the nineteenth century when their standard of living started to improve and social measures were taken to better their living conditions (Scholliers 1996; Lis & Vanthemsche 1995). Whether the expansion of fashion, consumerism and the multiple retail innovations in the nineteenth-century Low Countries served as an equalising factor or actively deepened existing social disparities is a matter to be taken up in future research.

Taxing the poor: social inequality as a political construct

Within the power balance of the urban world the middling sort of people had a strong voice, yet it was not the only one, nor necessarily the most dominant. The urban elites, looking for commercial and economic opportunities and prospects, were certainly not deprived of rent-seeking policies (Blockmans Chapter 7). Indeed, social inequality is to a large extent the product of policy, and this was no different in the pre-industrial cities of the Low Countries. Several chapters in this volume testify to the growing importance of the fiscal system in fostering urban inequality. Compared to Gross Urban Income, the overall fiscal pressure in the Low Countries was far from impressive (Janssens 1990), but two remarks need to be made. First, one can wonder whether state taxes accurately represent the total fiscal pressure, as many taxpayers also owed other dues, not least land and house rents. By their very nature, such dues increased social inequality through the redistribution of income based on existing political inequalities. Second, within urban society taxes were mainly regressive. In Chapter 9, Bruno Blondé, Jord Hanus and Wouter Ryckbosch explore the role of beer duties in sixteenth-century 's-Hertogenbosch. They conclude that the consumption taxes were extremely unbalanced compared to the proportion of wages in the urban income. For the lower classes beer taxes constituted a significant burden on their consumption. Consequently, indirect taxes on necessities fostered social unrest, as is evident from several riots in the sixteenth century. They also impeded the development of the Habsburg state, which met fierce resistance from local power holders in its efforts to establish more modern and equitable taxes. The short intermezzo of the Calvinist Republics illustrates how conscious policy makers at all levels were about the consequences of this fiscal architecture. In Chapter 10, Guido Marnef clearly shows how the shifting political power balance in the Calvinist Republic was oiled with a new social policy. While the bulk of the tax burden was collected through a path-dependent and regressive tax system, the mounting fiscal needs of the war in the rebellious cities were increasingly met through proportional and even progressive direct taxes. Unsurprisingly, after the conquest of Antwerp in 1585, the Habsburg government immediately abolished this modern tax system and returned to dominant indirect taxes. The Dutch Republic was, most probably, an exception by also adopting tax systems in which citizens contributed more in proportion to their socio-economic status ('t Hart & Limberger 2006). Yet, even here, the overall burden of proportional taxes remained very limited (Alfani & Di Tullio 2019). In the first half of the seventeenth century, taxes on land and capital existed in the Dutch Republic but were levied mostly at a flat rate. Meanwhile, up to 75 per cent of all tax revenues in Holland were raised by means of – regressive – consumption taxes on basic necessities. So if differences there were, they remained very limited (Prak 2005, 78).

Due to the regressive way in which it was absorbed, the growing fiscal pressure in the early modern Low Countries had a strong impact on income inequality. The effects were aggravated because only a minor share of urban and provincial taxes was reinvested in infrastructural improvements or services to society. The lion's share drained away to the owners of government debts. These creditors predominantly lived in cities and derived a substantial income from the interest on government debts. Moreover, a large part of this income was reinvested in the consumption of urban products and services, hence strengthening the redistributive effect of state taxes. In sixteenth-century 's Hertogenbosch and in the medieval cities of Flanders, the majority of annuities was held by citizens belonging to the middle and, especially, the upper classes (Chapter 9). Increasingly, the wealthy preferred to live in urban society, lured by the success of the urban behavioural model and the metropolitan fashion imperatives that permeated into Low Countries' society. In eighteenth-century Brabant, for instance, it was mainly the cities that attracted the rentiers, and the wealthier ones preferred cities with a vivid cultural and social scene, especially the bigger cities such as Brussels and Antwerp (Blondé 1998). This process continued during the nineteenth century when Brussels attracted many property owners from inside the country and from abroad (De Schaepdrijver 1999), who were also lured by the 'liberal' attitudes of the young kingdom and the well-established railway connections with major European metropoles such as Paris. In doing so, they contributed to the geographical redistribution of tax incomes, in the process sharpening differences between town and countryside, but also reallocating capital and central functions between smaller towns and larger cities.

No city is an island: urban hierarchies and town-countryside dimensions

The rise of the fiscal state not only propelled social inequality within the town walls, but also impacted upon relationships between town and countryside. Cities were often able to pass a considerable part of the mounting fiscal pressure on to the countryside, as is generally acknowledged for fifteenth-century Flanders. Moreover, in the current volume Thijs Lambrecht (Chapter 8) shows how citizens investing in the surrounding countryside accumulated fiscal exemptions in the process, thereby eroding the tax base of the rural economy. As a result, urban landowners were among the groups that profited most from the inequity of the fiscal distribution. Power asymmetries between town and countryside were not constant however: in the coastal part of Flanders, thirteenth-century peasant communities compelled urban landlords to contribute to the cost of flood protection by shifting the tax burden from land-use to landed property (Soens 2011). While declining rural bargaining power in the subsequent centuries increasingly benefitted urban landlords, by the eighteenth century a new cohesive class of large commercial tenant farmers in the coastal areas successfully lobbied for financial support from the state, distributing the substantial cost of flood protection over a much larger rural *and* urban population (Van Cruyningen 2017). Thus, institutional arrangements constantly interacted with shifting power configurations in fiscal allocations between town and countryside (Van Bavel, Curtis & Soens 2019).

On a more general level, the relationship between social inequality and the city cannot be studied by mapping inequalities at the individual town level only. In contrast to the most frequently adopted methodology for charting social inequality at the individual town level (De Keyzer Chapter 20), both urban hierarchies and town-countryside relations need to be taken fully into account when assessing the relationship between social inequality and the city. In the sixteenth century, for instance, Antwerp served as a major commercial gateway for the industrial products of the Low Countries. Yet weavers in Hondschoote and pin makers in 's-Hertogenbosch, to name but a few, often worked at the service of merchants operating from Antwerp, the commercial metropolis (Van der Meulen Chapter 2; Blondé 1987). In this respect, the high levels of Gross Urban Income in Antwerp owed a lot to the proletarianisation of labour elsewhere in the Low Countries and far beyond their boundaries (Blondé & Puttevils forthcoming).

In a similar vein, inequality was forged in town-countryside relationships. Relative price developments, for instance, determine shifting proportions of labour and wealth incomes, while they also correspond to shifting balances in the relative distribution of town-countryside incomes (Hohenberg & Lees 1985). The growth in Gross Urban Income in nineteenth-century Ghent, for example, resulted at least as much from the rapidly rising rent flow generated by the rural (and proto-industrialised) possessions of its citizens as from the industrial activities within the city (Kint 1989). In most cities of the Low Countries landed property remained associated with the urban elite and a minority of farming citizens (Vermoesen 2015). In very specific contexts, such as post-Black Death Ghent, landed property also became an important asset for a significant part of the urban population beyond the strict confines of the urban patriciate (Geens Chapter 12). The constant migration fluxes and the fact that newcomers coming from the surrounding hinterland provided a substantial part of the urban population inevitably led to out-of-town land ownership patterns. It remains to be seen whether many also actively included land – which they often inherited from relatives – into securing their supply of food. In some contexts, an integration of town and countryside might have provided particular layers in the urban social fabric with an opportunity to diversify both their income and provisioning strategies (Charruadas & Deligne 2019). This might have created new layers of inequality between those town dwellers whose access to land provided them with an additional buffer against recurrent food shortages and those who remained entirely dependent on the urban food market (Soens forthcoming). Of course, the ability of urban citizens to acquire land in the countryside also depended on the 'nature' of the rural economy. Within the Low Countries regional divergences in the social organisation of the rural economy – the social agro-system, as Erik Thoen (Thoen 2004) has labelled it – became more pronounced from the later Middle Ages onwards. The cohesiveness of the peasant community and the strength of its property rights in land also determined the opportunities for town dwellers to acquire land. Whereas in the polders of seventeenth-century Holland and Zeeland and the Groninger Oldambt half or more of the land was owned by urban landowners, in sixteenth-century inland Flanders this was around 20 per cent, and in Drenthe or the Land van Herve it even came close to zero. If peasant claims to land were strong, the expansion of urban landownership could be successfully contained, even at a short distance from major cities (Curtis 2016, 122-123).

In those regions where urban landownership was substantial, rent income fueled inequalities within the city, between town and countryside, and in the countryside. An intriguing example of the complexity of the dependencies and inequalities created by the requirement to pay rent is offered by the analysis of the urban manure trade in eighteenth-century Flanders by Pieter De Graef (Chapter 3). De Graef shows how mounting pressure of rent and declining income in proto-industrial industries pushed peasants into the use of urban manure as a fertilizer, thereby reinforcing a vicious circle of landholding fragmentation and mounting rental flows towards the city (Kint 1989). Apart from direct rental flows, urban traders also profited from the outsourcing of industrial production to the country-side, where part of the cost of labour was covered by smallholding-subsistence farming. Interestingly, this model of shifting part of the labour cost of industrial production to the countryside continued even after the demise of agricultural labour and rural industries in the late ninetenth century. The example of the village of Waremme in the province of Liège, elaborated by Scheepers, Polasky, Verhetsel and De Block in this volume (Chapter 5), shows how the spectacular expansion of the Belgian railway system, combined with the introduction of cheap workmen's tickets, allowed villagers to integrate 'urban' factory work into a traditional income-pooling household model where home food production helped to keep industrial wages low. At the same time the rural population was saved from the 'moral degradation' which was associated with city life. It was stimulated to continue living in small villages or towns, contributing to processes of urban decentralisation and urban sprawl, yet making any analysis of social inequality at the individual city level extremely short-sighted.

This history of late nineteenth- and early twentieth-century commuting also shows how town-countryside dynamics heavily affected migration patterns, which in turn strongly shaped urban inequalities. For centuries, cities were marked by the 'urban graveyard' effect. In towns the number of burials usually exceeded the number of baptisms, thus necessitating a constant influx of newcomers to fill the ranks of the deceased. Both mortality and fertility have a role to play. The idea of the 'filthy' pre-industrial city where unhealthy sanitary conditions paved the road for epidemic disease has been corrected significantly in recent literature (Rawcliffe 2013). Space in the early modern city was highly fragmented. For example, Van Kooten's contribution to this volume (Chapter 13) shows how households were segregated by income across and within neighbourhoods. So, it was not the city that was unhealthy, but rather the sanitary conditions in some districts of the city. Such 'environmental inequalities', combined with the unequal spread of low-income rural migrants, might have contributed to creating pockets of misery and unhealthy living conditions.

Apart from health inequalities, renewed attention has been paid to the impact of delayed marriage and female participation in the labour market. The number of immigrants marrying never or late was relatively high and the weaker social and economic position of these immigrants generally resulted in lower marriage statistics, thus in the low reproduction rate of urban populations. This stands in stark contrast to the 'core population' of the town. As long as the economic and cultural codes of the Low Countries' town were essentially corporate, not to say guild-based, such a pattern inevitably contributed to the increase in social inequality. Marriage was indeed a crucial threshold and cornerstone of the privileged master positions in guilds, and the moral, social and cultural codes related to guild membership were crucial in the rent-seeking strategies of urban middling groups as well (Stabel & De Meyer Chapter 15). By the late early modern period, the parameters of the urban demography had changed fundamentally. Yet, in the short run, the declining impact of the 'urban graveyard effect' did little to ease the proliferation of social inequality through migration. Indeed, traditionally nineteenth-century migration to cities is associated with a series of (perceived) societal challenges and problems, both reflecting real problems and middle-class anxieties. Hilde Greefs and Anne Winter have charted the demographic developments and migration movements which were clearly much more complicated than straightforward countryside-town relocations contributing to urbanisation. The most defining characteristic of nineteenth-century migration to towns in Belgium was not the way in which immigrants contributed to the replenishment of the lower ranks of urban society and eventually to the rate of urbanisation. Strikingly, an enormous army of internal migrants, and towards the end of the century also less affluent foreign migrants, continued to constitute a floating and unsettled demographic reservoir that could not easily be absorbed into urban society (Greefs & Winter Chapter 4). Unsurprisingly then, the moral panic that gained currency in the late nineteenth century focused on these particularly mobile groups, moving into and out of the city. It was mirrored in far more repressive vagrancy legislation and selective policing (De Koster & Vrints Chapter 19). These changing rural-urban relocations were also reflected in broader social policies, such as the organisation of social services which were an urban responsibility until deep in the nineteenth century. Urban administrators tried to reduce social costs by stricter admission conditions (for instance by lengthening the necessary residential period) and by recovering the costs at places of birth, which led to complex financial transactions between the countryside and the city during the nineteenth century (Van Damme 1990; Winter 2013).

As the absorption capacity of the big cities reached its zenith at the closure of the nineteenth century and infrastructural policies, particularly the extension of railway networks and tramways, reinforced the urbanisation processes of the countryside, more people moved to suburban districts (De Block & Polasky 2011). Such districts, whether industrial or rather marked as 'bourgeois' zones, shared one common feature: population growth. In the post-war period, some of these fringes, particularly those with an industrial character in the immediate surroundings of the big cities, were confronted with social problems which were for a long time identified as metropolitan problems, such as deteriorating living conditions and low levels of employment and education, as is also demonstrated in the chapters by Coenen (Chapter 6) and Clycq et al. (Chapter 21) in this volume.

Social inequalities as drivers of crises

Social inequality is to a large extent shaped by practices of governance, political desicions and the overall organization of the polities. Despite the attention recently paid in historical research to external shocks and calamities such as pandemics, warfare and revolutions as agents of change – or even 'levellers of inequality' (Scheidel 2016), the role for patterns of social inequality of political economy should not be ignored. While shocks are often grouped together under the single denominator of crisis, the mechanisms behind their effect on inequality (whether these were levelling or polarizing processes) differed greatly between and even within each type of event. Revolutions generally had a positive effect on the personal distribution of income and wealth, as ownership of the factors of production forcefully changed hands. During the French Revolution, properties of the Church were expropriated and sold off. Although the lion's share of land was bought by wealthy farmers and bourgeois families, thus merely passing ownership from one elite to another, at least some peasants were able to enlarge their holdings. More importantly, feudal dues and tithes were abolished, much to the benefit of lower income groups in the countryside (Morrisson & Snyder 2000). During the communist revolutions in China and Russia changes in ownership were even more radical. Agricultural lands and urban businesses of the elite and middling classes were confiscated, redistributed among lower income groups and, at a later stage, collectivised. Naturally, declining economic disparities do not equate to better living standards, as the mass starvation during the 'Great Leap Forward' illustrates (Dikötter 2010). Moreover, low income inequalities might obscure real inequalities. For example, luxury imports for Soviet party elites might have increased consumption inequality in a society where income differentials were minimal (Scheidel 2016).

Pandemics do not intervene directly in the ownership of the factors of production but, instead, have the power to fundamentally change the functional distribution of income, which leads in turn to a redistribution of personal incomes. The Black Death and the consequent recurrent plague waves released the Malthusian deadlock between rising demographic pressure and the declining marginal productivity of labour in fourteenth-century Europe. Labour became scarce at the same time as land turned into an abundant resource. Drastic changes in the rent-wage ratio theoretically benefitted the poorer income groups at the expense of the elite, reducing income inequality – at least temporarily. While the demographic crisis had severe consequences for urbanisation rates in many regions, such as England and the Republic of Florence, cities in the southern Low Countries recovered relatively fast thanks to increased immigration from the countryside. In this region, there were already strong ties between town and countryside, a large rural population, and weak control by lords over their tenants facilitated mobility (Thoen 2004; Stabel 1997). Mass emigration further exacerbated the differential fiscal capacity between communities. It is therefore not surprising that Thijs Lambrecht (Chapter 8) found multiple agreements between rural districts and cities concerning the taxability of migrants in the aftermath of the Black Death.

Warfare also impacts on economic inequality, mainly through direct changes in the personal distribution of income. In principle, wars have a tendency to destroy capital and people. As such they drive up the price of labour while destroying wealth-based sources of income. Yet the specific relationship between warfare and inequality is highly contingent and needs to move beyond simplistic one-to-one causations. Three chapters in this volume take up the challenge of confronting war-induced crisis with social inequality. Sam Geens (Chapter 12) discovered a paradoxical long-term consequence of the military conflict the city of Ghent was involved in at the end of the fourteenth century. Tellingly, the levelling effects of the political crisis were short-lived, as Geens could infer from probate inventory data. On the other hand, war did have a profound impact on wealth compositions. While the city of Ghent was saved from massive destruction, the countryside suffered badly. In the short run, this was problematic for the landowning urban elites, who saw their income from landed property collapse and were forced to invest in the rebuilding of tenant farms. In this way warfare was a powerful leveller. However, low land prices also stimulated urban investment in rural land, not only by the urban elites, but also by part of the corporative middle classes. In the longer run, warfare therefore increased the rent flows from the countryside to the city, while at the same time creating new inequalities within urban society, between a land-owning elite and higher middle class and a landless workforce (Lambrecht Chapter 8).

Warfare had a different effect in the case of the siege of Antwerp in 1584-1585, studied by Rogier van Kooten (Chapter 13). Massive emigration and economic decline after the conquest of the city by Spanish troops resulted in a significant decline in income inequality. This effect was geographically clustered, since segregated communities, both poor and rich, contributed disproportionately to this effect. As demonstrated by Heidi Deneweth in her contribution on the housing market in Bruges in the same period (Chapter 14), the urban poor and the lower middle classes did not necessarily profit from the collapse of the housing market in the wake of warfare. The urgent need to limit credit to 30 per cent of the total value of immovables and the structural impoverishment and indebtedness of the lower middle classes indeed reduced house ownership among the lower middling sort of people in late sixteenth-century Bruges. As a result, when prices recovered again early in the seventeenth century it was these people of modest means who increasingly transferred incomes to the house owners. In a similar context, Andrea Bardyn discovered that poor female landowners in particular fell victim to a property crisis in late fourteenth-century Brussels (Bardyn 2018).

Moreover, the contributions to this volume also confirm that inequality is not merely a dependent variable, but also an independent variable when assessing the occurrence and outcome of crises. High levels of inequality might provoke or intensify crises. In his provocative synthesis of the relationship between inequality and market development, Bas van Bavel (2016) conceived the expansion of market economies as cyclical, with the growth of factor markets fostering inequality and the concentration of wealth and power in the hands of a rent-seeking elite, which in the end proved detrimental for economic growth itself and unleashed violent conflict. Social equality was also one of the central ideals driving the French Revolution (Alfani & Frigeni 2016). In particular the mismatch between the economic and political power of the bourgeoisie, the detrimental economic position of the peasantry vis-à-vis the nobility and clergy, and the uneven distribution of taxes among those different classes gave rise to one of history's most famous revolutions (see also Chapters 8, 9 and 10). The French ideals influence policies even today, and social and political protest and upheaval were needed to narrow the gap between those who had and those who had not. They were also needed to distribute taxes more evenly among the population, which is also reflected in contemporary discussions.

Vice versa, the middle-class-inspired ideology and the checks on inequality which continued to characterise the Low Countries might help to explain why on balance the urban populations were often relatively well protected against major crises. As a recent analysis of famine history suggests, the urban Low Countries were seemingly successful in avoiding mortal famines at an early stage. They did so however by externalising part of the risk to the countryside, as was the case in the seventeenth-century Dutch Republic (Curtis & Dijkman 2019), or to the poorest groups in society, as recently demonstrated by Nicolas Barla (Barla 2019) in his analysis of famine in late medieval Mons and Lille. And even though the last big food crises in Belgium (outside periods of war) during the nineteenth century, such as the hunger crisis in Flanders during the 1840s, hit the population severely in some regions, the detrimental effects were once again slowed down by policy measures such as liberating the import of grain, adjusting bread prices and, above all, effective social policies (Vanhaute 2007; Beeckaert & Vanhaute 2019).

Thus, urban inequality constantly interacted with institutional arrangements to produce vulnerabilities and hamper or foster resilience (Van Bavel, Curtis & Soens, 2018). In that, the relationship between inequality and crisis has come full circle: from being the outcome, to a mediator and, finally, a cause.

Epilogue: lessons from the Low Countries?

The conclusions of the explorations in this voluminous book are anything but comprehensive. In fact, they cover a wide range of perspectives. By including access to justice, education, violence, cultures and ideologies of inequalities, this book highlights the multi-dimensional dynamics of urban inequalities (De Keyzer Chapter 20). Yet, too many key areas of such an integrated approach are unfortunately still non-existent (health, environmental (in)equality, gender relations, etc.). Moreover, as has already been said, the coverage of other critical topics was unbalanced from a thematic, geographic and chronologic perspective. This is regrettable since the book wants to show that no clear one-to-one relationships existed between different vectors of urban inequality, let alone that a prime mover can be detected. Urban ideology, for instance, offers a nice example. A good case can be made that a specific urban middle-class-inspired ideology originated in the Low Countries, building on the social, economic and political power of 'civil society'. Yet, this ideology often merely upholds an illusion, albeit a powerful one, rather than a reality. Such ideological frameworks sometimes compensated for structural underlying frictions in society (van der Meulen Chapter 2; Kint 1996). Not all determinants of social inequality necessarily move in the same direction, and even when they do so it is often with varying intensity or speed. Anyway, without avoiding the challenge of mapping long-term transformations in inequality, the broad approach that is advocated in this volume warns us not being trapped in easy teleological tell-tales dominated by ex ante conceived perceptions of social inequality (Bert de Munck Chapter 21). Thus, the fragmentation that marks this volume is more than a reflection of the unequal responses harvested after our first call for contributions; the fragmentation is also *essential*.

This does not provide us with an alibi for abandoning the greater issues that are at stake in the social inequality debate in academia and society today. The variety of essay subjects indeed helps us enormously in cautiously drawing conclusions, formulating some overarching hypotheses and raising challenging questions for future research. In the twentieth century, for instance, major crises (such as the two world wars) directly contributed to reducing economic inequalities. Indirectly the Second World War also shaped the conditions for a mixed economy and a tax and welfare policy that for decades would reduce inequality. Yet, this exploration of urban societies of the Low Countries shows that the 'benign' effects of warfare on social inequality were highly contingent on a series of conditions. More often than not, wars and long-lasting economic crises fundamentally impacted on social structures, albeit seldom in a clear-cut 'positive' way. Moreover, social inequality itself was a major cause of the differential effects of crises on groups in urban society. Whether or not citizens proved resilient to shocks and crises heavily depended upon their initial position at the outbreak of the calamity. This is evidenced by the fundamental redrawing of land and house ownership patterns and the long-lasting consequences thereof in the aftermath of such crises.

Secondly, this book again demonstrates that social inequality is a politically constructed choice, as is exemplified by the fiscal policies pursued by the urban elites in the early modern era. In both the northern and southern Low Countries, regressive taxes contributed to reproducing social inequalities. The frictions that arose from this system were considerable, hence the importance attached to more proportional (and even progressive) taxation under the short-lived experiments of the Calvinist Republics. Such conflicts also reveal the complex power play between social groups in urban society, and especially the intense yet varying political power exerted primarily by corporate organisations. While craft guilds generally suffered from a political loss of ground in the sixteenth century, even today 'civil society' is said to be a relatively powerful actor in Belgium and the Netherlands alike. In 2007-2008, the political leverage of the middle classes contributed to the protection of a social security that shielded the region from the worst effects of the financial crisis. Yet, these middle classes also disproportionately profit from tax and social welfare policies, a phenomenon commonly known as the 'Matthew effect' (Deleeck 1983), and they do so at the expense of the opportunities for the poor (Cantillon 2016, 250-255; Clycq Chapter 22). The essence of the Low Countries' paradox is perhaps that a river delta urbanisation contributed to policies of 'checks and balances' both between and within urban societies, while competition and cooperation were continuously leapfrogging each other. Yet, the social, cultural and ideological density of the urban middling sort that resulted from this process came at a cost. It often brought affluence, but it also drew strong lines of social and cultural demarcation between the urban middling sort and the people who fell outside it, such as the rural population, unskilled or low-skilled workers or various newcomers operating in the geographical, demographical, cultural and social periphery of urban society. Whether or not the problems some present-day migrant communities face in the urban environments are path-dependent on these age-old processes of inclusion and exclusion is far from clear, however. This question echoes to some extent the much-debated Polder-model myth in the Netherlands (Prak & Van Zanden 2013). Besides the teleological risk inherent in an interpretation that links centuries-old patterns of urbanisation to the social architecture of our society, such a general model would do little justice to the diversity of urban typologies and trajectories that have been revealed in this volume.

Our approach yielded a methodological contrast, indeed. On the one hand it increased the need for an in-depth contextualisation of social inequalities through case studies that look far beyond the processing of income proxies, urbanisation percentages, violence rates and other similar parameters that are sometimes lumped together in reductionist quanti-tative models. Indeed, historical and typological differences urge the researcher to tackle cases from a *sui generis* perspective with a wide variety of thematic and methodological perspectives. They probably also invite policy makers to cope with social challenges in a similar way: with a tailor-made approach. Yet, the need to tackle the individual city and to study it from an 'integrated social history' perspective, as Raymond Van Uytven and Wim Blockmans (1971) challenged us to do decades ago, was also offset by the need to zoom out and to look beyond the individual town. This book urges us to look at the multiple ways in which towns were connected both in an urban network and between town and countryside. Any claim on changing social inequality from the perspective of the individual urban settlement is doomed to be far-sighted. Instead, the extent to which divergent urban typologies and trajectories match the different regional agricultural systems of the Low Countries certainly deserves further scrutiny. The misfortune of the eighteenth-century Flemish peasant was intimately linked to the fortune of the urban rentier, who responded in gratitude by selling the industrious peasant his shit at a high price (De Graef Chapter 3). Yet, it is not only town-countryside dynamics that come into play: social inequalities were also forged in inter-urban asymmetries, as is evidenced by the thousands of poorly-paid labourers across the Low Countries who in the sixteenth century especially enriched the merchants in the commercial gateway of Antwerp.

The lure of an overarching argument putting the Low Countries at centre stage in an analysis of the interplay between urbanity and social inequality has been great. While raising a lot of doubts and questions, this book offers few definite answers. In the future, a more ambitious project will need to frame the multiple vectors creating social relationships in urban society in a more systematic way. In doing so, some under-explored dimensions (for instance health conditions, gender relations and consumption inequalities) would profit from preferential treatment. Furthermore, such a project would also require a comparative perspective, confronting different cities and time periods and their relation-ships with the wider regional and even international economy. Speaking of the latter, the urgency of a proper international comparative perspective in which the specificity of the Low Countries' paradox is really put to the test hardly needs to be advocated. Whether or not policy makers, economists and social scientists can immediately reap profits from such a historical exploration remains to be seen (De Munck Chapter 21). History as an academic discipline will never offer a mere toolkit for policy. The complexities revealed in this volume offer no prospects whatsoever for copy-and-paste answers and policies. Yet a nuanced historical understanding of the way in which cities and social inequalities historically interacted is indispensable for a fruitful public and policy debate.

References

Alfani, Guido, and Roberta Frigeni. 2016. "Inequality (Un)perceived: The Emergence of a Discourse on Economic Inequality from the Middle Ages to the Age of Revolution." *The Journal of European Economic History* 44 (1): 21-66.

Alfani, Guido, and Wouter Ryckbosch. 2016. "Growing apart in early modern Europe? A comparison of inequality trends in Italy and the Low Countries, 1500-1800." *Explorations in Economic History* 62: 143-153.

Alfani, Guido, and Francesco Ammannati. 2017. "Long-term trends in economic inequality: the case of the Florentine state, *c.* 1300-1800." *Economic History Review* 70 (4): 1072-1102.

Alfani, Guido, and Matteo Di Tullio. 2019. *The Lion's Share. Inequality and the Rise of the Fiscal State in Preindustrial Europe.* Cambridge Studies in Economic History. Cambridge: Cambridge University Press.

Attanasio, Orazio P., and Luigi Pistaferri. 2016. "Consumption Inequality." *Journal of Economic Perspectives* 30 (2): 3-28.

Baatsen, Inneke, Bruno Blondé, Julie De Groot and Isis Sturtewagen. 2018. "At home in the city: the dynamics of material culture." In *City and society in the Low Countries, 1100-1600*, ed. Bruno Blondé, Marc Boone and Anne-Laure Van Bruaene. 192-219. Cambridge: Cambridge University Press.

Barca, Fabrizio, Philip McCann and Andrés Rodriguez-Pose. 2012. "The case for regional development intervention: place-based versus place-neutral approaches." *Journal of Regional Science* 52 (1): 134-152.

Bardyn, Andrea. 2018a. *Women's fortunes. gender differences, property, and investment in late medieval Brabant.* Leuven: unpublished PhD thesis, KUL & University, of Antwerp.

Bardyn, Andrea. 2018b. "The gender distribution of immovable property ownership in late medieval Brussels (1356-1460)." *Continuity and Change* 33 (1): 29-57.

Beeckaert, Esther, and Eric Vanhaute. 2019. "Whose Famine? Regional Differences in Vulnerability and Resilience during the 1840s Potato Famine in Belgium." In *An Economic History of Famine Resilience*, ed. Jessica Dijkman and Bas van Leeuwen. 115-141. London: Routledge.

Blockmans, Wim, and Antheun Janse. 1999, *Showing Status: Representation of Social Positions in the Late Middle Ages.* Turnhout: Brepols.

Blockmans, Wim, I. De Meyer, J. Mertens, C. Pauwelyn and J. Vanderpijpen. 1971. *Studiën betreffende de sociale strukturen te Brugge, Kortrijk en Gent in de late 14de en 15de eeuw.* Heule: UGA.

Blondé, Bruno. 1987. *De sociale structuren en economische dynamiek van 's-Hertogenbosch, 1500-1550.* Vol. 74, *Bijdragen tot de geschiedenis van het Zuiden van Nederland.* Tilburg: Stichting Zuidelijk Historisch Contact.

Blondé, Bruno. 1996. "Economische groei en armoede in de pruikentijd. Het voorbeeld van de Brabantse steden, 1750-1780." In *Werkgelegenheid en inkomen. Referaten colloquium 30 jaar UFSIA*, ed. Carl Reyns. 343-358. Antwerp: Ufsia.

Blondé, Bruno. 1998. "Disparities in the development of the Brabantine urban network: urban centrality, town-countryside relationships, and transportation development." In *Recent Doctoral Research in Economic History*, ed. Clara Eugenia Núñez. 41-52. Madrid: Universidad nacional de educacion a distancia.

Blondé, Bruno. 2009. "Conflicting Consumption Models? The Symbolic Meaning of Possessions and Consumption amongst the Antwerp Nobility at the End of the Eighteenth Century." In *Fashioning Old and New. Changing Consumer Preferences in Europe (Seventeenth-Nineteenth Centuries)*, ed. Bruno Blondé et al. 61-79. Turnhout: Brepols.

Blondé, Bruno, and Raymond Van Uytven. 1996. "De smalle steden en het Brabantse stedelijke netwerk in de Late Middeleeuwen en de Nieuwe Tijd." *Lira Elegans* 6: 129-182.

Blondé, Bruno, and Ilja Van Damme. 2010. "Retail growth and consumer changes in a declining urban economy, Antwerp (1650-1750)." *The Economic History Review* 63 (3): 638-663.

Blondé, Bruno, and Jord Hanus. 2010. "Beyond Building Craftsmen. Economic Growth and Living Standards in the Sixteenth-Century Low Countries. The Case of 's-Hertogenbosch (1500-1550)." *European Review of Economic History* 14 (2): 179-207.

Blondé, Bruno, and Ilja Van Damme. 2013. "Early Modern Europe: 1500-1800." In *The Oxford Handbook of Cities in World History*, ed. Peter Clark. 240-257. Oxford: Oxford University Press.

Blondé, Bruno, and Wouter Ryckbosch. 2015. "In 'splendid isolation'. A comparative perspective on the historiographies of the 'material renaissance' and the 'consumer revolution.'" *History of Retailing and Consumption* 1 (2): 105-124.

Blondé, Bruno, and Jeroen Puttevils. 2020. "Antwerp in the Renaissance." In *Antwerp in the Renaissance*. Forthcoming. Turnhout: Brepols Publishers

Blondé, Bruno, Marc Boone and Anne-Laure Van Bruaene. 2018. *City and Society in the Low Countries (1100-1600)*. Cambridge: Cambridge University Press.

Blondé, Bruno, Frederik Buylaert, Jan Dumolyn, Jord Hanus and Peter Stabel. 2018. "Living together in the city: social relationships between norm & practice." In *City and Society in the Low Countries, 1100-1800*, ed. Bruno Blondé, Marc Boone and Anne-Laure Van Bruaene. 59-92. Cambridge: Cambridge University Press.

Cantillon, Bea, and L. Buysse. 2016. *De staat van de welvaartsstaat*. Leuven and The Hague: Acco.

Charruadas, Paulo, and Chloé Deligne. 2019. "Cities hiding the forests: wood supply, hinterlands and urban agency in the Southern Low Countries, 13th-18th centuries." In *Urbanizing Nature, Actors and Agency in the History of City/Nature Relationships*, ed. Tim Soens, Dieter Schott, Michael Toyka-Seid and Bert De Munck. 112-134. London: Routledge.

Childe, V. Gordon. 1950. "The Urban Revolution." *Town Planning Review*, 21: 3-17.

Corfield, P. 2013. "Cities in Time." In *Oxford Handbook to Cities in World History*, ed. Peter Clark. 828-846. Oxford: Oxford University Press.

Crouzet-Pavan, Elisabeth, and Elodie Lecuppre-Desjardin, eds. 2008. *Villes de Flandre et d'Italie (XIIIe-XVIe siècle). Les enseignements d'une comparaison*. Turnhout: Brepols.

Davis, M. 2005. *Planet of Slums*. London and New York: Verso.

De Schaepdrijver, Sophie. 1990. *Elites for the Capital? Foreign Migration to Mid-Nineteenth-Century Brussels*. Amsterdam: PDIS.

Decoster, André, Koen Dedobbeleer and Sebastiaan Maes. 2017. "Using fiscal data to estimate the evolution of top income shares in Belgium from 1990 to 2013." *Discussion paper series KU Leuven Faculty of Economics and Business*, DPS17.18.

De La Torre, Carlos. 2019. *Routledge Handbook of Global Populism*. London Routledge.

Denis, Britt. 2016. "In search of material practices: the nineteenth-century European domestic interior rehabilitated." *History of Retailing and Consumption*, 2:2, 97-112.

De Vries, Jan. 1984. *European Urbanization, 1500-1800*. London: Methuen.

De Vries, Jan. 2003. "Luxury in the Dutch Golden Age in Theory and Practice." In *Luxury in the Eighteenth Century. Debates, Desires and Delectable Goods*, ed. Maxine Berg and Elizabeth Eger. 41-56. Basingstoke: Palgrave Macmillan.

De Vries, Jan. 2008. *The Industrious Revolution. Consumer behavior and the household economy, 1650 to the present*. Cambridge: Cambridge University Press.

Dikötter, Frank. 2010. *Mao's great famine: the history of China's most devastating catastrophe, 1958-62*. London: Bloomsbury.

Engbersen, Godfried, Erik Snel and Monique Kremer, eds. 2017. *De val van de middenklasse? Het stabiele en kwetsbare midden*. The Hague, Wetenschappelijke Raad voor het Regeringsbeleid.

Faber, Jan A. 1980. "Inhabitants of Amsterdam and their possessions 1701-1710." In *Probate inventories. A new source for the historical study of wealth, material culture and agricultural development*, ed. Ad Van der Woude and Anton Schuurman. 149-156. Utrecht: HES.

Fjelde, Hanne, and Gudrun Østby. 2014. "Socioeconomic Inequality and Communal Conflict: A Disaggregated Analysis of Sub-Saharan Africa, 1990-2008." *International Interactions* 40, no. 5: 737-762.

Freedman, Paul. 1999. *Images of the medieval peasant*. Stanford, CA: Stanford University Press.

Glaeser, Edward L., Matt Resseger and Kristina Tobio. 2009. "Inequality in cities." *Journal of Regional Science* 49 (4): 617-646.

Haemers, Jelle, and Jan Dumolyn. 2013. "'Let each man carry on with his trade and remain silent'. Middle class ideology in the urban literature of the late medieval Low Countries." *Cultural and Social History* 10, no. 2: 169-189.

't Hart, Marjolein, and Michael Limberger. 2006. "Staatsmacht en stedelijke autonomie. Het geld van Antwerpen en Amsterdam (1500-1700)." *Tijdschrift voor sociale en economische geschiedenis* 3 (3): 36-72.

Hoffman, Philip T., David S. Jacks, Patricia A. Levin and Peter H. Lindert. 2002. "Real Inequality in Europe since 1500." *The Journal of Economic History* 62, no. 2: 322-355.

Hohenberg, Paul M., and Lynn Hollen Lees. 1985. *The making of Urban Europe, 1000-1950*. Cambridge, MA: Harvard University Press.

Janssens, Paul. 1990. "De achttiende eeuw: een lage maar zware belastingdruk." In *Drie eeuwen Belgische belastingen. Van contributies, controleurs en belastingconsulenten*, 37-122. Brussels: EHSAL. Fiscale Hogeschool Brussel.

Kaelble, Hartmut, and Mark Thomas. 1991. "Introduction." In *Income Distribution in Historical Perspective*, ed. Simon Brenner, Hartmut Kaelble and Mark Thomas. 1-56. Cambridge: Cambridge University Press.

Kint, A. 1996. "The Community of Commerce: Social Relations in Sixteenth-Century Antwerp." New York: unpublished PhD thesis, Columbia University.

Kint, P. 1989. *Prometheus aangevuurd door Demeter. De economische ontwikkeling van de landbouw in Oost-Vlaanderen, 1815-1850*. Amsterdam: VU Uitgeverij.

Kuznets, Simon. 1955. "Economic growth and income inequality." *American Economic Review* 45 (1): 1-28.

Lambrecht, Thijs, and Wouter Ryckbosch. Forthcoming. "Economic inequality in the Southern Low Countries during the late middle ages: a regional comparison." In *Economic inequalities in pre-industrial societies: causes and consequences*, ed. F. Ammanati. Florence: Florence University Press.

Lis, Catharina, and Hugo Soly. 1977. "Food consumption in Antwerp between 1807 and 1859: a contribution to the standard of living debate." *Economic History Review* 30 (3): 461-486.

Lis, Catharina, and Hugo Soly. 1979. Poverty and Capitalism in Pre-Industrial Europe. Bristol: The Harvester Press.

Lis, Catharina, and Guy Vanthemsche. 1995. "De sociale zekerheid in historisch perspectief." In *De sociale zekerheid verzekerd?*, ed. M. Despintin and M. Jegers. 23-69. Brussels: Scientific Publishers.

MacCulloch, Robert. 2005. "Income Inequality and the Taste for Revolution." *The Journal of Law & Economics* 48 (1): 93-123.

Marx, Ive, and Gerlinde Verbist. 2018. "Belgium, a poster child for inclusive growth?" In *Inequality and inclusive growth in rich countries: shared challenges and contrasting fortunes*, ed. Brian Nolan. 75-97. Oxford: Oxford University Press.

McKendrick, Neil. 1982. "The consumer revolution of eighteenth-century England." In *The birth of a consumer society: the commercialization of eighteenth-century England*, ed. Neil McKendrick, John Brewer and J. H. Plumb. 3-33. London: Europa Publications.

Mijnhardt, Wijnand. 2010. "Urbanization, culture and the Dutch origins of the European Enlightenment." *BMGN-Low Countries Historical Review*, 125 (2-3): 141-177.

Milanovic, Branko. 2016. *Global Inequality. A New Approach for the Age of Globalization.* Cambridge, MA: The Belknap Press of Harvard University Press.

Milanovic, Branko. 2018. "Towards an explanation of inequality in premodern societies: the role of colonies, urbanization, and high population density." *The Economic History Review* 71 (4): 1029-1047.

Morrisson, Cristian, and Wayne Snyder. 2000. "The income inequality of France in historical perspective." *European Review of Economic History* 4: 59-83.

Muchembled, Robert. 1978. *Culture populaire et culture des élites dans la France moderne (XVᵉ-XVIIIᵉ siècles): essai.* Paris: Flammarion.

Neves, Pedro C., Oscar Afonso and Sandra T. Silva. 2016. "A Meta-Analytic Reassessment of the Effects of Inequality on Growth." *World Development* 78: 386-400.

Piketty, Thomas. 2001. *Les hauts revenus en France au XXᵉ siècle.* Paris : Bernard Grasset.

Piketty, Thomas. 2013. *Le Capital au XXIᵉ siècle.* Paris: Seuil.

Pirenne, Henri. 1927. *Les villes du Moyen Age: essai d'histoire économique et sociale.* Brussels: Lamertin.

Prak, Maarten. 2005. *The Dutch Republic in the Seventeenth Century. The Golden Age.* Cambridge: Cambridge University Press.

Prak, Maarten, and Jan Luiten Van Zanden. 2013. *Nederland en het poldermodel. Sociaal-economische geschiedenis van Nederland, 1000-2000.* Amsterdam: Bert Bakker.

Royuela, Vincente, Paolo Veneri and Raul Ramos. 2014. *Income Inequality, Urban Size and Economic Growth in OECD Regions.* OECD Regional Development Working Papers 2014/10. Paris: OECD.

Ryckbosch, Wouter. 2012. *A consumer revolution under strain? Consumption, wealth and status in eighteenth-century Aalst (Southern Netherlands).* Antwerp: unpublished PhD thesis, University of Antwerp and Ghent University.

Ryckbosch, Wouter. 2015. "Economic inequality and growth before the industrial revolution: the case of the Low Countries (fourteenth to ninenteenth centuries)." *European Review of Economic History* 20 (1): 1-22.

Scholliers, Peter. 1996. *Wages, Manufacturers and Workers in the Nineteenth-Century Factory: The Voortman Cotton Mill in Ghent.* New York and London: Berg Publishers.

Scholliers, Peter. 2008. Food culture in Belgium. London: Greenwood Press.

Scholliers, Peter. 2014. *Geschiedenis van de ongelijkheid.* Berchem: EPO.

Segers, Yves. 2001. "Oysters and rye bread: Polarising Living Standards in Flanders, 1800-1860." *European Review of Economic History* 5 (3): 301-336.

Segers, Yves. 2003. *Economische groei en levensstandaard. Particuliere consumptie en voedselverbruik in België, 1800-1913.* ICAG Studies. Leuven: Leuven University Press.

Simmel, Georg. 1903. "Die Großstädte und das Geistesleben." In *Die Grosstadt. Vorträge und Aufsätze zur Städteausstellung*, ed. Theodor Petermann. 185-206. Dresden: Gehe Stiftung (*The Metropolis and Mental Life*. Repr. London: Sage, 1997).

Simmel, Georg. 1957. "Fashion." *The American Journal of Sociology*, 62 (6): 541-558.

Soens, Tim. 2011. "Floods and money. Funding drainage and flood control in coastal Flanders (13th-16th centuries)." *Continuity and Change*, 26 (3): 333-365.

Soens, Tim. Forthcoming. "Urban Agriculture and Urban Food Provisioning in pre-1850 Europe: towards a Research Agenda." *Jahrbuch für Geschichte des ländlichen Raumes/Rural History Yearbook*, 16.

Soly, Hugo. 1988. "Social Aspects of Structural Changes in the Urban Industries of Eighteenth-Century Brabant and Flanders." In *The Rise and Decline of Urban Industries in Italy and in the Low Countries (Late Middle Ages–Early Modern Times)*, ed. Herman Van der Wee. 241-260. Leuven: Leuven University Press.

Stabel, Peter. 2008. "Composition et recomposition des réseaux urbains des Pays-Bas au Moyen Âge." In *Villes de Flandre et d'Italie (XIIIe-XVIe siècle). Les enseignements d'une comparaison*, ed. Elisabeth Crouzet-Pavan & Ellodie Lecuppre-Desjardin. 29-63. Turnhout: Brepols Publishers.

Stabel, Peter. 1997. *Dwarfs among giants: the Flemish urban network in the Late Middle Ages.* Leuven: Garant.

Stabel, Peter. Forthcoming. *A Capital of Fashion. Guilds and Economic Change in Late Medieval Bruges.*

Stiglitz, Joseph E. 2013. *The price of inequality.* London: Penguin Books.

Sweezy, Paul M., and Maurice Dobb. 1950. "The transition from feudalism to capitalism." *Science & Society* 14 (2): 134-167.

Thoen, Erik. 2004. "'Social Agrosystems' as an Economic Concept to Explain Regional Differences. An Essay Taking the Former County of Flanders as an Example (Middle Ages-19th. Century)." In *Landholding and Land Transfer in the North Sea Area (Late Middle Ages-19th Century)*, ed. Bas J. P. van Bavel and Peter Hoppenbrouwers. 47-66. Turnhout: Brepols.

United Nations, Department of Economic and Social Affairs. 2020. *World Social Report 2020. Inequality in a Rapidly Changing World.* New York: United Nations.

Van Bavel, Bas. 2016. *The Invisible Hand? How market economies have emerged and declined since AD 500.* Oxford: Oxford University Press.

Van Bavel, Bas, Daniel Curtis and Tim Soens. 2019. "Economic inequality and institutional adaptation in response to flood hazards: a historical analysis." *Ecology and Society* 23(4): art. 30.

Van Cruyningen, Piet. 2017. "Sharing the cost of dike maintenance in the south-western Netherlands: Comparing 'calamitous polders' in three 'states', 1715-1795." *Environment and History* 23 (3): 363-383.

Van Damme, Dirk. 1990. "Onderstandswoonst, sedentarisering en stad-platteland-tegenstellingen. Evolutie en betekenis van de wetgeving op de onderstands woonst in België (einde achttiende tot einde negentiende eeuw)." *Belgisch Tijdschrift Nieuwste Geschiedenis* 21 (3-4): 483-534.

Van der Wee, Herman. 1971. "The Economy as a Factor in the Revolt of the Southern Netherlands." *Acta Historica Neerlandica* 5: 52-67.

Van der Wee, Herman. 1988. "Industrial Dynamics and the Process of Urbanization and De-urbanization in the Low Countries from the Late Middle Ages to the Eighteenth Century. A synthesis." In *The Rise and Decline of Urban Industries in Italy and in the Low Countries (late Middle Ages-Early Modern Times)*, ed. Herman Van der Wee. 307-381. Leuven: Leuven University Press.

Van Dijck, Maarten F. 2005. "Het verenigingsleven op het Hagelandse platteland. Sociale polarisatie en middenveldparticipatie in de 17e en 18e eeuw." *Tijdschrift voor Sociaal-Economische Geschiedenis* 2 (2): 81-108.

Vanhaute, Eric. 1999. "Het debat dat er geen was: sociale stratificatie in de geschiedschrijving." In *Docendo discimus: liber amicorum Romain van Eenoo*. 229-240. Ghent: Academia Press.

Vanhaute, Eric. 2007. "'So worthy an example to Ireland'. The subsistence and industrial crisis of 1845-1850 in Flanders." In *When the potato failed. Causes and effects of the "last" European subsistance crisis, 1845-1850*. Richard Paping, Eric Vanhaute and Cormac O'Grada, ed. 123-148. Turnhout: Brepols.

Van Uytven, Raymond, and Wim Blockmans. 1971. "De noodzaak van een geïntegreerde sociale geschiedenis. Het voorbeeld van de Zuidnederlandse steden in de late middeleeuwen." *Tijdschrift voor Geschiedenis* 84: 276-290.

Van Zanden, Jan Luiten. 1994. "Tracing the Beginning of the Kuznets Curve: Western Europe during the Early Modern Period." *The Economic History Review* 48 (4): 643-664.

Vermoesen, Reinoud, 2015. "Boerende stedelingen of verstedelijkte boeren. Een verkennend onderzoek naar Urban Farming in vroegmodern Antwerpen." *Tijdschrift voor geschiedenis* 128 (4): 533-553.

Wilkinson, Richard, and Kate Picket. 2010. *The Spirit Level. Why Equality is Better for Everyone.* London: Penguin Books.

Winter, Anne. 2013. "Settlement Law and Rural-Urban Relief Transfers in Nineteenth-Century Belgium: A Case Study on Migrants' Access to Relief in Antwerp." In *Migration, Settlement and Belonging in Europe, 1500-1930s: Comparative Perspectives*, ed. Steven King and Anne Winter. 228-249. New York: Berghahn.

PART II

The Urbanisation of Inequality

JIM VAN DER MEULEN

Get Rich and Try Dyeing

Cloth Production and Social Inequality in Town and Countryside (Sixteenth Century)*

Introduction

This chapter discusses a case-study that sheds light on the issue of social inequality in the pre-industrial Low Countries; more specifically in the county of Flanders during the sixteenth century. The analysis revolves around a comparison of three textile industries in relatively 'new' Flemish production centres: Armentières in the castellany of Lille, Hondschoote in the castellany of Bergues, and Nieuwkerke in the castellany of Bailleul. These textile centres are suitable candidates for a comparison because of their different institutional profiles, and because in each case inequality played a different role in the local cloth industry. As we shall see, only two of these centres witnessed social polarisation within the entrepreneurial community, and in only one of those cases does the evidence suggest an interrelationship between social polarisation and industrial decline. Thus, I will argue that social cohesion was a factor in the proper functioning of pre-industrial industries, but that its relative importance was contingent upon institutional factors. That being so, the impending analysis largely follows the work of Bas van Bavel, emphasising the connection between rising social polarisation and economic decline (van Bavel 2016).

However, an additional, methodological, aim of this contribution is to explore the subject of social inequality from a combined socio-economic and cultural perspective. The goal is to merge the current historiographical focus on inequality with the more recent research agenda on the cultural features of economic development set by Joel Mokyr (2018). Following his example, our analysis partly explores the impact of cultural-ideological aspects on local economies. This is not exactly a novel idea. In his seminal 1990 work on institutional arrangements and economic performance, Douglass North already pointed to the role of culture in shaping and maintaining norms of behaviour relating to market exchange (North 1999). Beyond institutional economics, there is a much older tradition

* I would like to thank Sam Geens, Bruno Blondé and Peter Stabel for commenting on an earlier draft of this contribution. I also wish to thank Kate Eliott for her educational corrections to the English. Any remaining mistakes are of course my own. This chapter was written while I was working on the ERC project *STATE – Lordship and the Rise of the State in Western Europe, 1300-1600* at Ghent University.

Jim van der Meulen • Ghent University

Inequality and the City in the Low Countries (1200-2020), ed. by Bruno BLONDÉ, Sam GEENS, Hilde GREEFS, Wouter RYCKBOSCH, Tim SOENS & Peter STABEL, SEUH 50 (Turnhout, 2020), pp. 45-62.

DOI 10.1484/M.SEUH-EB.5.120437

about the impact of historical 'moral' contexts on economic performance (Polanyi 1944; Thompson 1971). But economic historians have often been reluctant to incorporate these factors into their studies (a notable exception is Greif 2006). Mokyr's *A Culture of Growth. The Origins of the Modern Economy* lays promising groundwork for a *rapprochement* between the fields of economics and cultural history. In the book the author connects modern economic growth in the West to specific cultural features that emerged in Europe in the period between 1500 and 1800. A central role is given to 'cultural entrepreneurs' such as Francis Bacon and Isaac Newton. They shaped an intellectual climate, or a 'market for ideas', favouring innovations and progress. This cultural climate supposedly gained critical mass in Europe during the seventeenth century and was a crucial step towards the early modern Enlightenment(s) and Industrial Revolution (Mokyr 2013). In this chapter I want to examine what Mokyr's cultural-ideological focus can offer to empirical case studies of social inequality in pre-industrial societies.

To do so, the present chapter examines the relationship between ideals of entrepreneurship and the economic 'reality' of unequal entrepreneurial opportunities in sixteenth-century Flanders. Instead of the likes of Bacon and Newton, the focus will be on more conventional, economic entrepreneurs. One part of this examination consists of determining to what extent these entrepreneurs operated on an equal footing, using quantitative data. Another part consists of approaching them as 'buyers' on the market for ideas such as it existed in the Low Countries at this time. I have argued elsewhere that concerns for communal solidarity and the 'Common Good' were vital aspects in holding together the entrepreneurial community in the Flemish cloth centre of Nieuwkerke between the fourteenth and mid-sixteenth centuries (van der Meulen 2018). Here, Nieuwkerke will be compared to two other cloth centres. I wish to demonstrate how contemporary ideology interacted with economic practice in the textile trade.

The main protagonists are the so-called clothiers (*drapiers*): the key characters within these cloth industries in terms of entrepreneurship. Simply put, clothiers were the people who owned the fabric and oversaw its production process. In practice, their economic activities could range from hands-on involvement in manufacture to marketing the finished cloth wholesale on international markets (Lee 2018). These practical differences within one and the same occupational group, tied to differences in individual affluence, were instrumental in fomenting frictions over economic opportunities. This makes the clothier a suitable candidate to use to study (ideas about) social inequality within the late medieval economies of small urban production centres.

Thus, the goal of this chapter is threefold: first, to examine how sixteenth-century Flemish cloth entrepreneurs could partake in the market for ideas, specifically in relation to inequality; secondly, to gauge how these culture-specific ideas may have influenced social tensions within the three cloth industries in question; and, finally, to assess the impact of these ideological factors by supplementing the analysis with actual, quantifiable rates of unequal economic opportunity. The results suggest that the social and economic impact of pre-industrial ideology differed according to locally determined institutional frameworks. In other words, the present chapter supports Mokyr's notion that pre-Enlightenment ideology may have led European societies to 'activities that were not conducive to economic growth'. But it challenges his hypothesis that ideology was 'an autonomous force' in this regard (Mokyr 2018, 9).

'Urban middle class' ideas about entrepreneurship in sixteenth-century Flanders

The first half of the sixteenth century saw economic, political and cultural changes in the cities of the Low Countries, which were reflected in contemporary ideas about entrepreneurship and commerce. Crucial to the present discussion were the religiously laden but wider societal tensions that culminated in the Iconoclastic Fury of 1566 and the Dutch Revolt. As Peter Arnade put it: 'Iconoclasm began in the rough-and-tumble drapery centers of Flanders' Westkwartier … where craftsmen and laborers embraced Calvinism, imbuing it with their local concerns' (Arnade 2008, 125). The *Westkwartier* or 'Western Quarter' was a sub-region of Flanders, in the hinterland of the city of Ypres. Textile manufacture flourished in the countryside of this region in particular, taking off in the fourteenth century and petering out only in the later 1500s. Yet their industrial efflorescence caused some villages to develop population levels and economic orientations perhaps sooner labelled 'urban'. The cloth towns central to this study fall into that category. Two of them were located in the Western Quarter: Nieuwkerke, the largest settlement and manufacturing centre in the castellany of Bailleul, which produced relatively high-quality woollens; and Hondschoote, Flanders's prime example of a late medieval boomtown, producing light textiles of the variety called *sayetterie*. The third cloth town under scrutiny here is Armentières, which was located just outside the Western Quarter, in the Lys (or *Leie*, in Dutch) river area. The only one of the three centres officially to become a town, Armentières also produced the highest-grade fabrics of the three, made from a combination of English and Spanish wool (see Map 1).

In the Low Countries, those engaging in commercial enterprises such as the marketing of fabrics belonged to an ideologically ambiguous category. Merchants had traditionally been perceived as morally questionable figures, but their social esteem had risen in the period leading up to 1566. Accordingly, the wealthier Netherlandish cloth entrepreneurs had begun to identify with the mercantile occupation (calling themselves *coopman*). But, as we are about to see, clothiers at the lower end of the economic spectrum expressly identified with the poor or 'common' workers of their industry. The origins and development of this collective identification of late medieval artisans with humility and poverty – among other traits – are discussed in depth by Peter Stabel and Anke De Meyer (Chapter 15).

In the sixteenth century, tensions within the middle class between mercantile and craft identity show up in cultural expressions of the time. So, in 1561, the city of Antwerp organised a competition between the typically Netherlandish literary-cum-theatrical associations known as 'Chambers of Rhetoric', inviting Chambers from Antwerp itself and from the wider region. The organisers made clear from the start that the central theme of this theatrical event would be the social benefits of the merchant, which had to be addressed in some way in each Chamber's Prologue. The main intention was to instil Antwerp's population with the belief that the merchant was the linchpin of the city's economy. However, some associations took a more critical view. One of the Prologues even contained the vivid statement: 'Like rust on iron, as the moth harms, eats and nibbles through cloth, so merchants altogether damage the community' (Silvius 1562, 103; Vandommele 2011, 302-305). The literary competition of 1561 reflects attempts by members of Antwerp's commercial elite to convince the wider public of the pivotal role of trade in

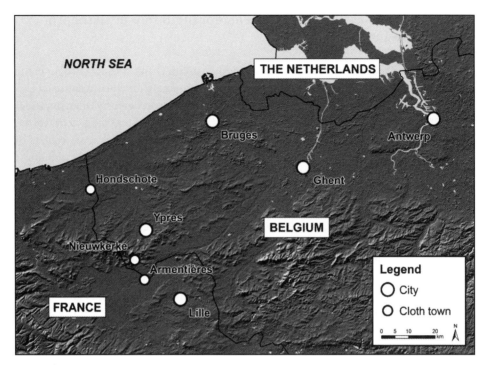

Map 1. The three cloth centres of Armentières, Hondschoote and Nieuwkerke in their modern locations. Made by Iason Jongepier, GIStorical Antwerp/Hercules Foundation

public welfare, even peddling an image of the city as a 'community of commerce' (Kint 1996). Central to a positive or negative judgment of trade was the extent to which merchants brought opportunities, not merely to fill their own pockets, but to benefit urban society as a whole. The first section of this chapter addresses the sixteenth century's tensions over this idea of inequality between rich merchant-entrepreneurs and their humbler fellows. The question here is how Flemish cloth entrepreneurs were able to buy, and in some cases resell, these notions about commerce versus community on the market for ideas.

The period between the end of the fifteenth century and the third quarter of the sixteenth was marked by swiftly rising literacy rates in Flanders and the Low Countries in general (Decavele 1992). Maintaining the analogy of a market for ideas, literate consumers had greater spending budgets, and their growing numbers increased the rate of exchange. The advent of the printing press gave rise to a wider distribution of 'books on the business arts' and literary culture alike (Eisenstein 1979). Quantifications of literacy rates for this period remain difficult, but the textile-producing settlements of Flanders scored particularly highly in this regard (Van Bruaene 2008). To take the cloth centre of Nieuwkerke as an example: it sported a Latin school, at least 26 known students at the University of Leuven between 1485 and 1569, and no fewer than two literary Chambers of Rhetoric. Several of Nieuwkerke's university students were probably clothiers or stemmed from families active in the cloth industry (Schillings 1954; 1966). This is perhaps unsurprising, since to read, write and cipher were useful abilities for entrepreneurs who wanted to keep some form of account of their business dealings. Moreover, although no information survives about who were active in Nieuwkerke's two literary associations, it is highly likely that clothiers comprised part of their memberships, too.

The evidence also suggests that master artisans and cloth entrepreneurs were active buyers, some even resellers, on the market for ideas in sixteenth-century Flanders. One of the better known Flemish Rhetoricians was Cornelis Everaert, who was active in the city of Bruges from the early to mid-1500s (Hüsken 2005). Everaert was a dyer and fuller by trade, just as one of his prominent predecessors, Anthonis de Roovere, had been a stone mason. Their plays breathe what Jelle Haemers and Jan Dumolyn have called the ideology of an 'urban middle class', consisting of those wedged in between wage earners and the patrician elite. This ideology hinged on the maintenance of social order, harmony between different trade groups, and the protection of political privileges (Haemers and Dumolyn 2013). Mokyr holds that the influence of the cultural climate on the economy takes precedence over the role of institutions (Mokyr 2013). But in the sixteenth-century Low Countries, the corporate framework largely shaped the platform for ideological exchange – although this runs the risk of becoming a chicken or egg dilemma, since one could argue that these institutions in turn derived from 'corporate' ideology, and so on (Dumolyn 2014).

Indeed, cultural-ideological interactions in this period cannot be entirely disentangled from exchanges of the economic kind. For example, corporate bodies of artisans in the cities of the Low Countries took part in public ceremonies intended to forge closer bonds between members of the urban community (Liddy and Haemers 2013). This connection between economic practice and ideological exchange is further illustrated by an account book belonging to the broker-hosteller Wouter Ameide, who conducted his business in Bruges in the late fifteenth and early sixteenth centuries (Stabel 1995b). The book consists almost exclusively of trade transactions brokered by Ameide in the early 1500s between international merchants and Flemish entrepreneurs. Among the latter are some clothiers from Nieuwkerke, as well as entrepreneurs from the Lys river area, near the town of Armentières. However, in two different places the ledger also contains crude notes about a literary event held in July of 1517, in which one of Nieuwkerke's Chambers of Rhetoric participated (SAB, Series 305, Journaal B, f. 200v°, 227v°). This is the first recorded instance of Nieuwkerke's presence at a rhetorical competition, in a ledger belonging to a broker who had commercial dealings with entrepreneurs from that cloth centre, and all this during the very period when Cornelis Everaert was promulgating his middle class ideology in the city of Bruges and beyond. It is circumstantial evidence, but still makes a case for the blending of commerce with ideological exchange, as well as the active involvement of the middling sorts from Flemish cloth centres in the market for ideas.

This sixteenth-century market for ideas will have been open to most cloth artisans and clothiers – although, as Stabel and De Meyer's contribution in this volume makes clear, the ideas and their channels of distribution largely hinged on masculine identities and contacts between male artisans (Chapter 15). As an itinerant business, the textile trade stimulated interactions between people from different towns, different countries, different religious persuasions. Clothiers from Armentières, Hondschoote and Nieuwkerke often travelled to and from various cities in the Low Countries to sell fabrics at fairs (van der Meulen 2018). With the establishment of an all-year-round market in the city of Antwerp, these business trips *avant la lettre* were monopolised more and more by the wealthier entrepreneurs, who could afford to be away from their workshops for extended periods of time (Stabel 2000). But the urban network stimulated frequent movements of people from one place to the next, thereby democratising the market for ideas. Even the poorer cloth entrepreneurs and artisans living in smaller villages could meet with foreign merchants who travelled to the Flemish countryside (e.g. RAG, Raad van Vlaanderen, Enkwesten, No. 3756). These economic interactions then facilitated the exchange of ideas, even contributing to religious dissent. As Natalie Zemon Davis put it: 'Protestant ideas were flowing with the fleece' (Davis 1983, 48).

Indeed, religious dissent is the most visible sign of ideological tension in sixteenth-century Flanders. Tellingly, the cloth industries of the smaller towns were hotbeds of Protestantism. During the 1560s, the attorney-general of Flanders actually used the records of Hondschoote's textile trade as his point of departure for the persecution of local heretics. At the same time, the warehouse and shop rented by the entrepreneurial corporation of Nieuwkerke in the city of Antwerp served as a hostel for Protestant sympathisers (Decavele 1975; Marnef 1996). In Nieuwkerke itself a native of the Flemish cloth town of Kortrijk was executed for his 'Lutheran' persuasion in 1529-30. His last words, as recorded by a judicial scribe, suggest that he must have read the 'forbidden books' found on his person, because he purportedly shouted: 'My lords, please do not give alms for … a Requiem Mass for my soul, for I require none!' (ADN, B Series, No. 5669, f. 6v°, 8v°). This Protestant sentiment apparently found a following in Nieuwkerke, because the only Rhetoricians' play to survive for that cloth centre, written a decade after the execution, contains a very similar passage (Erné and Van Dis 1982, vol. 1, 202):

> *Evangelical teacher:*
> Yea, and do not think that we may expect to benefit from
> Our works and merits (take this to heart),
> These costly funerals or testaments.
> Nor place hope in other people's long prayers,
> By monks or nuns, no matter the frequency;
> Nor perpetual masses. These things
> Cannot offer true consolation.

The printing of this and all other plays performed at the same 1539 literary competition in Ghent was subsequently proscribed by the authorities.

Nevertheless, the 'civic religion' in the towns of the Low Countries in this period, as elsewhere, shows a lot of continuity in its entrenchment in late medieval corporate ideology (Marnef and Van Bruaene 2018; Duffy 1992). Accordingly, competitions among the Chambers of Rhetoric sought to create a 'strong fiction of equality', both between members of associations from different settlements and between people belonging to the same occupational group. Still, in practice, there was also a lot of strife between Chambers, and the plays sometimes reveal an acute sense of wider societal tensions (Van Bruaene 2006). Everaert, for example, frequently discusses the harmful influence of foreign wars on the urban Flemish economy, the plight of the poor artisan, and the economic decline of the city of Bruges in general. As with the above-quoted judicial record from 1529-30, there is a certain transtextual affinity between the plays of these Netherlandish middle-class playwrights and the official records of internal strife within the cloth industries. Everaert's plays regularly feature allegorical characters with names like Common Trade (*Ghemeene Neerynghe*) and Poor Community (*Scamel Ghemeente*), portraying interactions between employers and wage workers characteristic of the late medieval urban economy (Haemers and Dumolyn 2013). Similar phrases appear, sometimes literally, in documented struggles over inequality within the cloth industries, which increased from the second quarter of the sixteenth century. During a conflict between some clothiers of Hondschoote in 1580, for example, the selfish actions of a small clique of merchant-entrepreneurs were offset against the interests of the 'poor community' (*schamel ghemeente*) (De Sagher et al. 1961, 536).

The discursive similarities between these legal industrial documents and literary texts fit with the tendency of Flemish urban rebels to use allegorical expressions in their political pleas (Dumolyn and Haemers 2012). Much like the plays of the literary associations, the industrial records of the Flemish cloth industries adopt a rhetoric emphasising the primacy of collective interests before those of the individual. On the one hand, this is self-evident because these documents were usually produced by representatives of corporate bodies of entrepreneurs. Like craft guilds proper, the mercantile-cum-industrial associations of clothiers – called *draperies* – held themselves out as embodying the local community (Dumolyn 2014). On the other hand, the phrasing suggests there were increasing cracks in these collectives from around the middle of the sixteenth century. The rhetoric casts blame on the selfish actions of a few wealthy entrepreneurs who tried 'to fill their own pockets' (*elcken om syn buerse te vullen*) (De Sagher et al. 1961, 360-61). In doing so, the industrial records echoed the literary *topos* of the covetous merchant, or 'moth in the cloth', favoured by urban middle-class Rhetoricians of the period.

Yet, although the clothiers of Armentières, Hondschoote and Nieuwkerke essentially bought similar ideologies, polarisation did not affect these settlements' cloth industries equally. To be sure, religious rebellion burst out in all three after 1566, indirectly contributing to serious economic setbacks for the Flemish textile trade in general. Like Hondschoote and Nieuwkerke, Armentières was purportedly 'infested' with Protestants and played a leading role in the Iconoclastic Fury (Duplessis 1991, 177, 211). But popular uprisings did not occur in any of the three textile centres until this ideological movement took off. When it did, the iconoclast crowd in both cities and countryside largely consisted of textile artisans. While sacking the city of Ypres, one of the leading rebels is reported to have shouted: 'Within three days, the journeymen and poor will be as rich as the masters and the wealthy!' (Arnade 2008, 131). This strongly suggests that religious ideas went hand in hand with socio-economic concerns, although which of the two was decisive remains hard to say (Marnef 1996, chapter 10).

Some cloth centres are more equal than others: Armentières and Nieuwkerke

Unlike in Armentières and Hondschoote, however, in Nieuwkerke industrial decline had already set in during the decade-and-a-half *before* the religious turmoil of 1566. In this same period, Nieuwkerke's clothiers were continuously quarrelling over their industrial regulations, with frequent references to the ideology of the Common Good. This loss of social cohesion shows a correlation with the industry's overall downturn: Nieuwkerke's output began to drop after 1550, coinciding with the most extended factional struggle recorded for the industry. Then again, the mere occurrence of conflicts between members of the entrepreneurial community on its own was not enough to extinguish an industry. The *sayetterie* of Hondschoote encountered similar strife over regulations (in 1557), but this did not coincide with an economic downturn; quite the contrary: the years leading up to the iconoclasm were marked by the highest trade volumes of the century (van der Meulen 2018; De Sagher et al. 1961, 478-496). Meanwhile, Armentières saw no recorded frictions over inequality within its entrepreneurial ranks. The clothiers in this town had their share of antagonism over regulations, but they always faced representatives of the artisans – usually the dyers – rather than their fellows. As in Hondschoote, Armentières's cloth industry remained more stable than that of Nieuwkerke during the 1560s and 1570s (De Sagher et al. 1951, 99-100). The question then becomes why ideology and social cohesion may have had a greater bearing on industrial performance in some places than in others.

I would argue that the answer lies in the institutional framework of the industry in question, specifically in its capacity to deal with (demographic) expansion. For its lack of a formal urban charter, Nieuwkerke's population grew explosively, from a little over 1,000 people in the second half of the fifteenth century to an 'urban' level of around 5,000 in 1550. Based on church records that are no longer available, an eighteenth-century priest even claimed that the village had had 11,000 communicants in the mid-sixteenth century, but that seems outrageously high (Geldhof 1974, 21). Whatever the exact number of inhabitants, the village probably lacked the proper infrastructure to accommodate all these new people. Indeed, some clothiers expressed a reluctance to let their children work outside the house, 'where they often learn the way of the tavern, keep bad company, wander around at night, play at dice, whore around, and utter blasphemies' (Decavele 1975, 561). Armentières saw a similar increase in its population between about 1500 and 1550. In 1533, the clothiers of Armentières claimed that their number had grown by 'half or a little bit more' since as recently as 1529 (De Sagher et al. 1951, 242). But the town was probably better equipped to deal with the expansion. In response to the 'ragrandissement et ampliation d'icelle ville', the government for instance enclosed an extra 20 *bonniers* of land in 1509 and constructed a new street in 1538 (AIA 1877, D Series, No. 52).

Moreover, in Armentières the different trade groups formed their own craft corporations, which guarded their memberships to some degree. This existence of craft guilds in Armentières was also an important factor in maintaining social equality within each trade group. Together with citizenship, guild membership was fundamental in creating a sense of responsibility to the wider community. Concomitantly, the urban corporations reinforced notions of equality to all, or at least to those fortunate enough to be granted membership (Liddy and Haemers 2013). On the industrial level, the 'corporative spirit' in Armentières led to an abundance of amendments to the regulations, which constitute most of the source material for this period (De Sagher et al. 1951, 99-100). This pushback by the craft guilds probably stimulated internal cohesion between the cloth entrepreneurs. After all, the clothiers had to form a united front if they were to ensure that the artisans' demands did not grow to such proportions that they became detrimental to profit margins. Moreover, the existence of craft corporations meant that separations between occupational groups were more clearly defined, as well as more successfully guarded. In general, the bylaws of Armentières's industry evince a preoccupation with collective interests over individual entrepreneurship that would make the Rhetoricians proud. For example, clothiers were not allowed freely to rent out or sell any unused looms that were in their possession, nor to deny these surplus tools to their fellows, 'because these looms shall be freely accessible (*communes*) to everybody in their turn, like all the other looms of the town' (De Sagher et al. 1951, 108). This vital role of skilled master-artisans may have contributed to middle-class ideas about equal opportunities seeping into the rulebook of the town's textile industry.

Armentières's greater level of institutionalised division of labour compared to those of Nieuwkerke and Hondschoote was partly a consequence of its costlier product. The more expensive the raw material, the more skill, or 'human capital', was required in handling it, and the greater the bargaining power of those who possessed this know-how (De Munck 2019). This also explains the superior position of the dyers' guild in particular, as dyeing was a highly technical skill, and one of the final – make or break – stages of textile production. Indeed, even in Nieuwkerke and Hondschoote, where the dyers were not formally organised into guilds, the dyeing process was a bone of contention between entrepreneurs. Rich clothiers tried to set their own workers on to it, but the smaller operators continuously strove to guard the independence of this craft stage. That they were usually successful suggests that even unincorporated dyers had great bargaining power (see below).

When we compare the limited quantitative evidence on entrepreneurial opportunities in Armentières and Nieuwkerke in this period, we find that inequality was indeed less pronounced in the former textile centre. The data for Nieuwkerke are based on one booklet listing the names of all clothiers whose fabrics passed official inspection for the accounting year of October 1564-September 1565 (ARB, Acquits de Lille, No. 1367/33). A comparable source, of ulnage accounts – records of the officials charged with measuring pieces of cloth – is available for Armentières, albeit for a period of merely a few months: February-May 1575 (De Sagher et al. 1951, 459-462). Based on the production outputs in these years, the rate of inequality was far higher in Nieuwkerke than it was in Armentières: The Gini coefficient for Nieuwkerke's industry in 1564-1565 was 0.54, while that of Armentières was 0.27 in early 1575. Note that in both cases the poll moment occurred at a time when the respective industries were just past their peak, but still prospering. Given the sharp difference in their rates of inequality at that stage, it is perhaps unsurprising that the poorer clothiers of Nieuwkerke had begun to raise concern over unequal opportunities on several occasions during the 1550s.

However, the entrepreneurial corporation of Armentières was clearly more exclusive than that of Nieuwkerke. More than half of Nieuwkerke's clothiers in 1564-65 had an output of fewer than 16 pieces of cloth for an entire year, whereas 83 per cent of clothiers in Armentières reached the same output in about three months in 1575! Meanwhile, the total production outputs of the two settlements did not differ much in the relevant years (both being in the neighbourhood of 10,000 per annum). This means that the higher production rates of the Armentières clothiers cannot be laid entirely at the feet of their industry's greater overall trade volume. Rather, the corporative organisation of the various manufacturing stages in the town meant that the entire production process had become strictly choreographed by the early sixteenth century. Armentières's industrial ordinance of 1510 is illustrative in this regard. It laid down the exact recipe for the proportions of various wool types in the production of 'ultra-fine' cloth (*oultrefin*), the town's signature fabric (De Sagher et al. 1951, 102-103). Because each clothier was allowed to operate with only a fixed amount of wool (the *taulx*), this regulation not only ensured the uniformity of the product, but also created a production ceiling per enterprise, thereby encouraging equality across the board. But these same statutory production quotas prevented the participation of minor operators who could not afford the very expensive (English) wool.

In Nieuwkerke a 'freer' form of entrepreneurship reigned. For one thing, access to raw materials and craft tools was not restricted in the same degree as in Armentières. Although this meant that rich entrepreneurs enjoyed a competitive advantage, it also gave manufacturers the opportunity to dabble in occasional entrepreneurship. This paradox probably explains the no fewer than 100 clothiers of Nieuwkerke with a production output of below five pieces in 1564-65; more than the total of 93 entrepreneurs active in Armentières in early 1575 (van der Meulen 2018). Back in 1462, the clothiers' corporation of Nieuwkerke had passed a bylaw stating that clothiers were allowed to combine their enterprises with only one manufacturing stage (either weaving, fulling or shearing). The exception was dyeing, which clothiers were expressly forbidden to have any part of. Yet, during the second quarter of the sixteenth century, the wealthier entrepreneurs had gradually whittled down these restrictions. Most conflicts about social inequality in this period revolved around attempts by the top clothiers to conduct the various production stages within their own workshops or to strike up illicit partnerships to the same effect. The Chamber of Accounts in the city of Lille – the official body charged with overseeing Nieuwkerke's industry after 1532 – upheld restrictions on how many and which craft stages were open to entrepreneurs and their partners. These rules slackened gradually, so that, where in 1462 clothiers had been allowed to engage in only one craft stage, by 1553 they were permitted to oversee three craft stages. Dyeing was still prohibited, though. This suggests that, despite there being no dyers' guild in the village, this craft group exerted some political influence. Meanwhile, the Chamber of Accounts provided the institutional backing to ensure that this production stage remained separate from the others (De Sagher et al. 1966, 112-113, 131-39, 149-76).

The relative, and increasing, inclusivity of Nieuwkerke's industry was a double-edged sword. The settlement was not officially a town and was therefore unable to impose entry barriers like mandatory local citizenship to aspiring entrepreneurs. In order to be recognised as a clothier or master artisan one simply had to be subject to taxes in the village (*taillable*) (De Sagher et al. 1966, 113). On the one hand, the influx of craftsmen and -women from outside was beneficial to the industry, because it created a larger labour reserve. On the other hand, the relatively open nature of the local cloth trade made it vulnerable to free riding, i.e. for people to profit from the reputation of Nieuwkerke's product without upholding the required standards. To make things more complicated, it appears that free riding was a problem among both the top producers and the smaller entrepreneurs. By 1550, wealthy merchant-entrepreneurs sought to bypass certain fees and inspections of their fabrics at the commercial outlets in the market cities. At the same time, poor operators pushed back against increased regulation of the quality of the wool they used in the production process. This freedom to improvise with raw materials had been a key competitive advantage of Nieuwkerke's industry. Unsurprisingly, the clothiers' corporation was sharply divided on how to address its problems without throwing the baby out with the bathwater.

This factional division of the clothiers' corporation or *draperie* became ideologically charged and turned into conflicts over unequal opportunities between the poor and the rich. First during the 1530s, and again in the 1550s, the faction that raised the issue of inequality termed themselves the 'common clothiers' (*communs drapiers*, or *ghemeene drapiers*), protesting measures by the industrial administration which favoured their richer fellows (De Sagher et al. 1966, 139-139, 156-176). We encounter similar invocations in other cities of the Low Countries around the same period: during the 1550s, the Antwerp brewer-entrepreneur Gilbert Van Schoonbeke was ousted from his position on the city council after hefty protests from other beer producers that he and a few others had pursued 'their singular profit and own benefit' (Soly 1968). In light of this event, it comes as no surprise that Antwerp's merchant elite actively strove to remould contemporary perceptions about commerce during the 1561 competition of the Chambers of Rhetoric (see above). But the small operators of Nieuwkerke dissociated themselves from the elite by styling themselves as 'common' clothiers. Furthermore, in doing so they were also implying that they represented the interests of the community as a whole (*ghemeente*). Whether they truly spoke for the majority is another question, but these clothiers clearly deemed appeals to middle-class ideology a powerful rhetorical tool in their negotiations.

Social polarisation was especially harmful in Nieuwkerke because the success of the corporation hinged on the participation of small artisan-entrepreneurs. In 1564-65, clothiers with an annual output of fewer than 50 pieces of cloth were still responsible for around half the village's total production volume. Despite Nieuwkerke's lack of craft guilds, middle-class manufacturers therefore still had a voice through their membership of the entrepreneurial community. So the formal institutional differences between Nieuwkerke and Armentières hide certain similarities on the informal level. The two industries mainly resembled each other through the comparable quality levels of their fabrics: in 1575, Nieuwkerke's product fetched 46-48*d* per ell, while Armentières served the top of the same market segment (60-85*d* per ell). Hondschoote's *sayetterie*, by contrast, cost only 10-25*d* per ell. Adequately to process expensive raw materials like the Spanish wool used in Nieuwkerke and the combination of Spanish and English wool used in Armentières, one needed training, skill and time (Thijs 1990; Munro 2005). As a consequence, even in a rural settlement like Nieuwkerke there was little opportunity for local peasant families to supplement their incomes by occasionally manufacturing cloth. This marks a contrast with other regions in Flanders and elsewhere, where so-called 'proto-industrial' by-employment in the linen industry was central to the subsistence of many rural families (Thoen and Soens 2015). Because of the skill threshold in Nieuwkerke, those clothiers who were essentially self-employed manufacturers did not have to compete with this cheap rural labour pool. Nor did 'rich' corporation members possess much more capital to insert into their businesses, or we would expect to see more than the mere eleven clothiers with production outputs of over 100 pieces in 1564-65 (van der Meulen 2018).

'Liberty' and social inequality

The situation in the textile centre of Hondschoote, with its lower-grade fabrics, was markedly different. As in Nieuwkerke, artisans living in Hondschoote were not organised into craft guilds. Also, if Nieuwkerke and Armentières witnessed demographic growth during the sixteenth century, Hondschoote certainly did: its estimated population peak in this period was *c.* 15,000. Like Nieuwkerke, Hondschoote did not have the physical infrastructure of a town and was probably unable properly to accommodate these slews of immigrants (Stabel 1995a; Decavele 1975). But there were two key important differences between Nieuwkerke and Hondschoote. First, the latter's main industry was *sayetterie*: a relatively cheap product that required less skill to produce. This detracted from the bargaining power of the manufacturers and small entrepreneurs. Secondly, in Nieuwkerke local clothiers controlled both manufacturing and marketing. In Hondschoote, by contrast, external merchant firms, mainly from Antwerp, bankrolled the local production process and oversaw trade (Coornaert 1930). This partly explains why discord over unequal entrepreneurial opportunities in Hondschoote contains more references to merchants rather than to rich clothiers, as in Nieuwkerke. The ideological rhetoric in one such conflict, in 1557, clearly echoes the self-fashioning of the disadvantaged entrepreneurs from the latter village. Yet here, those calling themselves the 'common' (*ghemeene*) clothiers complained about the avarice of 'merchants' (*cooplieden*) – recalling once more the familiar literary trope (De Sagher et al. 1961, 360-361). By the beginning of the seventeenth century, a small number of merchant dynasties from Hondschoote, in collusion with external firms, would come to completely dominate the production process and trade.

On the one hand, the case of Hondschoote demonstrates a well-known phenomenon, of the consequences of scale enlargement in the sixteenth century. Similar trends are attested to for other industries: merchant capital from Antwerp raised the scale of urban and rural manufacture in the Low Countries, thereby pushing down the local wage level. Social polarisation might arise in these places, but it had less of an impact because the problem was not rooted in local society but in the commercial metropolis (Lis and Soly 1979; Blondé 1987). The same applied to potential problems with housing in a settlement that must have been bursting at the seams. On the other hand, the smaller clothiers of Hondschoote still carried some political weight during the sixteenth century. Moreover, even in this 'puppet' industry of Antwerp, the local dyers managed to retain independent operations throughout the sixteenth century.

Data on individual cloth exports from Hondschoote clearly show the influence of scale enlargement between the middle and the end of the sixteenth century. These figures have been derived from tax lists of *sayetterie* fabrics exported from the cloth centre (De Sagher et al. 1961, 478-512). In other words, they give an impression not so much of the production component of the industry, but of the commercial side of entrepreneurship. Another caveat is that the involvement of Antwerp merchant firms distorts these figures. They should therefore not be taken as a proxy of social inequality in general. Still, they offer insights about inequality between the local commercial enterprises. The results are interesting for a number of reasons (Table 1). To start with, during the 1540s the rate of inequality between cloth exporters in Hondschoote was already a lot higher (Gini: 0.53) than in the clothiers' corporation of Armentières in 1575 (0.27), while it was roughly similar to that in Nieuwkerke's entrepreneurial community in 1564-65 (0.54). Again, however, this is a little bit like comparing apples and oranges.

More interestingly, the export figures indicate that the discontent expressed by the common clothiers of Hondschoote in 1557 coincided with an increasing gap between the top and bottom of local commercial enterprises. In a ten-year period, the rate of inequality

Table 1. Inequality between cloth exporters in 16th c. Hondschoote (own calculations based on DE SAGHER et al. 1961, 478-512)

	Gini coefficient	Total volume of *sayetterie* export (pieces)	No. of cloth exporters (n)
1 August 1544 – 1 August 1548	0.53	177,509	29
1 August 1554 – 31 July 1558	0.72	267,362	30
1 August 1564 – 31 July 1568	0.71	375,204	34
10 August 1587 – 10 August 1591	0.83	52,023	33

among cloth exporters had greatly increased, with the Gini coefficient rising from 0.53 to 0.72. Ten years later, this unequal situation remained virtually unchanged. Looking at the entire period from 1544 until the last decade of the sixteenth century, the figures show a steady increase in inequality. This trend built up more or less independently from the industry's overall trade volume. Although still impressive compared to the production peaks of Nieuwkerke and Armentières, by the end of the sixteenth century Hondschoote's cloth exports were at a low point. Contrary to other findings for the pre-industrial economy, the rate of inequality among Hondschoote's cloth traders actually peaked at this time despite this industrial downturn (Milanovic et al. 2011). This, too, may have been a consequence of the external involvement of the Antwerp firms. But in that case it is still noteworthy that their local puppets were unable progressively to exploit the industrial heyday of the mid-sixteenth century. Although inequality between the exporters was still increasing when the numbers rose from 40,000 to 45,000 fabrics per annum in the 1540s to *c.* 70,000 in the 1550s (Gini: 0.53-0.72), this unequal footing plateaued while the annual trade volume grew beyond the 90,000 mark in the 1560s (Gini: 0.72-0.71).

Leaving aside these figures at the very top of the cloth trade, the potential impact of ideology and social cohesion was reduced in Hondschoote through the nature of the textile centre's product. The textiles produced in Hondschoote, if not as inexpensive as linens, were still a lot cheaper than those in Armentières and Nieuwkerke. The lower skill premium resulting from this, coupled with the lack of craft guilds, made the labour market in Hondschoote way more competitive. That situation was further exacerbated by the rural context, because local peasants could supplement their incomes relatively easily by engaging in part-time weaving and other jobs. Moreover, the richer clothiers and merchants of Hondschoote could push their prices down because of their superior capital inputs and larger trade volumes: some of them commissioned fabrics in the 10-20,000 range. Small enterprises like those in Nieuwkerke could never survive in this economic climate. The result was a widening gap between rich and poor clothiers. Over time, the latter were proletarianised completely, mirroring other regional economies in this period (Lis and Soly 2008; Alfani and Ryckbosch 2016). At the other end of the spectrum stood a commercial elite consisting of only around 30 individuals out of a total number of inhabitants of *c.* 15,000. This made the inequality gap in Hondschoote even more pronounced in comparison with those of Nieuwkerke and Armentières, where the top economic layer was larger and the overall population smaller.

Still, even in Hondschoote the ideal of collective interests before those of the individual retained some rhetorical power at least until the end of the sixteenth century. The ideological precept was deployed in 1580 as a reason for maintaining, or rather restoring, the independence of dyeing operations in the cloth centre. Michel Godeschalck, Hondschoote's top merchant-clothier, complained about the industry's bylaw prohibiting him from owning his own dyeing workshops. He claimed this regulation ran 'counter to liberty', and 'also robbed him of the liberal faculties he possessed'. But the industrial officials claimed the exact opposite. The separation of dyeing operations and mercantile activity 'increases the business and liberty of the merchant, as well as [the inclination] of any man to invest his money in trade, seeing that he is served, and may profit, just as much as others'. In this case, the local magistrates actually sided with those calling themselves the 'common clothiers and merchants' (*smalle ende ghemeene drapiers ende cooplieden*), under the familiar rationale of protecting communal interests (*de ghemeente*). In their eyes, the superior economic power of a small group of wholesalers had given these entrepreneurs a 'competitive advantage' (*betercoop*), 'thereby disadvantaging and all at once ruining all others' (*daermede alle andere achter vente ghehouden ende t'eenemaele ghedestrueert*) (De Sagher et al. 1961, 536-538).

The episode of 1580 shows that neither ideology nor the local institutional context was entirely irrelevant to economic developments, even when an industry was in many ways controlled by external capital. To be sure, in the longer term these measures against unfair competition did little to stem the flow of increasing inequality at the absolute top. Indeed, in 1590 the rate of inequality between export enterprises had grown further still (Gini: 0.83). But dyeing remained an independently operated craft stage in Hondschoote. Merchant-entrepreneurs like Michel Godeschalck would probably look for other ways to subvert these restrictions, but they would have a hard time of it in this specific regard. In all three textile centres discussed in this chapter, the autonomy of dyeing operations emerges as a kind of last bastion of restricted entrepreneurship. Clothiers' attempts at vertical integration of the manufacturing process usually provoked a reaction from the artisans, but only the dyers were consistently able to safeguard their independence.

On the one hand, this may have had less to do with the latter's stronger ideological claims, and all the more with their superior negotiating position. As explained above, dyeing was the most technical production phase. It also required the greatest capital inputs of all manufacturing stages, since dyers' tools and installations, not to mention good tinctures, were very expensive. Accordingly, the masters of this craft were often entrepreneurs in their own right, ran larger operations, and had more capital at their disposal than, say, weavers or fullers. Moreover, unlike clothiers, they were allowed to process different types of textiles all in one workshop (Coornaert 1930). On the other hand, the dyers could not have preserved their independence on their own. The conflicts in both Hondschoote and Nieuwkerke make clear that dyeing could remain separate because clothiers, local magistrates and princely officers lent their support. The currency, if not necessarily the motivation, of that support was ideological claims that promoted collective interests and disavowed self-enrichment. So ideology did have an impact on economic performance in the sixteenth century, albeit one contingent upon the local institutional framework.

Conclusion

In his 1525 'Play of the High Wind and the Soft Rain' (*Tspel van den Hooghen Wynt ende Zoeten Reyn*), the Flemish playwright Cornelis Everaert displays his abilities as an astute observer of the economic realities of his day. A character called One (*Enich*), portrayed as a merchant, and an interlocutor called Many (*Menich*), dressed as a craftsman, discuss the unfavourable economic climate in the city of Bruges following on from recent wars. Their conversation makes clear that both are suffering losses in their lifestyles. However, it is equally clear who is bearing the brunt of the adversity: Many can no longer enjoy even the taste of beer, whereas One is apparently still in a position to appreciate the flavour of Rhenish wine (Hüsken 2005, 225-230). Their relative positions in the socio-economic hierarchy remain unaffected. But Many's lesser financial resilience means straddling subsistence level, while One is still sitting comfortably in an absolute sense. Everaert's social criticism is subtle and slightly opaque. To an extent, contemporary spectators and readers of the play were able to judge for themselves what they thought of the economic division between One and Many. Also, the economic adversity is principally blamed on external circumstances (in this case, war). Yet, upon experiencing the play one cannot fail to notice the glaring inequality reigning within the economy of sixteenth-century Flanders.

In this contribution, I have attempted to show that ideas like those of Everaert were derived from the economic practices of the day, but that the ideology these people espoused in their literary works was also 'consumed' by others. Textile artisans and cloth entrepreneurs were no exception, when one remembers that Everaert himself belonged to this category, and also bears in mind the tight bonds within the urban network. The industrial sources clearly echoed certain 'literary' ideas about proper entrepreneurial conduct, chiefly in their vilification of individual enrichment. These different kinds of sources reveal that social inequality was definitely perceived as a problem in the cloth industries of sixteenth-century Flanders. The social tensions that arose within this fluid profession were probably exacerbated by wider societal tensions (religious, political) that swept through the Low Countries during the 1500s.

Nevertheless, although we find similar ideological sentiments in all three cloth industries under discussion here, the potential impact of the dissent differed according to the local institutional context and nature of their product. So Joel Mokyr was partly correct in hypothesising that the ideology of pre-Enlightenment societies could place restrictions on economic development. Even in Hondschoote, where the industrial proceeds flowed out of the town and may therefore have been less conspicuous in local society, getting rich had its limits. As borne out by all three cloth centres, the final barrier to complete vertical integration of cloth manufacture was the independence of dyeing workshops. Rich clothiers were certainly ready to dye, but they were unable to gain lasting control of this process. Still, this was not a consequence of the 'autonomous' operating power of ideology, as Mokyr has suggested. Rather, whenever a small number of entrepreneurs sought to manage their own dyeing workshops, they were consistently thwarted by the resistance of the local entrepreneurial community. That resistance was ideology-powered but could be successful only if it followed the seams of the institutional framework.

Sources

Archival sources
Bruges, City Archives (SAB), Series 305, Journaal B.
Brussels, General State Archives (ARB), Acquits de Lille, No. 1367/33.
Ghent, State Archives (RAG), Raad van Vlaanderen, Enkwesten, No. 3756.
Lille, Departmental Archives Nord (ADN), B Series, No. 5669,
Source editions
N. N. 1877. *Inventaire Analytique des Archives Communales d'Armentières* (AIA). Lille : Imprimerie de Lefèbvre-Ducrocq.
De Sagher, H., et al., eds. 1951, 1961, 1966. *Recueil des documents relatifs à l'histoire de l'industrie drapière en Flandre. Deuxième partie. Le sud-ouest de la Flandre depuis l'époque bourguignonne,* 3 vols. Brussels: Académie Royale de Belgique. Commission Royale d'Histoire.
Erné, B. H., & Van Dis, L. M., eds. 1982. *De Gentse Spelen van 1539,* 2 vols. The Hague: Martinus Nijhoff.
Geldhof, J., ed. 1974. *Het handboek van P. J. Vandendorpe, pastoor van Nieuwkerke (1730-1806).* Bruges: Genootschap voor Geschiedenis.
Hüsken, W., ed. 2005. *De spelen van Cornelis Everaert. Opnieuw uitgegeven, van inleidingen, annotaties en woordverklaringen voorzien,* 2 vols. Hilversum: Verloren.
Schillings, A., ed. 1954, 1966. *Matricule de l'Université de Louvain,* vol. 3, vol. 4. Brussels: Paleis der Academiën.
Silvius, W., ed. 1562. *Spelen van sinne, etc.* Antwerp: Willem Silvius.

References

Alfani, G., and W. Ryckbosch. 2016. "Growing apart in early modern Europe? A comparison of inequality trends in Italy and the Low Countries, 1500-1800." *Explorations in Economic History* 62: 143-153.
Arnade, P. 2008, *Beggars, iconoclasts, and civic patriots. The political culture of the Dutch Revolt.* Ithaca, NY, & London: Cornell University Press.
Blondé, B. 1987. *De sociale structuren en economische dynamiek van 's-Hertogenbosch, 1500-1550.* Tilburg: Stichting Zuidelijk Historisch Contact.
Coornaert, E. 1930. *Un centre industriel d'autrefois. La draperie-sayetterie d'Hondschoote (XIVe-XVIIIe siècles).* Paris: Les Presses Universitaires.
Davis, N. Z. 1983. *The return of Martin Guerre. The brilliant historical and psychological study of imposture in a sixteenth-century French village.* Harmondsworth & New York: King Penguin.
Decavele, J. 1975, *De dageraad van de Reformatie in Vlaanderen (1520-1565).* vol. 1. Brussels: Paleis der Academiën.
Decavele, J. 1992. "Het culturele en intellectuele netwerk. De middeleeuwen en 16e eeuw." In *Het stedelijk netwerk in België in historisch perspectief (1350-1850). Een statistische en dynamische benadering. Handelingen,* 155-190. Brussels: Gemeentekrediet.
De Munck, B. 2019. "Artisans as knowledge workers. Craft and creativity in a long term perspective." *Geoforum* 99: 227-237.

Duffy, E. 1992. *The stripping of the altars. Traditional religion in England c. 1400-c. 1580* New Haven, CT: Yale University Press.

Dumolyn, J. 2014. "Guild politics and political guilds in fourteenth-century Flanders." In *The voices of the people in late medieval Europe. Communication and popular politics*, ed. J. Dumolyn et al., 15-48. Turnhout: Brepols.

Dumolyn, J., and J. Haemers. 2012. "'A bad chicken was brooding'. Subversive speech in late medieval Flanders." *Past and Present* 214 (February): 45-86.

Duplessis, R. 1991. *Lille and the Dutch revolt. Urban stability in an era of revolution, 1500-1582.* Cambridge: Cambridge University Press.

Eisenstein, E. 1979. *The printing press as an agent of change. Communications and cultural transformations in early modern Europe.* 2 vols. Cambridge: Cambridge University Press.

Haemers, J., and J. Dumolyn. 2013. "'Let each man carry on with his trade and remain silent'. Middle class ideology in the urban literature of the late medieval Low Countries." *Cultural and Social History* 10, no. 2: 169-189.

Greif, A. 2006. *Institutions and the path to the modern economy. Lessons from medieval trade.* Cambridge: Cambridge University Press.

Kint, A. M. 1996. *The community of commerce. Social relations in sixteenth-century Antwerp.* New York: Columbia University.

Lee, J. 2018. *The medieval clothier.* Woodbridge: Boydell & Brewer.

Liddy, C., and J. Haemers. 2013. "Popular politics in the late medieval city. York and Bruges." *English Historical Review* 128, no. 533 (August): 771-805.

Lis, C., and H. Soly. 1979. *Poverty and capitalism in pre-industrial Europe, 1350-1850.* Atlantic Highlands, NJ: Humanities Press.

Lis, C., and H. Soly. 2008. "Subcontracting in guild-based export trades, 13th-18th centuries." In *Guilds, innovation, and the European economy, 1400-1800*, ed. S. R. Epstein and M. Prak, 81-113. Cambridge: Cambridge University Press.

Marnef, G. 1996. *Antwerpen in de tijd van de Reformatie. Ondergronds protestantisme in een handelsmetropool, 1550-1577.* Amsterdam & Antwerp: Meulenhoff.

Marnef. G., and A.-L. Van Bruaene. 2018. "Civic religion. Community, identity and religious transformation." In *City and society in the Low Countries, 1100-1600*, ed. A-L. Van Bruaene et al., 128-161. Cambridge: Cambridge University Press.

Mokyr, J. 2013. "Cultural entrepreneurs and the origins of modern economic growth." *Scandinavian Economic History Review* 61, no. 1: 1-33.

Mokyr, J. 2018. *A Culture of Growth. The Origins of the Modern Economy.* Princeton, NJ: Princeton University Press.

Milanovic, B., et al. 2011. "Pre-industrial inequality." *The Economic Journal* 121, no. 551 (March): 255-272.

Munro, J. 2005. "Spanish *merino* wools and the *nouvelles draperies*. An industrial transformation in the late-medieval Low Countries." *The Economic History Review* 58, no. 3 (August): 431-484.

North, D. 1990. *Institutions, institutional change and economic performance.* Cambridge: Cambridge University Press.

Polanyi, K. 1944. *The Great Transformation. The political and economic origins of our time* New York: Farrar & Rinehart.

Soly, H. 1968. "De brouwerijenonderneming van Gilbert Van Schoonbeke (1552-1562). 1ste deel." *Revue Belge de Philologie et d'Histoire* 46, no. 2: 337-392.

Stabel, P. 1995a. "Demography and hierarchy. The small towns and the urban network of sixteenth-century Flanders." In *Small towns in Early Modern Europe*, ed. P. Clarke, 206-228. Cambridge: Cambridge University Press.

Stabel, P. 1995b. "Entre commerce international et économie locale. Le monde financier de Wouter Ameide (Bruges fin XVe-début XVIe siècle)." In *Public and private finances in the Middle Ages*, ed. M. Boone and W. Prevenier, 75-100. Leuven & Apeldoorn: Garant.

Stabel, P. 2000. "Marketing cloth in the Low Countries. Manufacturers, brokers and merchants (14th-16th centuries)." In *International trade in the Low Countries (14th-16th centuries. Merchants, organization, infrastructure. Proceedings of the international conference Ghent-Antwerp, 12th-13th January 1997*, ed. P. Stabel, B. Blondé and A. Greve, 15-36. Leuven & Apeldoorn: Garant.

Thompson, E. P. 1971. "The moral economy of the English crowd in the eighteenth century." *Past & Present* 50: 76-136.

Thijs, A. 1990. "Les textiles au marché anversois au XVIe siècle." In *Textiles of the Low Countries in European economic history. Session b-15. Proceedings Tenth International Economic History Congress. Leuven, August 1990*, ed. E. Aerts and J. Munro, 76-86. Leuven: Leuven University Press.

Thoen, E., and T. Soens. 2015. "The family or the farm: a Sophie's choice? The late medieval crisis in the former county of Flanders." In *Crisis in the Later Middle Ages. Beyond the Postan-Duby paradigm*, ed. J. Drendel, 195-224. Turnhout: Brepols.

Vandommele, J. 2011. *Als in een spiegel. Vrede, kennis en gemeenschap op het Antwerpse Landjuweel van 1561*. Hilversum: Verloren.

Van Bruaene, A.-L. 2006. "'A wonderfull tryumfe, for the wynnyng of a pryse'. Guilds, ritual, theater, and the urban network in the Southern Low Countries, ca. 1450-1650." *Renaissance Quarterly* 59, no. 2 (Summer): 374-405.

Van Bruaene, A.-L. 2008. *Om beters wille. Rederijkerskamers en de stedelijke cultuur in de Zuidelijke Nederlanden (1400-1650)*. Amsterdam: Amsterdam University Press.

Van der Meulen, J. (2018) "Corporate collective action and the market cycle of the cloth industry in Nieuwkerke, Flanders, 1300-1600." *Social History* 43, no. 3: 375-399.

PIETER DE GRAEF

Did Urban Manure Nourish the Country?

Social Consequences of Fertiliser Improvement in Eighteenth-Century Flemish Farming

Introduction

Over the past 150 years food production has witnessed enormous gains in land and labour productivity, unmatched by any agricultural progress in pre-modern times (Federico 2005). New crop varieties, crop protection, mechanisation, and primarily the introduction of artificial fertilisers have produced a breakthrough, sweeping away old limits to agricultural output (Broadberry 2015, 115).[1] In the capitalistic world system, nutrients – like so many other environmental resources – are reallocated on a global scale from (rural) peripheries to (urban) centres, thereby creating huge imbalances and very open nutrient cycles (e.g. feeding stuffs imported from Latin America in European stockbreeding). This global nutrient trade clearly engenders an unequal allocation of costs and benefits. In the Global South, the 'mining' of nutrients exhausts the soil and stimulates forest clearance. Plantations of soya rapidly exhaust the nutrients accumulated in the land after centuries or millennia of forest cover. The Global North profits from cheap access to nutrients, but also faces an excess of unwanted nutrients (manure) in some places, leading for instance to eutrophication of surface waters. Moreover, the cheap access to nutrients may favour large-scale industrial farming while disadvantaging family farms (Moore 2000, 123-157). For most agricultural scientists there is still no realistic alternative to high-intensity farming and global nutrient transfers. However, over the past decade, attention to alternative approaches has been growing. Such alternatives aim to resolve bottlenecks in food production starting from the principles of a circular economy (cradle to cradle), in which the processing of animal manure and reuse of urban organic waste as fertiliser in agriculture is championed.[2] The careful collection of human and animal waste in cities and its recycling in agriculture is often seen as the ultimate example of such 'circular waste economy', uniting town and

---

1 In England, for instance, annual growth rates remained below 0.5 per cent before 1700, rose to 0.93 per cent in the second half of the eighteenth century, but started to increase substantially only after 1870, with outstanding growth figures of 2.3 per cent per year in the period from 1946 to 1985.

2 The EU recently launched some legislative actions to stimulate the transition to a circular economy (e.g. the EU Fertilizers Regulation 2003/2003 has been changed in order to achieve free trade in fertilising products in order to encourage the closing of nutrient loops in the European food system). However, nutrient resources which are potentially available, such as sewage sludge, including struvite, and human excreta, are not yet targeted by the reviewed Fertilizers Regulation because of food safety concerns (cf. residues of pharmaceuticals, hormones etc.): de Boer & van Ittersum 2018, 28-29.

Pieter De Graef • University of Antwerp

Inequality and the City in the Low Countries (1200-2020), ed. by Bruno BLONDÉ, Sam GEENS, Hilde GREEFS, Wouter RYCKBOSCH, Tim SOENS & Peter STABEL, SEUH 50 (Turnhout, 2020), pp. 63-77.

  DOI 10.1484/M.SEUH-EB.5.120438

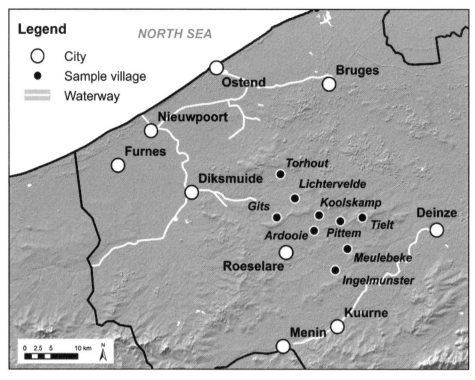

The distribution of off-farm fertilisers in inland Flanders (sample villages between Bruges and Courtrai). Edited by Iason Jongepier, GIStorical Antwerp.

countryside in a 'symbiotic relationship' (Tanner 2001, 130-136; Drangert 1998, 157-164). Both the urbanised core of the Low Countries before 1850 and the Yangtze delta in Ming and Qing China are often cited as regions where the recycling of human waste in agriculture reached unprecedented levels, seemingly providing an answer to the two major environmental challenges of pre-modern societies: the lack of fertiliser in agriculture and the insalubrious conditions of city life. A nutrient cycle was indeed generated in which (at least a part of) nutrients extracted from the soil at harvest and distributed to cities as food found their way back to the soil in the form of organic waste, such as kitchen refuse, animal dung and human excrement (van Zon 2012-2013, 41-67; Barles 2005, 28-47).

Nevertheless, such utopian representation of the town-countryside nexus in the past ignores the social inequalities and market imperfections which often contributed considerable noise to this 'harmonic' interplay (Massard-Guilbaud & Rodger 2011). Eighteenth-century Flanders offers the ideal testing ground to investigate the 'environmental inequalities' generated by the recycling of urban waste in the countryside. All over (western) Europe the eighteenth century offers an example of agricultural growth in a traditional economy. In many regions output growth was driven by labour input, and hence a declining productivity of labour. In Flanders this might have been complemented by a highly-developed 'science of fertilisers', including maximum recycling of urban organic wastes. It remains to be seen whether urban waste recycling indeed provided substantial output gains in agriculture. Moreover, as I will argue in this chapter, the allocation of costs and benefits was highly unequal, and the recycling of urban nutrients in agriculture exacerbated rather than mitigated both the inequalities between town and countryside and the inequalities in rural society.

Together with mechanisation, fertiliser improvement is considered quintessential to explaining the increasing productivity of land in the nineteenth and twentieth centuries (cf. contributions on modern farming in Thoen & Soens 2015). Existing historical research on pre-modern fertilisation is however limited and often fails to link manuring strategies and innovations with the specific features of agrarian production. Agricultural regions and individual farms might have known very different fertilisation strategies, depending on farm sizes, property rights and income strategies; in short, on the social organisation of agricultural production in a given region (the 'social agrosystem' as it has been labelled by Erik Thoen). This essay deepens our insight into the contribution of farmyard manure and compost recuperated on farms and, more specifically, of urban and industrial fertilisers brought from outside the farm to agricultural productivity and the livelihoods of the farming community in an era often labelled as a revolutionary period for pre-modern agriculture, namely the eighteenth century. These issues will be addressed through a study at micro level of one of the leading regions in terms of agricultural productivity in Europe at that time, namely the smallholding peasant economy of inland Flanders in present-day Belgium.

The Flemish Husbandry in context of growth

Research into one of the leading regions in terms of agricultural productivity in Europe, which maintained high yields per unit area of land against a background of ever more intensive input of labour – the smallholding peasant economy of inland Flanders – has pointed to the growing importance of off-farm-purchased manures in the course of the eighteenth and early nineteenth centuries, as had been attested to by contemporary agronomists and travellers (Goossens 1992; Dejongh 1999, 7-28). This region of very intensive agriculture and dense urbanisation seemed to be an area *par excellence* for this kind of 'environmental symbiosis' between town and countryside: human and industrial waste, an unwanted surplus of urban agglomerations, was 'transformed' into a resource when exported to the country. In this region dominated by smallholding families amidst a few larger holdings in each village, the rural economy was characterised by the combination of proto-industry and mixed farming. Since this provided it with possibilities for on-farm manure recuperation, it raises questions about the reasons behind the increasing application of urban and industrial fertilisers (Thoen 2001, 102-157).

The eighteenth century was a period of population growth in the Flemish countryside which gave rise to the fragmentation of peasant holdings. The possibilities of reclaiming more land were very limited by this time, while more labour input became available for the same amount of cropland. Fragmentation of holdings and the increase in available family labour were not isolated phenomena, but instead occurred in close relation to specific societal, political and economic constraints or opportunities, which could set in motion alterations in farming strategies. Together with labour-intensive cultivation methods (i.e. declining labour productivity), the increased attention to soil fertility led to the growth of physical productivity (i.e. higher yields per unit area of land) (Thoen & Soens

Table 1. Farm structures in the seigniory of Lichtervelde, eighteenth century

	1724	1750	1780
Number of exploitations	*381*	*393*	*477*
0-1 ha	36.0%	41.7%	50.9%
1-2.5 ha	19.2%	14.2%	13.8%
2.5-5 ha	18.1%	22.1%	17.8%
5-10 ha	17.3%	11.2%	10.5%
>10 ha	9.4%	10.7%	6.9%
Surface area (ha)	*1396.3*	*1394.9*	*1351.4*
0-1 ha	3.3%	3.8%	5.0%
1-2.5 ha	8.6%	6.6%	8.5%
2.5-5 ha	17.5%	22.5%	23.4%
5-10 ha	32.9%	21.7%	26.1%
>10 ha	37.7%	45.4%	37.1%

Source: State Archives Bruges, INV 129/16, *Archief van Lichtervelde (oud)*, no. 292-295.

2015, 1-8). In the course of the early modern period, fallow was gradually reduced (and almost entirely eliminated) whilst the cultivation of fodder crops was on the rise, a factor which contributed to increasing stable-feeding and hence increasing possibilities for the recuperation of farmyard manure. Still, off-farm fertiliser inputs were apparently on the rise and 'contributed to a new upswing in arable productivity' (Goossens 1992, 287-292). However, the causal link between off-farm manure and the rise in arable productivity is far from clear.

According to Guy Dejongh, the change in population numbers could be understood as a stress factor (for smallholdings) or as an opportunity (for large farmers), which gave rise to alterations in production strategies (Dejongh 1999, 7-28). Yet the impact of social property relations on agricultural production should not be overlooked. As rising population numbers in combination with limited supplies of land resulted in upward pressure on land prices, absentee landowners were inclined to split up their leaseholds and to set higher rents per unit area of land (Thoen 2001, 102-157; Vanhaute 2001, 19-40). In so doing, they further reinforced stress factors on small leaseholders caused by population growth, but they also increasingly whittled away the profit margins of large tenant farmers, which challenged the existing production strategies with their particular sets of resources.

Central in evaluating these challenges to production strategies and resource allocation (i.c. manuring with on-farm and off-farm fertilisers) is the specific agrarian structure within which eighteenth-century farming in inland Flanders occurred, and which was characterised by a highly unequal distribution of land among a majority of smallholding peasant families and a top layer of larger farmers, the latter having more than half of the village's arable land under the plough (Lambrecht 2002, 24). Table 1 illustrates this inequality between different layers of the rural community in our sample region – the seigniory of Lichtervelde, nowadays situated in the province of Western Flanders, Belgium. As in other regions characterised by numerous smallholdings (e.g. many regions in the north-east of France), production on small and larger farms in inland Flanders was framed within a system of unequal relations of exchange between these agrarian groups (Lambrecht 2003, 237-261; Vermoesen 2011, 147-151). Peasant families could make use of the horse teams of larger farmers to plough their plots of land or transport stuff (or have the larger cultivators do these tasks for them) in exchange for labour in the fields and farmsteads of these more well-to-do cultivators. Expressed in monetary terms, the labour peasant smallholders had to perform as payment for the services of large farmers was way above the equivalent cost price of these services, but was still cost-effective in terms of working time as compared to the situation where all the agricultural work on the smallholding had to be done by manual labour instead of animal traction. Thus, peasant smallholders had more time left to elaborate proto-industrial activities (Lambrecht 2003, 237-261). This proto-industrial income model in turn provided smallholders with funds that complemented their agricultural production and ensured that the reproduction cost of labour remained low. As a consequence, the large farms in inland Flanders had access to a cheap labour force, one which even expanded in the eighteenth century as a result of population growth. This very system of symbiosis or *convivium* between different strata of rural society, based on credit systems in the form of labour, goods and services, implied a coping mechanism for smallholding families in times of economic stress, because one of its effects was reducing risk (Vanhaute & Lambrecht 2011, 155-186). If the peasant classes of society indeed provided themselves with bought fertilisers, this means that they subscribed to commercial circuits, which could also have brought about unequal power relations, such as with urban entrepreneurs or rural intermediaries who might try to cash in on issues of information asymmetry as regards the supply of urban and industrial fertilisers.

Against the background of these social property relations and economic and societal stress factors, smallholding families and families farming on medium-sized and large holdings needed to make decisions about soil fertility maintenance and the purchase of off-farm fertilisers. Macro-level research has not been able to prove on which types of farms (large, medium-sized or small) and on which types of land (only on freehold property or on leasehold as well) the purchased off-farm fertilisers ended up. Nor was this research able to delve into agricultural practice in order to determine which kinds of fertilisers benefited which kinds of crops, let alone to gain a clear understanding of the role of social relations in fertility management as well as the social effects of certain manuring strategies.

A series of unique eighteenth-century appraisals of goods and chattels which have been preserved for several villages in the districts – castellanies – of Bruges and Courtrai (figure 1) allowed me to discover which types of on-farm and off-farm manures were used and to investigate the distribution of urban manure to smallholdings and large farms in a period of accelerating agricultural growth. This essay presents the conclusions from our visit to the fields and farmsteads in our sample villages in the castellany of Courtrai and the Franc of Bruges, situated in the very heart of the *Flemish Husbandry* region (see for more information on the specific methodology and description of our source material De Graef, 2017a, 379-410; 2017b, 25-61; 2019, 231-255). We can question the choice of different kinds of fertilisers, the reasons behind changing fertilisation patterns and the acquisition of extraneous fertiliser inputs, and the return of new fertilising strategies for different segments of the farming community, hence revealing the inequalities generated by manure.

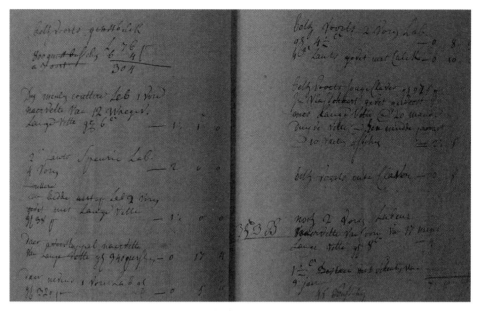

Figure 1. Appraisal or *prijzij* (i.c. part of the estimation of cultivated land)

Source: State Archives Courtrai, 905/6, no. 58, booklet 9, f. 373ᵛ-374ᵛ: appraisal of Joos De Vriendt, deceased in Meulebeke in 1758; appraisal recorded on 21 September 1758.

Rising use of off-farm fertilisers

In the second half of the eighteenth century the use of off-farm fertiliser inputs was clearly on the rise in our sample villages. All layers of the farming community – smallholders, medium-sized and large farmers – increased their application of the most popular off-farm fertilisers, namely urban night soil (or the content of urban privies), soap ashes or bleach ashes,[3] lime[4] and pigeon dung (cf. table 2). More arable land was dressed with these inputs and the intensity with which every hectare was fertilised with these soil improvers also increased. Apart from the general finding that off-farm fertilisers were increasingly applied on all categories of farms, the rise of liming and ash fertilising in the second half of the eighteenth century, compared to the first half, was what most stood out. In addition to the substantial increases in the use of ashes and lime on small peasant and cottage farms, fertilising with these soil improvers peaked on middle-small, medium-large and large farmsteads, where their use was nearly omnipresent in the decades after 1750. The increase in the usage of urban night soil was less pronounced. Growth in the dressing of fields with the contents of urban privies was observed for the peasant strata of the farming community. On medium-sized farms their application remained more or less constant, and on larger farms it was even downscaled. At the same time, when aggregate supplies of ashes and lime boomed, access to urban night soil should be framed within a story of reshuffling distribution in the countryside itself, rather than in large-scale increases in the urban supply.

---

3   i.e. ashes as the by-product of the combustion of wood or charcoal were themselves base materials for various industries like the bleaching industry, soap works and glassworks.

4   A soil conditioner that adjusts the soil pH to less acidic conditions.

Table 2. Users of off-farm fertilisers, overall application rates and the mean level of manuring intensity, 1720-1800

		1720-1749				1750-1800				
		N_{total}	N_{total} %	overall application rates (%arable land)	mean level of measuring intensity (wagons ha-1)	N_{total}	N_{total} %	overall application rates (%arable land)	mean level of measuring intensity (wagons ha-1)
Night soil	0-1 ha	8	35	22.9	3.7		15	29	51.7	8.2	
	1-2.5 ha	18	102	17.7	2.2		21	56	37.5	1.6	
	2.5-5 ha	31	79	39.3	2.5	10.9	18	33	54.6	2.6	21.9
	5-10 ha	17	44	38.7	2.0		12	23	52.2	2.1	
	>10 ha	12	29	41.4	2.8		7	16	43.8	0.5	
Figeon dung	0-1 ha	2	35	5.8	3		1	29	3.5	1.4	
	1-2.5 ha	6	102	5.9	0.9		11	56	19.7	1.9	
	2.5-5 ha	9	79	11.4	1	3.4	10	33	30.4	1	5.4
	5-10 ha	7	44	16	2.5		8	23	34.8	1	
	>10 ha	4	29	13.8	1.2		5	16	31.3	0.6	
Ashes	0-1 ha	2	35	5.8	0.2		11	29	38	4.1	
	1-2.5 ha	9	102	8.9	0.3		31	56	55.4	4.2	
	2.5-5 ha	10	79	12.7	0.3	6.6	27	33	81.8	4.2	7.5
	5-10 ha	12	44	27.3	0.8		19	23	82.6	5.3	
	>10 ha	15	29	51.8	1.4		15	16	93.8	5.1	
Lime	0-1 ha	0	35	0	0		3	29	10.4	1.6	
	1-2.5 ha	0	102	0	0		21	56	37.5	1.2	
	2.5-5 ha	2	79	2.6	0	4.6	19	33	57.6	4.6	4.6
	5-10 ha	1	44	2.3	0.3		19	23	82.6	4.9	
	>10 ha	3	29	10.4	0.2		15	16	93.8	3.8	
Off-farm inputs	0-1 ha	8	35	23			15	29	51.7		
	1-2.5 ha	22	102	22			35	56	62.5		
	2.5-5 ha	32	79	41			27	33	81.8		
	5-10 ha	20	44	46			20	23	87		
	>10 ha	17	29	59			1.5	16	93.8		

Source: database based on eighteenth-century appraisals of goods and chattels of the villages Meulebeke, Pittem, Ingelmunster, Tielt, Gits, Torhout and Lichtervelde: see P. De Graef, 2017a.

The increase in the use of off-farm fertilisers paralleled changing cultivation practices on the farm: on-farm compost and farmyard manure were applied in higher quantities on fewer hectares of arable land, the cultivation of soil-improving clover expanded,[5] and flax cultivation also tended to increase.[6] All of these changes fitted into a strategy of both smallholding peasant families and medium-sized and large farmers to cope with challenges they faced and opportunities they encountered.

Fertilisation strategies and the impact of the social organisation of agriculture

The in-depth analysis of the fertilisation strategies on the various types of farms in our sample region teaches us that these farms changed their manuring patterns as a response to the economic and societal context and the prevailing social relations within which agricultural production took place. Aggregate cereal yields as well as proto-industrial

---

5   From a mean share of clover of 8.5% of the arable land in the 1720s to more than 10% by the 1750s and to more than 20% by the end of the century: see De Graef 2017a, 379-410.

6   The mean share of flax for the total cultivated acreage increased from 8% in the 1720s to more than 10% in the second half of the eighteenth century: see De Graef 2017a, 379-410.

produce benefited from the higher levels of manuring intensity with on-farm farmyard manure and compost. This change in application of on-farm nutrients was combined with additional inputs of urban and industrial fertilisers and the extension of clover cultivation. Hence, the change in manuring practice added to the usual explanation for the increase in physical yields, namely the growing availability of agricultural labour (Dejongh 1999; De Graef 2019, 248-249).

The reasons behind the change in fertilisation patterns differed according to the various types of farming families. Falling linen prices and increasing prices for crude flax were the main incentives for smallholding families to increase their acreage under flax by changing their manuring strategy and buying additional fertiliser inputs (cf. figure 4). Hence they were able to produce more flax of their own for producing more linen in an effort to safeguard their proto-industrial revenues. Higher prices for crude flax and higher cereal prices in their turn were opportunities that motivated the larger farmers to optimise their fertilisation strategies. Both smallholding households and families on large farms faced the consequences of the increasing pressure on the land market (i.e. higher purchase prices of land due to population increase as well as increasing rents set by landowners who split up their leaseholds) (cf. figure 4) (De Graef 2017a). In the light of the growing importance of leasehold and the continuing increase in rental prices in the nineteenth century (Vanhaute 2001, 19-40), this factor must have had even greater influence in pushing smallholders as well as larger farmers to change fertilising patterns and adopt more off-farm fertiliser inputs.

The acquisition of off-farm fertilisers brought about significant costs (especially for the small cottage families when expressed per unit area of land), but if the use of these bought-in manures went hand in hand with a change in crop patterns (i.e. the extension of flax cultivation in particular) these efforts would pay off, as an analysis of income and expense models has shown (De Graef 2019, 247-253). Notwithstanding the fact that the situation for all layers of the farming community sharply deteriorated in the course of the eighteenth century, the balance sheets of rural households in the second half of the century would have been even worse if fertilising modes and rotation schemes had remained unchanged.

For the acquisition of off-farm fertilisers cottagers and peasant smallholders relied on the systems of reciprocal exchange with larger farmers on which rural society was based. The smallholders were able to transform part of the cash outlay needed for manure purchases into labour input on the holdings of larger farmers providing transport services, albeit at comparatively disadvantageous tariffs. In other words, cottage and peasant smallholding families raised their capital inputs – which they partly financed through labour input on larger holdings – in order to produce more linen (for which again more family labour was required), so that they could maintain their proto-industrial household model. Yet, even when the full extent of the unequal exchange relations was expressed in monetary terms and taken into account, the strategy of raising capital (fertiliser) inputs in combination with changing cropping patterns (especially more flax to increase proto-industrial income) paid off for the smallholding families already at minor increases in cereal output. Thus, buying off-farm fertiliser inputs became a compelling strategy to follow in order to make ends

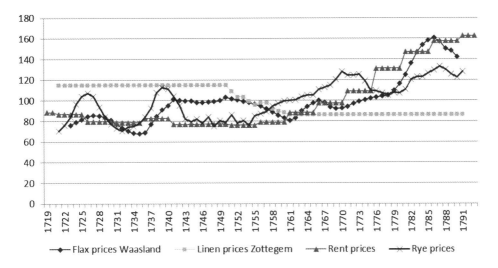

Figure 4. Price indices of flax, linen, rye (5-year moving average) and rents (5-year average), 1719-1792 = 100.

Source: De Graef 2016, 137.

meet in a social and economic context of increasing pressures on the survival algorithms of smallholding households.

The increased use of fertilisers was explained by developing a micro-level approach, starting from the fertiliser strategies of individual farm households, from small cottagers to middle-sized and larger holdings.[7] Such an approach can be a more than welcome complement to more aggregate, macro-level analyses of agricultural output and productivity. From such a micro perspective it becomes clear that rising cereal outputs in the eighteenth century were indeed linked to higher levels of manuring intensity, with nutrients recuperated on-farm in combination with higher inputs of off-farm fertilisers like lime and ashes, on the cereal fields of larger farmers (who were still responsible for the majority of cereal output) but also with higher inputs of urban night soil (and ashes) which (primarily) benefited flax cultivation. This allowed the smallholders and cottagers to continue their proto-industrial household model, thus keeping the reproduction cost of labour low. Low labour costs in turn favoured labour inputs on the larger holdings, which once again stimulated cereal outputs. As a response to the rhythms of the economic situation and the surplus extraction by landowners during a period of population growth and fragmentation of holdings, a green fertiliser revolution – so to speak – of changing fertilising patterns, characterised by more intensive use of on-farm pools of nutrients and higher levels of off-farm fertiliser inputs, was instigated from below. Yet, it increasingly became a compulsive strategy in the particular social and economic context of the *Flemish Husbandry* (De Graef 2017a).

---

7 Farm size categories: 0-0.5 ha, 0.5-1 ha, 1-2.5 ha, 2.5-5 ha, 5-10 ha, more than 10 ha.

Fertilisation strategies in areas of *grande agriculture*

In contrast to the larger farms in a region in inland Flanders still dominated by smallhold-ings, manuring strategies on large farms were quite different in the nearby region of coastal Flanders. This was a region of specialised cattle breeding and more extensive arable farming on large, market-oriented farms. In coastal Flanders, both manure from cities and excess livestock manure were either exported to the intensive husbandry of inland Flanders or redistributed amongst the large, specialised cereal-growing farms within the coastal region itself (figure 2). In other coastal regions in the Low Countries, also characterised by large-scale commercial farming, similar redistributive flows of livestock manure have been observed (Priester 1991, 233). The use of higher amounts of seed-corn per unit area of cereal land, the less intensive weed control and the greater importance of fallowing all point to the more extensive method of farming in the coastal plain as opposed to the intensive methods in inland Flanders.[8] The reason for this must be sought in the fact that the daily operations on the large commercial farms – often exceeding 50 hectares – were based on the labour input of agricultural day labourers. The labour costs were weighted against the returns and always kept as low as possible (Thoen & Soens 2015, 221-258). This labour-saving strategy was also reflected in the manuring practice (i.e. fields were manured only once every five or six years as compared to every two or three years on the large farms in inland Flanders) (van Cruyningen 2000, 189). As manuring was far less important in this large-scale, market-oriented farming region, little urban manure ended up on these farms.

Such differences in farming practices in general, and fertilising systems in particular, also existed in northern France and England. The large *fermiers* in the Île-de-France – the region surrounding Paris – and the large English capitalistic farms, with farms of up to 100 hectares and more, intensified their manuring efforts in the course of the sevententh and eighteenth centuries, but this intensification can hardly be compared to fertilisation standards in the smallholding economy of inland Flanders. In the latter region fallowing had virtually disappeared in the eighteenth century while the *fermiers* in the Île-de-France managed to reduce the amount of fallow from about a third of their farmland in the second half of the seventeenth century to approximately a quarter by the end of the eighteenth. At the same time the *fermiers* increased the amount of *prairies artificielles* (soil-improving crops like sainfoin, alfalfa or clover) and *refroissis* (legume cultivation on fallow) (Delmaire & Delleaux 2015, 196; Chevet 1999, 90). They also got more of the '*premier sole*' (i.e. the part of the triennial rotation devoted to winter cereals) fertilised but still stuck on a maximum of 33 per cent of the total cultivated acreage fertilised each year (compared to 42 per cent on the large farms in our sample region in inland Flanders) (Moriceau 1994, 423-426 compared to our database). Whilst the proportion of arable land dressed with farmyard manure remained quite constant over time on the large farms in the Île-de-France, more land was fertilised by folding sheep overnight in pens on the arable, known as '*parcage*' (Moriceau

---

8   Although this statement needs to be qualified because coastal Flemish agriculture continued to adopt some intensive cultivation practices (especially weeding) from its medieval past as a peasant region, which contributed to a relatively high productivity of land (van Cruyningen 2000, 176-178). It nevertheless seems to hold true for manuring activity.

1994, 423-426). This system of manuring was interesting for these large *fermiers* from a labour-saving perspective, which was also adopted on large farms in certain regions of the northern Low Countries and England (Brusse 1999, 290; Turner et al. 2001, 85). However, urban manure also increasingly ended up on the fields of the *fermiers* in the Île-de-France in the form of horse dung or *poudrette* (i.e. the result of drying and pulverising human waste, a process which gained importance at the end of the eighteenth century and really came into its own in the nineteenth) (Moriceau 1994, 660-661; Chevet 1999, 94). Street wastes and night soil from Paris were most popular on the smaller farms of urban and peri-urban horticulturalists and winegrowers, whereas the majority of processed/dried night soil or *poudrette* was sold to the larger *fermiers* in the Île-de-France or in regions which were opened up by rivers, canals or adequate road (or later railway) infrastructure (Herment 2017, 95-126) One of the main determinants for applying these fertilisers on the large farms was their cost price. Therefore, it can be assumed that the popularity of processed night soil on the large farms can at least partly be explained by the smaller amount of labour needed to manage this dried and pulverised fertiliser input in contrast to unprocessed forms of urban manure. Although applications in the region of the '*grande culture*' were on the rise, urban waste and (processed) night soil were still used in dribs and drabs, as Laurent Herment (2017, 95-126) has pointed out. Despite their efforts, the regions of large-scale commercial cereal farming in northern France and the Île-de-France did not reach the same yields as did regions like the Béthunois, Walloon Flanders and the north of Hainaut. These were regions where large *censier*-farmers co-existed with a broad range of small and medium-sized holdings, very much like the *Flemish Husbandry* (Delleaux 2012, 34-47). Like the Flemish large farmers, the large *censiers* in the latter regions could intensify their farming approach thanks to a large and low-cost labour pool (Delleaux 2012, 119). Although detailed research at farm level is currently lacking, I suppose that the large capitalist farmers in England – the prime movers behind the so-called Agricultural Revolution – ran their vast estates in broadly similar ways to their French counterparts in the Île-de-France as far as their fertility management was concerned. To follow a very intensive course of fertilisation purely on the basis of wage labour was not an option for them. They would have adopted off-farm fertilisers only after weighing the benefits (i.e. output increase) against the costs (i.e. the fertiliser cost price as well as the labour costs involved in the physical act of broadcasting). This can explain the restricted spread of certain off-farm fertiliser inputs such as yard dung, marl and ashes on these farms, as observed by Brunt (2007, 342) and Turner, Beckett and Afton (2001, 81-84).

To a certain extent, Patrick O'Brien and Jean-Michel Chevet were right when they argued that cultivators on both sides of the Channel (which we consider to be the North Sea area) had access to the same 'constricted options available to maintain and to improve crop yields' (O'Brien 1996, 219; Chevet 1999, 83-104). However, the way in which different types of farmers actually incorporated these options into their fertilising patterns differed widely from region to region. It was the regional structure of agriculture (with characteristics such as systems of reciprocal exchange between large and small farmers or the preponderance of wage labour on large farms, the availability of a cheap labour force, the specific proportion of smallholdings to large farms, the kinds of crops grown and their fertiliser requirements, etc.) in combination with specific institutional settings (such as the ownership rights over improvements made during tenancies) and the quality of transport between cities and their hinterlands that shaped the fertilising methods of various types of farmers as a response to challenges and opportunities.

Towards the edge of the *Flemish Husbandry*

As a reaction to the economic situation of declining prices in proto-industry and the (urban) landowners' efforts to nibble at profits by setting higher rents, turning to the use of off-farm fertilisers and intensifying farm production became a compelling strategy for farming households in inland Flanders in order to safeguard their survival strategies (in the case of smallholders) or maintain reasonable profit margins (in the case of larger farmers). This compelling strategy of continuously adjusting farming practice and trying to increase output in order to survive or maintain profits confirmed and reproduced existing unequal power balances between cultivators and landowners, between smallholding peasants and large farmers, and between the city and the countryside. The smallholders needed the transport facilities of the larger farmers to get the night soil, ashes and lime on their fields. The smallholding families therefore had to perform disproportionally extra labour on the farms of the latter. The surplus output, resulting from the improvement in fertilisation management, further incentivised the landowners to skim off profits, resulting in a substantial cash flow from countryside to city. Thus, the fertiliser improvement was one of the cornerstones of *Flemish Husbandry* that facilitated the continuing process of fragmentation of holdings until the system collapsed in the nineteenth century.

The fragmentation of holdings continued in the nineteenth century and the importance of leasehold amongst smallholders expanded against a background of ever-increasing land prices and rents. In the 1790s, rents represented 69 per cent of the total surplus extraction (i.e. rents and land taxes). The total amount of extracted surplus further grew as a result of the growing rental prices, which accounted for more than 80 per cent of the total surplus extraction by the mid-nineteenth century (Vanhaute 2001, 32-35). All of the productivity gains made in agriculture during the eighteenth and nineteenth centuries were pruned away by private landowners (Vanhaute 2001, 34-35). In the second quarter of the nineteenth century almost one fifth of the gross returns of agriculture were transferred to non-farming landowners. Some of these non-farming landowners lived in the city, the rest of them belonging to the rural nobility, the clergy or being village worthies.[9] As the expenditure pattern of the last three groups was also 'urban' to a large extent (luxury consumption), they also channelled rent to the city. Furthermore, the rural linen industry collapsed. The small farmers were time and again pushed into maximising the output of their land in order to maintain their survival algorithms as well as possible (Thoen & Vanhaute 1999, 290-292). From that point of view, the new fertiliser approach of the second half of the eighteenth

---

9 E.g. in the case of the province of eastern Flanders, Phil Kint was able to estimate that by 1850 no fewer than 35-45 per cent of income from landed property (in the form of rents) flowed from the countryside to the cities. Moreover, he estimated that income from rents was considerably larger than income from the burgeoning cotton industry in the first half of the nineteenth century in the city of Ghent: the total income from the cotton industry in Ghent around 1850 was estimated at 4 million Belgian francs, whereas the income from rents with respect to just the province of eastern Flanders was calculated to have amounted to 4.64 million Belgian francs (Kint 1989, 314-328).

century – based on intensive manuring with nutrients recuperated on-farm and applying additional urban and industrial fertiliser inputs – is most likely to have continued and to have been optimised in the course of the first half of the nineteenth century.

From the mid-nineteenth century rural production was severely hit by the crisis in the linen industry (i.e. declining prices and export problems) at the same time as the subdivision of holdings had reached its zenith. The system of reciprocal exchange came under stress since there were too few large farms to provide employment for the large number of, especially, cottage families (Thoen & Vanhaute 1999, 290-292). Moreover, new techniques such as machinery, artificial fertilisers and crop protection were gradually introduced on the larger farms, which reduced their need for agricultural labour. This change in agrarian structures, together with a range of other factors, ushered in the downturn of the re-use of urban organic waste, which had been a cornerstone of *Flemish Husbandry*. The system of co-existence between large and small farms, which was important for the supply of off-farm fertilisers to the smallholdings, was shaken to its foundations. Related to this factor, and due to the problems of the rural proto-industry, lots of smallholding cottagers had to leave the agricultural sector for urban factory work or for a life abroad. Furthermore, when new fertilisers (such as guano) were imported and artificial fertilisers began to be spread, urban organic waste increasingly became useless as a fertiliser due to new systems of waste disposal (i.e. water-based sewage systems) (e.g. Blomme 1992, 155-158). As a consequence, the manure trade from city to country gradually declined in importance in the second half of the nineteenth and the first half of the twentieth centuries.

The way in which large farmers and especially smallholders had improved their fertilisation strategies by the second half of the eighteenth century contributed to the delay in the downfall of the rural linen industry and the continuation of the proto-industrial household model, albeit at high costs. To state it boldly: the city sold its waste as manure at a high price and cashed in once more by increasing its share of agricultural and proto-industrial profits (i.e. the exponential rise in rents), which further provoked the countryside into applying more urban fertilisers. The use of off-farm fertilisers thus reproduced and enhanced the existing power relations between town and country as well as the ones within rural society itself. Hence the new fertiliser approach of the second half of the eighteenth century marked the onset of what has been labelled a 'rich agriculture and poor farmers' (Vanhaute 2001, 19-40). With an eye on the future, this historical essay makes clear that the way to a successful circular economy in the food and agriculture sectors does not just depend on closing the environmental loops of nutrient resources as well as possible. The social aspects of circularity should not be disregarded. In reaching a sustainable circular economy in the food and agriculture sectors, adequate attention should go to guaranteeing well-balanced social property relations along the value chain of nutrient recycling with a fair distribution of risks, costs and benefits among all actors involved.

References

Barles, Sabine. 2005. "A metabolic approach to the city: nineteenth and twentieth century Paris."
    In *Resources of the City. Contributions to an Environmental History of Modern Europe*, ed.
    Dieter Schott et al., 28-47. Aldershot: Ashgate.

Blomme, Jan. 1992. *The economic development of Belgian agriculture 1880-1980. A quantitative and qualitative analysis.* Studies in Belgian economic history 3. Brussels [publisher].

Broadberry, S., et al. 2015. *British Economic Growth, 1270-1870.* Cambridge: Cambridge University Press.

Brunt, Liam. 2007. "'Where there's Muck, there's Brass'. The Market for Manure in the Industrial Revolution." *The Economic History Review* 60, no. 2: 333-372.

Brusse, Paul. 1999. *Overleven door ondernemen. De agrarische geschiedenis van de Over-Betuwe 1650-1850.* AAG 38. Wageningen: Wageningen Universiteit.

Chevet, Jean-Michel. 1999. *La terre et les paysans en France et et en Grande-Bretagne. Du début du XVIIe siècle à la fin du XVIIIe siècle. Vol. II: Les hommes et la production.* Paris: Editions Messene.

De Boer, I., and M. van Ittersum. 2018. *Circularity in agricultural production. Mansholt lecture 2018.* Wageningen: WUR.

De Graef, Pieter. 2016. *Urbs in Rure? Urban manure and fertiliser improvement in 18th-century Flemish farming.* PhD dissertation: University of Antwerp.

De Graef, Pieter. 2017a. "A green revolution from below? A social approach to fertiliser use in eighteenth-century Flanders." *Continuity and Change* 32, no. 3: 379-410.

De Graef, Pieter. 2017b. "Food from country to city, waste from city to country. An environmental symbiosis? Fertiliser improvement in eighteenth-century Flanders." *Journal for the History of Environment and Society.* 2: 25-61.

De Graef, Pieter. 2019. "La valorisation des déchets urbains et l'amélioration des plans de fertilisation dans l'agriculture flamande du XVIIIe siècle." In *Fumiers! Ordures! Gestion et Usage des Déchets dans les Campagnes de l'Occident Médiéval et Moderne.* Actes des XXXVIIIes Journées Internationales d'Histoire de l'Abbaye de Flaran, ed. Marc Conesa and Nicolas Poirier, 231-255. Toulouse: Presses Universitaires du Midi.

Dejongh, Guy. 1999. "New estimates of land productivity in Belgium, 1750-1850." *Agricultural History Review* 47, no. 1: 7-28.

Delleaux, Fulgence. 2012. *Les censiers et les mutations des campagnes du Hainaut français. La formation originale d'une structure socio-économique (fin XVIIe-début XIXe siècle).* Namur: Presses Universitaires de Namur.

Delmaire, Bruno, and Fulgence Delleaux. 2015. "Northern France, 1000-1750." In *Struggling with the environment: land use and productivity*, ed. Erik Thoen and Tim Soens, 149-184. Turnhout: Brepols.

Drangert, J. 1998. "Fighting the urine blindness to provide more sanitation options." *Water South Africa* 24, no. 2: 157-164.

Federico, Giovanni. 2005. *Feeding the World. An Economic History of Agriculture, 1800-2000.* Princeton, NJ: Princeton University Press.

Goossens, Martine. 1992. *The economic development of Belgian agriculture: a regional perspective, 1812-1846.* Brussels: Koninklijke Academie voor Wetenschappen, Letteren en Schone Kunsten.

Herment, Laurent. 2017. "Vidanges et fertilisants. Le cas de la poudrette parisienne au milieu du dix-neuvième siècle." *Journal for the History of Environment and Society* 2: 95-126.

Kint, Phil. 1989. *Prometheus aangevuurd door Demeter. De economische ontwikkeling van de landbouw in Oost-Vlaanderen 1815-1850.* Amsterdam: VU Uitgeverij.

Lambrecht, Thijs. 2002. *Een grote hoeve in een klein dorp. Relaties van arbeid en pacht op het Vlaamse platteland tijdens de 18de eeuw.* Ghent: Academia Press.

Lambrecht, Thijs. 2003 "Reciprocal exchange, credit and cash: agricultural labour markets and local economies in the southern Low Countries during the eighteenth century." *Continuity and Change* 18, no. 2: 237-261.

Massard-Guilbaud, Geneviève, and Richard Rodger, eds. 2011. *Environmental and Social Justice in the City: Historical Perspectives.* Cambridge: The White Horse Press.

Moriceau, Jean-Marc. 1994. *Les fermiers de l'Île-de-France: l'ascension d'un patronat agricole (XVe-XVIIIe siècle).* Paris: Fayard.

Moore, Jason. 2000. "Environmental crises and the metabolic rift in world-historical perspective." *Organization and Environment* 13, no. 2: 123-157.

O'Brien, Patrick. 1996. "Path Dependency, or why Britain became an Industrialized and Urbanized Economy long before France." *The Economic History Review* 49, no. 2: 213-249.

Priester, Peter. 1991. *De economische ontwikkeling van de landbouw in Groningen 1800-1910. Een kwalitatieve en kwantitatieve analyse.* Historiae Agriculturae 24, Groningen.

Tanner, R. 2001. "The waste of human wastes. A discussion of a global ongoing loss of nutrient assets." *Human Ecology* 10: 130-136.

Thoen, Erik. 2001. "A 'commercial survival economy' in evolution. The Flemish countryside and the transition to capitalism (Middle Ages-19th century)." In *Peasants into farmers? The transformation of rural economy and society in the Low Countries (middle ages-19th century) in light of the Brenner debate,* ed. Peter Hoppenbrouwers and Jan Luiten van Zanden, 102-157. Corn publication series 4, Turnhout: Brepols.

Thoen, Erik, and Eric Vanhaute. 1999. "The 'Flemish Husbandry' at the edge: the Farming System on Smallholdings in the Middle of the 19th Century." In *Land Productivity and Agro-Systems in the North Sea Area (Middle Ages-20th Century),* ed. Bas van Bavel and Peter Hoppenbrouwers, 271-296. Corn publication series 2, Turnhout: Brepols.

Thoen, Erik, and Tim Soens, eds. 2015. *Struggling with the Environment: Land Use and Productivity.* 4th volume in the series Rural Economy and Society in Northwestern Europe, 500-2000. Turnhout: Brepols.

Turner, M., J. Beckett and B. Afton. 2001. *Farm Production in England 1700-1914.* Oxford: Oxford University Press.

Van Cruyningen, Piet. 2000. *Behoudend maar buigzaam. Boeren in West-Zeeuws-Vlaanderen 1650-1850.* AAG 40, Wageningen: Wageningen University.

Vanhaute, Eric. 2001. "Rich agriculture and poor farmers: land, landlords and farmers in Flanders in the eighteenth and nineteenth centuries." *Rural history* 12, no. 1: 19-40.

Vanhaute, Eric, and Thijs Lambrecht. 2011. "Famine, exchange networks and the village community. A comparative analysis of the subsistence crises of the 1740s and the 1840s in Flanders." *Continuity and Change* 26, no. 2: 155-186.

Van Zon, Henk. 2012-2013. "Cradle to cradle in het verleden: agrarisch hergebruik van stedelijk vuilnis in Nederland en omringende landen, 1800-2000." *Jaarboek voor Ecologische Geschiedenis*: 41-67.

Vermoesen, Reinoud. 2011. *Markttoegang en 'commerciële' netwerken van rurale huishoudens. De regio Aalst, 1650-1800.* Ghent: Academia Press.

Cities in Motion

Mobility, Migration Selectivity and Demographic Change in Belgian Cities, 1846-1910

Introduction

In collective memory and traditional historiography migration to nineteenth-century cities carries with it a powerful association with marginalisation and desperation. In this view, migration complicated, if not caused, the widening problems of urban overcrowding, poverty and social disintegration as cities grew at an unprecedented speed during Europe's transition from pre-industrial to industrial society. The uncontrolled immigration of record numbers of urban newcomers spurred middle class anxiety over the 'social question' by the close of the long nineteenth century – a disenchanting cocktail of slum formation, poverty, congestion, alcoholism, family abandonment and unemployment (Jackson 1997). The prospects that awaited nineteenth-century urban migrants were considered to have been bleak indeed, and their movements as guided more by despair than by any hope of betterment – as captured tellingly by the mid-nineteenth-century reflections of one of Dickens' protagonists as she observed migrants on their way to London: 'always … in one direction – always towards the town … towards which they seemed impelled by a desperate fascination … Food for the hospitals, the churchyards, the prisons, the river, fever, madness, vice, and death – they passed on to the monster, roaring in the distance, and were lost' (Dickens 1848). Also in nineteenth-century Belgium, uncontrolled migration to cities was often problematised in elite and middle-class opinion as fostering problems of urban poverty, disease, lawlessness and crime – especially during times of rural crisis, such as the 1845-47 crop failures and the depression of the 1870s and 1880s (Van Damme 1990). Conversely, researchers on social inequality often assume that the permanent influx of newcomers offset any internal dynamics of upward social mobility within urban populations, thereby perpetuating, if not widening, social inequality in cities (Ryckbosch 2010).

Migration historians have however in the past decades significantly nuanced the image of nineteenth-century urban migration as one-directional desperate moves by rural people uprooted in the transition from pre-industrial to industrial society. While migration rates did record unprecedented levels in the long nineteenth century, mobility patterns were much more complex than a one-off transfer of the population from the countryside to cities: people moved in many directions at different stages of their life courses (Moch 2003; Lucassen and Lucassen 2009; Pooley 2017). Moreover, most urban newcomers were not 'subsistence migrants', but were often positively selected in terms of

Hilde Greefs • University of Antwerp

Anne Winter • Vrije Universiteit Brussel

Inequality and the City in the Low Countries (1200-2020), ed. by Bruno BLONDÉ, Sam GEENS, Hilde GREEFS, Wouter RYCKBOSCH, Tim SOENS & Peter STABEL, SEUH 50 (Turnhout, 2020), pp. 79-102.

© BREPOLS 🏛 PUBLISHERS   DOI 10.1484/M.SEUH-EB.5.120439

human capital. An important group of those who settled in cities might be characterised as 'betterment migrants', and as such often fared better than their city-born counterparts (Sewell 1985; Williamson 1990; Winter 2009). The relationship between migration and urban growth was not simple cause and effect: cities not only welcomed growing numbers of newcomers in this period, but also recorded increasing levels of out-migration at the same time (Jackson 1997; Hochstadt 1999; Winter 2009; Eggerickx 2010). Since these urban patterns of immigration and emigration varied through time and space, they had a divergent impact on the composition of urban populations and shaped the face and fate of individual cities in different ways.

Urban historians have emphasised that the speed of urban growth differed between nineteenth-century cities: periods of accelerated growth alternated with periods of deceleration and sometimes even contraction, while not all cities prospered at the same time or to the same extent. Dynamics of economic expansion, driven by processes of industrialisation, are often considered the main explanation for differences in urban growth. However, recent historiography has emphasised that this relationship between industrialisation and urban growth was not straightforward. Some new industrial centres experienced exceptionally fast growth during the nineteenth century, but other centres did not – while service towns and port cities also recorded high increases in population (Lawton and Lee 2002). Distinct work opportunities probably represent a major explanation, but these did not affect all people in the same way, since labour markets were highly segmented according to gender, age, background and skill. In addition, the vicinity of other urban centres, acting as intervening opportunities in the decision processes of migrants, could hamper demographic expansion.

These observations illustrate that relations between mobility and migration on the one hand and urban growth and inequality on the other are still in need of further research. Belgian cities represent an interesting case because of Belgium's precocious industrialisation and urbanisation in the context of a long-standing urban tradition. The well-developed road and waterway networks, as well as the early development of a dense railway infrastructure, facilitated mobility both within the country and from neighbouring countries. Early industrialisation in Belgium was furthermore characterised by a so-called demographic paradox: the industrial centres in the southern or Walloon half of the country modernised in a sparsely populated region, while the Flemish part was densely populated but lagged behind economically (Vanhaute 2007; Eggerickx 2010). As industrialisation was, particularly in the early years, a labour-intensive affair, migration therefore represented a vital conduit for Belgium's industrial labour markets of the nineteenth century. Already characterised by a long-standing urban tradition, accelerated urbanisation went hand in hand with extreme housing shortages, growing inner-city poverty, the spread of disease, and increasing moral panics as the long nineteenth century progressed (Lis 1977; Van Damme 1990; Tollebeek et al. 2003). The urgency of the 'social question' reached a high point at its close, symbolised by the 1891 reform of social policy, which combined heightened repression of vagrancy and 'debauchery' with a firm belief in social re-education (Christiaens 1999; Vercammen 2014).

This chapter will not be able to provide any conclusive answers to the question whether and how migration contributed to rising social inequality and social deprivation in nineteenth-century cities. Such endeavours have to await the availability of studies and/or data that provide comprehensive insights into the social positions of migrants and locally-born town dwellers in a longitudinal and comparative perspective. Yet in the meantime we aim to at least provide some oblique indications on this central question by exploiting a range of data that have recently become available, and which allow us to explore further the demographic side of the relationship between migration and urban development. While this implies that this chapter's empirical findings are limited to a purely demographic perspective, they nevertheless have important implications for the social experience of urban migration in Belgium's long nineteenth century.

For such an undertaking, Belgium has the advantage of an early preoccupation with population registration and statistics: dynamic nominal population registers were in place in all municipalities from 1846 onwards, and were accompanied by ten-yearly censuses – of which the aggregate results were published in impressive volumes with municipal figures – and regularly published yearly statistics on the *Mouvement de la population,* i.e. numbers of births, deaths, in-movements and out-movements at the level of municipalities. Thanks to the recent digitisation efforts of the LOKSTAT and IMMIBEL projects,[1] these data are available in spreadsheet format, which allow for a quantitative analysis of different components of urban growth and dynamics of migration at city level. By comparing these figures on population and migration for several Belgian cities from 1846 to 1910, this chapter constitutes a first exploration of these data to unravel the dynamics and timing of changes in urban growth, migration and mobility in this transformative period. It does this by looking at population, migration and mobility levels in different types of cities, and combining them with insights from existing case studies. For this analysis we have selected a number of major cities with a long-standing urban tradition (Antwerp, Brussels, Ghent and Liège), a number of new centres that urbanised only in the nineteenth century in the wake of their spectacular industrialisation (Charleroi, Seraing), and a number of suburban municipalities surrounding major cities that gradually became integrated into the urban agglomeration during the nineteenth century (Borgerhout near Antwerp, Anderlecht near Brussels, Ledeberg near Ghent).

By looking at demographic change over time as well as at the levels of migration and turnover, the chapter aims further to explore the impact of migration and mobility on the growth and composition of urban populations in different settings. By comparing the relative contributions of native-born residents, internal migrants (moving within Belgium) and foreign migrants (born abroad) to demographic developments, the chapter aims to identify more clearly their relative weight in the changing urban populations of the nineteenth century. Since internal migrants have received most attention in Belgian historiography so far (Eggerickx 2010; Deschacht & Winter 2015), a last section will focus more specifically on the presence of foreigners to scrutinise their contribution to Belgian urbanisation. The overall aim of this chapter is to highlight the dissimilar behaviour of migrant groups in different urban settings, and to highlight how this resulted in a varied landscape in which the relationship between cities and migrants differed markedly according to local context.

---

1   *Historische Databank van Lokale Statistieken – LOKSTAT, University of Ghent* (http://www.lokstat.ugent.be), www.immibel.arch.be.

Demographic growth in different urban settings

Overall population increased significantly in Belgium over the nineteenth century, a general dynamic explained primarily by a combination of high fertility rates and declining mortality rates – making it one of the classic examples of the so-called demographic transition. The Belgian population rose from 4.3 million in 1846 to 7.4 million in 1910, with the largest increases recorded in cities and adjoining suburban areas (see also Deprez and Vandenbroeke 1989).

In 1846, only Ghent and Brussels had more than 100,000 inhabitants, later followed by Antwerp (1856) and Liège (1880) (Table 1). Antwerp was the city that recorded the strongest increase over the period, with a population exceeding 300,000 inhabitants by 1910. It was spurred by the marked expansion of maritime and commercial activities, which accelerated after the redemption of the Scheldt toll in 1863. Antwerp's role in the Atlantic economy was further strengthened by its function as the place of embarkation for hundreds of thousands of migrants to America and Canada (Veraghtert 1986; Lis 1986). The strong population growth was facilitated by the urbanisation of previously sparsely populated areas *extra muros* – that were juridically part of the urban territory and became more densely populated and functionally integrated into the urban fabric after the demolition of the city walls from the 1860s onwards. Brussels had no such *extra muros* areas that were part of the urban municipality and its territory remained more or less delimited by the *tracé* of its *ancien régime* walls – the so-called pentagon. Thus, population growth in the municipality of Brussels proper was necessarily limited, but adjacent municipalities experienced marked expansion during the nineteenth century as they increasingly became integrated into the Brussels agglomeration (Zitouni 2010; Eggerickx 2013). Located at the core of the Belgian kingdom, the attractiveness of Brussels proper was connected to its role as the capital city and as the administrative and financial heart of the industrialising country, while large-scale industrial employment was located mainly in the surrounding municipalities. Antwerp and Brussels, both centres of trade and service without much mechanised production, remained at the top of the Belgian urban hierarchy, with larger populations than more industrial cities such as Ghent (in Flanders) and Liège, Charleroi and Verviers (in the Walloon region) (Greefs, Blondé & Clark 2005).

Already early in the nineteenth century, Ghent experienced rapid modernisation of its textile industries, hosting the first completely integrated and mechanised cotton factories on the continent. This early industrialisation was accompanied by fast demographic growth in the early nineteenth century. In the Liège-Vesder region, the traditional woollen industry in Verviers was modernised under the impetus of the Cockerill family, who subsequently stimulated the development of iron processing and machine building in the Liège area, which developed into the major centre of modern metallurgy on the European continent. The strongest urban growth in Liège occurred in the first half of the century, when population increased from about 46,000 inhabitants in 1806 to nearly 76,000 in 1846. Since transport imperatives favoured location in the proximity of coal mines, however, a whole series of smaller metallurgy centres, such as Tilleul or d'Ougrée, expanded in the area and population growth spread over this whole area. A similar dynamic took place

Table 1. Population in selected Belgian municipalities, 1846-1910, in numbers

Municipality	1846	1856	1866	1880	1890	1900	1910
Antwerp	88487	102761	117269	169112	224012	272831	301766
Borgerhout	5347	7308	10884	20268	28882	37693	49333
Brussels	123874	152828	157905	162498	176138	183686	177078
Anderlecht	5966	7465	11580	22812	32311	47929	64137
Ghent	102977	108925	115354	131431	148729	160133	166445
Ledeberg	3597	4066	5606	10124	12362	14230	13999
Charleroi	7490	10702	11856	16372	20668	24460	28177
Liège	75961	89411	99129	123131	147660	157760	167521
Seraing	10540	16835	19451	27407	33495	37845	41015
Verviers	23363	27115	32011	40944	48907	49067	46948
Total Belgium	4337196	4529460	4827833	5520009	6069321	6693548	7423784

Italicized places are suburban districts

Source: Population censuses, 1846-1910. Database LOKSTAT, Quetelet Center, Ghent University.

in the Charleroi region, which became the centre of an industrial basin consisting of a northern part with coal-mining and glass-production and an eastern part with heavy industry, based on iron-melting and iron-processing (Van der Wee 1996). In the Charleroi region, population was spread over smaller industrial settings, situated around the coal mines and factories. This region as a whole experienced impressive demographic growth at a rate comparable to that recorded in suburban districts of the Brussels agglomeration, but even though Charleroi's population grew fast, it did not exceed 30,000 inhabitants during the nineteenth century (Eggerickx 2004).

Over time, the suburban districts surrounding the older cities started to grow rapidly. Around the middle of the century, Borgerhout (near Antwerp) and Anderlecht (near Brussels) had a population of more than 5,000 inhabitants, as did Ledeberg (near Ghent) from 1866 onwards. These suburban municipalities developed from quasi-rural villages to densely populated suburban – or arguably urban – districts in the later nineteenth century. Anderlecht was situated in the first belt round the city proper, which consisted of a more industrial zone (Anderlecht, Vorst, Molenbeek) and a more 'bourgeois' zone, all characterised by marked population growth during the nineteenth century (Eggerickx 2013). By 1910, the population of Anderlecht and Borgerhout had grown by a factor of 10.7 and 9.2 respectively, which was much higher than for instance that of Ledeberg, where population had multiplied by 3.8. From 1866 onwards, more people lived in Anderlecht and Borgerhout than, for instance, in the old city of Charleroi, Seraing and Verviers. Population growth in these suburban districts accelerated from the 1860s onwards and continued to rise during the period under study, while population growth slowed down in cities like Brussels and Ghent, whose growth was skimmed off by that of their suburban districts.

Migration, mobility and urban growth

Census results recorded among other things the number of people born within and outside the municipality in which they resided, and as such they provide cross-sectional information about the population composition at a given moment in time. We used the population figures of subsequent censuses to calculate inter-census average annual growth rates of the whole urban population and the contribution to this growth by migrants and locally-born residents respectively ('growth contribution rates'), i.e. that part of the inter-census average annual growth rate of the whole urban population that was attributable to the growth of this particular subpopulation.[2] These 'growth contribution rates' therefore give insight into the *net* demographic contribution of particular subgroups to overall urban growth between two censuses, but offer only static and indirect indications of the underlying dynamics of migration and mobility. We therefore complemented these cross-sectional data with dynamic data on annual immigration and emigration recorded in the *Mouvement de la population*. By comparing these gross indications of on-going mobility with net indications on population growth attributable to the increase in immigrants, it is possible to compare overall levels of immigration and emigration with their eventual impact on population growth – to compare flows with their impact on the stocks.

Graph 1 therefore expresses both average inter-census 'growth contribution rates' of migrants for different types of cities (against the right-hand axis) and annual rates of immigration and emigration (against the left-hand axis) between 1846 and 1910. Let us start with exploring the latter. A first observation is that overall immigration and emigration rates, i.e. the number of moves in and out of the city per 100 inhabitants, increased markedly and more or less consistently over time in all types of cities, reflecting a strong overall increase in mobility. While annual immigration was the equivalent of circa 2 per cent of the population in major cities in the 1840s, by the end of the century this had increased to no less than 10 per cent of the population. A second and closely linked observation is that emigration rates moved closely in tandem with immigration rates, indicating that they were two sides of the same coin. Existing research indicates that many of these emigrants were

---

2   We used data on population figures to calculate inter-census absolute increase and inter-census average annual growth rates for the whole urban population, and we used data on the number of locally-born and non-locally-born residents in the same censuses to calculate the inter-census absolute increase of non-migrant and migrant subpopulations respectively. By multiplying for each subgroup the share of their inter-census increase in the overall inter-census increase with the average annual growth rate of the whole urban population, we calculated what we called the 'growth contribution rates' of each subgroup. For example: the growth of Antwerp's population from 88,487 in 1846 to 102,761 represents a net increase of 14,274 inhabitants, the equivalent of an average annual growth rate of 1.5 per cent. This net increase of 14,274 was composed of a net increase of 8,550 Antwerp-born residents (from 57,078 in 1846 to 65,628 in 1856) and a net increase of 5,724 immigrant residents (from 31,409 in 1846 to 37,133 in 1856). Thus, the net increase in immigrants realised 40 per cent of the overall net increase, and Antwerp-born residents 60 per cent. Transposing these respective growth shares on the average annual growth rate of the whole population (1.5 per cent) results in immigrants contributing an average annual growth rate of 0.6 per cent and Antwerp-born residents one of 0.9 per cent. These 'growth contribution rates' therefore do not express the average annual growth rate of the subgroup itself (which could be heavily influenced by small base figures in smaller municipalities), but reflect that part of overall urban growth that can be attributed to the growth of this particular subpopulation – hence they allow us to compare not only the respective contributions to urban growth between different groups, but also their impact on overall urban demographic development.

also former immigrants (Pasleau 1993; 1994; Winter 2009), and the overall increase of both immigration and emigration rates together is therefore indicative of a marked increase in overall turnover of urban populations in the second half of the long nineteenth century. While these trends confirm observations on increasing mobility in existing literature, their extremely high levels indicate the importance of realising that unprecedented turnover was probably the most defining characteristic of the urban experience at the close of the long nineteenth century. By then, gross rates of annual mobility – i.e. the sum of both immigration and emigration rates – constituted the equivalent of no less than 20 per cent of the population in major cities such as Brussels and Antwerp, and no less than 30 per cent in suburbs and new industrial centres! In other words, urban populations were highly volatile by this time, with the equivalent of one fifth to one third of the population moving in and out of urban boundaries *each year*.[3] Conversely, the difference between emigration and immigration rates, i.e. the rate of net migration, remained remarkably stable throughout the period. This already indicates that notwithstanding the marked increase in migration levels, the direct demographic contribution of migration to urban population growth may not have changed very much over this period – something we will explore further below.

The even greater rates of mobility observed in suburbs and new industrial centres compared to older cities bring us to a third observation, which pertains to differences between city types. Although a general growth of mobility was observable in all cases, levels and trends varied according to city type. Suburban districts such as Borgerhout and Anderlecht recorded significantly higher rates of migration than their urban centres throughout the period, while new industrial centres like Charleroi and Seraing likewise overtook older cities in migration levels from at least the 1850s onwards. We know from existing research that mobility rates were indeed very high in industrial centres such as Charleroi and Seraing. They were part of a larger industrial basin with multiple centres between which labourers regularly relocated (Eggerickx 2004). Analysis of workers' *livrets* shows that nineteenth-century coalminers on average changed their place of work eighteen times in their career (Leboutte 1995). In Seraing, 20 to 30 per cent of the migrant population stayed in the city for less than one year, and often moved to and fro to nearby places (Pasleau 1993). These 'micro-mobilities' within industrial basins have been explained by a search for better jobs and higher wages, but also by the regular depletion of coal sites, which prompted these manual labourers to look for other work opportunities. In addition, these different nearby centres functioned as intervening opportunities in migration decisions and resulted in severe competition in a sector that experienced labour shortages throughout the entire nineteenth century (Caestecker 2008). Particularly during the 1846-80 period – with peaks in the wake of the 1845-47 subsistence crisis and of the

---

3   The underlying dynamics and geography of immigration and emigration are in themselves in need of more detailed research, but it is worthwhile pointing out that the marked increase in urban turnover is not solely an artefact stemming from the movement between city centres and the surrounding municipalities that increasingly became integrated into one urban agglomeration. One exploration of the nominal emigration registers for the city of Antwerp in combination with aggregate figures from the *Mouvement de l'état civil* indicates that in 1890 around 27 per cent of all recorded movement out of the city was towards one of its six surrounding municipalities (Borgerhout, Deurne, Berchem, Hoboken, Wilrijk, Merksem) (SAA (City Archives Antwerp). MA (Modern Archives), no. 74604: Register van afschrijving, 1888-91), while in 1855 this was 19 per cent (SAA, MA, no. 74784: Register van afschrijving 1852-55).

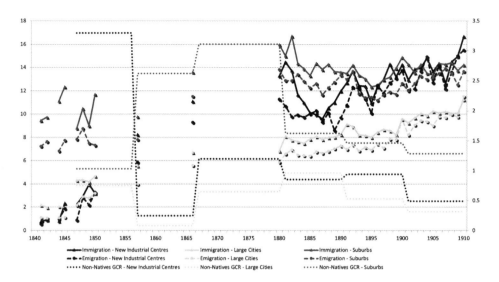

Graph 1. Immigration and emigration rates and inter-census annual growth contribution rates of non-native residents in selected Belgian municipalities, 1846-1910 (per 100 inhabitants)

Notes: Immigration and emigration rates against the left-hand axis. Inter-census annual growth contribution rates (GCR) against the right-hand axis. Source: Census figures & Mouvement de la Population collected by LOKSTAT & IMMIBEL projects.

economic boom of the early 1870s – these industrial centres experienced high levels of immigration and emigration (Eggerickx 2010).

Let us now move from analysing the *flows* (movement in and out of the city) to evaluating the eventual contribution of these migration flows to urban population growth. Already the relatively stable and small difference between immigration and emigration rates (i.e. the rate of net migration) has suggested that this contribution may not have changed very much over this period, and indeed may have remained relatively small. One way to explore this further is to compare the observed trend in immigration and emigration rates with inter-census growth contribution rates of the non-native population, which is expressed in Graph 1 against the right-hand axis. The comparison is not flawless, as immigration and emigration figures do not pertain solely to non-native residents (locally-born residents could move out of and into the city as well), but it is sufficiently indicative to highlight overall trends.

The most important observation is that with the exception of the 1846-56 period for new industrial centres and that of 1856-80 for suburban centres – to which we will return below – overall growth contribution rates of non-native residents remained relatively stable, and even displayed a decreasing trend after 1880, notwithstanding the marked increase in overall migration levels. While migration rates reached an all-time high then, immigrants' contribution to population growth decreased in the closing decades of the long nineteenth century. By 1900-10 non-native residents contributed an average annual growth rate of between 0.4 per cent (in older cities) and 1.2 per cent (in suburbs) of urban populations. While these contributions were far from negligible from the perspective of demographic growth, they were only a fraction of the overall immigration taking place, which in the absence of emigration would have contributed an average annual growth rate of 10 and 15 per cent respectively by this period. Indeed, the 'immigration yield', calculated as the ratio between inter-census growth contribution and overall immigration rates – something which, for lack of data, we can calculate consistently only after 1880 – was low and declined from an average of 11 per cent in the 1880-90 inter-census period, to 7 per cent for 1890-1900 and 5 per cent by 1900-10. In other words, the actual contribution of migrants to demographic growth was less than 10 per cent of overall immigration taking place at the close of the long nineteenth century – confirming yet again turnover rather than settlement as the main experience of urban migration in this period.

A second observation pertains to differences between city types. Throughout the nineteenth century migrants' contribution to population growth was more important in new industrial centres and suburbs than in older cities, as was the overall 'immigration yield'. Since overall absorption capacity – in terms of housing and income opportunities – was lower in existing urban centres, such centres offered less room for growth than new industrial and suburban areas whose populations were much smaller at the beginning of the period. In many cities the old city walls were demolished around mid-century, which further stimulated the integration of suburban districts into the urban agglomeration. Extreme housing shortage in the old city centres as well as large-scale urban building and sanitation projects pushed inhabitants out of the urban cores. This process was intensified by the construction of new transport infrastructure, such as canals (for instance the Charleroi canal in Brussels 1832), stimulating economic activity, and later tramways, stimulating mobility between suburban areas and the city. The absorption of new residents in suburban and new industrial municipalities appears to have been highest in the early decades of the period under consideration – with peaks in 1846-56 for new industrial centres and 1856-80 in suburbs – and likewise displayed decreasing immigration yields by the close of the long nineteenth century. Although in a first phase these municipalities therefore retained a relatively large share of newcomers,[4] by the later decades they were characterised by the same trends of increasing turnover as the larger cities, resulting in an overall convergence of the urban migration experience as highly temporary and unstable.

While the contribution of migration to urban growth was relatively small compared to the overall migration taking place, it still represented a major contribution to the growth of urban populations. Graph 2 represents the relative 'growth contribution rates' of locally-born residents, internal migrants and foreign migrants respectively between the different censuses, of which the sum makes up the overall average annual growth rate. Average annual growth rates of new industrial centres and suburbs were consistently considerably higher than those of older cities – which again can be related to their smaller starting population and greater room for expansion. Periods of particularly high growth with rates of more than 4 per cent were recorded in the earlier decades of the period under consideration: 1846-56 for new industrial centres and 1856-80 for suburban municipalities. Such very high growth rates were invariably spurred by the contribution of immigrants,

---

4   Calculations of immigration yields before 1880 are hampered by the fragmentary availability of immigration rates. If we make do with available figures, immigration yields were 37 per cent in the 1846-56 period (based on figures for 1847-50) and 9 per cent in 1856-66 (based on figures for 1857 and 1866), with very high levels for new industrial centres (+100 per cent) in 1846-56 and suburbs in 1856-66 (+24 per cent).

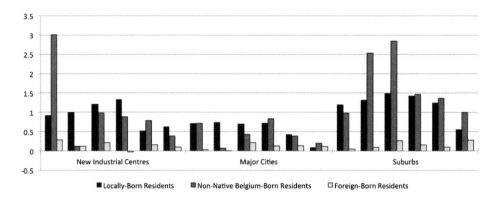

Graph 2. Growth contribution rates of locally-born and non-native residents in selected Belgian municipalities, 1846-1910

Note: each collection of three bars (black, dark grey and light grey) represents the growth contribution rates (GRC) of locally-born, non-native Belgium-born and foreign-born residents respectively for the six consecutive inter-census periods under study (from left to right in chronological order 1846-56, 1856-66, 1866-80, 1880-90, 1890-1900, 1900-10). The sum of each collection of three bars makes up the overall average annual growth rate for each of these inter-census periods per city type.

whose increase was responsible for 60-70 per cent of overall growth in these instances. Related to the earlier discussion on migration rates, it is clear that the contribution of migration was shaped more by immigration yields than by immigration rates. In other words, the most important determining factor for the contribution of immigration to urban growth in nineteenth-century Belgium was the retention of locals rather than the attraction of newcomers. As the former declined from the 1880s onwards, so did overall growth rates, notwithstanding increasing immigration rates. At the turn of the twentieth century, population growth slowed significantly in all types of cities. Declining settlement rates, as well as declining birth rates (Matthijs 2001), explain these shifting patterns.

The end result of these different dynamics is that the average share of non-native residents in the different types of cities increased only slightly over the period under consideration – from 49 per cent in 1846 to 52 per cent in 1910. For suburban districts and new industrial centres there was even no clear trend in this direction, as levels fluctuated from 54 per cent (1846) through 62 per cent (1856) down to 52 per cent (1910) in new industrial centres, and from 57 per cent (1856) through 64 per cent (1880) to 61 per cent (1910) in suburbs. Only in large urban centres was there a consistent but overall modest increase from 38 per cent (1846) to 45 per cent (1910). Over the whole period in all municipalities, then, an average of 50 per cent (in older cities) to 60 per cent (in suburbs and new industrial centres) of population growth was attributable to growth of the immigrant population – hence warranting the conclusion that migration was indeed a major contributor to urban growth, especially if we acknowledge that their presence probably had a knock-on effect on the growth of the 'local' population if they settled to form families. The main caveat, however, is to realise that this contribution was not the result of a simple one-off transfer of population between the countryside and cities, but a small residual of repeated moves in various directions in a context of high and increasing turnover.

The extreme mobility of people constantly moving in and out of cities, however, had a major impact on urban life and organisation, which is reflected, among other things, in the proliferation of urban 'hospitality infrastructure', as well as in the policing of specific neighbourhoods. Districts that housed many labourers or particularly mobile groups as well as streets in the vicinity of places of arrival and departure, such as railway stations, waterfront areas or lodging houses, were controlled more severely as the nineteenth century progressed (see also the contribution of De Koster and Vrints in this volume). This local preoccupation with controlling 'neighbourhoods of arrival' was mirrored in the growing efforts of both national and urban authorities to record, control and monitor migration in the long nineteenth century, in the context of which a dedicated bureaucratic administration to identify and register foreign newcomers was in place from 1834 onwards (Caestecker 2000). In order better to understand the interaction between cities and their mobile population, however, it is necessary to obtain more insight into the profiles of migrants in relation to the places under scrutiny.

Migrant selectivity: gender and distance

The census data do not allow us to differentiate between different types of migrants except for the distinction between internal and foreign migrants on the one hand and between men and women on the other. Yet in a comparative perspective these two distinctions help us to gain further insight into the dynamics of migrant selectivity at play. Men and women are often observed to have displayed distinct migration behaviour. According to Ravenstein's 'laws', women were very mobile, but engaged more in patterns of short-distance migration and often moved at a younger age, mostly before getting married (Ravenstein 1889). Men were also engaged in migration patterns at a somewhat older age and dominated longer-distance movements between cities. As such, men have often been depicted as 'pioneers', and women as 'following' in male footsteps, depending more on family networks and decisions in their migration behaviour. Recently, this traditional image of male dominance has been criticised by emphasising the presence of women in long-distance migration (Donato et al. 2011) and by focussing on their independence and own networks (Sharpe 2001; Hoerder & Kauer 2013).

As men and women operated in very different labour markets, gender balances in migration streams provide helpful indications of the extent to which they were attuned to local income opportunities. According to the typology of Leslie Page Moch (2003), cities of heavy industry, such as Liège and Charleroi in our sample, typically recruited predominantly men, whereas textile cities, such as Ghent, attracted more women – as a reflection of the gender-biased nature of their labour markets. Brussels and Antwerp belong to the category of commercial and service cities in Moch's typology, offering diversified income opportunities also for women, such as in domestic service, catering and retailing – next to, in the case of the port city Antwerp, mainly male-oriented port-related employment (Lee 1998; Lawton & Lee 2002). The sex ratios among non-native residents in our sample reflect the differences in labour market structure as Moch's typology predicts, confirming an overall selectivity of migration in relation to local employment structures (Graph 3). Over the whole period, men outnumbered women in the new industrial centres, while women were more numerous than men in the large cities. The suburban districts occupied a middle ground with relatively equal gender ratios – be they slightly biased towards women. Almost all city types, however, also displayed a growing feminisation of its immigrant population, most spectacularly so in the new industrial centres, where gender ratios decreased from 1.9 (Seraing) and 1.4 (Charleroi) in 1846 to 1.3 and 1.1 in 1910 respectively. This trend is indicative of a wider feminisation of migration in the course of the nineteenth century, in the context of which women also started to migrate over longer distances – something we explore further below.

The only indication about the origins and distances of the migrants in the data is the distinction between internal migrants (i.e. Belgium-born) and foreign-born migrants, but these already indicate important differences between the different city types regarding overall immigration distances. Firstly, as graph 2 above has already shown, the demographic contribution of foreign migrants was considerably higher in traditional centres than in suburbs and new industrial centres, confirming that large cities had a wider and much more diverse recruitment area than new industrial centres or suburbs. These new industrial centres, such as in the Charleroi and Liège basin, indeed attracted mainly short-distance migrants. In an early phase, many Walloon farmers moved in seasonal patterns to work in the coal mines and factories, after which the recruitment area enlarged to labourers from Eastern and Western Flanders and – for the Liège area – to German adjacent regions in the later nineteenth century (Oris 1997; Roels 2008; Caestecker 2008). Increasingly, a substantial and growing part of the labour force – especially from Flemish provinces – also commuted to work in the industrial basins on a daily or weekly basis, stimulated by the subsidisation of railway tickets to avoid large-scale population transfers (De Block & Polasky 2010; Schepers et al. in this volume). Secondly, even though the recruitment area of traditional cities was much more diversified, Ghent attracted many fewer foreign migrants than Brussels and Antwerp. Ghent was oriented much more towards industrial employment than Antwerp or Brussels, and as such resembled new industrial centres in the sense that its attraction remained limited mainly to Belgian migrants, especially from within the provincial boundaries of East Flanders (Scholliers 1996). Brussels, the administrative and financial heart of the country, was connected to the whole nation and, as such, recruited more migrants from everywhere in the country and beyond. For the two censuses in 1846 and 1856, the only ones that further distinguished among Belgian migrants between those born within or beyond provincial boundaries, Brussels was the only municipality where migrants from other provinces outnumbered those from within its own province. Thirdly, the growth of suburbs from the middle of the century onwards was driven primarily by internal migrants, often from the immediate surroundings and from the old city centre.

Internal Belgian migrants obviously outnumbered foreign migrants in all types of Belgian cities during the nineteenth century. Their migration during the nineteenth century was connected mainly to rural proletarianisation processes and their search for work in cities or in industrial basins, while their high mobility indicates that they moved from one place to the other to survive or at least improve living and working conditions. As urban growth slowed down everywhere at the end of the period, the contribution of foreigners became more important, and this was particularly so in the traditional cities. Over the 1846-1910 period, foreigners contributed on average 7 per cent of recorded urban

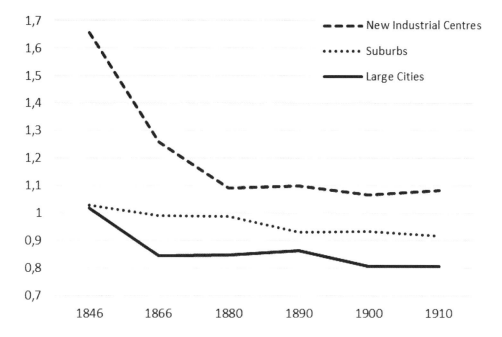

Graph 3. Sex ratios of non-native residents in selected Belgian municipalities, 1846-1910 (men:women)

Source. Population censuses, 1846-1910. Database LOKSTAT, Quetelet Center, Ghent University.

population growth in our sample, but this was considerably more in older cities (11 per cent) than in the new industrial centres (7 per cent) or in the suburbs (5 per cent), and by the end of the long nineteenth century they supplied no less than 27 per cent of the – by then relatively low – urban growth in the old cities.

Foreigners: changing profiles and background

Even though emigration surpassed immigration for the whole of Belgian territory until the last decade of the nineteenth century (Stengers 1978), foreign presence in Belgium increased over the period under consideration, particularly in the largest cities. Foreign-born residents represented around 2 per cent of Belgium's total population until 1866, and increased their share to 2.5 per cent in 1880 and 3.7 per cent in 1910. Their presence was concentrated primarily in border areas on the one hand and in the large traditional cities on the other hand. In 1910, no less than one quarter of Belgium's foreign-born residents lived in Antwerp, Brussels and Liège. Still, the share of foreigners in the urban population varied through time and space (Graph 4). For most of the period it was highest in Antwerp, falling from 9 per cent in 1846 to 6 per cent in 1866 and increasing again to 11 per cent by 1910. In Brussels, the evolution was from 7 per cent through 5 per cent to 11 per cent in the same censuses. In Liège, the proportion of foreigners increased gradually from 7 to 9 per cent between 1846 and 1910. In absolute numbers, most foreigners lived in Brussels until 1866, after which Antwerp took the lead. In comparison to other major cities, industrial

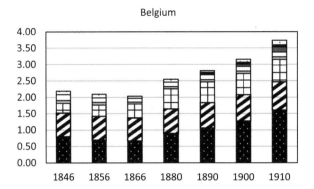

Belgium

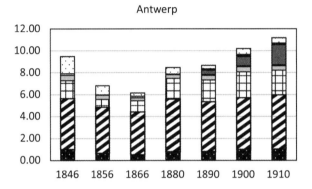

Antwerp

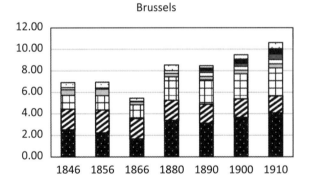

Brussels

☐ Other   ▨ Great-Britain

■ Italian & Swiss states   ▥ German states

■ Austria-Hungary & Russia   ▨ Netherlands

☐ Luxemburg   ■ France

Graph 4. Share of foreign-born residents in selected Belgian cities, 1846-1910

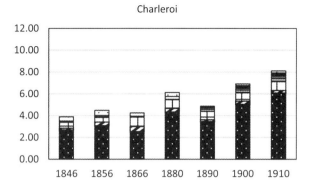

Charleroi

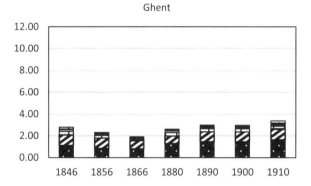

Ghent

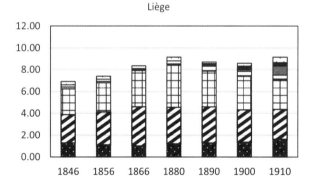

Liège

☐ Other   ☐ Great-Britain

■ Italian & Swiss states   ⊞ German states

■ Austria-Hungary & Russia   ▨ Netherlands

☐ Luxemburg   ■ France

Graph 4. Continued

Source. Population censuses, 1846-1910. Database LOKSTAT, Quetelet Center, Ghent University.
Note: For the period 1846-1880 the category "Other" includes "Italian & Swiss states" and "Austria-Hungary & Russia".

Ghent was far less attractive to foreigners, and its share of the population barely surpassed 3 per cent. In industrial centres in the Walloon part of the country, such as Charleroi and Seraing, foreign presence was also low, even though foreigners' share of the population in Charleroi exceeded that of Ghent, increasing from 4 to 8 per cent between 1846 and 1910. Suburban municipalities such as Borgerhout and Anderlecht likewise recorded much lower shares of foreign-born residents than their urban centres: between 3 per cent in 1846 and 5.5 per cent in 1910. Existing data indicate that many foreigners stayed only temporarily, so that their importance was probably greater than suggested by these cross-sectional data. Some very mobile groups, such as sailors, were moreover often not registered in population statistics, but surely influenced the 'cosmopolitan' atmosphere in particular urban districts (Loockx 2020).

The majority of Belgium's foreigners in the long nineteenth century were born in neighbouring countries. Over the period under consideration, the lion's share were born in France, the Netherlands, the German states and Luxemburg. By the turn of the twentieth century migration over longer distances, especially from Central Europe and Russia, was on the increase. Many of these migrants were Jews who fled their home countries in the wake of religious persecution and poverty (Caestecker & Feys 2010). Important differences continued to exist, however, in the origins of foreigners in different cities. French-born migrants dominated in Charleroi, while in Liège and Antwerp Dutch and German foreigners were far more important.

Geographical proximity was important to explain foreign migration patterns, especially for the Dutch in Antwerp, Germans and Dutch in Liège, and the French in Charleroi. By all indications, most of them came from adjacent border regions, and as such conceptually resembled regional migrants who happened to cross national borders and who were often less qualified or skilled (Winter 2009). For Brussels, situated in the centre of Belgium at a distance of at least 50 kilometres from the nearest border, such patterns of cross-border regional migration were less important – which explains the more diverse background of its foreigners. All large cities, however, recorded an increasing diversification of their foreign-born residents in the course of the long nineteenth century. By 1910, the proportion of residents who were born beyond neighbouring countries had risen to 26 per cent in Antwerp, 19 per cent in Brussels and Liège, and 14 per cent in Ghent, up from 22, 14, 7 and 12 per cent respectively in 1846. Conversely, their combined importance in the overall population of these four cities increased from 1 to 1.8 per cent on average, and even to 2.9 per cent in Antwerp. This was much less the case for suburbs and new industrial centres, where the combined importance of these long-distance migrants in total population never exceeded 0.9 and 0.7 per cent respectively.

Not only in terms of origins, but also with respect to social class, foreign presence in major cities became more diverse as the long nineteenth century progressed. Long-distance migration to cities had long been a selective affair, dominated by highly skilled, specialised inter-urban migrants involved in patterns of career migration (Poussou 1988; Winter 2009). Conversely, foreign migrants from nearby regions in cities located near borders typically resembled internal regional migrants in social profile, dominated by rural-born, low-skilled and less-specialised workers, as the migration of domestic servants from North Brabant to Antwerp illustrates (Verbruggen 2018). But labourers from the vicinity of Aachen to Liège, textile workers from Lille or Tourcoing to Ghent or German labourers in the Charleroi basin are also cases in point. Overall, around the middle of the nineteenth century, long-distance foreign migration was still a male-dominated affair of better-off social groups, such as German merchants in Antwerp or proprietors in Brussels.

The long-standing connection between migration distance and social class became severed in the later part of the long nineteenth century, resulting in growing numbers of people from modest backgrounds travelling longer distances. Although the census data do not provide indications of social background, in-depth research for Antwerp has revealed that foreign migrants from beyond border regions came to include more women, more rural-born and more unskilled or low-skilled workers by the late nineteenth century, and that they were recruited from an increasingly wider range of birth places (Greefs & Winter 2016). This process intensified in the run-up to World War I, when more people from Eastern Europe and Russia started to arrive at the port city (Feys & Caestecker 2010). The only oblique indication on a widening social profile that the census data provide for all cities under study is the disappearance of male dominance among foreigners: while the ratio of foreign-born men to women was still 133:100 in 1846, this declined markedly to only 87:100 in 1890 to eventually even out at 99:100 by 1910. This trend was strongest in large cities, and least marked in new industrial centres, where men remained dominant throughout.

These trends towards intensification, 'democratisation' and feminisation of long-distance migration in this period were fostered by the great expansion and improvement of means of travel and communication. Of major importance no doubt was the precocious expansion of the Belgian railway network and its integration into expanding cross-border European railway connections. Over time, train connections became faster, cheaper and more varied (Van der Herten 2004; De Block & Polasky 2011). Better overland connections together with the strong competition among transport companies and travel agencies caused a strong reduction in travel costs. At the same time, the improved distribution of newspapers, growing literacy rates and the activities of recruitment agencies facilitated and democratised access to information. Together, these changes accelerated and increased the movement of goods, information and people, which reduced the role of distance as a migration barrier and offered even less qualified and less skilled people the opportunity to move over longer distances.

While improving transport and communication means widened the migration fields from which particularly the larger centres recruited their foreign migrants by the later nineteenth century, the profiles of migrants recruited to each city remained distinct and influenced by local opportunity structures and transport networks. Port cities, such as Antwerp, provided many casual work opportunities in the informal sector and commanded wide transport connections, attracting many temporary and transient migrant groups of relatively distant origins, such as sailors or prostitutes at one end of the social spectrum (Loockx 2020; Greefs & Winter 2020), or merchants and business representatives at the more upmarket end (Greefs & Winter 2016). The majority of the growing number of foreign women in Antwerp worked as domestic servants. In the middle of the century domestic servants were recruited predominantly from adjacent regions abroad, of which the North Brabantine region was the most important. When the century progressed these domestic servants also began to migrate over longer distances and from a wider variety of urban and rural places (Verbruggen 2018; Debackere 2020). Also Brussels tended to recruit migrants of relatively distant origins, but of a more elitist nature, attracted primarily by the career opportunities and leisure facilities offered by the well-connected administrative and financial centre of the young Belgian kingdom (De Schaepdrijver 1999; Coppens 2017). In addition, the capital of course also exerted a large demand for domestic servants (Piette 2000). Inter-urban connections with other capital cities – next to Paris also London or Amsterdam – became more important as the century progressed. By this time, even suburban districts started to attract elite groups, but not foreigners so much, as the censuses indicate (Eggerickx 2013). Next to financial and administrative elites, the capital also attracted foreign intellectuals and exiles who sought refuge in 'liberal' Belgium (Coppens 2017). The less diversified opportunity structure of industrial centres such as Ghent, Charleroi and Seraing was less attractive to foreigners: less numerous, they continued to be recruited from relatively nearby regions and – at least for centres of heavy industry – dominated by men. These industrial cities offered more labour opportunities for low-skilled people and fewer opportunities for social mobility, compared to service and commercial centres such as Antwerp and Brussels. Likewise, suburban districts recorded relatively few foreigners and they came primarily from neighbouring countries – again reflecting that these often more closely resembled internal migrants both in social profile and migration behaviour.

The changes in the profiles and social backgrounds of foreign migrants are, for instance, reflected in changing expulsion practices of local and national authorities towards the end of the nineteenth century. While the law stipulated that expulsions of foreigners could be motivated by criminal misconduct, lack of means or social or political disturbance, the lion's share (77 per cent) of the 340,000 expulsions from Belgium in the 1835-1913 period took place by reason of vagrancy and lack of means – and mainly in the last decades. Particularly from the 1870s onwards, the number of expulsions from Belgium increased noticeably, doubling from at most 3,000 per year in the preceding decades to around 6,000 by the early 1880s, and peaking at *c.* 10,000 by 1890, when foreigners were included in the general legislative reform of 1891 on vagrancy and social policy (Coupain 2003; Feys 2019). While in earlier decades vagrancy laws and social policies seem to have been primarily directed towards Belgian migrants, attention shifted to include foreigners as well by the last quarter of the century, particularly as growing numbers of them were characterised by low social profiles and high mobility rates.

Conclusion

What, now, has this selective exploration indicated regarding the relationship between migration and urban development in Belgium's long nineteenth century? The most salient finding is that increasing turnover rather than simple immigration was the main defining characteristic of the urban migration experience in the second half of the long nineteenth century – which by its close had recorded gross migration rates equivalent to between one fifth and one third of the population *each year,* but was contributing less than 1.5 per cent in annual urban growth rates. This trend towards increasing mobility and turnover went hand in hand with a diversification in migrant background and the growing participation of women in urban migration. These trends towards diversification and feminisation were most marked in large cities, probably stimulated by their more diverse income opportunity structures and well-connected transport and communication networks. In the early decades of the period under consideration new industrial centres and suburbs still displayed strong absorptive capacities towards their newcomers, but as time progressed they were likewise characterised by growing turnover, resulting in a growing convergence of the urban migration experience. This implies that the most determining factor in the contribution of migration to urban growth throughout the period was the retention rather than attraction of newcomers. Yet, the actual impact of migration on nineteenth-century cities was probably determined more by the evolution of flows than their impact on stocks.

Together with the indications on declining migrant selectivity in terms of gender ratios, this growing turnover is indicative of a painful social transition in which growing numbers of people turned to migration to an extent that vastly surpassed the absorptive capacities of the urban economies, resulting in a vast expansion of the 'floating' population. While foreign migration had traditionally been a relatively upmarket affair, from the 1870s onwards growing numbers of foreigners from modest backgrounds added to the 'floating' population of Belgian cities, fostering increasing attempts at control and policing by local and national authorities. To the extent that migration contributed to social inequality in nineteenth century cities, then, it was not so much via the permanent replenishment of the poorest ranks of the urban population – as most of them were quick to move on – but via its contribution to the growth of an extremely unsettled population whose presence in cities was of a highly transitory nature, which must have represented acute challenges to the social fabric and in terms of social control and heightened social inequality. The moral panic on urban degeneration that characterised public debate by the close of the nineteenth century was therefore probably less engendered by the accumulation of destitute rural migrants in urban centres than by the growing transience and diversity of urban populations – which helps us better understand the central preoccupation with vagrancy legislation in the social policy reforms of the late nineteenth century.

Sources

Population censuses, 1846-1910. Database LOKSTAT, Quetelet Center, Ghent University.

Historical Statistics on International Migration in Belgium 1846-1910 – IMMIBEL (BRAIN-Belspo). State Archives in collaboration with Vrije Universiteit Brussel, University of Antwerp and Université Libre de Bruxelles, co-ordinated by Anne Winter.

SAA (City Archives Antwerp). MA (Modern archives). No. 74604: Register van afschrijving, 1888-1891; no. 74784: Register van afschrijving (1852-1855).

References

Caestecker, Frank. 2000. *Alien policy in Belgium. The creation of guest workers, refugees and illegal aliens*. New York & Oxford: Berghahn Books.

Caestecker, Frank. 2008. "Arbeidsmarktstrategieën in de Belgische mijnindustrie tot 1940." *Tijdschrift voor Sociale en Economische Geschiedenis* 5, no. 3: 30-52.

Caestecker, Frank, and Torsten Feys. 2010. "East European Jewish Migrants and Settlers in Belgium, 1880-1914: A Transatlantic Perspective." *East European Jewish Affairs* 40, no. 3: 261-84.

Christiaens, Jenneke. 1999. *De geboorte van de jeugddelinquent. België, 1830-1930.* Brussels: VUB Press.

Coppens, Alexander. 2017. *Tussen beleid en administratieve praktijk. De implementatie van het Belgisch migratiebeleid in negentiende-eeuws Brussel.* Unpublished PhD thesis: Vrije Universiteit Brussel and University of Antwerp.

Coupain, Nicolas. 2003. "L'expulsion des étrangers en Belgique (1830-1914)." *Belgisch Tijdschrift voor Nieuwste Geschiedenis* 33, no. 1-2: 5-48.

De Block, Greet, and Janet Polasky. 2011. "Light Railways and the Rural–Urban Continuum : Technology, Space and Society in Late Nineteenth-Century Belgium." *Journal of Historical Geography* 37, no. 3: 312-28.

Debackere, Ellen. 2020. *Welkom in Antwerpen? Het Antwerpse vreemdelingenbeleid, 1830-1880.* Leuven: Leuven Universitaire Pers.

Deprez, Paul, and Christian Vandenbroeke. 1989. "Population Growth and Distribution and Urbanisation in Belgium during the Demographic Transition." In *Urban Population Development in Western Europe from the Late Eighteenth to the Early Twentieth Century*, ed. R. Lawton and R. Lee, 220-257. Liverpool: Liverpool University Press.

Deschacht, Nick, and Anne Winter. 2015. "Rural Crisis and Rural Exodus? Local Migration Dynamics during the Crisis of the 1840s in Flanders (Belgium)." *Explorations in Economic History*, no. 56: 32-52.

Dickens, Charles. 1848. *Dombey and Son*, ed. 1995. London: Wordsworth Classics.

Donato, Katharine M., Joseph T. Alexander, Donna R. Gabaccia and Johanna Leinonen. 2011. "Variations in the Gender Composition of Immigrant Populations: How They Matter." *International Migration Review* 45, no. 3: 495-526.

Eggerickx, Thierry. 2004. *La dynamique démographique et la transition de la fécondité dans le bassin industriel de la région de Charleroi de 1831 à 1910.* Brussels: Académie Royale de Belgique.

Eggerickx, Thierry. 2010. "Les migrations internes en Wallonie et en Belgique de 1840 à 1939: un essai de synthèse." In *Histoire de La Population de La Belgique et de Ses Territoires*, ed. Thierry Eggerickx and Jean-Paul Sanderson, 293-336. Louvain-la-Neuve: Presses Universitaires de Louvain.

Eggerickx, Thierry. 2013. "Transition démographique et banlieue en Belgique: le cas de Bruxelles." *Annales de demographie historique* 126, no 2: 51-80.

Feys, Torsten. 2019. "Riding the rails of removal. The impact of railroads on border controls and expulsion practices." *Journal of Transport History* 40, no. 2: 189-210.

Greefs, Hilde, Bruno Blondé and Peter Clark. 2005. "The Growth of Urban Industrial Regions: Belgian Developments in Comparative Perspective, 1750-1850." In *Towns, Regions and Industries: Urban and Industrial Change in the Midlands, c. 1700-1840*, ed. Jon Stobart and Neil Raven, 210-227. Manchester: Manchester University Press.

Greefs, Hilde, and Anne Winter. 2016. "Alone and Far from Home. Gender and Migration Trajectories of Single Foreign Newcomers to Antwerp, 1850-1880." *Journal of Urban History* 42, no. 1: 61-80.

Greefs, Hilde, and Anne Winter, 2020. "Foreign Female Sex Workers in an Atlantic Port City. Elite Prostitution in Late Nineteenth Century Antwerp." In *Migrants and the making of the urban-maritime world,* ed. Christina Reimann and Martin Öhman. New York: Routledge (forthcoming).

Herten, Bart Van der. 2004. *België onder stoom: transport en communicatie tijdens de 19de eeuw.* Leuven: Leuven University Press.

Hochstadt, Steve. 1999. *Mobility and Modernity: Migration in Germany, 1820-1989.* Ann Arbor, MI: University of Michigan Press.

Hoerder, Dirk, and Amarjit Kaur, eds. 2013. *Proletarian and Gendered Mass Migrations: A Global Perspective on Continuities and Discontinuities from the 19th to the 21st Centuries.* Leiden: Brill.

Jackson, James Harvey. 1997. *Migration and Urbanization in the Ruhr Valley, 1821-1914.* Studies in Central European Histories. Atlantic Highlands, NJ: Humanities Press.

Lawton, Richard, and Robert Lee, eds. 2002. *Population and Society in Western European Port Cities, c. 1650-1939.* Liverpool: Liverpool University Press.

Leboutte, René. 1995. "Mobilité spatiale de la main d'œuvre dans les bassins industriels au 19ᵉ siècle. L'apport des livrets ouvriers." In *Les chemins de la migration en Belgique et au Québec. XVIIᵉ-XXᵉ siècles,* ed. Yves Landry, John A. Dickinon, Suzy Pasleau, Claude Desama, 155-163. Louvain-La-Neuve : Editions Academia-Erasme.

Lee, Robert. 1998. "The Socio-Economic and Demographic Characteristics of Port Cities: A Typology for Comparative Analysis?" *Urban History* 25, no. 2: 147-172.

Lis, Catharina. 1977. "Proletarisch wonen in Westeuropese steden in de 19de eeuw: van wildgroei naar sociale controle." *Belgisch Tijdschrift Voor Nieuwste Geschiedenis* 9, no. 3-4: 325-366.

Lis, Catharina. 1986. *Social Change and the Labouring Poor: Antwerp, 1770-1860.* New Haven, CT: Yale University Press.

Loockx, Kristof. 2020. "Migration, maritime labour, and family: the life course of Carel Hendrik Bloebaum, 1848-1916." In *Migrants and the making of the urban-maritime world,* ed. Christina Reimann and Martin Öhman. New York: Routledge (forthcoming).

Lucassen, Jan, and Leo Lucassen. 2009. "The Mobility Transition Revisited, 1500-1900: What the Case of Europe Can Offer to Global History." *Journal of Global History* 4, no. 3: 347-377.

Matthijs, Koen. 2001. *De mateloze negentiende eeuw: bevolking, huwelijk, gezin en sociale verandering.* Leuven: Universitaire Pers.

Moch, Leslie Page. 2003. *Moving Europeans: Migration in Western Europe since 1650.* 2nd ed. Bloomington & Indianapolis, IN: Indiana University Press.

Oris, Michel. 1997. "L'impact d'une dépression économique sur le champ migratoire d'une grande ville industrielle. L'expérience de Seraing entre 1857 et 1900." *Revue Du Nord* 79, no. 320-321: 531-548.

Pasleau, Suzy. 1993. "L'immigration des travailleurs à Seraing durant la seconde moitié du 19e siècle." *Annales de Démographie Historique,* no. 1: 227-250.

Pasleau, Suzy. 1994. "Les migrations internes en Belgique. Ruptures et continuités du XVIIe au XXe Siècle." In *Les migrations internes et à moyenne distance en Europe, 1500-1900,* ed. Antonio Eiras Roel and Ofelia Rey Castelao, 1: 179-204. Premier Conférence Européenne de La Commission Internationale de Démographie Historique (CIDH), Santiago de Compostella, 22-25/09/1993. Santiago de Compostella: Xunta de Galicia & CIDH.

Piette, Valérie. 2000. *Domestiques et servantes: Des vies sous condition. Essai sur le travail domestique en Belgique au 19ᵉ siècle.* Brussels: Académie Royale de la Belgique.

Pooley, Colin G. 2017. *Mobility, Migration and Transport: Historical Perspectives.* Basingstoke: Palgrave Macmillan.

Poussou, Jean-Pierre. 1988. "Mobilité et migrations." In *Histoire de la population française, Vol. 2: De la rénaissance à 1789,* ed. Jacques Dupâquier, 99-143. Paris: Presses Universitaires de France.

Ravenstein, E. G. 1889. "The Laws of Migration." *Journal of the Royal Statistical Society* 52, no. 2: 241-305.

Roels, Leen. 2008. "Buitenlandse arbeiders in de Luikse steenkoolmijnen, 1900-1974", *Tijdschrift voor Sociale en Economische Geschiedenis* 5, no. 3: 104-125.

Ryckbosch, Wouter. 2010. "Vroegmoderne economische ontwikkeling en sociale repercussies in de Zuidelijke Nederlanden: Nijvel in de achttiende eeuw." *Tijdschrift voor Sociale en Economische Geschiedenis* 7, no. 3: 26-55.

Schaepdrijver, Sophie de. 1990. *Elites for the Capital? Foreign Migration to Mid-Nineteenth-Century Brussels*. Amsterdam: PDIS.

Scholliers, Peter. 1996. *Wages, Manufacturers and Workers in the Nineteenth-Century Factory: The Voortman Cotton Mill in Ghent*. Oxford: Berg.

Sewell, William H. 1985. *Structure and Mobility. The Men and Women of Marseille, 1820-1870*. Cambridge: Cambridge University Press.

Sharpe, Pamela, ed. 2001. *Women, Gender and Labour Migration: Historical and Global Perspectives*. London: Routledge.

Stengers, J. 1978. *Emigration et immigration en Belgique au XIXe et XXe siècles*. Académie Royale des sciences d'outre-Mer. Classe des sciences morales et politiques. N.S; 46,5. Brussels: Académie royale des sciences d'outre-mer.

Tollebeek, Jo, Geert Vanpaemel and Kaat Wils, eds. 2003. *Degeneratie in België (1860-1940): Een geschiedenis van ideeën en praktijken*. Leuven: Leuven University Press.

Van Damme, Dirk. 1990. *Armenzorg en de staat. Comparatief-historische studie van de origines van de moderne verzorgingsstaat in West-Europa*. Ghent: S. N.

Van der Wee, Herman. 1996. "The Industrial Revolution in Belgium." In *The Industrial Revolution in National Context: Europe and the USA*, ed. Mikulas Teich and Roy Porter, 64-77. Cambridge: Cambridge University Press.

Vanhaute, Eric. 2007. "So Worthy an Example to Ireland. The Subsistence and Industrial Crisis of 1845-1850 in Flanders." In *When the Potato Failed. Causes and Effects of the Last European Subsistence Crisis, 1845-1850*, ed. Cormac Ó Gráda, Richard Paping and Eric Vanhaute. Turnhout: Brepols.

Veraghtert, Karel. 1986. "From Inland Port to International Port, 1790-1914." In *Antwerp: A Port for All Seasons*, ed. Fernand Suykens, 279-422. Deurne: MIM.

Verbruggen, Thomas. 2018. "Het Antwerpse en Brusselse rekruteringsgebied voor buitenlandse dienstmeiden (1850-1910)." *TSEG/ Low Countries Journal of Social and Economic History* 15, no. 2-3: 33-68.

Vercammen, Rik. 2014. "Leven aan de rafelrand? Landlopers en bedelaars in Belgische Rijksweldadigheidskolonies (1870-1930)." Unpublished PhD thesis: Brussels: Vrije Universiteit Brussel.

Williamson, Jeffrey G. 1990. *Coping with City Growth during the British Industrial Revolution*. Cambridge: Cambridge University Press.

Winter, Anne. 2009. *Migrants and Urban Change: Newcomers to Antwerp, 1760-1860*. Perspectives in Economic and Social History 1. London: Pickering and Chatto.

Zitouni, Benedikte. 2010. *Agglomérer. Une anatomie de l'extension bruxelloise (1828-1915)*. Brussels : Asp/Vubpress/ Upa.

INGRID SCHEPERS, JANET POLASKY, ANN VERHETSEL
AND GREET DE BLOCK*

Organising the Work-Home Split by the Urban-Rural Link

Transport Networks, Mobility and Urbanisation in Early Twentieth-Century Belgium

Mais, avec le progrès des moyens de transport (…) la ligne de démarcation entre les villes et les campagnes perd sa rigidité; politiquement et économiquement, urbains et ruraux deviennent égaux, sinon en fait, du moins en droit. Les murailles des villes sont démolies. Les barrières d'octroi commencent à tomber. Les relations se multiplient entre citadins et campagnards. Dès à présent, il apparaît comme vraisemblable que les cités de l'avenir seront bien moins de centres d'habitation que des agglomérations de monuments, des lieux de réunion ou de travail, des rendez- vous d'affaires, de plaisirs et d'études. Emile Vandervelde (1903, 298)

Introduction: fixing the mobile worker

During the second half of the nineteenth century the Belgian government established a synergetic relationship between infrastructure, mobility and housing policy, with the explicit intention of organising a far-reaching functional split between working and living (De Block & Polasky 2011). By the first decade of the twentieth century, a dense, mostly public, network of rails and light railways connected the smallest of hamlets in the countryside to virtually every city and industrial area in Belgium (Fig. 1). The intricate infrastructure network, in combination with a consistent mobility and housing policy of reduced train fares and cheap housing loans for workers, encouraged workers to commute between their homes in the countryside and work in factories and mines in urban and industrial centres (Polasky 2010; De Block & Polasky 2011). The increase in mobility facilitated by the network would fix the worker in place while he or she could 'participate' in national economic space.

Despite concentration of the agricultural crisis and accelerating industrialisation in certain cities and regions, infrastructure policy aimed to curb rural outmigration to industrial cores by organising a unique territorial balance between city and countryside. This spatial re-organisation instigated by infrastructure would transform agricultural labourers and

---

* corresponding author

| Ingrid Schepers, Ann Verhetsel and Greet De Block* • University of Antwerp

| Janet Polasky • University of New Hampshire

Inequality and the City in the Low Countries (1200-2020), ed. by Bruno BLONDÉ, Sam GEENS, Hilde GREEFS, Wouter RYCKBOSCH, Tim SOENS & Peter STABEL, SEUH 50 (Turnhout, 2020), pp. 101-121.

DOI 10.1484/M.SEUH-EB.5.120440

Figure 1 Top: The city: the light rail bringing workers and goods from the countryside into the monumental station square of the city of Namur / **Bottom:** The countryside: The small, rural village of Merkem hosts a busy flow of people and goods on the move from the countryside of South-West Flanders to the cities of Ypres, Roeselare, Diksmuide and Veurne / **Right:** The dense network of railways (black – thin lines) and light railways (greys – thick lines) in 1929.[1]

farmers into industrial workers while still permitting them to return home each day to their ancestral villages and 'consequently avoid the immoral influences of large population centers' (Jamar 22 April 1869, 765). Transport policy thus constructed a spatial fix – the networked home – accommodating industrialisation while safeguarding 'morals'. Catholic and Liberal policy makers also hoped to mitigate an upsurge of socialism. Socialists, some also supporters of the policy, expected that rooting the worker in the countryside would be a first step in the emancipation of the working class, as families could live a healthy life and grow their own food. They would be less dependent on the factory because they could change jobs freely without having to relocate. Appealing to divergent political aims, the spatial fix of 'the networked home' set up by late-nineteenth-century Belgian policy makers was rapidly adopted in laws and fully operationalised by the end of the nineteenth century (Polasky 2010; De Block & Polasky 2011).

Studies conducted at the time by foreign and Belgian observers demonstrated that the population density of most country villages remained constant or increased through the second half of the nineteenth century. '[T]he astonishing population density is maintained', Socialist Emile Vandervelde commented on the decentralisation of work-place and residence (Vandervelde 1900, 109). During the 1886-1906 period, in France 61 out of 87 *départements* had to contend with rural outmigration towards major urban

1   Image sources: Top Left: NMBS Archives – Fototheek – Z00262/Right: SNCV Report 1929.

centres, Vandervelde pointed out, while in Belgium only four out of 41 administrative areas faced permanent migration.

Whereas European metropolises such as Paris exponentially increased in size and number at the expense of villages or towns with a population of up to 50,000 (Hohenberg & Lees 1995, 222), in Belgium only the municipalities with a population of fewer than 2,000 decreased in the second half of the nineteenth century (Vandervelde 1900). Considering the general population increase of 54 per cent between 1846 and 1900, municipalities between 2,000 and 5,000 inhabitants grew by 29 per cent, between 5,000 and 10,000 by 79 per cent, and between 10,000 and 25,000 by 164 per cent (Van der Haegen 1982; Smets 1976, 9; see also De Block & Polasky 2011). Thus, the development of towns into massive *villes tentaculaires*, as the poet Emile Verhaeren called them, was averted in favour of the consolidation, and indeed urbanisation, of the countryside. Although in many small villages this increase meant a spatial status quo or a slight growth of only a couple of houses, the socio-economic setting changed drastically. The spatial rural-urban continuum set up by rails, mobility and housing policy instigated a socio-economic transformation deeply affecting almost all Belgian municipalities.

Industrial labourers were distributed over the entire Belgian territory. Geographer Omer Tulippe maps this transformation, showing the industrial population living in Belgian municipalities (Map 1). The highest ratio of industrial workers is located in urban as well as rural municipalities in and around the industrial basins, large perimeters surrounding towns and the border region of South-West Flanders, which was well connected to industrial northern France and Walloon provinces. Other than a few municipalities in West Flanders, Limburg and the Ardennes (see white - light grey on map 1), the ratio of industrial labourers was high in almost all rural municipalities.

'Scratch a Flemish industrial worker and you will find a farmer underneath', British sociologist Benjamin Seebohm Rowntree aptly stated in *Land and Labour: Lessons from Belgium* (Rowntree 1910, 18). Although studies of geographers like Tulippe showcase the work-home split (see also De Brabander 1983), socio-economic indicators such as occupations are not related to infrastructure networks and mobility. Nor do these studies explore what the ratios actually mean on the ground. How did the work-home split affect socio-spatial organisation?

At the turn of the twentieth century a number of publications analysed the socio-spatial landscape of Belgium resulting from this unique pattern of mobility. Emile Vandervelde, as well as foreign observers including Benjamin Rowntree and Patrick Abercrombie, heralded the conversion of the Belgian territory into the utopian rural-urban landscapes described by Pecquer, Proudhon, Owen and Howard, in which workers could live comfortably in the healthy countryside while earning a good wage in the city (Vandervelde 1903; Rowntree 1910; Abercrombie 1912). Not all social observers shared this optimism. August De Winne believed that labourers remained subjugated by ingrained social inequalities of *Poor Flanders*. Although the urban-rural link kept the population of the countryside from starving, it condemned them to long working days for little pay. Workers took the train at 4 am to commute to the factory or mine, only to return home after 9 pm (De Winne 1902, 161-162; see also Weber 2009). Moreover, several politicians criticised the rural-urban continuum for rendering the countryside and workers even more dependent on the city and its bourgeoisie. According to these critical voices, the national scheme propelled the transformation of cities as rivers were bricked over, avenues widened, and impasses levelled. The workers, in the words of

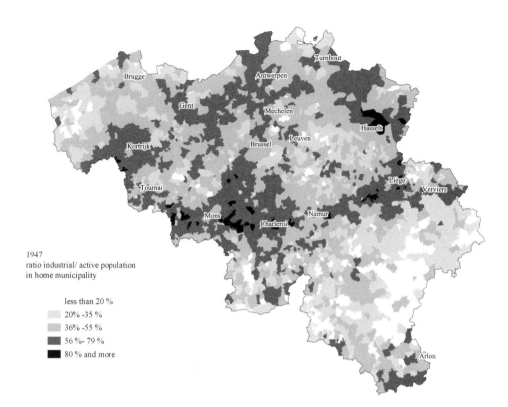

1947
ratio industrial/ active population
in home municipality

less than 20 %
20% -35 %
36% -55 %
56 %- 79 %
80 % and more

Map 1 Map based on census data of 1947 showing the ratio of industrial/active population. In almost all municipalities – urban and rural – at least 20 per cent of the active population are industrial labourers, with ratios of more than 56 per cent along industrial corridors and agglomerations. Large areas of countryside between cities and industrial zones hold ratios of over 36 per cent industrial labourers, especially in Flanders (northern area).[2]

a Socialist from Schaerbeek, were relocated like the Native Americans onto reservations outside the city, while Brussels underwent a Haussmannian make-over to accommodate the bourgeoisie (Commune de Schaerbeeck *Construction d'habitations* 1898).

Although these observations link the rail network with socio-spatial (re-)organisation, the accounts remain fairly speculative in nature and most of them are determined by a strong political agenda. This chapter will qualify and quantify these earlier statements and study the socio-economic and spatial effects instigated by the combination of transport, mobility and housing policy. Transport history, mobilities, historical geography and urban history all address aspects of transport, mobility and urbanisation relations. Yet, how infrastructural and spatial complexes are implicated in enabling or disabling mobilities, or how mobility relates to urbanisation and associated social inequalities, remains a blind spot (Moraglio 2017; Pooley

---

2   Image source: Authors' adaptation of map of *Atlas van België* (Brussels: Militair Geografisch Instituut) _ Map based on Omer Tulippe's study : Omer Tulippe, 'La population active en Belgique: localisation et mouvements. Etude préliminaire', *Les cahiers d'urbanisme* 17 (1954).

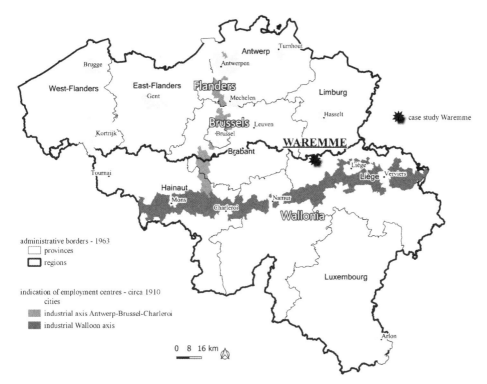

Map 2 Map based on Paul Olyslager's study (1947). It indicates the main industrial employment centres at the dawn of the twentieth century. It likewise visualises the location of the Waremme municipality situated in the countryside on the railway line that connects Liège with Brussels.

2017). In what follows we will study the interaction between infrastructure, motion and spatial transformation or, more specifically, the relationship between rails, commuting flows and urbanisation, with a focus on socio-economic transformation. National ambitions about societal transformation inscribed in nineteenth-century transport, mobility and housing policy (De Block & Polasky 2011) are confronted with socio-economic (commuting/occupations) and spatial (urbanisation and demographic rates) effects of the social engineering geared at organising a work-home split by constructing the urban-rural link. Did the railway network instigate nationwide rural-urban commuting, as demonstrated by mobility patterns and the distribution of occupations? And how did these dynamics 'land' on the ground or indeed relate to urbanisation? We will centre on the first systematic study of commuting on the Belgian railway network, published by Ernest Mahaim in 1910, to relate workers' mobility on the rail network to the geographical distribution of occupations in Belgium. In the second part we move to a smaller spatial scale to capture local spatial and socio-economic transformations, namely the municipality of Waremme situated in the countryside while linked to two major centres of employment by the Brussels-Liège railway line (see map 2).

Putting the work-home split to the test: Ernest Mahaim's early study of commuting

Ernest Mahaim (1865-1938) was hired by the University of Liège at the age of 27, with three degrees on his résumé – in law, political sciences as well as public and administrative law (Dechesne 1959). As he was a disciple of Emile de Laveleye, his teaching focused on political economy. As a young intellectual starting a career in academia at the time when positivism was in full development, his research was driven by an ambition to contribute to society (Wils 2005), and to the improvement of the condition of workers more specifically. He approached the topic with an enormous disciplinary breadth, including international law, statistics, commercial politics and sociology. His writing and (inter)national public service mainly addressed international public law. Along the way, he wrote the most comprehensive interdisciplinary publication on cheap workmen's tickets of the Belgian rail network, combining statistics and law with methods from the social sciences. Mahaim's *Les abonnements d'ouvriers sur les chemins de fer belges et leurs effets sociaux* (1910) was published and supported by the Institut Solvay, affirming its progressive, social sciences approach, guided by a strong societal engagement. This study can be interpreted as the scientific test of Vandervelde's hypothesis foregrounded in *L'exode rurale ou le retour aux champs* of 1903 (Dechesne 1959, 138), namely: that the railway network tempered rural outmigration and could even lead to 'a return to the fields' of the workers who were living in the city. In this rural-urban continuum, cities would become places of work and concentrations of monuments, while workers would live in the countryside. Workers would enjoy the benefits of the city while escaping the overcrowding of the capitalist *villes tentaculaires* (Vandervelde 1903).

Mahaim verified Vandervelde's analysis by studying the numbers and geographical distribution of the cheap workmen's tickets. The system of workmen's tickets dated from 1869. The Belgian government set a price that made it more beneficial for workers to maintain family life in the countryside than to live near their jobs. The prices were calculated based on an estimation of the costs of board and lodging outside the home, being approximately 85 cents a day, while the ticket prices depending on the distance travelled varied between 15 and 75 cents a day (Mahaim 1910, 7). The subscription system of cheap workmen's tickets was reformed several times, each time broadening the mobility opportunities permitted by these tickets. In 1869, the only formula available was a ticket for six round trips a week on special workmen's trains with a maximum distance of 35 kilometres. In 1896, seven different ticket categories existed, allowing daily and weekly travel in various combinations with a distance limit of 100 kilometres, except for two new categories introduced in 1896: labourers who just needed a one-way ticket for their daily journey to work (and returned with another mode of transport) could not travel more than 20 kilometres, while workers who needed only one round trip a week could travel as far as they wanted (Mahaim 1910, 11-12). Together with the system of cheap workmen's tickets, the idea of a policy for cheap housing loans was launched, stimulating workers to build their own houses in the countryside where land was affordable (Mahaim 1910, 8). It would take until 1889, with the general workmen's strike in 1886 as a strong impetus, before this idea was translated into law (Smets 1976, 46-47). However, in 1906 these two policies were fully implemented and thus their effects could be measured.

After an analysis of the legal framework of the workmen's tickets, Mahaim moved to the quantitative analysis of commuting, 'a social phenomenon of primary importance', which 'could

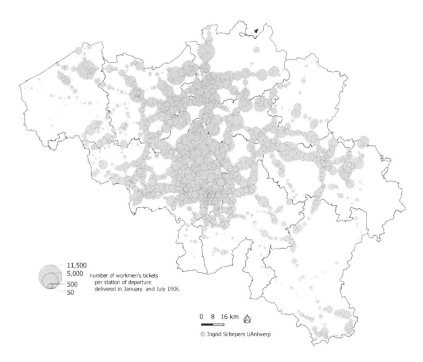

Map 3 The number and geographical distribution of workmen's tickets in Belgium (based on statistics of Mahaim 1910, 217-239).

no longer be ignored' (Mahaim 1910, VII). In addition to personal site visits and interviews of workers (Mahaim 1910, IX), his analysis is largely based on the data assembled by an administrator of the railways who sent a questionnaire to all stations of the public railway in 1906. Although at the time most of the network was public, a few lines were in concession to private companies. Some of these lines were situated in industrial regions, thus undoubtedly transporting many workers. For instance, without being able to verify the numbers, Mahaim described the crowded trains in the morning and the evening on the Namur-Liège line, running through the Walloon area of heavy industry and coal basins, exploited by the *Compagnie du Nord-Belge* (Mahaim 1910, 128-129). Notwithstanding that these private lines were excluded from the study, Mahaim's data are significant, to say the least. He collected data of 1,206 stations of which only 78 did not offer workmen's tickets, resulting in a total of 1,128 stations of the public network from which workers took the train to work (Mahaim 1910, 63). This density of railways and railway stations was unprecedented in Europe (Rowntree 1910), and so was their use. In the months of January and July 1906, 978,202 workmen's tickets were issued, turning Belgium into a massive labour market (see map 3). Except in the more peripheral areas of Limburg (north-east), the Ardennes (south) and West Flanders (south-west), large numbers of labourers commuted from their villages in the countryside to work in factories or mines.

Considering the difference in commuting behaviour of workers, ranging from full-time employed industrial workers commuting daily for 52 weeks a year to farmers working in industry only during the winter or workers returning home for the weekend or only every two weeks (Mahaim 1910; Demain 1919; Vliebergh, n.d.), Mahaim calculated an average of 20 weekly tickets a year per worker. This difference in commuting behaviour was not

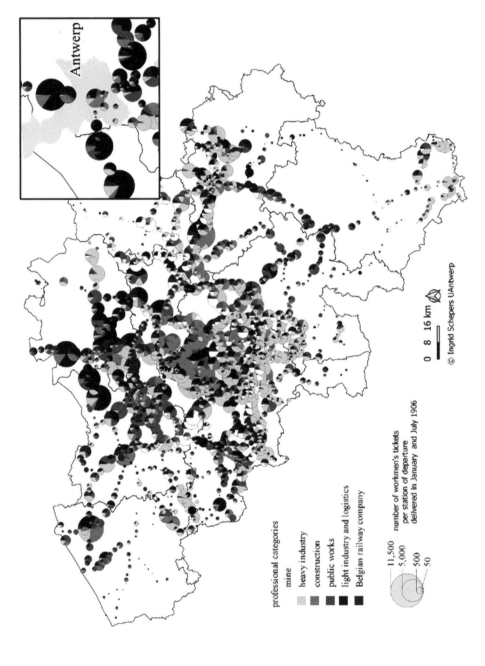

Map 4 Job categories of workers using the cheap tickets, issued at the station (based on statistics of Mahaim 1910, 217–239).

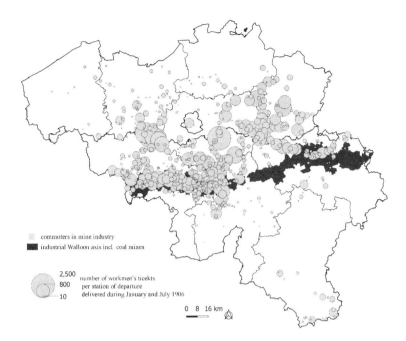

Map 5 Geographical distribution of the departure stations that issued cheap workmen's tickets for the commute to the mine industry in Wallonia. At the time of Mahaim's study the mine basins in Limburg were not yet in exploitation (based on statistics of Mahaim 1910, 217-239).

distributed evenly. An analysis of the kinds of tickets delivered shows that most workers living in the central area of the network commuted daily, and more peripheral areas had a higher ratio of labourers commuting weekly.

This difference in commuting intensity can be partly explained by the density and service of the railway network, but occupations with dispersed work locations have to be taken in consideration too. Map 4 shows the geographical distribution of workers according to six categories of work: coal mines, heavy industry, construction, public works, light industry and transport including port labour, and working for the Belgian railways. It is important to note that in principle a labourer was not trained, so he or she could be employed in any sector based on unskilled labour, be it in a factory, mine, port or construction. The map of workmen's tickets by departure stations reveals a few clear patterns of travel between home and place of work. For example, in the region of Antwerp we see high numbers of commuters to the port (black), but almost no mobility to mine basins (white).[3] Around Liège and the Mons-Charleroi axis there are a significant number of workers employed in heavy industry.

A correlation between tickets for daily commutes at the station of departure and the place of work shows that the average distance between departure station and work was 17.7 kilometres. If all tickets are included in the calculation, the distance increases to 19.1 kilometres, corresponding with a travel time of 45 minutes on the contemporary

---

3   Mahaim's study dates from before the mine basins in Limburg were exploited.

network (Mahaim 1910, 49-57). Yet, distance and time are not the only variables determining the mobility of workers. The Walloon mine sector employed workers from deep in the Flemish countryside (see map 5). The industrial census of 1910 confirms that commuting over long distances was highest in the mine sector, followed by heavy industry (metal) and construction, while the textile, food and paper industries employed more local labourers (Demain 1919).

L'exode rurale ou le retour aux champs? The case of Waremme

After having documented the magnitude and geographical scope of commuting on a national scale in 1906, Mahaim selected the station of Waremme for a case study as it had attracted his attention due to the high number of cheap workmen's tickets it issued. The data he gathered in 1908 are also of particular interest for studying the impact of commuting on rural outmigration, given that the catchment area of Waremme station (i.e. the area where the labourers who started their travel to work at Waremme station lived) corresponds to the profile prone to rural outmigration. It was located in the heart of a rural region, and 47 out of the 49 municipalities of the catchment area had fewer than 2,000 inhabitants, therefore being the category that was most affected by *l'exode rural* (Vandervelde 1900). Yet, the area was well served by light railways connecting small villages to the main railway line that gave direct access to industrial employment either in Liège or in Brussels, hence the high number of workmen's tickets delivered by the stationmaster of Waremme station during the first decade of the twentieth century. In addition, the irregular shape of Waremme's catchment area can be explained by the north-south orientation of the light railways (dotted lines, map 6) on the one hand and the presence of adjacent stations on the Brussels-Liège railway line (black line, map 6) on the other hand. As can be seen on the map, the number of commuters per municipality, visualised by the size of the circles, reflects the layout of the transport network: if the distance between the municipality and Waremme station increases, the number of commuters decreases, except for those municipalities that are well served by light railways, thereby giving easy access to the main station of Waremme. Within the catchment area, a travel distance of 16 kilometres at most separated the home from Waremme station (Mahaim 1910, 122).

Only a person who performed predominantly manual work, was paid by the day or piece and worked for an employer had access to cheap workmen's tickets (Mahaim 1910, 12). Consequently, categories like artisans, industrials, entrepreneurs, merchants, clerks, liberal professionals and employers were excluded. Two documents had to be produced, one by the employer and one by the chief of police or the mayor of the home municipality, testifying that the person holding the documents was indeed a wage worker. Furthermore, this status of wage labourer needed to be confirmed through a visit to the workplace performed by an official. After these formalities were completed and the station master had granted his permission, the name of the worker was entered into the station register. Every three years, the procedure had to be repeated (Mahaim 1910, 15-18). The name, occupation, home address and travel destination of all the labourers who were entitled to request a cheap workmen's ticket were recorded.

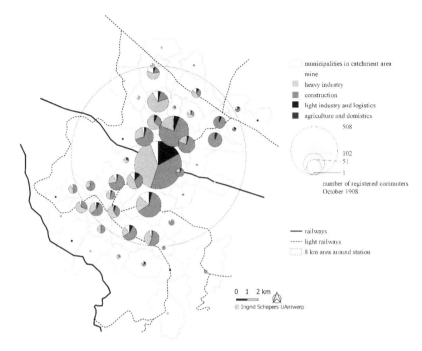

Map 6 Size of commuters per municipality and their occupations. All the municipalities within the circle are situated at a distance of eight kilometres at most from Waremme station (based on statistics of Mahaim 1910, 250-253).

So the register of Waremme station allowed Ernest Mahaim to research in depth the occupations exercised by the commuters in the catchment area. These data can be complemented with the information given by the industrial census of 1910. The 1910 census showcases commuting as an important societal phenomenon at the beginning of the twentieth century as, for the first time, the government ordered the inclusion of data on work-home mobility for every municipality. Per municipality, the number of commuters was recorded as well as their destination, occupation, gender and social profile. In addition, like the previous industrial survey of 1896, the census paid attention to the industrial activity located in the municipality itself. The two industrial surveys together thus enable a detailed inquiry into industrial employment in 1896 and 1910.

In 1908, 1,794 labourers were listed in the station register of Waremme. This impressive number explains its third place in the ranking of more than 1,000 stations that provided Ernest Mahaim with commuter data for January and July 1906. In comparison, the station register of the nearest city – Liège – noted only 1,190 workers for the same year, so 604 fewer commuters than Waremme station (Mahaim 1910, 122). As the city of Liège itself was a major labour market, the majority of these commuters were, according to Mahaim, workers who were sent out by their employers to perform a specific task in the countryside or other cities, workers who did not necessarily live in Liège. The industrial census of December 1910 confirms the importance of commuting for the inhabitants of Waremme station's catchment area. Forty-eight municipalities housed industrial workmen, but they

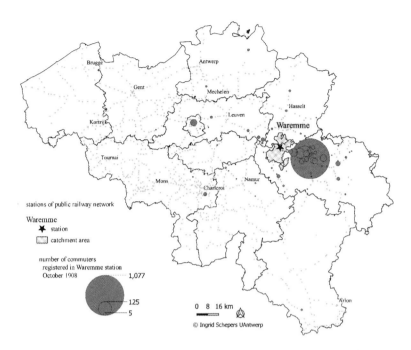

Map 7 Magnitude and geographical scope of the destinations reached by the workers living in the catchment area and registered in the station of Waremme in 1908 (based on statistics of Mahaim 1910, 250-253).

offered work to only 20 per cent of them, leaving the other 80 per cent dependant on the mobility offered by the transport networks to find work elsewhere (*Recensement de l'industrie et du commerce* 1910).

The majority of commuters recorded in the station register were oriented towards the agglomeration of Liège, some travelling further to Verviers and its surroundings. Other, but far less important, places of employment had the advantage of proximity: Ans, Bierset and even Remicourt, a village that was located in the catchment area of Waremme station. A small number of workers used the mobility opportunities offered by the railway network to their full extent: they went to Turnhout in the north of Antwerp, Appelterre in East Flanders or Saint-Vincent-Bellefontaine in the South of Luxembourg. Only a meagre 31 commuters had the capital city as their final destination which, for Mahaim, was a clear sign of 'unskilled labour, removing rural population from agriculture to industry' (Mahaim 1910, 123) (see map 7).

As the second industrial revolution advanced, the ubiquitous demand for unskilled labour meant a way out for rural residents who needed to supplement their agricultural activities with industrial work in order to obtain enough income to sustain themselves and their families (Bouché 1913). Historian Martina de Moor draws attention to income pooling (i.e. combining different occupations) as 'the key mechanism in the survival policy of the rural population' made necessary by the extreme fragmentation of farmland (De Moor 2001, 294). In 1896 rural residents in the catchment area of Waremme station predominantly turned to cottage or light industry to increase their household income.

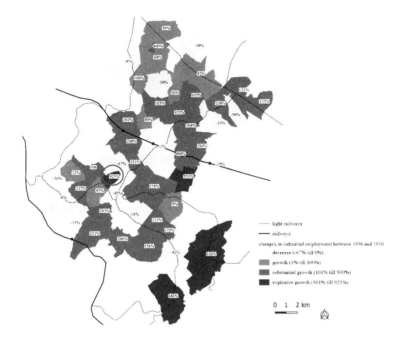

Map 8 The map is based on the industrial surveys of 1896 and 1910. It shows the changes in industrial employment per municipality between those dates. In total, the substantial growth of the industrial labour force surpasses the slight decrease of industrial workers in some municipalities.

Activities in metal, clothing, construction, wood and furniture, skin and leather industry were performed in almost all municipalities. Typically, the number of companies in these industry branches corresponded more or less with the number of 'non-workers' (i.e. a term used in the 1896 census to indicate people who ranked higher than the wage labourer (Demasure 2011, 31)), pointing to cottage industry. Correspondingly, the ratio of workers employed in these industry branches was very low. In contrast, the food industry employed 67 per cent of the workers (1,828 people) active in the catchment area of Waremme station.

In 1910 a different picture of the occupational activities emerges, because in the industrial census commuter numbers were registered next to local employment for every municipality. In general, the industrial employment in the catchment area of Waremme station increased by 41.9 per cent, giving work to 5,934 instead of 4,191 persons. It equalled the nationwide growth of 44.2 per cent. At the level of the municipalities, the results are more nuanced (see map 8). Although some municipalities accommodated fewer industrial workers, the majority experienced a significant increase. The most drastic one (925 per cent) manifested itself in Darion (163 inhabitants in 1910) where 41 people worked in an industrial occupation on the last day of December 1910, instead of the four people in October 1896; among them were 16 commuters.

A more even distribution, spatial as well as occupational, characterised the expansion of the industrial labour force. In 1896, for example, only two municipalities housed workers employed in the chemical industry, while this rose to 15 municipalities in 1910. The spatial distribution was even more prominent for the mining industry: from one to 38 municipalities. Graph 1 shows the occupational reorientation. A sharp decrease in employment in

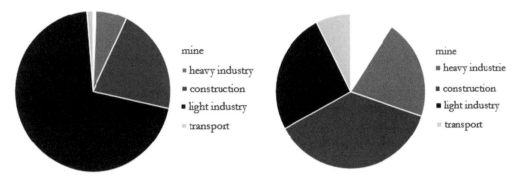

Graph 1. Professions census 1896 and 1910.

The graphs are based on the industrial surveys of 1896 and 1910. The different industry branches are grouped together in order to correspond with the occupation classification used by Ernest Mahaim. The importance of the food industry in the industrial employment of 1896 explains the predominance of light industry in the left graph.

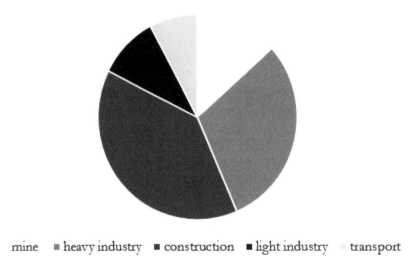

Graph 2. Commute data census 1910.

The graph is based on the industrial census of 1910. The majority of commuters had a job in mining, heavy industry or construction.

the food industry, from 49.7 to 9.8 per cent, next to a drop in the clothing industry, from 15.7 to 9.8 per cent, was accompanied by a standstill in the wood and furniture industry, which varied from 9.4 to 9.6 per cent. Thus the predominance of the light industry in 1896 dissolved in 15 years. This was compensated for by the increase of employment in other occupations, such as mining, heavy industry and construction.

It could be argued that increased employment in mining, heavy industry and construction is correlated with mobility flows, and indeed commuting, of wage workers as the places of work in these industrial branches were mainly situated outside the catchment area of Waremme station. Graph 2 confirms that commuting was indeed more prominent in these three branches compared to light industry. Furthermore, map 9 shows a strong correlation between a decrease in industrial employment per municipality and a decrease in the occupational importance of the food industry between 1896 and 1910. Or, put differently, only the municipalities with a high proportion of the food industry in 1896 demonstrated a slight decrease in industrial employment in 1910. However, the loss in employment per municipality was far less pronounced than the decline in available jobs in the food industry, thus indicating that wage labourers did find employment in other industrial occupations, or at least supplemented their income from agriculture with industrial work. The ability to find employment elsewhere due to the mobility offered by the railway network and the cheap workmen's tickets was especially important for peasant farmers or farm labourers who wanted to stay in their ancestral villages and partly live off the land, but had to turn to industrial occupations out of necessity, not as a full-time job but as a temporary occupation to supplement the family income (De Moor 2001, 294; Vliebergh n.d., 186).

This type of commuter also appears in the six categories of commuters discerned by Ernest Mahaim, who based his categorisation on the worker's choice of socio-economic strategy made possible by the railway network. First, the farmer who was bound to his land and turned to commuting only if absolutely necessary; second, the labourer-farmer who worked on the land in summer and on industrial sites in winter; third and fourth, the factory worker who saw commuting as a way of life and either was born in or migrated to the countryside; fifth, the skilled worker who was sent to work in different places for his boss; and, sixth, the semi-rooted who lived near his work but travelled home every week (Mahaim 1910, 139-143). This diversity in socio-economic motivations resonated in the information written down in the station register for the catchment area of Waremme station. Nearly 1,000 workers (54.9 per cent) commuted on a daily basis, while the rest returned home only once a week. Most of them were unskilled labourers employed in mines, heavy industry, construction or public works, making them highly flexible in combining agricultural activities in their own municipality with wage labour elsewhere, but skilled workers like painters, plumbers, carpenters and electricians also subscribed to the cheap workmen's tickets (Mahaim 1910, 122-124).

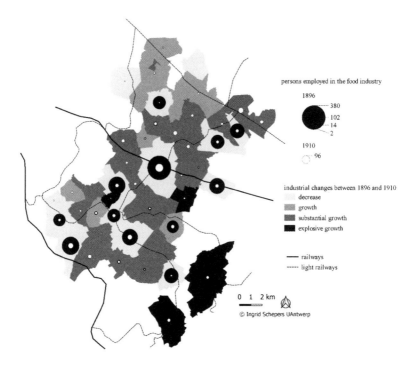

Map 9 The map is based on the industrial surveys of 1896 and 1910. It shows the strong spatial correlation between the sharp drop in employment in the food industry and the municipalities that accommodated fewer industrial workers in 1910 compared to 1896.

To conclude, and in line with Emile Vandervelde's expectations, rural outmigration was tempered because the loss in local industrial employment could be compensated for by commuting. As a result, the population in the catchment area of Waremme station grew by nearly 6 per cent during the first decennia of the twentieth century. Although this is below the national average of 10.9 per cent, it manifested itself in a region that was vulnerable for *l'exode rural* since 47 out of the 49 municipalities had fewer than 2,000 inhabitants. In general, in Belgium, rural villages of the size of Waremme shrank due to rural outmigration. However, the rail network introduced a new vector of spatial development. The number of households in the catchment area of Waremme station increased by 10.9 per cent while the number of houses grew by 11.7 per cent (*Recensement général* 1900; *Recensement général* 1910).

Although Waremme did not grow exponentially, the comparison of topographic maps shows that the rural village grew at a steady rate during the second half of the nineteenth century (see fig.2). As early as in 1867 a second centre developed around the railway station. In the following decades, the urban tissue was gradually filled in with housing. Even industry – a sugar refinery – settled next to the railway.

Figure 2[4] Topographic maps of Waremme for the years 1867, 1885 and 1903.

Discussion: the socio-economic effects of the rural-urban link

The researched period coincides with the transition to the second industrial revolution (Deneckere et al. 2013, 95), resulting in a nationwide industrial growth of 44.2 per cent between 1896 and 1910 (*Recensement général des industries et des métiers* 1896; *Recensement de l'industrie et du commerce* 1910), while at the same time full-time employment in the agricultural sector dropped from one third to little more than one fifth of the active population (De Moor 2001, 292). Furthermore, 1896 is the year in which the numbers of cheap workmen's tickets increased significantly (Mahaim 1910, 3), thereby establishing commuting as an integral part of the socio-economic strategies of the Belgian population. Thus, the occupational transformation between 1896 and 1910 provides insight into changes of socio-economic strategies in relation to the mobility of labourers as set up by transport policies stimulating mobility flows between the countryside as a place of residence and cities

---

4   Waremme XLI / 3 (1867) National Geographic Institute; Waremme XLI / 3 (1885) National Geographic Institute; Waremme 41 / 3 (1903) National Geographic Institute (consulted on http://www.cartesius.be).

and industrial sites as centres of work. Results clearly show that industrial employment increased significantly for most rural municipalities in the Waremme catchment area and that rural outmigration was very low, while the area went through a prominent reduction in the food and cottage industries. In a short period the occupational distribution shifted from predominant shares in light industry (the food and cottage industries) to large shares in mining and heavy industry located outside the catchment area. In the case of Waremme as well as for most of the Belgian territory large numbers of workmen's tickets were registered, allowing this fast and dynamic shift in occupational structure. Workers could choose from a wide variety of commuting schemes to accommodate their personal socio-economic strategies or needs, ranging from 'income pooling' with agricultural labour to full-time work in factories or mines, returning each day to their homes and families or hiring rooms in the city and returning for the weekend. The quantitative analysis thus substantiates the observations of reformers linking transport policy with commuting and countryside urbanisation. Emile Vandervelde concluded that the workmen's trains 'caused perhaps the most profound revolution ever in labour in Belgium in a quarter of a century' (Vandervelde 1903, 143). The national government had, by means of a ministerial decree, set out to fill the temporary demand for labour and ended up reorganising Belgian demographic patterns for the coming century. The workmen's train tickets instituted in 1869, together with the housing subsidies introduced in 1889, had encouraged workers to reside locally in villages spread throughout the Belgian countryside while allowing them to seek employment nationally. Even with declining agricultural employment, the population of the Belgian countryside remained stable through the First World War. Industrial employers continued to draw peasants and workers from a national labour market, just as the Liberal minister and Catholic deputy who co-operated on the original plan expected they would.

Unlike cities such as London where workers were stuck in urban quarters close to their jobs because commuting was too expensive and suburban houses were built for the elite, Belgian workers could remain in their ancestral villages or even move from the city to the countryside. Whereas in England only skilled workers could afford to commute and live in the suburbs (Polasky 2010, 176), in Belgium the cheap workmen's tickets targeted unskilled workers. As Bouché observed in 1913, commuting between city and countryside was the most profitable strategy as the wages in industry were high, rent and cost of living in the countryside were low, and transport costs were cheap. In 1910, the average wage per year in agriculture was 633 francs while in industry it was 1,125 a year (De Moor 2001). Vandervelde explained that a worker could afford to rent a house of four rooms in the countryside for 12.50 francs per month or even build a house with a cheap loan, while in Brussels it would cost 20 francs to rent much less and far more insanitary. Even with a train ticket costing 1.35 francs, the worker could still save (Vandervelde 1903, 223; Polasky 2010, 168).

In line with Vandervelde, we can conclude that rural outmigration was tempered and harsh social realities like, for instance, the workers' quarters in London were partly avoided by the institutionalised work-home split. In addition, transport and mobility policy gave workers flexibility in both socio-economic strategy and the workplace, making them more independent from factory owners. However, the idea that transport mobility increased social mobility and ultimately would lead to the emancipation of the working class, as Vandervelde hoped, remained a utopian thought. Yet the analysis does show that farmers were turned into industrial workers and most of them remained in the countryside, either as part-time agricultural workers or at least residing in a home with a garden with space for a vegetable patch.

Conclusion: organising the work-home split by the rural-urban link

Ernest Mahaim's study of the Belgian government's introduction of a national system of workmen's tickets on the railways and their social effects was truly pioneering. In addition to collecting quantative data, he asked questions about the experience of individual workmen as he mapped their movement from home to work. In his 1910 study, he studied the workmen's trains as social scientists would define mobilities in the twenty-first century, as 'a complex assemblage of movement, imaginings and experience' (Salazar 2016). Mahaim recognised that his study would not be definitive even if he compiled volumes of statistics from station masters and talked with countless working men in every Belgian province (Mahaim 1910, VII). Interested in grounding his study in the 'reality' of workmen's trains, he asked the women he found lined up on Sunday to buy a week's tickets about their husband's work. Mahaim never imagined that in fact the women were buying their own tickets. He was invested in the organisers' expectations that the workmen's tickets were designed to transport what Belgian deputy Kervyn de Lettenhove called 'the industrial classes', specifically working men, to work each day, returning every night to the countryside to 'what the English call home, that is to say what attaches a man not only to his nation, but also to his family, because after a day of labour, he finds such joy in the face of his wife and children' (de Lettenhove 1869, 735). Mahaim did not see the sizeable numbers of women commuting in patterns reported by a critic of the scheme and verified by census data (Demain 1919, 68; Polasky 2010, 162-181). There is still much to be done to understand the relationship not only of occupations, but also gender, among other factors, with infrastructure and mobility.

The Belgian experiment in controlling territory by engineering a network did not result in the assimilation of labourers into a homogeneous national citizenry, as Ernst Mahaim expected. He depicted commuters passing their evenings amidst the domestic peace of a family supper followed by time spent in the cultivation of a kitchen garden. Flemish workers travelling daily to Wallonia brought different populations into contact with each other. The workmen's trains that were intended to mould national citizens reinforced local identification by rooting the labourers and their families in their ancestral villages. The commuting Belgian workers travelled nationally, but they lived locally. Rather than 'cementing together a common nationality' (Mahaim 1910, 205), the trains contributed to the development of a regionalism that has come to define the federal Belgian state (Polasky 2010).

That said, mobility introduced by the scheme of workmen's tickets did effectively curtail the rural exodus, as planned. The second densest railway network in the world served to limit the urbanization that typically accompanied industrialisation. Instead of large metropolises, smaller cities dotted the territory. Half of the urban population lived in towns of fewer than 25,000 residents in 1910 (Van Ginderachter 2019, 15-16). Emile

Vandervelde observed from the window of the train, with some satisfaction, 'Nothing is more striking for the visitor who travels from London to Brussels than the contrast between the deserted pastures of Kent and animated fields bordering our major cities' (Vandervelde 1903, 138).

References

Abercrombie, Patrick, and A. Dumont (Transl.). 1912. *Bruxelles: étude de développement et de trace urbain.* Brussels: Editions de l'Emulation.

Bouché, Bart. 1913. *Les ouvriers agricoles en Belgique.* Brussels and Leipzig: Misch et Thron.

Commune de Schaerbeek. 1898. *Construction d'habitations à bon marché par la commune.* Brussels: Becquart-Arien.

De Block, Greet. 2011. "Designing the Nation. The Belgian Railway Project, 1830-1837." *Technology and Culture*, no. 52: 703-732.

De Block, Greet. 2014. "Planning Rural-Urban Landscapes: Railways and Countryside Urbanisation in South-West Flanders, Belgium (1830-1930)." *Landscape Research* 39, no. 5: 542-565.

De Block, Greet, and Janet Polasky. 2011. "Light Railways and the Rural-Urban Continuum: Technology, Space and Society in Late Nineteenth-Century Belgium." *Journal of Historical Geography*, no. 37: 312-332.

De Brabander, Guido. 1983. *Regionale structuur en werkgelegenheid. Een economische en geografische studie over de Belgische lange- termijn-ontwikkeling.* Brussels: Koninklijke Academie.

De Moor, Martina. 2001. "The Occupational and Geographical Mobility of Farm Labourers in Flanders from the End of the 19th tot the Middle of the 20th Century." In *Labour and Labour Markets between Town and Countryside (Middle Ages – 19th Century),* ed. Bruno Blondé, Eric Vanhoute and Michèle Galand, 295-304. Turnhout: Brepolis.

De Winne, August. 2001 (1902). *Door arm Vlaanderen.* Leuven: Van Halewyck.

Dechesne, L. 1959. "Notice sur Ernest Mahaim." *Biographie Nationale*, no. XLIII. Brussels: Bruylant.

Demain, H. 1919. *Les migrations ouvrières à travers la Belgique.* Leuven: Bomans.

Demasure, Brecht. 2011. *Rapport. Sociaal-economische streekstudie Midden- en Zuid-West-Vlaanderen (1840-1970). Een kritische analyse aan de hand van overheidsinstelingen.* Leuven: Centrum Agrarische Geschiedenis.

Deneckere, Gita, Tom De Paepe and Bruno de Wever. 2012. *Een geschiedenis van België.* Ghent: Academian Press.

Hohenberg, Paul, & Lynn Hollen Lees. 1996. *The Making of Urban Europe, 1000-1994.* Cambridge, MA: Harvard University Press.

Jamar, *Annales parlementaires (note 54) 1868-1869.* 22 April 1869.

Kervyn de Lettenhove, *Annales parlementaires.* 21 April 1869.

Mahaim, Ernest. 1910. *Les abonnements d'ouvriers sur les chemins de fer belges et leurs effets sociaux.* Brussels: Misch et Thron.

Moraglio, Massimo. 2017. "Seeking a (new) ontology for transport history." *The Journal of Transport History* 38, no. 1: 3-10.

Olyslager, Paul M. 1947. *De localiseering der Belgische nijverheid.* Antwerp: Standaard.

Polasky, Janet. 2010. *Reforming Urban Labor: Routes to the City, Roots in the Country.* Ithaca, NY: Cornell University Press.

Polasky, Janet. 2015. "Contemporary Urban Reform in London and Brussels." In *Cities Beyond Borders: Comparative and Transnational Approaches to Urban History,* ed. Nicolas Kenny and Rebecca Madgin, 113-130. Farnham: Ashgate Press.

Pooley, Colin. 2017. *Mobility, Migration and Transport. Historical Perspectives.* Cham: Palgrave.

Rowntree, Benjamin Seebohm. 1910. *Land and labour: Lessons from Belgium.* London: Macmillan.

Salazar, Noel B. 2016. "Keywords of Mobility: A Critical Introduction." In *Keywords of Mobility. Critical Engagements,* ed. Noel B. Salazar and Kiran Jayaram, 1-12. New York and Oxford: Berghahn.

Smets, Marcel. 1976. *L'avènement de la cité-jardin en Belgique. Histoire de l'habitat social en Belgique de 1830 à 1930.* Brussels: Mardaga.

Vandervelde, Emile. 1900. *Le propriété foncière en Belgique.* Paris: C. Reinwald.

Vandervelde, Emile. 1903. *L'exode rural et le retour au champs.* Paris: Alcan.

Van der Haegen, Herman. 1982. *West European Settlement Systems.* Leuven: KUL Geografisch Instituut.

Van Ginderachter, Maarten. 2019. *The Everyday Nationalism of Workers. A Social History of Modern Belgium.* Stanford, CA: Stanford University Press.

Vliebergh, Emiel. n.d. *Het Hageland. Bijdrage tot zijn ekonomische geschiedenis in de XIXe en in't begin der XXste eeuw.* Bruges: Houdmont-Carbonez.

Weber, Donald. 2009. "Werkmanstreinen en de geboorte van de moderne pendelaar, 1870-1914." *Brood & Rozen,* no. xiv: 131-148.

Wils, Kaat. 2005. *De omweg van de wetenschap: het positivisme en de Belgische en Nederlandse intellectuele cultuur, 1845-1914.* Amsterdam: Amsterdam University Press.

Ann Coenen

The City and the Parking Lot

Movement and Standstill on the 21ˢᵗ-century Urban Labour Market[*]

Introduction

There is wide agreement among scholars of inequality that urbanisation is associated with higher levels of inequality (Atkinson 2015; Behrens & Robert-Nicoud 2014; OECD 2015). While assessing levels of inequality on a local level is understandably difficult with limited historical sources, it is surprising that even contemporary sociological and economic studies rarely look below the national level. In Belgium, due to our intricate stratification of political competences most of the present-day administrative sources are available for the three regions (Flemish, Walloon and Brussels-Capital Region) and/or three communities (Flemish, French and German-speaking). However, as Belgium is a small country, existing contemporary research rarely goes into further detail, and when it does it focusses mainly on the differences between those regions. This has the benefit that we know from a wide range of official statistics that the Brussels-Capital Region – Belgium's largest urbanised area – indeed exhibits more pronounced labour market inequalities than the other regions: on the one hand, wages in Brussels are relatively high (Eurostat & Statbel 2018), and on the other hand (long-term) unemployment is also high compared to the rest of the country (Eurostat & Statbel 2019), leading to a higher risk of poverty than in the other regions. The Brussels-Capital Region also has a higher proportion of temporary contracts and of involuntary part-time or fixed-term work (Eurostat & Statbel 2019), while at the same time it has a smaller proportion of people in non-standard contracts (i.e. working in shifts, at night or during weekends) (Eurostat & Statbel 2018b).

There are however many types of cities in Belgium, each with specific forms of urbanisation, varying sizes, a presence of different economic sectors, etc. To answer the question whether present-day cities in Belgium are more unequal than its less-urbanised regions, I will use exhaustive administrative data on the working-age population in its capital, Brussels (divided into five sub-units based on average wage levels),[1] and in 16 other

[*] While taking full responsibility for the text, the author would like to thank Valérie Burnel, Marilyne De Spiegeleire, Valérie Gilbert, Marie-Laure Noirhomme, Frédéric Poupinel de Valence and Tom Bevers.

[1] The 'Brussels – very low incomes' subgroup consists of Sint-Joost-ten-Node, Sint-Jans-Molenbeek, Anderlecht and Schaerbeek. 'Brussels – low incomes' is made up of the municipalities of Brussels, Saint-Gilles, Koekelberg and Evere. 'Brussels – average incomes' includes Etterbeek, Forest, Jette and Ganshoren. 'Brussels – high incomes' groups together Sint-Agatha-Berchem, Ixelles and Woluwe-Saint-Lambert. Finally, Brussels – very high incomes' consists of the municipalities of Auderghem, Uccle, Watermael-Boitsfort and Woluwe-Saint-Pierre.

Ann Coenen • FPS Employment, Labour Market and Social Dialogue, and University of Antwerp

Inequality and the City in the Low Countries (1200-2020), ed. by Bruno Blondé, Sam Geens, Hilde Greefs, Wouter Ryckbosch, Tim Soens & Peter Stabel, SEUH 50 (Turnhout, 2020), pp. 123-138.

   DOI 10.1484/M.SEUH-EB.5.120441

Belgian municipalities (Antwerp, Mons, Bruges, Charleroi, Eupen, Genk, Ghent, Hasselt, La Louvière, Leuven (and Oud-Heverlee), Liège (including Seraing), Malines, Namur, Verviers, Vilvoorde and Wavre). The selected towns[2] are a mix of those with the largest number of inhabitants (Brussels, Antwerp, Ghent, Charleroi and Liège) and smaller ones, as research suggests that larger cities are associated with more elevated levels of social inequality (OECD 2015, 80; Van Hamme 2015, 11). They are also spread across the three regions and communities because, on average, the unemployment rate in the Walloon and Brussels-Capital regions has recovered much more slowly from the severe hit the Belgian labour market received during the oil crises of the 1970s. Lastly, the selection includes cities that form interesting case studies because of their specific economic situation or migration history (e.g. Verviers, Vilvoorde and Genk).

This chapter will analyse a range of contemporary inequalities. The wage dispersion will take up the smallest part, as harmonised data on income inequality are more limited and available only for the three regions. The main focus will be on the three main employment-related indicators (employment, unemployment and inactivity), as being employed is still the best protection against poverty and material deprivation. And while the exact relationship between unemployment and inequality is nuanced, there is wide agreement that (involuntary) unemployment leads to social exclusion and deteriorating living conditions (Atkinson 2015, 102). Where possible, I will also discuss the segmentation between qualitative and less qualitative jobs, with parameters such as job security, risk of poverty and the higher education premium. As Belgium has a traditionally highly heterogeneous labour market – where moderate income and wealth inequality go hand in glove with strong stratification in terms of labour market integration and job quality – the emphasis will be on those groups that are most vulnerable, i.e. particular groups of migrants and low-qualified persons. The largest part of the chapter is based on microdata retrieved from the Datawarehouse Labour Market and Social Protection (managed by the Crossroads Bank for Social Security – CBSS). On the basis of these administrative data (composed of variables that have been developed for the 2019 socio-economic monitoring, SPF Employment and Unia 2020), I will try to determine whether or not there is greater labour market segmentation in Belgian cities than elsewhere in Belgium, and in what type of cities this inequality is most obvious.

Income inequality

Income inequality continues to be the focus in inequality studies, and it is also the aspect that has been – and still is – studied with the most academic vigour. This is the case for Belgium as well. So while it is necessary to look beyond this indicator (De Keyzer Chapter 20), we cannot leave it out.

Belgium is one of only a few industrialised countries that has not experienced a substantial increase in income inequalities over the course of the last three decades (Van Rie & Marx 2013a, 126). This is remarkable given the differences between the regions

---

2   The selection was made in the context of the forthcoming *2019 Socio-economic monitoring report* (FPS Employment and Unia).

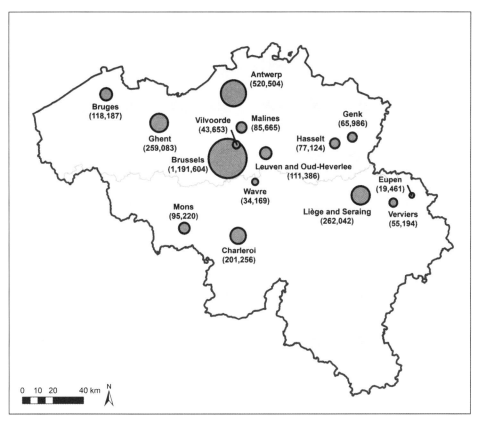

Map 1. Belgium including the 17 cities, with number of residents (1 January 2017)

Source: Statbel – Bevolking; NGI – Administrative Map version 3 – 1999, Statbel – 2006. Created by Iason Jongepier, GIStorical Antwerp (UAntwerpen/Hercules Foundation).

and communities. And it is even more remarkable because Belgium is a country with a very heterogeneous labour market, as will be shown below. It is probably crucial to note in this context that the main instruments of income distribution (social security and the bulk of taxation) have largely stayed in the hands of the central, federal government (Van Rie & Marx 2013a, 127). On top of that, the country's minimum wage system is one of the few offering effective dual protection against low wages: it combines a national statutory minimum with high levels of collective bargaining coverage and binding wage floors defined in sectoral agreements. Such systems have been proven to be associated with low wage inequality levels (Garnero et al. 2015). Survey data suggest that, while real average incomes increased, income inequality in Belgium remained fairly stable between 1985 and the late 2000s (Horemans, Pintelon et al. 2011; Piacentini 2014). However, an important caveat for present-day data on income is that they omit employer-provided non-wage benefits. Employer-provided fringe benefits that are fully or partially tax-exempt, such as luncheon vouchers and – most notably – company cars, are popular in Belgium, and tend to be strongly concentrated among the highest wage earners (Van Rie & Marx 2013a, 130).

But averages always cover up part of the story. Let us start with Brussels. The Brussels Capital Region is a major centre of economic activity, a fact which is reflected by higher average monthly gross wages than the rest of the country. Its average gross monthly salary is 17 per cent higher than the national gross monthly salary (Eurostat & Statbel 2018). Brussels moreover has a much higher GDP per capita than the other regions (Institute for National Accounts (INR-ICN) and Statbel). Yet its resident population is on average relatively poor and economically vulnerable (Van Rie & Marx 2013b, 9; Van Hamme et al. 2015). As we shall see below, the disparities in income correspond clearly to differences in labour market performance.

On the basis of the microdata from the CBSS, we can divide the Belgian population aged 18 to 64 into wage deciles (by region only), and then see whether the wage distribution in Brussels differs from the overall distribution of wages. This shows in particular that the share of people earning low wages (workers in the first three deciles of the distribution) is very high in Brussels: in 2016, 39.2 per cent of Brussels residents earned a low wage (as opposed to 30.8 and 27.0 per cent in the Walloon and Flemish Regions). The share of high wages (the three highest wage deciles) is also the lowest in Brussels, but here differences are small (respectively 28.3 per cent as against 28.7 and 32.3 per cent) (SPF Employment & Unia 2020, annex 7.4). This can in part be explained by the fact that Brussels has a younger population than the other regions (seniority has a strong impact on Belgian wages), but not entirely. When we focus on people with a migrant background (i.e. those who currently have a foreign nationality, had a foreign nationality at birth, or who have at least one parent with a foreign nationality (at birth)) we see that share of workers with low wages among this group is even larger in Brussels compared to other regions (SPF Employment & Unia 2020, annex 7.4). The same is true for people who have at best finished lower secondary education (SPF Employment & Unia 2020, annex 7.9). In short, for groups which have in general a higher than average percentage of low wage earners (people of foreign origin and those with poor qualifications), distribution is even more skewed in Brussels than it is elsewhere in Belgium.

As has been said, income-related indicators have many caveats – as will be discussed later in this volume – but we can start by complementing them with poverty indicators. Unfortunately, the official risk of poverty indicators calculated on the basis of the EU-SILC survey (by Eurostat and Statbel) are unreliable for the Brussels Capital Region due to small sample sizes. Nonetheless, as we know that those who work have a very low risk of poverty in Belgium (5 per cent), while those who are unemployed have a very high risk (49 per cent) (Van Lancker 2019, 115) and as more people are unemployed in Brussels (an unemployment rate of 13.1 per cent compared to 5.8 per cent for the total Belgian population in 2018), the risk of poverty is probably also higher than in the rest of the country.

Data on wealth inequality are strikingly scarce compared to those on income distribution. Historical research is hindered by the frequent methodological changes over time and the scarcity of sources, and these problems have surprisingly even worsened in recent decades due to fiscal choices (Coenen 2017). Belgium is not alone in facing this problem, but it is one of the few Western European countries that were not included in Piketty's seminal work (Piketty 2013). Koen Dedobbeleer has pointed out the problems with the official data series for Belgium. He writes: 'For our country even the most recent 43 years are a puzzle of available data. For now, they could by no means always be collected on a uniform basis' (Dedobbeleer 2016, 49).

Demographic differences between Belgian cities

Fortunately, in terms of socio-economic position (employment, unemployment and types of inactivity) we have detailed data on a wide range of Belgian cities. Thanks to the existence of the Datawarehouse Labour and Social Protection, Belgium is blessed with an abundance of data on the demographic and socio-economic characteristics of Belgian residents (all those registered in the national register) between 2008 and 2016.[3] Belgium is a highly heterogeneous society, where moderate income and wealth inequality go hand in glove with strong segmentation in the labour market, due to processes of compartmentalisation between high-status well-paid jobs and more flexible jobs with low status and wages (Peck 1989). (Non-EU) Immigrants, low-skilled and older workers in particular can often be found in unfavourable conditions (more short-term contracts, higher unemployment and jobs with lower wages (SPF Employment & Unia 2020, ch.2)). In this chapter I will focus on two groups: people with a migrant background and people who have not finished secondary school. The labour participation gaps for these groups are strikingly high in Belgium compared to other EU member states (European Commission 2019).

Migrants in particular face many challenges such as limited labour market participation, lower labour quality and precariousness. Even though they form a very diverse group, they are also more often over-qualified for their jobs, and this is particularly the case in Belgium (European Commission 2019; OECD 2017; OECD 2017b). In 2016, 31.1 per cent of the Belgian population aged 18 to 64 years was of foreign origin (including foreign national and first- and second-generation Belgians).[4] When we divide the population (18-64 years old) per city into origin groups, it is clear at a glance that there are major differences between populations in Belgian cities. While Bruges (the biggest city in the province of West Flanders) has only a 14 per cent share of people of foreign origin (again, all generations taken together), there are several other Belgian cities (in particular Antwerp, Brussels, Charleroi, Genk, La Louvière, Liège and Vilvoorde) with shares of more than 50 per cent. The four municipalities of Brussels with the lowest average incomes (i.e. Saint-Josse-ten-Noode, Molenbeek, Anderlecht and Schaerbeek) have by far the largest proportion of inhabitants of foreign origin (81 per cent).

The people of foreign origin (excluding the unknowns) can then be further broken down according to their migration background. Again, the populations in the various cities do not have the same composition. A number of cities have a noticeably high proportion of people who have not (yet) acquired Belgian nationality, but who are registered in the National Register (whether for more or less than five years). In the case of Leuven (the capital of Flemish Brabant and home to the main campus of Belgium's biggest university) and of the municipalities of Brussels with high and very high wage levels, this amounts to a share of more than 60 per cent of people of foreign origin. Brussels, Ghent and Leuven are also the cities with the youngest populations in our sample. The high proportion of recent entrants, their relatively young age and high level of education (as we shall see below) all

---

3   Earlier data are available for some variables, but not for origin or migration background.
4   On top of this, 6.4 per cent of people have non-determined origin, mainly because it is impossible to determine the nationality at birth of one or more parents.

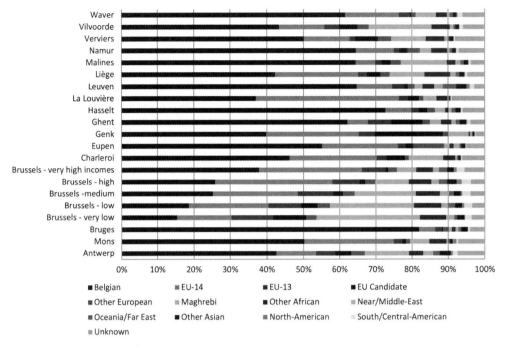

Figure 1. People aged 18-64 by origin, by city (2016)

Source: Annexes to SPF Employment and Unia 2020. Calculations by the author.

lead to the conclusion that a large number of them are either (former) students of higher educational institutions or associates of international companies and organisations.

Genk, located in the Flemish province of Limburg, has by far the highest proportion of second-generation migrants, which is not surprising given the important groups of foreigners (including Poles, Italians and Turks) who have been attracted to work in the Genk coalmines since the 1920s. Even though demand for these workers was high, their integration did not go as smoothly as one might assume (Beyers 2007). This long migration history is also reflected in the high proportion of people of over 55 among non-EU originals in Genk.

The second main characteristic of important challenges on the Belgian labour market is the level of education (European Commission 2019; OECD 2017). The demographic composition according to this variable is again cross-tabulated with the variable origin (grouped into Belgium, EU Member States, and non-EU countries). This is done because it allows for an intersectional analysis of the labour market indicators below.

In all of the 17 cities we find the largest proportion of holders of at most a certificate of lower secondary education to be people of non-EU origin, followed by those of EU origin and, finally, Belgians. The opposite is true for higher education graduates: people of Belgian origin are most likely to have completed higher education, followed by those of EU origin. An exception is the city of Mons (located in the Walloon province of Hainaut), where the proportion of highly educated people of non-EU origin is slightly higher than that of

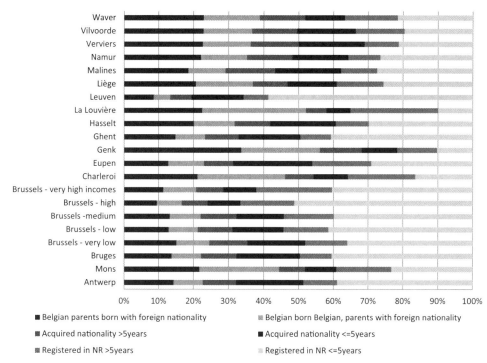

Figure 2. People of foreign origin (18-64 years old) by migration background, by city (2016)

Source: Annexes to SPF Employment and Unia 2020. Calculations by the author.

EU-origin. The highest proportion of low-skilled (i.e. at most lower-secondary education) people of non-EU origin is found in Verviers, Antwerp, Charleroi, Liège, Eupen and the municipalities of Brussels with the lowest income levels. There is also a relatively high proportion of low-skilled people of EU origin in these cities. In Charleroi, the proportion of people who have at most finished lower secondary education is remarkably high for all residents, including those of Belgian origin. In Genk and Verviers the proportion of higher education graduates among non-EU originals is the lowest, and in Charleroi and La Louvière the proportion of highly qualified people is very low in general. These four cities all have a rich industrial past, and so, during the twentieth century, blue-collar workers from Southern and Eastern Europe were actively recruited to come and work in their local industries (especially coal and steel), sectors that have shrunk considerably in the most recent decades, thus leaving a group of people without higher education in a context of dwindling demand for low-skilled workers.

The highest proportion of residents with a higher education diploma can be found in the municipalities of Brussels with high and very high salary levels, and in Leuven. These are also the cities with the highest proportion of master's degrees among people of non-Belgian origin. Leuven is moreover the city with the highest proportion of people who have obtained a PhD: 4.0 per cent of 25-64-year-olds have obtained a PhD, compared to only 0.6 per cent for the whole of Belgium. Charleroi, Genk, La Louvière and Verviers have the smallest shares of master's degree holders and PhDs among people of foreign origin.

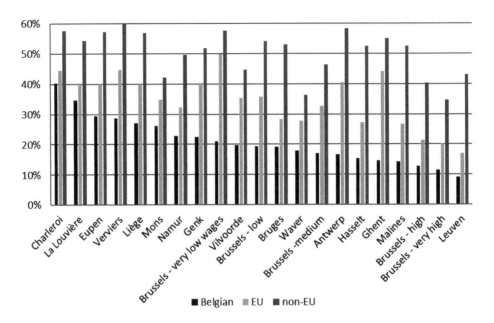

Figure 3. Proportion of 25-64-year-olds who have at most obtained a certificate of lower secondary education by origin, by city (2016)[6]

Source: Annexes to SPF Employment and Unia 2020. Calculations by the author.

Unequal labour market outcomes

When it comes to the labour market participation in the cities under scrutiny, it comes as no surprise that in all of them the employment rate of people of Belgian origin is higher than that of those of EU origin, which in turn is higher than that of those of non-EU origin (as is the case in all of Belgium (SPF Employment & Unia 2020)). The same holds true for the employment rate of low-skilled (at most lower secondary school) as opposed to medium (higher secondary) and highly skilled (higher education) people. However, it is remarkable that the levels vary considerably between cities, as does the size of the gap between the different groups of residents.

On average (for the total population aged 20-64), Bruges, Malines, Hasselt and Vilvoorde (all located in Flanders) have the highest employment rates. In 2016 the laggards were the municipalities of Brussels with very low and low wages, Charleroi, Liège and Verviers, as well as the municipalities of Brussels with high wages.[6] When we look at the employment rate just of non-EU originals, Verviers, Eupen, Liège, Mons and Charleroi

---

5   Without unknown levels of education.
6   In the case of the municipalities of Brussels, we have to make an important correction. Some 30,800 people are wrongly recorded as inactive in the administrative data. They work for international institutions in Brussels, and for the most part they are of EU origin. The employment rate of the EU originals in the entire Brussels Region is thus about 10 percentage points higher than calculated on the basis of administrative data. Most employees of international institutions live in the municipalities of Brussels, Ixelles and Etterbeek (Desiere, Struyven, Cuyvers & Gangji 2018).

(Walloon Region) perform worst. We know that the labour markets of the latter cities have experienced major disruption in recent decades. Especially during the oil crises of the 1970s and 1980s there was huge job loss in industry from which the region never fully recovered. Just like the mining regions in the north of France or the former industrial leaders in Britain (like Newcastle and Sheffield), they experienced great difficulty in reconverting their economies when their former economic strongholds started to languish. However, with the exception of Eupen and Verviers, these are not the cities where the gap between persons of non-EU and Belgian origin is most important. The employment gap is the largest in Leuven (possibly because a larger proportion of people of foreign origin live there as students or guest lecturers/researchers, or work for international institutions in the Brussels region) and the smallest in Bruges (where all employment rates are relatively high). It is possible that certainly people who migrated only recently are more often employed through informal channels, which factor bars them from social security or decent working conditions. In brief, the average employment rates per group, often explained by the general economic context of cities, and the width of the gaps at first glance do not seem to correlate.

Although the gap between people of Belgian and non-EU origin is important everywhere, it is, in all cities, smaller in 2016 than it was in 2008. In Bruges in particular, the difference in employment rates has decreased sharply. While the employment rates of Belgian-origin residents in Bruges have not changed, people with a migrant background, particularly those from recent EU member states, have revealed higher employment rates in 2016 compared to 2008. In Charleroi, La Louvière, Wavre and Vilvoorde the employment gap is also relatively small. In the case of the first two cities, this is mainly because the 'Belgians' have very low employment rates as well. In the case of Wavre, the rates are close to each other at an average level and in Vilvoorde they are at a relatively high level (with, moreover, an underestimation for the employment rate of EU originals (due to the fact that those working for international organisations are not subjected to Belgian social security; Desiere et al. 2018)).

Brussels has almost the largest employment gap between those who completed lower secondary education at best and holders of higher education degrees. Given that, the advantage gained from higher education, the so-called higher education premium, is greater than on average. However, the relatively low wage levels of highly skilled migrants in Brussels and the sectors in which they work suggest that their skills match the jobs they end up in less often than in the case of nationals (SPF Employment & Unia 2020; Tuccio 2019; Jacobs et al. forthcoming).

Unemployment rates again vary widely between Belgian cities, but everywhere non-EU nationals have the highest unemployment rate by far, as do poorly qualified people. In a number of cities the gap between Belgian and non-EU-origin inhabitants even widened between 2008 and 2016, particularly in Mons, Bruges, the (very) high-wage municipalities of Brussels, Leuven and La Louvière. Verviers has by far the highest unemployment rate among people of non-EU origin, as well as the highest proportion of people with lower secondary education at best. Leuven, on the other hand, has the lowest unemployment rate among residents of non-EU origin, but also the highest proportion of higher education graduates. The fall in unemployment in all cities between 2010 and 2016, however, was accompanied by a significant increase in the number of people who depend on social

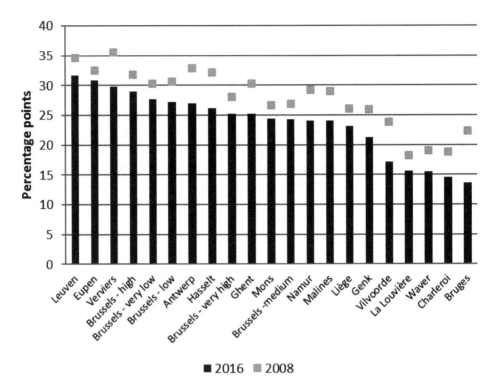

Figure 4. Employment rate gap between people of Belgian and non-EU origin (20-64), per city (2008/2016), in percentage points

Source: Annexes to SPF Employment and Unia 2020. Calculations by the author.

welfare benefits, and this was the case even in the best-performing cities, although to a lesser extent (Van Hamme 2015).

In terms of unemployment, the level of education seems to be more decisive than other variables in determining someone's chances in the labour market, and the level of education seems to go hand in glove with the (past) economic structure of the city: former heavy industrial towns tend to have more low-skilled inhabitants than cities with a more diverse mix of economic sectors, adding to a negative spiral of worsening economic prospects. The situation in Brussels, where the unemployment rate is not particularly low, even in the richer municipalities – despite the very high level of education in the municipalities with high and very high wages – nuances this conclusion a little, although even in Brussels the unemployment rate decreases with the increase in salary and education levels.

Unlike the previous two indicators, the inactivity rate (i.e. the proportion of people neither in employment nor looking for employment within the population aged 25-64)[7] is not always the lowest for people of Belgian origin. In Charleroi, people originating from an EU member state are doing slightly better in terms of inactivity. In the municipalities of Brussels with high or very high wages, they have a slightly higher inactivity rate than

---

7   Inactive people under 25 are mostly still studying.

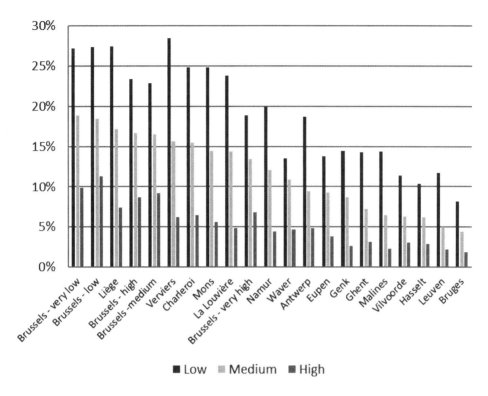

Figure 5. Unemployment rate of 18-64-year-olds by education level, per city (2016)

Source: Annexes to SPF Employment and Unia 2020. Calculations by the author.

people of non-EU origin, but this is again explained by the underestimation of the activity rate of EU members working for the international institutions (Desiere et al. 2018).

Eupen and Verviers have the highest inactivity rate among people of non-EU origin (in part due to unregistered cross-border work, but this applies to all origins); Vilvoorde, Bruges and Wavre have the lowest. The gap between people of Belgian and non-EU origin is smallest in Bruges (where all groups have a low inactivity rate) and in Charleroi (where both Belgian and non-Belgian originals have very high inactivity rates). The gap is the largest in Leuven, where some of the foreign inactives are presumably still studying or have an international employer, followed by – again – Verviers. Verviers is one of the smallest cities in the sample, yet it clearly faces a number of major labour market challenges. While the general situation can largely be explained by the specific background of old industrial cities and their path-dependent developments, aggravated by the traditionally low level of geographical mobility in Belgium (European Commission 2018), there is no obvious explanation of why inequalities are as large in Verviers. Both its residents of non-EU origin and people of Belgian origin have a rather poor educational profile. Moreover, the proportion of recent newcomers, who face additional labour market obstacles such as language and unaccredited degrees, is not particularly high.

'Inactivity' is a category that consists of a very diverse set of circumstances, some of which have much more favourable characteristics (e.g. entitlement to benefits) than others.

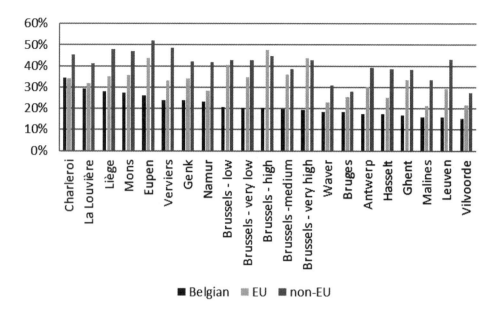

Figure 6. Inactivity rate of 25-64-year-olds by origin, per city (2016)
Source: Annexes to SPF Employment and Unia 2020. Calculations by the author.

Therefore it is interesting to take a closer look at the group of inactive people in the cities. This is possible for only a limited number of cities: i.e. Antwerp, Brussels, Charleroi, Ghent, Liège, Malines, Genk and Namur. For the others, the numbers are too limited. But even from this reduced sample it is clear that there are striking differences between cities when it comes to unequal labour market positions.

Career breaks and time credit are arguably the most favourable inactive positions. They can be used only by people who have been in employment for a sufficient amount of time, and in many cases provide access to financial benefits, for example in case of parental or carer's leave. This system is much more popular in Flemish than in Walloon cities, and is most frequently used in the municipalities of Brussels with very high wages. Everywhere, people of Belgian origin use them more often than those of foreign origin, and highly skilled more than low skilled. This is easily explained because, in order to take a career break, you must have a stable job and sufficient savings to bridge a period with a reduced income.

Among inactive people aged 55-64, Namur, Malines, Genk and Ghent have the largest proportion of retired people. While people of Belgian origin usually have the largest proportion of retired persons, in Genk the difference between natives and people of foreign descent is the smallest. The system of early retirement with company top-up (also known as 'bridging pension') is also most common among people of Belgian origin, except in Charleroi, Liège and Genk, where the over-55s of EU origin are the most frequent beneficiaries. It is no coincidence that these are three cities with a rich industrial past, but where various restructurings and collective dismissals have taken place in recent decades, involving many people of Italian and Polish descent.

Lastly, in the case of inactives receiving social welfare benefits, which function as a final safety net, the differences between the cities are again huge. The proportion of people depending on social welfare benefits is especially high in the Brussels municipalities with very low and low wage levels, and in Liège. In Genk and Malines the share is the lowest. Everywhere, people of non-EU origin have a higher proportion of social welfare beneficiaries than those of Belgian origin, and so do the low-skilled. The cities with the highest rate of social welfare dependence are precisely those where unemployment rates are highest. This is easily explained as Belgium has a relatively high proportion of (very) long-term unemployed, who after some years become completely detached from the labour market and risk becoming dependent on social welfare. For people with a migrant background, the situation is even more complex; they often enter the labour market in precarious contracts – in particular short-term or temporary agency work – that do not give access to unemployment benefits when contracts come to an end (de Wilde 2017). However, there are again some very striking differences in the size of the gaps between origin groups. In Charleroi, the proportion of social welfare beneficiaries is almost as high among people of Belgian origin as among those of non-EU origin, while in Liège that of non-EU originals is twice as high. In Ghent and Antwerp the gap is even bigger, albeit at a lower level.

By looking at Brussels at five different salary levels, it becomes clear that there are major differences even within a single urbanised area, as earlier research on disadvantaged urban areas has shown (Van Hamme et al. 2015; Dujardin et al. 2008). Strangely enough, this is hardly the case for Brussels' residents of Belgian origin. Of course, due to the construction of these five groups, their salary levels differ, but in the five groups of municipalities the employment, unemployment and inactivity rates of people of Belgian origin are virtually the same. What does differ, however, is the situation of people of foreign origin. For many, there are differences of around 20 percentage points in employment rates depending on the municipality in which they live. In the case of people of Near/Middle Eastern origin, the level of employment is twice as high in very high-wage municipalities as it is in very low-wage municipalities.

To synthesise the main gaps in the Belgian labour market that we identified above, the following figure contains – per city and for the total Belgian population aged 20-64 – the employment rate gaps (in percentage points) between higher education graduates and people with lower secondary schooling at most, and between those of Belgian and non-EU origin.

The Figure shows that, while in some cities inequalities in labour participation are indeed higher than on average in Belgium, this is certainly not always the case. Moreover, a city with, for example, a large gap between the employment rates of the highly and poorly qualified (Mons has the largest gap) does not necessarily have the largest gap between natives and migrants. One should thus be very careful when using synthetic indices: cities with a similar score on an overall inequality index are not necessarily faced with the same underlying problems. And, as Brussels shows, relatively high income levels can certainly hide the existence of groups with sizable disadvantages. Even when different dimensions (for example high unemployment and poor education) are clearly very strongly related, there is no perfect agreement. So even though cities generally have a more diverse population and a longer history of migration than rural areas, it is clear

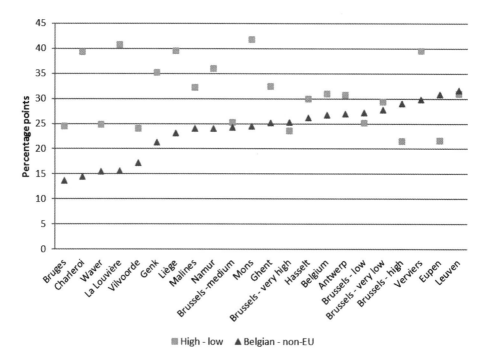

Figure 7. Employment rate gap (in percentage points) between higher education graduates and people with lower secondary schooling at most, and between those of Belgian and non-EU origin (2016)

Source: Annexes to SPF Employment and Unia 2020. Calculations by the author.

that Belgian cities are highly heterogeneous, with gaps of very different sizes for specific target groups. Economic misfortune largely explains the general welfare level, but it does not necessarily lead to growing inequality.

Conclusion

Several Belgian cities are confronted with greater diversity and larger inequalities than Belgium on average, but their inequality levels differ greatly, as this chapter has shown. Size does not necessarily matter when it comes to the level of inequality, as in the case of Verviers for example. The level of education, the proportion of newcomers, as well as economic history and the general welfare level mostly explain average labour market outcomes. However, the major differences between groups within the same city and the strongly varying sizes of those gaps are difficult to explain. Even in cities with excellent labour market performance some groups are left behind, while cities with generally poor labour market performance can have very small gaps between different groups (as in Charleroi) or – again – very large discrepancies (Verviers). In all cases, the situation has often not improved much in the last decade. The way to explain these differences will definitely include looking to history, but not just by examining economic trajectories of cities or demographic changes. A more conclusive explanation for the level of inequality lies in human and political choices. The city level provides the best perspective for including them in future research on inequality.

References

Atkinson, Anthony. 2015. *Inequality What Can Be Done?* Cambridge, MA: Harvard University Press.

Behrens, Kristian, and Frédéric Robert-Nicoud. 2014. "Survival of the Fittest in Cities: Urbanisation and Inequality." *The Economic Journal* 124, no. 581 (December 2014): 1371-1400.

Beyers, Leen. 2007. *Iedereen zwart. Het samenleven van nieuwkomers en gevestigden in de mijncité Zwartberg 1930-1990.* Amsterdam: Aksant.

Coenen, Ann. 2017. "Charting the development of wealth inequality in the Netherlands since 1950: an on-going quest." *TSEG* 14, no. 2: 11-28.

Corluy, Vincent, and Gerlinde Verbist. 2010. *Inkomen en diversiteit: onderzoek naar de inkomenspositie van migranten in België.* Antwerp: University of Antwerp.

Dedobbeleer, Koen. 2016. *Piketty for Belgium: Onderzoek naar de haalbaarheid en reconstructie van de reeksen van 1970-2013.* Ghent: University of Ghent.

De Graef, Pieter. 2016. *Urbs in rure? Urban manure and fertiliser improvement in 18th-century Flemish farming.* Doctoral dissertation: University of Antwerp.

Desiere, Sam, Ludo Struyven, Dries Cuyvers and Amynah Gangji. 2018. "De internationale tewerkstelling: eindelijk aanwezig in de arbeidsmarktstatistieken." *BISA FOCUS* no. 24 (May 2018).

De Vos, Dietert, and Hildegarde Van Hove. 2017. *De loonkloof tussen vrouwen en mannen in België. Rapport 2017.* Brussels: FPS Employment, Labour and Social Dialogue.

de Wilde, Marjolijn. 2017. "The social legitimacy of targeted welfare: attitudes to welfare deservingness." In *The Social Legitimacy of Targeted Welfare*, ed. W. van Oorschot et al. Cheltenham: Edward Elgar Publishing.

Dujardin, C., H. Selod and I. Thomas. 2008. "Residential Segregation and Unemployment: The Case of Brussels." *Urban Studies* 45, no. 1: 89-113.

European Commission. 2018. *2017 Annual report on intra-EU labour mobility.* January 2018, Brussels: European Commission.

European Commission. 2019. *Country Report Belgium 2019.* Brussels: European Commission.

Garnero, Andrea, S. Kampelmann and F. Rycx. 2015. "Minimum Wage Systems and Earnings Inequalities: Does Institutional Diversity Matter?" *European Journal of Industrial Relations* 21, no. 2: 115-130.

Gurvil, Clément. 2010. *Les Paysans de Paris Du Milieu Du XVe Au Début Du XVIIe Siècle.* Paris: Honoré Champion.

Horemans, J., O. Pintelon and P. Vandenbroucke. 2011. *Inkomens en inkomensverdeling op basis van Belgische enquêtegegevens: 1985-2007.* CSB-bericht. Antwerp: Centrum voor sociaal beleid Herman Deleeck.

Jacobs, Valentine, Benoît Mahy, François Rycx and Mélanie Volral. Forthcoming. "The Heterogeneous Effects of Workers' Countries of Birth on Over-education." *Applied Economics.*

Marx, Ive, and Gerlinde Verbist. 2018. "Belgium: A Poster Child for Inclusive Growth?" In *Inequality and Inclusive Growth in Rich Countries: Shared Challenges and Contrasting Fortunes*, ed. B. Nolan. Oxford: Oxford University Press.

OECD. 2017. *OECD Economic Surveys: Belgium 2017*. Paris: OECD Publishing.

OECD. 2017b. *How's life? 2017: Measuring Well-being*. Paris: OECD Publishing.

OECD. 2015. *The Metropolitan Century: understanding urbanization and its consequences*. Paris: OECD Publishing.

Peck, Jamie. 1989. "Labour Market Segmentation Theory." *Labour & Industry* 2, no. 1: 119-144.

Piacentini, M. 2014. "Measuring Income Inequality and Poverty at the Regional Level in OECD Countries." *OECD Statistics Working Papers* no. 2014/03. Paris: OECD Publishing.

Piketty, Thomas. 2013. *Le capital au XXIe siècle*. Paris: Seuil.

SPF Employment and Unia. 2017. *Socio-economische Monitoring: arbeidsmarkt en origine 2017*. Brussels: SPF Employment.

SPF Employment and Unia. 2020. *Socio-economische Monitoring: arbeidsmarkt en origine 2019*. Brussels: SPF Employment.

Tuccio, M. 2019. "Measuring and assessing talent attractiveness in OECD countries." *OECD Social, Employment and Migration Working Papers* no. 229. Paris: OECD Publishing.

Van de Walle, Tineke. 2019. *Van twee wallen eten? De stadsrand als overgangszone tussen stad en platteland in de late 15de en 16de eeuw : casus Oudenaarde*. Doctoral dissertation: University of Antwerp.

Van Hamme, Gilles, Taïs Grippa, Pierre Marissal, Xavier May, Isaline Wertz and Maarten Loopmans. 2015. *Dynamiek van de buurten in moeilijkheden in de Belgische stadsgewesten*. Brussels: POD Maatschappelijk Integratie.

Van Lancker, Wim. 2019. "Tewerkstelling en armoede: vier lessen om het aandeel baanloze gezinnen te verminderen." In *OVER.WERK Tijdschrift van het Steunpunt Werk* 1/2019.

Van Rie, Tim, and Ive Marx. 2013a. "Belgium: When growing background inequalities meet resilient institutions." In: *Changing inequalities and societal impacts in rich countries: thirty countries' experiences*, ed. B. Nolan et al. Oxford: Oxford University Press.

Van Rie, Tim, and Ive Marx. 2013b. *Growing inequalities and their impacts in Belgium*. GINI Country report for Belgium (March 2013).

Data series*

Eurostat and Statbel. 2019. *Labour Force Survey 2018 (LFS)*.

Eurostat and Statbel. 2019b. *European Union Statistics on Income and Living Conditions 2018 (EU-SILC)*.

Eurostat and Statbel. 2018. *Structure of earnings survey 2017 (SES)*.

Eurostat and Statbel. 2018b. *Labour Force Survey 2017 (LFS)*.

Statbel. 2018. *Population per municipality 2017*.

---

*   All indicators used are available on: https://www.employment.belgium.be/moduleDefault.aspx?id=21166

PART III

Politics of Inequality

WIM BLOCKMANS

The Impact of Urban Elites' Political Participation on Economic Policy in the Low Countries 1100-1600

Introduction

For a couple of decades, adherents of the New Institutional Economics have emphasised the impact institutional factors have on economic growth. With regard to representative institutions, empirical data about the whole of Europe during the *ancien régime* showed that the intensity of parliamentary activity was important 'for subsequent economic development' (Van Zanden et al. 2012, 837, 847, 860). It has been generally acknowledged that representative institutions came into being during the eleventh to fourteenth centuries, as a response to the specific interests of citizens, and in some regions also those of peasants. It remains less clear, however, whether the extension of political participation emanated solely from the initiative of benevolent rulers including the 'third estate' whenever they felt an urgent need for military and financial aid and political support. Recent research has demonstrated that the earliest representative meetings to include the third estate were initiated by communities of citizens and peasants seeking protection against arbitrary violence perpetrated against them by the aristocracy. In the kingdom of Aragon, the principality of Catalonia and in Languedoc these meetings were supported by the peace movement launched by the bishops, and they occasionally found royal acquiescence. In the process, citizens also made other demands, directly addressed to the king, such as that he observe customary rights or the stability of the currency, which was considered beneficial for the economy (Bisson 2009, 544-545).

This chapter aims to show that the broad variety of institutional settings on a territorial and inter-regional level, initiated by mercantile groups in the most dynamic urban centres of the Low Countries, contributed to economic development. A question to be examined further is what effects economic growth and some extension of political participation had on social inequality. Among medievalists, it has been known for generations, as a matter of course, that merchant guilds and hanses were set up by merchants in particular cities or groups of cities for the purpose of securing and even monopolising their trade on particular routes. They aimed at setting rules of conduct for their members and accommodating internal conflicts, as well as providing rules for non-members. In the twelfth century, the merchants of Ghent controlled the profitable connection between Cologne and England on the rivers Scheldt and Rhine through an association which they called *hansa*. That name referred to the fee that warranted a member's trustworthiness as a business partner. The Ghenters imported wine from the Rhine valley in exchange for English wool and Flemish cloth. From the second half of the century onwards, the shippers from Cologne took care

Wim Blockmans • Leiden University

Inequality and the City in the Low Countries (1200-2020), ed. by Bruno BLONDÉ, Sam GEENS, Hilde GREEFS, Wouter RYCKBOSCH, Tim SOENS & Peter STABEL, SEUH 50 (Turnhout, 2020), pp. 141-152.

    DOI 10.1484/M.SEUH-EB.5.120442

to stop shippers from Ghent from sailing upstream along the Rhine and themselves to connect with England directly. Probably under this pressure, the Ghent traders concentrated on the overland connection in the thirteenth century.

Similarly, the merchants of the (then) Flemish city of Saint-Omer trading with the British islands and France offered their protection to those who paid the entry fee to the merchant guild and tried to monopolise that trade. In return, merchants who were associated through paying the *hansa* were allowed the same privileges as the citizens of the leading city in the group. It must have been in reaction to such practices of dominant cities that count Philip of Alsace in 1180 and 1183 expressed his will that the burghers of the towns of Damme and Biervliet, which he had newly founded, would not be subjected to the 'customs that my merchants call *hansa*'. In 1180, he 'sharply admonished all merchants and burghers of his territories… not to require his citizens of Damme to pay the *hansa*, wherever they may meet them'. In 1183, the count sharpened his will into a prescription, but in the end it was the merchants of major cities who controlled the trade routes. Count Philip of Alsace, who visited the Holy Land several times, may have observed the utility of maritime harbours there, and in his own county he built at least five of them, and maybe even that of Calais, between 1163 and 1183. In doing so, he displayed a keen interest in economic policy, which at some points conflicted with the vested interests of the merchant elites of his established cities. The first observation to be made about the earliest merchant guilds is thus that local protectionism prevailed, and that each of them aimed at monopolising routes.

In the thirteenth century, Cologne's merchants regularly appeared in Ghent on their way to England as members of their own *hansa*. The Flemish practice of organising hanses did not disappear, and eventually it spread beyond the borders of Flanders. In the 1270s, merchant guilds were mentioned in the neighbouring cities of Middelburg and Mechelen, and in 1308 the Antwerp guild levied *hansa* fees on outsiders willing to participate in long-distance trade. The payment itself was called *hansari* and the leader of the Middelburg guild was called the *Hansegraaf*. We can thus distinguish two organisational levels, local and interregional, which were closely interconnected, local membership being a precondition for accession to the larger network. The merchant guild as a guarantee for more secure trade also proved an asset because of the risk that a merchant abroad could be held responsible for his fellow townsmen's debts. Reprisals were the most effective way to pressurise foreign partners. City aldermen frequently had to mediate in such cases in order to prevent them from escalating.

A similar loosely structured association was formed, probably between 1212 and 1241, among a number of local merchant guilds in Flanders which traded with England and Scotland. Bruges and Ypres were the leading partners, while Saint-Omer, Douai and Ghent remained outside it. Membership of the local merchant guild was a condition for inclusion in this so-called Flemish Hanse of London. Given the higher capital flows involved, the association was more socially exclusive than older merchant associations. Commercial transactions had expanded considerably, and the number of participating local guilds had increased. The Hanse of London took the inter-urban organisation of international merchants to a higher level. It functioned as a powerful instrument for defending Flemish interests and solving disputes as quickly and smoothly as possible. Membership of the Flemish Hanse of London was a requirement for being a Bruges alderman, a fact which clearly demonstrated the very close connection between merchants' interests and the city government. Within the cities, the merchant elite strengthened its supremacy thanks to their inter-urban organisation which effectively prevented striking labourers blacklisted in their own cities from seeking employment elsewhere.

Fairs, held at fixed dates for a few weeks at a time, became a major institutional framework for increasing commercial activity through Europe. Those held at Lille and Ypres, two major Flemish centres of cloth production, were first mentioned in a very precise chronicle written in 1127-1128 about the extraordinary events occurring that year. The author, Galbert of Bruges, described precisely the international character of these fairs and the special guarantee of peace provided by the count of Flanders (Galbert 2013, 32-33, 39, 48, 147).

> At that time [2 March 1127] merchants from all the realms around Flanders had poured into Ypres for the feast of Saint Peter's Chair and all the markets were being held there, and they were buying and selling in all security under the peace and protection of the most pious count. Merchants from the realm of the Lombards had come to the fair and were there then. ...
>
> Last August 13 [1127], and thus on the feast of Saint Peter in August, while the fair was being held in Lille, when the count wanted to seize one of his serfs in the marketplace there and had ordered him to be seized, the citizens of Lille rushed to arms, chased the count and his men out of the town, beating those from the court and casting the Normans [the count's troops] down into the swamp, and injured many of the ones and the others. The count immediately besieged Lille on every side and forced the citizens to hand over fourteen hundred silver marks, thinking they might be made peaceful again at least this way.

At the time of Galbert's writing, 1128, these two fairs appeared to him to be well-established institutions attracting merchants from various countries, including those from 'the realm of the Lombards'. Peace had been guaranteed by a previous count, and the citizens of Lille considered it to be inviolable even by the count and his men. In the course of that century, three more towns and the city of Bruges came to be included in a cycle of fairs covering most of the year and linking the most southern location, Lille, directly with the harbour system at the North Sea.

At the same time, or even somewhat earlier, fairs had developed around Troyes, where the counts of Brie and Champagne held their splendid court. Their location on the Seine and its tributaries, and the counts' protection made the Champagne fairs the most convenient stopping places for Italian merchants on their way to Paris and further north. Its most western town, Lagny, was located at a short distance from Saint Denis, ten kilometres north of Paris, where the famous *Foire du Lendit* was held. Conversely, as early as 1137 merchants from Arras owned a particular house in Troyes which had storage facilities for their merchandise. The counts provided a stable currency that was used massively in Italy and elsewhere, and standardised weights, internationally renowned as 'troy weights', which were used in Paris and as far north as London. They negotiated with the neighbouring dukes of Burgundy and counts of Flanders to ensure the security of the merchants and their goods on their way to the fairs and on their return. They levied a moderate toll which they used gradually to organise a system of overseers and courts to deal with the enforcement of contracts. In the course of the thirteenth century, the regularity of the fairs had evolved into a cycle of six periods of six weeks each, held in four towns in Champagne (Troyes, Provins, Bar-sur-Aube and Lagny) throughout the year. The cycle fitted seamlessly with another cycle of fairs, organised in Flanders itself. These events boosted local industries and trades as much as they facilitated the international economy. The order and regulation of the fairs created trust between partners coming from great distances. The wardens of the Champagne fairs held registers of the written agreements, while the aldermen of Ypres issued thousands of *chartes-parties,* standardised documents issued in two or three copies written on a single piece of parchment and cut up in two or three by a jagged line, to be handed out to the parties, and one to be kept in the city archive; that allowed the aldermen's court to act as an efficient last resort for trade disputes. Italian merchants, operating in companies and profiting from a favourable balance of payments, started to provide commercial credit for fixed periods ending at the next fair, a few months later, often in the other region, Champagne or Flanders. In their turn, Flemish merchants were also regular visitors to the circuit of English fairs where the wool market was concentrated. In this way, an extensive system of commercial exchanges gradually came into being. It arose in the trust networks created by local and regional associations, and by the mid-thirteenth century it had extended from Central Italy to the Rhineland, France and England. As the Flemish merchants had been closely connected with Italian partners at the fairs of Champagne, the overland route between Siena and the English wool fairs and London seemed well secured throughout the thirteenth century (Spufford 2002, 143-152).

At some time before 1230, a group of merchants from a total of 22 towns, 16 of which were in the counties of Flanders, Ponthieu and Vermandois, associated with neighbouring cities such as Tournai, Cambrai, Valenciennes and Huy to regulate their activities at the fairs of Champagne. Arras was top of the list. In 1230, their association appeared to be well established, as 'the wise men assembled in Champagne' mediated in a dispute between merchants from Cambrai and Bologna. Trying to manage commercial conflicts quickly, informally, by negotiation, mediation and expert advice was the preferred method by which all types of merchants' associations typically dealt with the interest of the continuity of the trade. This association, known as the 'Hanse of XVII cities' (the number was purely symbolic), united merchants belonging to a variable number of cities in eight principalities, facilitating trade in the Champagne fairs on the basis of economically sound principles.

All these institutional arrangements were aimed at creating a secure environment for the merchants travelling with their valuable goods over long distances and putting themselves at risk of being robbed by local armed bands in foreign lands. Merchants started to organise their solidarity groups on a local basis and gradually extended them as their business expanded and more people became involved. The initiative was theirs, and the agreements with territorial rulers gave them protection beyond the limits of their own cities. There can be no doubt that merchant guilds, hanses and fairs created systems of security and trust that fostered commercial expansion, especially during the twelfth and thirteenth centuries, when territorial pacification was all but achieved.

The great majority of the thousands of contracts issued by the Ypres aldermen during the second half of the thirteenth century were credit operations concluded by common people in the city and its environs, middle class small producers and craftsmen. Local money-lenders made three quarters of the contracts, which represented 47 per cent of their total value. Only 39 per cent of their transactions were connected with the periods of the fairs. The fairs included all kinds of people, agents from Italian companies as well as ordinary producers and consumers. Martha Howell recently studied these documents in detail and could distinguish different tiers of credit operations. In terms of the value of the loans, merchants from Lucca, Piacenza and Florence stood out as providers of English wool to local craftsmen, followed by exporters from England, La Rochelle, Lübeck and Cahors. Their deals reached average amounts equivalent to up to 36 years' worth of earnings of a semi-skilled labourer. This top tier of international merchants provided nearly 46 per cent of the total value of the credit operations enacted between 1249 and 1291 (Howell 2019, 7, 19, 23).

When it came to trade agreements with other territorial units, it was no longer the merchant guilds but the city aldermen who came to the fore, especially in politically sensitive situations. Even if aldermen and guild members certainly belonged to the same elite families and the institutions were strongly interwoven, the distinction between merchant guilds and city governments mattered. In a period of instability of the count of Flanders' position, the 'six cities of Flanders' negotiated agreements with King John of England in 1208 and 1209, the second of which concerned relations with La Rochelle. In the thirteenth century the 'aldermen of Flanders', *scabini Flandrie*, became the standard expression when referring to the association of the five major cities of the county (Dhondt 1977, 72-77). They were actively involved in monetary policy, a matter in which rulers needed the expert advice and collaboration of the merchants (Wyffels 1967, 1134-1141). The information available to us becomes more detailed from the 1280s onwards, from which time some accounts of the city of Bruges in which the purposes of aldermen's journeys to other places were mentioned have been preserved. In that period, several times per year (and probably more often, as they probably met in Bruges as well) they discussed economic matters such as trade relations with English and Spanish partners, the cloth trade, textile production and financial transactions with the count and the king of France. The exceptional role of the *scabini Flandrie* was obviously derived from the economic and demographic development of their cities, which reached its apex towards 1300. The proximity of the major cities facilitated frequent contacts, as the longest distance, that between Douai and Ghent or Bruges, was around 120 kilometres. The cities, as well as individual citizens, provided the counts with important loans, allowing them in 1281 to run up debt of up to 200 per cent of comital income. The counts' net revenues around 1300 were less than those of the cities of Ghent and Bruges put together, which explains the prince's need to collaborate with the urban patricians.

Since the early twelfth century, the Low Countries have been characterised by relatively high urbanisation. If we look more closely, however, we find that significant regional variation always existed with regard to the levels and the chronology of the development between the various principalities of the region, as it did between countries and regions in Europe in general. Major cities arose earliest in the county of Flanders, initially in its southern parts which, from 1191, became the county of Artois. Arras was clearly the core of an international network that was highly active in textile production and trade in the fairs of Champagne and also directly in northern Italy. Its population has been estimated at 35,000 (Castellani & Martin 1994). Most of these cities probably had 20,000 to 30,000 inhabitants, while the largest among them reached even much higher population levels. The estimations are based on data from the fourteenth century, when important losses happened through the great famine, revolts and warfare, and the plague. Bruges may then have had a minimum of 46,000 inhabitants, Ghent around 65,000 (Brown & Dumolyn 2018, 98).

Neighbouring Brabant, which was not directly on the sea, developed later; its urban network initially grew along the overland route from Cologne to the North Sea. The major cities of Louvain and Brussels became prominent by the end of the thirteenth century, though the rank-size hierarchy remained fairly static until Antwerp's spectacular growth took place from the 1480s onwards. Around 1560, that metropolis reached a population of more than 100,000. Its success gave an impetus to Zeeland, the out-port of which was Arnemuiden near Middelburg. Amsterdam also profited from Antwerp's rise, as its harbour was a gateway for the fast-growing grain trade from the Baltic. By 1530 it had grown to having 30,000 inhabitants, and from then onwards it became clearly predominant over all other cities in the county of Holland. In contrast, in the early fourteenth century northern Italy had, besides the metropolises, another eight cities with populations of between 40,000 and 60,000, and a dozen with more than 20,000 residents. Even on a sub-regional scale variation was noticeable, as is demonstrated by the rapid growth between 1480 and 1585 of Antwerp as a metropolis and its network of surrounding towns, while the south-eastern areas of the duchy of Brabant including Louvain lost their dynamism and probably saw many of their young inhabitants migrate towards the booming centres in the north.

The percentage of the total population living in towns is revealing, but the concept of 'urban potential' in a region, defined not by political borders but by population density, might offer a more precise indicator. Jan De Vries demonstrated that around 1500 the highest level of urban potential was attained by Venice, at that time the largest city in Europe, against which he plotted all other selected cities with at least 10,000 inhabitants. The next highest levels of urban potential were in areas of northern Italy around the Po valley, with Milan and Genoa as the outlying metropolises, the Gulf of Naples and the south-western regions of the Low Countries (De Vries 1984, 151-172).

The issue of the urbanisation level was central to the argument van Zanden and others have developed about the role parliamentary activity might have played in fostering urban development before the French Revolution. This point is exactly the one I would like to make. The authors considered it as a 'proxy for economic development' and concluded that 'parliaments by acting as "constraints on the executive" had a positive effect on urban development' (Van Zanden 2012, 860). The point is, in my view, first that the emancipation of citizens (and peasants in Catalonia, Languedoc and elsewhere) was a social movement 'from below' of 'associative power', as Thomas Bisson labelled it; and, second, that town dwellers did not always need a king or prince to 'establish' an institution apart from the prince's great council of clerics and aristocrats. Citizens and peasants themselves chose in what pragmatic way they might achieve their goals. The question is now how far the political role of urban governments continued to serve mercantile interests in the fourteenth and fifteenth centuries, when new emancipatory groupings of craftsmen arose and in some cities succeeded in getting access to the councils.

Mercantile Interests in the Political Arena

John Munro has extensively shown how frequently the concerns of the Merchants of the Staple at Calais were on the English Parliament's agenda during the last decades of the fourteenth century. Reports from the Tower Mint officials were discussed, petitions were submitted, and the Staplers also made their voice heard directly. The crown issued a ban on the export of all bullion and coins during the English war with France in 1299, a ban which needed to be repeated many times, particularly in 1335, now through Parliament, as merchants tended to circumvent such draconic measures. Under Richard II, the short-term financial interests of the crown tended to undermine the Staplers' monopoly of the export of wool to the continent, but at the same time the English merchants felt they had been harmed by the debasement of the Burgundian gold coins, which had attracted bullion to the Low Countries. The concept of the Balance of Trade was expounded as early as 1381 in a report by a Mint official to Parliament, as discussions on monetary policy had a direct impact on trade regulations and fiscal arrangements in the harbours (Munro 1973, 7-8, 23, 44-47, 54).

In Flanders and Artois, on the 'Burgundian' side of the North Sea, the tension between the citizens' commercial interests and their duke's dynastic policies was even more obvious. The Anglo-French war disrupted Flemish maritime trade and the regular provisioning of the county's important textile industry with valuable English wool. From October 1387 onwards, Bruges merchants who were closely connected with English colleagues as well as with high officials started negotiations with the Merchants of the Staple in Calais. These talks were conducted by the aldermen, especially those of Bruges, on behalf of the Four Members of Flanders. This consortium continued the tradition established in the thirteenth century by the *scabini Flandrie*, adapted to the political reality of their time. The consortium was now made up of the governments of the three major cities and the rich rural territory in coastal Flanders. The guild revolution in the early years of the century had prompted the substantial participation of craft guilds in urban administrations. However, as the trade relations between England and Flanders had a direct impact on the whole textile industry, the craftsmen understood that, under the prevailing circumstances, the best advocates of the welfare of their business were the well-connected anglophile mercantile circles in Bruges. Violent conflicts occurred repeatedly in the main cities, especially since the silver content of the Flemish currency was reduced by three quarters between 1337 and 1383. The workers in the textile industry were the most active in protesting against the loss of their purchasing power, but, in the meantime, the real reduction in the cost of wages enabled the export trade to hold on against the fierce English and other competitors (Van Werveke 1968b, 244; Van Werveke 1968c, 266; Brown & Dumolyn 2018, 283-290). The city governments' negotiations about commercial relations went on for years, and at some stages also included the duke's councillors. They reached some temporary arrangements, but the final trade agreement between England and Flanders could be concluded only in 1407. It served both sides' commercial interests, avoiding the dynastic sensitivities. The whole process, lasting 20 years, had been steered by the commercial interest groups on both sides, more effectively on the Flemish side than on the English one. It was neither the princes and Parliament (dominated by the rural interests of the aristocracy and gentry) on the English side, nor the Three Estates of Flanders on the Flemish side, that held control, but the mercantile interest groups in London, in direct contact with their counterparts in the Flemish leading cities, represented in the 'Members of Flanders' (Prevenier 1973, 482-489).

The pattern revealed under these extreme circumstances in the most populated and economically dominant county of Flanders can further be observed, albeit in more moderate forms, in the three other highly urbanised and commercialised principalities in the Low Countries, Brabant, Holland and Zeeland. Even if major cities were less dominant there they nevertheless took the lead, on their own initiative having frequent and rather informal meetings of their representatives. Their system differed fundamentally from that in the essentially rural counties of Artois and Hainaut, where the prince fixed the meetings of the assemblies of the Three Estates at his convenience and on the agenda were topics of his choice, as was the case in most such formal assemblies elsewhere in Europe. The urbanised areas, however, were far more dynamic and connected with other regions through their long-distance trade routes. They dealt with their vital interests, such as supplies of grain and of raw materials for their industry, as well as the protection of their trades. They were prepared to send deputations abroad to negotiate with the Hanse cities, to England, Scotland and even to Spain. Fundamentally, urban governments took care of typically urban interests, including those of artisans, in so far as their leaders had a voice in the urban councils. As public institutions, they represented the whole population, at least in principle, while the older merchant guilds and hanses had been concerned only with their own profit. If they managed to agree on a common policy, the capital cities' influence could be very effective, for example in banning the import of English cloth from Flanders, in forbidding grain exports in years of shortage, or negotiating the restoration of regular trade relations with external partners, of whom the English and German Hanse were the most prominent. Holland's cities successfully opposed the levy of a 10 per cent tax on trade and 1 per cent on exports in 1543-1545, arguing that 'trade had to be free' and that Hanseatic ships loaded with grain would bypass the Low Countries. As the Dutch merchant fleet was deeply involved in transit trade between the Baltic and the North Sea and Atlantic coasts, they would have been hurt more than the merchants in other provinces, which explains why the government did not impose it again in Holland after the strong resistance to it and poor revenue obtained from it in 1543 (Tracy 1985, 85-91).

Urban governments typically represented local interests, and the aldermen and councillors found it difficult to agree with policies aiming at a more general and greater interest but conflicting with the common perception of their immediate utility. In Flanders, and in some major cities of Brabant after the later fourteenth (Leuven) or early fifteenth century (Brussels), the large councils included leaders of the craft guilds. In extreme cases, the crowds bypassed their leaders and expressed their views by means of collective protests in the form of petitions or, more vehemently, in outright uprisings during which violence might occur. The major cities frequently pursued differing policies for the sake of their local affairs, which hampered or even halted their common activities. The cities of Holland agreed to wage a common war against the Hanse in 1438-1441, but Dordrecht claimed not to have to contribute to its costs, as its trade was primarily focused on the rivers.

It is possible to describe the representative activities of cities in figures. They show a world of difference between them and rural territories such as Artois and Hainaut, where the prince summoned the Three Estates once or twice a year in the fifteenth and sixteenth centuries, primarily for his fiscal or military needs. The towns which participated in these meetings were relatively small, while the landed interests of the clergy and aristocracy were huge. No mention is made of separate meetings of just cities, and the commercial city of Valenciennes managed to maintain an independent position within the county of Hainaut. Zeeland and Guelders held an intermediate position with regard to their level of

Table 1. Frequency of meetings of cities and assemblies of estates in Holland.

	Meetings	Yearly average
1400-17	179	10
1418-32	356	24
1433-76	1,540	35
1477-94	807	45
1506-15	329	34
1544-71	1,014	36
1575-88	2,942	210

commercialisation and the size of their towns; this is reflected in the number of around ten meetings per year which were registered there (Stein 2017, 54-59).

The contrast with the highly urbanised regions is striking. The frequency of meetings is the first major difference, their composition the second, the agendas of the meetings the third. The influence of the clergy and the aristocracy remained real in the duchy of Brabant, for which an earlier period has been studied. All in all, 1,610 meetings were recorded between 1355 and 1430, making an average of 22 per year. Together or separately, the clergy and aristocracy participated in 25 per cent of all the meetings from 1383 to 1430, but the number of their separate meetings remained at a modest 2 per cent. Matters of trade and currency constituted 21 per cent of all the subjects mentioned (Uyttebrouck 1975, 447-462, 465, 772-909).

Table 1 gives the numbers of meetings of the cities and States of Holland, including their deputations to the States General and foreign authorities, for the periods for which the sources have already been analysed. The frequency of meetings remained fairly constant at around 35 between their incorporation into the Burgundian composite state in 1433 and the beginning of the Revolt in 1572. There was intensified activity only in the turbulent period after the death of Duke Charles of Burgundy in 1477. Between 1477 and 1494, the six capital cities participated in more than 91 per cent of all the meetings, the smaller towns in 31 per cent and the knights in 17 per cent (Kokken 1991, 135-136). Between 1506 and 1515 seven to ten noblemen were summoned to the assembly of the estates, and most of the frequent attenders held high offices on behalf of the prince (Ward 2001, 109-113). Clergy never participated, as the few important religious houses were female.

The average number of 35 meetings per year happened to apply also to the activities of the Four Members of Flanders and other representative formations during the period from 1385 to 1506, when a total of 4,055 meetings of all types were held, ranging from small informal consultations between two or three capital cities to mass participation in the plenary sessions of the States General of the Low Countries. In the course of a few years between 1429 and 1435, Duke Philip the Good doubled his possessions in the Low Countries and changed his alliance with England to one with France. In the following years, he first subdued a revolt in Bruges, and another one in Ghent, the largest and richest cities of all his territories, giving a clear demonstration of his supremacy. The fundamental cause of the Bruges revolt in 1436-1438 was the damage inflicted on the Flemish economy by the English bullionist policy and the duke's change of dynastic alliance. The latter provoked an English trade boycott and a military invasion (Munro 1973, 93-126). The duke reacted by trying to lay siege to the English staple city of Calais, and to blockade its harbour. He called for the mobilisation of the guild militias, which complied reluctantly even though they felt damaged by the English economic policy of earlier years. Moreover, their military value had become questionable. The siege soon became a disaster as the blockade of the harbour failed. The returning Bruges militias felt betrayed by their duke as well as by their city government, which was dominated by the merchant class and some wealthier craftsmen. The militias took their frustrations out on the out-port of Sluis, from which the conflict escalated and led to Bruges' submission to the duke, after a year and a half of revolt (Dumolyn 1997, 108-115, 147-181).

The Ghent war appears to have been deliberately provoked by the duke, who intended to impose a salt tax. It lasted from 1449 to 1453 and turned into a large-scale military conflict. These two periods of revolt severely disrupted the cohesion between the Four Members, as they marked the fact that the extension and centralisation of Burgundian power steadily reduced the cities' freedom of action. The number of meetings gives a clear indication of this trend: between 1385 and 1435 the Four Members held on average 42 meetings per year, several of these overlapping in time. Missions to foreign trading partners lasted months, while normal business at home went on. Between 1386 and 1400, representatives of the Four Members went on no fewer than 37 diplomatic missions abroad, mostly with the aim of restoring or initiating commercial agreements after the revolt had disrupted relations in the preceding years. Twenty-five of them were missions to the German Hanse, others were aimed at the creation of settlements of the Genoese and Catalan nations in Bruges or the management of commercial disputes (Blockmans 1978, 176-177, 196-202, 463-522, 545, 598-601).

In the half century preceding the Anglo-Burgundian war and the consequent Bruges revolt, the Four Members' own initiatives clearly contributed to the 'golden age of Burgundy'. Forty-six per cent of the subjects mentioned in their meetings concerned economic affairs, ranging from the re-establishment of disrupted trade agreements with the Hanse and the English after 1385 to mediation of incidents between foreign merchants. Monetary policy and commercial and industrial regulation were among the matters they frequently discussed with commercial partners, foreign authorities as well as with government officials and the duke himself. Between 1436 and 1506, however, the average number of meetings fell to only 27 per year; the proportion of assemblies of estates increased, as did the agenda items put forward by the government, mainly concerning fiscal and military requests. The total number of meeting days dropped by 23 per cent, from 373 days per year until 1435, to 286 thereafter, mainly due to the smaller number of economic missions abroad.

Conclusion

It is clear that mercantile interest groups played an initiating role in creating optimal conditions for the economic expansion of the later Middle Ages in the Low Countries. During the twelfth and thirteenth centuries, private associations organised the protection of trade, seeking the support of princes to secure the overland routes. From the thirteenth century onwards, associations of urban governments took the lead in an ambitious economic policy, negotiating and facilitating regional and long-distance trading relations, controlling monetary policy, and seeking to manage international conflicts on a private as well as dynastic level. The political participation of the governments of major cities in policy making on the level of the principalities could not prevent monarchs from waging wars for purely dynastic purposes or manipulating currency for their own profit. Neither was the participation of representatives of the major guilds of Flemish cities sufficient to protect textile workers' wages from the effects of repeated monetary devaluations. Nevertheless, their political presence did contribute to the awareness of the social effects of policies. Their interventions were primarily protectionist in character, such as banning the import of English cloth into Flanders or forbidding the export of grain in years of poor harvests. As discussed in the next chapter (Lambrecht Ch. 8), urban interest groups generally upheld the repartition of tax revenue for their own benefit and they were in a position to trade their agreement with new subsidies off for substantial reductions in their own contribution (Blockmans 1978, 414-421). The interests of traders prevailed over those of workers, citizens over countrymen, landowners over farmers. It is on the experience of these representative institutions that the United Provinces developed their daring economic innovations.

References

Bisson, Thomas N. 2009. *The Crisis of the Twelfth Century. Power, Lordship, and the Origins of European Government.* Princeton, NJ: Princeton University Press.

Blockmans, Wim P. 1978. *De volksvertegenwoordiging in Vlaanderen (1384-1506).* Brussels: Kon. Vlaamse Academie.

Blockmans, Wim. 2018. "Fairs in Northern France and the Low Countries, 1200-1600." In *Europäische Messegeschichte 9.-19. Jahrhundert*, ed. Markus A. Denzel. 115-123. Cologne etc.: Böhlau Verlag.

Blockmans, Wim. 2020. *Medezeggenschap. Politieke participatie in Europa vóór 1800.* Amsterdam: Prometheus.

Blondé, Bruno, Marc Boone and Anne-Laure Van Bruaene, eds. 2018. *City and Society in the Low Countries, 1100-1600.* Cambridge: Cambridge University Press.

Brown, Andrew, and Jan Dumolyn, eds. 2018. *Medieval Bruges, c. 850-1550.* Cambridge: Cambridge University Press.

Carolus-Barré, Louis. 1965. "Les XVII villes. Une Hanse vouée au grand commerce de la draperie." *Académie des Inscriptions et Belles-lettres*,109. Paris: 20-31.

Castellani, M.-M., and J.-P. Martin, eds. 1994. *Arras au Moyen Age. Histoire et littérature.* Arras: Presses Universitaires.

Dhondt, Jan. 1977. "Les origines des États de Flandre." *Standen en Landen* I (1950): 3-52, reprinted in Jan Dhondt, *Estates or Powers. Essays in the parliamentary history of the southern Netherlands from the XIIth to the XVIIIth century*, ed. Wim Blockmans. 25-53. *Standen en Landen*, LXIX. Heule: UGA.

Galbert of Bruges. 2013. *The Murder, Betrayal, and Slaughter of the Glorious Charles, Count of Flanders,* trans. and ed. Jeff Rider. New Haven, CT, and London: Yale University Press.

Gelderblom, Oscar. 2013. *Cities of Commerce: the Institutional Foundations of International Trade in the Netherlands, 1250-1650.* Princeton, NJ: Princeton University Press.

Howell, Martha. 2019. "Credit networks in a late medieval industrial giant: the case of Ypres." *Past & Present,* 242: 3-36.

Kokken, Henk. 1991. *Steden en Staten. Dagvaarten van steden en Staten onder Maria van Bourgondië en het eerste regentschap van Maximiliaan van Oostenrijk (1477-1494).* The Hague: HHR.

Koopmans, J. W. 1990. *De Staten van Holland en de Opstand. De ontwikkeling van hun functies en organisatie in de periode 1544-1588.* The Hague: HHR.

Laurent, Henri. 1935. *La draperie des Pays-Bas en France et dans les pays méditerranéens (XIIe-XVe siècles).* Paris: Droz.

Munro, John. 1973. *Wool, Cloth and Gold. The Struggle for Bullion in Anglo-Burgundian Trade 1340-1470.* Brussels and Toronto: Editions de l'Université de Bruxelles.

Prevenier, Walter. 1973. "Les perturbations dans les relations commerciales anglo-flamandes entre 1379 et 1407." In *Economies et sociétés du Moyen Age. Mélanges Edouard Perroy.* 477-497. Paris: Publications de la Sorbonne.

Ogilvie, Sheilagh. 2011. *Institutions and European Trade. Merchant Guilds, 1000-1800.* Cambridge: Cambridge University Press.

Spufford, Peter. 2002. *Power and Profit. The Merchant in Medieval Europe.* London: Thames and Hudson.

Stabel, Peter. 2008. "Composition et recomposition des réseaux urbains des Pays-Bas au bas Moyen Âge." In *Villes de Flandre et d'Italie (XIIIe-XVIe siècle),* ed. Élisabeth Crouzet-Pavan and Élodie Lecuppre-Desjardin. 29-63. Turnhout: Brepols.

Stein, Robert. 2017. *Magnanimous Dukes and Rising States. The Unification of the Burgundian Netherlands, 1380-1480.* Oxford: Oxford University Press.

Tracy, James D. 1985. *A Financial Revolution in the Habsburg Netherlands. Renten and Renteniers in the County of Holland 1515-1565.* Berkeley, CA: California University Press.

Uyttebrouck, André. 1975. *Le gouvernement du duché de Brabant au bas moyen âge (1355-1430).* 2 vols. Brussels: Univ. Libre de Bruxelles.

Vries, Jan de. 1984. *European Urbanization 1500-1800.* London: Methuen.

Ward, James Paul. 2001. *The Cities and States of Holland (1506-1515).* Leiden: unpublished PhD thesis, Leiden University.

Werveke, Hans van. 1968a. "Das Wesen der flandrischen Hansen." In Hans van Werveke, *Miscellanea Mediaevalia.* 88-103. Ghent: Story.

Werveke, Hans van. 1968b. "De economische en sociale gevolgen van de muntpolitiek der graven van Vlaanderen (1337-1433)." In Hans van Werveke, *Miscellanea Mediaevalia.* 243-255. Ghent: Story.

Werveke, Hans van. 1968c. "Currency Manipulation in the Middle Ages: the Case of Louis de Male, Count of Flanders." In Hans van Werveke, *Miscellanea Mediaevalia.* 254-267. Ghent: Story.

Wyffels, Carlos. 1967. "Contribution à l'histoire monétaire de Flandre au XIIIe siècle." *Revue belge de philologie et d'histoire,* XLV: 1113-1141.

Wyffels, Carlos. 1991. "De Vlaamse hanzen opnieuw belicht." In *Academiae Analecta. Mededelingen van de Koninklijke Vlaamse Academie voor Wetenschappen, Letteren en Schone Kunsten van België, Klasse der Letteren,* 53. Brussels: Kon. Vlaamse Academie.

Zanden, Jan Luiten van, Eltjo Buringh and Maarten Bosker. 2012. "The rise and decline of European parliaments, 1188-1789." *Economic History Review* 65: 835-861.

THIJS LAMBRECHT

Si grant inégalité?

Town, Countryside and Taxation in Flanders, c. 1350 – c. 1500

Introduction

In 1476, Charles the Bold ordered a commission to re-evaluate the existing fiscal system to allocate taxes between settlements in the rural district of Bruges. According to the mandate the tax system was unfair, as some communities were vastly overtaxed relative to their demographic and economic situation. The *'grant inégalité'* resulting from this skewed distribution of taxes needed to be addressed swiftly (Buntinx 1965, 169). This example illustrates that, as fiscal extraction increased, specific challenges and tensions arose concerning the geographical allocation of taxes. In this particular case, the issue that needed to be addressed was their inter-settlement distribution. As meticulous research on fiscal systems in the county of Flanders during the late medieval period abundantly illustrates, this region was a hotbed of conflicts, tensions and clashes between regions concerning the division and allocation of taxes (Blockmans 1978; Zoete 1990). One of the patterns that emerged from this research was the almost endemic character of rural-urban fiscal conflicts. The three largest Flemish cities in particular – Ghent, Bruges and Ypres – pursued an aggressive and pro-active strategy to protect the fiscal interests of their citizens vis-à-vis the inhabitants of the surrounding countryside.

This chapter draws its inspiration from a thought-provoking essay by Wim Blockmans on taxation and social inequality in the Low Countries between the thirteenth and sixteenth centuries (Blockmans 1987). In a sweeping analysis Blockmans claimed that increased state taxation unequivocally contributed to the rise of social inequality. The urban tax system pressed hard on the budgets of the labouring classes in many parts of the Low Countries. As most of the urban revenue was raised through indirect taxes on popular and essential food items and beverages, taxation in urban settlements had a regressive character. As a result, urban tax systems have been identified as one of the main drivers of rising economic inequality in the Low Countries (Blondé, Hanus & Ryckbosch 2018). Additionally, Blockmans identified a second group that fell victim to the increased fiscal demands of the state. Next to the urban labourer, the peasantries were also exposed to increased state surplus extraction compared to other social and occupational groups. In contrast to the cities, this was not the result of the specific mechanics and nature of fiscal organisation, but a consequence of the skewed rural-urban distribution of state taxes. Rural communities and their representatives were no match for the dominant cities and urban elites made active use of their political weight to shift the rising costs of state formation

Thijs Lambrecht • Ghent University

Inequality and the City in the Low Countries (1200-2020), ed. by Bruno BLONDÉ, Sam GEENS, Hilde GREEFS, Wouter RYCKBOSCH, Tim SOENS & Peter STABEL, SEUH 50 (Turnhout, 2020), pp. 153-167.

   DOI 10.1484/M.SEUH-EB.5.120443

onto the countryside. The over-taxation of the countryside relative to urban settlements has been confirmed by subsequent research.

In recent years research has emerged that indicates that late medieval and sixteenth-century rural Flanders experienced a deepening of inequality. The inequality statistics for parishes around Bruges clearly illustrate a rise in wealth and income inequality (Dombrecht & Ryckbosch 2017; Lambrecht & Ryckbosch 2020). These upward trends in economic inequality are inextricably linked to access to land and property structures. Indeed, the interlinked processes of farm engrossment and proletarianisation go a long way in explaining these trends, but are far from conclusive. Although many historians agree that the rural sector was more heavily exposed to state surplus extraction compared to the urban economies in late medieval Flanders, and some have even speculated about the role and impact of increased state taxation on the dynamics of farm engrossment (Thoen & Soens 2008, 966), taxation is not included in these explanatory models of rising economic inequality in the countryside.

In this short essay I want to delve more deeply into some of the complexities of rural-urban fiscal organisation and lift the veil on the mechanisms that contributed to this skewed geographical allocation of taxes in late medieval Flanders. As I will illustrate, reviewing fiscal systems from both an urban and a rural perspective adds an additional layer of complexity to both the topics of urban and rural inequality. With particular reference to urban fiscal systems, the rural perspective makes clear which urban groups tended to benefit from spatial fiscal inequality. Also, the urban perspective allows us to gain more insight into the potential effects of urban fiscal privileges on rural settlements and the size of their tax base. In the limited scope of this article, I have restricted my analysis to the period from 1350 to 1500 in particular, and directed the geographical focus on the western part of the county of Flanders.

The Transport of Flanders

The fiscal-institutional background against which many of the tax conflicts between cities and rural districts materialised in late medieval Flanders was the so-called 'Transport of Flanders'. The Transport was originally designed as a repartition scale to allocate the fines and taxes that emanated from the Franco-Flemish peace treaty of Athis-sur-Orge in 1305. The Transport fixed the relative contribution of each urban settlement and rural district for all (external and internal) fiscal obligations resulting from the peace treaty with the French. After experimentation with different scales during the 1300s and 1310s, a more permanent solution was adopted in the 1320s (van Werveke 1950; Buntinx 1965). To date, we do not know which factors were taken into account to draft this original scale. A number of historians, from Henri Pirenne onwards, have assumed that – at least with respect to the cities – the scale largely reflects the demographic and economic strength of each settlement (Stabel 1997, 45-52). Therefore, the fiscal hierarchy emanating from this scale can probably serve as a reliable proxy for the urban economic hierarchy during the early fourteenth century. During the last quarter of the fourteenth century there was increased pressure to revise the Transport as it no longer reflected the geographical distribution of the population and economic resources. The combined effects of war, outbreaks of plague and flooding in the second half of the fourteenth century necessitated an updated repartition scale taking into account the new demographic and economic geography of the county. During the last quarter of the fourteenth century (and possibly earlier in some regions) a modified scale with adjusted quota was used, but no official revision had taken place (Prevenier 1960). Although plans were already forged in 1395 to update the Transport, the revision would not start until 1408 (Buntinx 1968). The revision of the Transport was an important political event, as it created a new fiscal hierarchy and would become the future standard for allocating taxes winthin the county.

In contrast to the first Transport, the revision of 1408 is much better documented. In particular for the rural districts and settlements, we have some indications as to how the commissioners proceeded in fixing the relative share of villages. One factor that was taken into account was population. In the report on the hearth census of 1469 in the small town of Poperinge the local bailiff added information on the number of houses and hearths at the time of the revision of the Transport.[1] This strongly indicates that a general hearth census was undertaken in 1408 in light of the revision. Population, however, was not the only factor taken into account. A hitherto unknown document sheds more light on the criteria adopted by the commissioners to determine the fiscal share of rural settlements. For the Pays of Waas, a rural district located in the north-eastern part of the county, a seventeenth-century copy survives of a census-like operation related to the revision of 1408.[2] This document lists the total surface area of the cultivated land, and the number of farmsteads and communicants for each settlement in that district. From this document we can infer that factors other than population were taken into account. Whereas the number of communicants served as a reliable proxy for population, the number of farmsteads and the land they cultivated indicates that rural economic structures also determined the share of each settlement. In addition to this this census-like information, the commissioners also requested tax lists to inform them about the number of taxpayers (Zoete 1990, 68). Finally, we have rare late fifteenth-century testimony from the aldermen of the rural district of Furnes with respect to the operations undertaken in 1408 to revise the Transport. In one of their numerous complaints and petitions about the over-taxation of their district, the aldermen declared that the share of the district in the Transport of 1408 was determined on the basis of the number of houses, the quality and quantity of the agricultural land and, finally, the income and profit (*'prouffit et gaing'*) that accrued to the rural population (Ronse 1854, 374). The combination of this fragmentary evidence suggests that the commissioners had relatively detailed information at their disposal about local and regional differences in demographic and agrarian structures from which they could proceed to draft a new repartition scale. More research is required to determine how these different variables (population, farmsteads, land) were ultimately used to fix the share of each rural settlement, but overall we can safely speculate that the fiscal share of each parish as set out in the Transport of 1408 is a reliable reflection of its relative demographic, agricultural and economic worth. With respect to the cities the situation is more complex. As has been noted by Peter Stabel, the Transport also served a political agenda, in particular for the large

---

1   Archives Départementales du Nord, *Série B*, nr. 195/39.
2   State Archives Ghent, *Hoofdcollege Land van Waas*, nr. 18.

Flemish cities like Ypres, Bruges and Ghent. The large share of each of these cities not only is indicative of their prosperity vis-à-vis smaller urban settlements and rural districts, but also served as a justification for their political power within the county (Stabel 1997, 46). The three largest Flemish cities, therefore, were probably overtaxed in relation to their economic strength in the Transport of 1408.

Although the modus operandi of the commissioners appointed to review the Transport in 1408 might seem objective and transparent, there were a number of problematic issues that the new repartition scale did not address. First, as can be inferred from the nature of the data collected for the rural settlements, the Transport made no allowance for any potential local and regional differences in the distribution of taxable rural income. Whereas the information at their disposal might have given them a reliable estimate of the relative wealth/income of each village from which they could proceed to determine the relative taxable income, they did not take into account how this income was distributed within villages and, more fundamentally, between town and countryside. The rationale of the Transport for the rural settlements was based on the implicit assumption that all rural income accrued to those living in the countryside. To the extent that rural-urban transfers were absent from the assessments of the urban tax quotas – and at present there is no evidence to the contrary – the Transport was blind to potential regional differences and temporal changes in the rural-urban transfers of rural income. Significantly, the new Transport did not take into account that part of the rural income that was diverted to cities through either direct exploitation or leasehold. This constituted a structural weakness of the repartition scale and method, in particular from the perspective of the countryside. To what extent this omission was a deliberate strategy adopted by the cities is difficult to determine at this stage. In any case, the absence of any consideration of rural-urban income transfers in assessing the share of each locality proved to be directly beneficial to cities with extensive landholdings in their hinterlands in particular. Second, the Transport also implicitly assumed that all inhabitants in the villages contributed to taxes or, at least, that there were no substantial differences between regions in the relative number of taxpayers. In contrast to other principalities of the Burgundian Low Countries, such as Hainaut and Brabant, the number of tax-exempt poor households was not taken into account. Also, the logic of the Transport assumed that all residents contributed to local taxes. Herein lies a significant structural weakness of the Transport: it was based on stability in the number of taxpayers and did not make any allowance for the possibility that some taxpayers would not contribute to the full of their fiscal potential due to their privileges or legal status. In sum, the commissioners who designed the new Transport assumed somewhat naïvely (1) that all rural income accrued to the rural population, and (2) that all residents in rural settlements would contribute to taxes. As evidenced by the large number of fiscal conflicts that emerged between towns and rural districts over these issues in the years following the revision of the Transport, this was not the case.

Although the Transport revision of 1408 got the proverbial seal of approval from the large Flemish cities, these political bodies pursued multiple and diverse strategies either to escape their fiscal obligations or to extend their tax base. This is particularly well documented for the city of Ghent. Research on the city accounts indicates that Ghent only rarely succeeded in paying its contractual share as determined by the Transport. The city of Ghent had agreed to pay some 13.775 per cent of all taxes imposed by the

Burgundian rulers on the county of Flanders, but in reality rarely paid its full share. Until the 1460s, Ghent paid only about one-third of its theoretical share. Although the situation improved during the last decades of the fifteenth century, the city of Ghent rarely met its fiscal commitments as stipulated in the Transport of Flanders. The city was able to negotiate substantial reductions throughout the fifteenth century (Boone 1990, 57-60; Ryckbosch 2007, 32-39). Ghent was not the only city that was successful in obtaining substantial reductions that were in violation of the fiscal equilibrium established by the Transport. Ypres, for example, succeeded in securing a substantial reduction of 50 per cent of its share in 1474. In this particular case, Ypres' reduced share was redistributed among the neighbouring smaller cities and rural districts. Although this was not a general rule, the urban reductions in the Transport frequently resulted in increased taxation of the countryside (Blockmans 1978, 414-421). To a certain extent these reductions compensated for the relative overtaxation of Ghent, Bruges and Ypres in the Transport. However, the magnitude of these reductions was so vast that they resulted in the relative overtaxation of the countryside. Moreover, fiscal reductions were only one of the many ways in which Flemish cities used their political power and leverage to reduce the overall tax burden for their populations. Cities such as Ghent were also successful, for example, in imposing taxes on their surrounding hinterlands (or '*kwartier*'), resulting in a direct rural-urban transfer (Boone 1990, 154-158). In addition to these official state-sanctioned reductions and deviations from the Transport, cities also pursued other strategies that served to strengthen the fiscal urban bias.

Urban landholding

As has been noted by a number of historians, late medieval Flanders was characterised by extensive landholding of urban citizens and institutions in their surrounding hinterlands. Although there were regional differences, this extension of urban capital and investment in land gained momentum during the second half of the fourteenth and fifteenth centuries (Thoen 2001; and for a recent overview see Boone 2015). One of the regions characterised by a structural and long-term penetration of urban capital in the countryside was coastal Flanders. As Tim Soens and Erik Thoen's meticulous research has shown, the rural polder settlements bordering the North Sea experienced a profound transformation of their property structures between the fourteenth and sixteenth centuries. This transformation was characterised by a growing share of urban landholding in the countryside. Peasant landowners encumbered with debts and heavy taxes to protect their land from flooding were forced to abandon and subsequently sell their holdings to urban institutional and lay landowners. The net result of this transition was a profound internal restructuring of rural communities in this region. Small peasant landownership dwindled, and land was concentrated in the hands of urban non-resident landlords who leased their newly acquired landed assets to aspiring medium and large tenant farmers. The concentration of urban landownership in this part of the county was also gradually accompanied by a restructuring of farm sizes. As evidenced by the records of large landowners in coastal Flanders, leasehold land was increasingly monopolised by yeomen farmers. This double transition of both property rights and farm engrossment resulted in a structural population decline

(Soens 2009, 73-206; Thoen & Soens 2015, 195-224). This transition was also observed by contemporaries. In the late fifteenth century a contrast was already drawn between the rural district of Kassel, where smallholdings and impoverished peasants dominated the landscape, and the coastal parishes in the vicinity of Bergues, where holdings varying between 15 and 75 hectares were frequently encountered (Diegerick 1859, 210). In 1495, a German traveller observed that the farmsteads north-east of Bruges were inhabited by rich farmers who made a good living from specialising in cattle breeding (Ciselet & Delcourt 1942, 52).

The transition to a new societal model closely resembling agrarian capitalism also had fiscal implications. The fiscal articulation of the property, farm and demographic transition of coastal Flanders has not hitherto received any systematic treatment. One of the most informative late medieval documents on this topic is the hearth census from 1469 executed in the rural district of Furnes. In that year the Duke ordered a systematic census of hearths throughout the county of Flanders in light of a revision of the Transport of Flanders (Blockmans 1978, 416-417). Although the hearth census was executed in most of the county, this administrative effort did not result in a revision of the Transport. The report on the hearth census for the district of Furnes stands out because it contains additional information on rural communities and their inhabitants. Whereas most other reports listed only the number of households paying taxes and the fiscal poor, the reports for the rural parishes in the district of Furnes also contain information on the social structure of parishes, farm size and landownership. The local communities in this region deliberately used the operation of the hearth census to voice their concerns and frustrations about the fiscal consequences of changing patterns of landownership and population decline. From some of these reports it is possible to collect more information about the nature of the property transitions that characterised coastal Flanders and their effects on rural communities during the fifteenth century (Zoete 1990, 55-133).

Although the report was published in extenso some 30 years ago, it has rarely been used by rural historians to assess the impact of the late medieval transition that characterised coastal Flanders. Table 1 summarises the information found in the reports of some 12 villages located in the polder region of Furnes (in the western part of the county). For these villages the reports contain sufficient reliable and standardised data for us to be able to infer some details about the social and economic structures of these communities. The first group identified by the bailiff in the report consists of the so-called 'hiritiers'. This category of rural dwellers can be identified as having working owner-occupied farms: households predominantly working in agriculture on land they owned. Unfortunately, more detailed information about this group is in most cases absent from the report. The only indication we have about their social and economic background comes from the report of the village of Izenberge. Here, the bailiff counted 30 'hiritiers' of whom half owned less than 2.7 hectares of land. This seems to suggest that this group of rural dwellers consisted predominantly of smallholders who probably combined small-scale agriculture with other activities (probably wage labour) to eke out a living. The second category distinguished in the census consisted of leaseholders. In contrast to the 'hiritiers' they did not own the farms they worked, but leased their land from (in many cases) multiple landlords. In some parishes, a distinction was made between tenants who leased land from ecclesiastical institutions (such as abbeys, monasteries, almshouses, churches and

Table 1. Social structures and population in the rural district of Furnes (northern part), 1469.

	Oostduinkerke	Ramskapelle	Pervijze	Eggewaartskapelle	Avekapelle	Steenkerke	Wulpen	Leisele	Wulveringem	Houtem	Izenberge	Bewesterpoort	Total
Owner-occupiers	4	2	2	2	1	4	6	60	8	38	30	4	161
Leaseholders	30	39	25	16	13	32	51	112	26	61	32	28	465
Religious landowner	7	13	5	3	1		3					3	
Lay landowner	23	26	20	13	12		48					25	
Labourers	10	22	3	11	6	11	14	32	13	18	19	10	169
Poor	4	14	12	11	5	11	8	60	20	36	9	6	196
Total	48	77	42	40	25	58	79	264	67	153	90	48	991
Empty houses	2		3				1			3			
Hearths *c.* 1400-1410	?	96	94	47	39	72	111	358	100	192	113	61 or 62	

Source: calculated from Zoete 1990, 118-133.

poor relief institutions) and those who leased their lands predominantly from laymen. As can be seen from Table 1, the tenants of religious institutions constituted a minority within the group of leaseholders. The vast majority of tenants leased their holdings and land from laymen. Again, the report does not contain much information about the social backgrounds of these tenants. In some cases they were described as poor or impoverished ('*povres censiers*'), but there are no more details. The only group for which we can obtain more information is the ecclesiastical tenants. For a number of parishes we can reconstruct the land owned by ecclesiastical institutions and the corresponding number of tenants (see Table 2). As can be seen from the table, the average surface area of the land leased by these tenants was relatively high by late medieval standards. In five parishes, tenants holding land from ecclesiastical landlords leased 53.76 hectares of land on average. In some cases, we know that farms owned by ecclesiastical landlords must have exceeded 100 hectares. In the parish of Beoosterpoort, for example, the abbey of Saint Nicolas owned 242.2 hectares of land which was farmed by only two tenants. This strongly suggests that this group of tenants held large holdings and can be identified as rural economic elites. The third group identified by the bailiff consisted of those who inhabited the parish but had almost no direct access to land. They were described as landless, and in many cases they were associated with poverty. This group probably contained not only labourers, but also craftsmen and tradesmen. Finally, the census also reports those who were deemed too poor to contribute anything to the taxes. These were surviving on a combination of charitable donations and assistance from the parish poor relief institutions.

Table 2: Ecclesiastical landownership in the rural district of Furnes, 1469.

	Tenants (n)	Total surface (ha)	Ha/tenant
Oostduinkerke	7	249.94	35.7
Pervijze	5	318.10	63.6
Wulpen	3	227.21	75.74
Stuivekenskerke	4	234.49	58.62
Oostkerke	1	45.44	45.44
Total	20	1075.18	53.76

Source: calculated from Zoete 1990, 118-133.

This four-fold social structure consisting of small owner-occupiers, tenant farmers, landless labourers and poor was probably not unique to this region. The same groups can be encountered in other regions of the Low Countries. What characterised the rural district of Furnes was the relative proportion of each of these social groups. As can be seen from Table 1, leaseholders were already by far the most dominant group in this region. In 1469, they accounted for nearly half of the households (46.92 per cent) in these villages. The number of owner-occupiers and labourers was almost identical: both these groups made up 16 to 17 per cent of the population. The poor, finally, accounted for 19.8 per cent of the number of households. Their share in the overall population was probably lower than their share of households due to the smaller size of their households. The data extracted from the hearth census of 1469 strongly indicate that this region had already experienced a profound property transition. The dominant position of tenants and the small number of owner-occupiers (for each owner-occupier there were approximately three tenants) suggests that most of the land was worked under contracts of leasehold. Many reports indicate that the land leased by tenants belonged to non-resident landowners in particular. In the absence of detailed cadastral information about ownership structures in their parishes, the villagers could offer no more than a sketchy picture of non-resident landholding in most cases. The parishes of Gijverinkhove and Vinkem claimed that one third of the land in their parishes was owned by non-residents. In the parish of Oeren, this share was estimated at two thirds. In some parishes more detailed information was provided. Reninge, for example, claimed that 2,000 gemeten or some 900 hectares was owned by non-residents. Lampernisse, finally, provided the most detailed information: only 6.25 per cent of the surface of the village (200 out of 3,200 gemeten) was still in the hand of local residents; the rest was owned by non-resident landowners. Some parishes not only reported that these non-residents owned a substantial share of land within their parish boundaries, but also added that these were generally the most productive and valuable plots. The information provided by the parishes on non-resident landownership is impossible to verify. Quite possibly, communities such as Lampernisse deliberately overestimated the level of urban and ecclesiastical landownership to add weight to their arguments.

Although expropriation at the expense of local peasantries constituted a dominant and recurrent theme in these reports, the change in the rural-urban distribution of property as such was not considered a major problem. Rather, the wider fiscal effects of these property changes was a contentious issue for these communities. According to their evidence, the effects were twofold. First, the change in ownership structures had resulted in population decline. Nearly all parishes provided data on the number of inhabited dwellings some 60 to 80 years earlier. A comparison with the hearth census data indicates that these parishes witnessed a substantial population decline between *c.* 1400-1410 and 1469. Overall, the number of hearths in this district had declined by some 25 per cent (see also Table 1). Although we must treat these estimates with some caution, they fit within the pattern of structural population decline in the coastal regions during this period (Dombrecht 2014, 60-74). In the eyes of the peasantries, this demographic trend was inextricably linked to the growth of non-resident landownership. Non-resident owners were accused of deliberately dismantling existing holdings and lack of investment in the upkeep of farmsteads. Urban landlords, it seems, were primarily interested in acquiring land, and not so much in the houses and farm buildings that required frequent and costly maintenance and repairs (Ronse 1854, 374). As the inhabitants stated, many of the existing farmsteads had been reduced to ruins or were uninhabitable. As a result of these landlords' policies, the number of habitable dwellings dropped and population declined. The net effect of this transition was a decline in the tax base of these communities. The demographic reality of 1469 no longer corresponded with that of the start of the fifteenth century. In the early fifteenth century these villages had still been more populous, which also partly justified their share in the Transport of 1408. Between 1408 and 1469 the number of taxpayers had dropped as a result of landlords' policies, but their share in the Transport remained unaltered.

In addition to a shrinking tax base, the communities also complained about the decline of taxable wealth and income in their communities. This too was directly linked to changes in the distribution of landownership. The transition from ownership by local residents to leasehold from non-residents resulted in the reduction of taxable income. The growing share of leasehold within these villages had the effect of transferring rural income beyond the borders of these communities where it could safely escape taxation. In some cases, rural communities could provide remarkably detailed information about the size of these transfers. In Reninge, for example, the villagers reported that ecclesiastical landowners enjoyed a joint annual income of 1459 pounds parisis from landownership in their parish, but that they contributed nothing to local taxes (*'qui riens n'y paient'*). However, whereas non-resident owners did not contribute directly to local taxes, their tenants certainly did. Land owned by non-residents (burghers or religious institutions) was as liable to taxation as owner-occupied land. Leaseholders were taxed on the income they earned within the community. There are, however, some indications that leaseholders were taxed at a lower rate than owner-occupiers. Because leaseholders had to share their income with a landlord, they enjoyed a smaller share of the profits compared to owner-occupiers with identical farms. Unlike owner-occupiers, they could subtract rent payments from their taxable income (Zoete 1994, 65). Leasehold land as such was not privileged and leaseholders did not enjoy fiscal immunity. However, because leasehold reduced the net taxable income of a community, the transition from ownership to leasehold had fiscal implications as it resulted in higher taxes for owner-occupiers. The decline in taxable income as a result of the extension of leasehold was represented by these communities as one of the great drawbacks of the rise of non-resident ownership.

Similar complaints were voiced in other regions of the Burgundian Low Countries. A similar tax survey undertaken in Walloon Flanders in 1449 points to the same challenges and problems. In this region too, rural communities addressed and identified the fiscal implications of increased non-resident landownership in relation to taxable income (Depauw 2000, 247-270). The reports contain dozens of examples of downward adjustment of taxes as a result of changes in ownership. The reports confirm that tax quotes of individual farms were reduced substantially when the farms were no longer owner-occupied (see the numerous examples in Derville 1983). Leaseholders enjoyed only part of the income generated by a farmstead and therefore paid a smaller contribution to local taxes compared to an owner-occupier. In Flanders, these issues would not be resolved until the start of the sixteenth century. From the 1520s onwards rural taxes were raised increasingly in direct proportion to the land that was used and irrespective of whether the land was owner-occupied or leased (Maddens 1978).

When the bailiff of Furnes finished his hearth census report, he summarised his two main findings and impressions. First, the number of households ('*feux*') and farmsteads ('*mannoirs*') had dropped significantly during the last 60 to 80 years. Second, ecclesiastical institutions and urban residents had greatly expanded ('*ont fort acquis*') their landholdings in this district (Zoete 1990, 133). In this particular context there were also marked fiscal implications. The decline in the number of taxpayers combined with the reduction of taxable income probably resulted in increased fiscal pressure compared to in other regions that did not witness such a progressive transition to leasehold. Quite possibly, this exposure to higher fiscal pressure contributed to the demise of the small owner-occupier in the region of Furnes.

Direct exploitation

As illustrated in the previous section, income from leasehold was largely shielded from taxation. In the context of coastal Flanders, where leasehold would become the dominant agrarian contract, this brought about increased fiscal pressure for the resident populations. In the specific context of declining population, expansion of leasehold and rising taxation, coastal populations were undoubtedly exposed to higher levels of state surplus extraction. Although most urban landlords and ecclesiastical institutions probably leased their land to tenants, other forms of agricultural exploitation can be encountered in this region. In contrast to other regions in Flanders, there is clear evidence that some of the urban owners did not lease their farms, but engaged in direct exploitation.

One of the characteristic features of urban-rural relations in the western part of the county is the many formal agreements on the taxability of urban residents. What such agreements address in particular is the exposure of urban dwellers to rural taxes on land they worked and cultivated themselves. These bilateral agreements stipulate the terms under which urban residents – having invested working capital in agricultural holdings in the countryside and employing agricultural labour – were expected to contribute to taxes raised in the countryside. In the western part of the county these bilateral agreements start to surface from the middle of the fourteenth century. The timing is probably not coincidental and could hint at increased emigration from countryside to city in the decades following the outbreak of plague in 1349. Recent research has suggested that cities were able to recover fast from the demographic impact of the Black Death as a result of increased rural-urban migration. One of the documents used to substantiate this claim is an agreement struck between the rural district of Furnes and the city of Nieuwpoort in April 1350 in which reference is made to migration from the villages of Leke and Klerken during and after the plague (Roosen & Curtis 2019, 51). This agreement, however, also deals with the fiscal consequences of migration between town and countryside in this part of the county. Around the same period, the rural district of Furnes also agreed terms with the city of Furnes on the issue of taxability of urban and rural residents. In this particular agreement, urban dwellers enjoyed some unusual privileges. Citizens of Furnes who resided within the walls of the town could still temporarily move to and work in the countryside without being liable for taxation in these rural communities. In other words, this category of urban citizens enjoyed fiscal immunity in the countryside. This fiscal immunity, however, was restricted to the harvest and sowing seasons. If they lived and worked in the countryside outside these seasons, they were expected to contribute to the taxes raised by the rural communities (Ronse 1854, 299-301). Another agreement, between the city and the rural district of Bergues dated 1365, contained almost identical stipulations. Here too, urban residents had the right to live outside the city walls during the harvest and sowing seasons. In this agreement, the exact duration of each season was specified for the first time: the fiscal exemptions enjoyed by urban dwellers were restricted to three periods, each consisting of 40 days. Again, any extension of this period exposed urban citizens to contributing to rural taxes (Bonenfant, Bartier & van Nieuwenhuysen 1965, 562-564). As the fourteenth century progressed, such agreements became more detailed. For example, the agreement between the city of Lo and the district of Furnes (1396/97) specified the exact dates on which each period of 40 days started. Also, this particular agreement contained a justification for these recurrent short-term urban-rural migrations. Urban dwellers did not move temporarily to the countryside to work as labourers on farmsteads or to sell their labour, but to till their own land. As the agreement between Lo and the district explicitly stated, urban dwellers moved to work on the land they owned in the countryside. During these periods they prepared the soil to sow summer and winter grains and to bring in their harvest (Ronse 1854, 322-324). These agreements, in other words, clearly indicate that permanent residence in the city was not incompatible with direct exploitation of rural land. In this part of the county, rural-urban migration did not result in abandoning rural land or agricultural activities altogether. On the contrary, it seems to indicate that urban residents still maintained strong links with the surrounding countryside. The most informative document on these practices is the agreement between the city of Ypres and the district of Furnes from 1397. From this agreement we can infer that the rural district of Furnes had tried to tax citizens of Ypres engaging in direct exploitation in rural parishes in Furnes. Ypres strongly objected to the fiscal claims of Furnes and claimed that its citizens enjoyed fiscal immunity throughout the county. As with other cities, the rural district of Furnes was forced to make some concessions. In addition to the three periods of 40 days' residence, Ypres was able to secure additional privileges. The citizens of Ypres could hire and employ servants to work on their farms in the countryside. However, as employing wage labourers entailed supervision ('*omme te zien hoe hare mesniede haer goed verwaren*'), it was necessary for these citizens to control and inspect the work of their labour force on a more frequent and regular basis. Therefore, citizens of Ypres were also entitled to stay on their farms for two to three days consecutively outside the three agricultural seasons (Ronse 1854, 325-326).

In the absence of other reliable sources and data about direct exploitation of rural land by urban citizens, it remains difficult to gauge the scale and frequency of this phenomenon. However, the fact that cities bargained for fiscal immunity for their citizens working the land themselves or making use of wage labourers suggests that this mode of agricultural exploitation was perhaps more common than historians have traditionally assumed. In this case, it raises a number of important observations. First, it would lend support to the hypothesis that rural-urban migrants consciously held on to their land or actively bought land as part of a food security strategy to counter the frequent supply disturbances and shortages encountered during the second half of the fourteenth century (Stabel 2005). Also, the existence of a group of urban dwellers moving periodically to the countryside suggests that inter-sectoral mobility was not unknown in late medieval cities. In this region, some urban dwellers were also active part-time in the agricultural sector. In any case, these agreements firmly challenge the notion of a strict occupational and economic divide between town and country in the western part of the county.

Some issues related to urban fiscal privileges and full or partial tax exemptions have remained untouched in this chapter, but are equally relevant to this discussion. The outburghers of the three largest Flemish cities, for example, also enjoyed considerable fiscal privileges and exemptions. The privileged fiscal position of outburghers of Ghent and Bruges well into the late fifteenth century also contributed significantly to the fiscal urban bias that we can observe in late medieval Flanders. Outburghers resided in the countryside on a permanent basis but were either exempt from taxes or taxed a at lower rate compared to other rural residents. Although outburghers gradually lost their privileges in the late fifteenth and early sixteenth centuries, they constitute an important element of the significant rural-urban fiscal inequality (Blockmans 1978, 425-432; Blockmans 1996).

Conclusion

This exploration of rural-urban fiscal relations between city and countryside in the western part of Flanders during the late middle ages has largely confirmed existing narratives about the Flemish urban bias in terms of state taxation. As in other Flemish regions, rural communities and their representatives were impotent vis-à-vis the political strength of the Flemish cities. The Burgundian rulers and administration were unable to shield the countryside from relative over-taxation. More research is required to measure and quantify these rural-urban fiscal transfers. Because the frequency and intensity of state taxes increased during this period – in particular during the later decades of the fifteenth century – rural communities experienced profound fiscal pressure. According to the aldermen and rural communities of Furnes these social and geographical fiscal imbalances exacerbated and fuelled the ongoing process of peasant expropriation and – as they testified in 1478 – rich burghers ('rycke lieden') from the cities of Ghent, Bruges, Ypres, Lille, St-Omars, Furnes and Diksmuide seized this opportunity to expand their landholdings in the countryside (Ronse 1854, 366). This process would continue throughout the sixteenth century and the region of Furnes would transform into one of the regions with the highest level of leasehold within the Low Countries (see van Bavel 2009 for a comparative view). This does not mean that increased state taxation would result in increased peasant expropriation elsewhere. The rise of the fiscal-military state was particularly hard to absorb in regions experiencing a more long-term transformation of land and farm structures. In coastal Flanders, increased state taxation did not lie at the origins of this process, but simply reinforced and accelerated existing dynamics. Although more detailed research is required, fifteenth-century state taxation can probably be added to the list of factors that contributed to the gradual dismantling of these peasant societies and their transformation into commercial large-scale tenant farming communities.

The focus on the western part of the county has also shown that certain groups within urban society clearly profited from this rural-urban fiscal inequality. Income accruing to urban dwellers from both leasehold and direct exploitation was not taxed. This probably acted as an important incentive for wealthy burghers to invest in land. Urban dwellers with extensive landholdings in the countryside, therefore, undoubtedly emerge as those who gained most from this geographical fiscal inequality. Landowing urban elites enjoyed low taxes within their cities and could reap the full financial benefits of their investments in the countryside. This was not a temporary or short-lived privileged fiscal position, but extended well into the early modern period. Admittedly, the revision of the Transport during the early sixteenth century would bring an end to some urban privileges. For example, outburghers lost their fiscal privileges and rural land exploited directly by urban dwellers was now liable to taxation (Maddens 1978). However, by and large urban landowners were able to prolong and even cement their late medieval fiscal privileges as rental income was not taxed. As this chapter has illustrated, late medieval urban middling groups and elites were extremely skillful in constructing a fiscal environment that was essential for their successful social reproduction, in both town and countryside.

References

Blockmans, Wim. 1978. *De volksvertegenwoordiging in Vlaanderen in de overgang van middeleeuwen naar nieuwe tijd (1384-1506)*. Brussels: Koninklijke Academie voor Wetenschappen, Letteren en Schone Kunsten van België.

Blockmans, Wim. 1987. "Finances publiques et inégalité sociale dans les Pays-Bas aux XIVe-XVIe siècles." In *Genèse l'Etat moderne. Prélevement et redistribution*, ed. J.-P. Genet and M. Le Mène, 77-90. Paris: Editions CNRS.

Blockmans, Wim. 1996. "De tweekoppige draak. Het Gentse stadsbestuur tussen vorst en onderdanen, 14de-16de eeuw." In *Qui valet ingenio. Liber amicorum aangeboden aan dr. Johan Decavele,* ed. Joris De Zutter, Leen Charles and André Capiteyn, 27-37. Ghent: Stichting Mens en Kultuur.

Blondé, Bruno, Jord Hanus and Wouter Ryckbosch. 2018. "The Predatory State? Urban Finances, Politics and Social Inequality in Sixteenth-Century 's-Hertogenbosch." In *Entrepreneurs, Institutions and Government Intervention in Europe (13th-20th Centuries). Essays in honour of Erik Aerts*, ed. Brecht Dewilde and Johan Poukens, 101-115. Brussels: Academic and Scientific Publishers.

Bonenfant, Paul, Paul Bartier and Andrée van Nieuwenhuysen. 1965. *Ordonnances de Philippe le Hardi et de Marguerite de Male du 16 octobre 1381 au 31 décembre 1393*. Brussels: SCT.

Boone, Marc. 1990. *Geld en macht. De Gentse financiën en de Bourgondische staatsvorming (1384-1453)*. Ghent: Maatschappij voor Geschiedenis en Oudheidkunde te Gent.

Boone, Marc. 2015. "Les villes de Flandre et leurs campagnes: état de la question et pistes de recherches." In *I paesaggi agrari d'Europa (secoli XIII-XV)*, 513-535. Rome: Viella.

Buntinx, Willy. 1965, *Het Transport van Vlaanderen (1305-1517): bijdrage tot de geschiedenis van de financiële instellingen van het graafschap Vlaanderen*. Ghent: Unpublished MA Dissertation.

Buntinx Willy. 1968. "De enquête van Oudenburg. Hervorming van de repartitie van de beden in het graafschap Vlaanderen (1408)." *Handelingen van de Koninklijke Commissie voor Geschiedenis* 134: 75-138.

Ciselet, Paule, and Marie Delcourt. 1942. *Monetarius. Voyage au Pays-Bas (1495)*. Brussels: Office de Publicité.

Depauw, Claude. 2000. "La fuite devant la taille ducale en Flandre Wallonne." In *Hainaut et Tournaisies; regards sur dix siècles d'histoire. Receuil d'études dédiées à la mémoire de Jacques Nazet (1944-1996)* ed. Claire Billen, Jean-Marie Duvosquel and André Vanrie, 247-270. Brussels: Archives et Bibliothèques de Belgique.

Derville, Alain. 1983. *Enquêtes fiscales de la Flandre Wallonne, 1449-1549. Tome Ier: l'enquête de 1449*. Lille: Commission Historique du Nord.

Diegerick, Isidore. 1859. *Inventaire analytique et chronologique des chartes et documents appartenant aux archives de la ville d'Ypres: tome quatrième*. Bruges: Vandecasteele-Werbrouck.

Dombrecht, Kristof. 2014. *Plattelandsgemeenschappen, lokale elites en ongelijkheid in het Vlaamse kustgebied (14de-16de eeuw). Case-study: Dudzele ambacht*. Ghent: Unpublished PhD thesis.

Dombrecht, Kristof, and Wouter Ryckbosch. 2017. "Wealth inequality in a time of transition: coastal Flanders in the sixteenth century." *Tijdschift voor Sociale en Economische Geschiedenis* 14: 63-84.

Lambrecht, Thijs, and Wouter Ryckbosch. 2020. "Economic inequality in the rural Southern Low Countries during the fifteenth century: sources, data and reflections." In *Economic inequality in pre-industrial societies: causes and effects*, in press. Florence: Firenze University Press.

Maddens, Niklaas. 1978. *De beden in het graafschap Vlaanderen tijdens de regering van keizer Karel V (1515-1550)*. Heule: Standen en Landen.

Prevenier, Walter. 1960. "De beden in het graafschap Vlaanderen onder Filips de Stoute (1384-1404)." *Belgisch Tijdschrift voor Filologie en Geschiedenis* 38: 330-365.

Ronse, Edmond. 1854. *Jaerboeken van Veurne en Veurnambacht. Tweede deel*. Furnes: Bonhomme.

Roosen, Joris, and Daniel Curtis. 2019. "The 'light touch' of the Black Death in the Southern Netherlands: an urban trick?" *Economic History Review* 72: 32-56.

Ryckbosch, Wouter. 2007. *Tussen Gavere en Cadzand. De Gentse stadsfinanciën op het einde van de middeleeuwen (1460-1495)*. Ghent: Maatschappij voor Geschiedenis en Oudheidkunde te Gent.

Soens, Tim. 2009. *De spade in de dijk? Waterbeheer en rurale samenleving in de Vlaamse kustvlakte (1280-1580)*. Ghent: Academia Press.

Stabel, Peter. 1997. *Dwarfs among giants. The Flemish urban network in the late middle ages*. Leuven-Apeldoorn: Garant.

Stabel, Peter. 2005. "Het grondbezit van stedelingen op het platteland. Enkele bedenkingen bij het onderzoek in het graafschap Vlaanderen in de late middeleeuwen." *Handelingen van de Geschied- en Oudheidkundige Kring van Oudenaarde* 42: 11-30.

Thoen, Erik. 2001. "A 'commercial survival economy' in evolution. The Flemish countryside and the transition to capitalism (middle ages-19th century)." In *Peasants into farmers. The transformation of rural economy and society in the Low Countries (middle ages – 19th century) in light of the Brenner debate*, ed. Peter Hoppenbrouwers and Jan Luiten Van Zanden, 102-157. Turnhout: Brepols.

Thoen, Erik, and Tim Soens. 2008. "The social and economic impact of central government taxation on the Flemish countryside (end 13th-18th centuries)." In *Fiscal systems in the European economy from the 13th to the 18th centuries,* ed. S. Cavaciocchi, 957-971. Florence: Firenze University Press.

Thoen, Erik, and Tim Soens. 2015. "The family of the farm: a Sophie's choice? The late medieval crisis in Flanders." In *Crisis in the later middle ages: beyond the Postan-Duby paradigm,* ed. John Drendel, 195-224. Turnhout: Brepols.

van Bavel, Bas. 2009. "The emergence and growth of short-term leasing in the Netherlands and other parts of Northwestern Europe (eleventh-seventeenth centuries). A chronology and a tentative investigation into its causes." In *The development of leasehold in northwestern Europe, c. 1200-1600*, ed. Bas van Bavel and Phillipp Schofield, 171-213. Turnhout: Brepols.

van Werveke, Hans. 1950. "Les charges financières issues du traités d'Athis (1305)." *Revue du Nord* 32: 91-93.

Zoete, Antoine. 1990. "De haardtelling van 1469 in Veurne-ambacht." *Handelingen van de Koninklijke Commissie voor Geschiedenis* 156: 55-133.

Zoete, Antoine. 1994. *De beden in het graafschap Vlaanderen onder de hertogen Jan zonder Vrees en Filips de Goede (1405-1467)*. Brussels: Koninklijke Academie voor Wetenschappen, Letteren en Schone Kunsten van België.

BRUNO BLONDÉ, JORD HANUS AND
WOUTER RYCKBOSCH

The Rise of the Fiscal State?

*Urban Finances, Politics and Social Inequality in Sixteenth-century 's-Hertogenbosch**

Introduction

Recent endeavours to map and better understand pre-industrial economic inequality through comparative studies offer a single straightforward conclusion: social inequality was on the rise between 1500 and 1800 virtually everywhere in Europe, Portugal being a notable exception (Reis 2017). Intriguingly, economic inequality grew both in countries that were marked by rapid economic growth and urbanisation, as well as in economies that faced (relative) stagnation and decline. And even though far from all mechanisms behind the growth in inequality are by now transparent, it seems safe to suppose that rather than the growth of incomes, the functional distribution of income and sectoral shifts in the economy played a significant role in the process of growing economic inequality. For the Low Countries Wouter Ryckbosch recently documented the role played by the decline in the wage rate relative to overall incomes and the concentration of capital ownership as two related key explanatory variables in the ongoing process of deepening social disparities (Ryckbosch 2016). Further, without being able conclusively to prove this claim, he mentioned the importance of the institutional context, in particular of the process of state formation.

The rise of the central state has often been credited with contributing to economic growth because of its role in protecting property rights, while it might not have contributed equally to the protection of the landless and labouring masses. On the contrary, the expanding financial needs of the fiscal state were largely met by means of regressive taxation, as is commonly recognised in literature on the rise of the fiscal state (Blockmans 1987; Yun-Casalilla & O'Brien 2012; Alfani & Ryckbosch 2016; Alfani & Di Tullio 2019). In the cities of the Southern Netherlands the lion's share of urban revenues was raised through indirect taxation (Janssens et al. 1990; Aerts 2013, 405-408). The highest revenue from these retail and consumption taxes came from taxes (excises) on foods and beverages with a high demand inelasticity, such as beer or bread-making grain (Aerts 1998). Meanwhile, on the expenditure side, the heavy debt burden contributed to the redistribution of income

---

* This article is a revised version of Blondé, Hanus and Ryckbosch 2018. The authors wish to thank Wim Blockmans, Marc Boone, Brecht Dewilde, Sam Geens, Johan Poukens and Catharina Lis and Hugo Soly for their stimulating comments and suggestions for corrections.

Bruno Blondé, Jord Hanus • University of Antwerp

Wouter Ryckbosch • Vrije Universiteit Brussel

Inequality and the City in the Low Countries (1200-2020), ed. by Bruno BLONDÉ, Sam GEENS, Hilde GREEFS, Wouter RYCKBOSCH, Tim SOENS & Peter STABEL, SEUH 50 (Turnhout, 2020), pp. 169-182.

DOI 10.1484/M.SEUH-EB.5.120444

in favour of those with the means to invest financial capital. Hence, at least within urban societies, public finances may have contributed to the production of social inequality. Since a considerable share of these urban public revenues ultimately served the needs of the central state, the rise of the fiscal-military state can probably be seen as a causal factor in the deepening of inequality during the early modern era (Tilly 1985). In more general terms, pre-modern states have recently been recast as characterised by a combination of 'high levels of elite predation with low levels of public goods provision', and it is therefore no surprise that the collapse of political states was described by Walter Scheidel as one of the four 'great levellers' of history (Scheidel 2016). Such is also the hypothesis strongly put forward by Guido Alfani and Matteo Di Tullio (Alfani 2015, 1088-1089; Alfani & Di Tullio 2019, 145-189). Based on extensive evidence from Venice and a comparative reading of the secondary literature for Europe, Alfani and Di Tullio ascribed a pivotal role to the rise of the fiscal state and its regressive taxation in the reproduction of economic inequality.

Yet, while all authors appear to be in agreement about the underlying regressive character of urban fiscalism and the rising fiscal pressure throughout the early modern period, the 'fiscal state' hypothesis seems hard to square with the particular situation of the southern Low Countries. Of the southern Low Countries the French traveller Dérival de Gomicourt observed in the eighteenth century that 'the farmer [there] neither suffers the yoke of arbitrary taxation as in France nor the burden of taxation as in England' (quoted in Janssens 2012). In fact, the tax burden in this region remained low – unlike in most other parts of Western Europe – and it continued to be low throughout the nineteenth century (Van de Perre 2003). For sixteenth-century Leuven, for instance, Raymond Van Uytven stressed the comparatively low fiscal and financial pressure (Van Uytven 1961, 486-487). In this university town the total income of the urban treasury in 1550 stood at 2.25 guilders per inhabitant, which corresponds to a fiscal pressure of 11 skilled summer wages per inhabitant (Scholliers 1975b). In eighteenth-century Lier, moreover, the fiscal pressure stemming from beer taxes equated to only three to seven daily summer wages for every household (Aerts 2014, 65-67). At first sight these and similar calculations do not suggest that regressive urban fiscality was a 'main driver of inequality growth' in the southern Low Countries (Alfani & Di Tullio 2019, 174).

Thus, the central question of this contribution is straightforward. Can we empirically assess the impact of regressive fiscalism on the reproduction of social inequality in the early modern town? And how are we to understand the political dimension involved in fiscal policy at the local level? The rise of the fiscal state is a well-documented phenomenon, but how conscious were early modern town governments of the distributional impact of their fiscal policies? Was the awareness of fiscal fairness limited to only 'fraud' and 'fiscal exemptions', which were seen to erode the ideal of the 'common good', or did it also include the structural implications of the financial policies on social stratifications (Aerts 2014, 65-67)?

In search of a case study: 's-Hertogenbosch

For several reasons, the city of 's-Hertogenbosch offers an excellent case study for tackling these complex issues. The history, historiography and sources available for this Brabantine town allow for an exploration of the problems raised above. 's-Hertogenbosch was a middle-sized urban economy in the sixteenth-century Habsburg Netherlands. With about 20,000 inhabitants by 1550 (Van de Laar 1969; Blondé 1987, 49-55) the town not only fulfilled important central-place functions, but was also firmly integrated into the growth of the Antwerp market (Van der Wee 1963). The commercial metropolis functioned as a major gateway for several export industries, among which linen production, knife-making and pin production figured prominently (Hanus 2014, 59-96). In 's-Hertogenbosch, as elsewhere, consumers bore the brunt of the urban fiscal burden, and beer drinkers mostly so (Blondé & Limberger 1998). However, in 's-Hertogenbosch the financial challenges for the town government were exceptionally high. The town was situated near the frontier of the prolonged military conflicts of the Habsburgs, which resulted in exacting pressure on the coffers of the town's mint. It is no coincidence that due to this situation the city produced a series of direct taxation lists that have already been widely used to estimate the levels and evolution of gross urban income and social inequality. Overall, income inequality in sixteenth-century 's-Hertogenbosch, as it turns out, was marked by stability, albeit at a staggeringly (yet for pre-industrial standards not exceptionally) high level (Hanus 2014, 141). Moreover, on several occasions the financial constraints of the city obliged the policy makers to make deliberate and explicit choices as to the financial and fiscal strategies that were to be pursued. The exceptional financial urgency provoked fierce debates and sometimes even popular unrest, which offer historians a unique insight into the ideology of different actors on the political scene (Blondé 1990).

Fiscal justice, tax reforms and the threat of an urban revolt

In 1547 's-Hertogenbosch faced the threat of a popular revolt against the town magistracy: in the words of the priest and chronicler Willem Molius it was a '*periculosa admodum plebis tumulteratio adversus magistratum et rectores*' (City Archives 's-Hertogenbosch/ Stadsarchief 's-Hertogenbosch (hereafter SAH), MS 8083). In the preceding years the town government had raised capital to fulfil its financial obligations to emperor Charles V by selling *renten* or public annuities. In such transactions a creditor bought an annual *rente* payment of typically one eighth to one twelfth of the purchase price. The main difference from a loan is that the principal was never repaid and the *rente* was paid for the rest of the buyer's life (hence *lijfrenten*). In the case of perpetual annuities (*erfrenten*), the buyer bought an everlasting annual allowance. Even though pre-industrial mortality rates were much higher than they are today, it is easy to see how this system could quickly spiral out of control when, especially in a time of low inflation such as the fifteenth and early sixteenth centuries, too many annuities were sold with insufficient margins for their annual costs to be covered by regular tax incomes – potentially even forcing town governments to issue new annuities to raise the funds required to fulfill the annual returns on older annuities.

This happened in 's-Hertogenbosch in the early sixteenth century, and again around the middle of the century. By 1547, the interest burden had overtaken the regular incomes of the town treasury. The financial conundrum became so great as to endanger the further payment of the *beden* to the central state. These *beden*, in particular the 'extraordinary' *beden*, were the subsidies paid by the provinces – in this case the Estates of Brabant – to the central Burgundian-Habsburg war coffers, and they had been the root cause of the town's pecuniary predicament.

The town magistracy intended to cope with this situation by raising the tariffs of the different excise duties that were collected in the town. However, the deans of the guilds that were represented as a third body in the town's government fiercely resisted this idea. Instead, they advocated the organisation of a series of direct and proportionate taxes in order to cope with the extraordinary financial needs of the time. Alarmed by the imminent danger of a revolt, Mary of Hungary, the governess of the Habsburg Netherlands, intervened in support of the magistracy's point of view. The threat of a military intervention decided the matter. The plans for proportional direct taxation, as advocated by the representatives of the guilds, were dismissed as unrealistic (*nyet practicable*) (SAH, Old Archives, Resoluties A1 (1552-56)). Thereafter, excise tariffs were raised considerably, and their collection was sublet to private entrepreneurs, rather than their being collected by state-appointed officials (Jacobs 1986, 174). Even though the available sources remain silent about the new tax tariff structures, the impact of the governess' intervention must have been considerable. While beer excise duty yielded about 16,000 guilders in the year preceding the fiscal reform, in the 1547/48 accounting year almost 25,000 guilders were raised. And while the total revenue from excise duties was less than 29,000 guilders in 1546/47, it jumped to 32,301 guilders and 41,221 guilders in 1547/48 and 1548/49 respectively. Cynically enough, the meagre 2,364 guilders that were raised via direct taxation based on the rental value of houses in 1547/48 offered only a minor consolation prize compared to the upsurge of taxes on necessities, such as beer and grain (Munro 2008). Quite strikingly, the wine tax – mostly a consumer prerogative of the richer inhabitants (Van Uytven & Blondé 1987) – was probably left untouched, since the revenue (5,439 guilders in 1547 and 5,808 guilders in 1549) did not grow substantially. As such, the urban elites did not contribute proportionately to achieving sound public finances (Hanus 2007, 128).

State formation and the debt burden

The threat of social confrontation and the efficient intervention of the governess prevented an outbreak of social revolt comparable to the one 's-Hertogenbosch had experienced more than 20 years earlier, in 1525. At that time, a *krijters* ('criers') revolt had indeed broken out in very similar circumstances (Van Uytven 1986). Charles V had required an extra *bede* which the political elite had wished to finance through raising excise duties. Not only did the rebels temporarily abolish some excise duties, they also invited representatives of religious institutions with fiscal privileges to contribute to the town's finances. The pillaging of the cellars of the Dominicans betrays an idea of 'fiscal justice' on the part of the revolting people. Much of the popular rage was directed at the clergy, which had refused to contribute to the town's finances. In that case as well, the governess, Margaret of Austria, had hastened to help the city and restore social order. On 12 August, Charles V not only fined the city an extra contribution of 12,000 guilders, but also imposed a new governmental structure that eroded the political power of the guilds and strengthened the plutocratic nature of the town government (Kuijer 2000, 299-309).

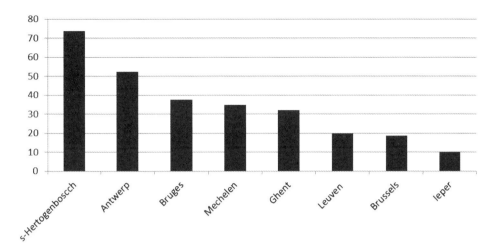

Figure 1. Public debt/value house stock (in %) for the top of the Flemish and Brabantine urban hierarchy (Mechelen included), 1569

Source: P. Stabel and F. Vermeylen, *Het fiscale vermogen in Brabant, Vlaanderen en in de heerlijkheid Mechelen: de honderste penning van de Hertog van Alva (1569-1572)* (Brussels, 1997) 25, 34, 39, 62, 88, 90, 92, 103, 218.

Why then was 's-Hertogenbosch, a seemingly healthy urban economy and society in one of the richest regions of early modern Europe, so vulnerable to fiscal revolts? Did the urban tax burden have a role to play in this? Perhaps an indication of 's-Hertogenbosch's peculiar financial situation can be found in the relative weight of debt in the urban economy. Thanks to the hundredth-penny tax levied by the Duke of Alva in 1569, we are well informed about the rental value of the immovable stock of several cities. In this levy houses were assessed at one sixteenth of their value and urban bonds at one twenty-second. In order to demonstrate the precarious position of the town government, it is sufficient to examine the ratio between the value of immovable stock and the public debt burden. While the absolute volume of *renten* sold by, for instance, the city of Antwerp was markedly bigger, the estimated value of outstanding public urban *renten* in 's-Hertogenbosch was enormous compared to the value of its immovable stock. This disproportionate debt burden dates back to the late fifteenth century, when the excessive demands of the Burgundian state began to make themselves felt, and the direct consequences of the wars with Gelderland, in which 's-Hertogenbosch functioned as a frontier town, further aggravated the situation.

As *renten* were issued on the *corpus* of the town, the private possessions of citizens served as collateral. Thus, in the event of failure to pay the annuities, merchants ran the risk of being arrested and having their merchandise confiscated. Given these serious consequences, how did the city succeed in burdening itself to such an extraordinary degree? During the first decade of the sixteenth century the town – governed by a special crisis management team of '*goede mannen*' – circumvented the need to raise money on the credit market by organising several direct taxes. Yet from 1511-12 onwards the city started selling *renten* again. It did so notwithstanding the fact that the outstanding payment arrears already exceeded the regular annual income by over 60 per cent. Population growth, economic development and inflation certainly helped to alleviate the (relative) financial pressure in the following years, but eventually the continuous sale of annuities and the war-induced claims of the central state resulted in the precarious financial situation of 1547. It is striking that the urban magistrates never encountered any difficulty in raising the considerable amounts of money needed to make ends meet. Even though getting itself into massive debt, the town succeeded in continuously selling *renten* at a very low, competitive interest rate (Hanus 2007, 35-40). Even from the 1530s onwards when the urban finances were increasingly running into problems, interest rates did not soar.

The resilience of the urban credit market can be understood only when the global affluence of the city and its inhabitants is taken into account. On the one hand, the social stratification of 's-Hertogenbosch was indeed marked by an unequal division of income and wealth. On the other hand, the city harboured a very diverse and relatively affluent middling layer of craftsmen servicing the local and export markets (Blondé 2004; Blondé & Hanus 2014). Table 1 shows the living standards of the population of 's-Hertogenbosch at various income levels in relation to the number of so-called baskets of consumer goods that a particular income could buy. The interpretation of the resulting figures is that a welfare ratio (WR) of 1 implies that the earned income sufficed 'respectably' to feed and clothe a household consisting of two adults and two children (Allen 2001). A welfare ratio of 0.6-0.7, for example, should allow for a respectable lifestyle for a smaller family of a childless couple or a single-parent household with one or two children. A one-person household could survive decently at a welfare ratio of 0.4 or even 0.3, given the diseconomies of scale for several types of expenditure this situation brings with it. On the other hand, in the early modern Low Countries the subsistence basket cost about one third of the respectable consumer bundle. In other words, a welfare ratio of 0.3 should have sufficed to offer bare bones food and shelter for a family of four. For singles in early modern Europe welfare ratios as low as 0.1 still allowed survival, albeit only barely so (Hanus 2014, 154).

As table 1 points out, the income situation in the lower income brackets of society was anything but glorious. However, while up to 40 per cent of the town's population did not earn enough to sustain a family of four respectably, numerous households in these income brackets were probably smaller, comprising a large number of single-parent households. Strikingly enough, discretionary income among the middling sort of people rose rapidly. It seems reasonable to assume that their capacity to save rose in a similar fashion. Unsurprisingly then, among the buyers of public bonds we encounter not only very rich burghers, but also a considerable number of people of more modest means, especially from the middling ranks of society (Hanus 2007, 47-116).

Moreover, the burden of the urban debt on the Gross Urban Income (GUI) was a surprisingly limited one, as can be inferred from Jord Hanus' estimations (see table 2). Not only was the relative weight of the indirect taxes limited to roughly 4 to 6 per cent of GUI. The money was also never really lost to the urban economy, since the town treasury distributed it immediately to the owners of the urban debt, who were predominantly residents of the city or of its immediate surroundings.

Table 1. Absolute income distribution in 's-Hertogenbosch expressed in Allen Welfare Ratios, 1502-1636

	1502-1503	1512-1513	1552
P10	0.0	0.1	0.1
P20	0.2	0.3	0.3
P30	0.4	0.5	0.6
P40	0.7	0.9	1.0
P50	1.4	1.5	1.4
P60	2.2	2.4	2.3
P70	3.8	3.9	4.1
P80	6.1	7.1	6.9
P90	13.5	14.7	15.3
P95	25.0	26.6	27.5

Source: Hanus, *Affluence and inequality*, 155.

Table 2. Gross Urban Income, per capita Gross Urban Income and key indicators of the urban finances of 's-Hertogenbosch, 1502-52

	1502/03	1512	1547	1552/53
Estimated Gross Urban Income (GUI) in fl.	372,000	511,000	585,000	832,000
Per Capita GUI in fl.	24.1	31.3	32.9	44.1
Total income town treasure (Idem, as % of GUI)	42,100 (11.0)	41,619 (8.1)	63,654 (10.9)	72,788 (4.9)
Total revenue from excises (Idem, as % of GUI)	23,352 (6.3)	29,180 (5.7)	32,301 (5.5)	36,012 (4.3)
Total revenue from beer excises (Idem, as % of GUI)	12,087 (3.2)	16,946 (3.3)	24,300 (4.1)	20,678 (2.5)
Payment of annuities (Idem, as % of GUI)	25,024 (6.7)	22,011 (4.3)	+/- 34,000 (5.8)	33,500 (4.0)
Cumulative amount of arrears (idem, as % of GUI)	99,350 (27.0)	54,330 (11.0)	42,533 (7.0)	65,179 (8.0)

Urban finances and social inequality: a factor endowments approach

The city of 's-Hertogenbosch was a comparatively rich city, gifted with a solid credit market in which both the elites and the middling layers of society actively took part. Admittedly, the town paid a high price for its particular role in the state-formation process, as the wars waged by the Burgundian-Habsburg state affected the town profoundly. At no point in time, however, did this directly or indirectly erode its economic resilience. In fact, our analysis shows that the 'brutal' tax reform of 1547 discussed above did little more than align the tax revenues again with the grown nominal GUI, so that the fiscal burden remained relatively constant compared to the evolution of the average income. How then can we explain the fact that the urban finances provoked such serious social unrest? The answer is at once social, political and economic. By closely looking at the functional distribution of income rather than at GUI estimates and the personal distribution of income, a much better insight into the real impact of urban finances upon urban society can be gained.

In the following estimation (table 3), the share of wage labour in the economy is deduced by starting from the theoretical premise that 'pure' household labour incomes equal at most the unskilled labourer wage rate. All (labour) earnings above that level reflect various forms of capital investments. In the absence of detailed data on the composition of household labour income in sixteenth-century Holland, Jan Luiten van Zanden assigned 150 per cent of an unskilled wage rate to every household (Van Zanden 2002). On the basis of the same presupposition a similar calculation was made for 's-Hertogenbosch in the sixteenth century, but with a downward correction for those households that – according to the tax lists – earned less than the estimated 150 per cent of unskilled labour wage in a year. This scenario applied to about half of households. In order to estimate the wealth and property incomes, we have relied on the empirical data and guesstimates produced by Hanus. The residual category is then equated to 'profits'. This includes the extra income above the unskilled labourer wage level earned by craftsmen and shopkeepers, and the skill premium for skilled wage labourers.

In order to examine the impact of the indirect tax burden not on the aggregate income, but on the estimated incomes of the lower social groups which were primarily dependent on wage labour for their incomes, the above estimations are tentative. If we compare the indirect (para)fiscal pressure not with the total GUI, but with the estimated wage labour income alone, it increases to a staggering 30 per cent. However, this figure also includes the revenue from the excise duties on wine, which was presumably consumed more by richer inhabitants than by the labouring share of the population (Van Uytven & Blondé 1987). While the beer tax in 1512-13 yielded nearly 17,000 guilders, the wine tax collection produced a considerable 4,351 guilders. Between 1500 and 1566 the wine excise duty yielded on average about 28 per cent of the beer tax. Moreover, beer excise duties also included taxes on export, and charged beers differentially on the basis of quality and strength. Moreover, consumer patterns differed greatly across social categories, hence also the impact of layered consumption taxes on urban incomes (Hanus 2013). As a result of these complicating factors it is impossible to calculate an exact social breakdown of the fiscal pressure. Nevertheless, it is clear that in 1512 approximately 45 per cent of households received an income that was less than the annual wages of a fully employed unskilled labourer. By the middle of the century 39 per cent of households were still in a similar situation. For these people, the fiscal pressure on beer consumption and production was indeed considerable: beer duties accounted for 15-18 per cent of the wage income earned in town, and this must have hit the social layers in the bottom 40 per cent of urban society particularly hard. Even with the broad margins of error that come with these kinds of speculations, it is clear that the urban financial policies must have exerted an important pressure on the ability of a large minority of the town's population to enjoy a respectable discretionary income, and to save for future setbacks or expenditure.

Table 3. Functional distribution of Gross Urban Income and key financial indicators, 1512 and 1552-53

	1512	1552-53
Gross Urban Income	511,000	832,000
Estimated Wage Income in %	18	16
Estimated Capital Income in %	35.5	41.3
Estimated Entrepreneurial Profits and Skill Premium in %	46.5	42.7
Excises as % of Estimated Wage Income	31%	27%
Beer Excises as % of Estimated Wage Income	18%	15%

Throughout the sixteenth century 's-Hertogenbosch was marked by a stable social structure. Yet behind this apparent stability dynamic forces were at play. While overall economic inequality stabilised, under the surface the fiscal policy helped to tip the balance in favour of capital, and to the detriment of both labour income and entrepreneurial profit. Clearly this policy contributed to the production of social inequality. In principle, the demand for bread and beer is highly price and income inelastic. Yet, the fiscal pressure on beer production and consumption grew so strongly that beer excise duties and consumption started to lag behind per capita GUI development. This indicates that either urban residents were increasingly reducing their calorific intake through beer or that they were beginning to rely more on smuggled beers or on consumption outside the city's liberty. Either way, it cannot be ruled out that the organisation of 's-Hertogenbosch's urban finances impeded the development of the brewing industry.

The redistributive role played by the transfer of economic surplus from consumers in general to a more socially exclusive group of rentiers thus seems clear. Nevertheless, it would be wrong to ascribe the financial strategy of urban policy makers solely to their own self-interested rent-seeking behaviour (Boone 2003, 5). In 's-Hertogenbosch a large share of the public debt was owned by the town's inhabitants. Although a few big investors proved crucial in buying annuities, the broad middling sorts of people were active on the market for annuities as well. The latter often tended to buy life annuities (that were, given the high risk for the creditor, more difficult to acquire on the private market), often sold on one or two lives. Richer burghers, on the other hand, tended to buy perpetual or hereditary annuities. While life annuities produced a higher return, perpetual annuities survived after the death of the annuity buyer, a mechanism that provided more modest inhabitants with sufficient means to survive, but that in the longer term contributed to a differential intergenerational redistribution of capital as well. Yet, the market for government bonds provided people of the middling layers in society with the means to acquire a safe (though on an individual basis often limited) source of income from capital.

Rent-seeking and coercion?

The above estimations shed a different light on the tense social relationships that marred 's-Hertogenbosch. In the middle of the *Krijtersopstand*, the urban revolt of 1525, representatives of the guilds in the urban government reproached the political elite of the town for being too eager to earn the favour of the Emperor and acquire official functions for their own offspring, rather than to serve the 'common good' of the town (Schuttelaars 1998, 98). The danger of a new revolt in 1547 was, again, averted by the threat of coercion. When Mary of Hungary considerably raised the (beer) taxes, she did little more than to bring them level again with the GUI of the town. However, discussions in the early 1550s clearly reveal how sensitive the representatives of the urban guilds in the town government were to issues of 'fiscal justice'. In 1551, for instance, Charles V sanctioned the Estates of Brabant to contribute an extraordinary 400,000 guilders. While the political elite preferred to sell annuities, which could be covered by indirect taxes, the guilds' representatives in 's-Hertogenbosch pleaded in favour of an extraordinary direct tax. They requested a *buidelgang* or direct tax, in which every inhabitant would contribute in proportion to his social and economic status. As in 1547, the political elite rejected this idea as 'impracticable' – indeed even today a long-standing and oft-repeated argument against the organisation of (unwanted) wealth taxation. However, the city would eventually give in and organise an extraordinary tax. In 1553 the town received about 36,000 guilders through indirect taxes, 13,000 guilders via the selling of annuities and about 21,500 guilders via the aforementioned proportionate income tax. In the last, the upper 10 per cent of the population contributed more than half of the total tax revenue, the poorer half of the population contributed next to nothing.

's-Hertogenbosch had quite a tradition and experience in organising similar direct taxes. Especially in the first decade of the sixteenth century, a considerable portion of the money needed to cope with the mounting financial stress was raised through the levy of a series of *gemene zettingen* or 'common taxes'. Most likely it was Duke Philip the Fair himself who had had a decisive hand in the financial strategy to clean up the urban finances and cope with urgent military needs through this special form of crisis taxation (Hanus 2014, 295).

Caution is required when interpreting the social and political fractures that ran through sixteenth-century 's-Hertogenbosch. Even though the representatives of the guilds in the middle of the sixteenth century belonged to the plutocratic town elite, this did not prevent them from pursuing a fiscal policy that was, relatively speaking, beneficial mostly to the bottom half of the urban social hierarchy (Blondé 1990, 72-73). It is unclear to what extent their position was inspired by an economic rationale, thoughts of moral economy and the pursuit of the common good, political calculation, personal interest (perhaps as drinkers of stronger beers) or fear of unrest and social instability. Yet whatever the underlying motivations, it is hard to deny that all actors were well aware of the underlying social consequences of the urban financial policy. Nor could it reasonably be believed that direct taxation was '*impracticable*'. In fact, not only did 's-Hertogenbosch organise a series of such taxes at the start of the sixteenth century, these did not impede the rapid economic growth of the town at the time.

Last but not least, the fiscal pressure on the GUI was limited. Yet, through the institutional organisation of tax collection and the relative strength of local vested interest groups, the Habsburg monarchy ultimately failed to mobilise the fiscal potential of its core economies. In effect the Southern Netherlands fell victim to a process of increasing political inequality (Van Bavel 2016, 195-200). Perhaps unwittingly, Charles V himself contributed to this process by the systematic marginalisation of the power of guilds in urban governments. In doing so, the emperor supported the political environment that allowed for a policy that fostered social inequality and obstructed the urgent need for fiscal reform and modernisation in the Low Countries, as the Duke of Alva would soon find out (Grapperhaus 1982).

Conclusion

Beer excise duties in sixteenth-century 's-Hertogenbosch weighed heavily upon the urban economic and social fabric. As argued above, the town fell victim to a very particular financial stress in the late fifteenth and sixteenth centuries. As a frontier city it paid a high price for the wars that shaped the formation process of the Habsburg state. Yet 's-Hertogenbosch was not necessarily an exception to the rule. In Antwerp during the 1530-45 period, the 'big excise duties' monopolised about 80 per cent of all urban revenue ('t Hart & Limberger 2006, 41-45). In the commercial metropolis the per capita (para)fiscal pressure reached 2.5 guilders. This equals a tax burden of, roughly speaking, 14 to 16 summer daily wages for an unskilled labourer. If only the big excise duties are included, the per capita fiscal pressure still approached 2 guilders, or about 11 to 13 summer daily wages (Scholliers, 1975, 165). In Leuven as well, as we indicated above, around 1550 the total town income equalled 2.25 guilders per inhabitant, corresponding to 11 summer wages for a skilled labourer per inhabitant, and no fewer than 20 daily summer wages for an unskilled labourer (Scholliers 1975b). For 's-Hertogenbosch the total fiscal revenue around 1552 equated to 13 daily summer wages for an unskilled labourer; the total income of the urban treasure in 'normal' years around this benchmark about 14.5 wages. Too little is, unfortunately, known about the social breakdown of the beer and wine taxes. Nor do we possess sufficiently detailed and stratified household composition and consumer expenditure data to really simulate the consequences of fiscal policies on a micro level. Yet, the available proxies indicate that at least wage labourers in the bigger Brabantine towns may have experienced fiscal pressure that was similar to that recorded in 's-Hertogenbosch (Munro 2008, 973-1026). In all likelihood, throughout the Brabantine urban network the impact on income redistribution was significant as well. In the context of prevailing wage stickiness and price inflation, Hugo Soly concluded that the proletariat paid the social costs of economic growth (Soly 1983, 118). We can now safely add that the sixteenth-century wage labourer also may have paid the costs of warfare, local politics and state formation. In short, social inequality was not just the result of changing economic structures, sectoral shifts and factor endowments. As is the case today, social inequality was also policed through the local (re)distribution of income via taxation. In the pre-industrial Low Countries beer taxes were at the very heart of that process.

At this stage it is impossible to extrapolate from the sixteenth-century experience and verify whether or not this regressive taxation helps to explain the enduring or even growing social inequality in the seventeenth and eighteenth centuries (Janssens 1990). Even though by the eighteenth century fiscal pressure in the southern Low Countries was still low in comparative terms, the way in which urban taxes were levied continued to distribute its burden unequally. Moreover, in the long run the social impact of the fiscal institutions and policies was reinforced by the growing proportion of the population that depended upon wages for its household income and that was particularly vulnerable to consumption-based excise duties. Within the city walls the rise of the fiscal state and the process of proletarisation will have reinforced one another.

Although more research is needed to unravel the impact of fiscal redistribution on social inequality and economic growth in the early modern Low Countries, in the sixteenth century, the impact of regressive taxation, hence of the rising fiscal state, on the reproduction of social inequality was probably considerable.

References

Alfani, Guido. 2015. "Economic inequality in Northwestern Italy: a long-term view (fourteenth to eighteenth centuries)." *The Journal of Economic History* 75 (2015) 1058-1096.

Alfani, Guido, and Wouter Ryckbosch. 2016. "Growing apart in early modern Europe? A comparison of inequality trends in Italy and the Low Countries, 1500-1800." *Explorations in Economic History* 62 (2016) 143-153.

Aerts, Erik. 1998. "Het hoofdelijk bierverbruik in de Zuidelijke Nederlanden (ca. 1400-1800). Enkele kanttekeningen." In *'Proeve 't al, 't is prysselyck.' Verbruik in Europese steden (13de-18de eeuw,* 43-60. Antwerp: Ufsia. Departement Geschiedenis.

Aerts, Erik. 2013. "Economische interventie van de centrale staat in de Spaanse en Oostenrijkse Nederlanden (1555-1795)." In *Gouvernance et administration dans les provinces belges (XVIe-XVIIIe siècles),* ed. Claude De Moreau de Gerbehaye, Sébastien Dubois and Jean-Marie Yante, 399-452. Brussels: Archives et Bibliothèque de Belgique.

Aerts, Erik. 2014. "Stedelijke overheidsregulering van een vitale sector. De bierfiscaliteit te Lier (1400-1800)." In *Overheid en economie. Geschiedenissen van een spanningsveld,* ed. Bruno Blondé, Henk de Smaele, Hilde Greefs, Ilja Van Damme and Maarten Vanginderachten, 55-74. Brussels: ASP.

Allen, Robert. 2001. "The great divergence in European wages and prices from the Middle Ages to the First World War." *Explorations in Economic History* 38 (2001) 411-447.

Blockmans, Wim. 1987. "Finances publiques et inégalité sociale dans les Pays-Bas aux XIVe-XVIe siècles." In *Genèse de l'état moderne prélèvement et redistribution. Actes du colloque de Fontevraud 1984,* ed. Jean-Philippe Genêt and Michel Le Mené, 77-90. Paris: Editions du CNRS.

Blondé, Bruno. 1987. *De sociale structuren en economische dynamiek van 's-Hertogenbosch, 1500-1550.* Tilburg: Stichting Zuidelijk Historisch Contact.

Blondé, Bruno. 1990. "De saneringspogingen van de Bossche stadsfinanciën in de eerste helft van de 16de eeuw: spiegel van een politieke, sociale en economische realiteit?" *Gemeentekrediet van België. Driemaandelijks tijdschrift* 44 (1990) 63-75.

Blondé, Bruno. 2004. "Bossche bouwvakkers en belastingen. Nadenken over economische groei, levensstandaard en sociale ongelijkheid in de zestiende eeuw." In *Doodgewoon. Mensen en hun dagelijks leven in de geschiedenis,* ed. Bruno Blondé, Bert De Munck and Filip Vermeylen, 45-62. Antwerp: Ufsia.

Blondé, Bruno, and Jord Hanus. 2010. "Beyond building craftsmen. Economic growth and living standards in the sixteenth-century Low Countries. The case of 's-Hertogenbosch (1500-1550)." *European Review of Economic History,* 14, 179-207.

Blondé, Bruno, Jord Hanus and Wouter Ryckbosch. 2018. "The predatory state? Urban finances, politics and social inequality in sixteenth-century 's-Hertogenbosch." In *Entrepreneurs, institutions& government intervention in Europe (13th-20th centuries). Essays in honour of Erik Aerts*, ed. Brecht Dewilde and Johan Poukens, 101-115. Brussels: Academic and Scientific Publishers.

Blondé, Bruno, and Michael Limberger. 1998. "Van Bourgondische welvaart tot Antwerpse schaduw? Het bierverbruik te 's-Hertogenbosch in de vijftiende en de zestiende eeuw." *Bijdragen tot de Geschiedenis* 81 (1998) 71-89.

Boone, Marc, Karel Davids and Paul Janssens. 2003. "Urban public debts from the 14th to the 18th century. A new approach." In *Urban public debts. Urban government and the market for annuities in Western Europe (14th-18th centuries)*, ed. Marc Boone, Karel Davids and Paul Janssens, 3-24. Turnhout: Brepols Publishers.

Coppens, Herman. 1992. *De financiën van de centrale regering van de Zuidelijke Nederlanden aan het einde van het Spaanse en onder Oostenrijks bewind (ca. 1680-1788)*. Brussels: Koninklijke Akademie voor Wetenschappen, Letteren en Schone Kunsten van België.

Grapperhaus, Ferdinaned. 1982. *Alva en de tiende penning*. Zutphen, Walburg Pers.

Hanus, Jord. 2007. *Tussen stad en eigen gewin. Stadsfinanciën, renteniers en kredietmarkten in 's-Hertogenbosch (begin zestiende eeuw)*. Amsterdam: Aksant.

Hanus, Jord. 2013. "Real inequality in the early modern Low Countries: the city of 's-Hertogenbosch, 1500-1660." *Economic History Review*, 66, 733-756.

Hanus, Jord. 2014. *Affluence and inequality in the Low Countries. The city of 's-Hertogenbosch in the long sixteenth century, 1500-1650*. Leuven: Peeters Publishers.

t Hart, Marjolein, and Michael Limberger. 2006. "Staatsmacht en stedelijke autonomie. Het geld van Antwerpen en Amsterdam (1500-1700)." *Tijdschrift voor Sociale en Economische Geschiedenis*, 3, 41-45.

Jacobs, Beatrix C. M. 1986. *Justitie en politie in 's-Hertogenbosch voor 1629. De bestuursorganisatie van een Brabantse stad*. Maastricht: Koninklijke Van Gorcum BV.

Janssens, Paul. 2012. *Taxation in the Habsburg Low Countries and in Belgium, 1579-1914*. Cambridge: Cambridge University Press.

Janssens, Paul, Hilde Verboven and Albert Tiberghien. 1990. *Drie eeuwen Belgische belastingen. Van contributies, controleurs en belastinconsulenten*. Brussels: EHSAL. Fiscale Hogeschool Brussel.

Kuijer, Pieter T. J. 2000. *'s-Hertogdom. Stad in het Hertogdom Brabant, ca. 1185-1629*. Zwolle: Waanders.

Munro, John. 2008. "The Usury Doctrine and Urban Public Finances in Late-Medieval Flanders (1220-1550): Rentes (Annuities), Excise Taxes, and Income Transfers from the Poor to the Rich." In *Fiscal Systems in the European Economy from the 13th to the 18th centuries*, ed. Simonetta Cavaciocchi. 973-1026. Florence: Fondazione Istituto Internazionale di Storia Economica "F. Datini".

Reis, Jame. 2017. "Deviant behaviour? Inequality in Portugal 1565-1770." *Cliometrica* 11, 297-318.

Ryckbosch, Wouter. 2016. "Economic inequality and growth before the industrial revolution: the case of the Low Countries (fourteenth to nineteenth centuries)." *European Review of Economic History* 20, 1-22.

Scheidel, Walter. 2016. *The Great Leveler: violence and the history of inequality from the stone age to the twenty-first century*. Princeton, NJ: Princeton University Press.

Scholliers, Etienne. 1975a. "De lagere klassen. Een kwantitatieve benadering van levensstandaard en levenswijze." In *Antwerpen in de XVIde eeuw*, 161-180. Antwerp: Genootschap voor Antwerpse Geschiedenis.

Scholliers, Etienne, 1975b. "Le pouvoir d'achat dans les Pays-Bas au XVIe siècle." In *Album aangeboden aan Charles Verlinden ter gelegenheid van zijn dertig jaar professoraat*, 305-330. Ghent: Universa.

Schuttelaars, Anton. 1998. *Heren van de raad. Bestuurlijke elite van 's-Hertogenbosch in de stedelijke samenleving, 1500-1850*. Nijmegen: Nijmegen University Press.

Tilly, Charles. 1985. "War making and state making as organized crime." In *Bringing the state back in*, ed. Pieter. B. Evans, Dieter Rueschemeyer and Thedra Skocpol, 169-186. Cambridge: Cambridge University Press.

Van Bavel, Bas. 2016. *The invisible hand? How market economies have emerged and declined since AD 500*. Oxford: Oxford University Press.

Van de Laar, A. J. M. 1969. "Schatting van het aantal inwoners van 's-Hertogenbosch in de zestiende eeuw." *Varia Historica Brabantica*, 3 (1969) 115-131.

Van De Perre, Stijn. 2003. *De Lasten van de Macht. Fiscaal Beleid in Belgi. (1830-1914)*. Brussels: KUB.

Van der Wee, Herman. 1963. *The growth of the Antwerp market and the European economy (fourteenth-sixteenth centuries)*. The Hague: Nijhoff.

Van Uytven, Raymond, 1961. *Stadsfinanciën en stadsekonomie te Leuven van de XIIe tot het einde der XVIe eeuw*. Brussels: Akademie Wetenschappen, Letteren en Schone Kunsten.

Van Uytven, Raymond. 1986. "'Altyt siet dat eynde aen!' Een gedicht over de 'Krijtersopstand' te 's-Hertogenbosch in 1525." In *Cultuurgeschiedenis in de Nederlanden van de Renaissance naar de Romantiek*, ed. Anne-Marie Van Aelst, 337-355. Leuven: Acco.

Van Uytven, Raymond, and Bruno Blondé. 1987. "Wijnverbruik te Antwerpen en 's-Hertogenbosch in de zestiende eeuw." In *Liber amicorum Dr.J¬ Scheerder. Tijdingen uit Leuven over de Spaanse Nederlanden, de Leuvense universiteit en Historiografie*, 107-126, Leuven: KUL. Vereniging Historici Lovanienses.

Van Zanden, Jan-Luiten. 2002. "Taking the measure of the early modern economy: historical national accounts for Holland in 1510/14." *European Review of Economic History* 6, 131-163.

Yun-Casalilla, B., and Patrick O'Brien, eds. 2012. *The Rise of the Fiscal States: A Global History, 1500-1914*. Cambridge: Cambridge University Press.

GUIDO MARNEF

An Experiment of Social Equality?

The Case of the Calvinist Republic in Antwerp (1577-1585)*

Introduction

On 8 November 1577, the burgomasters and aldermen – who formed the core of the Antwerp city administration – made a remarkable complaint in the Broad Council. They had heard that some people were daring more and more to discredit them among the citizenry. One of the rumours was 'that they [those of the citizenry] once had been betrayed by the lords and that they were at the point to betray them again. Furthermore, the lords oppressed the commune and they did not advocate their justices'. It was clear that the burgomasters and aldermen cast a critical glance at the deans of the craft guilds who constituted a separate unit in the Broad Council. They assured everyone present that they wanted to maintain their authority 'not to serve any particular interest but only out of love for the common welfare'.[1]

The statements just mentioned were made in a period of profound political turmoil. A few months earlier the Spanish garrison had been expelled from the Antwerp citadel and the Antwerp city fathers had joined William of Orange's rebellious movement (Marnef 1987, 2010). On 22 December 1577, a renewal of the city's magistracy was organised under the supervision of the rebellious States-General. In practice, William of Orange had a strong hand in the election process. Earlier in the year he had declared that the Netherlands needed reliable politicians 'who were good patriots, far from every form of ambition and avarice, only paying attention to the common welfare'.[2] There was, however, not only a process of political change but also a clear shift in the social policy conducted by the Antwerp city government. This social policy, I will argue in this chapter, was embedded in a specific framework of political decision making. The way in which the body politic was organised, the social recruitment of the political representatives and the political and ideological choices could influence and to a large extent steer a city's social policy and social stratification (compare Stiglitz 2013 and Blondé, Hanus and Ryckbosch 2018). In the second part I will focus on the fiscal policy of the new Calvinist regime. The domain of fiscal policy was indeed the avenue par excellence to influence the social fabric within

---

* A more fully elaborated and annotated version of this chapter will be integrated in my book on the Calvinist Republic in Antwerp.

1 City Archives Antwerp (Henceforth: SAA), *Privilegekamer*, 1658, f. 161r°-163r°.

2 William of Orange to the States-General, 1 February 1577, in: National Archives Kew, *State Papers*, 70/13: 1062.

Guido Marnef • University of Antwerp

Inequality and the City in the Low Countries (1200-2020), ed. by Bruno BLONDÉ, Sam GEENS, Hilde GREEFS, Wouter RYCKBOSCH, Tim SOENS & Peter STABEL, SEUH 50 (Turnhout, 2020), pp. 183-197.

                    DOI 10.1484/M.SEUH-EB.5.120445

urban society: it could contribute to the production of social inequality or direct urban society towards more social equality.

A new political regime

In late medieval and early modern Europe, a city's institutional framework was in most cases the result of two factors. One was the power relationship between city and overlord resulting in the granting – but also the revocation – of privileges. The other factor was social relations and tensions within the urban community. The outcome of these two elements determined to a large extent who was in power and what kind of power they could exercise. The power balance could change over time. Collective actions and other forms of urban protest could lead to a broader participation of urban society, although this could be short-lived. At the same time, a mighty overlord could curtail the power of an ambitious and autonomy-driven city council (Friedrichs 2000). Antwerp was one of the four capital cities of the duchy of Brabant – a province that had displayed a strong constitutional tradition since the fourteenth century. In the sixteenth century, Brabantine cities continued to cherish their charters and privileges when they were put under pressure by a centralising Habsburg monarchy (Marnef 2007). As a mighty commercial metropolis, Antwerp succeeded fairly well in maintaining her autonomy although there were more and more infringements during the first decade of Philip II's reign. As in most European cities, the city council – called the *magistraat* or magistracy – was the engine of the daily administration and political decision-making process. The two burgomasters and 16 or 18 aldermen serving in this body were renewed annually. The Regent and the central government in Brussels chose the aldermen from a list submitted by the city council. In practice, a small group of interconnected noble or semi-noble families played a dominant role in the city council. In particular marriage into one of these established political dynasties could open the field for representatives of new families. Merchants rarely found their way on to the city council and craftsmen, who had acquired a fixed number of seats in some neighbouring towns, were altogether absent (Marnef 1996, ch. 2; Everaert 2019).

There was, however, still room for broader political representation. In a recent book, Maarten Prak (Prak 2018, ch. 2) emphasised that forms of citizen participation in the political and administrative processes of medieval and early modern towns were much more common than is usually acknowledged. He refers to the existence of Common or Broad Councils – a kind of general assembly advising the town or city council – to the inclusion or consultation of citizen representatives – often guild deans – in core government institutions, and to direct or indirect elections for municipal office. Using two data sets covering European cities and towns in the medieval and early modern period,[3] Prak argues that guilds were represented in the city councils of nearly half of the towns with a concentration in the southern part of Germany and the southern Low Countries. Broad Councils also existed in nearly half of the towns but there was no clear geographical

---

3   Based on Wahl 2015 who included 104 towns and on Prak 2018, appendix 1 pp. 80-88, which contains data about urban representative institutions in 1500 and 1700 in the large towns and cities of seven European countries.

pattern here. At the same time, the database reveals a peak in the number of representative institutions around 1500. In the sixteenth and seventeenth centuries a process of gradual decline took place. Yet in many places informal political participation emanating from guilds, neighbourhoods and civic militias continued to play a role. The Dutch Republic offers an interesting case in point. There, the civic militias served as platforms for the articulation of political claims and as vehicles for citizen agency in general (Prak 2018, chs. 5 and 7). In the Holy Roman Empire a number of cities supporting the Protestant Reformation movements gained power at the expense of the territorial overlord, although in the long term most of them proved unable to safeguard their autonomy and independence (Schilling 1992, ch. 1).

In Antwerp, too, political and religious change went hand in hand once the city joined the Revolt in 1577. The institutional framework rapidly underwent profound changes while many more citizens were involved in the political decision-making process. To start with the city council or magistracy, the profile of the burgomasters and aldermen altered significantly. This was already clear with the first renewal of the magistracy in December 1577. Most city fathers were still Catholic but their social profile was different. Many representatives of the traditional ruling families had been removed and several newcomers or *homines novi* made their entrance on the city council. When we bring together the information about all the city fathers appointed during the Calvinist Republic, we see that all the traditional elite families except one disappeared from the city council. Henceforth, new leaders dominated the political arena. The majority of them were Calvinist and university trained while several belonged to the commercial class (Marnef 2010, 27-29).

The burgomasters and aldermen active on the city council represented broader segments of urban society than did their predecessors. Yet, a larger social representation was primarily achieved in the Broad Council. This council consisted of four branches: the magistracy as the first; the ancient or former aldermen as the second; the four headmen (*hoofdmannen*) and 26 wardmasters (*wijkmeesters*, two for each of the 13 wards) as the third; and the deans of the craft guilds as the fourth. The wardmasters – mostly rich merchants – represented the well-to-do citizenry, while the deans of the guilds gave a voice to the aspirations of the urban middle classes. The Broad Council was not a new institution. Prior to the Revolt of 1577, it had been convoked from time to time, especially when the central government was in need of extra money (Kint 1996, 314-315; Marnef 1996, 17-18; Masure 1986, esp. 59-60). During the Calvinist Republic, however, the Broad Council developed from its early beginning into a nearly permanent assembly. At the same time, the Council's jurisdiction broadened significantly. The members of the Council not only deliberated about financial and fiscal matters but dealt with a huge variety of topics, including the many political and religious issues which were at stake during the Dutch Revolt.

Another body that gave more weight to the Antwerp citizenry in the political decision-making process was the civic militia. One of the first decisions the Antwerp city fathers took after the expulsion of the Spanish garrison was to raise a permanent civic militia. A city ordinance of 12 December 1577 regulated all aspects of the civic militia's organisation and functioning (Génard 1864a, 189-211). The ordinance was issued and proclaimed by the city council but had been drafted under the supervision of William of Orange and – not unimportant – with the advice of the Broad Council. The civic militia consisted of 80 companies of 200 citizens each. In principle, all male citizens aged between 20 and 60 qualified for incorporation. An 81st company consisting of 200 young men was added as a separate unit. Each company was headed by a captain who commanded a number of minor officers. Next to the civic militia there were six shooting companies or *schuttersgilden* comprising 100 men each. In general, the shooting companies were considered a kind of civic elite troop. Members of these companies were all Antwerp citizens but free of service in the civic militia.

During the Dutch Revolt, the captains of the civic militia and the deans of the shooting companies were often consulted when the city governments had to take important decisions, and this also happened during the Antwerp Calvinist Republic. The captains and deans were not involved in the political decision-making process in an institutional or structural way. Nevertheless, the city council more than once asked their opinion when important issues were at stake. For instance, the captains and deans gave their advice about the eternal religious peace of 1579, the abolition of the public exercise of the Catholic religion in 1581 and the negotiations about the capitulation in 1585.[4] In one way the captains and deans were treated as if they too were members of the Broad Council.

It is beyond doubt that the quasi-permanent Broad Council and the mainly informal but real impact of the civic militia and the shooting companies created a broader social underpinning of the urban political fabric. There is however one element that we have to take into account: during the Calvinist Republic Antwerp became more and more a divided society. During the first years of the republic, most Catholics joined the new regime and the rebellious movement. Catholics too had indeed suffered from the Spanish policy. The terrible effects of the Spanish fury of 1576 were still in everyone's minds, Catholics and Protestants alike. Yet, soon after the early years, there was a forceful politico-religious polarisation closely connected to the course of the Dutch Revolt. Catholics increasingly alienated themselves from a revolt that threatened the chances of practising their own religion. The Calvinists, on the other hand, began to see Catholics more and more as politically unreliable. As a consequence, in the city council, the Broad Council and the companies of the civic militia Catholics and Protestants started to perceive each other as opponents. In the craft guilds, there were in 1580-81 serious discussions and even power struggles between Catholics and Protestants, especially on the occasion of the annual election of the deans (see e.g. Serrure 1859-1860). Similar struggles took place in other civic corpora. In most cases, the Protestants, and especially the Calvinists, won because they could rely on the military power in and around the city. As a consequence, we may assume that the representative bodies active during the Calvinist Republic more and more represented the Protestant part of the urban population. Yet, the gradual process of a Calvinist take-over of power does not rule out the fact that the representative administrative bodies took decisions which were favourable for both Protestants and Catholics, especially in the social domain. This brings us to the second part of this chapter.

---

4   I refer here to my forthcoming book on the Calvinist Republic in Antwerp.

Fiscal inequality in late-medieval and early modern cities

The profound changes in the institutional framework entailed that the social policy of the Antwerp city government was no longer the preserve of a small and self-interested elite. This new situation created opportunities for a shift in the fiscal policy conducted by the Calvinist regime. This fiscal policy concerned and touched all inhabitants within the city walls and may therefore serve as an indicator for the overall social policy.

We can understand the complex domain of fiscal policy and practice only if we look at the situation prevailing before the start of the new regime. An important feature of the tax system in the late medieval and early modern cities was that indirect taxes were completely dominant (see also ch. 9). These regressive taxes, commonly called *accijnzen* or excises, were retail and consumption taxes levied on foods and beverages, i.e. grain and beer. In other words they concerned essential products consumed by the rich, the middle classes and the poor people alike. Yet, the last category had to spend a much bigger part of their income on primary consumption. As a consequence, taxes on beer and grain hit the rank and file people much harder than the rich. Furthermore, some privileged categories in urban society, such as the clergy, were often exempted from these indirect taxes. In the fourteenth and fifteenth centuries indirect taxes in the towns of the southern Netherlands produced between 63 and 98 per cent of the global urban income (Blockmans 1987, 77-79, esp. table 1; also Van Uytven 1982, 242, table 6). The situation in sixteenth-century Antwerp was completely in line with these late-medieval figures. In 1531-42 the taxes on beer, wine and grain realised on average 80.6 per cent of the city's income ('t Hart and Limberger 2006, 41-43, 67-68).

The growing fiscal demands of the central state further increased the tax burden. This process started as early as in the fifteenth century under the Burgundian dukes, who put more pressure on the cities through a number of subsidies or *beden*. In the cities this caused an increase in public debt and a steady rise in the already high level of excises. It is hardly surprising that the expanding tax burden, which put constant pressure on real household income, led to several tax revolts such as those of Bruges (1436-38) and Ghent (1447-55) (Blockmans 1987, 83-90; Tracy 1994, 576-578). In the duchy of Brabant, there were tax revolts in 's-Hertogenbosch (1525) and Brussels (1528 and 1532) (Van Uytven 1986; Marnef 2001, 88-90). How sensitive the issue of the rising tax burden was became equally clear in Antwerp in 1554. When Charles V asked for new subsidies in order to finance his ongoing wars a social uprising started in the summer. People belonging to the urban middle classes and simple workers voiced grievances that were clearly connected to the economic and social malaise of the early 1550s. In particular, Gilbert van Schoonbeke's brewery monopoly and the way beer excises were collected were targeted. Some people cried that the excise collectors were 'villains and blood boozers' who stripped the skin off their bones. Hugo Soly emphasised that the representatives of the urban middle classes were the real engine behind the social protest but, at the same time, they did not want to unite with the discontented workers (Soly 1970). The social protest movement of 1554 also revealed that there were widespread rumours about the corruption of the acting ruling class, which was prepared to collude with an industrial monopolist such as Gilbert van Schoonbeke. In this regard, the rumours spread in November 1577 that the commoners 'once had been betrayed by the lords and that they were at the point to betray them again', undoubtedly referring to the social uprising of 1554.

Towards a more equal society? The fiscal policy of the Calvinist regime

The fiscal policy conducted by the Antwerp city government during the Calvinist Republic is well documented since it was the subject of many proposals and discussions in the Broad Council. Furthermore, it is possible to check whether the four members or branches of the Broad Council expressed opinions which were typical for the social layers they represented. The Broad Council had already met before the citadel was liberated from its 'Spanish' garrison at the beginning of August 1577. In July 1577, the members of the Council pleaded for the departure of the garrison and wanted to take the city's defence into their own hands.[5] This issue returned once the citadel had been liberated and the city government followed the rebellious movement of the States-General and William of Orange. Requests by the States-General to contribute to the financing of the war immediately reached the agenda of the Broad Council and they would continue to do so over the next eight years. It was certainly not by accident that from the very beginning the deans of the guilds present in the Broad Council coupled political claims with the approval of new taxes and loans.[6]

When we look at the decisions taken by the magistracy and the Broad Council we see that they indeed developed a new fiscal policy. A leading principle that often returned in the arguments underpinning the decisions was that the strongest shoulders had to carry the heaviest burden. This principle was present in a capital imposition proclaimed by the States-General at the end of 1577 in order to pay for the foreign regiments which had to leave the Low Countries. The tax rate was established not on someone's wealth but on status and social hierarchy, and included members of the clergy, the nobility and the third estate. Bishops, abbots and high-ranking noblemen were taxed by an amount ranging from £100 to £600, while artisans of modest standing paid 7 *schelling*.[7] It is not clear to what extent this capital imposition was levied, but the long list reveals how the administration of the rebellious States-General developed a strong sense for gradual hierarchy in both cities and countryside.

The idea of taxation according to status was also present in a list of *generale middelen* proposed by the States-General in order to carry the burden of war. This list was in fact a package of different taxes to be levied on a variety of products. On 15 March 1578, the magistracy introduced this tax proposal in the Broad Council and immediately started the discussions.[8] The list of *generale middelen* contained, among other things, a luxury tax on

---

5   SAA, *Privilegekamer*, 1658, f. 104v°-105v°, 106r°-107r° (19-24 July 1577).

6   Ibid., f. 123 ff. (September and October 1577).

7   The complete list is printed in *Lijst gepubliceerd in Personele ende gewillige contributie* (1577), and is also in SAA, *Privilegekamer*, 1658, f. 88r°-101r°. An analysis is in Dambruyne 2002, 349-355. The amounts are in guilders or pounds *artois* of 40 *groten* Flemish.

8   SAA, *Privilegekamer*, 1658, f. 220v°-232v°. The opinion of the deans of the guilds is in ibid., f. 233v°-236v°. See also the published list: *Listen vande generale middelen* (1578).

wearing silk clothes. The underlying idea was that while conspicuous luxuries could not be banned, they certainly deserved extra taxation. The arguments for the introduction of this new tax contained a social vision with even an anti-Spanish flavour: '[k]nowing that the pomposity planted by the Spaniards in these lands is so excessive and so rooted in the people through their abundances and costly attire of silk, so that it is nearly impossible to distinguish the mistress from the servant, the noble woman and noble man from the burgher and the tradeswoman, exceeding among them in pride and bombastic behavior'.[9] The proposed ordinance contained a long list of categories of clerical and lay people, each with the accompanying taxation payment, ranging from 100 guilders for a bishop to 3 guilders for a servant or his widow. The burgomasters and aldermen were prepared to consent to its levy for one year but suggested some modifications indicating that the imposition of a sumptuary tax was a delicate balance. For the *rentier* class, for instance, they suggested a distinction between those who were powerful and who had thus far worn silk clothes and those of little authority who had not worn silk. The deans of the guilds were thinking on the same lines although they suggested using discretion while collecting the tax. Unfortunately, the sources left do not allow us to assess how such a complex sumptuary tax was put into practice. In any case, the opinion of the deans of the guilds seems to confirm the observation that in sixteenth-century Antwerp silk was certainly not the monopoly of the elite, but was also well spread among the urban middle groups. This wider distribution undoubtedly made the tax on silk clothes attractive for the tax system of the *generale middelen*. (Blondé et al., forthcoming)

The two taxes introduced by the States-General in 1577 and 1578 show that there was a deliberate aim to limit fiscal exemptions as much as possible. It was especially the clergy – male and female – who were targeted. A similar concern comes to the fore during the deliberations in the Broad Council. On 27 January 1578, for instance, the deans of the guilds argued that no one, lay or clerical, should be exempt from taxes. On the contrary, everyone had to contribute according to his quality. Only those who lived off alms qualified for exemption.[10] The religious peace proclaimed by the Antwerp city government in June 1579 stipulated that the clergy were subject to the civil authorities and that they had to contribute to indirect taxes, direct taxes as the 10th and 100th penny taxes, and to all other duties (Prims 1954, 41). At this point, the new regime achieved a break with the past. The clergy's fiscal exemptions were however an old problem in urban society, as they conflicted with the 'moral economy' of the urban community. Already in the medieval period lay people were complaining that they had to pay taxes on the beer they consumed while the clergy, especially the better-off parish clergy and those belonging to the rich male monasteries, were not taxed on their large quantities of quality beers and wines (Van Uytven 1968, 96-98).

Another instrument used by the city government in order to call upon the wealthiest in urban society was the technique of forced loans. These forced loans were attractive when the city had to raise money in a short time span. In theory, the city fathers promised to reimburse all contributors. In practice, this promise was far from certain since the city

---

9 The quotation in SAA, *Privilegekamer*, 1658, f. 225v°-226r°.
10 Ibid., f. 203v°.

Table 1: Forced loan of 52,000 guilders consented to in October 1579

N of people	Amount paid	Total
15	1000	15,000
25	400	10,000
60	200	12,000
100	100	10,000
100	50	5000

administration constantly lacked money. Strictly speaking, forced loans were not direct taxes, but they serve as interesting indicators for the social choices made by city governments in times of financial crisis. The number of people who had to contribute and the amounts they had to pay are particularly revealing. A forced loan brought together by a small elite or one which the urban middle classes had to contribute was the result of different policies (Dambruyne 2002, 457-467).

In October 1579, the Broad Council consented to a forced loan of 52,000 guilders to be paid during three consecutive months. The extra money was necessary for the payment of regiments in the service of the States and active around Antwerp. The forced loan was divided among 300 people, 'being the most principal and the most famous citizens and merchants residing in the city'. The 300 people were divided into five wealth categories, each having to contribute a specific amount for three consecutive months.[11]

The first and richest category consisted of 15 people paying in all 15,000 guilders. In other words, the top 5 per cent of contributors paid 29 per cent of the entire loan. In category five, we see the opposite: 100 people or just one third of the total had to pay 5,000 guilders or 9.6 per cent of the total. Though we cannot compare the tax burden with the actual wealth of the people contributing, the fiscal principle nevertheless seems clear: the strongest shoulders had to carry the heaviest burden. The 15 richest contributors were all merchants or merchant companies. In the other four categories the merchant class was still completely dominant. With a total of 300 contributors, the forced loan of 1579 was aimed at a small financial elite, especially when we compare it with the forced loan of 1574. In 1574, the Antwerp city fathers levied a 400,000 guilder loan to which 2,036 people contributed. The amounts collected varied from 2 to 8,000 guilders (Marnef 1996, 9-10). In Ghent, two forced loans levied by the Calvinist regime in 1578 had 1,558 and 561 contributors (Dambruyne 2000, 462). To put the figures for Antwerp and Ghent in perspective we must of course take the overall population figure into account. Antwerp may have had between 80,000 and 90,000 inhabitants in 1574-79 and Ghent a good 40,000 in 1578 (Van Roey 1795, 96, 99, 101; Dambruyne 2001, 54-55).

It is interesting to see that the forced loan met fierce resistance and led to animated discussions in the Broad Council.[12] It was especially the deans of the craft guilds who

11   The list of the payments of the 300 is in SAA, *Rekenkamer*, 1823, f. 2 ff., SAA, *Privilegekamer*, 1656, f. 160v°-168v°, and State Archives Antwerp, *Fonds stad Antwerpen*, 3, f. 216-227. The list is partly published in Prims 1942-43, I, 188-191.
12   SAA, *Privilegekamer*, 1656, f. 145v°-157v°.

pleaded for the continuation of the forced loan. They argued that the merchants involved were wealthy enough to pay their share of the loan. In February 1580, the collection was resumed. If necessary, the captains and their civic militia were mobilised to force unwilling contributors to pay. The operation was successful. With an amount of 149,000 guilders collected the financial goal of the forced loan was almost completely achieved. 149,000 guilders was a substantial amount of money if we realise that in 1580 indirect taxes on beer totalled 282,000 guilders and those on wine 82,000 guilders (Van Aelst 2000, appendixes). Upon payment individual contributors received a written statement promising reimbursement, but it is unclear to what extent this was actually done.

The new city regime also tried to follow the principle of contributing according to wealth with a series of direct taxes levied from late 1577. To meet the financial demands of the States-General, eager to find 600,000 guilders in 1578, the magistracy proposed to organise a direct tax that would be collected on a weekly basis. While the poorest 3,000 households would be exempted, the remaining 10,000 households were supposed to pay, but in accordance with their social standing. On 25 January the magistracy, the old *schepenen* or aldermen and the wardmasters reached an agreement on a new proposal that was approved two days later by the representatives of the guilds.[13] The results of the initial proposal and the final agreement are captured in table 2. Strikingly enough, the negotiations with the guild representatives did not result in a lowering of the tax rates for the lower social groups and the middling layers of society. Nor did the Broad Council wish to enlarge the group of poor households that were exempt from taxation. Indeed, even though, judging from the nominal and real house rent evolution, the Antwerp economy was already shrinking slightly, by no means were the relatively affluent and numerous middle classes of Antwerp society fundamentally affected in 1578. Conversely, however, in the final resolution the richest households carried significantly higher weight in the final tax burden, shifting the overall Gini-coefficient from 0.48 to 0,61 (figure 1).

These direct taxes of different types and techniques were mainly based on the value of immovable property. Owners of the property had to pay half of the tax and the tenants the other half. In the last years of the Calvinist Republic there was a social correction with two thirds to be paid by the owners. Especially during the period of the siege of Antwerp (July 1584–August 1585), the number of taxes on property grew significantly. Not all the direct tax accounts have been preserved but, based on the registers that have survived, we can conclude that the direct taxes raised more than 900,000 guilders. Even for a city like Antwerp this represents an enormous amount of money. These direct taxes were of course more 'just' than the indirect taxes, since the wealthy owners paid the bulk. Furthermore, a substantial part of the urban population was exempt because it was considered too poor to contribute. We know for instance that 4,635 people contributed to the direct taxes levied from November 1584 until April 1585, which means that around 75 per cent of the households were exempt (Van Aelst 2000, ch. 5; Van Roey 1968, 243-249).

The figures about 1584-1585 confirm the very difficult social circumstances experienced within the Antwerp city walls during the siege by Alexander Farnese and his Spanish army (Jongbloet-Van Houtte, 1986). It is therefore dangerous to conclude on the basis of this

---

13   SAA, *Privilegekamer*, 1658, f. 188v°-190v°, 202.

Table 2. Tax rates for the 'weekgeld' in 1578 in *stuivers*[14]

No. of households	Proposal Magistracy	Final decision of the Broad Council
3000	0	0
1000	1	1
1000	2	2
1000	3	3
1000	4	4
1000	6	6
1000	8	8
1000	10	10
1000	12	15
1000	14	20
500	16	30
400	16	40
100	16	60

exceptional situation that in sixteenth-century Antwerp there was a social polarisation process that led to the contraction of the middle groups (Dambruyne 2000, 504-505; Soly 1993, 38). Social relationships at the beginning of the Calvinist Republic are undoubtedly much more relevant to the sixteenth century. At that moment the ratio between those who could contribute to the direct tax of January 1578 and those who could not was precisely the opposite of that of 1584-85 indicating the existence of vital social middle groups.

The tax-related evidence presented above makes clear that the regime of the Calvinist Republic achieved a fundamental change in fiscal policy. The traditional focus on indirect taxes on retail and consumption was complemented by a variety of direct taxes. Here, the principle was that taxes were paid according to status and wealth. Another element, underscoring once again the new policy, is that the indirect taxes levied on daily consumption products were reshuffled. Taxes on common, cheaper beers were lowered and taxes on the better beers and on wine rose (Van Aelst 2000, ch. 4; compare Van Uytven 1961, 113-115). There is no doubt that there is a strong link between the new tax policy and the broader representativeness of the city government. It was especially the deans of the craft guilds who pushed in the Broad Council for a fairer tax system. The suggestion that the Calvinist Republics in the Southern Netherlands moved towards a less guild-based conception of the body politic (De Munck 2018, 103) therefore finds no supporting evidence in the case of the Antwerp Calvinist Republic. From 1577 onwards, the deans of the craft guilds played an important and often crucial role in the Broad Council, especially when fiscal matters were discussed.[15]

---

14   20 *stuivers* = 1 guilder.
15   The socio-political role of the craft guilds has already been emphasised by Soly 1983, 129-130.

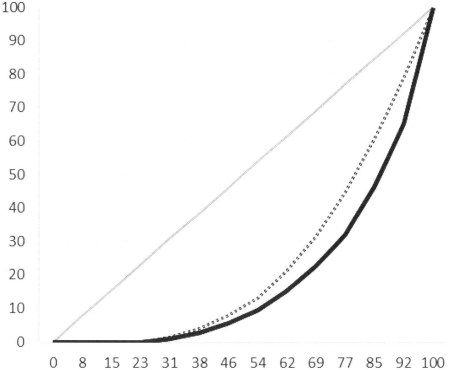

Figure 1. Fiscal burden *weekgeld* 1578, comparison of the initial proposal of the city magistracy with the final agreement reached in the Broad Council

The new tax policy however did not prevent the citizens of Antwerp from having still to pay a lot of taxes, probably more than they had done before, although the efforts were better divided over the urban society. One of the main features of the early modern tax system is that taxes were levied on the basis of the anticipated expenses and the accumulated debt. The circumstances of war caused a constant demand for money. Antwerp significantly contributed to the maintenance of the army equipped by the rebellious States. At the same time, the military needs of the city had to be covered. The building and maintenance of new fortifications, the purchase of munitions and the building of new forts around the city of Antwerp needed a constant flow of money.

Yet, there are indications that there was in general a willingness to contribute. This willingness can undoubtedly be linked to what specialists of present-day tax systems call 'tax compliance'. They argue that in societies with a transparent political and economic organisation, tax morale will be high (Prak 2018, 76, 79, with references). Something similar can be seen in Antwerp during the Calvinist Republic. New taxes were proclaimed only after they had been discussed and consented to in the Broad Council. The deans of the guilds more than once stated that they were prepared to approve the taxes proposed 'if they were consented and levied in a general way'. By a general way they meant with the consent of the different bodies or branches of the Broad Council. Through this representative negotiation process the new taxes gained legitimacy in urban society. For the actual organisation and collection of the taxes the Antwerp city government could rely upon a sophisticated citizens' network: the captains and their civic militias. Also, at this level, the active involvement of citizens was helpful. The contrast with the situation in the late 1560s and the early 1570s is in any case striking. At that time, the Duke of Alva launched his new tax system based on real wealth and property. Historians agree that Alva's tax system was modern and fairer than what existed in the Low Countries (Grapperhaus 1982, 291-293). Yet his new tax system met heavy resistance because it was imposed and associated with a regime of repression and terror.

There is perhaps yet another element that was favourable to the new taxes: until 1583 the evolution of living standards was positive. Wages were relatively high and prices were under control. Here, too, the new regime conducted a social policy. The prices of basic consumer products were capped at a certain level so that they remained within the reach of the common people (Van Aelst 2000; Scholliers 1960, 142-143).

Conclusion

We can conclude that the Calvinist Republic was a successful experiment in social fairness. The new political regime and the new institutional framework open to different layers of urban society followed a different and more just fiscal policy. Many extraordinary taxes levied to finance the ongoing war were conceived and introduced by the States-General. Often, the Antwerp city government reluctantly accepted these taxes 'out of love for the fatherland and the common cause'. In the Broad Council there was however room to discuss how the new taxes should be implemented. The extensive records of the proceedings of this Council amply demonstrate how most members pleaded for a tax distribution that took into account the status and wealth of their citizens. From 1583 onwards there are indications that the States of Brabant came more and more to the fore when new taxes had to be levied (Génard 1864b). Maybe they came to play a role similar to that of the States of Holland which succeeded in creating a centralisation of the fiscal policy at provincial level (Fritschy 2003, 68-70). A few years later, however, Antwerp's contribution to the Revolt came to an end, so we cannot check whether there was a parallel evolution over the long term.

Another point we may not overlook in evaluating the fiscal policy of the new regime is that the Calvinists who gradually seized power were a minority. Yet it is undeniable that their social policy was also favourable to rank and file Catholics. It is however difficult to pinpoint how they matched a favourable social policy with an oppressive religious policy, especially in the later years of the Calvinist Republic. But that the social policy of the new Calvinist regime generated sympathy among Protestants and Catholics is undeniable. The new approach of the Calvinist regime is the more obvious when we compare it with what happened immediately after the city's capitulation in August 1585. With the new Catholic regime returned the dominance of the small group of elite families. They immediately raised the indirect taxes on beer – even on the cheaper beers – and on grain (Van Aelst 2000, 109-112).

References

Blockmans, Wim. 1987. "Finances publiques et inégalilté sociales dans les Pays-Bas aux XIVe-XVIe siècles." In *Genèse de l'état moderne : prélèvement et redistribution*, ed. J.-P. Genet and M. le Mené, 77-90. Paris: Éditions du CNRS.

Blondé, Bruno, Jeroen Puttevils and Isis Sturtewagen. Forthcoming. "Silks and the 'Golden Age' of Antwerp." In *Antwerp in the Renaissance*, ed. Bruno Blondé and Jeroen Puttevils. Turnhout: Brepols.

Blondé, Bruno, Jord Hanus and Wouter Ryckbosch. 2018. "The predatory state? Urban finances, politics and social inequality in sixteenth-century 's-Hertogenbosch." In *Entrepreneurs, Institutions and Government Intervention in Europe (13th – 20th centuries). Essays in honour of Erik Aerts*, ed. Brecht Dewilde and Johan Poukens, 101-115. Brussels: ASP.

Dambruyne, Johan. 2001. *Mensen en centen. Het 16de-eeuwse Gent in demografisch en economisch perspectief*. Ghent: Maatschappij voor Geschiedenis en Oudheidkunde.

Dambruyne, Johan. 2002. *Corporatieve middengroepen. Aspiraties, relaties en transformaties in de 16de-eeuwse Gentse ambachtswereld*. Ghent: Academia Press.

De Munck, Bert. 2018. *Guilds, Labour and the Urban Body Politic. Fabricating Community in the Southern Netherlands, 1300-1800*. New York & London: Routledge.

Everaert, Janna. 2019. "Power in the Metropolis. The Impact of Economic and Demographic Growth on the Antwerp City Council (1400-1550)." *Urban History* 46: 1-21.

Friedrichs, Christopher R. 2000. *Urban Politics in Early Modern Europe*. London & New York: Routledge.

Fritschy, W. 2003. "A 'financial revolution' reconsidered: public finance in Holland during the Dutch Revolt, 1568-1648." *Economic History Review* 56/1: 57-89.

Génard, Pieter. 1864a. "Ordonnantien van het Antwerpsch Magistraat, rakende de godsdienstige geschillen der XVIe eeuw." *Antwerpsch Archievenblad* 3: 1-463.

Génard, Pieter. 1864b. "Verzameling getiteld: Collegiale Actenboecken van 1583-1585." *Antwerpsch Archievenblad* 5: 151-472.

Grapperhaus, F. H. M. 1982. *Alva en de tiende penning*. Zutphen: De Walburg Pers.

Jongbloet-Van Houtte, Giselle. 1986. *Brieven en andere bescheiden betreffende Daniël van der Meulen 1584-1600*. Vol I: *augustus 1584 – september 1585*. The Hague: Instituut voor Nederlandse Geschiedenis.

Kint, A. M. 1996. "The Community of Commerce: Social Relations in Sixteenth-Century Antwerp." Unpublished Ph.D. thesis, New York: Columbia University.

Lijst gepubliceerd in Personele ende gewillige contributie ende medegeldinge byde drye Staten van Brabant, geconsenteert totte tegenwoirdelijcke nootelicheyden. Ter ordonnantien vande Heeren die Staten generael. 1577. Brussels: Michiel van Hamont.

Listen van de generale middelen gheresolveert by zijn Alteze/ mijn Heere den prince van Orangnien/ den Raedt van State/ ende de generale Staten. 1578. Antwerp: Christoffel Plantijn.

Marnef, Guido. 1987. "Brabants calvinisme in opmars: de weg naar de calvinistische republieken te Antwerpen, Brussel en Mechelen, 1577-1580." *Bijdragen tot de Geschiedenis* 70: 7-21.

Marnef, Guido. 1996. *Antwerp in the Age of Reformation. Underground Protestantism in a Commercial Metropolis 1550-1577*. (The Johns Hopkins University Studies in Historical and Political Sciences, 114th Series, n°1). Baltimore, MD, & London: Johns Hopkins University Press.

Marnef, Guido. 2001. "The towns and the revolt." In *The Origins and Development of the Dutch Revolt*, ed. Graham Darby, 84-106. London & New York: Routledge.

Marnef, Guido. 2007. "Resistance and the Celebration of Privileges in Sixteenth-Century Brabant." In *Public Opinion and Changing Identities in the Early Modern Netherlands. Essays in Honour of Alastair Duke*, ed. Judith Pollmann and Andrew Spicer, 125-139. Leiden: Brill.

Marnef, Guido. 2010. "The process of political change under the Calvinist Republic in Antwerp (1577-1585)." In *Des villes en révolte. Les Républiques urbaines aux Pays-Bas et en France pendant la deuxième moitié du XVIe siècle*. (Studies in European Urban History 1100-1800), ed. Monique Weis, 25-33. Turnhout: Brepols.

Masure, Thierry. 1986. "De stadsfinanciën van Antwerpen 1531-1571. Een poging tot rekonstruktie." Unpublished Master's thesis, Ghent: University of Ghent.

Prak, Maarten. 2018. *Citizens without Nations. Urban Citizenship in Europe and the World c. 1000-1789*. Cambridge: Cambridge University Press.

Prims, Floris. 1942-43. *Beelden uit den cultuurstrijd der Jaren 1577-1585*, 2 vols. Antwerp: Bureel der Bijdragen tot de Geschiedenis.

Prims, Floris, ed. 1954: *Register der Commissie tot onderhoud van de Religionsvrede te Antwerpen (1579-1581)*. Brussels: Paleis der Academiën.

Schilling, Heinz. 1992. *Religion, Political Culture and the Emergence of Early Modern Society. Essays in German and Dutch Society*. (Studies in Medieval and Reformation Thought, vol. L). Leiden: Brill.

Scholliers, Etienne. 1960. *De levensstandaard in de XVe en XVIe eeuw te Antwerpen*. Antwerp: De Sikkel.

Serrure, C. P. 1859-60. "Peeter Heyns. Het schoolwezen te Antwerpen in 1579 en 1580." In *Vaderlandsch Museum voor Nederduitsche letterkunde, oudheid en geschiedenis*, ed. C. P. Serrure, vol. III, 293-404. Ghent: E. Hoste.

Soly, Hugo. 1970. "Economische vernieuwing en sociale weerstand. De betekenis en aspiraties der Antwerpse middenklasse in de 16de eeuw." *Tijdschrift voor Geschiedenis* 83: 520-535.

Soly, Hugo. 1983. "De dominantie van het handelskapitalisme: stad en platteland." In *Geschiedenis van Vlaanderen van de oorsprong tot heden*, ed. Els Witte, 105-179. Brussels: La Renaissance du Livre.

Soly, Hugo. 1993. "Sociale relaties in Antwerpen tijdens de 16[de] en 17[de] eeuw." In *Antwerpen verhaal van een metropool 16[de]-17[de] eeuw*, ed. Jan Van der Stock, 37-47. Ghent: Snoeck-Ducaju.

Stiglitz, Joseph. 2013. *The Price of Inequality*. London: Penguin.

't Hart, Marjolein, and Michael Limberger. 2006. "Staatsmacht en stedelijke autonomie. Het geld van Antwerpen en Amsterdam (1500-1700)." *Tijdschrift voor Sociale en Economische Geschiedenis* 3/3: 36-72.

Tracy, James D. 1994. "Taxation and State Debt." In: *Handbook of European History 1400-1600. Late Middle Ages, Renaissance and Reformation*. Vol. I, ed. Thomas A. Brady, Heiko A. Oberman and James D. Tracy, 563-588. Leiden: Brill.

Van Aelst, Tim. 2000. "De Antwerpse stadsfinanciën tijdens de Calvinistische Republiek (1577-1585)." Unpublished Master's dissertation. Ghent: University of Ghent.

Van Roey, Jan. 1968. "De correlatie tussen het sociale-beroepsmilieu en de godsdienstkeuze te Antwerpen op het einde der XVIe eeuw." In *Sources de l' histoire religieuse de la Belgique. Moyen âge et Temps modernes.* (Bibliothèque de la Revue d'Histoire Ecclésiastique, fasc. 47), 239-257. Louvain: Publications Universitaires.

Van Roey, Jan. 1975. "De bevolking." In *Antwerpen in de XVIde eeuw*, 95-108. Antwerp: Genootschap voor Antwerpse Geschiedenis.

Van Uytven, Raymond. 1961. *Stadsfinanciën en stadsekonomie te Leuven van de XIIe tot het einde der XVIe eeuw*. Brussels: Paleis der Academiën.

Van Uytven, Raymond. 1968. "Wereldlijke overheid en reguliere geestelijkheid in Brabant tijdens de Late Middeleeuwen." In *Sources de l' histoire religieuse de la Belgique. Moyen âge et Temps modernes.* (Bibliothèque de la Revue d'Histoire Ecclésiastique, fasc. 47), 48-134. Louvain: Publications Universitaires.

Van Uytven, Raymond. 1982. "Stadsgeschiedenis in het Noorden en Zuiden." In *Algemene Geschiedenis der Nederlanden*, ed. D. P. Bok et al., vol. II, 188-253. Haarlem: Fibula-Van Dishoeck.

Van Uytven, Raymond. 1986. "*Altyt siet dat eynde aen!* Een gedicht over de krijtersopstand te 's-Hertogenbosch in 1525." In *Cultuurgeschiedenis in de Nederlanden van de Renaissance naar de Romantiek*, 337-354. Leuven & Amersfoort: Acco.

Wahl, Fabian. 2015. "Participative Political Institutions and City Development 800-1800." (EHES Working Papers in Economic History, n° 73). Hohenheim, available at http://www.ehes.org/EHES_73.pdf.

GRIET VERMEESCH

Law Courts and Social Inequality in the Cities of the Eighteenth-Century Low Countries

Introduction

In the 1554 edition of his very influential volume *Praxis Rerum Criminalium* on criminal legal practice in the Low Countries the eminent lawyer Joos de Damhouder included a large number of illustrations. Damhouder actively endorsed the inclusion of illustrations depicting crimes and scenes from criminal judicial proceedings, bringing him great commercial success. The book went through numerous editions throughout the early modern period and was translated and read across Europe. The illustrations however also served another, less pecuniary purpose. As the 2016 exhibition in Bruges on 'The Art of Law' abundantly documented, art depicting the law helped to set an example to judges, lawyers and the wider public. The 1562 edition accordingly included an additional artwork, 'The description of worldly justice' (*Mundanae Justiciae Declamation*) which expressed the way magistrates were to act in a society characterised by vast social inequality. Sitting on a throne, Justitia has one blindfolded face looking at a small group of *personae miserabilis* – poor, widows and orphans – on her left, and another non-blindfolded one looking at a number of affluent citizens on her right. In the accompanying text, Damhouder elucidates that the judge should keep a sharp eye on the actions of the moneyed, and act compassionately towards poor and vulnerable people (Monballyu 2016). The theme of *miserabiles personae* is a familiar one in the bible, where one was ordered to treat them kindly, and in law (see for instance Deuteronomy, 24:17), inspiring – for instance – free legal aid to the poor in early modern lawcourts (Brundage 1992). All in all, the principal quality of justice, according to its iconography, was impartiality, and detachment from moneyed interests.

Judging from research which has been carried out in the past few decades on the social history of law in early modern Europe, the ideals of impartial justice lenient to the poor suggested in the writings of lawyers and in the iconography of law contrasts with reality. The law was fundamentally hierarchical and inequality before the law was institutionally anchored. Noblemen and clergymen enjoyed the privilege of being heard in special courts and different bodies of law applied to different social groups. In addition, quite a few seminal social history works have corroborated that legal practice furthered existing social hierarchies. Especially for eighteenth-century rural England, there is a strong historiographic tradition of demonstrating the ways in which the legal system buttressed the interests of the propertied classes and at times brutally clashed with lower social groups who had vastly different notions of justice. The background to these legal criminal practices was the gradual replacement of traditional economies with market economies and profound social change, which jeopardised the relative stability of social relations (see

Griet Vermeesch • Vrije Universiteit Brussel

Inequality and the City in the Low Countries (1200-2020), ed. by Bruno BLONDÉ, Sam GEENS, Hilde GREEFS, Wouter RYCKBOSCH, Tim SOENS & Peter STABEL, SEUH 50 (Turnhout, 2020), pp. 199-209.

  DOI 10.1484/M.SEUH-EB.5.120446

for instance Thompson 1993; Brewer & Styles 1983; Hay et al. 1975). For other countries such interpretation reminiscent of social conflict theory was elaborated as well. Antony Crubaugh has, for instance, emphasised that seignorial law courts in eighteenth-century south-western France were largely inaccessible to ordinary people, and were mostly brought into play by members of the elite to have a hold over defendants lower on the social ladder (Crubaugh 2001, 47, 56). However, his interpretations have been convincingly challenged (Hayhoe 2008; Garnot 2005). As Julius Ruff underlines in a survey on the history of crime in early modern Europe, we must be careful not to consider the law as 'a one-way flow of the normative power of the state … downward to society' (Ruff 2001, 105). Both criminal and civil courts largely depended on the participation of the population at large, and claimants and witnesses in judicial proceedings did not necessarily belong to the elites or solely represent elite interests. Current historiography (for example Vermeesch et al. 2019) often emphasises wide participation in litigation and describes the early modern law court as a forum that was intensely used by remarkably broad social groups.

This essay embraces the recent interpretations that judicial proceedings were a service that was 'consumed' by inhabitants, who belonged to broader sections of society. It builds on the research that has been conducted in the past decade on the uses and accessibility of law courts in the early modern Low Countries. It claims that law courts were indeed used by broader sections of the urban communities. Middling groups in particular constituted an important clientele for the courts. However, there was a marked threshold which excluded the major proportion of urban dwellers from civil litigation. In addition, the practices regarding legal aid to the poor suggest that the socially broad uses of justice do not negate the fact that judicial proceedings served to reproduce social hierarchies. Recent research on criminal legal practices however suggests broader uses of justice across social boundaries. All in all, the chapter advises caution in straightforwardly ascribing social inclusiveness to early modern urban institutions of dispute settlement.

The clientele of early modern civil law courts

In 1681, an elderly woman was questioned in Brussels by two officials of the Council of Flanders as part of an investigation into the misconduct of lawyer Philip Vrijleven at an urban court of the city of Ghent. While they wanted only some information from her in order to find another, more indispensable witness, she was overawed by the two officials. She refused to give them her name or to swear to her evidence. Never before had she sworn an oath and she was terrified 'that the devil would then seize her, and if she would have given her name, she would perhaps be tortured'. Clearly, the woman had little experience of the law, and it terrified her. In view of her age, the two officials left her in peace.[1] This short anecdote illustrates the obstacles ordinary people could encounter when facing the law and lawcourts in the early modern period. While historians nowadays emphasise how people from all walks of life found their way to court, the distress of the old woman

---

1   Rijksarchief Gent, Raad van Vlaanderen, inv. nr. 22372 Philips Vijlevens, proc. voor de schep. van ghedeele van Gent: uitoefening van functie van notaris zonder admissie – vervalsing van handtekens – bedrog als proc. – omkoping van getuigen – verkrachting – bedreigingen. 1679-82.

suggests that we should not over-state such views. For her, courts were part of a repressive culture she preferred to keep at distance.

Nonetheless, courts do not seem to have been such distant peculiarities for urbanites, at least in geographical terms. Notwithstanding processes of state formation and centralisation, the prime forum of most judicial proceedings in the Low Countries was firmly located at the local level. This was the case for both criminal and civil disputes, in both the Habsburg Low Countries and the Dutch Republic. Criminal legal practice was characterised by pronounced fragmentation, with a multitude of local courts meting out capital punishment. Appeal to courts on higher geo-institutional levels – such as the provincial Councils – was generally ruled out (Monballyu 1991). For civil matters there was an even greater multitude of judicial forums, corresponding to the fact that the number of criminal cases was dwarfed by the enormous number of civil interpersonal disputes. Another important difference from criminal proceedings was the fact that appeal to higher courts was possible. These higher courts tried only a fraction of the cases that were heard at the local level, yet they were clearly important for the exemplary function of their proceedings and sentences. In cities a wide range of institutions for dispute settlement generally existed alongside the emblematic bench of aldermen, where aldermen sat as judges. For the seventeenth-century Dutch city of Leiden, Aries van Meeteren has for instance detailed the rich array of dispute settlement bodies, including guilds, notaries, civil guards, neighbourhood associations and churches. The city government actively promoted such bodies of 'infrajudicial' conflict settlement to reduce the burden on urban courts and to encourage the settlement of disputes out of court. It also set up separate summary courts for specific types of disputes, for instance the peacemaker court to deal with disputes relating to sums of less than 100 guilders (in the eighteenth century). Another example is the commission for neighbourly disputes which typically dealt with boundary disputes. These courts operated in the grey area between formal and informal justice and considerably lightened the case load of the Bench of Aldermen (Meeteren 2006). During the long sixteenth century, cities across the Low Countries took similar measures to meet the enormous demand for dispute settlement. Many, for instance, set up small claims courts to relieve the pressure on their benches of aldermen and to avoid the often superfluous use of intricate and expensive judicial proceedings that generally governed the course of hearings by the bench of aldermen. The city of Brussels in 1585 set up a so-called Burgomaster's roll to deal with the innumerable petty disputes brought before the aldermen (Godding 2002). Antwerp's urban court accommodated various 'rolls', i.e. lists that every week were filled with cases. The Wednesday roll and – after 1685 – the 'small roll of the amman' were reserved for small claims, to be settled without the help of legal representatives (Laenens 1953).

To what extent did various social groups have dealings with these extensive urban judicial infrastructures and how did this evolve during the seventeenth and eighteenth centuries, concomitant with increasing social inequality? Historians tend to assume that legal records offer an exceptionally broad and socially differentiated illustration of early modern society (see for instance Deceulaer et al. 2014). Examination of the clientele of local courts in early modern England has indeed confirmed such generally widespread social inclusiveness of law courts, at least the inexpensive ones. For example, Craig Muldrew asserted that the borough court of seventeenth-century King's Lynn was amply used by all social categories, including the poorest, which made it 'a surprisingly egalitarian and accessible institution' (Muldrew 1993, 36). Similar inclusiveness was established for the summary courts of the justices of the peace, who arbitrated on petty disputes. Peter King emphasised that 'the summary courts were the arena in which the vast majority of the population experienced the law' (King 2004, 128).

However, there are indications that matters were different in the cities of the Low Countries. There, civil judicial records in all probability reflect a more biased representation of social relations in the early modern town. For instance, the poorest sections of the urban populace had much less access to civil courts, including the cheapest and most accessible ones. This has been established for the small claims court in mid-eighteenth-century Leiden. At first glance, the so-called *Vredemakers* seemed to have a particularly low threshold, in view of the fact that its procedure was markedly quick, operated almost free of charge, and did not use complex legal arguments. Nonetheless, cross linking of fiscal records with the *Vredemakers'* registers showed that the court scarcely attracted claimants from among the lower 60 per cent of households (Vermeesch 2015b). The court was accessible only to inhabitants with confirmed citizenship, and appears to have been massively used by Leiden's higher middle groups and elites (Van Meeteren 2006). In view of the importance of immigrants among the population of early modern towns, limiting access to citizens only excluded large sections of the urban population from the services of this small claims court, as purchasing citizenship was a costly affair.

Reinoud Vermoesen has conducted a spatially comparative examination of small claims filed at the bench of aldermen in the small town of Aalst during the second half of the eighteenth century. He notably examined whether inhabitants of the suburbs of Aalst used the bench of aldermen to the same extent as those who lived within the city walls. He showed that inhabitants from the suburbs used this court much less frequently, even though they were as numerous as the 'urbanites'. He suggests that this is to be explained by the fact that 'suburbanites' consisted of comparatively more (recent) immigrants. It appears that they had less inclination to seek legal recourse (Vermoesen 2017). Ans Vervaeke's research on litigation in the eighteenth-century Liberty of Bruges showed that lower social groups did have recourse to the Bench of Aldermen, situated in the city of Bruges, yet did so considerably less often than their demographic weight would suggest. Cross linking of judicial records with fiscal and demographic data has revealed that middling groups and elites were the prime users of this local court during the eighteenth century (Vervaeke 2018). To be sure, this court had jurisdiction over a fairly large geographical area and was not an urban court, even though it was situated in the centre of Bruges. Nonetheless, this research indicates that the social inclusiveness of early modern courts should not just be assumed.

The fact that lower social groups and – as the article by Vermoesen suggests in particular – migrant groups participated much less in litigation in all probability reflects their limited participation in credit relations. To be sure, not all migrants belonged to the lower social groups. The ubiquity of credit relations in early modern society has been thoroughly examined both internationally and in the context of the Low Countries (Willems 2009). It was such relations that led to the majority of legal actions at local civil courts. More often than not, such legal action was taken first and foremost to officialise informally extended credit. As Bart Willems has suggested for eighteenth-century Antwerp, shopkeepers were less inclined to extend informal credit to the then growing number of households who were wage-dependent. Strikingly, the proportion of cases relating to credit extended for the sale of goods decreased concomitant with growing wage-dependence in the second half of the eighteenth century (Willems 2009, 221-222). Heidi Deneweth has similarly suggested reduced access to credit of lower social groups, which further exacerbated poverty (Deneweth 2011). This may explain the absence of lower social groups in the urban civil courts in the eighteenth century. Important thresholds existed, yet in all probability lower social groups also had less ground for entertaining the disputes that dominated court business.

Legal aid to the poor in civil justice

All in all, the social and economic position of claimants and defendants is difficult to assess. There are few (reliable) indications in the judicial records about social profiles. The painstaking and time-consuming effort to crosslink the names of litigants with fiscal records, as was done for the towns of Kings Lynn, Leiden and the Liberty of Bruges, is more often than not impracticable. Another way to observe the relationship between the group of impecunious urbanites and local courts is through the study of legal aid granted to *personae miserabilis*, as depicted in the Damhouder illustration described at the start of this chapter. The practices and discussions regarding entitlement to free legal aid reveal how contemporaries reflected on the accessibility of their courts to lower social groups and how dedicated they were in fulfilling the biblical ideals depicted in the iconography of law. Ultimately, it reveals the expectancies about which social groups were supposed to be able to take legal recourse, and which were not.

Legal aid to the poor had been considered a work of mercy by St Augustine, and had been practised by clergymen since the twelfth century (Brundage 1988). In canon law, it implied entitlement to summary proceedings without the need for legal spokesmen to limit the cost of judicial proceedings. By the sixteenth century, such practices had been adopted by secular courts as well. Charles V included a stipulation regarding legal aid to the poor in the 1531 general ordinance on civil procedure. Article 21 stated that all court employees and legal spokesmen were expected to assist poor claimants and defendants 'for the love of God', in the same way as they would help richer clients. Urban law courts across the Low Countries similarly offered such help to poor litigants, or – to be more precise – required their staff and legal spokespeople to help the poor free of charge. After a petition for free legal aid was granted, urban courts often assigned to the case a legal spokesman, who was expected to register the costs incurred and have them paid by the losing party (Vermeesch 2014, 693-694). Some courts assigned their most junior lawyers to serve poor litigants, or randomly delegated such services to all the lawyers affiliated to them (Nauwelaers 1947, 336).

It appears that a comparatively small number of households petitioned for free legal aid. In eighteenth-century Leiden, only between three and 18 such petitions were filed annually, out of a population of over 30,000 inhabitants. This is a very small number of petitions, in view of the fact that 60 per cent of the population paid hardly any taxes because of their poverty (Vermeesch 2014). In Antwerp, an extensive collection of registers for the early modern era detailing many thousands of petitions has been preserved. The registers also included requests for free legal aid, and more often than not such petitions were filed free of charge as well. The analysis of all these 'free of charge' petitions for a number of sample years during the eighteenth century shows that only between 2 and 4 per cent of all petitions were typically filed without charge. This figure is strikingly low in view of the massive poverty rates in eighteenth-century Antwerp (Vermeesch 2015a). No wonder that the existence of such aid was hardly studied for so long – it reveals itself to have been a fairly marginal phenomenon.

Nonetheless, in some contexts it could be an important avenue by which to gain access to the courts for people belonging to the lower rungs of society. This is interestingly the case in eighteenth-century Leiden, where free legal aid was typically requested by and granted to unmarried mothers in the context of paternity cases. Civil cases relating to debts or other more standard interpersonal disputes only occasionally led to requests for free legal aid. In Leiden, therefore, free legal aid seems to have been reserved for one, very specific kind of dispute (Vermeesch 2014). There is no doubt that most of these women belonged to the poorest subsections of Leiden society. For instance, many of them were householders who received poor relief, and the burden of an illegitimate child must have been a challenge in such modest living conditions. The aldermen rather willingly bestowed help on these mothers in the hope of having putative fathers assume responsibility, and thus saving the local poor relief from feeding extra mouths. The mothers accordingly appear to have been rather successful in their cases. However, it would be wrong to assume that all women in such dire circumstances simply found their way to the courts. In fact, only a small fraction of unmarried mothers actually filed petitions for free legal aid and thus made use of the court to pressurise putative fathers. Comparative research between litigating and non-litigating mothers shows that the latter similarly disputed with putative fathers, but did not cross the threshold to the Bench of Aldermen. Those who did represented a particular, somewhat 'privileged' subsection of the Leiden poor. They were often recipients of local poor relief and belonged to the dominant Dutch Reformed Church. The findings for Leiden suggest that these poor women found their way into court when encouraged by members of the middling sort – like poor masters or members of the consistory – who had a stake in alleviating the pressure on poor relief funds. This is telling for the relationship between the poorest members of society and urban courts – taking legal action was not at all readily open to the poor, even if it was obtainable for free (Vermeesch 2016).

Free legal aid was a vastly different phenomenon at the Bench of Aldermen in eighteenth-century Antwerp. Here, aid was rarely solicited in paternity cases. It rather served claimants and defendants who had disagreements about debts, inheritances and alimony, involving rather sizeable claims. The nature and pecuniary scope of these cases already indicates that litigants petitioning for free legal aid did not come from households which knew structural poverty. Analysis of the rhetorical strategies used by the petitioners confirms that many of the requests for free legal aid stemmed from newly impoverished people, formerly belonging to the middling sort, who were on the verge of losing their economic independence. They often emphasised that their poverty was recent and had arisen unexpectedly. Petitioners for free legal aid were by their own account victims of downward social mobility, and they asked the aldermen to help mitigate their dire new circumstances. The few petitioners who mentioned their employment were usually not wage labourers. The few exceptions emphasised how their dependence on wages was humiliating and stemmed from sheer necessity. These rhetorical ploys served to convince the city government to grant free legal aid to reverse their fortunes. These petitioners shared a similar social background with the members of staff of the urban court, as well as with the lawyers who acted as scribes and legal spokesmen. Many of these lower officials typically belonged to the petty bourgeoisie who had similar worries about downward mobility. The petitions were habitually written by urban scribes and lawyers who thus helped other citizens whose situation mirrored their own anxieties. The fact that free legal aid to the poor – also in the form of petitioning free of charge – was largely dependent on the willingness of scribes to grant it helps to explain the marginal scope of such aid (Vermeesch 2015a).

Social inequality and the chasm between middling groups on the one hand and wage-dependent poor on the other is at the fore of the rhetoric pertaining to legal aid to the poor. Here, poverty is conceptualised as a lack of independence that enables households to entertain credit relations that are at the centre of the lives of the middling sort. The urban governments appeared to be rather indulgent towards these poverty-stricken households. Consistent with other kinds of poor relief to so-called shamefaced poor, legal aid was intended to confirm social hierarchies rather than to remedy social inequalities (Cavallo 1991; Lis 1986, 116-127, 132-133).

The uses of criminal law

All in all, lower social groups seem to have been less involved in civil litigation than recent historiography on the inclusiveness of early modern law courts would have us believe. What, then, was the interaction between criminal courts and lower social groups in the urban context? In international historiography, criminal law has been the subject of analyses referring to social conflict theory much more than has civil law. Historiography on urban criminal law in the Low Countries also echoes such interpretations. As was elaborated above, criminal law was first and foremost executed at the local level, and local judges had far-reaching autonomy to hear cases and to mete out punishments. Historiographic apprehensions about the arbitrary authority of the *ancien regime* judge have been partly fuelled by the late eighteenth-century reform movement of criminal law that proclaimed the principles of – amongst other things – equality before the law (Monballyu 2014, 17-25). The fact that some social-political groups were heard at particular courts was also a source of criticism in the sixteenth century. For instance, disapproval was expressed as early as the sixteenth century about the fact that clerics who were suspected of a criminal offence were typically tried by much more lenient church courts. In the eighteenth century, enlightened mistrust of such judicial inequality become more intense (Put 2005).

Research on the alleged arbitrariness of local criminal courts has however established that, despite the autonomy of local magistrates, justice was meted out surprisingly consistently. Florike Egmond has affirmed that the extensive fragmentation of criminal courts and jurisdictions in the Low Countries did not lead to inconsistent justice. It did, however, lead to some inequality before the law. Even though they were not entirely without rights, town dwellers who lacked local roots or a fixed residence tended to have fewer entitlements, could be arrested more quickly, and were often exposed to summary justice (Egmond 1989, 14; 2001, 29). Xavier Rousseaux has similarly rejected the idea that criminal justice was a means whereby elites gained leverage over less privileged inhabitants. Based on examination of the small town of Nivelles during the seventeenth century, he comes to similar conclusions to Egmond. There was a clear difference in the handling of local suspects as opposed to immigrants. The latter were less protected by juridical procedures and had the disadvantage of lacking a local social network (Rousseau 2001). In fact, mobility and perceived delinquency appear to have often gone hand in glove in the context of high levels of migration between countryside and cities and between cities.

In the past decade, interpretations of criminal justice have however not exclusively focussed on suspects and the convicted. Drawing on the concept of 'uses of justice', historians have increasingly paid attention to the victims, that is, the people who made sure criminal procedures were begun (Dinges 2004; Garnot 1999). This is a challenging exercise, as source materials do not always allow the identifying of off-the-record protagonists in a context where criminal proceedings were formally started by the bailiff. Nonetheless, research that was conducted recently has shed light on this fascinating theme and helped to assess the accessibility of such services to people of modest means. Research into the theme of crime and gender in early modern Holland has for instance documented the approachability of criminal courts for dealing with marital issues, unruly family members and alcohol abuse, or with rowdy neighbours. Claimants accessed them in a strategic way, bringing into play different urban courts depending on the nature of the dispute (Van der Heijden 2004, 2013, 2015). In eighteenth-century Antwerp, petitions for locking up bothersome family members also increasingly came from lower social groups (Lis & Soly 1996). Criminal proceedings against unmarried couples for fornication could similarly be used by pauper women to pressurise putative fathers (Kamp & Schmidt 2018). These findings infer that households belonging to the lower rungs of society did find their way to criminal courts. These courts plausibly attracted a socially more diverse clientele than civil courts did. This brings us again to the comparison of the well-studied English summary courts that appeared more socially inclusive than the small claims courts studied in the Low Countries. Summary courts typically heard misdemeanours that would be labelled criminal offences in the Low Countries. All in all, the small claims courts in the Low Countries – which typically dealt with disputes relating to credit – are not very comparable to the English Justices of the Peace. This shows the difficulties there are in comparing and extrapolating the accessibility of early modern forums for dispute settlement across time and space.

Conclusion

Social historians have dealt with the question of how the judiciary related to the social hierarchies of early modern Europe in different ways in the past few decades. Whereas older historiography assessed that (criminal) justice was used to confirm social hierarchies, recently historians have tended to emphasise the participatory nature of justice, and the fact that broad groups in society found their way to the courts. This chapter has advised caution in straightforwardly assuming that people from all walks of life participated in litigation. There was a marked threshold for using civil courts, even the very cheap ones which utilised summary procedures. In all probability, this reflects the limited participation of wage-dependent households in informal credit relations, and their marked distance from middling groups where such credit relations were at the core of social bonds. Whether the limited inclination of wage-dependent households to access civil courts is also due to difficulties in overcoming perceived social distance to the courts is difficult to assess. On the one hand, it is striking that only limited sections among the group of single mothers in mid-eighteenth-century Leiden found their way to court in paternity conflicts. I have hypothesised that this particular group was encouraged by its social betters to take legal action, which hints that for most pauper women such action was difficult to take. On the other hand, research into the uses of criminal justice and petitioning for the forced confinement of unruly household members suggests that the distance to the city government could indeed be overcome. The relative absence of lower social groups in civil litigation records then mostly reflects the lack of disputes eligible for arbitration, as lower social groups did not have the social bonds that were so central to the lives and relations of urban middling groups and elites. As examination of legal aid to the poor reveals, the *personae miserabilis* depicted in the iconography of the law belonged to middling groups, and they were in danger of joining the ranks of wage-dependent paupers that crowded the cities in the Low Countries.

References

Brewer, John, and John Styles. 1983. *An Ungovernable People. The English and their Law in the Seventeenth and Eighteenth Centuries*. London: Rutgers University Press.

Brundage, James A. 1988. "Legal Aid for the Poor and the Professionalization of Law in the Middle Ages." *The Journal of Legal History* 9, 169-179.

Brundage, James A. 1992. "Widows as Disadvantaged Persons in Medieval Canon Law." In *Upon My Husband's Death. Widows in the Literature and Histories of Medieval Europe,* ed. Louise Mirrer, 193-206. Ann Abror, Michigan: University of Michigan Press.

Cavallo, Sandra. 1991. "Conceptions of Poverty and Poor Relief in Turin in the Second Half of the Eighteenth Century." In *Domestic Strategies. Work and Family in Italy and France (17th-18th centuries,* ed. Stuart J. Woolf, 148-199. Cambridge: Cambridge University Press.

Crubaugh, A. 2001. *Balancing the Scales of Justice. Local Courts and Rural Society in Southwest France, 1750-1800*. University Park: The Pennsylvania State University Press.

Deceulaer, Harald, Sébastien Dubois and Laetizia Puccio, eds. 2014. *Het Pleit is in de Zak! Procesdossiers uit het Ancien Regime en hun Perspectieven voor Historisch Onderzoek*. Brussels: Algemeen Rijksarchief.

Deneweth, Heidi. 2011. "A Fine Balance. Household Finance and Financial Strategies of Antwerp Households, 17th-18th centuries." *Tijdschrift voor Sociale en Economische Geschiedenis* 8, no. 4: 15-43.

Dinges, Martin. 2004. "The Uses of Justice as a Form of Social Control in Early Modern Europe." In *Social Control in Europe 1500-1800*, ed. Herman Roodenburg and Pieter Spierenburg, 159-175. Columbus, OH: Ohio State University Press.

Egmond, Florike. 1989. "Fragmentatie, Rechtsverscheidenheid en Rechtsongelijkheid in Noordelijke Nederlanden tijdens de Zeventiende en Achttiende eeuw." In *Nieuw Licht op*

Oude Justitie. Misdaad en Straf ten Tijde van de Republiek, ed. Sjoerd Faber, 9-23. Muiderberg: Coutinho.

Egmond, Florike. 2001. "Recht en Krom. Corruptie, Ongelijkheid en Rechtsbescherming in de Vroegmoderne Nederlanden." *Bijdragen en Mededelingen tot de Geschiedenis der Nederlanden* 116, no. 1: 1-33.

Garnot, B. 1999. *Les Victimes, des Oubliées de l'Histoire?* Dijon: Presses Universitaires de Dijon.

Garnot, B. 2005. "Une Rehabilitation? Les Justices Seigneuriales au XVIIIe siècle." *Histoire, Economie et Société* 24, no. 2: 61-72.

Godding, Philip. 2002. "Comment la Justice Echévinale a pu Faire Face aux Besoins de Villes en Expansion: le Cas du Brabant (XIIe-XVIIIe siècles)." In *Les Acteurs de la Justice, Magistrats, Ministère Public, Avocats, Huissiers et Greffiers (XIIe-XIXe siècle),* ed. René Robaye, 7-13. Namur: Presses Universitaires de Namur.

Hay, D, P. Linebaugh, J. G. Rule, E. P. Thompson and C. Winslow. 1975. *Albion's Fatal Tree: Crime and Society in eighteenth-century England.* London: Pantheon Books.

Hayhoe, Jeremy. 2008. *Enlightened Feudalism. Seigneurial Justice and Village Society in Eighteenth-Century Northern Burgundy.* New York: Boydell & Brewer, University of Rochester Press.

Heijden, Manon van der. 2004. "Punishment vs. Reconciliation: Marriage Control in Sixteenth- and Seventeenth-century Holland." In *Social Control in Europe 1500-1800,* ed. Herman Roodenburg and Pieter Spierenburg, 55-77. Columbus, OH: Ohio State University Press.

Heijden, Manon van der. 2013. "Women, Violence and Urban Justice in Holland, ca. 1600-1838." *Crime, History and Societies* 17, no. 2: 71-100.

Heijden, Manon van der. 2015. "Domestic Violence, Alcohol Abuse and the Uses of Justice in Early Modern Holland." *Annales de Démographie Historique* 130, no. 2: 69-85.

Kamp, Jeannette, and Ariadne Schmidt. 2018. "Getting Justice: a Comparative Perspective on Illegitimacy and the Uses of Justice in Holland and Germany, 1600-1800." *Journal of Social History* 51, no. 4: 672-692.

King, Peter. 2004. "The Summary Courts and Social Relations in eighteenth-century England." *Past and Present* 183, no. 1: 125-172.

Laenens, Charles. 1953. *De Geschiedenis van het Antwerps Gerecht.* Antwerp: Van de Velde.

Lis, Catharine. 1986. *Social Change and the Labouring Poor. Antwerp, 1770-1860.* New Haven, CT, and London: Yale University Press.

Lis, Catharina, and Hugo Soly. 1996. *Disordered Lives. Eighteenth-Century Families and their Unrule Relatives.* Cambridge: Polity Press.

Meeteren, Aries van. 2006. *Op Hoop Van Akkoord. Instrumenteel Forumgebruik bij Geschilbeslechting in Leiden in de Zeventiende Eeuw.* Hilversum: Verloren.

Monballyu, J. 1991. "Het Onderscheid tussen de Civiele en Criminele en de Ordinaire en de Extra-ordinaire Strafrechtspleging in het Vlaamse Recht van de 16de eeuw." In *Misdaad, Zoen en Straf. Aspekten van de Middeleeuwse Strafrechtsgeschiedenis in de Nederlanden,* ed. Herman Diederiks and Herman Roodenburg, 120-132. Hilversum: Verloren.

Monballyu, Jos. 2014. *Six Centuries of Criminal Law. History of Criminal Law in the Southern Netherlands and Belgium (1400-2000).* Leiden: Brill.

Monballyu, Jos. 2016. "Joos de Damhouder, een Brugs Jurist met Internationale Invloed." In *De Kunst van het Recht. Drie Eeuwen Gerechtigheid in Beeld,* ed. Stefan Huygebaert et al., 107-119. Tielt: Lannoo.

Muldrew, Craig. 1993. "Credit and the Courts: Debt Litigation in a Seventeenth-Century Urban Community." *Economic History Review* 46, no. 1 : 23-38.

Nauwelaers, Jules. 1947. *Histoire des Avocats au Souverain Conseil de Brabant, vol 1*. Brussels: E. Bruylant.

Put, Eddy. 2005. "Standenongelijkheid in Strafzaken: Geestelijken voor Zuid-Nederlandse en Luikse Officialiteiten (16de-18de Eeuw)." In *Recht in Geschiedenis. Een Bundel Bijdragen over Rechtsgeschiedenis van de Middeleeuwen tot de Hedendaagse Tijd. Aangeboden aan Prof. Dr. Ferdinand Vanhemelryck*, ed. Jaak Ockeley et al., 285-296. Leuven: Davidsfonds.

Rousseaux, Xavier. 2001. "Tensions Locales et Menaces Exterieures. Criminalité et Repression Dans la Region Nivelloise Durant la Seconde Moitié Du XVIIe Siècle." In *Crimes, Pouvoirs et Sociétés (1400-1800). Anciens Pays-Bas et Principauté de Liège*, ed. Marie-Sylvie Dupont-Bouchat and Xavier Rousseaux, 111-146. Kortrijk: Heule.

Ruff, Julius R. 2001. *Violence in Early Modern Europe 1500-1800*. New Approaches to European History. Cambridge: Cambridge University Press.

Thompson, E. P. 1993. *Customs in Common. Studies in Traditional Popular Culture*. New York: The New Press.

Vermeesch, Griet. 2014. "Access to Justice: Legal Aid to the Poor at Civil Law Courts in the Eighteenth-Century Low Countries." *Law and History Review* 32, no. 3: 683-714.

Vermeesch, Griet. 2015a. "'Miserabele Personen' en hun Toegang tot het Stadsbestuur. Pro Deo Petities in Achttiende-eeuws Antwerpen." *Tijdschrift voor Sociale en Economische Geschiedenis* 12, no. 4: 1-27.

Vermeesch, Griet. 2015b. "The Clientele of an Eighteenth-century Law Court. An Analysis of Plaintiffs and Defendants at a Small Claims Court in the Dutch City of Leiden, 1750-1754." *Social History* 40, no. 2: 208-229.

Vermeesch, Griet. 2016. "The Legal Agency of Single Mothers: Lawsuits over Illegitimate Children and the Uses of Legal Aid to the Poor in the Dutch Town of Leiden (1750-1810)." *Journal of Social History* 50, no. 1: 51-73.

Vermeesch, Griet, Manon van der Heijden and Jaco Zuijderduijn, eds. 2019. *The Uses of Justice in Global Perspective, 1600-1900*, Abingdon and New York: Routledge.

Vermoesen, Reinoud. 2017. "Suburbs en Klachten. Burgerlijke Vorderingen in de Stad Aalst en haar Buitenwijken Tijdens de Periode 1750-1800." *Stadsgeschiedenis* 12, no. 2: 137-156.

Vervaeke, Ans. 2018. *Met Recht en Rede(n). Toegang en Gebruik van Burgerlijke Rechtbanken in het Brugse Vrije (1670-1795)*. Brussels: Unpublished PhD thesis, Free University of Brussels.

Willems, Bart. 2009. *Leven op de Pof. Krediet bij de Antwerpse Middenstand in de Achttiende Eeuw*. Amsterdam: Aksant.

PART IV

Shocks, Crises and Inequality

SAM GEENS

The Great Destruction of People and Wealth

The Impact of the Ghent Revolt on Wealth Inequality in the Last Quarter of the Fourteenth Century

Introduction

From 1379 to 1385 the citizens of Ghent revolted against the Counts of Flanders, Louis of Male and his successor Philip the Bold, whose centralisation politics tried to curb the autonomy of the city. The conflict quickly escalated as other towns allied themselves to one of the belligerents. Numerous battles and sieges were fought across the entire county, but no clear victor emerged. In contrast to the limited political consequences, the economic impact of the war was immense. According to historian James Murray (Murray 2005, 18), it was the 'most destructive civil war in the war-torn history of fourteenth-century Flanders'. And the contemporary chronicler Jean Froissart believed it would be at least 100 years before the county recovered from the violence. Froissart states that Count Louis of Male hesitated to wage war because he predicted 'great destruction of people and wealth' (Croenen & Romanova 2013, 10r-v). The present chapter examines one specific effect on the city of Ghent. Did the popular revolt result in a fundamental redistribution of wealth between citizens?

In recent historiography, warfare has been seen as an important driver of economic (in)equality (consisting of disparities in income and wealth). Together with epidemics and natural disasters, it is often cited as one of the few events able to trigger a significant and longlasting decline in inequality. The rationale behind this hypothesis is much in line with the aforementioned reservations of the count. War destroys capital. Because capital is generally concentrated at the top of society, the fortunes of the elite are most affected. War also destroys lives. According to classic economic theory, substantial population losses may change the relative prices of factors of production. As labour becomes scarcer wages will increase. Because poorer groups are generally more dependent on labour income, they will profit at the expense of elites, who are more likely to be employers. In sum, scholars believe that war has a strong levelling effect by reducing top wealth levels and increasing bottom income levels (Scheidel 2017, 113-210; Milanovic 2018, 1030; Alfani, Schaff & Geirok 2017, 28-30).

Although the theory seems compellingly straightforward, the real impact of warfare is more complex and diverse. Indeed, very few wars in the course of history did significantly reduce inequality, while others have, in fact, contributed to increasing it. The effect seems to be largely dependent on the unit of analysis and the nature of the conflict (Scheidel 2017, 196-199; Coşgel & Ergene 2012, 318-321; for a case study on the importance of the unit

Sam Geens • University of Antwerp

Inequality and the City in the Low Countries (1200-2020), ed. by Bruno BLONDÉ, Sam GEENS, Hilde GREEFS, Wouter RYCKBOSCH, Tim SOENS & Peter STABEL, SEUH 50 (Turnhout, 2020), pp. 213-229.

    DOI 10.1484/M.SEUH-EB.5.120447

of analysis, see also Van Kooten Chapter 13). In pre-industrial Europe traditional warfare was mostly limited in scope, often involving a relatively small body of specialised soldiers fighting each other (mobilisation rates rarely exceeded 1.5 per cent of an empire's population before 1900: Onorato, Scheve & Stasavage 2014, 458-460). In an empire-wide perspective, such battles caused only marginal destruction of wealth and people. Exceptions do exist however. The best-known example is the Thirty Years War (1618-48). The prolonged and violent warfare between all major European powers combined with a severe outbreak of plague in 1627-29 devastated the Holy Roman Empire and its population, causing a 10 per cent reduction in wealth inequality on average. Only after a century did inequality again reach its pre-war levels (Alfani, Schaff & Geirok 2017, figure 6; Scheidel 2017, 335-342; Pfister forthcoming). In a more indirect way, warfare increased disparities in the long run through taxation, especially during the early modern period. As taxation was often regressive, the rise of fiscal-military states accentuated the tendency towards the concentration of wealth (Alfani & Di Tullio 2019).

On a regional or local level the direct impact of warfare is more frequently observed. Depending on the extent of destruction, the level and method of wealth extraction, and the goals of the belligerents, the results may vary. For instance, the Vikings raiding north-western Europe in the ninth century were chiefly interested in acquiring riches. The pillaging of towns, such as the sacking of Paris in 845, probably reduced wealth inequality within the affected regions. At the same time, inequality in Norse societies may have increased due to the unequal distribution of returned loot (Barett 2008). The objective and outcome were very different when their Norman descendants invaded England in 1066. For William the Conqueror and his followers, land and power were the main price. William replaced the English aristocracy by confiscating their lands and redistributing them amongst 200 of his loyal, and probably already wealthy, vassals. Landholding became concentrated in fewer hands, which must have increased inequality in many regions (Thomas 2008, 67-71).

Whereas the effect of traditional pre-industrial warfare is primarily mediated through the actions of an external specialised force, the impact of popular uprisings is more ambiguous as destruction comes from within and involves a broad layer of society.[1] During the Ghent revolt, the urban militias were, as we will see, primarily composed of craftsmen from every trade, thus involving a broad spectrum of the professional population. Although scholars have devoted a lot of attention to the role of inequality in promoting popular uprisings (e.g. MacCulloch 2005; Cederman, Gleditsch & Buhaug 2013; Fjelde & Østby 2014), few studies have documented the evolution of inequalities during and after the conflict. A comprehensive study of 128 contemporary countries found that intrastate warfare temporarily widened income disparity because of the cutbacks in social spending, the disruption of labour markets and the breakdown of agricultural production. Five years after the war income levels gradually reached their pre-war levels thanks to the revival of the

---

1 Popular uprising is defined in this chapter as violent intrastate conflict between two or more parties, of which at least one includes a significant share of the common population. It comprises revolts, insurrections, rebellions, resistance and civil wars. Such a broad conceptualisation is preferred since a clear distinction between the types of intrastate warfare is lacking in the literature and multiple types can occur during one conflict. In the case of Ghent, the war started as a resistance, but escalated into a revolt with occasional elements of civil warfare. Historians have consequently used a multitude of terms to describe the revolt.

economy and distributive politics (Bircan, Brück & Vothknecht 2017). These mechanisms do not apply to all conflicts, however. For example, the exact opposite trend is visible for the Spanish Civil War (1936-39). Income inequality narrowed during the conflict and witnessed an upsurge during its aftermath due to General Franco's policies (Prados de la Escosura 2008, 303-304).

For wealth inequality and pre-modern times the number of observations is even more limited and they have rarely, if ever, been the primary focus of research. Walter Scheidel (Scheidel 2007, 329-333; 2017, 206-207) argues that disparities grew during the revolts at the end of the Roman Republic (first century BCE) because the benefits of confiscations were mainly distributed among a select group of supporters. In contrast, in the late 40s BCE, expropriations and the introduction of progressive taxation transferred wealth into the hands of the large citizen army as compensation for its service. Due to a lack of quantitative sources the impact on total inequality remains obscure, but the abolition of taxes and the downsizing of the citizen army during the peace which followed suggest that the consequences were only temporary. Guido Alfani (Alfani 2010, 532-533), employing annual tax records for the Italian city of Ivrea, reports no impact of the Piedmontese Civil War (1638-42) on wealth distributions even though Ivrea was besieged and the countryside ravaged. Unfortunately, he does not explain this anomaly.

If any general conclusion can be deducted from this literary overview, it is that our knowledge of the impact of warfare is still limited despite the bold claims often made about its levelling potential. This is especially true for (pre-modern) popular uprisings. The few observations suggest no predetermined effect, as outcomes varied from no effect to increasing or decreasing inequality. Yet they do seem to agree that any redistribution was reversed within a decade following the end of the hostilities. In the following paragraphs I will argue that, by focusing on general evolutions of inequality measures such as the Gini coefficient, scholars have underestimated the transformative power of warfare. In line with previous studies, inequality in Ghent decreased significantly during the revolt of 1379-85 and increased soon afterwards to pre-war levels. However, as we will see, the destruction of the Flemish countryside provided its urban middle classes with the opportunity to acquire substantial amounts of land. The multiplication of absentee landowners probably tempered intra-urban disparities in the long run but, at the same time, it increased urban-rural inequality. However, before we do so, the nature and causes of this particular uprising as well as the sources and methodology used need to be addressed in more detail.

The Ghent revolt (1379-85)

In the county of Flanders and, by extension, the Low Countries, the recurrence of popular uprisings was exceptionally high between the twelfth and nineteenth centuries. According to Wim Blockmans (Blockmans 1988), there was a long tradition of citizens opposing central authority and themselves seizing power whenever their privileges were threatened. Following the same logic, Charles Tilly (Tilly 1993, 52-78) labelled the Low Countries the 'home of bourgeoisie revolt'. The long-term evolution of the causes of this and the development of rebellious repertoires have been the subject of ample studies and do not need to be repeated here in great detail. Instead, we limit ourselves to the specific context that gave rise to the Ghent revolt of 1379-85.

In the fourteenth century, the traditional Flemish industry in light and cheap textiles, which had brought great wealth and power to the cities, was in economic decline. Intra-urban rivalries for political control and the rising cost of living due to coin devaluation compounded the crisis. Unemployment and poverty increased, especially in the city of Ghent, where almost half of the population worked in the textile sector. At the same time, cities in the Low Countries, until then characterised by the dichotomy between wealthy merchant-entrepreneurs and a proletarianised labour force, underwent profound societal change with the emergence of a strong middling group of skilled artisans (Stabel forthcoming). As a result, the Ghent economy gradually reoriented itself towards the international market for luxury woollens, towards the domestic markets for (new) consumer goods to provide for the increased demand generated by the middling group, and towards the regional grain trade. The last was especially important to cushion, but never offset, the effects of the industrial crisis. In the first half of the fourteenth century, the city had acquired the right to act as the exclusive trading hub for all grain transported over the Lys and Scheldt rivers thanks to its advantageous location at the confluence of both waterways. As many cities in the county of Flanders and the duchy of Brabant were dependent on grain imported from northern France, the trade proved to be very profitable (Nicholas 1987). It can roughly be estimated that between 149,130 and 437,615 hectolitres of grain annually passed through Ghent during the late 1380s, enough to feed up to 120,000 adults.[2]

In 1379, Count Louis of Male authorised the city of Bruges to dig a canal towards the Lys. For Ghent, such a bypass posed a serious threat to its all-important grain trade. When diggers reached the territory of Ghent, an urban militia responsible for maintaining law and order, called the *Witte Kaproenen* (White Hoods), stopped the construction by force. The count agreed to withdraw his support for the canal on the precondition that the *Witte Kaproenen* were disbanded. This demand was typical for Louis' centralisation politics, which used inter-city rivalries to curtail urban privileges and enlarge comital jurisdiction. When bailiff Roger of Outerive, the representative of the count in Ghent, arrested a member of the White Hoods, the already tense situation spiralled out of control. The citizens rose up and assassinated the bailiff. One month later, many towns and cities had already joined the revolt or were forced to do so by the Ghent militia. Six years of bloody war ensued. The French king had to intervene three times with a large force to help his vassal, the count of Flanders, restore order (see section 3 for a more detailed course of events). But even then, no clear victor emerged. The peace treaty of 1385 simply affirmed the status quo by pardoning Ghent on all counts (de Muynck 1951).

The popular nature of the revolt is evident from the large number of citizens who took up arms. According to the contemporary chronicler Jean Froissart, allegedly up to 100,000 men had gathered from all over the county to fight Louis of Male at the height of the uprising. For the city of Ghent, the reported figures vary between 3,000 and 12,000 per expedition (Froissart 2013, 17r-64v; Miller & Coenen 2013, 101r-180v). Naturally, we should

---

2   Caclulations based on the lowest and highest volumes reported for the toll on grain trade in Dendermonde. According to David Nicholas (Nicholas 1978, 247-258), these volumes account for only half of the original amount that was entering upstream Ghent, so we have doubled all the figures from Dendermonde.

not put too much weight on the exact figures as they are crude estimates by an author who did not participate in the warfare and was being paid by an opponent of the revolt, Guy II of Châtillon. Froissart was perhaps inclined to exaggerate the Flemish threat in order to magnify the deeds of his employer. Therefore using his lower estimate for Ghent, we can guestimate a mobilisation rate of about 24 per cent of the able-bodied men or about 6 per cent of the total urban population based on the maximum number of men that could be mustered in the city in 1357 (i.e. 12,260 men: Van Werveke 1975). Such mobilisation rates might seem high for a pre-modern society, but much was at stake for the citizens during the revolt. When Ghent came under siege in 1381, even the young were called upon to defend their home. Froissart informs us that the age restriction of the recruits, normally between 20 and 60 years old, was reduced by five years (Froissart 2013, 61r; for age restrictions in the militia see Haemers & Verbist 2008, 291).

The involvement of a large proportion of the urban population is also reflected in the social profile of the combatants.[3] The fourteenth-century militia of Ghent comprised four groups. First, the lion's share of men was recruited from the craft guilds. The city housed 58 guilds, from low to highly skilled occupations, and membership implied military service in times of need. How many men each guild had to muster depended on its size, importance and financial abilities. Second, a smaller contingent was selected from the commercial elites, the *poorterij*. Given their wealth, they often provided the cavalry or simply paid a fee to be absolved from service. A third group consisted of hired professional soldiers, sometimes in the permanent service of the city, and paramilitary organisations such as the shooting guilds and the already mentioned White Hoods. Lastly, a multitude of men joined the militia even though they were free of conscription: engineers, drivers, foragers, etc (Haemers & Verbist 2008; Stabel 2011).

Sources and methodology

To map the evolution of wealth disparity in Ghent we employ probate inventories. Compared to tax registers, the most frequently used source for medieval inequality, they offer only a sample of the population rather than a cross-section, making it more difficult to estimate the distribution of the total population. Both sources are often socially biased, excluding groups of people at the top and bottom. Despite these drawbacks, probate inventories have already been successfully used by other scholars to produce assessments of wealth in historic societies (Lindert 1986; Canbakal & Filiztekin 2013). They have the advantage of providing a comprehensive picture of household assets and their composition. Tax registers, on the other hand, generally record only a single sum based on vague criteria. Moreover, the former tend to be more abundantly available, allowing for more frequent observations.

For the city of Ghent, probate inventories are preserved for the entire period between 1349 and 1789 (Municipal Archives Ghent, Oud Archief Stad Gent, series 330), making them one of the oldest and most complete series in Europe. They originate from the

---

3 We rely on the composition of the militia during other expeditions because the only quantitative source for the revolt, confiscations of landed property, suffers from too many methodological issues (Van Oost 1975).

Table 1. Wealth levels in the probate inventories of Ghent (1371-1400).

	Sample period		
	1371-75	1379-85	1395-1400
Total observations (N)	391	635	477
Median wealth (in kg silver)	10.11	12.65	9.17
Min wealth (in kg silver)	0.33	0.43	1.47
Max wealth (in kg silver)	557.97	455.55	575.24
Gini coefficient	0.68	0.58	0.67

custom of recording inheritances bequeathed to orphans, minor citizens who had lost one or both parents. Friends and family gathered before the aldermen to declare the possessions and appoint a guardian responsible for managing those assets within 40 days of death. Registration was not as uncommon as one would think since mortality rates were relatively high and emancipation quite late (the age of majority was 25 or when someone married). The fourteenth-century inventories represent on average 10 per cent of all married adult deaths according to Liliane Wynant (Wynant 1973, 50) and about 5 per cent of all adult deaths based on the urban mortality rates calculated by Peter Stabel for medieval Flanders (Stabel 1997, 119).

Certain groups are systematically excluded. The precondition of orphanhood implies that those without children, like clergymen or unmarried singles, do not show up in our analysis. The other precondition, citizenship, is less problematic. As in many other Flemish cities, citizenship in Ghent was free and thus, in theory, the inventories could include all social layers. In practice, the lower classes with limited to no assets did not register their inheritance as a fee of 40 deniers Flemish groats (the equivalent of four days of skilled work) had to be paid to the aldermen. Nevertheless, the level of recorded wealth (see table 1) seems to hint at a rather inclusive source with minimal values equal to 147 grammes of silver or 15 days of skilled work. At the upper end of society, the high nobility is also under-represented as they used their own courts to settle and register inheritances. Lower nobility, mostly daughters married to rich traders or merchants, are however well recorded (8.55 per cent of all inventories).

We employed the summaries of all fourteenth-century inventories compiled by Liliane Wynant (1989) to construct a database. To assess the impact of the popular uprising we have selected three sample periods, comprising the pre-war conditions (1371-75), the revolt (1379-85), and the situation after a decade (1395-1400). In total, the database contains 1,503 inventories. Generally, the probate inventories list information on annuities, chattels, liquid assets, houses and land, though the level of detail may vary from one to another. We have calculated the value of every component based on the inheritance laws (partible and impartible goods were recorded differently) and the reported value (sales, rents, leases). If no monetary assessment of a particular asset was given, the median value of all similar assets with a value in other inventories of the sample period was used as a proxy (for a more detailed description of the calculations see Espeel & Geens forthcoming, appendix 3). In a quarter of the inventories (n=389; 25.9 per cent) the surviving spouse chose not to register the inheritance, but instead paid a fee, called *afkoop*, to the heirs. While this practice obscured the composition of assets, it can be used to calculate total wealth.

The illusion of unchanging wealth inequality

At first glance, the Ghent Revolt seems to confirm the levelling theory of warfare when comparing Gini coefficients, a measure between zero and one, whereby a higher value represents more inequality. Table 1 reports a significant decrease in Gini coefficient (-15 per cent) between the sample of 1371-75 (Gini=0.68) and the revolt (0.58). Yet, the levelling impact of warfare was severely limited in time. Within years, inequality reached its pre-war levels. The Gini coefficient of our next sample period, only ten years later, is almost identical (Gini=0.67) to that of the first sample. At a general level, the case of the Ghent Revolt is thus consistent with earlier observations about the fleeting effects of popular uprisings. However, this traditional methodology of comparing a single measure over a prolonged time obscures important changes both during and after the war ((for a theoretical discussion on the shortcomings of general measures see chapter 20. How was city life?). While the latter will be discussed in the next section, the former is analysed below. Tracing year-to-year fluctuations in inequality and wealth levels has the downside of making samples less robust due to limited observations (on average, n = 91). We therefore focus on trends rather than absolute values and employ multiple measures of disparity (see Graph 1B and C). Drawbacks notwithstanding, an in-depht analysis of the different war events has the potential of untangling its complex and ambiguous impact on people's possessions.

The Ghent Revolt can be divided into three phases based on their different effects on wealth levels and disparities. The first phase, running until the spring of 1380, encompasses the conquest of the county by Ghent and its allies. After the assassination of the bailiff (see section 1), the revolting citizens pillaged several of the count's residences in the neighbourhood. A militia was sent to capture Ypres, gathering support along the way. The city, one of the three largest in the county together with Ghent and Bruges, was a potential ally as it had also suffered from centralisation politics and economic decline. When the rebels arrived, commoners of Ypres forced the count's soldiers out. Together with the Ghent militia, they marched onwards to Bruges. Here, too, some citizens were sympathetic to the revolt and refused to take up arms against those of Ghent. Fearing repression, a large proportion of loyalists, mostly wealthy merchants, fled the city, leaving control in rebel hands. Taken by surprise by the speed of the revolt, the count managed to fortify and hold only the cities of Dendermonde and Oudenaarde. In the winter the outnumbered Louis of Male agreed to a peace treaty (for these and following details about the course of the revolt see de Muynck 1951; Murray 2005, 16-38; Vaughan 2009, vol. 3, 413-510; Froissart 2013).

Graph 1A plots the evolution of median and average wealth levels, representing the fortune of the middle classes. Then, two graphs depict the evolution of wealth inequality in the three sample periods. Graph 1B employs the share of wealth owned by the top 10 per cent and the Gini coefficient. Graph 1C shows how much more the top 10 per cent of society owned compared to the bottom 10 per cent, the so-called decile dispersion ratio. All graphs show a significant increase during the first phase. Median and average values reached their highest level in 1380, while disparities widened by approximately 15 per cent. Such an evolution is in line with the theory that inequality increases within the victor's society (see introduction). The first phase of the revolt was indeed a clear success for Ghent as it met little resistance and confiscations of property from loyalists brought wealth to the rebels. One possible explanation for the simultaneous increase in both the Gini coefficient and the decile dispersion ratio is the way these confiscations were handled. Just as during the revolts at the end of the Roman Republic (Scheidel 2007 and 2017; see introduction), benefits may have been distributed unevenly among the different classes in Ghent, disproportionately rewarding those at the top.

The newly acquired riches were however short-lived. The tide turned when Louis of Male broke the peace in the spring of 1380. During this second phase, Ghent was on the defensive. A comital army was mustered to recapture all the revolting cities. By the autumn Ghent stood alone. The count tried to besiege and starve the city. Troops from both sides ravaged the countryside during one of the several skirmishes, especially near the city, the Vier Ambachten in the north and near Dendermonde and Oudenaarde in the south-east. The situation became dire by 1382. Driven by famine, the Ghent militia made a desperate sortie towards Bruges. Taken by surprise, the disorganised comital forces were defeated. Louis of Male, residing in Bruges, barely managed to escape to northern France. While the victory motivated other towns to rejoin the revolt, it also infuriated the French child king who was facing multiple other revolts in his kingdom. One of his uncles and regents, Philip the Bold, who was married to the daughter and heiress of the count, convinced him to react strongly upon the expulsion of one of his wealthiest vassals. To secure his inheritance, Philip led a large army towards Flanders and crushed the revolutionaries at Westrozebeke on 27 November. Harsh repression followed: Kortrijk was plundered, rebel leaders were beheaded, and Bruges had to pay high fines. Ghent, on the other hand, escaped retaliation as winter forced the French troops back home.

In stark contrast to the start of the revolt, the second phase caused massive destruction. Wealth levels declined sharply (graph 1A), especially for the cream of society, as is evident from their decreasing share of total wealth (graph 1B). Lower classes were apparently less affected, resulting in lower inequality (graph 1B and C). The heterogenous impact can be explained through differences in wealth composition. Probate inventories of lower classes (QU1) were mainly composed of capital and houses (representing 70.6 per cent of the total value), assets concentrated in the city. Those of the higher classes contained more land (29 per cent of the total value for QU5 vs. 18.2 per cent for QU1) and annuities (26.6 per cent vs. 1.5 per cent). Whereas the city itself was spared from destruction, the war had been devastating for the countryside. The inventories report multiple burned farmsteads. Land values had dropped to one third of their pre-war levels (Thoen 1988, 879-886). Moreover, ongoing warfare hindered farmers from working the land and citizens from collecting leasehold rents. Debts and annuities were likewise difficult to collect (Nicholas 1987, 11-16). These evolutions were detrimental to the wealth of the higher classes. A wave of plague in 1380-82 possibly reinforced the levelling process. Scholars generally associate pandemics with decreasing inequality (Alfani 2017, 1095-1099) but, for the case of Ghent, the precise impact of plague is impossible to assess as mortality from disease cannot be discerned in the probate inventories.

Wealth and inequality in the probate inventories of Ghent, 1371-1400 (n=1,503)

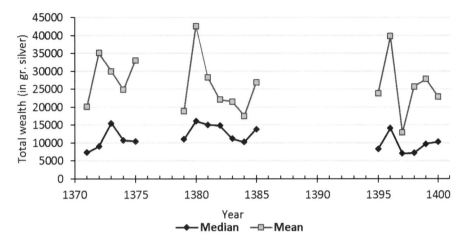

Graph 1A. Total wealth levels

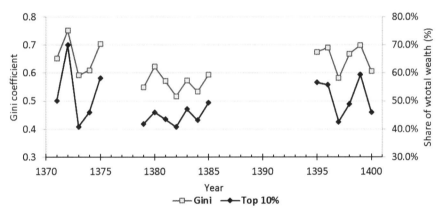

Graph 1B. Wealth inequality

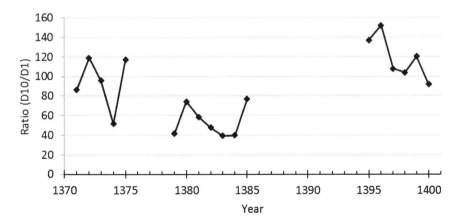

Graph 1C. Wealth ratio between top and bottom 10%

During the third phase, the uprising became overshadowed by the Hundred Years' Wars. In the spring of 1383, the English invaded the county under the guise of a crusade against Clementists. In practice, the severe disruption of the all-important wool trade to Flanders due to French embargoes was a more decisive motive (Lloyd 1977, 225-230). After English troops had conquered several coastal towns, the militia of Ghent joined them to besiege Ypres, which failed miserably. The militia returned home and captured the city of Oudenaarde while the French army was too preoccupied with repelling the English. Early in 1384, Louis of Male died and was succeeded by the already mentioned Philip the Bold, duke of Burgundy. This change brought no end to the conflict as hostilities flared up again over the control of Oudenaarde. In a bold move to take Bruges by surprise, the Ghent militia captured the port town of Damme, which controlled the Zwin estuary between Bruges and the North Sea. This loss was a disaster for the French, who were planning an invasion in England from the estuary. The royal army was immediately diverted to Damme, but the Ghent militia escaped and the damage was already done. The Four Offices, north of Ghent, were pillaged as retaliation before the royal army was disbanded. Philip the Bold now understood that he could not afford an enemy at home during an invasion of England. He therefore proposed a peace treaty, pardoning Ghent on all accounts in exchange for its renunciation of the English alliance. On 18 December 1385 the war finally ended.

With the exception of the Vier Ambachten, destructions in the proximity of Ghent were limited during the final phase of the war. The trade embargoes on English wool were however catastrophic for the already suffering urban economy. Production in the textile industry must have slumped due to a lack of raw materials. With declining income for a large share of the population median and average wealth levels declined (Graph 1A). Disparities widened as higher classes were comparatively less dependent on labour, since they had more diversified income streams, including more annuities and rents (see wealth compositions QU5 above; graph 1B and C). These trends continued after the peace treaty. Apparently, lower classes had more problems in recovering from the warfare (the share of wealth owned by D1-3 dropped by half between 1379 and 1400, whereas those of D8-10 increased). Inequality measures accordingly achieved their pre-war levels (graph 1B). The similarities in inequality before and after the revolt however mask the negative impact of the conflict and the struggling economy. Median wealth levels declined to an all-time low (graph 1A), while the decile dispersion ratio soared to unprecedented heights in the last decade of the fourteenth century (graph 1C).

The spoils of war: changes in landownership

In spite of all the negative consequences of the revolt, it also provided some opportunities. The extensive destruction of the countryside around Ghent (see section 3) resulted in severe disruption of the land market. Prices dropped by two thirds and recovered only slowly over the course of two decades (Thoen 1978; Thoen 1988, 879-886). Citizens who had some resources to spare could buy land at favourable rates. Such assets were seen as safe investments even in normal years. Since the urban economy had suffered greatly during the uprising, investments in the countryside probably appealed to an even larger share of the population when the war was finally over. Furthermore, the increased migration from the countryside to Ghent during the revolt might have positively affected the amount of land owned by citizens, if the migrants settled and acquired citizenship (Nicholas 1987, 12).[4]

The average size of all lands reported per probate inventory confirms this hypothesis. In the first sample period, 1371-75, the average size was 5.07 hectares (see table 2A). During the revolt, the figure decreased to 3.58 hectares. (-29 per cent) because of confiscations and destructions. If this trend is representative for the entire countryside of Ghent, this would imply that at least one quarter of the cultivated acreage was affected by warfare. According to Erik Thoen, pre-war levels of cultivation would not be reached until the turn of the century. At that time, the average size of land owned per citizen with a probate inventory had more than doubled, namely to 7.46 hectares in the sample period of 1395-1400. Even compared to the higher levels of the first sample, this figure is remarkably high (+47 per cent). In sum, the war indirectly transferred a substantial part of wealth from the countryside to Ghent (for the evolution of urban landholding in coastal Flanders see Lambrecht Chapter 8).

Map 1 locates all land recorded in the inventories for the pre- and post-war sample periods. Quantitative evolutions between sample periods are given per administrative district (castellany) in table 2A. In general, clear regional disparities in the land acquisitions by Ghent citizens can be observed. A first group of districts is characterised by temporary increases in landownership during the revolt. This trend is found in castellanies not neighbouring Ghent (other in table 2A) and, even more pronounced, in the Franc of Bruges, albeit the share of these castellanies in the total acreage remained limited compared to others (from 3 per cent of the total before the conflict to 9 per cent during the war). Immigration of revolutionaries is the most plausible explanation here. The increased landownership in the Franc of Bruges for example, was concentrated around Eeklo, a town that was probably sympathetic to the revolt given its intimate social and commercial ties with Ghent (Nicholas 1989). The second group of districts consists of castellanies that witnessed a rapid restoration after extensive destruction during the revolt, resulting in relatively stable acreage over the whole period. This was the case in Kortrijk and Oudenaarde (a total growth of respectively 0 per cent and -6 per cent). The last group comprises castellanies with strong growth rates, especially after the war. Here, increasing investments rather than immigration must have been the primary driver, considering the timing. While investments increased in already established markets, they were even stronger in regions where pre-war acreage had been limited, such as in the Vier Ambachten (+473 per cent) and the Land of Waas (+197 per cent). One possible explanation for choosing these districts might be their geographical location. The castellanies with strong growth rates are those situated farthest from the crown lands of France, which made them, in theory, more resilient to French invasions.

Remarkably, the explosion of absentee landownership by citizens was not primarily driven by the elites. In fact, the top of society was less inclined to invest in the countryside or migrate from it after the war. The likelihood of reporting landed property in their probate inventories declined by about 6 per cent between 1385 and 1400 (see QU5 in table 2B). Those

---

4   *Buitenpoorters* (citizens living in the countryside) were not recorded in the probate inventories and therefore have no impact on the evolution of landownership (Thoen 1988, 25).

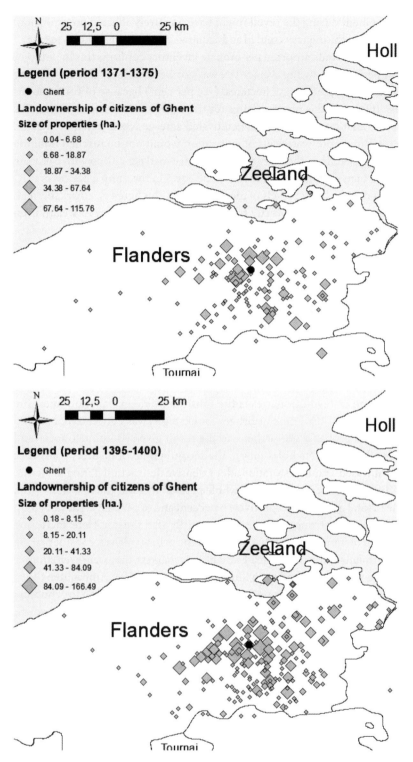

Map 1. Geographical distribution of landownership by citizens in 1371-75 and 1395-1400.

Source: Stef Espeel and Sam Geens, map 1.

Table 2A. Geographical distribution of landownership by citizens per castellany (1371-1400)

Castellany	Average size per inventory (in hectare)					
	1371-75	Growth	1379-85	Growth	1395-1400	Total growth
Franc of Bruges	0.007	1830%	0.137	-93%	0.010	41%
Courtrai	0.415	-91%	0.038	934%	0.392	-6%
Oudburg	2.683	-31%	1.852	81%	3.343	25%
Oudenaarde	0.165	-52%	0.079	109%	0.166	0%
Land of Aalst	1.320	-31%	0.916	132%	2.126	61%
Land of Dendermonde	0.059	10%	0.065	161%	0.169	186%
Land of Waas	0.138	63%	0.225	197%	0.667	385%
Vier Ambachten	0.123	-27%	0.090	473%	0.514	318%
Other	0.161	9%	0.175	-55%	0.078	-51%
TOTAL	5.072	-29%	3.576	109%	7.464	47%

Table 2B. Landownership in the probate inventories of Ghent per quintile (1371-1400)

Quintile	Reporting land (% within quintile)			Median size (in hectare)		
	1371-75	1379-85	1395-1400	1371-75	1379-85	1395-1400
QU1	33.8%	37.3%	23.9%	0.53	0.67	0.89
QU2	40.3%	37.6%	47.0%	1.34	1.54	1.43
QU3	55.9%	46.3%	70.4%	2.45	3.59	3.3
QU4	72.2%	65.8%	77.6%	4.37	4.01	7.69
QU5	95.3%	94.8%	88.9%	20.9	16.05	25.76

who did report such assets, however, owned significantly more (+23.2 per cent by hectare) compared to pre-war levels. As a result, the top of society still held approximately three quarters of all land owned by citizens despite increasing access to those assets for a large part of the population. Indeed, increasing investment and, to a lesser extent, immigration of landowners is visible for all but the lowest classes (QU2-4), especially for middle groups: the likelihood of reporting land increased from 46.3 per cent to an impressive 70.4 per cent for QU3! The size of those assets remained relatively stable, suggesting a democratisation rather than a specialisation of the investment pattern. For the lowest classes (QU1) the detrimental impact of the Ghent revolt can once again be attested to as the likelihood of reporting land in probate inventories declined by about 10 per cent.

Conclusions

Despite bold claims being made about the longlasting levelling effect of warfare, popular uprisings do not seem to fit this model, even when, as in the case of the Ghent revolt, a large share of the population was involved and destruction was extensive. We observed varying trends during the conflict, suggesting once again that warfare has no predetermined effect, but is rather dependent on the nature of the events. Inequality initially increased, possibly due to the uneven distribution of gains from confiscations, then decreased significantly afterwards because of destruction of the wealth of elites, and moved back upwards as the economic damage affected lower classes disproportionally in the last phase. Taken as a whole, the period of the revolt stands out as one of low inequality but, in the long run, our results seem to confirm earlier observations about the limited impact of popular uprisings. After only a decade, disparity had returned to its pre-war levels. However, looking beyond general measures of inequality revealed important shifts in the distribution of a certain type of wealth.

Landownership among the citizens of Ghent increased significantly after the peace treaty of 1385. Favourable prices, caused by the large-scale destruction of the countryside, and a slumbering urban economy, compounded by the trade embargoes during the war, attracted many citizens to invest in the countryside rather than the city. Immigration from the countryside probably contributed to this trend, but geographical differences suggest only a limited and temporary effect. The boom in landownership after the revolt was mainly driven by the middle classes. Consequently, the war of 1379-85 did have long-term effects on inequality. A share of wealth was transferred from the countryside to the city. Without information on the profile of the sellers it is hard to estimate whether disparities accordingly widened within village communities or merely passed from one absentee owner to another. Likewise, there are not the sources to generalise the case of Ghent to the whole county, though in certain areas, such as in Ypres, conditions were similar.

For the city of Ghent, the widespread ownership of land probably helped to keep inequality between the middle classes and elites more in check. Given that land prices and leases reached new heights while wages remained relatively stable during the fifteenth century, disparities between the two classes would have been greater if the former had not gained access to those assets (Thoen 1988, 879-886; Munro 2005, 1038-1076). A tax register of 1492, albeit not directly comparable to the sources used here as it pertains to income rather than wealth, still shows a relatively low Gini coefficient (0.55) a century later (Blockmans 1973). On the other hand, the fortunes of those at the bottom of society had been negatively influenced by the revolt. Since they owned no land, the gap with the other classes probably further increased and remained difficult to bridge thereafter. In this sense, disparities in late medieval Ghent resembles those of contemporary Belgium: a strong and large middle class that is relatively closed to the poorer strata (Kuypers & Marx 2016). The war of 1379-85 thus played an important part in shaping inequalities in the long run through a fundamental shift in wealth composition among the different classes.

References

Alfani, Guido. 2010. "Wealth Inequalities and Population Dynamics in Early Modern Northern Italy." *Journal of Interdisciplinary History* XL, no. 4 (Spring): 513-549.

Alfani, Guido. 2017. "Long-term trends in economic inequality: the case of the Florentine state, c. 1300-1800." *The Economic History Review* 70, no. 4 (Winter): 1072-1102.

Alfani, Guido, and Matteo Di Tullio. 2019. *The Lion's Share: Inequality and the Rise of the Fiscal State in Preindustrial Europe*. Cambridge: Cambridge University Press.

Alfani, Guido, Felix Schaff and Victoria Gierok. 2017. "Economic inequality in preindustrial Germany: a long-run view (fourteenth to nineteenth centuries)." *Dondena Working Papers* 110: 1-46.

Barrett, James. 2008. "What caused the Viking Age?" *Antiquity* 82: 671-685.

Bircan, Çağatay, Tilman Brück and Marc Vothknecht. 2017. "Violent Conflict and Inequality." *Oxford Development Studies* 45, no. 2 (Summer): 125-144.

Blockmans, Wim. 1971. "Peiligen naar de sociale strukturen te Gent tijdens de late 15e eeuw." In *Studiën betreffende de sociale strukturen te Brugge, Kortrijk en Gent in de 14e en 15e eeuw*, ed. Wim Blockmans et al., 215-262. Heule: UGA.

Blockmans, Wim. 1988. "Alternatives to monarchical centralisation: the great tradition of revolt in Flanders and Brabant." In *Republiken und Republikanismus im Europa der frühen Neuzeit*, ed. Helmut Koenigsberger, 145-154. Munich: Oldenbourg.

Canbakal, Hülya, and Alpay Filiztekin. 2013. "Wealth and Inequality in Ottoman Bursa, 1500-1840." Unpublished conference paper, Houston, TX: The Political Economy of the Muslim World.

Cederman, Lars-Erik, Kristian Skrede Gleditsch and Halvard Buhaug. 2013. *Inequality, Grievances, and Civil War*. Cambridge: Cambridge University Press.

Coşgel, Metin, and Boğaç Ergene. 2012. "Inequality of Wealth in the Ottoman Empire: War, Weather, and Long-Term Trends in Eighteenth-Century Kastamonu." *The Journal of Economic History* 72, no. 2 (Summer): 308-331.

Croenen, Godfried, and Natasha Romanova, eds. 2013. Koninklijke Bibliotheek Brussel, ms. II 2552. In *the Online Froissart*, ed. Peter Ainsworth and Godfried Croenen, version 1.5. Last modified 2013. https://www.hrionline.ac.uk/onlinefroissart.

de Muynck, Raymond. 1951. "De Gentse Oorlog (13749-1385). Oorzaken en karakter." *Handelingen der Maatschappij voor Geschiedenis en Oudheidkunde te Gent* V: 305-318.

Espeel, Stef, and Sam Geens. Forthcoming. "Feeding Inequalities: the role of economic inequalities and the urban market in late medieval food security. The case of fourteenth-century Ghent." In *Disuguaglianza economica nelle società preindustriali: cause ed effetti*. Atti delle settimane di studi 53. Florence: Firenze University Press.

Fjelde, Hanne, and Gudrun Østby. 2014. "Socioeconomic Inequality and Communal Conflict: A Disaggregated Analysis of Sub-Saharan Africa, 1990-2008." *International Interactions* 40, no. 5 (Autumn): 737-762.

Froissart, Jean. 2013. "Chroniques de France, d'Angleterre et des païs voisins." Translated by Keira Borrill. In *the Online Froissart*, ed. Peter Ainsworth and Godfried Croenen, version 1.5. Last modified 2013. https://www.hrionline.ac.uk/onlinefroissart.

Haemers, Jelle, and Botho Verbist. 2008. "Het Gentse gemeenteleger in het laatste kwart van de vijftiende eeuw: een politieke, financiële en militaire analyse van de stadsmilitie." *Handelingen der maatschappij voor geschiedenis en oudheidkunde te Gent* 62: 291-325.

Kuypers, Sarah, and Ive Marx. 2016. "Social concertation and middle-class stability in Belgium." In *Europe's disappearing middle class? Evidence from the world of work*, ed. Daniel Vaughan-Whitehead, 112-159. Cheltenham: Edward Elgar Publishing.

Lindert, Peter. 1986. "Unequal English Wealth since 1670." *Journal of Political Economy* 94, no. 6 (Winter): 1127-1167.

Lloyd, Terrence. 1977. *The English Wool Trade in the Middle Ages*. Cambridge: Cambridge University Press.

MacCulloch, Robert. 2005. "Income Inequality and the Taste for Revolution." *The Journal of Law and Economics* 48, no. 1 (Spring): 93-123.

Milanovic, Branko. 2018. "Towards an explanation of inequality in premodern societies; the role of colonies, urbanization, and high population density." *The Economic History Review* 71, no. 4 (Winter): 1029-1047.

Miller, Hartley, and Godfried Croenen, eds. 2013. Besançon, Bibliothèque municipale, MS 865. In *the Online Froissart*, ed. Peter Ainsworth and Godfried Croenen, version 1.5. Last modified 2013. https://www.hrionline.ac.uk/onlinefroissart.

Munro, John. 2005. "Builders' Wages in Southern England and the Southern Low Countries, 1346 -1500: A Comparative Study of Trends in and Levels of Real Incomes." In *L'Edilizia prima della rivoluzione industriale, secoli XIII-XVIII*, ed. Simonetta Cavaciocchi. Atti delle Settimana di Studi e altri convegni 36: 1013-1076.

Murray, James. 2005. *Bruges, Cradle of Capitalism, 1280-1390*. Cambridge: Cambridge University Press.

Nicholas, David. 1978. "The Scheldt trade and the 'Ghent War' of 1379-1385." *Bulletin de la Commission royale d'histoire* 144: 189-359.

Nicholas, David. 1987. *The Metamorphism of a Medieval Town. Ghent in the Age of the Arteveldes, 1302-1390*. Leiden: Brill.

Nicholas, David. 1989. "The Marriage and the Meat Hall." *Medieval Prosopography* 10:1 (Spring): 23-52.

Onorato, Massimiliano, Kenneth Scheve and David Stasavage. 2014. "Technology and the Era of the Mass Army." *The Journal of Economic History* 74, no. 2 (Summer): 449-481.

Pfister, Ulrich. Forthcoming. "Economic Inequality in Germany, *c.* 1500-1800." In *Disuguaglianza economica nelle società preindustriali: cause ed effetti*. Atti delle settimane di studi 53.

Prados de la Escosura, Leandro. 2008. "Inequality, poverty and the Kuznets curve in Spain, 1850-2000." *European Review of Economic History* 12: 287-324.

Scheidel, Walter. 2007. "A Model of Real Income Growth in Roman Italy." *Historia: Zeitschrift Für Alte Geschichte* 56, no. 3 (Autumn): 322-346.

Scheidel, Walter. 2017. *The Great Leveler. Violence and the History of Inequality from the Stone Age to the Twenty-First Century*. Princeton, NJ: Princeton University Press.

Stabel, Peter. 1997. *Dwarfs among giants: the Flemish urban network in the late Middle Ages*. Leuven: Garant.

Stabel, Peter. 2011. "Militaire organisatie, bewapening en wapenbezit in het laatmiddeleeuwse Brugge." *Revue belge de philologie et d'histoire* 89, nos. 3-4 (Autumn): 1049-1073.

Stabel, Peter. Forthcoming. *A Capital of Fashion. Guilds and Economic Change in Late Medieval Bruges*.

Thoen, Erik. 1978. "Oorlogen en platteland. Sociale en ekonomische aspekten van militaire destruktie in Vlaanderen tijdens de late middeleeuwen en de vroege moderne tijden." *Tijdschrift voor Geschiedenis* 91: 363-376.

Thoen, Erik. 1988. "Landbouwekonomie en bevolking in Vlaanderen gedurende de late Middeleeuwen en het begin van de Moderne Tijden." Unpublished PhD thesis, Ghent: Rijksuniversiteit Gent.

Thomas, Hugh. 2008. *The Norman Conquest: England After William the Conqueror*. Lanham, MD: Rowman & Littlefield.

Tilly, Charles. 1993. *European revolutions, 1492-1992*. Oxford: Blackwell Publishers.

Van Oost, Angeline. 1975. "Sociale stratifikatie van de Gentse opstandelingen van 1379- 1385. Een kritische benadering van konfiskatiedokumenten." *Handelingen der maatschappij voor geschiedenis en oudheidkunde te Gent* XXIX: 59-92.

Van Werveke, Hans. 1975. "Het bevolkingscijfer van de stad Gent in de 14[de] eeuw. Het laatste woord?" *Studia Historica Gadensia* 195: 449-465.

Vaughan, Richard. 2009. *Philip the Bold: The Formation of the Burgundian State*. Vol. 3. London: Faber and Faber.

Wynant, Liliane. 1973. "Peiling naar de vermogensstructuur te Gent op basis van de staten van goed 1380-1389." In *Studien betreffende de sociale strukturen te Brugge, Kortrijk en Gent in de 14e en 15e eeuw*, ed. Wim Blockmans et al., 48-138. Heule: UGA.

Wynant, Liliane. 1989. *Regesten van de Gentse Staten van Goed*. Brussels: Koninklijke Commissie voor Geschiedenis.

ROGIER VAN KOOTEN

Levelling Through Space?

The Redistributive Capacity of Demographic Decline in Antwerp's Darkest Hour (1584-1586)

Introduction

Warfare can be a powerful leveller. After centuries of increasing wealth inequality, the First and the Second World Wars coincided with a fundamental reshuffling in the distribution of wealth. Apart from the direct destruction of movable and immovable capital, desperate states finally introduced substantial taxes on wealth and income from capital. And warfare sacrifices created the political leverage needed to elaborate and consolidate the post-1950 welfare state (Piketty 2014). Walter Scheidel, who studied the history of human inequality from the end of the last Ice Age, even claims that *only* catastrophic societal disruptions like warfare (and to a lesser extent famines and epidemics) were able to interrupt the otherwise autonomous and unstoppable process of rising inequality (Scheidel 2017). Not every war, plague or earthquake, however, was a levelling crisis. The more a crisis penetrated society as a whole by disrupting the functioning of a community and mobilising people and resources, the stronger and more sustainable its effects on the redistribution of wealth and income. As Scheidel demonstrates, history provides us with plenty of opportunities to study this 'levelling' mechanism in more detail. However, most studies stay on macro level, following the long-term evolution of Gini or Theil coefficients on country, region or city level without really understanding the redistributive dynamics underneath the surface. As I will argue in this chapter, a spatial approach to urban inequality might offer a better understanding of the interaction between warfare and inequality. Space allows us to move the scale of analysis from the city as a whole to different districts or households within the city which might have witnessed highly contrasting experiences of welfare and inequality in the wake of disruptive warfare. Moreover, these divergences might shed light on the dynamics driving the presumed 'levelling' characteristics of warfare. The observation of intra-urban divergences in welfare and inequality changes might reflect the pre-existing vulnerability of particular groups and districts to disruption following warfare. If the impact of warfare mainly affects households and districts with particular features, the levelling effect of warfare may be the result of these specific features. Space thus allows us to uncover drivers of inequality changes.

This contribution will use 1584 Antwerp as a case study to investigate how sudden *demographic decline*, predominantly mass emigration following a period of prolonged (civil) warfare and famine, affected social topography and intra-urban *spatial inequality*. House rental values will be used as proxy for income distributions. According to several

Rogier van Kooten • University of Antwerp

Inequality and the City in the Low Countries (1200-2020), ed. by Bruno BLONDÉ, Sam GEENS, Hilde GREEFS, Wouter RYCKBOSCH, Tim SOENS & Peter STABEL, SEUH 50 (Turnhout, 2020), pp. 231-249.

 DOI 10.1484/M.SEUH-EB.5.120448

scholars house rental values are often our best proxy of residents' economic wellbeing, although we should keep in mind that the percentage of household budget spent on housing is inversely proportional to household income, and house rental values will therefore understate the real economic inequality (Hanus 2013, 743, Alfani and Ryckbosch 2016, 143-153, Soltow and Zanden 1998). However, since only relative redistribution effects of depopulation are of primary concern here, house rental values are satisfactory for the purpose of this contribution.

Two questions will be addressed. First, how do we measure spatial inequality in 1584 Antwerp? This question is closely related to the field of residential segregation, but not necessarily the same. Second, how did the demographic shock of 1586 change Antwerp's socio-spatial stratification or, in other words, did inequality level through space?

Antwerp in 1584

In Europe the period between approximately 1550 and 1650 was extremely violent. The Eighty and Thirty Years' Wars and the Italian Wars joined forces with plague and famine and disrupted life in many cities in the Low Countries, the German lands and the Italian peninsula. Antwerp around 1584 provides a unique case study from this period. In the sixteenth century, it was a real merchant capitalist 'boom town'. Between 1495 and 1568 Antwerp's population more than doubled from 48,000 to more than 100,000 and also the number of houses doubled. This resulted in a real 'Megalopolis' accounting for 42 per cent of the total urban population (cities above 5,000 inhabitants) in Brabant (Soly 1978, 95-97, Van der Wee and Materné 1993, 20). In his study of the entreprises of Gilbert Van Schoonbeke Hugo Soly unveiled how real property speculation and exploitation became widespread in the wake of this rapid expansion (Soly 1977). No less than 80 per cent of all houses were rental houses, a very high percentage compared those in Ghent (53 per cent in 1571) and Bruges (66 per cent in 1583) around the same period (Deneweth 2007, 537). Although Antwerp had passed its demographic and economic peak around 1565, in 1582 the city was still one of the largest cities north of the Alps (almost 84,000 inhabitants) and certainly by far the most important city of the Low Countries.

In 1584 the city had already experienced two decades of religious disruptions between Catholics and mainly Calvinists, starting with the 'Beeldenstorm' in 1566 (Marnef 1996). Between 1577 and 1584 Antwerp was the capital of the Calvinistic Republic. In 1579, King Philip II appointed Alexander Farnese as governor of the Habsburg Netherlands to reconquer the rebellious cities. After a siege of more than a year, on 17 August 1585 Antwerp surrendered. This did not imply the end of hardship for the population. Farnese's *reconciliation terms* gave the non-Catholic citizens of Antwerp four years to convert to Catholicism or sell their property and leave the city (Van Roey 1985, 78). The continuing war with the provinces in the North after 1585 and the blockade of the Scheldt sharply reduced the opportunities for trade. The reduced access to international markets and supplies also hit local industries, especially textiles (Thijs 1987, 99). Additionally, the summers of 1585 and 1586 were extremely wet and harvests failed

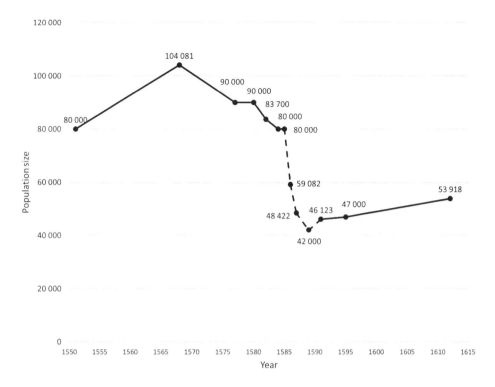

Figure 1: Antwerp's depopulation gains momentum in 1585 by war, famine and migration

Source: (Van Roey 1975)

widely. The destruction of many farms in the surrounding countryside by plundering armies further reduced the food supply (Thijs 1987, 99). As a consequence, there was hunger and the price of bread grains in Antwerp (the major food component in those days) skyrocketed (Scholliers 1955, 80-103). In sum, a cocktail of calamities created a true societal disruption and caused a massive migration of people to the German lands, England and the rebellious provinces in the North (Briels 1978, Asaert 2004) (figure 1). This catastrophic course of events sets the stage for our study of intra-urban spatial redistribution of inequality.

Reconstructing Antwerp 1584: methodology and sources

Worried by the mass emigration and the impending food crisis in 1586, the city magistrate ordered two inspections, one in in May and one in October (Scholliers 1960, 57-58, 195-198). The heads of neighbourhoods visited their patches street by street, counting families, their grain stocks and registering vacant houses. The results of eight of the 13 wards visited in the October have survived in detail. These are a fairly representative sample of the city as a whole, covering both central and peripheral areas. These data were integrated into a socio-spatial reconstruction of 1584 Antwerp.

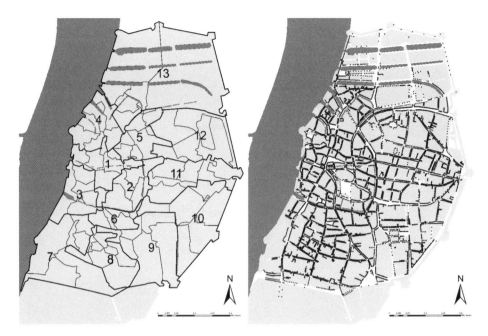

Figure 2: Mapping of Antwerp in 1584: 12,500 properties, almost 13,500 households in 13 wards and 79 neighbourhoods

Early modern fiscal sources should be interpreted with care if used for the reconstruction of social stratifications, since most are incomplete or provide biased information. Regularly, inhabitants below certain wealth criteria or houses below certain values were excluded from tax lists (Blondé 1987, 21-31, Dambruyne 2002, 363). Fortunately, the 1584 data are extremely complete, detailing even the smallest back alleys and households in extreme poverty.

In 2017 the GIStorical Antwerp II project[1] reconstructed 1584 Antwerp on household level using a Geographical Information System (GIS). This created a 'historical laboratory' in the true sense, combining house rental values, house ownership, occupational data, wealth taxation and even the religious belief of almost 13,500 households (Bavel and Curtis 2015, 1-32, Janssens and Jongepier 2015, 49-62). Indispensable for this study was the 'Kadastrale Ligger van Antwerpen (1584-1585)' (Degueldre 2011).[2] Since detailed cadastral maps did not exist before 1830, only some of the houses could be located accurately. The others were interpolated using a technique called 'linear referencing'.[3] This was possible because the city tax officers walked through the streets in clear traceable directions. Based on the

1   University of Antwerp / Hercules Foundation, see https://www.uantwerpen.be/gistorical-antwerp/.
2   The 'Kadastrale Ligger' is based on several underlying sources like the 'Register inhouden[de] de huysen ende woonyngen bevonden inden I. II. III. IIII. V. VI. en[de] VII. wycken deser stadt van Antwerpe[n]. 1584', several fiscal sources and the neighbourhood registers, which altogether detailed owners, tenants, house rental values and property taxes and were supplemented, using other sources, with professions, house names and house features. We are very grateful to Dr. Heidi Deneweth of the Vrije Universiteit Brussel (VUB) for the conversion of the 'Kadaster' to Excel, which reduced our processing time significantly.
3   Based on two corner houses the computer positions the intermediate houses by equal distribution. This means that the houses are positioned in the right order but not necessarily according to their size and the distance between them. For more information about linear referencing see https://desktop.arcgis.com/en/arcmap/10.3/

ward books (wijkboeken), covering the evolution of house ownership in the period of roughly 1560-1795[4] and the French cadaster from 1796[5] (the first to use house numbers), quality checks were carried out on the linear reference results. Since most of Antwerp's street patterns and housing blocks were more or less 'frozen' between 1585 and 1800 many links could be established between sixteenth-century descriptions and eighteenth-century registrations. Figure 2 shows the results of this mapping process:

Socio-spatial patterns of income and inequality

For a long time urban social geography was dominated by the models of Gideon Sjoberg and James Vance. Sjoberg claimed that in pre-industrial cities political and religious elites tended to concentrate in the city centre, whereas James Vance stressed the rising importance of location in relation to price determination on the urban real property market in times of growth. According to Vance, the growing competition for 'premium' locations in the busiest spots in the city centre was eventually followed by a relocation of the wealthy in the outskirts of town (Sjoberg 1965, Vance 1971, 107-111). This would result in segregation patterns on the level of zones or wards. As long as one's perspective is city level, these models hold fairly well. But, with respect to pre-modern cities, other authors have drawn our attention to the large diversity at neighbourhood and street level (Langton 1975, 21-22). According to Clé Lesger and Marco van Leeuwen, it is predominantly at the level of frontages that residential segregation existed, the rich generally occupying the houses facing the main streets and the poor the back alleys (Lesger and Leeuwen 2012, 354). Although this allowed great inequality within short radius, according to some scholars it also enhanced neighbourhood cohesion and facilitated mutual support (Lis and Soly 1993, 1-30).[6]

Before investigating whether late sixteenth-century Antwerp conformed to one of these models, we first have to analyse inequality in house rental values on the level of the city as a whole. This analysis is based on the 12,192 households in the inhabited and assessed houses.[7] The median house rental value was 30 Carolus guilders and inequality ratios using Gini and Theil coefficients were respectively 0.48 and 0.41, comparable to cities like Bruges or 's-Hertogenbosch (Ryckbosch 2015, 8).

To put these inequality levels in perspective a comparison can be made with nearby Ghent (Dambruyne 2001, 54, 2002, 363-368)[8] (Table 1). The median house rental value of 30 Carolus guilders in Antwerp is more than double the value of 1571 Ghent, whereas nominal wages in Antwerp (skilled artisans) were only 23 per cent higher than in Ghent

---

guide-books/linear-referencing/what-is-linear-referencing.htm. An interesting example of pre-cadastral reconstruction in GIS is a study by Anne Galanaud about socio-spatial consequences of plague in medieval Dijon (Galanaud 2009).

4   FAA – PK2256-2278 (Wijkboeken Ketgen), PK2279-2303 (1st series), PK2304-PK2328 (2nd series).

5   FAA – 12#4262 – 12#4265, MA#2631.

6   It is therefore remarkable that, according to some scholars, post-modern cities are on the way back to fragmentation and that this may lead to social breakdown (Alves 2016, 413-414).

7   The citadel was excluded because of its specific military character.

8   Using a comparable source based on very complete house rental values.

Table 1: rental values (in guilders) and inequality scores in sixteenth-century Antwerp and Ghent

	Population	Median	Average	Total value
Antwerp (1584)	80,000	30	50.4	613,143.60
Ghent (1571)	39,200	12	16.4	136,912.00

Sources: 1584 GISdatabase and (Dambruyne 2002).

Table 2: inequality in house rental values: percentage of households per decile in Antwerp and Ghent

	Bottom					Top				
% households	10%	20%	30%	40%	50%	50%	40%	30%	20%	10%
Antwerp (1584)	1.62	4.24	7.87	12.4	18.2	81.8	74.5	65.4	53.6	36.0
Ghent (1571)	2.0	5.4	9.4	14.5	20.9	79.1	71.3	61.2	48.7	31.5

Sources: 1584 GISdatabase and (Dambruyne 2002)

(Dambruyne 2002, 375). The high prices of land reflect the extraordinary character of Antwerp as a merchant capitalist boom town. Does this also mean that Antwerp's population was much more polarised than that of Ghent or other cities in the southern Low Countries? Based on house rental values, this conclusion is not obvious (Table 2). More than one third of the house rental value of Antwerp in 1584 was concentrated in the hands of only 10 per cent of the households. In contrast, the bottom 50 per cent accounted for only 20 per cent of the aggregated rental value. However, the differences with Ghent are not impressive: the overall picture is fairly similar. In other words, Antwerp distinguishes itself more by the extraordinarily high level of house rent, and less by the internal allocation among different types of households.

But, as we claimed in the introduction, aggregate levels of inequality may hide significant variations in income and wealth levels between different parts and social groups of the city. Spatial analysis in GIS allows us to investigate house rental values and inequality distributions on different geographical levels. In line with Lesger and Van Leeuwen, the analysis of Antwerp was focused on the lowest level of geographical classification, the 79 neighbourhoods, and on individual households at the level of streets and buildings. First, medians of house rental value were calculated for all of the 79 neighbourhoods. Then, a cluster and outlier analysis was performed to calculate statistically significant clustering of neighbourhoods based on these median values.[9] This analysis indicates whether the apparent similarity (a spatial clustering of either high or low values) or dissimilarity (a spatial outlier) is more pronounced than one would expect in a random distribution (the null hypothesis). Figure 3 suggests a centre-periphery dispersion, although outliers within the rich central cluster like the 'Guldenberg' area (1), an infamous brothel district, indicate that Sjoberg's model offers some explanation

---

9   Using a fixed distance band of 400 metres. For more information about cluster and outlier analysis (Anselin Local Moran's I) please refer to https://pro.arcgis.com/en/pro-app/tool-reference/spatial-statistics/cluster-and-outlier-analysis-anselin-local-moran-s.htm.

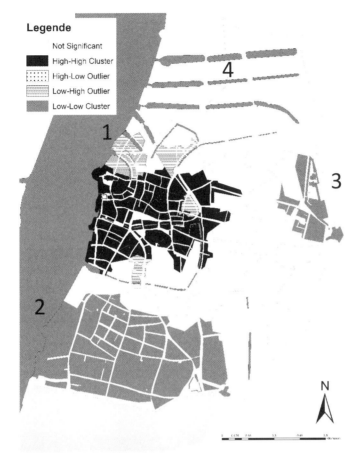

Figure 3: Clustering income levels at neighbourhood level

but hides many exceptions. We also find rather homogenous poor areas in typical slums in the south like St.-Andries (2) and the Kauwenberg (3) in the north-east. On the other hand, based on their position close to the city wall, several neighbourhoods were expected to cluster on low medians but did not. This was the case, for instance, in the Nieuwstad (4). This neighbourhood in the north-west corner of the city had a relative high income level because of its many high-value breweries, along with many small dwellings, bleacheries, dyeries and shipyards.

According to Lesger and van Leeuwen, one of the main features in the social topography of pre-modern cities was the concentration of high-income households along the main streets to the city gates. Therefore, the same cluster and outlier analysis was carried out at household level (Figure 4).

Apart from the many outliers in the clustering at frontage level, figure 4 discloses that the overall pattern in figure 3 appears to be more diverse at household level. In particular the gathering together of rich households along main streets like Kipdorp, Lange Nieuwstraat, Meir (5) and Huidevetterstraat/Gasthuisstraat (6) between the city gates and the city centre stands out, as do breweries in the Nieuwstad (4).

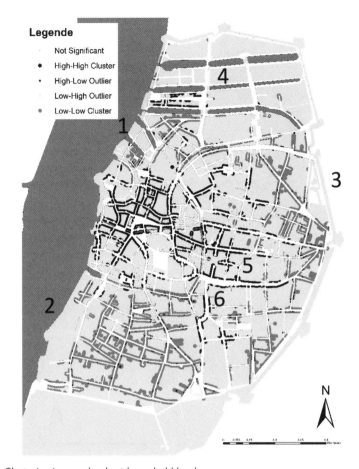

Figure 4: Clustering income levels at household level

Internal neighbourhood inequality

In pre-industrial societies, rising welfare was often accompanied by rising inequality (Soltow and Zanden 1998). Some authors have claimed that this is also the case for inequality within social groups or between spatial entities (Blondé 1987, 90-91, Carmo and Carvalho 2013, 44-45). We would therefore expect neighbourhoods with high median income levels to be more unequal internally than those with low income levels. Or, in spatial terms, we would expect neighbourhoods with high levels of inequality to be in the wealthy centre of town and the low inequality neighbourhoods in the poor periphery. As in the case of the median values, the GIStorical 1584 database allowed us to assess intra-neighbourhood inequalities with Gini coefficients varying between 0.22 and 0.5.

But, surprisingly, the clustering of neighbourhoods based on their internal inequality led to an almost opposite pattern to that of clustering based on median house rent levels (Figure 5). Generally speaking, neighbourhoods tended to be rather equal in the south-west of the city and unequal in the north-east, including the newly developed 'Nieuwstad' (4)

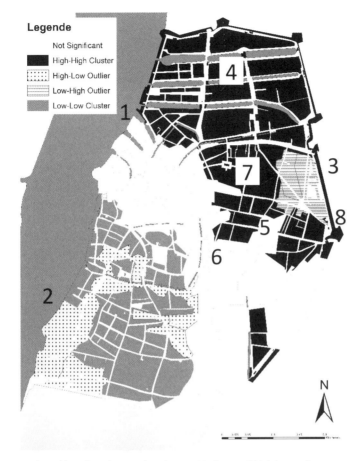

Figure 5: Internal neighbourhood inequality clustered in low and high inequality zones

and the area around the 'Nieuwe Waag' and the 'Keizerstraat' (7). The Molenberg (8), too, although a very poor ghetto with many back alleys close to the Kipdorp gate, finds itself in the unequal zone because of the relatively high house rental values along the Kipdorpstreet. In each zone, however, outliers could be found, like the 'Kauwenberg' area (3) in the north-east, which was a relatively equal and very poor neighbourhood within an unequal cluster, and some neighbourhoods in the area of Saint Michael's abbey in the south-west along the main exit street (Kloosterstraat and Boeksteeg), these being relative unequal within a zone of mostly equal (and poor) neighbours. Additionally, the city centre, being the most expensive part of the city, also shows little or no significant neighbourhood inequality at all.

So the preliminary conclusion at this point is that in Antwerp in 1584 there seems to be no clear relationship between affluence and inequality at the neighbourhood level: both rich and poor neighbourhoods could have relatively equal or unequal distributions of house rent values. This shows that in certain parts of the city residential segregation, of both poor and rich, was more dominant than in others. Based on figure 4, the presence of main streets, important public buildings and economic zones recently developed by Gilbert van Schoonbeke, like the Nieuwe Waag, the grain market and the brewery district in the Nieuwstad seems to be an important 'disturbing' factor (Soly 1977).

The next section will explore the spatial dimension of inequality in more depth. How important are spatial differences in the explanation of overall inequality?

Decomposing spatial inequality

When we compare the internal inequality distribution with the city level inequality, the majority of the neighbourhoods score much lower than the total for the city itself (Figure 6). Just four neighbourhoods are more unequal than the city of Antwerp as a whole. Clearly, overall city inequality is not just the average of decentralised or subgroup inequality.

Further analysis is possible, using a method used in development economics. According to Ravi Kanbur and Anthony Venables, spatial inequality can be defined as '[t]he contribution of variation in per capita income across spatial units to income variation across all individuals' (Kanbur and Venables 2005, 8). This means that total inequality can be divided into two variables: inequality *within* the spatial units of study (Within Group Inequality or WGI) and inequality *between* the averages of the spatial units (Between Group Inequality or BGI) or TI = WGI + BGI. The division of inequality into spatial groups can only be done by using a decomposable inequality indicator. The Theil coefficient is widely used for this purpose (Alfani 2010, 541-543, Ryckbosch 2010, 49-50).

This decomposition method (Mussard, Seyte, and Terraza 2003, 1-6) has been applied to the 13 wards and 79 neighbourhoods of Antwerp.[10] How important were spatial differences in economic inequality in the explanation of overall inequality in Antwerp 1584? WGI and BGI have been calculated for wards and neighbourhoods as spatial groups (Table 3).

At the ward level, BGI explains 21.7 per cent of Antwerp's total inequality, whereas the other 78.3 per cent is explained by inequality within the wards. Additionally, at the smaller geographic level of the neighbourhood, BGI already contributes more than one third of overall inequality. A decrease in the size of spatial groups produces in most cases less variation within the group and higher differences between the groups (Elbers et al. 2005, 45).

An important implication of WGI-BGI decomposition in table 3 is that it provides average values for WGI and BGI based on the combined contributions of 79 neighbourhoods to overall urban inequality. This does not mean that every neighbourhood contributed the same share (Elbers et al. 2005, 46). It is possible to calculate the exact contribution of each individual neighbourhood to overall city inequality, but this goes beyond the purpose of this chapter.

We now have, for the first time, a complete insight into the spatial dimension of inequality in Antwerp in 1584. It provides us with the perfect starting point for evaluating the importance of space in possible redistribution processes in the wake of Antwerp's demographic catastrophe.

---

10   The software used can be found at Program for Dagum's Gini Index Decomposition, University of Ottawa and Lameta, University of Montpellier, http://www.lameta.univ-montp1.fr/online/gini.html.

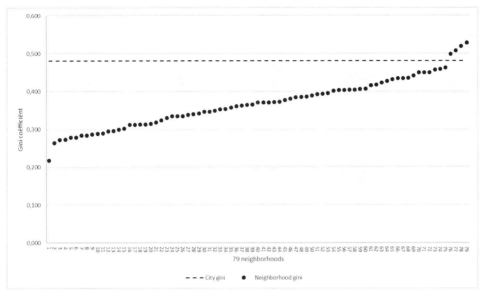

Figure 6: inequality within neigbourhoods (GINI). Just four neighbourhoods out of 79 were more unequal than the city as a whole

Source: 1584 GISdatabase.

Table 3: Within Group Inequality (WGI) versus Between Group Inequality (BGI) in Antwerp 1584: decreasing size of spatial groups increases Between Group Inequality

Group level	# groups	Theil	WGI	%	BGI	%
City	1	0.408	0.408	100	0	0
Ward	13	0.408	0.319	78.3	0.089	21.7
Neighborhood	79	0.408	0.259	63.6	0.149	36.4
Household	12.149	0.408	0	0	0.408	100

Source: 1584 GIS database.

Levelling through space?

While Alexander Farnese and his soldiers enjoyed their victory dinner on the famous wooden bridge across the river Scheldt (Strada 1655, 489-490), large parts of the Antwerp population prepared for departure. Between August 1585 and December 1589 40,000 people left the city, of whom almost 31,500 did so already in the first year. The visitation records of October 1586 give us the vacant houses in eight of the 13 wards or 49 of the 79 neighbourhoods. Based on (assessed) empty houses, 1,454 disappeared households and their characteristics were matched in the database and plotted in GIS (Figure 7).

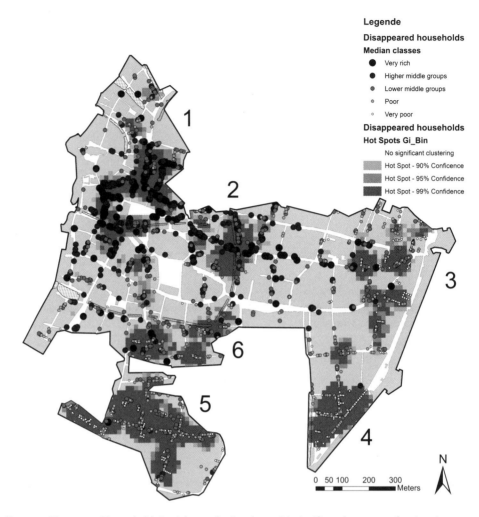

Figure 7: Disappeared households in eight wards, October 1586: significant hot spots of emigration.

To identify significant clustering an Optimized Hot Spot analysis was carried out on the departed households.[11] A Hot Spot analysis indicates whether the spatial clustering of features observed is more pronounced than one would expect in a random distribution (the null hypothesis). Figure 9 shows these hot spots or clusters. Cluster one is in the richest area of Antwerp close to the former stock exchange and the city hall; cluster two is located along the St. Katelijnevest close to the new stock exchange. Clusters three, four and five are in the periphery: in ward eight, and in the outskirts of wards ten and 11. The latter areas are situated close to the city wall. The visitation report also confirms that these areas had many empty dwellings and were once populated by outcasts or 'zeker arm

---

11   How Hot Spot Analysis (Getis-Ord Gi*) works, Environmental Systems Research Institute, Inc. (ESRI), https://pro.arcgis.com/en/pro-app/tool-reference/spatial-statistics/h-how-hot-spot-analysis-getis-ord-gi-spatial-stati.htm and https://pro.arcgis.com/en/pro-app/tool-reference/spatial-statistics/optimized-hot-spot-analysis.htm. In this case, the 49 neighbourhoods were used as polygons of analysis (bounding polygons).

Table 4: Emigration and inequality: comparing the emigrated households and those who stayed behind with regard to house rent value in Carolus guilders (median and average) and inequality ratio's (interquartile, Gini and Theil).

	Median	Average	Interquartile	Gini	Theil
Antwerp 1584	30.0	50.4	42	0.481	0,408
8 wards 1584	37.5	56.0	50	0.472	0,383
8 wards: disappeared households 1586	30.0	47.2	43	0.503	0,438
8 wards: remaining households 1586	40.0	58.2	52	0.463	0,368

Sources: 1584 GISdatabase and FAA GA4827/T1098.

volck bedelders ende bedelaersen [...].[12] Finally, cluster number six largely covers ward six, south of the Lombardenvest and along the Everdijstraat, an area mostly inhabited by impoverished low skilled artisans.

Before enquiring into the spatial redistribution effect of the emigration, we will first have a closer look at the social stratification of the 1,454 households which had left their houses by the end of 1586 (Table 4).

Overall, median house rent value was lower for the disappeared households (30 guilders) compared to the overall population of the eight wards in question (37.50 guilders), and clearly lower than the house rent value of the households still in Antwerp in 1586 (40 guilders).[13] Inequality within the group of disappeared households, both in Gini (+6.6 per cent) and Theil (+14.4 per cent), was higher. This indicates that emigration particularly affected the top and the bottom deciles, while middle groups tended to stay behind more often. The result was a small decrease in overall inequality in 1586 (Gini: 0.472 to 0.463 and Theil 0.383 to 0.368), indicating that the population collapse had a modest levelling effect thanks to the changed composition of the post-crisis population. The use of deciles (Table 5) discloses that, indeed, the top deciles reduced their share of house rent value, while the share of the lower deciles rose. Overall the top 50 per cent lost, the bottom 50 per cent gained. The top 5 per cent decreased most, to 21.1 per cent of the total house rent value in 1586 (compared to 24.0 per cent in 1584).

How did this affect the importance of space in the inequality distribution? For that, we have to return to the decomposition of overall inequality. We performed the same inequality decomposition calculation, but now using only the eight wards and 49 neigbourhoods within the visitation area. First we wanted to know how the depopulation changed the overall inequality decomposition (Table 6).

Both at ward (+5.1 per cent) and neighbourhood level (+7.3 per cent), the inequality within the spatial units became more important in explaining overall inequality. On the other hand, the polarisation between wards and between neighbourhoods decreased.

---

12   FAA – GA4827, Ward 10, 5th quarter, folio 4.
13   Man-Whitney test, p<0,05.

Table 5: The social distribution of rental values in 1584 and 1586 (% of total rental value per population decile)

Deciles	Bottom					Top						
	10%	20%	30%	40%	50%	50%	40%	30%	20%	10%	5%	1%
1584 total	1.6	4.2	7.9	12.4	18.2	81.8	74.5	65.4	53.6	36.0	22.9	6.9
8 wards 1584	1.6	4.2	7.8	12.5	18.3	81.7	74.3	64.8	52.3	34.4	24.0	5.8
8 wards 1586	1.7	4.5	8.2	13.0	19.1	81.0	73.4	63.9	51.3	33.7	21.1	5.1
%	104.2	105.1	104.2	103.6	104.1	99.1	98.8	98.6	98.2	98.0	87.9	87.9

Sources: 1584 GISdatabase and FAA GA4827/T1098.

Table 6: Levelling through space: decreasing inequality between neighbourhoods (1586 compared to 1584).

	1584 (shares in %)		1586 (shares in %)		Change in %	
Level	WGI	BGI	WGI	BGI	WGI	BGI
8 Wards	74.3	25.7	78.1	21.9	+5.1	-14.8
49 Neighborhoods	58.9	41.1	63.2	36.8	+7.3	-10.5

Sources: 1584 GISdatabase and FAA GA4827/T1098.

Figure 8: Depopulation concentrates in predominantly (very) poor and (very) rich but also relatively segregated neighbourhoods causing the maximum levelling effect in space

This can also be seen on the map (figure 8). The match with clusters of disappeared households is obvious. Specifically, rich and poor but relatively equal and consequently segregated neighbourhoods were targets of the depopulation, causing their inequality contributions to drop (rich neighbourhoods) or rise (poor neighbourhoods). In contrast, diverse (unequal) neighbourhoods were more resilient.

Conclusion

The history of inequality often concentrates on long-term evolutions of inequality at the level of entire countries, regions or cities, without really exploring the redistributive dynamics behind them. The aim of this contribution was to find out whether a spatial approach to urban inequality could offer a better understanding of one of the mechanisms, sudden demographic decline, in causing shifts in inequality. Space allowed us to move the scale of analysis from the city as a whole to wards, neighbourhoods or even households. For the city of Antwerp in the late sixteenth century we observed a large socio-spatial diversity within, but also between, neighbourhoods. First, we found that Antwerp's income, based on house rental values, was more or less distributed according to the Sjoberg model, with rich neighbourhoods concentrated in the center and poor neighbourhoods predominantly along the southern periphery. Based on the expectation that inequality rises with rising income levels, we expected the inequality level of individual neighbourhoods to decrease from the centre to the periphery. But this pattern was absent in large parts of the city. In particular the strong residential segregation of rich neighbourhoods in the centre caused very low inequality rates within those neighbourhoods. On the other hand, meso-segregation along main streets all the way to the city gates and the construction of new public and economic hot spots could cause relatively high inequality in peripheral neighbourhoods. Both phenomena led to the 'disturbance' of the expected pattern of rising affluence, causing rising inequality.

Perhaps the exceptional size of Antwerp – according to pre-industrial European standards – and its explosive demographic growth in the course of the sixteenth century might explain why the differences between neighbourhoods were more obvious than observed in most other European towns in the same period. A similar hypothesis was put forward and confirmed for seventeenth-century Amsterdam by Lesger and van Leeuwen (Lesger, van Leeuwen, and Vissers 2013, 74, 92-93, 100). Periods of rapid expansion allowed urban elites to create living environments according to their wishes and protect these (e.g. by specific regulations) from negative externalities and the settlement of unwelcome social groups. This is how the canal belt in seventeenth-century Amsterdam developed as a new residential elite quarter. In the case of Antwerp, however, rapid urban expansion resulted not so much in new purely residential elite quarters but in combinations of economic hot spots and housing. The Nieuwe Waag and the brewery district are just a few of the many examples created by the famous urbanist Gilbert van Schoonbeke (Soly 1977). But there may be another explanation for the existence of elite residential segregation in Antwerp. By far the most affluent (median house rental value of 140 Carolus guilders) and one of the most segregated neighbourhoods (internal Gini of only 0.27) was north of the Grote Markt close to the former stock exchange, encompassing the Lange en Korte Doornikstraat,

Hofstraat and Oude Beurs. This was not a newly created area like the Amsterdam canal belt, yet it had been able to develop and maintain an elite character and low internal inequality. Although the trading activities had moved to the new stock exchange in the 1530s, the inhabitants had a great interest in preserving their living environment since the values of their houses and their status depended on it (Lesger, van Leeuwen, and Vissers 2013, 94). And, perhaps because the busy trading activities had moved to the new stock exchange, congestion was reduced and living conditions improved.

After exploring Antwerp's socio-spatial configuration, we looked for distinctive spatial redistribution effects following the massive exodus of 1586. By October 1586, the demographic shock alone had already had a modest but clear levelling effect, both socially and spatially. Overall, Gini and Theil coefficients decreased slightly. Since emigrants were concentrated in the higher and lower strata of the population, the overall distribution became more equal. Spatially, 1584 Antwerp already contained several large poor and rich segregated neighbourhoods. The segregation made these neighbourhoods vulnerable in the depopulation process. This was visible through clear clusters of emigrants in these relatively poor and rich segregated areas. Consequently, this reduced the inequality between neighbourhoods and increased the relative importance of internal neighbourhood inequality.

These preliminary findings need to be analysed further, for example with socio-professional characteristics, to see how income segregation was associated with the vulnerability of specific social groups. Finally, this study covered only the impact of demographic decline, leaving all other variables stable. Further research is also needed to include other variables in the analysis, such as the evolution of standards of living, property redistribution and revaluation or the impact of fiscal policies.[14] Mass emigration led to the collapse of the housing market, both for rentals and sales, with severe redistribution effects. The destruction of the rural hinterland by marauding armies resulted in the collapse of urban rental income, but also in opportunities for speculative investment in real property (See Geens Chapter 12, Deneweth Chapter 14). This all contributed to the (post-)crisis redistribution of wealth and income. And finally, some households might have relocated within the city, and this might also have had a significant impact on the redistribution of income levels.

Sources

Primary Sources
Felix Archive Antwerp (FAA):
PK2256-2278: Wijkboeken Ketgen
PK2279-2303: Wijkboeken 1st series
PK2304-PK2328: Wijkboeken 2nd series
12#4262 – 12#4265: Gevelplan wards 1-4
MA#2631: Gevelplan kadastrale legger
GA4827: Burgerlijke Wacht – Generale Monstering (Ward 3, 4, 8 and 10)
T1098: Tresorij – Visitatie van het koren (Ward 1, 2, 6 and 11)

---

14   Marnef's contribution in this volume gives a good insight into how fiscal policies, as result of political negotiation, hit social groups differently.

IB3017: Insolvente Boedel Gilbert van Schoonbeke – several 'sommieren overslach'.

T1105: Tresorij – Somier van[de] visitatie van[de] xiii wijcken van persoone[n] oft mo[n]den deser stadt en[de] de provisie van[de] Graene[n] daer toe sijn viii May 1586. Item de 21. Octob[er] 1586.

References

Alfani, Guido. 2010. "Wealth Inequalities and Population Dynamics in Early Modern Northern Italy." *The Journal of Interdisciplinary History* 40 (4): 513-549.

Alfani, Guido, and Wouter Ryckbosch. 2016. "Growing apart in early modern Europe? A comparison of inequality trends in Italy and the Low Countries, 1500-1800." *Explorations in Economic History* 62: 143-153.

Alves, Sónia. 2016. "Spaces of inequality: It's not differentiation, it is inequality! A socio-spatial analysis of the City of Porto." *Portuguese Journal of Social Science* 15 (3): 409-431.

Asaert, G. 2004. *1585. De val van Antwerpen en de uittocht van Vlamingen en Brabanders*. Tielt: Lannoo.

Bavel, Bas van, and Daniel Curtis. 2015. "Better understanding disasters by better using history: Systematically using the historical record as one way to advance research into disasters." *CGEH Working Paper Series* 68: 1-32.

Blondé, Bruno. 1987. *De sociale structuren en economische dynamiek van 's-Hertogenbosch 1500-1550*. Edited by H. F. J. M. van den Eerenbeemt, A. H. Bredero, Th. M. Frijthoff, K. F. E. Veraghtert and P. H. Winkelman. Vol. 74, *Bijdragen to de geschiedenis van het zuiden van Nederland*. Tilburg: Stichting Zuidelijk Historisch Contact.

Briels, J. 1978. *De Zuidnederlandse immigratie 1572-1630*. Haarlem: Fibila Van Dishoeck.

Carmo, Renato Miguel do, and Margarida Carvalho. 2013. "Multiple disparities: earning inequalities in Lisbon." *Landscape and Geodiversity* (1): 36-45.

Dambruyne, Johan. 2001. *Mensen en centen. Het 16de-eeuwse Gent in demografisch en economisch perspectief*. Vol. 26, *Verhandelingen der maatschappij voor geschiedenis en oudheidkunde te Gent*. Gent: Maatschappij voor geschiedenis en oudheidkunde te Gent.

Dambruyne, Johan. 2002. *Corporatieve middengroepen. Aspiraties, relaties en transformaties in de 16de-eeuwse Gentse ambachtswereld*. Vol. 28, *Verhandelingen der Maatschappij voor Geschiedenis en Oudheidkunde te Gent*. Gent: Academia Press.

Degueldre, Gilberte. 2011. *Kadastrale ligger van Antwerpen (1584-1585) proeve van reconstructie op de vooravond van de scheiding der Nederlanden*. 14 vols. Antwerpen: Felix Archief.

Deneweth, Heidi. 2007. "The Economic situation and its influence on building and renovating in Bruges during the 16th-18th centuries." *Mélanges de l'Ecole française de Rome. L'économie de la construction dans l'Italie moderne* 119 (2): 531-544.

Elbers, Chris, Peter Lanjouw, Johan Mistiaen, Berk Özler, and Kenneth R. Simler. 2005. "Are Neighbours Equal? Estimating Local Inequality in Three Developing Countries." In *Spatial Inequality and Development*, edited by Ravi Kanbur and Anthony J. Venables, 37-60. New York: Oxford University Press Inc.

Galanaud, Anne. 2009. "Demographie et societe a Dijon a la fin du moyen-age (1357=1447) a partir d'une analyse informatique des registres des comptes de l'impot des marcs." Docteur en histoire PhD, Sciences de l'Homme et Société, Université de Franche-Comté (tel-01166860).

Hanus, Jord. 2013. "Real inequality in the early modern Low Countries: the city of 's-Hertogenbosch, 1500-1660." *The Economic History Review* 66 (3): 733-756.

Janssens, Ric, and Iason Jongepier. 2015. "GIStorical Antwerp : historisch GIS als laboratorium voor de stadsgeschiedenis." *Stadsgeschiedenis* 10 (1): 49-62.

Kanbur, Ravi, and Anthony J. Venables. 2005. "Spatial Inequality and Development." In *Spatial Inequality and Development*, edited by Ravi Kanbur and Anthony J. Venables, 3-11. New York: Oxford University Press Inc.

Langton, John. 1975. "Residential Patterns in Pre-Industrial Cities: Some Case Studies from Seventeenth-Century Britain." *Transactions of the Institute of British Geographer* 65: 1-27.

Lesger, C., M. H. D. van Leeuwen, and B. Vissers. 2013. "Residentiële segregatie in vroeg-moderne steden. Amsterdam in de eerste helft van de negentiende eeuw*." *Tijdschrift voor Sociale en Economische Geschiedenis* 1: 71-101.

Lesger, Clé, and Marco H. D. Van Leeuwen. 2012. "Residential Segregation from the Sixteenth to the Nineteenth Century: Evidence from the Netherlands." *Journal of Interdisciplinary History* 17 (3): 333-369.

Lis, Catharina, and Hugo Soly. 1993. "Neighbourhood Social Change in West European Cities. Sixteenth to Nineteenth Centuries." *International Review of Social History* 38: 1-30.

Marnef, Guido. 1996. *Antwerpen in de tijd van de Reformatie. Ondergronds protestantisme in een handelsmetropool 1550-1577*. Amsterdam / Antwerpen: Meulenhoff / Kritak.

Mussard, Stéphane, Françoise Seyte, and Michel Terraza. 2003. "Decomposition of Gini and the generalized entropy inequality measures." *Economics Bulletin* 4 (7): 1-6.

Piketty, Thomas. 2014. *Kapitaal in de 21ste eeuw*. Amsterdam: De Bezige Bij.

Ryckbosch, Wouter. 2010. "Vroegmoderne economische ontwikkeling en sociale repercussies in de Zuidelijke Nederlanden. Nijvel in de achttiende eeuw." *Tijdschrift voor Sociale en Economische Geschiedenis* 7: 26-55.

Ryckbosch, Wouter. 2015. "Economic inequality and growth before the industrial revolution: the case of the Low Countries (fourteenth to nineteenth centuries)." *European Review of Economic History* 20 (1): 1-22.

Scholliers, E. 1955. "De levensstandaard der arbeiders op het einde der 16e eeuw in Antwerpen." *Tijdschrift voor Geschiedenis* 68: 80-103.

Scholliers, E. 1960. *De Levensstandaard in de XVe en XVIe eeuw te Antwerpen*. Antwerpen: Uitgeverij de Sikkel N. V.

Sjoberg, Gideon. 1965. *The Preindustrial City. Past and Present*. London: The Free Press.

Soltow, Lee, and Jan Luiten van Zanden. 1998. *Income and wealth inequality in the Netherlands 16th-20th century*. Amsterdam: Het Spinhuis.

Soly, H. 1977. *Urbanisme en Kapitalisme te Antwerpen in de 16de eeuw. De stedebouwkundige en industriële ondernemingen van Gilbert van Schoonbeke., Historische Uitgaven Pro Civitate – Reeks in-8°*. Brussel: Gemeentekrediet van België.

Soly, H. 1978. "De Megalopolis Antwerpen." In *De Stad Antwerpen van de Romeinse tijd tot de 17de eeuw. Topografische studie rond het plan van Virgilius Bononiensis 1565*, edited by L. Voet, G. Asaert, H. Soly, A. Verhulst, F. De Nave and J. Van Roey. Brussel: Gemeentekrediet België.

Strada, Famiano. 1655. *Het Tweede Deel Der Nederlandtsche Oorlogen*. Rotterdam: Andries van Hoogen-huyse.

Thijs, A. K. L. 1987. "De Contrareformatie en het economisch transformatieproces te Antwerpen na 1585." *Bijdragen tot de Geschiedenis* 70 (1-2): 97-124.

Van der Wee, Herman, and Jan Materné. 1993. "De Antwerpse wereldmarkt tijdens de 16de en 17de eeuw." In *Antwerpen. Verhaal van een Metropool. 16de-17de eeuw*, edited by Jan van der Stock, 19-31. Antwerpen: Snoeck-Ducaju & Zoon.

Van Roey, Jan. 1975. "De bevolking." In *Antwerpen in de XVIde eeuw*, 95-108. Antwerpen: Genootschap voor Antwerpse Geschiedenis.

Van Roey, Jan. 1985. *De val van Antwerpen 17 augustus 1585 – voor en na*. Antwerpen: De Dageraad pvba.

Vance, J. E. 1971. "Land assignment in the pre-capitalist, capitalist and post-capitalist city." *Economic Geography* (47): 101-120.

HEIDI DENEWETH

Real Property, Speculation and Housing Inequality

Bruges, 1550-1670

Introduction

The financial and housing crises of 2007 and 2008 sparked a renewed interest in the causes and consequences of crises. In particular the impact of rising inequality worried social scientists. It was feared that disproportionate social inequality, undermining the position of the middle class, might threaten societal stability and check economic growth. The same concerns stimulated historians to investigate the causes and – to a lesser extent – consequences of rising inequality in the past (Blondé, Hanus & Ryckbosch 2018; see also ch. 9 in this book). The link between inequality and economic growth was particularly high on the agenda. In the last decade, the research group around Guido Alfani has collected a large number of data on wealth inequality in Italy and Europe in a longitudinal perspective (Alfani 2015, online 2019). After Lindert (Lindert 2000a and b) had already rejected Kuznets' hypothesis (Kuznets 1955), which says that inequality rose during the first phase of economic growth but would decline again once a certain level of development had been achieved, Scheidel demonstrated that Europe had witnessed only three periods of declining inequality in its entire history: after the collapse of the Roman Empire, after the Black Death, and after both World Wars (Scheidel 2017). During all other periods, inequality was constantly on the rise. Furthermore Alfani stressed that it proves difficult to point out exact causalities since different forces were acting in different periods and places, and 'similar trends might have had deeply dissimilar underlying causes'. He therefore pleaded for new research that should look 'for complex and more case-specific explanations instead of trying to devise simple universal laws' (Alfani online 2019, 20).

In this chapter, I will investigate a single case – Bruges between 1550 and 1670 – in order to expose the mechanisms behind increasing wealth inequality in that particular period. My focus will be on the housing market, for three reasons. First, real property was one of the main components of wealth in early modern societies, hence, changes in property patterns might explain divergent trends in inequality. Second, real property was one of the ways of gaining access to financial markets in the sense that owners' access to larger and longer-term loans was facilitated because of their property that could be used as collateral. When used for productive investments, this contributed to economic growth. After the real property bubbles of 2007-08, house prices dropped below mortgage levels, prompting creditors to take measures to recoup as much of their capital as possible, or to seize and

Heidi Deneweth • Vrije Universiteit Brussel

Inequality and the City in the Low Countries (1200-2020), ed. by Bruno BLONDÉ, Sam GEENS, Hilde GREEFS, Wouter RYCKBOSCH, Tim SOENS & Peter STABEL, SEUH 50 (Turnhout, 2020), pp. 251-268.

  DOI 10.1484/M.SEUH-EB.5.120449

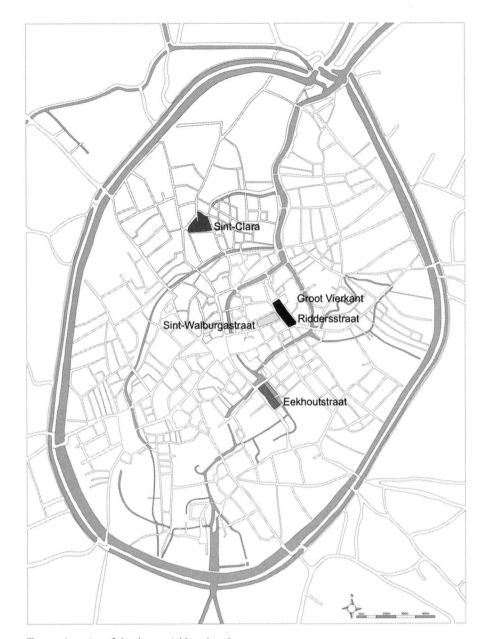

Figure 1 Location of the three neighbourhoods
Source: Deneweth (2008a)

auction properties and convert them into rentals. The resulting shift in property rates can also result in increasing inequality. Third, substantial research by Wouter Ryckbosch on inequality in the early modern Low Countries has been based on fiscal sources concerning the rental value of houses, unique sources that are comparable over time and space. Combining these with other sources, Ryckbosch found that inequality was the consequence of a changing functional distribution of income favouring capital over labour. The early modern period was not only characterised by an increasing concentration of property, but (income from) property was also better protected by urban governments than income from labour (Ryckbosch 2016; see also van Zanden 1995). Indeed, governments were far more lenient towards house-owners and their investment behaviour, even in periods when tenants were the ones who needed protection. I will therefore pay attention to housing/ income ratios as well.

Literature on wealth inequality attributes a significant role to housing, but how exactly demand and supply on the housing market itself triggered inequality is less clear. Bruges is an interesting case in which to study these phenomena since economic change and high inflation undermined the purchasing power of the working classes and forced them to switch from owned to rented houses. Here, income inequality caused housing inequality. When the severe food crisis around 1580 was over, a massive emigration in 1585 caused house prices to drop, and wages doubled around 1600, one would expect that this would have countered the housing crisis and that lower social groups would eventually acquire property again. This was not the case because the elites were already massively investing in housing at that time. Their financial dealings and speculation reshuffled the housing market and property patterns, and drove house prices beyond the reach of workers' households. In this period, it was the dynamics on the real property market itself that induced higher housing inequality.

In what follows I will first introduce the case of Bruges with attention to economic and demographic variables, and present the research for this case study. I will then describe the nature and frequency of transactions on the housing market and their interaction with the financial market between 1550 and 1670. Since the aggregate level tends to flatten out divergent patterns for different submarkets, I will use a micro-historical analysis of three socially different neighbourhoods to explain different investment patterns and shifts in property patterns leading to increasing inequality.

Bruges

Bruges had been the main gateway for international trade and the main financial centre of Western Europe until a shift in the international trade routes and networks made Antwerp a better gateway from the end of the fifteenth century onwards. Still, both cities continued to operate as complementary ports throughout the sixteenth century, and international trade remained important until 1585, when the Scheldt connection to the North Sea was blocked during the Dutch Revolt (Brown & Dumolyn 2018; Bertels et al. 2011). During the seventeenth century, alternative connections with the ports of Ostend and Dunkirk made Bruges an important node in a network of waterways connecting the seaports with the hinterland of the southern Netherlands. The 1660s witnessed a short revival of international trade with the construction of a new trade basin, wharves and warehouses in the north of Bruges, the establishment of a new Chamber of Trade and Commerce, and the founding of the Greenland Company (whaling), all in 1665. Although trade volumes remained below those of Bruges' heyday in the late Middle Ages, the city continued to play a central role in transhipment and regional trade (Ryckaert et al. 1999).

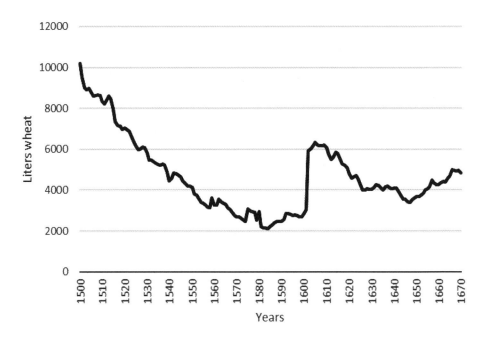

Graph 1 Real wage (in litres of wheat) of master masons in Bruges, 1500-1670

Annual income of a master mason (Scholliers 1965a, 87-160) in litres of wheat (Verhulst 1965, 2, 3-70).

Bruges' second pillar was the textile industry which provided the bulk of exports. Around 1500, competition from rising textile centres in Brabant and neighbouring regions in the County of Flanders prompted product innovation and differentiation, which eventually created a shift from cloth to cheaper woollens and linen. Structural changes based on subcontracting and lower wages allowed the textile sector to survive. Craft guilds, however, never acquired a strong position in these new sectors and the incomes of linen workers were substantially lower than those of cloth workers (Vermaut 1974). Apart from textiles, luxury products such as tapestries, paintings, printed books and silver and golden objects were also highly sought after on the international markets until the sixteenth century, when they gradually faded away in early modern Bruges (Stabel forthcoming).

Whereas merchants and entrepreneurs profited from the reorientation and partial recovery of Bruges' economy until the 1670s (see also ch. 16 by Inneke Baatsen), the lower classes fell on hard times. The decline of international trade in the early sixteenth century had reduced employment in supporting sectors such as packing, weighing and transport. At the same time, increasing competition from the cottage industry undermined employment in the preparatory sectors of the textile industry, whereas the shift from cloth to linen production required less employment in the finishing sectors. The main problem, however, was the rapid deterioration in purchasing power during the sixteenth century (graph 1). Around 1500, craftsmen in Bruges still earned the highest wages in the Low Countries, and an estimated 45 per cent of the population lived in their own houses (Deneweth, Leloup & Speecke 2018). Sticky wages and high inflation during the sixteenth century let the purchasing power drop by 75 per cent (Blockmans 1998). Inflation was

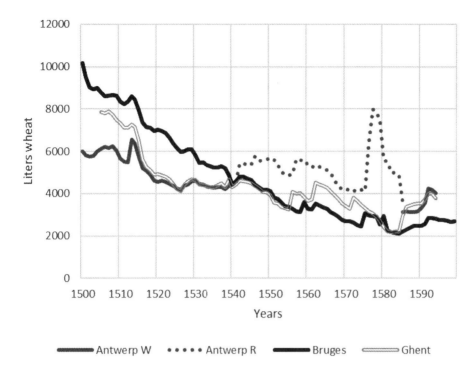

Graph 2 Comparison of real wages in Antwerp, Bruges and Ghent in the sixteenth century

Annual real wages of master masons in litres of wheat: Bruges: Verhulst 1965, 2, 3-70; Scholliers 1965a, 87-160; Antwerp: Scholliers 1960; Ghent: Toch 1973, 4, 326-400; Scholliers 1965b, 353-461. Full information on wheat prices (W) for Antwerp was not available. Since rye prices (R) are often defined in a fixed correlation to wheat prices, I reconstructed hypothetical wheat prices (based on rye) for Antwerp.

high all over the Low Countries, but wages in Antwerp and Ghent were adjusted earlier and more substantially than those in Bruges. When, around 1540, real wages in Bruges dropped below those in Antwerp and Ghent (graph 2), master craftsmen left Bruges for better opportunities elsewhere. At the same time, structural changes in the textile industry attracted many lower skilled workers from southern Flanders, Hainaut and Artesia (Vermaut 1974; Thoen 1994; Deneweth 2011). These opposite migration trends gradually changed the social composition of the population, whereas the impoverishment of the lower social groups remaining in Bruges started to erode the position of the middling groups as well. Local producers and shopkeepers saw their sales volumes and profit margins drop to unprecedented levels (Dewitte & Viaene 1977, 66; compare with Van der Meulen, ch. 2 in this book). A grain crisis and extreme dearth around 1580 drove purchasing power to an absolute minimum. This coincided with the Calvinist Republic (1578-84) when Bruges, just like Ghent and Antwerp (compare Rogier van Kooten, ch. 13), revolted against Spain. Soon afterwards, Farnese reconquered the rebellious cities and Spain left their inhabitants the choice between (re)converting to Catholicism or leaving the country. In 1585, about one third of the population left Bruges, a decline from 38,000 to 25,000 inhabitants, partly for ideological reasons but mainly because of diminishing job opportunities and poor living standards (Deneweth 2010). It would take almost 15 years for the Bruges economy to recover and for population numbers to start to rise again, mainly by attracting low-skilled textile workers. Bruges' population reached 35,000 again in 1680, but already around 1600 wages were adjusted to the same levels as those in Antwerp and Ghent. The purchasing power almost tripled, compared to the crisis of 1580, but remained at only 60 per cent of what it had been around 1500. During the first half of the seventeenth century, it would decline again, however, with about one third (graph 1).

The question is how these economic and social changes in general, and the demographic crisis of 1585 in particular, impacted on property patterns and housing inequality. To answer this question, I first investigated the evolution of housing values and property patterns between 1583 and 1667, based on tax registers on housing values (Deneweth, Leloup & Speecke 2017, 2018). Second, I used the so-called *registers van de zestendelen*, a pre-cadastral source, to study the frequency and nature of land transactions, mainly sales, mortgages, sequestrations and public auctions. At the time of research, all transactions between 1580 and 1800 were integrated in a database for 23 per cent of all houses (1,875 out of 8,129), spread over the city centre and peripheral zones. Third, I made an in-depth analysis of the evolution of a sample of about 150 houses distributed over three neighbourhoods, with different locations (figure 1) and different socio-economic profiles. All notarial deeds relating to these houses were used to calculate the relationship between mortgages and property prices, and between housing and rental prices (Deneweth 2008a). Although this sample is very small, it provides a first impression of the price evolution for different housing categories, which is quite exceptional for the early modern period.[1]

Housing values, property rates and inequality

The tax registers on housing values were adjusted to real market prices in 1583 and 1667. They mention all housing values as a fixed percentage of the market price, respectively 6.25 and 5.0 per cent. Since rental fees were usually calculated in the same way, all housing values offer a representative image of the entire housing market (residential properties and rentals) for both years. A third tax register is available for 1382, although only for the administrative section of St James. We do not know the exact rate between housing values and market prices for that year, but the spread of housing values can be extrapolated with some reliability because all administrative districts extended from the central market square to the city walls and equally covered elite neighbourhoods, important access roads and poor neighbourhoods. Ryckbosch demonstrated that inequality in the housing market in Bruges diminished slightly with Gini coefficients of 0.49 (1382), 0.46 (1583) and 0.45 (1667) (Ryckbosch 2016 and online appendix). Based on a tax register of 1394-96, Stabel (forthcoming) demonstrates that St James was one of the more equal districts, with a Gini of 0.35 versus 0.4 and 0.44 in other parts of the city. This means that housing inequality in Bruges was declining in early modern Bruges, which is counter-intuitive in light of the social and economic context sketched earlier. Ryckbosch stipulated that an increasing

---

1   The only exception is Eichholtz and Lindenthal (2014) for early modern Amsterdam, based on a similar research methodology.

concentration of property was one of the explanatory factors. Indeed, the percentage of owners living in their own houses dropped from 43 through 34 to 27 per cent. But what caused this concentration? Variety in housing was reduced as well: variation coefficients of houses declined from 1.55 in 1382 through 1.01 in 1583 to 0.95 in 1667 (Deneweth, Leloup & Speecke 2018, 27). Could it be that housing values do not reflect changing inequality that well, and that the housing market itself was one of the main catalysts of changing inequality instead?

Two important trends in the housing market can be discerned. In 1382, many houses in the city centre and along the main entrance roads were already constructed in stone and masonry, in combination with (partly) wooden façades. Most roofs were covered with durable, more fireproof materials, which made housing in the city centre quite expensive. The urban periphery, on the other hand, had very modest houses, often a combination of wood and loam, with straw roofs. Since these cheaper building materials kept housing prices down, access to property was easier for the lower social groups. During the Late Middle Ages, the purchasing power of craftsmen was quite high in Bruges, certainly when compared to other cities. Stimulated by urban fire prevention measures and subsidies, both residential owners and investors renewed or renovated their houses. By 1583, all houses were of brick construction with hard and fireproof roofing, although some kept their often highly decorated wooden façades until the nineteenth century. The change in building materials was one of the reasons for the diminishing variation in housing prices, although changing demand must have impacted on them as well. The strong erosion of the purchasing power of the lower social classes also affected the lower middling groups in the second half of the sixteenth century. This must have increased demand for cheap houses and, as a result, also raised relative prices in the lower segment of the market, therefore causing the variation in prices to decline. Sources are lacking for this period, but we can document a similar trend much better for the following period.

Our focus, indeed, is on the period between 1583 and 1667, when a second important trend can be identified in the dynamics of the property market itself. During that period, the concentration of property further increased from 34 to only 27 per cent of owners living in their own houses. Remarkably, median housing values increased from 480 to 1,680 Flemish groats, an increase with a factor of 3.5. Taking into account that housing values represented respectively 6.25 and 5.0 per cent of house prices, this means that median market prices in reality increased from 7,680 to 33,600 Flemish groats, a nominal increase of a factor of 4.4. This increase had nothing to do with new building materials, new construction techniques or new housing types, but was nothing more than the outcome of the dynamics of the housing market itself (Deneweth 2020).

This rapid surge in housing prices is quite surprising, given that in 1585 one third of the population left Bruges for new opportunities elsewhere. At least one third of all houses, but also many warehouses and workshops, were vacated at that time, which must have led to falling housing prices at first. We would have expected that the combination of falling house prices and increasing purchasing power as soon as nominal wages doubled in around 1600 (graph 1) would have led to improved access to housing and increasing property prices again. This was not the case; on the contrary, many households of the lower middling groups and below moved from their own homes to rented accommodation, whereas newcomers continued to prefer rental housing since they remained highly mobile.

On the other hand, wealthier groups extended their investments in property. These trends are well documented by our micro-analysis of neighbourhoods.

The micro-analysis of three neighbourhoods (figure 1), each with a different socio-economic composition, clearly shows that property patterns evolved very differently according to location and the social identity of their inhabitants. The first housing block (*Riddersstraat*) belonged to an elite neighbourhood in the city centre where most houses had very high housing values and were inhabited by mayors, councillors, merchants, lawyers, clergymen and rentiers. Contrary to the aggregate trend, the percentage of residential owners increased from 37 to 47 per cent. They invested in the expansion of their residences by joining houses into larger units and converting adjacent houses into stables, coach houses, kitchens and living quarters for servants. As a consequence, the number of individual houses declined from 35 (1550) to 25 (1667). The second neighbourhood (*Eekhoutstraat*) was situated along one of the main entrance roads, close to the city centre, and was inhabited by guild officials and master craftsmen – in 1550 mainly leather workers, later craftsmen of mixed occupations. The housing values were quite high (upper middle class). Property rates were exceptionally high in the 1580s but declined from 51 to a still impressive 44 per cent of residential owners in the 1670s. The number of houses in two adjacent housing blocks declined from 42 to 37, merely due to the conversion of former rental houses into warehouses, workshops or larger housing units along the side streets. The third housing block (*Sint-Clarastraat*) was more peripheral to the city centre, housing values belonged to the second lowest quintile, and the houses were inhabited by weavers, tapestry weavers, journeymen and labourers. The number of houses declined from 53 to 33 units between 1550 and 1667, partly due to the consolidation of former plots into larger units and partly due to the demolition of former rental houses. Property patterns witnessed a dramatic decline from 74 to only 25 per cent of resident owners (full details in Deneweth 2020).

An in-depth analysis of what exactly happened during the period under discussion establishes very divergent trends, originating from different causes: shifts in supply and demand for housing, urban regulations related to vacancy, manipulation of the supply side of the rental market, and different forms of speculation and investment in property. The timing of these processes was different, but subsequent trends reinforced each other. On the one hand, higher middling groups and elites profited from the massive emigration and falling housing prices by acquiring better located houses, extending their residences, and improving their personal comfort. Lower social groups, on the other hand, lost their property at first, but should have been able to improve their position once the economy rebounded and housing prices were still reasonably low. This was not the case, because investment strategies and speculation by the higher social strata drove prices up so fast that they were no longer affordable for labourers and craftsmen. Let us first focus on the housing situation of the lower social groups.

Crisis, mortgages and sales

Whereas craftsmen in Bruges had earned the highest wages in the Low Countries around 1500, and a presumed 45 per cent of the population still inhabited their own houses around

1550, the end of the sixteenth century was a bitter period for labourers and lower middling groups. Sustained sticky wages and high inflation, together with the extreme dearth around 1580, brought their purchasing power down to an absolute minimum. The prolonged crisis had consumed the few savings they had, if any, and induced high indebtedness, especially among lower (middling) groups in neighbourhoods such as the *Sint-Clarastraat*. In those streets, most houses were relatively small in 1583, but they still had their own gardens. Their rental values were in the second lowest quintile, but they were affordable for the lower middling groups, since 74 per cent of all houses were inhabited by their owners. On closer inspection, however, the situation was less rosy. Many households could ill afford even the basic foods and they had postponed maintenance works on their houses for many years, indicating that they were now on the verge of poverty. Several houses were in such a bad state of repair that they were eventually sold for the value of the land and with a note that the new owner could re-use the building materials that could be recovered from the ruins.[2]

Additionally, many owners had accumulated arrears of rent and annuity payments at a time when they needed additional loans or credit most urgently. It must be stressed that most creditors did not manifest immediate predatory behaviour in the crisis of the late 1570s. For instance, many ecclesiastical institutions owned rents and annuities that the original landlords had donated to them during the Middle Ages. Since 1304, it had been forbidden to adjust existing rents to current market prices and these rents therefore represented only a very small percentage of the total value of the houses (Gilliodts-van Severen 1874-75, 1, 314). Nevertheless, several owners accumulated arrears for many years without any reaction from the institutions. Private creditors who had granted informal loans or loans on collateral were also quite lenient towards their debtors during this crisis. Unfortunately, the crisis lasted for a long time and at one point creditors had to intervene in order not to lose their priority claims: within three years for non-mortgaged and informal credit, within ten years for all forms of mortgaged credit (including land rents). The period during which most creditors needed to initiate sequestration and auctions in order not to lose their priority claims unfortunately coincided with a crisis of a different kind.

From 1585 onwards, the mass emigration of at least 13,000 people not only destabilised the economy and the labour market, but it also created an enormous gap in the housing market in which house prices declined by 40 to 50 per cent (graph 3 a, b). The decline was most noticeable in the category of cheap houses which were the first victims of over-mortgaging, as we can see in the block near *Sint-Clarastraat*. To modern standards, over-mortgaging means that the mortgage exceeded the value of the house. For early modern cities, however, this should be interpreted differently. Mortgages did not usually exceed 30 per cent of the house price. This was the customary rule in medieval Paris (Godding 1960, 227), but such rules lack any legal basis in the Low Countries. Still, this rate seems to have been an implicit norm there as well, which must be explained by the high occurrence of other personal and non-mortgaged debt. Society thrived on credit and every household had personal debts for consumption, rent, taxes and small personal loans, all secured by the person and the

---

2   CAB, OA, 198, *Klerken van de vierschaar,*186, f. 21r, 24 September 1601 (houses NIK/0843 and 844).

A General image

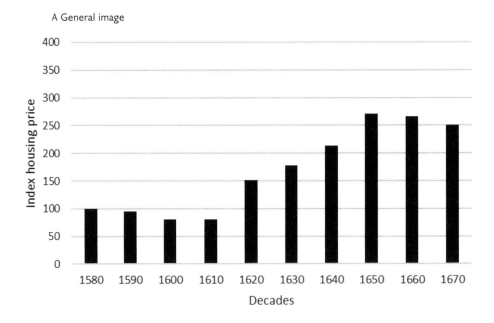

B Cheap houses

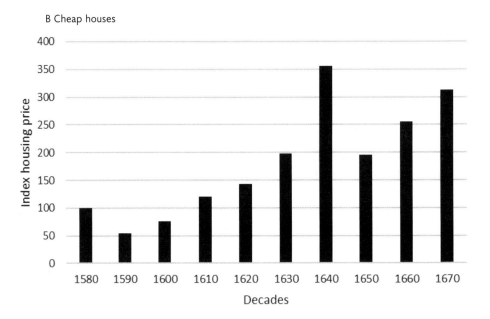

Graph 3 Prices of houses

3.A. Based on a sample of 462 sales (1580s-1670s) in the three neighbourhoods under discussion. Sale prices could be reconstructed for 196 sales.

3.B. Based on a sample of 100 sales of cheap houses. Sale prices could be reconstructed for 49 sales. Obviously, the trend is only indicative for the market.

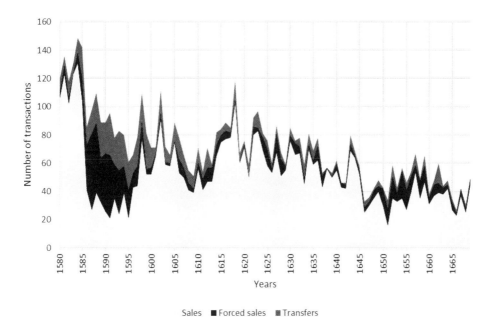

Graph 4 Sales, forced sales and transfers (1580-1670)

The number of property transfers relates to a sample of 23 per cent of all houses in Bruges (1,875 out of 8,129). Between 1580 and 1670, the total number of sales was 6,070, forced sales 1,085 and transfers of property rights 847. For full details see Deneweth 2008a, 562-622 (sales), 697-714 (forced sales), 717-729 (transfers of property rights).

goods of the debtor (Muldrew 1998; Stabel forthcoming). The remaining 70 per cent of the housing value can be considered as security for the creditors of non-mortgaged credit (Van Bochove, Deneweth & Zuijderduijn 2015). In Bruges, the average mortgaged debt during the 1580-1800 period equalled 27 per cent of the housing value. As soon as the weight of mortgages rose from an average 24 per cent of the housing price in the 1580s to 34 per cent in the 1590s, creditors were in a higher state of alert and proceeded to sequestration more easily, the more so since their maximum terms for intervention after the crisis of the 1580s were reached as well. The impact of sequestrations and auctions was never as high as it was during the 1585-95 period (graph 4).

This in turn, created an additional supply of houses and led to further declining housing prices, with ever higher rates of over-mortgaging. The *tRoot Hertkin* inn along the *Sint-Clarastraat* might be an extreme example. It changed owners 15 times between 1580 and 1630, in both voluntary sales and enforced auctions, while two parts of the garden were sold to neighbours. In 1620, the mortgage reached no less than 79 per cent of the value of the house, which kept the creditors of the successive owners in a high state of alert. Since buyers took over existing mortgages, they only had to make a very small down payment for the house, but soon found out that they were also incapable of paying the required interest on the mortgage, which left them without money for the maintenance works needed. The turnover of real property was high in these neighbourhoods, and the quality of lower-class housing deteriorated even more. Eventually, this particular inn, together with seven adjacent houses, was demolished for the construction of a new house intended for a higher-class investor.[3]

In lower class neighbourhoods, the combination of a prolonged period of declining living standards and extreme dearth around 1580, and of accumulated debts and falling housing prices proved to be detrimental for many small owners who were eventually forced to switch from owned to leased property. In this first phase, a large supply of housing created fertile ground for property concentration. But who bought property and for what purpose?

Investments and speculation lead to increasing inequality

Mayors, councillors, public servants, merchants, guild governors and entrepreneurs who decided to stay in Bruges were less affected by declining living standards. Many could fall back on their assets or income from business and investments. As a matter of fact, the enormous number of empty properties and the collapse of property prices at the end of the sixteenth century offered them the right opportunities to resettle in well-located neighbourhoods and expand their residences and workspaces. The micro-study of the *Riddersstraat* revealed that this former nucleus of international trade had become a residential neighbourhood in the sixteenth century. It was conveniently located near the *Burg,* where the administration of the city, of the Liberty of Bruges and of the bishop were all concentrated, a perfect location for the elites. Some owners profited from the property crisis of the 1580s to acquire houses there, or to expand existing residences and gardens, and reconvert adjacent houses into stables or coach houses. In the third case-study property patterns along the *Eekhoutstraat,* one of the main entrance roads to the old city centre, were analysed. The favourable commercial location ensured that none of these houses remained vacant for too long. They were in high demand from master craftsmen and shopkeepers and they were, therefore, never joined into larger units. Vacated houses in the side streets or backstreets, on the other hand, were often converted into workshops or warehouses. Both neighbourhoods maintained relatively high levels of residential owners throughout the seventeenth century, with 47 and 44 per cent in 1667, well above the urban average of 27 per cent (Deneweth 2020).

While the first years after the emigration shock of 1585 offered wealthier groups the opportunity to (re)settle in better locations or expand their own residences, soon afterwards they began to detect additional investment and even speculation opportunities in real property. The narrow definition of 'speculation' is 'to buy or sell in expectation of profiting from market fluctuations', but a more general definition is 'assuming a risk in hope of future gain' (Merriam Webster online dictionary). This future gain was expected on two levels: rent and sales.

The rental market seemed to be a good investment opportunity since small owners were massively switching to leased property. Since the general supply of housing was still too high, and thus housing prices were low, several investors took action to manipulate

---

3   CAB, OA, series 198, 713, f. 111 and f. 155; 69, p. 469; 775, f. 176; 1108, f. 184; series 138, Sint-Niklaas, f. 1477.

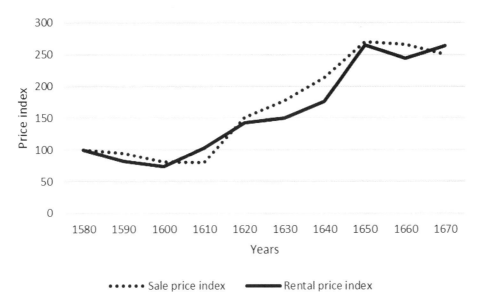

Graph 5 Comparison of sale price and rental price indices

This sale price index is based on a small sample of 196 houses and should be considered as indicative of a trend rather than representative of the entire market. Full details are in Deneweth 2008a, 609-618. The rental price index is based on Masson 1972, 3-94.

the rental market. Urban regulations, being promulgated in the – perhaps too optimistic – expectation that Bruges would be repopulated in the near future, forbade the demolition of houses.[4] Reality, however, differed from the norm, and we observe a divergent evolution between the city centre and peripheral neighbourhoods. In the city centre empty or existing rental houses in well-located neighbourhoods, such as the side streets of *Riddersstraat* and *Eekhoutstraat*, were joined into larger units, simply by making an additional opening between two houses on the upper floors. This had nothing to do with extending houses and creating more comfort for the residing owners as was the case with elite housing, but was meant to preserve the existing patrimony of rental houses. Even if the total number of houses declined, these larger units generated higher prices. It was often master crafts-men in construction who bought existing houses, joined them together, leased them for a couple of years and sold them again. In peripheral neighbourhoods, on the contrary, poorly maintained houses were simply demolished, integrated into neighbouring plots, or retained by the owners in the hope of future development (Deneweth 2008a, 253-303). A second evolution was not directly linked to speculation but eventually reinforced it. Since wars and looting in the countryside had driven many religious communities to their urban refuges, the spirit of the Counter Reformation stimulated them to build new convents and expand their domains in surrounding lower-class neighbourhoods. This was quite obvious around the *Ten Duinen* abbey in the north-east of Bruges, but several other

---

4   First proclamation: CAB, OA, series 120, reg. 1, f. 352 (1499); repeated in CAB, OA, series 120, reg. 9, f. 276v (1587), reg. 10, f. 375 (1602), reg. 11, f. 66 v (1605).

convents incorporated adjacent houses as well (Deneweth 2008b). The result of both evolutions was that by 1600 the demand for and supply of houses had adjusted again, and this finally countered the drop in housing prices.

In this very same period, between 1600 and 1620, the textile industry started to revive, wages in other sectors were adjusted to similar levels to those current in Antwerp and Ghent, and textile workers from southern Flanders and northern France started to repopulate Bruges, even if it was at a slower pace than hoped for. These immigrants were often lower skilled workers who could not afford their own houses and did not really intend to buy one, since they formed highly mobile groups which travelled between textile centres according to employment opportunities (Junot 2012). As a result of changing demographics, rental prices started to rise again, and investors were rewarded for their patience (graph 5). Since housing prices would soon follow the same trend, especially after the wages of master craftsmen had doubled, others realised that it was the right moment to buy cheap houses and make nice returns from rent, or from future sales. Unfortunately, the few prices I could collect for that period are insufficient to document speculation by buying and selling, but the combination of rising prices (graph 3) and high activity on the market for sales (graph 4) justifies this hypothesis that should be corroborated by future research.

Since wage adjustments in Bruges coincided with a period of declining food prices, we would expect an improved standard of living in combination with low housing prices to lead to more investment by the lower middling groups as well. This was not the case, for three main reasons. First, the previous crises of the sixteenth century (sustained declining living standards and an extreme dearth around 1580) had induced high indebtedness on the personal level. This not only affected the creditworthiness of possible buyers but made it also increasingly difficult to make the required down payments, since mortgages had to remain around 30 per cent. Second, the manipulation of housing supply and investments by the higher social groups drove house prices up much faster than labourers and master craftsmen could afford, especially in the market segment of cheap houses (graph 3b). The impact was disastrous for them. Wages of masons, for example, doubled at the beginning of the seventeenth century, from 3,024 to 6,048 Flemish groats for a bricklayer's assistant, and from 6,048 to 12,096 Flemish groats for a master mason. House prices, on the other hand, increased by a factor of 4.4 between 1580 and 1670. Whereas a bricklayer's assistant needed 1.6 annual incomes to purchase a cheap house in the 1580s, he needed 5.4 annual incomes to buy the same house in 1670. Obviously, it took him many more years before he could save the necessary amount for his deposit. Even if wages doubled, the cost of living increased much faster. Where a bricklayer's assistant spent 7 per cent of his annual income on a median rent in the lowest quintile of houses in 1580, he paid 11.2 per cent in 1670; a master mason's rent budget for houses in the second lowest quintile rose from 5.4 to 7.9 per cent of his annual income. One would expect that this was not that bad in the light of doubled wages. However, considering that during the first half of the seventeenth century food prices rose again by 49 per cent, and prices for combustibles tripled (firewood) or even quadrupled (peat), their savings capacity was severely affected, which is clearly reflected in property rates. The number of households living in their own houses dropped from 43 per cent in 1382 (perhaps a bit more around 1500) to 34 per cent in 1583 and a mere 27 per cent in 1667 (Deneweth 2008a). A third reason was the result of speculation. Wealthier families had invested in property with the purpose of leasing it. Although some of them must have profited from buying and selling in the period of fast rising housing prices, most families preferred to lease their property. This is clear from the average period of ownership of cheap housing which increased from 10 years for houses acquired in the 1580s to 39.4 years for houses purchased in the 1630s. Compared to the housing price at the date of purchase, the return from further increasing rents was quite lucrative. On the other hand, even if craftsmen were willing to buy a house – many of them were lower skilled and highly mobile migrants working in the textile sector – the opportunities to do so were much fewer from the 1630s onwards since wealthier investors were active on this very same market and drove housing prices up faster than craftsmen could afford. These three trends reinforced each other and led to a sustained concentration of property that was not countered once the crisis of the late sixteenth century was over.

Conclusion

Rental values of houses have often been used as indicators for changing income inequality over time or for differences in inequality between cities, often departing from the notion that everyone lives in the house he can afford (Ryckbosch 2016). Ryckbosch already suggested that rental values were perhaps not always representative of incomes, especially during periods of concentration of property. This case study of Bruges, with micro-studies for different neighbourhoods and social groups, has demonstrated that changes in the housing market itself prompted housing inequality.

During the Late Middle Ages, the introduction and wider use of new construction materials such as brick and tiles (instead of wood and straw) made housing more expensive and less accessible for the lower social groups. During the early modern period, investment strategies by wealthier groups, combined with a certain degree of manipulation of supply and demand on the housing and rental markets, influenced housing prices. However, it was the speculation strategies of wealthy investors that drove these prices up beyond the reach of the lower social (middling) groups. The differential price evolution of different housing categories reduced price variations on the housing market, suggesting that housing or income inequality was diminishing, whereas the social reality was that (rental) housing became more expensive and less accessible for the lower social groups, which was shown by the dropping property rates. This makes us question the representativeness of housing values of income inequality. The focus should be on changes in the housing market itself.

Concentration of property is indeed an important factor, but this can happen only in a context in which owners are willing or have been forced to sell their houses. Sixteenth-century Bruges witnessed the right circumstances for a larger supply on the housing market. Shifts in international trade and structural changes in textile production led to a slowdown in economic growth (especially when compared to Antwerp) and to social polarisation. Opposite migration trends (emigration of middling groups and immigration of labourers) gradually changed the social composition of the population. These processes eventually favoured the market for rental housing. The biggest problem, however, was the successive crises (see also Friedrichs 1975) that undermined the position of the lower social groups: a sustained decline in real wages, the erosion of the savings capacity, the extreme dearth around 1580, and the mass emigration of 1585 that not only destabilised the labour market but also created such a vacancy on the housing market that prices dropped. This in turn caused the over-mortgaging of houses and finally resulted in major shifts on the property market. We can compare this mechanism very well to what Thijs Lambrecht described in this book (Chapter 8). In his case study, it was increased taxation that undermined the purchasing power and savings capacity of lower social groups in the countryside.

Whereas the very much reduced purchasing power of lower social groups in Bruges prompted housing inequality at the end of the sixteenth century, this process was not countered when, around 1600, the wages of craftsmen and labourers doubled in a period when housing prices were still low. Unfortunately, the indebtedness of lower social groups was still such that they could not react in time, and the investment and speculation strategies of wealthy groups drove housing prices up too fast and took them beyond reach of many. Since rental prices usually reflect housing prices, the rapidly increasing rents took up an increasing share of the budget, which reduced the savings capacity once again. Dynamics in the housing market itself caused further inequality. Very similar mechanisms have been established by Thijs Lambrecht (chapter 8) and Sam Geens (chapter 12). Lambrecht demonstrated how increased taxation resulted in the loss of land formerly owned by lower social groups. It was urban elites who were the first to invest in this land. Sam Geens found that after wars the destruction of property (and lives) in the countryside opened up similar opportunities for urban elites to invest in land. In both cases the resulting concentration of property induced higher inequality as well.

Alfani (online 2019) has pointed to the institutional context as an explanatory factor in processes of inequality. The same link between institutions and inequality also resonates from Griet Vermeesch's chapter 11 in this book. She stipulates that lower courts could have been accessible for lower social groups, but it was exactly these groups that participated less frequently in court cases, the majority of which concerned credit relations. Institutions have not been the subject of my research, but it is clear that the urban authorities and existing legal systems mainly protected property and creditors, not tenants and debtors. For a large part of the population, it was regrettable that nothing was done to combat the excesses of speculation or to provide affordable social housing for workers. The lack of intervention reinforced the processes of inequality.

References

Alfani, Guido. 2015. "Economic Inequality in Northwestern Italy: a Long-Term View (Fourteenth to Eighteenth Centuries)." *Journal of Economic History* 75, no. 4 (December): 1058-1096.

Alfani, Guido. Online 2019. "Wealth and Income Inequality in the Long Run of History." In *Handbook of Cliometrics*, ed. Claude Diebolt and Michael Haupert. Berlin: Springer. https://doi.org/10.1007/978-3-642-40458-0_29-1.

Bertels, Inge, et al., eds. 2011. *Antwerpen. Biografie van een Stad*. Antwerp: De Bezige Bij.

Blockmans, Wim. 1998. "'Fondans en Melencolie de Povreté'. Leven en Werken in Brugge 1482-1584." In *Brugge en de Renaissance. Van Memling tot Pourbus*, ed. Maximiliaan Martens, 26-32. Bruges: Stichting Kunstboek.

Blondé, Bruno, Jord Hanus and Wouter Ryckbosch. 2018. "The Predatory State? Urban Finances, Politics and Social Inequality in Sixteenth-Century 's-Hertogenbosch." In *Entrepreneurs,*

Institutions & Government Intervention in Europe (13th-20th Centuries). Essays in Honour of Erik Aerts, ed. Brecht Dewilde and Johan Poukens, 101-115. Brussels: ASP.

Brown, Andrew, and Jan Dumolyn, eds. 2018. *Medieval Bruges c. 850-1550*. Cambridge: Cambridge University Press.

Deneweth, Heidi. 2008a. "Huizen en Mensen. Wonen, Verbouwen, Investeren en Lenen in drie Brugse Wijken van de Late Middeleeuwen tot de Negentiende Eeuw." Unpublished PhD thesis. Brussels: Vrije Universiteit Brussel.

Deneweth, Heidi. 2008b. "De Identificatie van Enkele Verdwenen Straten nabij de Potterierei in Brugge." *Brugs Ommeland* 48, no. 4 (October): 222-227.

Deneweth, Heidi. 2010. "Een Demografische Knoop Ontward? Brugse Bevolkingscijfers voor de Vroegmoderne Tijd." *Handelingen van het Genootschap voor Geschiedenis* 147, no. 1: 3-48.

Deneweth, Heidi. 2011. "Migratiebeleid, Armenzorg en Arbeidsmarktregulering. Brugge in de Zestiende Eeuw." In *Werken aan de Stad. Stedelijke Actoren en Structuren in de Zuidelijke Nederlanden 1500-1900. Liber Alumnorum Catharina Lis en Hugo Soly*, ed. Margo De Koster et al. 103-118. Brussels: ASP.

Deneweth, Heidi. 2020. *Goede Muren Maken Goede Buren. Verbouwingen en Buurtleven in Brugge (1500-1800)*. Bruges: Genootschap voor Geschiedenis.

Deneweth, Heidi, Ward Leloup and Mathijs Speecke. 2017. "Visualising Urban Change. Bruges (Belgium) 1300-1700." In *Mapping Urban Changes. Mapiranje Urbanih Promjena,* ed. Ana Plosnić Škarić, 336-363. Zagreb: Institute of Art History.

Deneweth, Heidi, Ward Leloup and Mathijs Speecke. 2018. "Een Versteende Ruimte? De Impact van Stedelijke Veranderingsprocessen op de Sociale Topografie van Brugge, 1380-1670." *Stadsgeschiedenis*, 13, no. 1: 19-40.

Dewitte, Alfons, and Antoon Viaene. 1977. *De Lamentatie van Zeghere van Male: Brugge na de Opstand tegen Spanje, 1590*. Bruges: Gidsenbond.

Eichholtz, Piet, and Thies Lindenthal. 2013. "That's What We Paid for It. The Spell of the Home Purchase Price through the Centuries." Working paper, version of 23 January 2013. http://www.cgeh.nl/sites/default/files/That%27s%20what%20we%20paid%20for%20it_2013-01-21_TL.pdf

Friedrichs, Christopher R. 1975. "Capitalism, Mobility and Class Formation in the Early Modern German City." *Past and Present,* 69, no. 4 (November): 24-49.

Gilliodts-van Severen, Louis. 1874-1875. *Coutumes des Pays et Comté de Flandre. Quartier de Bruges. Tome second. Coutumes de la ville de Bruges*. Brussels: Gobbaerts.

Godding, Philippe. 1960. *Le Droit Foncier à Bruxelles au Moyen Age*. Brussels: ULB – Institut de sociologie Solvay.

Junot, Yves. 2012. "Heresy, War, Vagrancy and Labour Needs: Dealing with Temporary Migrants in the Textile Towns of Flanders, Artois and Hainaut in the Wake of the Dutch Revolt (1566-1609)." In *Gated Communities? Regulating Migration in Early Modern Cities,* ed. Bert De Munck and Anne Winter, 61-80. Farnham: Ashgate.

Kuznets, Simon. 1955. "Economic Growth and Income Inequality." *American Economic Review* 45, no. 1 (March): 1-28.

Lindert, Peter H. 2000a. "Three Centuries of Inequality in Britain and America." In *Handbook of Income Distribution*, ed. Anthony B. Atkinson and François Bourguignon, 167-216. London: Elsevier.

Lindert, Peter H. 2000b. "Making the Most of Capital in the 21st Century." NBER Working Paper no. 20232, National Bureau of Economic Research, Cambridge, MA.

Masson, Freddy. 1972. "Huishuren te Brugge (1500-1796)." In *Dokumenten voor de Geschiedenis van Prijzen en Lonen in Vlaanderen en Brabant, XVe-XVIIIe eeuw,* ed. Charles Verlinden et al., 3, 3-94. Bruges: De Tempel.

Muldrew, Craig. 1998. *The Economy of Obligation. The Culture of Credit and Social Relations in Early Modern England.* Basingstoke: Palgrave.

Ryckaert, Marc, et al., eds. 1999. *Brugge: de Geschiedenis van een Europese Stad.* Tielt: Lannoo.

Ryckbosch, Wouter. 2016. "Economic Inequality and Growth Before the Industrial Revolution: the Case of the Low Countries (Fourteenth to Nineteenth Centuries)." *European Review of Economic History* 20, no. 1 (February): 1-22; https://academic.oup.com/ereh/article/20/1/1/2465267. Online appendix.

Scheidel, Walter. 2017. *The Great Leveler. Violence and the History of Inequality from the Stone Age to the Twenty-First Century.* Princeton, NJ, and Oxford: Princeton University Press.

Scholliers, Etienne. 1960. *Loonarbeid en Honger. De Levensstandaard in de XVe en XVIe Eeuw te Antwerpen.* Antwerp: De Sikkel.

Scholliers, Etienne. 1965a. "Lonen te Brugge en in het Brugse Vrije (XVe-XVIIe eeuw)." In *Dokumenten voor de Geschiedenis van Prijzen en Lonen in Vlaanderen en Brabant, XVe-XVIIIe Eeuw,* ed. Charles Verlinden et al., 2, 87-160. Bruges: De Tempel.

Scholliers, Etienne. 1965b. "Lonen te Gent (XVe-XIXe eeuw)." In *Dokumenten voor de Geschiedenis van Prijzen en Lonen in Vlaanderen en Brabant, XVe-XVIIIe Eeuw,* ed. Charles Verlinden et al., 2, 353-461. Bruges: De Tempel.

Stabel, Peter. Forthcoming. *A Capital of Fashion. Guilds and Economic Change in Late Medieval Bruges.* Oxford: Oxford University Press.

Thoen, Eric. 1994. "Immigration to Bruges during the late Middle Ages." In *Le Migrazioni in Europa (secc. XIII-XVIII). Atti della "Venticinquesima Settimana di Studi", 3-8 maggio 1993,* ed. Simonetta Cavaciocchi, 335-353. Prato: Istituto Internazionale di Storia Economica F. Datini.

Toch, M. 1973. "Prijzen uit Gentse Instellingsrekeningen (16de Eeuw)." In *Dokumenten voor de Geschiedenis van Prijzen en Lonen in Vlaanderen en Brabant, XVe-XVIIIe Eeuw,* ed. Charles Verlinden et al., 4, 326-396. Bruges: De Tempel.

Van Bochove, Christiaan, Heidi Deneweth and Jaco Zuijderduijn, 2015. "Real Estate and Financial Markets in England and the Low Countries, 1300-1800." *Continuity and Change* 30, no. 1 (May): 9-38.

van Zanden, Jan Luiten. 1995. "Tracing the Beginning of the Kuznets Curve: Western Europe During the Early Modern Period." *Economic History Review* 48, no. 4 (November): 643-664.

Verhulst, Adriaan. 1965. "Prijzen van Granen, Boter en Kaas te Brugge Volgens de 'Slag' van het Sint-Donatiaanskapittel (1348-1801)." In *Dokumenten voor de Geschiedenis van Prijzen en Lonen in Vlaanderen en Brabant, XVe-XVIIIe Eeuw,* ed. Charles Verlinden et al., 2, 3-70. Bruges: De Tempel.

Vermaut, Joseph. 1974. "De Textielnijverheid in Brugge en op het Platteland, Westelijk Vlaanderen voor 1800: Konjunktuurverloop, Organisatie en Sociale Verhoudingen." Unpublished PhD thesis, Ghent: University of Ghent.

PART V

Cultural and Consumer Dynamics of Inequality

Craft Guilds as Vectors of Middle-Class Values

Introduction. Craft guilds, guild identities and social inequality

The cities in the late medieval Low Countries went through a rollercoaster of social change from the late thirteenth century onwards. Urban growth in the central middle ages, when the southern Low Countries became with Italy the most densely urbanised region of Europe, was the result in the principalities of Flanders, Walloon-Flanders, Artois, Brabant and, at a later stage, even to a certain extent in Holland of the industrial deployment of textile industries (woollen cloth) in particular. Economic development was founded on almost industrial capitalist relations in the thirteenth century between extremely wealthy merchants and entrepreneurs and semi-proletarianised textile workers. But towards 1300 industrial change in many cities also transformed these highly polarised social relations. By then small-scale entrepreneurs were better placed to safeguard quality control in an industry ever more oriented towards producing high-quality fabrics. These clothiers (or drapers), usually craftsmen themselves, replaced the elite merchants and entrepreneurs as pivotal figures of industrial organisation. Instead of social polarisation between the extreme wealthy with direct access to political power and their poor labour force, cities tended to become less unequal, harbouring strong middle groups, which were able to force the traditional mercantile elites into differing levels of power sharing. Moreover, because of de-industrialisation and lower employment levels in textile manufacture, the proportion of semi-proletarianised workers declined significantly in most larger cities. In particular cities which lost part of their textile industries and started to focus on the manufacture of and trade in consumer goods, catering for the stronger middle groups, tended to be characterised by lower inequality in the fourteenth century, when the first data allow us to assess, be it very roughly, fiscal inequality. An overall reduction of inequality rates was therefore particularly strong in the more commercial cities such as Bruges, where transformation towards luxuries and fashion was more radical than in the traditional industrial cities, such as Ypres and Leiden, that still focused on textiles (Stabel forthcoming). The economic transformation towards luxury textiles, luxuries and consumer goods went hand in hand with a phenomenon that would define urbanity in the centuries to come: the coming of age of craft guilds as pivotal institutions in the urban corporative fabric.

In this changing social landscape, identities started to matter. Guilds aspired to political power as much as guildsmen aspired to achieve a particular position in urban society, by maximising income but also by acquiring status in society at large. Even from the analysis of early guild statutes it is clear that particular social identities were appropriated and performed from the moment guilds came of age in the late thirteenth century. It is less clear, however, to what extent they were also appropriated and put to use by the individual guild members themselves. Statutes and collective expressions of group identities are

Peter Stabel and Anke De Meyer • University of Antwerp

Inequality and the City in the Low Countries (1200-2020), ed. by Bruno BLONDÉ, Sam GEENS, Hilde GREEFS, Wouter RYCKBOSCH, Tim SOENS & Peter STABEL, SEUH 50 (Turnhout, 2020), pp. 271-287.

 DOI 10.1484/M.SEUH-EB.5.120450

one thing, social practices and experiences at the level of the social actor quite another. Scholarly attention has recently focused on how individual guildsmen identified themselves and with what kind of values they wanted to be associated (Dumolyn & Haemers 2012). In this chapter we want to point to particular collective identities that started to appear in thirteenth- and early fourteenth-century statutes, and how these were taken over by individual guild members.

In particular, the ways in which guildsmen presented themselves before a court of law prove useful in this respect. Guild identity must have mattered a lot to people who depended on the craft guilds for their livelihoods and for their social, cultural and religious networks. Moreover, because urban society was built on a multitude of often very different guilds ranging from craft guilds to military guilds and religious fraternities and because guilds carried a lot of weight in urban polity from the fourteenth century onwards, guild identity was important and most of all also very familiar, not only for the in-crowd of the members of the craft guilds, be they masters or journeymen, but also for urban society at large. But, of course, craft guilds constituted very heterogeneous groups of men (and only occasionally women). One guild could differ substantially from another in scope, in workshop organisation, in the access to social, economic, cultural and symbolic capital of the various members, and in their involvement in city politics, hence not all markers of guild identity must have suited everyone in similar ways.

Shifting identities and the emergence of the guilds before 1300

The period around 1300 witnessed a dramatic shift of labour identities in textile manufacture in many textile cities of the Low Countries. As the industry in the big industrial cities changed under market pressure from a massive producer of all kinds of woollens to a more selective producer of ever more refined and more expensive woollens, the balance of power within urban communities shifted in favour of the middle classes of skilled craftsmen and retailers. As a result the traditional mercantile and landowning elites had to compromise and share access to political power in cities such as Mechelen, Ypres and Gent, the most successful cloth cities in the southern Low Countries. The elites in the guilds therefore not only started to control manufacture, in the early 1300s they also started to influence the political levers of power that decided on economic organisation. As master craftsmen – in the first instance a select group of wealthier entrepreneurs – could achieve this pivotal role in urban society, they started almost at once to adapt the existing systems of organising labour markets, putting much more emphasis on the actual and often very hands-on labour relations inside the workshop or between workshops. As a result labour markets were increasingly formalised in order to facilitate strategies of small entrepreneurs. In the process the social and economic status of wage workers became more rigid (and gradually even their hold on guild politics diminished as well in favour of the masters, the small guild entrepeneurs). Labour markets were increasingly segmented, as journeymen (skilled and apprenticed guild workers), apprentices (young people learning the trade on the workshop floor), members of the household of the entrepreneur and finally unfree labour (unskilled workers or workers whose skills were not as such formally recognized in guild hierarchies operating largely outside the guild framework) were attributed specific roles in an ever more regulated guild economy. Yet, paradoxically, the implementation of these rigid labour controls was not just about market segmentation, the controls were also aimed at facilitating entrepreneurial strategies of the guild elites, the guild masters. These were given considerable freedom to tap into labour reserves as they saw fit. Labour time and relations on the workshop floor between employers and employees were strictly defined by guild statutes, but leverage was put in the hands of the guild masters who could employ one or another category of workers in function of labour shortages and their business strategies. The equilibria of power in the workshop fundamentally shifted in their favour. The guild masters lacked the financial, social, economic and even political power the thirteenth-century merchant-entrepreneurs had been able to mobilise. They made up for it by using an institutional framework, the guilds and the guilds' willingness to engage in the organisation of labour markets, to compensate for this deficiency. The craft guilds and their complex regulatory framework were crucial therefore for enforcing new social relations, while stimulating guild masters' agency in economic organisation (Stabel 2016, 159-180).

In order to facilitate these processes, guilds also seem to have simultaneously adopted a set of values that placed more attention on moral behaviour and strict hierarchies among guild members. Labour identities as a consequence also shifted considerably. The strict opposition between the fruits of manual labour and mercantile just profit made room for a hierarchical labour market. The former was negatively perceived, the latter positively. In the second half of the thirteenth century, the so-called pre-guild period, manual labour was still described by the mercantile elites in Mechelen as the 'despicable trades' (*fallacis officiis*). The politically powerful merchants preferred to keep labour identities in the dark, and they were only very rarely mentioned in the statutes and privileges of the cloth industry. But gradually in the late thirteenth century the regulatory framework was increasingly defined in moral terms. The new economic position of masters, journeymen, apprentices (all of them framed within the context of guild membership) and of the unfree workers (from members of the household to workers who were not indentured), of employers and employees was continuously linked to particular associations referring to a moral consensus of what work was and workers were. To a certain extent there was an economic reason for this. Construction of quality that was crucial for guaranteeing market transparency in an economic system that capitalised on high added value and collective guild control, was achieved through the guildsman's identity. It was the (male) master's and his (male) employers' reputation that guaranteed the quality of the product made or sold. And the construction of this quality also occurred through allegedly masculine values of self-restraint, trustworthiness and decency. Women were in the process ousted from the manufacturing process in most key economic activities. And even the mercantile activities of the workshop, contacts with suppliers of raw materials and with customers, were more and more restricted to either men or women albeit firmly embedded in the male-dominated household. The patriarchal household very much came to the fore in this period. The guild revolution was in many ways also a revolution of gender roles.

These dramatic changes left their imprint on the image and self-image of the guildsmen, and sometimes this happened almost immediately. When from the 1270s changing economic orientation forced cloth entrepreneurs in Ypres, Ghent and Mechelen to abandon mass production of all types of cloth, the statutes of the emerging guilds became to some extent a compromise between merchants' and craftsmen's identities and strategies. In Mechelen, one of the many large cloth cities, were wealthy merchant-entrepreneurs who, gathered in the local merchant guild of the wool trade (*wollewerck*), had made strong claims to political power and moral authority, the authority of the craft guilds, the organisations of the already mentioned 'despicable trades', for controlling industrial manufacture were slowly and very reluctantly recognised. But already at this early age, some of the rulings point in the direction of a regulatory environment that fully fledged craft guild organisation would achieve in the course of the fourteenth century. In the 1270 statutes of the Mechelen cloth workers, the training of apprentices was restricted to a limited circle of relatives or people of good name and conduct, which must have limited to no small extent competition among skilled artisans and must at the same time have reinforced their bargaining power with the mercantile elites. Moreover, seemingly strange 'moralistic' notions already in this early regulation must not be interpreted as a way for the ruling elites to force a bunch of craftsmen into adopting 'civilised behaviour'. They were probably not top-down arrangements. In the course of the fourteenth and fifteenth centuries these rulings would be part of the construction of a master craftsman's identity, and so they must be interpreted as such in the late thirteenth century as well. Reputation was to be one of the cornerstones of guild ideology; it was of essence for even the survival of the guild master's workshop. It was the instrument used to pursue social, economic and political aspirations, from setting standard qualities to maintaining relations of trust and credit. Hence fines for not wearing decent (of course woollen) dress during work for both employers and employees (masters and journeymen) and bans on living with prostitutes or on not paying (drinking) debts in due time can be seen as instruments in building a guildsman's reputation in a period when reputation was of key strategic importance to the success of the industry as a whole. It was a cornerstone in their competition with the urban elites for political and economic power.

From the 1300s on ever more refined systems of controlling guild behaviour were introduced almost everywhere, in particular in those cities where guilds achieved access to political power. Fines were levied on excessive drinking, on promiscuity and illicit sexuality, on gambling, not to mention far worse undesirable behaviour such as theft, fighting and cheating which was often put an end to by the guilds themselves in close collaboration with the urban authorities. Breaching a set code of behaviour was more and more considered unacceptable for a guildsman's proper behaviour. Fines of various kinds were intended to promote the moral decency that was expected of guildsmen, masters, apprentices and journeymen alike. Reputation and respectability were at the heart of the construction of guild identity. If guild masters and their employees were to act as a beacon of trustworthiness in a market characterised by ideas of a just price and asymmetrical access to information about the market itself and the products that were manufactured and traded, their behaviour should be beyond reproach. High moral values were reflected in high-quality products and in the prices guild masters could ask. In pre-industrial guild society, middle-class values of modesty, reliability, truthfulness and hard work entered the realm of the economy. A moral economy was not only about social and economic justice and equal opportunity, it was much more about identity and the alleged superiority of guild ideology in constructing urban society at large. This process fundamentally changed the social equilibrium in the manufacturing cities of the Low Countries. The rise of the middle classes, considered by many as one of the fundamental developments in the social history of late medieval and early modern cities of the Low Countries, is, therefore, intrinsically linked to the rise of new mentalities, of new moral codes.

See you in court! Guildsmen before a court of law

When brought before a court of law, guildsmen could actively adopt and deploy identifications and presentations of the self linked to their own collective guild identity and draw explicitly on their position as members of the guild, in the knowledge that these identities would be understood by all. These markers of guild identification, however, were also in dialogue with other identity markers (loyalty to the prince, charity, religious sensitivities and observance of religiously inspired moral codes, etc.) and with other identifications such as age (De Meyer 2014). The specific cocktail of identifications therefore reveals how guild identities related to other identities as well. Processes of self-fashioning before courts of law were also geared towards pragmatic behaviour in order to achieve particular goals. They needed to be reconciled with the legal and social expectations of the court. Moreover, because self-representation differed according to the situation, the performance of social identities was analysed in two very distinct judicial spheres, namely in fifteenth-century civil court cases and in criminal cases at a higher judicial level. In the former, guildsmen played on familiar territory. The city's aldermen, the main mediators of urban peace, were partly recruited from guild networks and their role in the civil proceedings in the city was primarily geared towards keeping the peace and defending social order. Proximity was the key to the success of the urban legal system and access to the legal system was relatively easy and cheap; proceedings were relatively fast, direct and efficient. This is also true for Bruges, a city which boasted more than 50 craft guilds, and, above all a city in which cloth manufacture was less dominant than in other similar cities of Flanders and Brabant, like Ypres, Ghent, Arras, Douai, Mechelen and Leuven. Civic identity in the late medieval cities of the Low Countries was to a large extent drenched in ideas of guild honour, and this was true for Bruges as well (Black 1984). Looking at court cases in the registers of the civil court of mid-fifteenth century Bruges, we can see that guild identifications were constantly invoked and that there was continuous reference to the legal framework that defined guild life, the statutes and privileges of the associations (Bruges City Archives - SAB, series 157, registers of 'civil justice').

For criminal cases, pardon letters for convicted criminals were taken as a starting point. These were issued by the prince (the Burgundian dukes in the fifteenth and the Habsburg rulers in the sixteenth centuries) and, of course, princely justice was well beyond the reach of the urban authorities (and therefore of the guilds). In contrast to urban criminal courts, guildsmen found themselves here on unfamiliar territory. The deployment of markers of guild identity is, therefore, telling for the way guildsmen used concepts and behaviour linked to guild life in fashioning themselves in contexts that are not directly associated with guild activity itself. The logic of pardon cases brought before the distant duke was, of course, very different from legal proceedings in the familiar urban setting. The individual guildsmen did not come before a court of law presided over by their peers, but before a strange court presided over by officials, increasingly also scholars of law, representing the prince himself. The expected result depended not primarily upon close scrutiny of guild and urban statutes and upon the involvement of networks of guildsmen they could activate, but upon the prestige, power and grace of the prince and his close collaborators. As a result, the discourses in the pardon letters were very layered, and to understand the strategies used by guild members as well as others the internal logic of the source itself must be addressed (Gauvard 1991; De Meyer 2014).

But besides this discourse of princely sovereign power, the pardon letters also contain the discourse of the wrongdoer, who had to convince the duke and his entourage of his worthiness to be forgiven (Arnade & Prevenier 2015). To achieve such a result, the subject had to strategically raise those aspects of his layered 'self' that established that he truly deserved the duke's favour. Being an ideal subject and a worthy person are returning tropes. The self-fashioning required implied activating those identities and networks available to him (and only very occasionally to her) that were useful for the convicted person to get what he wanted, and for the ducal entourage to use as an appropriate argument to explain this particular occasion for demonstrating the prince's forgiveness. Social status (and therefore access to the duke's attention) was, of course, of crucial importance, but it is striking that princely pardon reached practically all layers of society, from the poor and needy to noble and bourgeois elites, and among them also many guildsmen. As such, princely pardon seemingly ignored social status, age or gender – a rare unrestricted option in an age structured along social hierarchies (Gauvard 1991, 47). The relatively open access to princely pardon entails that the identification of a person by referring to his or her status, networks and reputation was important, but, above all, that an appropriate narrative – a carefully moulded plausible tale – had to be told that fashioned the wrongdoer as a stereotypical victim and allowed the duke to grant pardon (Davis 1987, 7-15; Prevenier 2004, 961-964). The narrative in the pardon letters is, therefore, also a strange mixture of legal process and the self-fashioning of petitioners.

The urban theatre of law: moulding social identities among peers

The civil court cases do not contain 'direct speech acts' and give at best only a short summary of the arguments (Stabel forthcoming). But besides the legalistic arguments that are based on an investigation of statutes, privileges and customary law we sometimes find traces of the arguments advanced by the parties in the final rulings. The arguments of both parties often addressed more or less directly the legislative and customary framework that regulated guild life. It is however not only the arguments, but also the strategies of self-fashioning, that touch the fundamental logic of the guild system. All the civil cases involving guildsmen have in common that the moulding and reproduction of guild identity was of the utmost importance. But at the same time not all markers of guild ideology were activated all the time and by everyone to the same degree. As argued elsewhere, guild litigation was at the heart of the guild system in the cities of the Low Countries (Stabel 2004). It is through permanent negotiation processes and through loopholes and inconsistencies in the regulatory environment that guild economies were able to thrive and adapt to new circumstances. No wonder that references to the statutes and the framework of guild and city custom and law were ubiquitous in the arguments before the aldermen.

The nature of civil law in a city such as Bruges was accusatory. The bench of aldermen decided on complaints by one party and its role was mostly that of an arbitrator. The aldermen's main task was to interpret the guild statutes and urban customary law, and to make changes if required. In fact, many court cases had run their course elsewhere. Merchants, guilds, even neighbourhoods and, of course, kin had their own informal (and sometimes even formal) ways of trying to solve conflict amongst themselves. It was often at the time when no such solution could be found that the bench of aldermen intervened (and they were sometimes, in the case of the foreign merchants in Bruges, clearly reluctant to do so). Not that such cases were considered as less crucial than those brought before the same bench as a criminal court of law (at this stage both via an accusatory procedure in the so-called *doorgaande waarhede* and as part of an inquisitory process, when the city's bailiff was involved). People's livelihoods or their wealth, their access to particular social and economic networks etc. could indeed depend upon the verdict of the aldermen.

In the middle of the fifteenth century, Bruges and its neighbouring satellite port of Sluis seem to quarrel constantly over issues of trade and manufacture. As most of the international trading ships arrived in Sluis (from where the merchandise was carried in small boats across the canal system to Bruges itself), the Bruges guild and city authorities were under threat of a potentially formidable competitor. Thus Bruges tried to limit the economic activities that could be organised in Sluis to port-related activities and to discourage international merchants from supplying themselves with goods in Sluis (Dumolyn 1997). In 1449 the guild of the Bruges old cloth sellers, one of the most important retail guilds in the city, took the case of old cloth seller Thomas Moreel to the Bruges court (SAB, Civil Justice, 1, 76v-77r.). The guild officials had convicted Thomas, who had been a former guild member in Bruges before he left the city for Sluis, to a huge fine of £50 parisis (100 days' wages of a skilled craftsmen) for having left the city without paying the taxes due to the city and the guild. Why Thomas had gone to Sluis is unknown, but his business interests must have remained largely in Bruges itself, because the Bruges guild complained (and fined him another £50) that he still maintained his old activities in Bruges, this time illicitly because he was a 'foreigner in Bruges' (*vreemde inder stede van Brugghe*). In his defence Thomas claimed that he wanted to become a Bruges citizen again and asked if his membership of the Bruges guild could be reactivated. Thomas argued that he was and always had been an honest guild member (in both Sluis and Bruges). Dual guild membership, in even more than one city was not that unusual in late medieval urban society. He claimed to be of 'modest means' (*schamelen staet*) and he begged 'unassumingly' (*omoedelike*) for re-entry into the Bruges guild. For this he would need the 'grace' (*gratie*) of the guild and the city authorities. His argument did not much impress the aldermen. In the end all the fines to which he had been condemned by the Bruges guild had to be paid and for his re-entry in the guild he would have to pay an additional entry fee.

The arguments put forward by Thomas Moreel clearly referred to specific attitudes, to what it really meant to be a guildsman. When needing the good 'grace' – a strange notion in guild terminology, because it was usually linked to the power of the prince – the process of self-fashioning seemingly required both modesty and poverty. Obedience to the guild authorities was felt to be crucial, although clearly in this case Thomas had broken all the rules by leaving without paying the taxes and returning to do his trade in Bruges without being a guild member. A very similar case in August 1454 opposed furrier Jan Meeus, who had moved from Bruges to the nearby town of Damme, to the Bruges furriers' guild. The same kind of self-fashioning before the court was Jan's strategy: he begged for comprehension in all 'modesty' to the city and the guild; he counted upon their 'grace' to do the right thing; he was 'poor and lived modestly' (*in soberen ende cleenen staet*); and he was prepared to return to Bruges and join the guild to be taken up in their midst again (SAB, Civil Justice, 2, 33v).

But poverty and modest status were by no means the only ways of self-fashioning for guildsmen in civil court cases. Association with other qualifications seems to have been as important. A very interesting court case from March 1453 opposed two groups of *patijnmakers*, manufacturers of wooden shoes (SAB, Civil Justice, 1, 318r-318v). The longstanding conflict –there were earlier verdicts of the Bruges aldermen in 1421 and 1441– was about the market stalls of the guildsmen. It was the tradition that the guildsmen with the longest experience as masters would be allowed to participate in a lottery for 18 market stalls close to the old cloth hall on the central Market square. The younger guild members would have to make do with other, less well located stalls further away from the core market activities. They were allowed to participate in the lottery only once one of the 18 older members had died or left the trade. In short, they had to wait their turn. Two concepts of the guild come into conflict in this case. On the one hand, guilds were notionally proud of giving their members (or at least the masters) equal access to economic opportunity; on the other hand, hierarchy (in this case decided by seniority) was as much part of guild life. The arguments of both parties are revealing of the self-fashioning of guild members. The younger members stressed the equality of membership and the fact that they were all Bruges citizens and as 'free' (meaning as much guild members) as their older colleagues. The argument even has a financial side to it: the 18 market stalls were maintained at the expense of the guild and all masters participated equally in the costs. In the end, the aldermen decided that the hierarchy was allowed to persist, but that the costs involving the 18 market stalls would be paid only by those who effectively held the stalls.

The same day –and this is certainly no coincidence– the older *patijnmakers* protested before the aldermen against the arrival of a younger colleague, Pieter Van den Dake, who had been allowed to participate in the lottery for the said 18 stalls. It is likely that the Van den Dake case had triggered the abovementioned litigation. Young Pieter had married the widow of an older guildsman, Pieter de Hekelare, and he had taken over his new wife's claim to one of the privileged stalls. Here again the notions of experience, old age and trustworthiness pop up in the guildsmen's arguments. Van den Dake had only recently become a manufacturer of wooden shoes, and, therefore, he did not deserve one of the good stalls, so the older masters argued. All this was, of course, spiced with sex, as the suspicion clearly behind the older guildsmen's arguments was that the younger Van den Dake had married the widow because of the profit he might expect from the marriage by taking over the deceased master's workshop and market stall. Respectability and trustworthiness were at the heart of a guildsman's identity. This time, however, the old guild members did not win their case. The widow's right was a key issue in all guild statutes of Bruges and Pieter van den Dake was, as the new master in an 'old' workshop (owned by his new wife), entitled to one of the good stalls (SAB, Civil Justice, 1, 318v).

The identity of guildsmen and their self-fashioning before a court of law were, of course, highly dependent upon the status of skill. In a dispute between the Bruges linen weavers and tapestry weavers in March 1453, two linen manufacturers were accused of manufacturing fabrics that normally would have been the prerogative of the tapestry weavers. The officials of the tapestry weavers clearly pointed out that their tools and techniques were very different from those of the linen weavers (*anderen engiene ende instrumenten*), and that, therefore, the work 'belonged to their own guild' (*toebehoorde haerlieder ambochte*). They argued further that such was 'the custom in Bruges' (*usancie binnen der stede van Brugghe*) and in other famous tapestry producing cities in the Low Countries, like Tournai and Brussels. A common guild identity beyond the city walls and even across the borders of the County of Flanders became an argument for a Bruges court of law. The aldermen decided to go for a compromise, forbidding a guildsman from doing work which belonged to another guild, but allowing him to do this if the craftsman was a member of both guilds (SAB, Civil Justice, 317v).

Solidarity was equally high on the agenda of guild identity. Breaching solidarity, either by achieving illicit profit at the expense of colleagues or by not getting involved in the collective activities of the guild (funerals, meals, religious celebrations), was often invoked when guild officials brought guild members before the city courts. When in 1454 butcher Lodewijk Breydel (a member of one of the leading butchers' families in the city and probably a descendant of the famous Jan Breydel who fought at the battle of Courtrai in 1302) insulted the guild officials (*ruuden worden*), he was required to make amends, not only by paying a fine to the city and the guild authorities, but also by asking publicly for forgiveness, paying for two large candles in the guild's chapel and going on a pilgrimage to Rome (SAB, Civil Justice, 2, 20r). Guild solidarity pops up, therefore, time and again in many cases brought before the aldermen. People talk about the 'common craft' (*ghemeenen ambochte*) as the institution that could guarantee all of its members fair access to markets for raw materials and manufactured goods. In November 1455 a dispute within the Bruges belt-makers' guild about labour relations between different specialist craftsmen was settled by the aldermen. The main argument of the parties concerned was that among guildsmen 'peace and love' (*pays ende minne*) should reign. The different occupations within the guild should also take turns in leading the guild.

Sometimes this solidarity needed to be implemented with the help of the aldermen. In March 1455 the Bruges aldermen had to act upon the request of the officials of the fish peddlers (*buerdenaers*). They were less formally organised than the formal and hereditary guild of the fishmongers (*viscoopers*), who sold their fish in the fish market. Members of the fraternity had become reluctant to pay their dues to the guild (1 penny for each basket sold for the maintenance of the chapel of St Josse) and to the guild's charity ('to sustain sick fish peddlers': *omme de verweicte buerdenaers mede te sustineirene*). The arguments were, as ever, centred on a common understanding of the basic qualities of the guild: it was solidarity among the members that constituted the essence of the guild. Trust is good, control is better, however. Henceforth, so the aldermen ruled, the guild money had to be kept in a chest with two keys, one held by the guild officials and the other by the aldermen themselves (SAB, Civil Justice, 2, 103v).

Self-Images in hours of need

The construction of the self was expressed differently in the pardon letters, and it is not only the legally convincing arguments that were recorded. In order to legitimise the prince's grace (and not to jeopardise the rule of law) most letters contain a well-crafted account of misfortune and coincidence that typically begins with the petitioner's daily business and builds towards a violent and often fatal confrontation. Petitioners constantly stressed that they neither intended nor initiated the acts in question and that the acts were caused by 'passion' (*chaude colle*) or accidental circumstance. To achieve a favourable outcome (and to give the ducal administration reason to grant a pardon) the juridical account needed to be skewed in favour of the supplicant, while remaining close enough to legal truth (Barthes 1982, 11-17). To forge the profile of a victim, the petitioner's account had to be exculpatory without casting doubt on the prince's justice. Hence a crime had to be admitted while the account was stuffed with justifications for what had occurred. Explaining the socially acceptable causes of violence and creating the image of a law-abiding perpetrator were the essence of a successful pardon-seeking letter (Arnade & Prevenier 2015). But discourses were not just aimed at explaining the act (anger, passion, drunkenness, self-defence, etc.), they were also aimed at presenting an image of the perpetrator who wanted princely pardon. Twenty-four pardon letters involving guildsmen could be found for fifteenth-century Bruges and 60 for Mechelen in the fifteenth and sixteenth centuries, and these constituted respectively 40 and 45 per cent of all pardon letters for those cities (Baatsen & De Meyer 2014, 23-39).

Most petitioners from Bruges and Mechelen, guild members and non-guild members alike, used similar elements to mould their stories and fashion themselves as stereotypical victims. As a rule, they had reacted to insults, were no longer in control of their actions or acted in self-defence. The great majority of pardon letters in our sample were granted for acts of manslaughter (see also for France Gauvard 1991, 22-24). This uniformity is not necessarily linked to the way people fashioned themselves before a court of law. The notions of self-defence, of anger, insult and reputation are legal grounds in respect of which all accused could ask for the leniency of the court. It is possible that in the construction of the pardon letters they were used almost automatically by clerks to transform a 'misdeed' (*villain fait*) into an excusable 'act' (*beau fait*) and help the petitioners to put a plausible story forward to the prince (Gauvard 1991, 67). Other arguments focus on the unpremeditated and unintentional character of the offender's deed (*sans penser aucune malice*), while elaborating on how the victim had in fact provoked the offender.

One of the petitioners, Gillekin Kerssavent, a young butcher from Mechelen, and Genkin Schoof, probably also a Mechelen butcher, had dinner together with some colleagues in the *La Tasse* tavern on a Monday night in July 1474. After their dinner they went to a brothel called *De Bonten Osse* where a fight broke out between Genkin and a Hannekin Colbrant (the diminutive forms point to the fact that these were all still young men: Dupont 2001 and 2012). After breaking up the fight, Gillekin left the scene, not suspecting that another fight would occur only moments later. Shortly after his departure, Genkin caught up with him and shouted out, 'Brother, I am wounded, he has killed me' (*Ha frere, je suis navré, il m'a tué*). He begged Gillekin to take his revenge on the perpetrator, the aforesaid Hannekin. Gillekin acted accordingly out of 'recklessness and hot anger' (*malvais corage et de chaude colle*) and, being 'angry and very drunk' (*eschauffé et avoit bien beu*), he stabbed Hennekin in the neck with his dagger. Although physicians labelled the wound as not life-threatening, Hannekin nonetheless died because, the petitioner claimed, of the lack of proper care.

Throughout the narrative, the petitioner is identified as an exemplary, impeccable and humble subject. He is the real victim because he acted only out of uncontrollable anger caused by seeing the injuries of his companion who, by using the notion of brotherly love, appealed to what must have undoubtedly been a forceful guild image (Farr 2001, 264). There is little doubt that the brotherly feelings expressed by Genkin were built on their shared occupation and their joint membership of the guild. It is also likely that it was this feeling of solidarity and mutual assistance that resulted in the fatal outcome. The use of the reference to fraternity was, therefore, strategically added to make the action more understandable for the court, but it referred above all to genuine ideas about guild solidarity (Prak 1996, 255-280). In the pardon-seeking letter the terms 'hot anger' (*chaude colle*) and *eschauffé* (literally 'warmed up') are used explicitly at least four times and their meaning is carried throughout the narrative.

Sudden anger, an emotion that undermined and eventually swept aside self-control, was a well-known juridical concept. The influential fifteenth-century Flemish legal writer Philippe Wielant considered anger with self-defence as a mitigating factor. Its frequent use in most pardon letters allowed the duke to excuse manslaughter (Arnade & Prevenier 2015; Monballyu 1995, 196-197), but, nonetheless, guildsmen were inclined to use this notion slightly more often than other petitioners. Similarly the notion of self-defence, and in particular the annoying disturbance of their daily activities, as a cause for the sudden explosion of violence appears more frequently in the pardon letters of guildsmen than in those of other petitioners. Drunkenness (ranked with gluttony) was, with anger, another circumstance that was often invoked in criminal law to explain the crime. It is striking, however, that drunkenness and lust were invoked less frequently in pardon letters issued to guild members, possibly because professional and personal honour was part of the guild canon and expected of members by both the guild authorities and society at large (see also Prevenier 2012, 266). Strikingly measures against drunkenness (and the fact that bills for drink would not be paid) and against adulterous relations and promiscuity (with prostitutes) were also integrated into guild statutes. The integration of this 'persuader' in of Gillekin Kerssavent's pardon letter can as such be explained by his youthfulness. Drunkenness and uncontrolled sexual activity were circumstances that return frequently in the pardon letters of younger people. Getting drunk was inextricably part of medieval youth culture and could help, therefore, to establish the unpremeditated nature of Gillekin's crime (De Meyer 2014).

If explaining the circumstances of the crime was already sensitive to being a member of a guild (or to being of a particular age), the identifications intended to sketch the particular social, psychological or occupational profile of the perpetrator were even more related to guild identity (De Meyer 2014; Baatsen & De Meyer 2014). When taking a closer look at Gillekin Kerssavent's parden-seeking letter, we can see that he presented himself as a 'a young journeyman about to get married, a butcher and citizen of Mechelen' (*jeune compaignon a marier, bouchier, demourant en ceste notre ville de Malines*) and as a person 'never convicted before of any misdeed, blame or reproach' (*ne convaincu d'aucun villain cas, blasme ou reproche*). These characteristics, even though they represent his personality, rely on a set of prescriptive, conventional and stereotypical identifications. Although for example servants and other non-guild members also included in their pardon letters their status as burghers of a particular city, members of crafts guilds did so in significantly greater numbers (two and a half times more than non-guildsmen described themselves as citizens of Mechelen). Equally important for the self-fashioning of guild members are the fact that they were married (more than twice more than non-guild members) and had the care of children (more than three times more), the patriarchal household being the cornerstone of economic organisation and guild identity. Only occasionally did guilds – for example the Bruges manufacturers of rosaries – require their members (or rather their masters) to be married, but for self-identification before a court of law marriage was an important feature of guild identity nonetheless. More surprisingly, reputation was not a particularly strong guild identifier: almost half of all guildsmen invoked their social reputation, but one third of the other petitioners did so as well. In contrast to other petitioners, guildsmen did not include having connections in high places and the fact that they were 'loyal servants' of the duke is less pronounced in their identification strategy.

It is therefore general identifiers related to the household (married, children to take care of) and the urban community (citizenship) that seem particularly powerful, not so much references to reputation.[1] Combined with notions of solidarity with fellow guildsmen these identifications point to the responsibility guildsmen had in society, for their families, for their fellow guild members and for the urban community as a whole. This is confirmed by particular identifications that have to do with their status as people who worked hard for their income. Many of the identifications linked the notion of having to support a family with the fact that the petitioners were earning their livelihoods through hard work. Although the notion of industriousness is used only sparingly by guild members (and almost not at all by others), it is their status as wage earners or earning a livelihood through hard work that sets them apart from others, as much as being part of a group that required acts of solidarity with fellow members (these qualifications were almost never used by non-guild members). One quarter of all guild members used this in their pardon letters, while it is almost completely absent in the other pardon letters. Moreover hard labour is typically combined in the letters with the notion of poverty. Being seen as poor is a qualification that can also be found in other letters, but it is used substantially more often in those written for guild members (more than twice as likely as for non-guild members).

The term 'poor' (*povre*) was, as we have seen, also widely employed in the civil court cases. It looks quite paradoxical because the fifteenth and sixteenth centuries were a period, after all, when poverty was increasingly moralised and poor relief was gradually limited to those who belonged to a fading number of 'deserving poor' (Lis & Soly 1979). In a pardon letter for Joos Ritsaert, a butcher in Bruges, we can read about the petitioner that he was a 'poor butcher' (*povre home bouchier*). This must have been quite an unusual combination. The Bruges butchers, partly because of the hereditary nature of their trade, traditionally belonged to the economic and financial elites of the city (Van Werveke 1942, 14-15). According to Claude Gauvard, who has studied the French royal pardon letters, the use of the term 'poor' has to be interpreted as 'a moral connotation … anticipating the transformation of a criminal into a humble subject' (Gauvard 1991, 400-410). Being

---

1   In the following analysis only the published quantified data for Mechelen will be discussed: the identifications mentioned in De Meyer 2014 are much more detailed than in the case of Bruges. The results are summarised in the annex.

branded as poor and modest seems, therefore, in particular for guildsmen to be a strategy of fashioning identity that was considered as particularly suitable for requesting a favour. Ritsaert used his guild identity in the most explicit manner by referring specifically to guild hierarchy. He was a 'free butcher' (*franc boucher*) after all, which distinguished him from his victim Hannekin van Bassevelde, who was 'just' a butcher's boy. Furthermore he stressed in his letter the fact that by his honest occupation not only did he provide a public service for his fellow citizens, but also escaped poverty and hardship: he was a modest craftsman and a man of good and honest conduct who plied his trade to make a decent living (*homme de bonne et honneste vie, faisant son dit mestier et gaignant son pain au moyen diceluy le mieulx que possible*). But this is clearly at odds with the nature of the butcher's trade in Bruges. Access to the trade was limited to only a small number of families, and sons usually took over from their fathers. This advantage, in combination with the increased consumption of meat in the late middle ages, made the butcher's trade a highly profitable one. Moreover, Ritsaert's identification as a 'free' butcher places him among the 17 elite butcher families with direct access to stalls in the meat hall. The Ritsaert family regularly provided members for the bench of aldermen of Bruges throughout the fifteenth century. It is therefore safe to assume that Joos must have belonged to the economic and political elite of the city (Baatsen & De Meyer 2014). Hence, the phrasing 'making a living as best as he could' in the context of an elitist and probably very wealthy butcher must be interpreted as a well-considered strategy rather than as a well-founded concern about the living conditions of guildsmen. The argument of poverty is very significant: guildsmen linked themselves to the modest lifestyle of people struggling to make a living for themselves and their families. Labour is associated with effort. If the changing attitudes towards the poor in the late medieval period were real enough, the poor were however not just on the receiving end. Their role was not only passive (Stabel forthcoming). For a long time the medieval ambiguities towards the poor survived, and linking poverty to guild identity did not constitute a problem. In their arguments before the urban courts of law and even before the prince directly, guildsmen did not hesitate to utilise their own poverty, real or imagined, to get things going their way. Poverty and bourgeois values of hard work and respect for hierarchy did not have to coincide all the time. On the contrary a modest demeanour and hard-working life to make ends meet were very much associated with guild identities. Guild members prided themselves on being poor, even when they were not. Poverty, or the image of poverty rather, was still an honourable thing. In other words, poverty was, contrary to what the rhetoric of the early humanists suggests, not necessarily associated with idleness. When a (probably wealthy) Bruges butcher claimed that he was a poor man who had to work in order to feed his family, poverty was not necessarily a shameful condition. It was not yet the antithesis of work, as it would be in the sixteenth century.

In the same case one of his fellow butchers assisting Joos Ritsaert, Hendrik Codde, represented himself as a peaceful man who made a living from his trade (*homme paisible, vivant de son dit mestier*). The key word is, of course, 'mestier', the guild occupation that defines the life of a guildsman. In 1470 the Bruges fishmonger George Uuten Kelnaire was courting a girl while drinking together with his fellow guildsmen in their favourite tavern the *Bree Steegere* (ADN, B1694, fol. 47-48v). When 'his' girl said she was leaving to visit her mother, George became suspicious. He followed her and saw her entering another tavern, the *Mint*, where she met another man, Simon Joos. The inevitable happened; a fight broke out with Simon and his companions. Injured, George returned to his favourite haunt and told his fellow guildsmen what had happened. Again the notion of solidarity among guildsmen pops up. Hearing his account, three or four fellow fishmongers accompanied him to the *Mint* and a row started with the company Simon was in. Daggers were drawn and George wounded Simon to 'save his life' (*pour garder sa vie*). Because the wounds were not cared for properly, Simon died a few months later and George was banished from Bruges. Although there is no record of the actions George's co-workers took in the tavern, the fact that they accompanied him there after hearing his report and that they held their daggers at the ready indicates that they would have been prepared to fight, if necessary, in order to help their companion to resolve the quarrel. In another case in November 1490 two painters were involved (ADN, B1707, 1 and B1708, 19). Lieven Meuckins from Antwerp had joined Heyn Kaerle from Mechelen for supper in an inn. They were accompanied by various 'honourable men' (*gens de bien*). Both were wage-earning painters (*compaignons* or journeymen). Heyn got into a violent dispute with a servant at the tavern, who accused him of not having paid his share of the bill. Fearing that Heyn would get injured, Lieven came to his rescue, took a sword from one of the tables and followed him to make sure everything would be all right. He found Heyn alone but still greatly enraged outside the tavern without a trace of the servant and gave him the good advice to go home rather than fight things out. But the inevitable happened and a fatal fight ensued. As a member of a collective it was a guildsman's duty to maintain his professional and personal honour in order to uphold the integrity and good reputation of his guild. This included giving good advice, but in the end standing by your 'brother' in his hour of need was of the utmost importance for upholding collective values, even when it involved violence and breach of the duke's peace.

Conclusion

The late middle ages were a period of dramatic social change. As urban economies transformed from all-encompassing cloth manufacture to luxury textiles and consumer goods, new middle groups, most of them organised into craft guilds, started to control the urban manufacturing and retailing networks. In many cities guilds also managed to gain access to political power. In this change new sensitivities about social and cultural standards in society started to gain importance. Economic change went hand in hand with new moral codes that were adopted by guildsmen and were also quickly put to use in their competition in urban society with other groups. The moral values attributed to all true guildsmen to a large extent legitimised the stronger social position of the urban middle classes in late medieval urban society. Guild statutes combined new approaches to organising labour and product markets with a new morality. The complex social system of late medieval cities, with its multitude of associations and often conflicting loyalties, required individuals and social groups to flaunt their social identities depending upon social status and circumstance. So members of craft guilds adopted particular identification strategies when confronted with courts of law. They were inclined to use the ideological constructs that defined guild life and that were built on solidarity and the guildsman's reputation of poverty and modesty, hard work and trustworthiness. In their own urban environment these were often used very explicitly but, as the pardon letters of the Dukes of Burgundy demonstrate, guild rhetoric also found its way into non-urban princely courts, where it became part of the petitioner's identity as the loyal subject.

Appendix

The Princely Pardon Letters for Mechelen 15th-16th century (source De Meyer 2014). Elements of identifications and self-fashioning (%)
    (identity of the petitioner = a: guildsman; b: non guildsmen; c: all petitioners; d: identifications of guildsmen vs. non guildsmen (=a/c)

Table 1 The circumstances of the crime

	A Guildsman	B Non guildsman	C Total	D A/C
(N)	(60)	(75)	(135)	
anger	46,7	29,3	37,0	1.6
self-defence	40,0	26,7	32,6	1.5
daily routine	10,0	5,3	7,4	1.9
pleasure	13,3	13,3	13,3	1
without suspicion	11,7	8,0	9,6	1.5
drunkenness	10,0	10,7	10,4	0.9
lust	6,7	10,7	8,9	0.6

Table 2 Identifications of the petitioner

	A Guildsman	B Non guildsman	C Total	D A/C
(N)	(60)	(75)	(135)	
Wage-earner	23,3	1,3	11,1	17.5
occupational solidarity	16,7	1,3	8,1	12.5
care of children	53,3	16,0	32,6	3.3
citizen	40,0	16,0	26,7	2.5
married man	60,0	25,3	40,7	2.4
poor man	26,7	12,0	18,5	2.2
man of reputation	45,0	34,7	39,3	1.3
industrious man	5,0	4,0	4,4	1.3
man of reason	13,3	21,3	17,8	0.6
well connected	0,0	12,0	6,7	-

Abbreviations

ADN B Archieves départementales du Nord, série B
SAB : City archives of Bruges

References

Arnade, Peter, and Walter Prevenier. 2015. *Honor, vengeance, and social trouble: pardon letters in the Burgundian Low Countries.* Ithaca, NY: Cornell University Press.

Baatsen, Inneke, and Anke De Meyer. 2014. "Forging or reflecting multiple identities? Analyzing processes of identification in a sample of fifteenth-century letters of remission from Bruges and Mechelen." *Revue du Nord* 30: 23-39.

Barthes, Roland. 1982. "The Reality Effect." In *French Literary Theory Today,* ed. Tzevetan Todorov: 11-17. Cambridge: Cambridge University Press.

Black, Antony. 1984. *Guilds and Civil Society in European Political Thought from the Twelfth. Century to the Present.* Ithaca, NY: Cornell University Press.

Blockmans. Wim. 1971. "Nieuwe gegevens over de gegoede burgerij van Brugge in de 15de eeuw." In *Studiën betreffende de sociale strukturen te Brugge,* ed. Wim Blockmans et al. Heule: Standen en Landen.

Davis, Natalie Zemon. 1987. *Fiction in the archives.* Stanford, CA: Stanford University Press.

Dumolyn, Jan. 1997. *De Brugse opstand van 1436-1438.* Kortrijk: Standen en Landen.

De Meyer, Anke. 2014. *'Tot synder goeden fame ende name'. De 'self-fashioning van Mechelse en Brugse stedelingen in de laatmiddeleeuwse en vroegmoderne genadebrieven.* Antwerp: unpublished PhD thesis, University of Antwerp.

Dumolyn, Jan, and Jelle Haemers. 2012. "A Bad Chicken was Brooding: subversive speech in Late Medieval Flanders." *Past and Present* 214: 45-86.

Farr, James R. 2001. *Artisans in Europe 1300-1914.* Cambridge: Cambridge University Press.

Dupont, Guy. 2001. "Van Copkin over Coppin naar Jacob. De relatie tussen de voornaamsvorm en de leeftijd van de naamdrager in het Middelnederlands op basis van administratieve bronnen voor het graafschap Vlaanderen, einde 14de-midden 16de eeuw." *Naamkunde* 33: 111-218.

Dupont, Guy. 2012a. "Le temps des compositions. Pratiques judiciaires à Bruges et à Gand du XIVe au XVIe siècle (Partie I)." In *Préférant miséricorde à rigueur de justice: Pratiques de la grâce (XIIIe-XVIIe siècles),* ed. Bernard Dauven et al.: 53-95. Louvain-la-Neuve: Presses universitaires de Louvain.

Dupont, Guy. 2012b. "Le temps des compositions. Pratiques judiciaires à Bruges et à Gand du XIVe au XVIe siècle (Partie II)." In *Amender, sanctionner et punir. Recherches sur l'histoire de la peine, du Moyen Âge au XXe siècle,* ed. Marie-Amélie Bourguignon et al.: 15-47. Louvain-la-Neuve : Presses universitaires de Louvain.

Gauvard, Claude. 1991. *De grace especial: Crime, état et société en France à la fin du Moyen Âge.* Paris: Publications de la Sorbonne.

Lis, Catharina, and Hugo Soly. 1979. *Poverty and capitalism in pre-industrial Europe.* Hassocks: Harvester Press.

Monballyu, Jos, ed. 1995. *Filips Wielant. Verzameld werk I. Corte instructie in materie criminele.* Brussels: Paleis der Academiën.

Prak, Maarten. 1996. "Individual, corporation and society: the rhetoric of Dutch guilds (18th C.)." In *Individual, corporate and judicial status in European cities (late middle ages and early modern period)*, ed. Marc Boone and Maarten Prak: 255-280. Leuven: Garant editors.

Prevenier, Walter. 2004. "Les multiples vérités dans les discours sur les offenses criminelles envers les femmes dans les Pays-Bas méridionaux (XIVe et XVe siècles)." In *Retour aux sources. Textes, études et documents d'histoire médiévale offerts à Michel Parisse*, ed. Sylvain Gouguenheim et al.: 955-964. Paris: Picard.

Prevenier, Walter. 2012. "The notions of honor and adultery in the fifteenth-century Burgundian Netherlands." In *Comparative Perspectives on history and historians: Essays in memory of Bryce Lyon (1920-2007)*, ed. David Nicholas et al. Michigan: Medieval Institute Publications.

Stabel, Peter. 2004. "Guilds in the late medieval Low Countries: myth and reality of guild life in an export-oriented environment." *Journal of Medieval History* 30: 187-212.

Stabel, Peter. 2016. "The Move to Quality Cloth. Luxury Textiles, Labour Markets and Middle Class Identity in a Medieval Textile City. Mechelen in the Late Thirteenth and Early Fourteenth Centuries." In *Europe's rich fabric: the consumption, commercialisation, and production of luxury textiles in Italy, the Low Countries and neighbouring territories (fourteenth-sixteenth centuries)*, ed. Bart Lambert and Katherine Anne Wilson: 159-180. Farnham: Ashgate-Routledge.

Stabel, Peter. Forthcoming. A *capital of fashion. Guilds and economic change in late medieval Bruges.*

Van Werveke, Hans. 1942. "Ambachten en erfelijkheid." *Mededelingen van de Koninklijke Vlaamsche Academie voor Wetenschappen, Letteren en Schoone Kunsten van België*, 51: 14-15.

INNEKE BAATSEN

In Haste for Better Taste?

The Social Effects of Changing Dining Cultures in Fifteenth- and Sixteenth-century Bruges

Introduction

'The inhabitants of Bruges are sympathetic and more polite, more artfully gifted and more cheerful than most other inhabitants of Flanders. They have a refined and extraordinarily well-mannered attitude and they are eagerly prepared to invite strangers into their houses and respect their guests' habits and customs' (De Keyser 2010, 129).

Thus reads a passage from the famous travelogue kept by Thomas Platter (1574-1628) written after visiting Bruges in 1599. Hospitality seems to have been a remarkably positive feature of the Bruges population, as reported by several other visitors to the city, and this in periods of both prosperity and decay. Monetarius (1447-1508) for example praised the social skills of Bruges inhabitants and the fine manner of welcome given by Jan Franck, who offered him a place to stay in his house (Ciselet & Delcourt 1942, 43-49). Also, while celebrating Bruges' hospitality, Pero Tafur (1410-1487) wrote that 'in this city, nations from all over the world, be they friend or foe, dined together at the same table, (De Keyser 2010, 194). The travelogues emphasised that not only public but also private domestic sociability had become important in offering opportunities to communicate and negotiate a family's social status to the invited table guests. One of the most social activities organised within the confines of the house was the organization of dinner parties. During the dinner event, social codes were to be followed to act and behave in the required 'proper' manner. Such propriety allowed one to build an image of creditworthiness, necessary to make business agreements or to conclude commercial contracts. Yet the material setting, the tableware and dishes served were also part of a household's social identity and status. This chapter explores the importance of dining rooms over the course of the fifteenth and sixteenth centuries, connecting changes in material culture and taste preferences to the disruptive social dynamics of Bruges. It will be especially interesting to test the resilience of the city's middling ranks, whose wealth and success were closely interwoven with a changing socio-economic climate.

In the late middle ages craftsmen, artisans and local merchants constituted the majority of these middling ranks. Due to Bruges' pioneering gateway function for international trade, high-end retail, luxury products and fashion, the urban middling ranks gained a uniquely powerful position which was reflected in their wealth and social status. However, this dependence on commercial success equally put urban society under severe pressure when economic and political shifts occurred. From the 1440s to the 1590s, the successful

Inneke Baatsen • University of Antwerp

Inequality and the City in the Low Countries (1200-2020), ed. by Bruno Blondé, Sam Geens, Hilde Greefs, Wouter Ryckbosch, Tim Soens & Peter Stabel, SEUH 50 (Turnhout, 2020), pp. 289-307.

DOI 10.1484/M.SEUH-EB.5.120451

economic gateway had turned into an economically devastated, depopulated town as a result of political troubles, famine, and subsequent commercial setbacks. This was a gradual process, for although the movement of international commerce from Bruges to Antwerp has been the topic of intense debate, it has been emphasised that the city maintained its status as an important commercial centre until well into the sixteenth century (Van der Wee 1963; Blondé et al. 2007). To those living in the 1540s and 1550s, there were indeed still signs that there was prosperity ahead and the future seemed bright. Nonetheless the fact remains that in 1544 it was estimated that 25 per cent of Bruges' population lived below the poverty line (Deneweth 2002, 91). Shifts in international trade and craftsmanship benefited the local elites and entrepreneurs, while the majority of the population was plagued by poverty by reason of a reduction in real wages and a rising cost of living. This majority was no longer composed of skilled artisans and shopkeepers, but unskilled and proletarianised wage labourers, leaving a considerably smaller group of middle class shopkeepers (Deneweth 2010, 47).

Meanwhile, new fashions in cheaper materials started to introduce more affordable luxuries, causing socially more inclusive consumption by offering inexpensive alternatives available to a broader spectrum of the urban population (De Vries 2003, 41-56). In this age of humanism, when table etiquette started to proliferate and the global economy brought new foods, new material goods and new cultural models to Bruges, it becomes very interesting to look at how these novelties were adopted and made use of in a deteriorating socio-economic urban setting. In becoming essential assets for negotiating social status, the characteritics of domestic conviviality present themselves as very good proxies for a household's sociability, depending on its ability to live up to the required material, spatial and social requirements attached to the performance of this conviviality. Did the middling ranks succeed in reaffirming and renegotiating their social status and urban identity by means of a new material dining culture? The analysis of the changes in domestic dining culture offers welcome new insights into how changes in materiality went hand in glove with changing social codes and the renegotiation of social boundaries.

An estate to die for?

The household perspective of domestic dining cultures requires the thorough analysis of a unique source: the household inventory. Detailed household inventories in Bruges are available from the fifteenth century, keeping their unique detailed character until at least the 1620s. As result, 502 inventories, covering the fifteenth and sixteenth centuries, were analysed in a relational database and distributed over five sample periods (see Figure 1 below). Due to the many inconsistencies in the process of registration by the urban magistrates, comparison between household inventories over a longer period is complex, requiring in some cases only a careful, selective use of inventories when investigating a specific topic.[1] However, in order to identify changes in how social groups were dealing with new material dining cultures, we needed a valid proxy for social stratification covering

---

1   For instance, in trying to assess changes in the function and decoration of dining rooms, all inventories that are not structured according to a house's room sequence, were omitted from the sample for analysis.

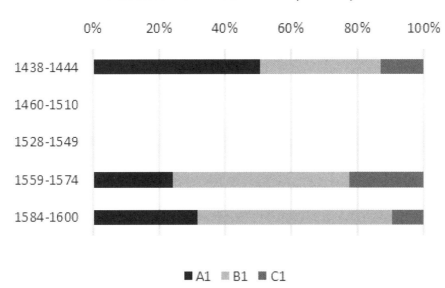

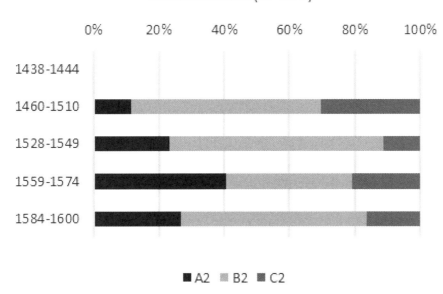

Figure 1. Stratification of Bruges household inventories |N=497|

Source: Database of inventories © Inneke Baatsen, Julie De Groot & Isis Sturtewagen

the whole period. Consequently we applied a complex stratification method consisting of the number of household items (or, rather, groups of items, hence RUC means Record Unit Count), and compared these with the number of rooms and the household's position in the few tax registers we have for sixteenth-century Bruges (Baatsen 2016). In order to assess changing dining culture strategies of the middling ranks over time, a control group was used to ensure that our samples represented a relatively comparable share of Bruges' society in both centuries. Previous research on late medieval Flemish and Brabant society, has ascertained that middling layers mostly comprised artisans and shopkeepers (De Meyer 1971; Blondé et al. 2018, 82-89). Because the occupational status of a sufficient number of households was known for each sample period, a smaller control group of 'middling rank' households could be defined through selecting artisans and shopkeepers. Then we calculated the median and quartile values for the RUC of this control group. Consequently, the wealthiest and poorest quartiles were separated from this generic control group, resulting in a group of households representing the statistical 'core' of the middling layers of Bruges society and thus being as close as possible to what must have been the middling ranks in each sample period. As can be seen from Figure 1, this group has been labelled the 'B group', while the 'A group' represents the lower middle to poorer ranks of society and the 'C group' denotes the higher middle ranks and urban elites. In subdividing the stratification into two categories (post mortem and confiscation inventories), we avoid the risk of ignoring source-specific characteristics when conducting broader analyses.

This allows for comparison between confiscation and post mortem inventories over a longer timespan, which is attested to by a unique example from confiscation and post mortem inventories belonging to one family yet drafted in two different periods. Because of an outstanding debt to Adriaen Codde, fishmonger Lowijs Maleghys was visited on 7 March 1560 by two of the city's appraisers to take inventory of the entirety of Lowijs' movable estate. Besides his furniture, bedding, tableware and kitchen accoutrements, they also registered a barge tied up in the city's canals (*reien*).[2] Still a young bachelor in 1560, Lowijs owned a house of six rooms in the Wijngaerdplaats in Bruges (Fig. 1), which included a dining room and a kitchen. Evidently Lowijs was able to prevent seizure of his estate, because a document drafted more than three decades later indicates that he still lived in the same property. Just before Christmas 1595, he lost his wife Gheeraerdine Floris after a marriage of 30 years and a property inventory taken at her death ensured that her inheritance could be safely and properly distributed to her heirs.[3] Gheeraerdine's inventory reveals how both Lowijs' kitchen and dining room – still in the same house at the Wijngaerdplaats – had become stuffed with goods over the 35 years, especially the range of tableware and kitchen equipment had grown in size. Interestingly, we can recognise some household objects in Gheeraerdine's estate as having already appeared in Lowijs' home in his bachelor days. For instance, the painting of the Last Supper (*een avontmael*) was on display in the couple's dining room (*camere*), where it had seemingly hung for the past 35 years.

---

2   City Archives of Bruges (hence CAB), Old Archives (hence OA), Serie 198, n° 216 – Jan Digne (1560-1561), f. 280.
3   CAB, OA, Serie 207, Staten van Goed, 1st Series, 441.

Figure 2. Map of Bruges by Marcus Gheraerds (1563)

In blue: Lowijs Maleghys's house, © www.magisbrugge.be, picture by Elien Vernackt

The unique inventories from the Maleghys family further validate the proposed stratification. In both 1560 and 1596, the household belonged to the higher middle ranks and elite (C), which is moreover attested to by the fact that their property was very large (seven rooms), their landed estate (including some fishing ponds) quite vast and their RUC among the highest quartile (Baatsen 2016, 71). This demonstrates how the methodology applied also assesses and overcomes source-technical and chronological differences, thus offering a unique view on long-term trends in the lower, middle and higher ranked Bruges families' material culture. In the following pages, the material possessions that were part of a household's dining and cooking culture will moreover be linked to additional source material, that being contemporary Dutch cookbooks and table etiquette literature in order to ensure a better interpretation of the function and use of the 'static material culture' in inventories.

Fleshing out material imprints of taste

Notions about the colour, taste and display of food were equally connected to social codes, offering society a guideline for distinguishing between high and low status cooking and dining. In late medieval dining culture, the combined and generous use of spices like saffron, nutmeg and grains of paradise was an example of conspicuous consumption at the table, because spices were commonly considered exclusive luxuries (Freedman 2008). But when the social signal function of spices started to dwindle by the end of the fifteenth century, the social importance of both spice use and spice preferences seemed to change in the course of the sixteenth century. The fashion of dining underwent change, and so too did the socially significant role spices played in it. By reconstructing changing perceptions of 'proper' taste via fifteenth- and sixteenth-century Dutch cookbooks, it has become clear that people indeed started to shy away from heavily spiced food. Sharp and tangy spice combinations did not lose out in popularity because of their cost, but because their flavour went out of fashion and thus no longer fitted into the common taste palate. The majority of late-medieval seasoning was moreover concentrated in tangy, piquant sauces. So it comes as no surprise that Dutch cookbooks document a marked, steady drop in the relative importance of sauce recipes from the sixteenth century onwards, and simultaneously indicate that the use of complex spice mixtures used in these sauces reduces significantly. The sauce bowl (sausier) was the table tool par excellence in which to serve sauces. It comes as no surprise, then, that Bruges household inventories show that the possession of sauce bowls reduces dramatically from the fifteenth to the seventeenth centuries. This consumer change seemed moreover quite inclusive, as it was seen in inventories from all social ranks. This highlights an important shift in dining preferences and the social codes at the dinner table. Yet when heavily spiced sauces slowly lost favour at dinner, other aspects of the dinner table started to gain in importance in communicating social status.

The social function of dinner was highly dependant on its setting and character. It is therefore important to emphasise that a dinner in a household was marked by a difference between everyday mealtimes and more exceptional, exclusive dinner occasions. If a family possessed some beautiful silver plates and crystal glasses, this did not mean that they used this tableware every day. This exceptional use added to the exclusive character of the mealtime at which such special tableware was brought out. From this point of view the possession of wine vessels becomes interesting. By looking at the possession of wine glasses or beakers over the course of the period, we see a marked decline among the lower (A) and middling (B) ranks, suggesting that wine consumption became far more exclusive. Whereas in the 1530s 40 per cent of middle ranked households (B) still owned such drinking vessels, only 8 per cent of this group mentions wine glasses in the 1560s and no household in the final decades of the century had such exclusive drinking vessels. Even among the wealthy elites (C), the possession rate drops from 60 per cent in the fifteenth century to 40 per cent in 1600, but the differences between lower, middling and elite groups are remarkably high.

Wine had definitely become more of a luxury by the end of the sixteenth century. Richard Unger estimated per capita wine consumption in Bruges at 100 litres per person per year in 1420, but in less than two decades, this had dropped to only 25 litres (Unger 1998). The collapse of local wine production and withdrawal of the Habsburg court from Bruges (1492) only worsened the situation. In 1583, one stope (ca. 2,187 litres) of Rhenish wine cost as much as 54.66 d. Fl., allowing a master mason to buy only half a stope or less with his daily wage (estimated at 26 d.Fl.). Meanwhile, beer consumption had risen considerably. This indicated a shift in the psychology of the consumption of drinks, with wine consumption becoming more of a social signifier than it had been before and even among the more well-off families it was reserved for special occasions only. Indeed, while travelling through the southern Low Countries the Spanish courtier Vincente Alvarez reported in 1548 that common people drank no wine unless they were receiving guests or at organised banquets (cited in Van Uytven 2001, 20). For instance, in their school rules it was written that the teachers (not the students) from the Bruges Beghard School for poor orphaned boys were served wine only on exceptional occasions (Van Male 1690 [1555]). In his manual to the governors of the school, Zegher Van Male further stated that the school boys were served roasted or boiled meat only on Sundays, while they had to do with a simple vegetables stew, bread and cheese during the remainder of the week. On feast days, like Shrove Tuesday or Saint Laurence's Day, ox flesh was added to the pottage, and at Easter the children were served lamb, eggs and sweet milk with white bread and beer.

Van Male's *Spieghel Memoriael* points to the way life alternated between everyday meals, feasting and fasting. It offers a unique insight into the diet of the more modest layers of Bruges society and contrasts sharply with the exemplary 'everyday family dinner' that was described in Noël Van Berlaimont's conversation manual from 1520 (Van Berlaimont 1900 [1520]). This manual describes a succession of salad, salted meat, vegetables or meat broth accompanied by bread and mustard. Pastries, pies, roast pork, rabbit, partridge and hare completed the meal while wine was advised as a drink and cheese and fruit were served at the close. The conversation manual, of course, was aiming at improving language skills and therefore describes an ideal meal with as much variety as possible. But this high degree of variety was in most Bruges families a far cry from reality. A varied meal moreover required sophisticated kitchen equipment. When looking into their cooking and roasting infrastructure, social differences also become obvious here.

The possession of roasting spits gives an indication of the ability to prepare, roast and consume large lumps of meat. As can be gleaned from Figure 3, the possession of roasting spits in every period was marked by social differences. Although differences between the lower (A), middle (B) and higher (C) social ranks remain considerable in all sample periods, we notice a clear drop in the sixteenth century for both the poorer (A) and mid-dling (B) groups. This indicates that the lower layers and middling ranks were less able to serve (and possibly also to buy) meat when compared to the most affluent (C) families. Research on consumption patterns in the Low Countries has already indicated that meat consumption started to decline in the sixteenth century due to the high cost of living and soaring grain prices (Soens & Thoen 2010). The possession of roasting pits should not immediately be considered to be a reflection of actual meat consumption, but it indicates that the roasting of large lumps of meat became far less affordable and far more socially exclusive as the sixteenth century proceeded. In its final decades, the most affluent families (C) moreover owned on average four roasting spits, whereas both the middling (B) and poorer (A) families had on average only one spit at their disposal.

For the remainder of the hearth equipment, too, a similar pattern of social polarisation can be discerned, although here it becomes clear that the sophistication and possession rate of other hearth tools rose for the middle ranks (B), suggesting that they were keeping up quite well with the growing variety in hearth accouterments. Grills, used for roasting or grilling small pieces of fish, meat and fruit, gained in popularity as did waffle irons. We defined 'hearth low' tools as iron tripods to rest cauldrons and kettles on or other tools that were to be placed in the burning embers of the fire, while 'hearth high' covers equipment for lowering or raising kettles and frying pans by means of a bar and adjustable pot hooks. These adjustable tools were among the lower ranks (A) the most frequently owned hearth

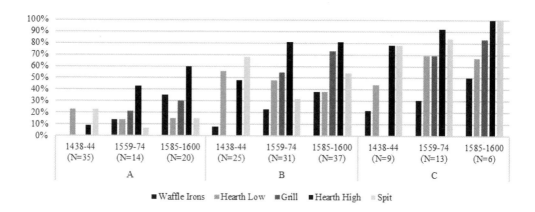

Figure 3. Percentage of households with hearth equipment in post mortem inventories |N=190|.
© database of inventories IB, JDG & IS.

equipment. In comparison with the middling ranks and more affluent groups, they lacked lower hearth tools, grills, and certainly roasting spits.

The most straightforward observation is perhaps on the sophistication and variety of domestic infrastructure for preparing food. Social differences were strongly reflected in the degree of sophistication of a family's hearth equipment, and the same conclusion can be drawn from an analysis of cooking equipment. Especially striking is for instance the difference in the possession rate of skillets among the lower ranks (A). Though rising over the course of the centuries observed, only 45 per cent of poorer families possessed skillets in the final decades of the 1500s. Families in this group owned on average one skillet, while the average among the middling groups was three and most of the elite families (C) even possessed more than four skillets. Moreover, in the more affluent households skillets appeared to be designed for specialised preparations, like a skillet to simmer fruit or onion, for baking pies, etc. Most skillets mentioned in the inventories were made of cast iron, suggesting that less well-off households could probably also count on ceramic alternatives. Yet this still does not contradict our statement that, when one was climbing the social scale, the range and sophistication of cooking infrastructure significantly broadened. At the end of the sixteenth century, Bruges' middle ranks definitely could not keep up with the urban elites in terms of cooking culture, yet they were far ahead in terms of sophistication and variety of their equipment when one looks at the impoverished lower ranked households.

Performance of refinement and individuality

The ability to perform and align with a socially desirable taste at the table also seems to have been closely related to the materiality of tableware objects. In the fifteenth century, the economic (financial) value and social hierarchies of tableware were closely interwoven, meaning that silver and pewter tableware because of their high intrinsic material value were out of reach of poorer Bruges households. But this picture changed in the sixteenth century, when fragile ceramic majolica dishes and fine glass drinking vessels joined the ranks and blurred the vested value system (Blondé 2002). Their low intrinsic value did not match their social appreciation as exclusive luxuries. Broken or damaged pewter could still be sold for a considerable price, while broken majolica or glass had lost all its value when broken. When proceeding from the fifteenth to the sixteenth century, the tableware collections of Bruges families were all marked by a sustained rise in material diversity, yet the differences between the social categories remain very clear as well.

This is a remarkable observation when we take into account the deep economic crisis that hit Bruges families in the sixteenth century. In the 1580s, the cost of living had reached previously unseen levels, the high cost of daily bread severely curbed households' purchasing power and forced families to make decisions about what to buy and what not to. It is not difficult to imagine that these circumstances could have kept families from buying new pewter tableware, or even compelled households to sell their pewter in order to make ends meet. When comparing the earliest sample period (1438-44) with the third quarter of the sixteenth century (1559-74), the lower ranks (A) in particular seem to have been less frequent pewter owners. The number of households that owned silver tableware dropped as well, except for the highest, most affluent families (C). The persistence of the late sixteenth-century crisis probably not only hindered the acquisition of (mostly pewter) tableware, but also made people pawn their platters or sell their pewter for cash in order to avoid debt or worse. Enmeshed in debt and threatened by confiscation, some people had good practical reasons for choosing to pawn their pewter. If we compare this to the fifteenth century, pewter and silver tableware possession had now become much more socially polarised. Yet still we see an increase in material variety.

While pewter and silver remained investments for the future, ceramics and glass became firm competitors. One could argue that these breakables – available in multiple shapes, qualities and functional types – were in all likelihood a welcome alternative when pewter was not within a family's financial reach. But the inventories suggest that these 'new' material media should not unequivocally be considered as cheaper substitutes. On the contrary: apart from silver, the majolica and glass tableware were the most exclusive owned items in the inventories of the late sixteenth century. The very low percentages of these 'new' material media among the lower social groups (A) suggest that they were not purchased as cheaper alternatives to pewter tableware but for other purposes, like refinement and aesthetic appeal.

Especially telling is the appearance of specialised furniture in which to store tableware from the sixteenth century onwards. Gradually, the ownership of one or more pewter cupboards (*tinschaprades*) became widespread among families of all social categories. Such a cupboard suggests that the household had a considerable amount of pewter table- and kitchenware, enough to fill a complete cupboard with pewter objects alone. First mentioned at the beginning of the sixteenth century, glass cupboards (*glazenberden*) were also making their appearance in households. Figure 4 indicates that the ownership of both glass cupboards and pewter cupboards was also marked by social differences. Yet it equally becomes clear that at the waning of the century glass cupboards' ownership became more exclusive. This is also linked to the location of this piece of furniture. Pewter cupboards were nearly always found in the kitchen, whereas glass cupboards were kept in more exclusive and intimate dining quarters. The appearance of glass cupboards most

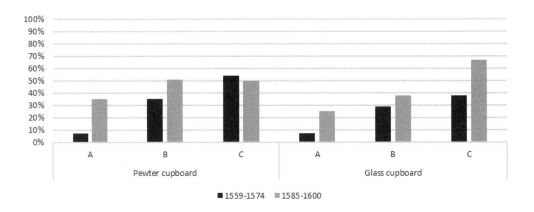

Figure 4. Pewter cupboards and glass cupboards in post mortem inventories (N=190)

Source: Database of inventories © IB, JDG & IS.

obviously evidences that a desire for breakable yet refined drinking vessels was reconfiguring families' tableware collections.[4]

Nevertheless, the archaeological record warns against making exaggerated statements on changes in materiality, for it has offered abundant material evidence of glass, wooden and ceramic tableware in both the fifteenth and sixteenth centuries (De Groote 2014; Caluwé 2006). But proceeding to the sixteenth century, innovations in production processes created on the one hand standardised, cheap glass vessels and ceramic dishes, while on the other hand the import of Mediterranean tin-glazed ceramics (majolica) and Venetian crystal glass via the port of Bruges introduced new types of products and new standards for aesthetics and craftsmanship. This introduction of high-end luxurious breakable tableware allegedly influenced the way appraisers made their inventories. Whereas appraisers in the fifteenth century ignored the great numbers of ceramics and glass that were presumably present in households, the same types of breakables seem to have caught their attention more in the sixteenth century. This sudden appearance of glass and ceramics therefore indicates three important shifts. First, it signals a change in the appreciation of breakable and relatively 'cheap' materials. Second, it suggests a widening of the quality range within the individual categories of ceramics and glass, where the appearance of new products with remarkably high quality finishing and requiring high-end craftsmanship like tin-glazed majolica and crystal glass reconfigured the established appreciation of glass vessels and ceramic tableware. Third, due to improvements in the production process, standardised production of the less-luxurious breakable table utensils resulted in a greater and cheaper output that could have prompted less affluent families to buy these products.

The appraisers did not record poor quality glass and ceramics, and therefore it remains difficult (and dangerous) to make assumptions based on the absence of certain objects. Many of the poorer households (A) were not able to acquire the high-quality decorative and aesthetically pleasing ceramics, but they were certainly capable of buying some

---

4   CAB, OA, Serie 207, Staten van Goed, 1st Series, 441.

standardised glass beakers or local earthenware cups, bowls and skillets. The fact that the bulk of cheaper glass was omitted from the inventories is substantiated by the presence of many 'empty' glass cupboards in the late sixteenth century, for in this period the desire for high-end crystal and Antwerp 'façon' glass was reconfiguring fashion standards and taste, narrowing the attention of appraisers towards these 'valuable' pieces only. Nevertheless, though glass vessels slowly came within the reach of the middle and lower social ranks, this did not mean that differences between social groups narrowed. Glass tableware on the one hand provided a relatively cheap substitute for the expensive silver and pewter cups for the lower social orders, while on the other hand it provided a solution to meet the new demands of design, 'sprezzatura' and 'diligenza' promoted by the Italian Renaissance and so desired by the higher social ranks of urban society (Rublack 2013, 41). This illustrates not only how art and design became valued differently but also, and perhaps more importantly, how the dining culture of Bruges' households was influenced and partly even shaped by a rush towards a growing consumption of new, cheaper and breakable consumer goods. This rush was not fair competition however, as the finest pieces clearly were a privilege for the urban elites only. The fine majolica pieces were only to be found among some middling (B) and higher (C) ranked households, and even significantly concentrated among the households of wealthy foreign merchants.

Overall, the evidence presented thus far has shown that the changes in tableware possession were deeply entrenched in the social and economic world of Bruges society. Though pewter tableware became less easy to acquire for the poorer and lower middling ranks, this did not exclude these households from participating in contemporary dining culture, as is suggested by the archaeological record. On special occasions, more prosperous households could even rely on catering services to temporarily update their dinner equipment. Such was the case with Lowijs Maleghys, who still needed to reimburse Jacques Hughelijnck after having hired silverware.[5] A lack of silverware among the tableware collection of the Beghard School for poor children in Bruges likewise caused Zegher van Male to stipulate that the wives of the six governors needed to bring some table equipment for the annual feast of Sint Lauwereins in August (Van Male 1690 [1555], 101-102). An individual napkin, a silver cup and trencher were to be provided for each diner. Significantly, these luxuries were not provided for the children but only for the small company of the governors and their wives.

Perhaps the most interesting innovation is this growing desire to acquire meaningful sets of tableware, a feature that becomes more pronounced in the sixteenth century. This holds true especially for small, individual trenchers (*teljoren*), which seem to have been acquired more consistently in sets of six, 12 or 18. Individual pewter or wooden trenchers became more popular as dinner equipment from the sixteenth century onwards. Hence, it is tempting to see this tendency to buy standardised 'complete' sets of individual plates as a prelude to the popularity of seventeenth-century china services which always comprised six, 12 or 18 pieces. It convincingly points to an increasingly standardised table layout and indicates that a new fashion of conviviality, one that emphasised individuality, had entered the vocabulary of table manners. As such, both the material refinement of domestic table equipment and individual plate-use had become important proxies of social status.

---

5   'Item Jacques Hughelijnck den zelver smit esmen schuldich van ghehaelde zelverwerck de somme van ...'

Performance of manners and domestic conviviality

The fact that Bruges families started to acquire trenchers in sets at approximately the same time as Desiderius Erasmus's humanist writings on table manners and table settings started to proliferate is best not considered as a mere coincidence. As early as in the fifteenth century we can trace important changes in Bruges' dining customs. Most debates on dining customs have pointed to Erasmus's '*De civilitate*' (1530) as a key turning point in the history of table manners, and they are indeed right to argue that his discourse on table etiquette introduced a new way of communicating proper table manners to the audience (Chartier 1987, 77). Erasmus's writings moreover perfectly fit into the socio-cultural transitions of the sixteenth century as described by Mikhail Bakhtin, who argued that the public unifying character of banquets and guild meals started to dwindle in the sixteenth century. Public meals were slowly replaced by a more private and intimate manner of dining, accompanied by stricter, more specific table manners (Bakhtin 1984, 4-18).

Yet sixteenth-century table manners were predicated on earlier customs. The 'Book of morals' (*Boec van Seden*, 1290), Jan van Boendale's 'Mirror for laymen' (*Der Leken Spieghel*, 1330) and the 'Instructions on courtesy' (*Leere van Hoveschede*, 1470) were already concerned with correct dining practices. Viewed from a thematic perspective, the principles advanced by '*De civilitate*' greatly resembled those discussed in 'Table manners' (*Manieren alsmen over tafel zal hantieren*, 1496), which gave individuality, bodily hygiene and the proper use of tableware much greater attention than previous table prescriptions. But Erasmus's text is more explicit on what from his humanist point of view constituted proper behaviour. Starting in the sixteenth century, humanist culture provided more technical advice that could immediately be translated into practice at the dinner table. This can be partly explained by the fact that humanist manuals were often composed as a dialogue between master and student. Hence table etiquette was structured in a more practical way, and their clear and simple language targeted a much broader audience (Cotman 2004, 55-66; Bryson 1998, 29). Erasmus's didactic literature also indicates a change in the perception of table manners. Good manners at the table were now considered as a performance of rational or reasonable behaviour, which had become an essential prerequisite of a civilised person and an externalisation of good virtue. The changing tone of table manners indicated new fashions of social distinction, implying new rules for Bruges households to respect when displaying social status. An analysis of a small sample of influential Dutch conduct manuals spanning the fifteenth and sixteenth centuries, reveals interesting textual shifts in the admonition.[6] The translation by the manuals of the Latin '*civile*' or civility into not one but many Dutch concepts, like 'polite' (*beleeft*), 'civil' (*borgerlick*), 'honourable' (*eerbaer*) or 'proper' (*fatsoenlyck*) moreover indicates an ever-stronger emphasis on self-fashioning, self-restraint and personal virtue (Elias 2001 [1932], 149). As the fifteenth century came to an end, the range of topics discussed by the Dutch dining manuals seems to have widened. The emphasis now was on individuality and personal cleanliness at the table.

In the 'Vocabulary' (*Vocabulaer*) of 1500 it is deemed highly 'shameful' (*scande ende bescaemtheyt*) to eat or drink before emptying your mouth. The word 'shame' (*schande*)

---

6   For a detailed analysis see Baatsen 2016, ch. V.

is the most frequently used adjective for labeling aberrant, unsuitable behaviour at the table in the 'Table manners' tract from 1496. When we read through the precepts in the Dutch translation of Erasmus's *'De civilitate'* (*Goede manierlijcke zeden*, 1546) we find that the word 'shame' is still frequently used, but other adjectives gain in importance. The word is moreover used just once in the 'Guidelines for the Dutch schoolmaster' (1591) and in the 1678 edition of Erasmus's *'De civilitate'*, the latter text preferring the use of adjectives like 'dishonourable' (*oneerlijck*) and 'improper' (*ongeschikt*). The shifts in the frequency of using more personal words like 'dishonourable' and 'improper' next to shame and shamefulness illustrate the changing educational strategy that was developed by humanist writers in the sixteenth century. This strategy was far more concerned with constructing personal boundaries between proper and improper conduct, while offering a practical toolkit to recognise, signal and judge the behaviour of other diners as transgressive with implications for their social status.

Most interestingly, late fifteenth-century manuals start to use the word 'peasant-like/rustic' (*boers/dorper*), which can be understood as non-urban. The 'Instructions on courtesy' (*Leere van Hoveschede*, 1470) already warn their readers not to talk in 'a village-like manner' (*dorperlicke sprake*) during conversations over dinner. In the 1562 edition of the French-Dutch dictionary by Joos Lambrecht (*Naembouck*), the word *'boers'* is explained as an 'incapable and unwanted person' (*onbecaem ende onghewenst mensche*) and explained as equal to rustic, uncivil and mad. The popularity of the concept of 'rustic' (*boers*) shows how knowledge of new table manners and refined behaviour discursively created a set of power relations through judging specific habits and actions as non-compliant with the expected rules on behaviour at the dinner table. The Latin word *'incivile'* was in most cases translated as 'uncivilised' (*onfatsoenlijk*), but also once mentioned as 'impolite' (*onbeleeft*). However, 'impolite' was in all other cases a translation of the Latin word *'inurbanum'*, which can in fact also be translated as 'not urban', or 'not civil', thus equal to incivility. 'Incivility', although easily translated into French conduct literature as *'incivilité'* or English manuals as 'incivility', does not seem to have immediately found one specific Dutch translation, but rather came to be associated through its translation with multiple concepts, like 'rustic' (*boers*), 'improper' (*onfatsoenlijck*) and 'impolite' (*onbeleefd*).

This discursively constructed contradiction between urban and non-urban values in table manners also demonstrates how a change in table manners aligned with a search for new codes of sociability by urban social groups to mark (new) social boundaries. The same vocabulary was used to sharpen the social boundaries within the city as well. Material culture was not unimportant in this process of redefining social boundaries, for the practice of the new rules of propriety also required specific material objects. Late fifteenth-century manuals already started to pay attention to table utensils, but Erasmus further expanded on this concern by emphasising the proper use of 'helping hands' in a far greater proportion of the precepts. The possession of these necessary tools for mediating proper table manners is therefore revealing.

As argued earlier in this chapter, there was a general tendency among Bruges households from the 1550s onwards to acquire individual trenchers (*teljoren*) in sets of six, 12, 18 or more pieces. Also, as illustrated by the graph above, the ability to do so was marked by social boundaries. Because wooden and ceramic trenchers were often omitted from inventories, the incidence of the actual possession of individual sets of trenchers presumably must have

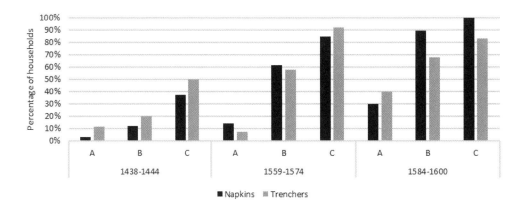

Figure 5. Napkins and individual trenchers |N=189|.

© Database of inventories: IB, IS & JDG

been higher. This suggests that the less well-off families (A) could equally participate in the new trend of individuality propagated by humanist table etiquette, even though it be via poorer quality ceramics or treen. But social differences were also very pronounced in the use of another 'helping hand': aside from individual trenchers, Erasmus's manual prescribes that on every trencher there should be placed a napkin (Van Vloten 1864, 346). When charting the proliferation of napkins in Bruges, it appears that the possession rate of these individual pieces of (mostly) linen closely follows the possession rate of trenchers: a rise in possession among all social groups. As with the trenchers, though possession rates were growing, the social differences remained high between the lower ranked households (A) on the one hand and the wealthier families (B-C) on the other. Of course, differences in quality of linen were high, allowing richer households to articulate their wealth with napkins of damask, silk or with '*panie*' decoration. And because the poorest quality of linen was often not specified individually, the actual possession rate of napkins could have been higher. However, the median number of individual napkins owned indicates substantial differences between all groups. Whereas the lower ranks (A) owned on average 4.5 napkins and 11 trenchers at the end of the sixteenth century, the middling groups (B) owned 19 napkins and 12 trenchers. It was the higher middling ranks and urban elites (C) that owned dazzling numbers of napkins (121) and trenchers (34), and were as such perfectly equipped to organise dinner parties in their homes with the right, proper tools for individuality and cleanliness. For, indeed, the rise in napkin use indicated a change in bodily hygiene as well, whereby individual linen replaced the common tablecloth as a receptacle for filth and bodily fluids (De Staelen 2007, 354-355). Just as outlined in the books of manners, napkins and trenchers signal new requirements for individual cleanliness, which had become an aspect of individual constraint and personal propriety at the table. From the fifteenth to the sixteenth centuries we observe an overall intensification in the possession and use of tableware related to individual cleanliness. Moreover, the drop in the possession of sauce bowls can be understood in this light as suggestive of a declining habit of dipping one's food in a shared sauce bowl. Both books of manners and inventories thus clearly allude to the same transformation in dining practices. Though presumably not ignorant of the new social codes in dining, the lower social ranks in Bruges were less able to acquire the table tools necessary for practising these more refined manners. This does not mean they were eating from a shared plate, but it underlines that they had less or limited access to sophisticated and expensive tableware and table linen when compared to the middling ranks and urban elites.

Importantly, the fact that rules were formulated to discourage the touching of food with bare hands should not be considered as a translation of actual constraint, but rather as a *need* formulated by contemporary society and inspired by cultural ideals to limit behaviour that was – perhaps ironically – still very much practised at that moment. It is interesting that sixteenth-century didactic literature became ever more focused on dining as a venue – or even a laboratory – where new social codes were tested and evaluated. In other words, it was at the table that the social guidelines were most needed (Romagnoli 1999, 328).

According to Mikhail Bakhtin, the forms of sociability and the ritual of eating both became relegated to the private area of the house during the sixteenth century (Bakhtin 1984, 4-18). This emphasis on *domestic* conviviality was celebrated in late sixteenth-century Flemish family paintings, displaying households among their expensive tableware and luxurious table linens. If one browses through the pages of Albrecht Dürer's travelogue (1520-21), it strikes one how often he is invited to the houses of friends for an intimate dinner party or sumptuous banquet, in both Bruges and Antwerp.[7] The inventories show that Bruges houses over the course of the sixteenth century developed a very layered and differentiated domestic conviviality, and that the manner of sophistication was – quite obviously – related to the size of the dwelling. Some general trends could be traced, such as, for instance, in the use of kitchens. Even in the early 1400s, the majority of the inventories describe rooms where the family organised dinner. Moreover, kitchens were used almost exclusively for cooking. Yet, this would change. The kitchen (*keuckene*) evolved in the sixteenth century from a functionally specialised room into a multifunctional space for dining. A growing hierarchy in exclusivity among convivial dining spaces paralleled this refurnishing into 'dining kitchens' in the Bruges house (Baatsen, Blondé & De Groot 2014). Medium-sized dwellings (four to five rooms) and large houses (six to nine rooms) especially seem to have been keen to equip a separate convivial room, away from the kitchen. This ability to organise everyday mealtimes and more exceptional dinners in different rooms slowly became a new aspect of social status. Within the constraints of domestic space, Bruges families across the social scale tried to create a special room reserved exclusively for dining, with sleeping and cooking activities banished to other locations. Yet even fancier and more socially exclusive seemed to have been the ability to have more than one location in the house for dining, allowing the family to select a room in accordance with the social importance of the dinner party. This hints at a tendency to better attune domestic space to mealtimes. The importance of domestic dining is moreover backed by an analysis of the material setting of the dining room. When calculating the relative spread of display items and decoration, these were significantly more (and more often) found in dining rooms than in other rooms. Dining rooms were equipped to host more people than household

---

7   Dürer, *Tagebuch der Reise in die Niederlande.*

members alone, and had an important signal function as well. In Lowijs Maleghys' house the dining room – with its massive fireplace, five paintings, nine sculptures and silver cupboard – outshone all other rooms in material splendour. Though there was dining furniture in other rooms, too, it was the dining room that undeniably contained the most valued material objects in order to convey social status and family identity (Goldstein 2016, 145-146). Although dining rooms were far from new by the sixteenth century, the change is in the importance of engaging domestic space in making this room the most important and suitable room for domestic sociability and welcoming guests. In the banishing of more trivial, everyday dining activities to other rooms of the house, the dining room acquired a more exclusive character. Yet the ability to do that depended on the available domestic space a household could employ in providing such a room. And this was, again, highly dependent upon a family's financial means and social status.

Finally, the inventories document a small and intimate dining room rather than a large dining hall, as most dining rooms included fewer than seven chairs. This correlates with an observation of the changing nomenclature of the dining room used by the appraisers of the inventories. Especially in the late fifteenth and early sixteenth centuries, the word 'eetcamere' (literally 'eating room') was preferred to be used to indicate principal dining rooms. But from the 1550s onwards, the Dutch nomenclature of the dining room starts to decline in popularity. Instead, the name 'salette' became more popular yet also more exclusive (Vandenbroeck 1990, 90-150; De Laet 2011, 111-112). A comparative analysis of the Dutch names used by the appraisers for all dining rooms indicates that at the start of the seventeenth century 'eetcamere' had disappeared from the appraisers' vocabulary. At that time, many rooms were still fitted out as dining rooms (mostly labelled 'front room' (voorcamere) or 'room' (camere)), but only the largest dwellings seem to have had the prerogative of having a salette.[8] Apparently the houses of the lower ranks and most of the middling ranks were not as able as those of the urban elites to include a salette. Even among the higher middling people, like Lowijs Maleghys, the salette remained an exclusive feature. The diminutive suffix of salette moreover suggests that these convivial spaces were rather small, intimate rooms. Borrowed from the Italian 'salotto', it was moreover connected to the Italian humanist culture and hence reflected – just as crystal glass and majolica did – the fashion of sprezzatura and diligenza. The label of salette can perhaps best be considered as a new way of branding those dining rooms that were best fitted for the practice of the humanist dining ritual or convivium. And Erasmus's table manners were obviously an intrinsic part of that practice. It can even be surmised that, just as in dining etiquette, people started to shy away from literally referring to the act of eating, which is so explicitly present in the word 'eetcamere' and can explain its disappearance at the close of the century. Instead, people preferred to refer to the social function and exclusive character that the dining ritual had come to signify by borrowing from humanist vocabulary words like salette. However the rules applied to the use of this terminology were far stricter and thus far more socially exclusive, even for the middle and higher middling ranks. They signalled a new set of social and material expectations connected to the dinner party.

---

8   For the final sample period (1585-1600), 17 per cent of houses with four to five rooms, 27 per cent of houses with six to nine rooms and 29 per cent of families living in houses with more than nine rooms. For more information on calculation of Bruges house sizes, see Baatsen 2016, 233).

Conclusion

By the end of the sixteenth century Bruges' domestic dining culture had become more polished, more refined, more sophisticated and more varied. Cultural and conceptual frameworks changed, fashioning a new specific palate of taste (in a material, spatial and spice-related way) that came to be associated with a specific moral quality. This moral quality, in turn, became a necessary ingredient in upward social mobility. It became a challenge for the lower and middling ranks of society to keep up with the new codes of social propriety, especially when considering their proletarianisation and impoverishment after the 1550s. Nevertheless, the dining culture of the middling ranks was not to be called unequivocally poor. Although middle-class households were unable to keep up with the luxurious dining culture of the urban elites, as had been the case in previous centuries, they were far ahead of the lower middle and poorer ranks in Bruges.

The importance of spices dwindled as the sixteenth century came to an end, while meat consumption and wine drinking became more exclusive. Table manners and associated tableware seem to have replaced spices as social signifiers, implying that the performance of individuality became more important. An ever-wider choice of materiality options for tableware signalled more options for discriminating between different social statuses. Although cheaper materials and standardisation in tableware – like individual dinner plates and glass beakers – offered the chance for the lower urban ranks (A) to keep pace with the new trends, it was the exclusive high quality ceramics and glass (like maiolica and crystal glass) next to diversity and quantity that came to reflect social status.

The changing definition of dining rooms moreover points to a reorientation away from the act of eating itself towards the social conventions, (domestic) spatial requirements and material mediators surrounding food consumption. The set of required expectations needed fully to indulge in the social benefits of the dining ritual had definitely become more complex, while the social gaps between the lower, middling and higher social ranks had widened. The shifting nuances in Middle Dutch nomenclature are, in that light, a very explicit reference to this process, because eventually they also reveal this ever more pronounced trend of judging and negotiating social status at the table.

At the beginning of this chapter, Thomas Platter might not have been wrong to generalise about hospitality as a shared quality of all Bruges' inhabitants, because we see even among the families with very small houses an urge to equip part of their domestic space with dining facilities. But social expectations changed during the decades of the 1500s. While the majority of Bruges households were certainly not excluded from participating in *general* new trends with respect to individual plate use, spice use and hygiene, the sixteenth century became an age in which especially the poorer and lower middling ranks (A) had difficulty living up to a much more articulated set of material, spatial and qualitative expectations. The resilience of the middling ranks (B), however, remains remarkable. While dealing with the economic setbacks curbing their purchasing power they still seemed to be able and eager – albeit from a second position with respect to the urban elites – to invest in new fashion accoutrements in order to communicate their social status.

References

Baatsen, I. 2016. *A bittersweet symphony. The social recipe of dining culture in late medieval and early modern Bruges (1438-1600)*, unpublished PhD-dissertation UAntwerpen, Antwerp.

Baatsen, I., B. Blondé and J. De Groot. 2014. "The kitchen between representation and everyday experience" In *Trading values in early modern Antwerp / Nederlands kunsthistorisch jaarboek 64*, ed. C. Göttler, B. Ramakers and J. Woodall, 162-185. Leiden: Brill.

Bakhtin, M. 1984. *Rabelais and his world*. Bloomington: Indiana University Press.

Blondé, B. 2002, "Tableware and changing consumer patterns. Dynamics of material culture in Antwerp, 17th-18th centuries." In *Majolica and glass from Italy to Antwerp and beyond: the transfer of technology in the 16th-early 17th century*, ed. Sarah Jennings and Johan Veeckman. 298-311. Antwerp: Stad Antwerpen.

Blondé, B., O. Gelderblom and P. Stabel. 2007. "Foreign merchant communities in Bruges, Antwerp, and Amsterdam (1350-1650)." In *Cultural exchange in Europe, 1400-1700*, ed. S. Turk Christensen et al. 154-174. Cambridge: Cambridge University Press.

Blondé, B., F. Buylaert, J. Dumolyn, J. Hanus and P. Stabel. 2018. "Living together in the city: social relationships between norm and practice." In *City and society in the Low Countries, 1100-1600*, ed. B. Blondé, M. Boone and A. Van Bruaene. 59-92. Cambridge: Cambridge University Press.

Bryson, A. 1998. *From courtesy to civility. Changing codes of conduct in early modern England*. Oxford: Oxford University Press.

Caluwé, D. 2006. "The use of drinking vessels in the context of dining and communal meals. Some preliminary thoughts drawn on archaeological evidence from medieval and post-medieval periods in Flanders and the Duchy of Brabant (Belgium)." *Food & history (Revue de l'institut Européen d'histoire et des cultures de l'alimentation 4/1*: 279-304.

Chartier, R. 1987. "From text to manners. A concept and its books: *civilité* between aristocratic distinction and popular appropriation." In *The cultural uses of print in early modern France*, ed. L. Chochrane. 71-109. Princeton, NJ: Princeton University Press.

Ciselet, P. and M. Delcourt. 1942. *Monetarius. Voyage aux Pays-Bas (1495)*, Brussels: Office de publicité.

Cotman, F. 2004. "De didactische methode van de laatmiddeleeuwse conversatieboekjes en hun navolgingen." *Handelingen koninklijke Zuid-Nederlandse maatschappij voor taal- en letterkunde en geschiedenis 58*: 55-66.

De Groote, Koen. 2014. *Middeleeuws aardewerk in Vlaanderen*. Relicta monografieën 1. Brussels: VIOE.

De Keyser, Joey. 2010. *Vreemde ogen. Een kijk op de Zuidelijke Nederlanden, 1400-1600*. Antwerp: Meulenhof/Manteau.

De Laet, V. 2011. *Brussel binnenskamers. Kunst- en luxebezit in het spanningsveld tussen hof en stad, 1600-1735*. Amsterdam: Amsterdam University Press.

De Meyer, I. 1971. "De sociale structuren te Brugge in de 14de eeuw." In *Studiën betreffende de sociale structuren te Brugge, Kortrijk en Gent in de 14de en 15de eeuw*, ed. P. Blockmans et al. 7-78. Heule: UGA.

De Vries, Jan. 2003. "Luxury in the Dutch Golden Age in theory and practice." In *Luxury in the eighteenth century*, ed. Maxine Berg and Elizabeth Eger. 41-56. London: Palgrave Macmillan.

Deneweth, H. 2002. "Brugge zoekt en vindt alternatieven." In *Brugge,* ed. Valentin Vermeersch. 86-103. Antwerp: Mercatorfonds.

Deneweth, H. 2010. "Een demografische knoop ontward? Brugse bevolkingscijfers voor de vroegmoderne tijd." *Handelingen van het genootschap voor geschiedenis te Brugge* 147/1.

De Staelen, C. 2007. *Spulletjes en hun betekenis in een commerciële metropool: Antwerpenaren en hun materiële cultuur in de zestiende eeuw.* Unpublished PhD-dissertation, Antwerpen: Universiteit Antwerpen.

Elias, N. 2001 [1932]. *Het civilisatieproces. Sociogenetische en psychogenetische onderzoekingen.* Amsterdam: Boom Uitgevers.

Freedman, P. 2008. *Out of the East. Spices and the Medieval Imagination.* Yale: Yale University Press.

Goldstein, Claudia. 2013. *Pieter Bruegel and the culture of the Early Modern Dinner Party.* Aldershot: Ashgate.

Romagnoli, D. 1999. "'Mind your Manners'. Etiquette at the Table." In *Food. A culinary history from antiquity to the present*, ed. Jean-Louis Flandrin and Massimo Montanari. 328-338. New York: Columbia University Press.

Rublack, U. 2013. "Matter in the Material Renaissance." *Past & Present* 219/1: 41-85.

Soens, T., and E. Thoen. 2010. "Vegetarians or carnivores? Standards of living and diet in late Medieval Flanders." *Le interazioni fra economica e ambiente biologico nell'Europa preindustriale. Secc. XIII-XVIII – Economic and biological interactions in pre-industrial Europe from the 13th to the 18th centuries.* 495-527. Prato: Prato Institution Internazionale di Storia Economica 'D.Datini'.

Tafur, Pero. 2005 [1926]. *Travels and adventures, 1435-1439*, trans. M. Letts. London: Routledge.

Unger, Richard W. 1998. "Beer, wine and land use in the late medieval Low Countries." *Bijdragen tot de Geschiedenis* 81: 327-337.

Van Berlaimont, Noël. 1900 [1520]. *Vocabulaire van nyeus gheordineert. Ende wederom gecorrigeert om lichtelic Francois te leren lesen scriven ende spreken…, printed in Antwerp by Willem Vorsterman, 1520,* Antwerp: s.n.

Van der Wee, Herman. 1963. *The growth of the Antwerp market and the European economy (fourteenth-sixteenth centuries)* 3 vols. Leuven: Nijhoff.

Van Male, Z. 1690. *Den speghel memoriael sprekende van 't gouvernement van den godshuuse ten bogaerde anno XVc LV.* ed. A. Schoutet as "Een beschrijving van de Bogardenschool te Brugge omstreeks 1555." Bruges: Stadsarchief.

Van Vloten, J. 1864. "Levensmanieren naar een handleiding der 16de eeuw." *De Dietse Warande* 6. 337-361. Amsterdam.

Van Uytven, Raymond. 2001. *Production and consumption in the Low Countries, 13th-16th centuries,* Aldershot: Ashgate Publishing.

Vandenbroeck, P. 1990. "De salette of pronkkamer in het 17de-eeuws Brabantse burgerhuis. Familie- en groepsportretten als iconografische bron, omstreeks 1640-1680." *Monumenten, landschappen en archeologie.* 8/6: 41-62.

WOUT SAELENS

Comforts of Difference

Social Inequality and the Material Culture of Energy in Eighteenth-Century Ghent*

Introduction

On 8 May 1780 the official appraiser of Saint Peter's parish in Ghent visited the house of Therese Philippine Roelandt, the late widow of Pieter Antone Baillius who had died shortly beforehand and left one minor child.[1] The visitor was appointed by the city aldermen and was burdened with the task of listing all the goods he encountered in Therese's home. The village of Saint Peter's, where Therese and Pieter had lived, was an impoverished neighbourhood that long kept its rural appearance at the edge of the city walls. Here a lot of poor textile bleachers lived and worked in the fields of Saint Peter's abbey where bleached linens were put to be dried. Therese and Pieter probably lived off their work in textile bleaching as well. Sure enough, their probate inventory leaves a rather sad impression. As there was no listing of any differentiation in rooms, although this had become the custom by that time, Therese and Pieter's home probably had only one room. The inventory was drawn up *pro deo*, a measure that was reserved for those who could not afford the costs involved in the probate process. In the end, the appraiser estimated the total of their possessions at 20 pounds and one shilling.[2] Despite their impoverished living circumstances, Therese and Pieter owned at least one basic element of comfort: an iron stove. Providing more warmth for a given quantity of fuel than a traditional fireplace, the stove became popular among the well-to-do in eighteenth-century Ghent, from whom it would gradually trickle down to the lower strata in urban society. By the end of the century, however, most poorer contemporaries of Therese and Pieter were still condemned to burning dirty coal – the dominant fuel at the time – in a fireplace or, in some cases, straight on the floor, turning the domestic environment into smoky discomfort. Therese and Pieter also owned a little brazier ('*conforken*') which was probably used for cooking, and had two candlesticks for lighting.

The limited distribution of elementary comforts of warmth and light in Therese and Pieter's home stood in sheer contrast to the contents of the probate inventory of Robert

* I wish to thank Bruno Blondé, Peter Stabel and the reviewers for their valuable comments. Thanks to Kate Eliott for correcting my English.

1 The following description is based on City Archives Ghent (hereafter: SAG), series 332, no. 772/12.

2 This corresponded to about 160 daily wages of an average building labourer in eighteenth-century Flanders (Vandenbroeke 1982).

Wout Saelens • University of Antwerp – Vrije Universiteit Brussel

Inequality and the City in the Low Countries (1200-2020), ed. by Bruno BLONDÉ, Sam GEENS, Hilde GREEFS, Wouter RYCKBOSCH, Tim SOENS & Peter STABEL, SEUH 50 (Turnhout, 2020), pp. 309-327.

DOI 10.1484/M.SEUH-EB.5.120452

Jan Moerman which had been drawn up a couple of months earlier.[3] Robert, a man who belonged to the richest segments of urban society, had died on 15 December 1779. Two tailors were appointed as appraisers and were taken round Robert's house by his widow, Maria Theresia Robette, in order to make an inventory of all their possessions – a process that took several days to complete. In Robert's office the two men found a stove, and so did they in the kitchen, in Maria's bedroom and in another small, private room. The four comfortable stoves Robert and Maria owned were probably much more elaborate than the one stove found in the home of Pieter and Therese. Each stove of the former was appraised at a little over two pounds, while in the latters' home the second-hand value of the stove was only ten shillings and a half.[4] Eight braziers, of which three were silver table braziers, further spread warmth through the house.

Continuing their tour, the appraisers found that fireplaces, not stoves, heated the more representative rooms of Robert and Maria's city *hôtel*. Operating them was a hard and dirty job, but these fireplaces clearly did not have just a practical function. In the dining room (*'eetplaetse'*) two pictures with gold-plated frames hung from the chimney, while two candlesticks on the mantelpiece provided extra light. In the adjacent room – the *'groote salette'* or parlour – the mantelpiece was decorated with a set of chinaware, a mirror and two sconces. Such fashionable fireplaces were a sign of good taste, wealth and status. In these places of domestic sociability, (physical) comfort and energy efficiency were for the richer members of society outweighed by reasons of conspicuous consumption. Here, in the 'frontstage' areas of everyday life, we usually find luxurious candlesticks and occasionally impressive chandeliers for illumination, while the more intimate 'backstage' areas were equipped with simpler lighting objects like candle pans and lamps.[5] Even the fuels used were socially polarised in this respect. Although the two coal scuttles that were found next to one of their stoves reveal that Maria and Robert were certainly not reluctant to use this fossil fuel as it indeed provided more thermal comfort, they clearly still preferred their fireplaces to be burning wood.

Why did Maria and Robert in some cases still favour a fireplace over a stove? Why did they not engage any further in the desire for more domestic comfort? Did the lasting importance of the fireplace not contradict the 'rational' belief in modernity and other bourgeois values such as the concept of cleanliness that prevailed at the time? Did it not go against the 'utility-maximising' individual that was born out of the consumer revolution? The multiple meanings attached to the stove, the fireplace and other objects of thermal comfort illustrate, as I will argue in this chapter, how household energy transitions and their material culture were fundamentally shaped by the social conditions in which consumers acted. Coal had long been considered to be an inferior fuel for the poor. Firewood, on the other hand, was cleaner, burned more pleasantly, and had long been preferred by those who could still afford it. Stoves also did not always match very well with the appropriate decorum which dictated how the domestic interior should be organised. Although the spread of new energy technologies reached all sectors of urban society, I will try to show that the comforts of warmth and light were not equally distributed among households of different classes and often conflicted with older, status-oriented consumer behaviour. In

---

3   SAG, series 332, no. 771/7.
4   Corresponding to c. 16 and c. four daily wages of an average skilled labourer, respectively.
5   On the distinction between the 'frontstage' and 'backstage' areas of everyday life see Goffman 1959.

the background of a modernising consumption model based on physical comfort, convenience and pleasure, the fireplace, among other markers of wealth, remained crucial for 'respectable' and 'genteel' burghers in a growing industrial centre like Ghent to distinguish themselves from the more ordinary sort of people.

Access to energy for warmth and light is key to experiencing a decent and comfortable quality of life. Most historians will agree that a household's access to energy and ownership of heating and lighting equipment, along with other basic necessities such as food, clothing and bedding, is a crucial proxy in measuring material wellbeing in the past. Classic standard-of-living studies have indeed almost invariably included fuels in their consumer price indices for reconstructing historical real wages. In his long-term overview of wages and prices in European cities, Robert C. Allen (Allen 2001), for instance, based his pre-modern consumer price index on a variety of foods, linen, candles, lamp oil and fuel. In addition, energy historians have pointed to the importance of changes in fuel usage – particularly of coal – for material living standards. According to Tony Wrigley, an energy revolution – or the increasing use of coal rather than wood for industrial purposes as well as domestic heating – in early modern England led to 'warmer rooms and the construction of brick chimneys', allowing households 'to live in greater comfort than their parents and grandparents' (Wrigley 2016, 81).[6] Similarly, in a recent article on the impact of fuel availability on English cooking habits during the industrial revolution, David Zylberberg (Zylberberg 2015) concluded that households in coal-rich regions were better off than those living in regions of peat or wood.

Much like the debate on pre-industrial living standards, the history of energy has long been suffering from (neo-)Malthusian pessimism. The history before the industrial revolution has been seen as some sort of an *histoire immobile* characterised by energy poverty and falling living standards due to population pressure. Writing an economic history of the world population through the lens of energy, Carlo M. Cipolla did not hesitate to describe all pre-industrial societies as being inherently constrained by scarcity: '[i]n all agricultural societies of our past we find that, mainly because of limitations of energy sources known and exploited, the great mass of people can hardly afford to satisfy anything but the more elementary needs – food, clothing, and housing, and even these at rather unsatisfactory levels' (Cipolla 1962, 61). The pessimist idea that the early modern economy was unable to generate growth was gradually altered from the 1980s on. Proof of profound early modern change was now to be found in consumption and material culture. Since Neil McKendrick (McKendrick 1982; McKendrick, Brewer & Plumb 1982) penned his seminal thesis of a 'consumer revolution' occurring in eighteenth-century England, many historians have accounted for the radical growth of material welfare by means of a new, more market-oriented consumption model in the course of the early modern period (Trentmann 2016). The pleasures of this new material world were to become increasingly accessible to and desired by a growing group of 'industrious' consumers, even when – paradoxically – real wages were dropping. The democratisation of consumption eventually undermined the traditional social hierarchies and moral constraints on the 'old luxury'. Instead of aiming for grandeur, exquisite refinement and distinction, the 'new luxuries',

---

6   A similar observation was made by Kander, Malanima & Warde 2013, 189.

as Jan de Vries (de Vries 2003, 2008) called them, allowed for a more popular indulgence in comfort, convenience and pleasure. Claiming new consumer behaviour as either the result or the cause of economic modernisation, the consumer and industrious revolutions alike ultimately diminished the pessimist overtone of the classic standard-of-living debate.

Although the consumer and energy revolution theses have hardly ever been confronted with one another, in a way the transition from Malthusian pessimism to Smithian optimism in the economic historiography on early modern consumption resembles Wrigley's (Wrigley 1988, 2010, 2016) transition from an 'organic' to a 'mineral economy'. According to this model, the shift to fossil energy enabled the early modern economy to break the spell of stagnation and to embark on a trajectory of energy abundance. In the same way as the consumer revolution liberated the economy from its traditional moral constraints on consumption, the substitution of coal for wood freed the economy from its organic energy constraint, prompting social and economic amelioration, progress and improvement for all strata in society. Indeed, the two historiographies share a similar sentiment of optimism that could be placed under the umbrella of what De Vries (De Vries 1994, 253) has dubbed 'the revolt of the early modernists'.

In its turn, however, the belief in economic progress bringing 'substantial benefit to all members of society' and 'narrowing the social distances', as McKendrick (McKendrick 1982, 20), De Vries (De Vries 2008, 54) and Wrigley (Wrigley 2010, 56) would want it, has been deemed by recent research into the history of consumption and material culture to be too much of an optimistic interpretation. While scholars like Colin Campbell (Campbell 1987), Peter Earle (Earle 1989) and Woodruff D. Smith (Smith 2002) have already linked changes in early modern material culture to the rise of bourgeois class-consciousness and the construction of a distinct urban middle-class identity, the main protagonist of the consumer revolution has implicitly or explicitly always been a more or less 'active searching', liberated agent (Bianchi 1998). In more recent years, the work of Bruno Blondé (Blondé 2001, 2009) and Wouter Ryckbosch (Ryckbosch 2012) has touched upon the historical relationship between consumption and power from the perspective of underlying social and economic structures. They have pointed out that, much like the old luxuries, new products of mass consumption like hot drinks were equally important in producing and reproducing social inequalities within the material culture of urban households. While they surely were introduced among all classes of consumers in society, colonial groceries like tea, coffee, chocolate, sugar and tobacco – and their associated material culture of tin-glazed earthenware – at the same time offered new opportunities to convey status, show wealth and strive for distinction through conspicuous ostentation. In a similar vein, historians like Michael Kwass (Kwass 2006, 658) and John Styles (Styles 2007, 181-211) have attributed such elements of 'transformed inequality' to new fashions in dress and accessories such as the wig.

Most of these accounts of early modern consumption inequalities have however, like the consumer revolution thesis itself, focussed on material cultures of luxury, novelty and fashion rather than on comfort. While John E. Crowley (Crowley 1999, 2001) saw the rise of a more comfortable lifestyle as being materially exemplified by the spread of better heating and lighting, the role of comfort has most usually been described as a discourse among contemporaries that reconceptualised the very ideas of 'necessity' and 'luxury'. In such discourse, signifiers like 'comfort', 'convenience' and 'ease' provided a more neutral and socially acceptable language for the consumption of luxuries, deriving it from its traditional overtones of excess and inequality (Kwass 2003, 94; Odile-Bernez 2014). Thus, comfort became a very marker of (early) modern consumer culture and its aspirations of equity, freedom and egalitarianism. But did a new emphasis on physical comfort really abolish older definitions of domestic amenity giving priority to social status, as Crowley has suggested (Crowley 2001, 3)? Did such elementary comforts as heating and lighting extend equally into all reaches of society?

By drawing on probate inventory evidence, this chapter will study how an 'invention of comfort' in eighteenth-century Ghent was socially differentiated. Ghent was one of the first places on the Continent to adopt the English mineral model which, after 1750, would quickly make the shift to coal (Ryckbosch and Saelens 2019). It experienced economic growth through commercialisation and budding industrialisation, and thus possessed all the features needed for becoming an economy of 'high mass consumption'. At the same time, however, within this climate of growth various historians have exposed growing levels of inequality, not only in Ghent but in the whole of the urban Low Countries as well (Ryckbosch 2016). In what follows below, I have studied material cultures of energy as they can be gleaned from a sample of probate inventories, in the background of these social delineations in eighteenth-century Ghent.[7] First to be discussed will be the social distribution of the broader assemblages of home heating and lighting within the material culture of comfort as well as the changes in fuel consumption that accompanied them. Then, the chapter will zoom in on two of the most important energy technologies: the stove and the fireplace; and relate how both were socially dispersed among and culturally defined by different layers in urban society.

The social distribution of home heating and lighting

To what extent did the consumer revolution and its subsequent 'invention of comfort' climb down the social scale? In their classic probate inventory-based studies, Lorna Weatherill and Mark Overton et al. insisted that in seventeenth- and eighteenth-century Britain there was no such thing as a 'humble consumer society' and that consumer change was limited to the urban middling groups and above (Weatherill 1988, 191-194; Overton et al. 2004, 165-169). Within the confines of the probate inventories' social scope, most case studies have, however, revealed a rich world of goods that spread across a wide spectrum of households. The diffusion of new luxuries like hot drinks, mirrors and majolica, in particular, was broadly carried out over all social groups, even in times of economic decline and pauperisation (Wijsenbeek-Olthuis 1987, 230-235; Blondé & Van Damme 2010). Yet again, very few studies have explicitly directed their attention to 'the poor'. An early exception was Cissie Fairchilds' (Fairchilds 1993) study on the distribution of populuxe goods in eighteenth-century Paris. She argued that the disappearance of guild restrictions on production and of traditional sumptuary laws opened up an entire market of new middle- and lower-class consumers. Likewise, Anne McCants (McCants 2008 and 2013)

---

7   390 Ghent probate inventories were analysed spread over four sample periods: 1674-87 (82 inventories), 1730-31 (99), 1780-83 (106) and 1830-31 (103).

has noted that 'luxury' articles like coffee and tea and porcelain were gradually becoming socially more inclusive as they descended the social ladder. Since probate inventories suffer from a very well-known social bias towards the 'middling sorts of people', broadly defined, these studies could not shine their light upon the very poor (nor will this study do so). They have nevertheless shown how new material cultures reached at least those 'sub-average' social strata that fell below the proper middle class.

Could such a process of democratisation also be observed for the comforts of home heating and lighting? By the late seventeenth century 62 per cent of the lowest quartile of inventoried households in Ghent owned at least one type of primary heating which could heat an entire room (i.e. a fireplace or stove: see table 1). This would rise steadily to 88 per cent in 1780, only to decline again to around 70 per cent in the first half of the nineteenth century. This is fairly consistent with the findings of Craig Muldrew (Muldrew 2011, 182) that 60 to 75 per cent of inventoried labourers in eighteenth-century rural England owned at least one hearth. Secondary heating such as braziers, bed warmers and foot stoves could be carried around the house for additional warmth. The rise of these heating items would prove even more impressive, easily doubling their presence throughout the period studied – although still only half of the poor inventories would mention one or more smaller energy objects. As for household illumination, a similar overall trend appears. Except for a brief stint in 1780, the share of the lowest rank of inventories owning lighting objects would increase from 62 to 92 per cent. Although their richer counterparts clearly took the lead, the poorer households would also thus experience an improvement in their material comfort in terms of heating and lighting.

Take, for instance, the examples of the two poorest inventories in the samples of 1680 and 1780. The furniture recorded in the home of Anthone Arnout, a single man who had died in the summer of 1680, consisted of only a chest, two racks and two bad ('*quaede*') chairs, but it did not include a table, a cupboard or a bed.[8] His inventory mentioned neither plates nor cutlery. The presence of a couple of bottles and beer mugs suggests that Anthone's assemblage of tableware was limited to the bare essentials. In terms of heating and light, he owned a couple of candles and a ton of coal. Anthone did not own any utensils for keeping a good fire going and probably burned his fuel straight on the floor of his single-roomed house. Nor was there any candlestick recorded which could be used to hold a candle in place. A century later, Joanne Wille, who at the time of probating had to take care of three small children after her husband had died in February 1781, lived in more comfortable circumstances.[9] Like Anthone, she lived in a one-roomed dwelling. Unlike his, however, her home featured at least a proper hearth along with some equipment to operate it. The light from the hearth's fire was augmented by a mirror that was hung above the chimney. Lighting her home was further facilitated by two candlesticks. Other aspects of material culture were more elaborate (though still modest) as well. Joanne had a bedstead with a straw mattress to sleep on, while two cupboards allowed her to put away the bedding and other household linen. Food could be prepared in an iron pot hung in the fireplace, and was served at the table on some tin-glazed earthenware plates. The presence of a tea kettle also

---

8   RAG, old notary archives (NOT1), no. 589.
9   SAG, series 332, no. 778/11.

Table 1. The ownership of heating and lighting objects among inventoried households in Ghent per social group (percentage of inventories and median number of objects per inventory).

		1680	1730	1780	1830
Primary heating					
	'Poor'				
	Spread (in %)	62	67	88	68
	Quantity (> 0)	1,5	1	1	1
	'Middling'				
	Spread (in %)	88	73	100	98
	Quantity (> 0)	1	2	2	2
	'Rich'				
	Spread (in %)	100	100	100	100
	Quantity (> 0)	3	3	4	5
Secondary heating					
	'Poor'				
	Spread (in %)	21	17	35	48
	Quantity (> 0)	1	1	1	1
	'Middling'				
	Spread (in %)	45	45	81	79
	Quantity (> 0)	1	1	1	1
	'Rich'				
	Spread (in %)	73	100	92	84
	Quantity (> 0)	2	3	2	2
Lighting					
	'Poor'				
	Spread (in %)	62	67	54	92
	Quantity (> 0)	1,5	1	1	3
	'Middling'				
	Spread (in %)	86	80	89	100
	Quantity (> 0)	2,5	2	3	5
	'Rich'				
	Spread (in %)	100	96	100	100
	Quantity (> 0)	4	6	7	10

Note: 1680: N 'lower' = 29; N 'middling' = 42; N 'upper' = 11. 1730: N 'lower' = 24; 'middling' = 51; N 'upper' = 24. 1780: N 'lower' = 26; N 'middling' = 54; N 'upper' = 26. 1830: N 'lower' = 25; N 'middling' = 53; N 'upper' = 25.

Sources: SAG, Minuten van staten van goederen, series 320, nos. 159, 184, 187-188, 192-193, 199-200, 532-543, 770-782; RAG, Old notary archives, NOT1; RAG, New notary archives, NOT622-653.

suggests that hot drinks were occasionally consumed. All these material pleasures could be conveyed to a domestic environment that provided decent warmth and light. In only a century it appears from these two cases that material comfort had indeed democratised and trickled down towards the more ordinary ranks in society.

Despite the obviously increasing inclusion of the poor, the relative differences between the lower and upper social groups would not just evaporate. Not only did the relative spread of thermal comfort among the poorer households consistently lag behind, the poor also owned fewer energy objects compared to their richer counterparts. Within the middle and upper ranks of the sample the spread of (primary and secondary) heating and lighting would rise to be included in practically all inventories by the end of the eighteenth century. While the bottom 25 per cent of households had only a median number of one fireplace or stove throughout the entire period, the middling sort would quickly add one additional source of primary heating during the eighteenth century. This average reinforces the findings of previous research. Annick Pardailhé-Galabrun (Pardailhé-Galabrun 1988, 235-236), for instance, found an average number of two fireplaces among Parisian households. The richest of the inventories studied here would even expand this number from three to five. Due to spatial and energy constraints, poorer households were often forced to concentrate most of their daily activities in the proximity of the light and warmth of the kitchen. The difference in the number of primary heating sources was important indeed, as it allowed richer households to expand their everyday activities into rooms other than the kitchen. The domestic life of the less fortunate, on the other hand, was often spatially limited, as poorer households lived in smaller dwellings or rented single apartments in larger buildings.

The spread of smaller heating objects, too, was socially skewed towards the upper classes. In the late seventeenth and early eighteenth centuries, braziers and bed warmers could already be found in about 75-100 per cent of the top 25 per cent of households. Towards the end of the eighteenth century the middling groups would gradually catch up with the richer inventories, but the lower strata never succeeded in doing so. With regard to illumination, all social groups managed to share in a quasi-doubling median quantity of objects. However, since the median number of lighting items of a richer household was still three times that of a poorer household, the dispersion of light would, once again, surely not lead to a 'narrowing of the social gaps'. Moreover, the materiality of such smaller energy objects was often seen as a grateful source of ostentation. Braziers, candlesticks and candle snuffers among the rich were regularly made out of silver, while their material, if known, in poorer inventories was usually copper, pewter, or iron. Likewise, the most conspicuous forms of lighting such as luxurious chandeliers or girandoles that held two or more candles and thus provided light from more than one angle were only to be found among the richest inventories.

Household energy transitions in social perspective

Owning a fireplace or stove was one thing; keeping them fuelled was quite another. Since poorer households did not often store wood or coal and rather purchased their fuels on a daily basis during wintertime, the ownership of fuels among the lower-ranked inventories was remarkably low. Overall, there was a steady increase among all social categories in the percentage of inventories registering fuels throughout the seventeenth to nineteenth centuries. This suggests that coal indeed allowed a wider and more democratic spread of energy. And this democratisation of energy was clearly stimulated by a drop in the price of coal in the middle of the eighteenth century (Ryckbosch & Saelens 2019). However, the presence of fuel energy remained socially differentiated. Whereas at least three quarters of the middle- and upper-ranked inventories mentioned fuels, only about 20 to 40 per cent of the poorer households owned them – except for an exceptional 58 per cent in 1780. When people were too poor to purchase their own firewood, coal or candles, they could always go to their local inn, tavern or coffeehouse, where a fire was roaring and where cooked food was served (Roche 1997, 149). But even when they had some fuel stored, the volume recorded by appraisers was consistently lower as compared to that of their richer counterparts. Indeed, the median appraised value of recorded fuels in the bottom-, middle- and top-ranked inventories reached 1 lb., 1.5 lb. and 2 lb. – which would have corresponded to about a half, one and one and a half *stères* of firewood, respectively.

In terms of fuel transitions, there were also some social differences. The household consumption of coal in Ghent was already rising before the middle of the eighteenth century, even though it would become cheaper than firewood only after that time. We can observe such a growth only among the better-off. These groups used coal quite substantially already in the late seventeenth and early eighteenth centuries. They did so as a complementary source of energy to firewood which remained the most important one. Only after 1750, when the price of coal fell below that of firewood, would the vast majority of households quickly make the change to fossil fuels, the spread of which rose at an astonishing rate from 10 per cent in 1730 to 93 per cent in 1780 among the lower inventories. Though taking the lead in the adoption of coal, the richer households were also the ones which stuck longest to firewood. Within the group of inventoried households that owned fuels, the spread of firewood had by 1780 already dropped to 40 per cent among the poorer ones, whereas 91 per cent of the richest households still heated their homes with wood.

Similar trends could be discerned in other regions as well. In the northern Low Countries, for instance, where peat has long served as a very cheap source of energy, expensive fuels like firewood and coal were especially to be found in richer inventoried households, whereas peat remained the only fuel accessible to labouring households (Wijsenbeek-Olthuis 1987, 450-451; Schuurman 1989, 229). In early modern England the opposite was true. Here, coal had been the cheapest fuel already since the sixteenth century and had as such long been a typical fuel for the poor (Cavert 2016). The British historian John U. Nef (Nef 1966 [orig. 1932], 196) noted already that the poor 'could less afford to pay the extra price required to obtain wood' and 'had to content themselves with a less pleasant fuel'. As the example of Maria and Robert in the introduction illustrated, wealthy households in eighteenth-century Ghent have long used different types of fuel interchangeably. Probably they preferred coal for its high energy-intensity, while firewood was valued more for its 'graceful' character. After all, the rich had better access to a wider variety of fuels. Also peat, for instance, the price of which was highly inflated because of exhaustion in eighteenth-century Flanders, could occasionally (and exclusively) be found among the well-to-do.

Bourgeois comfort: the stove

Usually borrowing a more cultural perspective, various scholars have already suggested that newly introduced commodities and their material nature typically signalled the values of the new consumer culture that came to be in the seventeenth and eighteenth centuries. Woodruff Smith (Smith 2002), for instance, saw in coffee and tea a material manifestation of the 'sobering' character of the respectable urban bourgeoisie. Likewise, Brian Cowan (Cowan 2005) interpreted the popularisation of coffee as part of a culture of curiosity established by an elite of 'virtuosi' who had a particular taste for the new. In a similar way the stove, perhaps even more than coffee and tea, corresponded well with the rationality that constituted the cultural identity of the rising middle classes. Exemplifying efficiency, convenience and cleanliness, the stove has indeed been placed at the heart of the invention of comfort. While the fireplace had always been an important source of heating and lighting in the historical home, the introduction of the stove has been interpreted by historians as a more radical shift in the improvement in domestic comfort. According to Raffaella Sarti (Sarti 2002, 92), stoves allowed for a 'more rational exploitation of a heat source', enabling households to heat entire rooms more effectively. In a similar vein, Anton Schuurman (Schuurman 1992) noted that the typical domesticity of the Dutch urban bourgeoisie, which in the nineteenth century gradually spread over the countryside as well, would have been hard to imagine without the introduction of the stove. For Daniel Roche, in his *History of Everyday Things* (Roche 1997, 144-145), the difference between fireplace and stove indeed marked the very difference between mere necessity and pleasurable comfort.

Was it also those consumers of 'bourgeois virtue' who in eighteenth-century Ghent took on the role of tastemakers in the adoption of the stove and subsequently pushed a new culture of comfort down the social scale? Figure 1 surely suggests such a pattern. The very first stoves in Ghent households can already be observed in the late seventeenth and early eighteenth centuries, but only among the upper crust of the sample. In its initial stages, the stove was adopted particularly by the top 25 per cent of households. It was only during the second half of the eighteenth century and later that the bulk of the urban population would gradually become involved in this new material culture of comfort. Stoves were fairly expensive, but still not out of the reach of ordinary people. Its median (second-hand) value in the sample of probate inventories was 1 lb. of Flemish *groten* – the equivalent of about 8 daily wages of an average building labourer in eighteenth-century Flanders (Vandenbroeke 1982) – and its price would start to decrease after 1780.[10] Economic historians of consumption have usually ascribed consumer change to a long-term decline in the prices of consumer durables (Shammas 1990, 96-100) and it seems that a reduction in price also played an important role in the democratisation of the stove in eighteenth-century Ghent. Combined with the growing availability of cheap coal, both the manufacture and diffusion of the stove would eventually become more popular. In the long term, comfort thus became cheaper.

Ryckbosch (2012) already saw in the diffusion of hot drinks, clocks and bedsteads in early modern Aalst a typical example of a 'Veblenesque' trickle-down effect. Such a process

---

10   In 1780 the median stove was appraised at 1 lb. 4 s., while in 1830 this had dropped to 0 lb. 17 s.

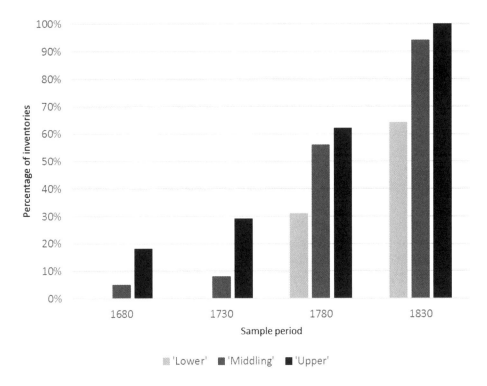

Figure 1. The social distribution of the stove in Ghent.

Note: 1680: N 'lower' = 29; N 'middling' = 42; N 'upper' = 11. 1730: N 'lower' = 24; 'middling' = 51; N 'upper' = 24. 1780: N 'lower' = 26; N 'middling' = 54; N 'upper' = 26. 1830: N 'lower' = 25; N 'middling' = 53; N 'upper' = 25.

Sources: SAG, Minuten van staten van goederen, series 320, nos. 159, 184, 187-188, 192-193, 199-200, 532-543, 770-782; RAG, Old notary archives, NOT1; RAG, New notary archives, NOT622-653.

of emulation also seems to have presented itself in the case of the popularisation of the stove in eighteenth-century Ghent, where this new consumer product was first introduced into the middling and upper parts of the social hierarchy and gradually spread downwards from there. By the late eighteenth century the stove had already become an integral part of an urban middle-class identity with its emphasis on bourgeois comfort. Take, for example, the home of Francis Van der Haegen, a master shoemaker and prototypical member of the 'middling sort of people', as it was depicted in the probate inventory of his late wife († 1781).[11] As 'the room which saw the least change' in the eighteenth century (Earle 1989, 296), Francis' kitchen may still have been equipped with a fireplace which fittingly suited a cooking culture directed at the boiling, stewing and smoking of food (Pennell 2016, 70-81). Also in the front room, where guests were usually accommodated, a nicely decorated open hearth could be encountered – a feature that was more in line with conventions of genteel status, almost literally 'opening' a world of politeness and good taste (cf. infra). In the back room, on the other hand, there was a stove. Here, Francis and his family could sit

---

11   SAG, series 332, no. 778/13.

comfortably warm at one of the two tables that were placed there and perhaps enjoy some tea served in one of the cups and pots related to the consumption of hot drinks that were listed by the appraisers. Judging from the many plates, spoons, forks and other tableware, they gathered here for dinner as well. The two writing desks also suggest that Francis, his wife and three small children could sit down in the back room to study or read, which was more pleasant for the fingers, which stiffened less quickly in the evenly distributed warmth of a stove, especially when fuelled by coal. A second stove was stored on the attic and could be moved around the house in the winter as an additional heating element. The fact that they owned candlesticks, lamps and candle pans, which could be backed with a couple of mirrors, meant that the Van der Haegen family enjoyed the genteel leisure of entertainment after dark. In their aspirations of creating a *warm* domestic environment, Francis' family, like most of the urban bourgeoisie in eighteenth-century Ghent, were clearly cosy in the private comforts of their home.

The genteel elegance of the fireplace

The fireplace has long been considered a very symbol of domestic life and intimacy. A main source of both warmth and light, the hearth became the heart of the home – a central element of domesticity and a centre of gravity for conviviality which people could gather around. This was also a psychological issue, for the fireplace, unlike the stove, showed a visible and 'living' fire which had a tremendous effect on the symbolic representation of the home (Sarti 2002, 95-96). In the words of Pardailhé-Galabrun (Pardailhé-Galabrun 1988, 332-333), 'fire was synonymous with the hearth and home in the language of times, and the fireplace, because of its multiple uses, was an essential pole of attraction in the home'. It is no accident that contemporary architects were often first and foremost concerned with the design and decoration of the fireplace as the main focal point of a room (Thornton 1984, 15). Even by the late nineteenth century, when central heating and ventilation were already quite advanced, interior decorators still maintained that open fireplaces were the only acceptable form of heating since 'the good taste and *savoir-vivre* of the inmates of a house may be guessed from the means used for heating it' (Wharton and Codman 1898, 87). According to specialists in historical architecture such as Christopher Gilbert and Anthony Wells-Cole (Wells-Cole 1985) the early modern fireplace was indeed a 'fashionable fireplace'. Contrary to the tenacious belief that the history of domestic heating has been just a matter of mere necessity, the home's fire could equally have been embedded in a culture of luxury, ostentation and elegance. In this respect, the fireplace fitted best with Smith's (Smith 2002) culture of gentility, a cultural context that embodied the status hierarchy of early modern society and all its codes of well-controlled manners that came with it.

Because of their inefficiency, most hearths had primarily been places to cook at and only secondarily were they used for heating (Braudel 1983, 299). Braziers were then usually brought in for their mobile energy as they could be carried around rooms where warmth was needed. In genteel milieus fireplaces that were placed in rooms other than the kitchen were therefore often loaded with decorative features. Fireplaces were more evenly distributed over each social group than the stove. Before 1800 the majority of households, even the poorer ones, owned at least one hearth (see figure 2). But social differences remained:

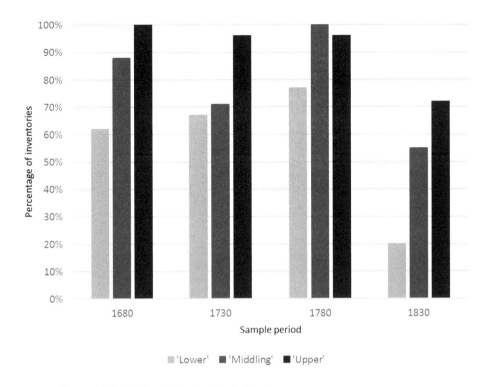

Figure 2. The social distribution of the fireplace in Ghent.

Note: 1680: N 'lower' = 29; N 'middling' = 42; N 'upper' = 11. 1730: N 'lower' = 24; 'middling' = 51; N 'upper' = 24. 1780: N 'lower' = 26; N 'middling' = 54; N 'upper' = 26. 1830: N 'lower' = 25; N 'middling' = 53; N 'upper' = 25.

Sources: SAG, Minuten van staten van goederen, series 320, nos. 159, 184, 187-188, 192-193, 199-200, 532-543, 770-782; RAG, Old notary archives, NOT1; RAG, New notary archives, NOT622-653.

while practically all middle- and upper-ranked households owned a few fireplaces, no more than 75 per cent of their lower-ranked counterparts had one fireplace at best. This does not necessarily mean that one quarter of the poorer families did not have a fireplace or chimney; they did not have any equipment to enable them to use it more effectively and probably lit fire straight on the floor. The social differences became more apparent, however, when the hearth's popularity gradually started to decline during the second half of the eighteenth century. Tellingly, richer families were much more inclined to stick to this traditional type of heating, even after the stove had already become the most common source of warmth. By 1830, over half of the middling inventories and about three quarters of the upper inventories still recorded hearth equipment, even when architectural attention was gradually beginning to shift from the fireplace to the ceiling (Thornton 1984, 150). Poorer households, on the other hand, as soon as they had switched over to the stove, quickly abandoned the use of the fireplace.

Rather than a practical instrument, the fireplace long remained a site of ornament, signifying wealth and status among the upper classes. Whereas the stove could be perceived as an investment in comfort, the fireplace guaranteed an investment in notions of hierarchy and order. The decorative role of the hearth could be seen as a means of demonstrating conspicuous consumption and distinction. Theoretically drawing from the relational sociology of Pierre Bourdieu, Hester Dibbits (Dibbits 2010) has described *pronken* or flaunting as a performative practice of reflecting and creating social and cultural distinctions. Putting (new) luxuries such as glazed earthenware, porcelain, chintzes, gold and silver on display was a way of exhibiting the aesthetic sensibilities, refined taste and polite behaviour that a respectable family was keen to demonstrate. And such a practice was not very different to the conspicuous world of the old luxury. According to Smith (Smith 2002, 25-62) older views of status defined by gentility were made to intersect with a new, broader cultural context of bourgeois respectability in which the link between status and consumption was now conveyed by 'taste' instead of birth. In a similar vein, Blondé and Ryckbosch have convincingly argued that the culture of drinking coffee and tea easily fitted into already existing cultural and behavioural codes of early modern urban society with all its opportunities for distinction, thus quickly lending itself to 'conspicuous tea display' (Blondé & Ryckbosch 2015; Ryckbosch 2012, 252-257).

Genteel behaviour expressed itself through material culture – in dress, in dining, in social rituals, but also in architecture and interior decoration.[12] Often heaped with a wealth of ornament, the chimneypiece was a preferred site for display and conspicuous consumption. Mirrors gradually replaced paintings as the most important form of decoration and often deserved a place on the mantelpiece (Blondé 2002b, 385-386). Hung above the chimney, huge mirrors not only exhibited new forms of proper decorum, they were also more tactile and functional – multiplying the light and creating the illusion of spatial enlargement. In the dining room of Susanne Cornelis († 1780), wife of the wealthy textile merchant Joannes Josephus Delanotte who lived in the *Paddenhoeck* in the centre of Ghent, a mirror was strategically placed above the central wood-burning fireplace and accentuated the hearth's prominence in the room. Covered in a mantel cloth of printed cotton, the chimneypiece was equipped with a set of shiny chinaware and other tin-glazed crockery, four copper candlesticks and two sconces, and a bird cage.[13] In Susanne and Joannes' dining room, the fireplace was the most felicitous place to put a world of luxury goods on display for others to see.

In a way, of course, such status-led consumption was also a form of comfort. In a recent article Jon Stobart and Christina Prytz (Stobart & Prytz 2018) have shown that the emotional and non-material dimensions of comfort dominated the concerns of elite households at the end of the eighteenth century. Creating an appropriate setting for 'polite' domestic sociability in the most 'civilised' manner was best achieved by inviting 'genteel' company to sit by a fashionable, well-ornamented fireplace. This was social rather than physical comfort, as Crowley would have described it. While bringing warmth and light to rituals of consumption that were carried out during teatime or at the dinner table, the fireplace at the same time symbolised power and status. It is no accident that we usually find a fireplace in representative rooms such as the dining room, the parlour or the best room, while the stove was more likely to be found in smaller, private rooms (Saelens 2019). Although often blessed with domestic servants for the dirty and full-time job of

---

12   Compare for instance to ch. 16, written by Inneke Baatsen, on dining culture in fifteenth- and sixteenth-century Bruges.

13   SAG, series 332, no. 773/1.

dealing with the fireplace,[14] the material practices of the hearth obviously conflicted with other domestic ideals such as idleness and cleanliness (Cowan 1983, 61-68; Denis 2016, 104). Unlike the 'bourgeois comfort' of a stove, the 'genteel fireplace' was more a matter of appearance. In affluent circles, notions of public elegance and private comfort often went hand in hand.

Conclusion

In eighteenth-century Ghent, one of the first coal-fired cities on the European Continent, households of all social strata within a population of probate inventories managed to make their domestic environment more comfortable in terms of heating and lighting. As it appears, the cheapening of energy because of the greater availability of coal as well as new fuel technologies becoming less expensive led to the democratisation of standards in thermal comfort. After being introduced into the richer households, coal and the new material culture of comfort that came with it – in the form of the stove, for instance – gradually reached out to the bottom of the social hierarchy as well. In this respect, both McKendrick and Wrigley, among other Smithian optimists, were right that economic modernisation would eventually be materially beneficial to all in society. However, this did not imply that comfort was equally distributed. The poorer households usually lagged behind as the spread of new heating and lighting technologies gradually trickled down the social ladder, while at the same time the relative gaps between rich and poor remained the same or widened even further. Even if a poor city-dweller already lived in a house of more rooms, most of his or her daily activities were necessarily concentrated in one and the same room – usually the kitchen where the hearth stood. Richer households, on the other hand, augmented their primary sources of warmth from two to even five more heated rooms. Together with an abundance of candles, lamps and mirrors, this significantly increased the opportunities of wealthy families for domestic leisure, sociability and work.

The stove was a new consumer product that was quickly adopted by the well-to-do. Its 'rational' character gradually pushed bourgeois domesticity from intimacy, leisure and ease towards – in the words of Rybczynski (Rybczynski 1987, 231) – 'mechanically aided comforts' which stressed efficiency and convenience. Even when this invention of comfort as symbolised by the rise of the stove was widely flourishing and the consumer revolution was set to replace the traditional hierarchies embedded in the old luxuries, the open fireplace still kept its relevance in the seventeenth to nineteenth centuries as a means of social distinction. While the stove exemplified the beginning of a new era in domestic comfort, the fireplace resembled a genteel and fashionable way of heating. In a time of growing sensibility towards privacy – homes increasingly being divided into more, smaller and functionally specialised rooms – middle-class and elite householders were also concerned about their public image. Genteel behaviour required tasteful surroundings. The social elites in eighteenth-century Ghent therefore developed a hybrid material culture of energy that often conflicted with the ideal of cleanliness and private comfort.

---

14 The number of rich households with domestic staffs in Ghent was rising during the period being studied: 18 per cent in 1680, 17 per cent in 1730, 23 per cent in 1780, and 48 per cent in 1830.

Especially in the public and frontstage rooms of their homes, these households have long wasted energy for reasons of conspicuous consumption. In the distribution of thermal comfort among the rich we can observe a manifestation of what Bruno Blondé (Blondé 2009) has called 'conflicting consumption models'. The fireplace – with its prominent chimneypiece – was both a lived and representational space by which one could easily imagine a self-evident claim to gentility; all the while silver tea braziers, candlesticks, snuffers and extinguishers could charm guests at the table. 'Comfort' clearly embodied different dimensions: the stove provided physical comfort, while the fireplace, more in line with the polite expectations and tasteful manners of respectable and genteel burghers, provided social comfort. A means to aspire to distinction, the comforts of the upper classes were indeed comforts of difference.

Primary sources

State Archives Ghent (RAG), Old notary archives, NOT1.
State Archives Ghent (RAG), New notary archives, NOT622-653.
City Archives Ghent (SAG), series 332, Minuten van staten van goederen, nos. 159, 184, 187-188, 192-193, 199-200, 532-543, 770-782.

References

Allen, Robert C. 2001. "The Great Divergence in European wages and prices from the Middle Ages to the First World War." *Explorations in Economic History* 38: 411-447.

Bianchi, Marina, ed. 1998. *The Active Consumer. Novelty and Surprise in Consumer Choice.* London: Routledge.

Blondé, Bruno. 2001. "Indicatoren van het luxeverbruik Paardenbezit en conspicuous consumption te Antwerpen (zeventiende-achttiende eeuw)." *Bijdragen tot de Geschiedenis* 84 (4): 497-512.

Blondé, Bruno. 2002a. "Tableware and changing consumer patterns. Dynamics of material culture in Antwerp, 17th-18th centuries." In *Majolica and Glass from Italy to Antwerp and Beyond. The Transfer of Technology in the 16th-Early 17th Century*, ed. Johan Veeckman, 295-311. Antwerp: Stad Antwerpen.

Blondé, Bruno. 2002b. "Art and economy in seventeenth- and eighteenth-century Antwerp: a view from the demand side." In *Economia e arte secc. 13-18*, ed. Simonetta Cavaciocchi, 379-391. Prato: Le Monnier.

Blondé, Bruno. 2009. "Conflicting consumption models? The symbolic meaning of possessions and consumption amongst the Antwerp nobility at the end of the eighteenth century." In *Fashioning Old and New: Changing Consumer Preferences in Europe (Seventeenth-Nineteenth Centuries)*, ed. Bruno Blondé, Natacha Coquery, Jon Stobart and Ilja Van Damme, 61-80. Turnhout: Brepols.

Blondé, Bruno, and Wouter Ryckbosch. 2015. "Arriving to a set table: the integration of hot drinks in the urban consumer culture of the 18th-century Southern Low Countries." In

Goods from the East: Trading Eurasia, 1600-1800, ed. Maine Berg, 309-327. London: Palgrave Macmillan.

Blondé, Bruno, and Ilja Van Damme. 2010. "Retail growth and consumer changes in a declining urban economy: Antwerp (1650-1750)." *Economic History Review* 63 (3): 638-663.

Braudel, Fernand. 1983. *The Structures of Everyday Life: The Limits of the Possible*. London: Collins.

Campbell, Colin. 1987. *The Romantic Ethic and the Spirit of Modern Consumerism*. Oxford: Blackwell.

Cavert, William M. 2016. *The Smoke of London: Energy and Environment in the Early Modern City*. Cambridge: Cambridge University Press.

Cipolla, Carlo M. 1962. *The Economic History of World Population*. Harmondsworth: Penguin.

Cowan, Brian. 2005. *The Social Life of Coffee: The Emergence of the British Coffeehouse*. New Haven-London: Yale University Press.

Cowan, Ruth Schwartz. 1983. *More Work for Mother. The Ironies of Household Technology from the Open Hearth to the Microwave*. New York: Basic Books.

Crowley, John E. 1999. "The sensibility of comfort." *The American Historical Review* 104 (3): 749-782.

Crowley, John E. 2001. *The Invention of Comfort: Sensibilities and Design in Early Modern Britain and Early America*. Baltimore, MD: Johns Hopkins University Press.

Denis, Britt. 2016. "In search of material practices: the nineteenth-century European domestic interior rehabilitated." *History of Retailing and Consumption* 2 (2): 97-112.

De Vries, Jan. 1975. "Peasant demand patterns and economic development. Friesland, 1550-1750." In *European Peasants and Their Markets. Essays in Agrarian Economic History*, ed. William N. Parker and Eric L. Jones, 205-266. Princeton, NJ: Princeton University Press.

De Vries, Jan. 1994. "The industrial revolution and the industrious revolution." *The Journal of Economic History* 54 (2): 249-270.

De Vries, Jan. 2003. "Luxury in the Dutch Golden Age in theory and practice." In *Luxury in the Eighteenth Century: Debates, Desires and Delectable Goods*, ed. Maxine Berg and Elizabeth Eger, 41-56. Basingstoke: Palgrave Macmillan.

De Vries, Jan. 2008. *The Industrious Revolution: Consumer Behavior and the Household Economy, 1650 to the Present*. Cambridge: Cambridge University Press.

Dibbits, Hester. 2010. "Pronken as practice. Material culture in the Netherlands, 1650-1800." In *Luxury in the Low Countries: Miscellaneous Reflections on Netherlandish Material Culture, 1500 to the Present*, ed. Rengenier C. Rittersma, 137-158. Brussels: Pharo.

Earle, Peter. 1989. *The Making of the English Middle Class: Business, Society and Family Life in London, 1660-1730*. London: Methuen.

Fairchilds, Cissie. 1993. "The production and marketing of populuxe goods in eighteenth-century Paris." In *Consumption and the World of Goods*, ed. John Brewer and Roy Porter, 228-248. London: Routledge.

Gilbert, Christopher, and Anthony Wells-Cole. 1985. *The Fashionable Fire Place, 1660-1840*. Leeds: Leeds City Art Galleries.

Goffman, Erving. 1959. *The Presentation of Self in Everyday Life*. Garden City, NY: Anchor Books.

Kander, Astrid, Paolo Malanima and Paul Warde. 2013. *Power to the People: Energy in Europe over the Last Five Centuries*. Princeton, NJ: Princeton University Press.

Kwass, Michael. 2003. "Ordering the world of goods: consumer revolution and the classification of objects in eighteenth-century France." *Representations* 82 (1): 87-116.

Kwass, Michael. 2006. "Big hair: a wig history of consumption in eighteenth-century France." *The American Historical Review* 111 (3): 631-659.

McCants, Anne E. 2008. "Poor consumers as global consumers: the diffusion of tea and coffee drinking in the eighteenth century." *Economic History Review* 61 (1): 172-200.

McCants, Anne E. 2013. "Porcelain for the poor. The material culture of tea and coffee consumption in eighteenth-century Amsterdam." In *Early Modern Things: Objects and Their Histories, 1500-1800*, ed. Paula Findlen, 316-341. London: Routledge.

McKendrick, Neil. 1982. "The consumer revolution of eighteenth-century England." In *The Birth of a Consumer Society. The Commercialisation of Eighteenth-Century England*, ed. Neil McKendrick, John Brewer and John Harold Plumb, 9-33. London: Europa Publications.

McKendrick, Neil, John Brewer and John Harold Plumb. 1982. *The Birth of a Consumer Society. The Commercialisation of Eighteenth-Century England*. London: Europa Publications.

Muldrew, Craig. 2011. *Food, Energy and the Creation of Industriousness. Work and Material Culture in Agrarian England, 1550-1780*. Cambridge: Cambridge University Press.

Nef, John U. 1966 [1932]. *The Rise of the British Coal Industry*. London: Frank Cass & Co. Ltd.

Odile-Bernez, Marie. 2014. "Comfort, the acceptable face of luxury: an eighteenth-century cultural etymology." *The Journal for Early Modern Cultural Studies* 14 (2): 3-21.

Overton, Mark, Jane Whittle, Darron Dean and Andrew Hann. 2004. *Production and Consumption in English Households, 1600-1750*. London and New York: Routledge.

Pardailhé-Galabrun, Annick. 1988. *La naissance de l'intime: 3000 foyers parisiens, 17e-18e siècles*. Paris: Presses Universitaires de France.

Pennell, Sara. 2016. *The Birth of the English Kitchen, 1600-1850*. London: Bloomsbury Academic.

Roche, Daniel. 1997. *Histoire des choses banales: naissance de la consommation dans les sociétés traditionelle (17e-19e siècle)*. Paris: Fayard.

Rybczynski, Witold. 1987. *Home: A Short History of an Idea*. New York: Penguin.

Ryckbosch, Wouter. 2012. "A consumer revolution under strain: consumption, wealth and status in eighteenth-century Aalst (Southern Netherlands)." Unpublished PhD thesis, Antwerp: University of Antwerp.

Ryckbosch, Wouter. 2016. "Economic inequality and growth before the industrial revolution: the case of the Low Countries (fourteenth to nineteenth centuries)." *European Review of Economic History* 20 (1): 1-22.

Ryckbosch, Wouter, and Wout Saelens. 2019. "Towards an energy revolution in Flanders and Holland? Energy consumption and the industrial revolution in Ghent and Leiden (*c.* 1600-1850): a comparison." *Afscheidssymposium Ben Gales* – International Workshop (Groningen, 29 November 2018).

Saelens, Wout. 2019. "The spatial organisation of home heating and lighting in eighteenth-century Ghent and Leiden." *Energy in the Early Modern Home: The Material Culture of Heating, Lighting and Cooking* – International Workshop (Antwerp, 19-20 September 2019).

Sarti, Raffaella. 2002. *Europe at Home: Family and Material Culture, 1500-1800*. New Haven, CT: Yale University Press.

Schuurman, Anton J. 1989. *Materiële cultuur en levensstijl. Een onderzoek naar de taal der dingen op het Nederlandse platteland in de 19e eeuw: de Zaanstreek, Oost-Groningen, Oost-Brabant*. Wageningen: A. A. G. Bijdragen.

Schuurman, Anton J. 1992. "Is huiselijkheid typisch Nederlands? Over huiselijkheid en modernisering." *Bijdragen en Mededelingen betreffende de Geschiedenis der Nederlanden* 107 (4): 745-759.

Shammas, Carole. 1990. *The Pre-Industrial Consumer in England and America*. Oxford: Clarendon.

Smith, Woodruff D. 2002. *Consumption and the Making of Respectability, 1600-1800*. New York: Routledge.

Stobart, Jon, and Christina Prytz. 2018. "Comfort in English and Swedish country houses, c. 1760-1820." *Social History* 43 (2): 234-258.

Styles, John. 2007. *The Dress of the People: Everyday Fashion in Eighteenth-Century England*. New Haven, CT: Yale University Press.

Thornton, Peter. 1984. *Authentic Decor: The Domestic Interior, 1620-1920*. London: Weidenfeld and Nicolson.

Trentmann, Frank. 2016. *Empire of Things. How We Became a World of Consumers, from the Fifteenth Century to the Twenty-First*. London: Allen Lane.

Vandenbroeke, Chris. 1982. "Prijzen en lonen als sociaal-economische verklaringsvariabelen (14e-20e eeuw)." *Handelingen der Maatschappij voor Geschiedenis en Oudheidkunde te Gent* 36: 103-137.

Weatherill, Lorna. 1988. *Consumer Behaviour and Material Culture in Britain 1660-1760*. London and New York: Routledge.

Wharton, Edith, and Ogden Codman, Jr. 1898. *The Decoration of Houses*. London: B. T. Batsford.

Wijsenbeek-Olthuis, Thera. 1987. *Achter de gevels van Delft. Bezit en bestaan van rijk en arm in een periode van achteruitgang (1700-1800)*. Hilversum: Verloren.

Wrigley, E. A. 1988. *Continuity, Chance and Change: The Character of the Industrial Revolution in England*. Cambridge: Cambridge University Press.

Wrigley, E. A. 2010. *Energy and the English Industrial Revolution*. Cambridge: Cambridge University Press.

Wrigley, E. A. 2016. *The Path to Sustained Growth: England's Transition from an Organic Economy to an Industrial Revolution*. Cambridge: Cambridge University Press.

Zylberberg, David. 2015. "Fuel prices, regional diets and cooking habits in the English industrial revolution (1750-1830)." *Past & Present* 229 (1): 91-122.

MAARTEN F. VAN DIJCK

Violent classes?

Interpersonal Violence and Social Inequality in Mechelen, 1350-1700

Introduction[1]

The sources do not give us the exact day of the year, nor do we know whether the following incident happened in the morning, the afternoon or at the end of the day, but we do know that Jehan Verberct accidentally killed Jehan Govaerts sometime between 1542 and 1544. Both perpetrator and victim were citizens of Mechelen, and they probably knew each other quite well. The manslaughter committed by Jehan Verberct is an example of most killings in the Low Countries during the early modern period. Homicides were seldom the result of an evil well-considered plan, but were the unintended result of everyday conflicts. Jehan Verberct and Jehan Govaerts met each other on the fatal day in a tavern in Mechelen. They played dice for money while ordering a couple of beers. The gambling started in good spirit, but the two men got into an argument about the outcome of the game and they started to insult each other. Jehan Verberct felt offended, took a bread knife and stabbed Jehan Govaerts.[2] The latter died from his injuries two or three hours later.

This story is typical of the violent interactions which occurred every day in late medieval and early modern cities in Europe. Not all of them resulted in a dead body, but homicide rates in the past were far higher than today. Manuel Eisner showed that homicide rates in late medieval Europe reached levels as high as between 15 and 60 per 100,000 inhabitants. The average was somewhere around 30-40 per 100,000 inhabitants. The subsequent decline in homicide rates was a linear process, interrupted only by periods of general upheaval, such as the turbulent second half of the sixteenth century and the revolutionary years between 1780 and 1840. This evolution started in England and the Low Countries, but homicide rates would decline all over Europe from the early modern period until today. At the beginning of the twenty-first century, homicide rates in Europe varied somewhere between 0.4 and 2 per 100,000 inhabitants (Eisner 2014).

Violent tavern conflicts – such as the abovementioned brawl between Jehan Verberct and Jehan Govaerts – did not completely disappear after the sixteenth century, but they were already less common compared to 100 years earlier. Changing cultural repertoires of different social groups not only transformed the frequency of manslaughter; it also had

---

1 I would like to thank the editors of the book and the anonymous reviewers for their useful comments on an earlier version of this chapter.
2 National State Archives Brussels, Audit-Office, Registers, n° 15,667, f. 5r°.

Maarten F. Van Dijck • Erasmus University Rotterdam

Inequality and the City in the Low Countries (1200-2020), ed. by Bruno BLONDÉ, Sam GEENS, Hilde GREEFS, Wouter RYCKBOSCH, Tim SOENS & Peter STABEL, SEUH 50 (Turnhout, 2020), pp. 329-342.

 DOI 10.1484/M.SEUH-EB.5.120453

an impact on the nature of day-to-day interpersonal violence. As a result, the social status of aggressors changed dramatically during the early modern period. The criminal records described Jehan Verberct as a 'poor man', and in his case this was not just a stereotypical platitude used by Jehan to placate the judicial authorities (Gauvard 1991, 400-410; Stabel Ch. 15). A taxation list of 1544 proves that Verberct belonged to the poorest 10 per cent of the population.[3] While perpetrators belonging to the elite dominated violence in the late medieval times, elite violence gradually became less common and Jehan is an example of this evolution.

Studies on thirteenth-century Bologna, fourteenth-century Lyon and fifteenth-century Constance show that the social elite was often over-represented in the group of late medieval perpetrators of manslaughter. By contrast, several studies on nineteenth-century crime make clear that in this period the lower classes dominated the manslaughter figures. The chronology of this transition is less clear, though. One study claims that this change started in England in the sixteenth century, while data on France show that this transformation occurred in the eighteenth century (Eisner 2003). Long-term studies on the social backgrounds of crimes are still non-existent (Eisner 2003, 117), and as a result the timing and mechanisms of this evolution are still unclear.

The timing of the transformations in the Netherlands is particularly crucial because the Low Countries were – together with England – the European region where homicide rates started to decline earlier than elsewhere. In our view, high levels of social control due to population density and the presence of middle-class associations in cities are crucial to understanding the long-term decline in manslaughters in both regions. From the thirteenth century at least, urban authorities developed a strong tradition of regulating social life in the Low Countries, long before states tried to control the everyday life of their citizens. The growth of urban associations was another important factor because those corporations not only strengthened social bonds, but also discouraged participation in blood feuds and penalised disagreement between members (Van Dijck 2006; 2009). This emphasis on the role of the urban middle classes is in line with earlier research on table manners that suggested that these groups were at least as important for the refinement of manners in the Low Countries as the nobility (Blondé 2002, 295-311).

Meanwhile seminal studies on the decline of interpersonal violence mainly focus on the role of the elites. Sociologist Mark Cooney claims that the pacification of the aristocracy is responsible for the decline in homicide rates in the western world, even though the available evidence for such a claim is rather limited and far from conclusive (Cooney 1997). Eisner's research on regicides in Europe between 600 and 1800 is at this moment the only long-term empirical study on the decline in elite violence. Yet, his research is on only the highest nobility; it does not shed light on the use of violence in urban elites, nor does it tell us anything about the evolution of violent behaviour in other social groups (Eisner 2011). A study by Conrad Gietman seems to confirm Cooney's and Eisner's conclusions for the Low Countries. He pointed to the extremely high levels of violence amongst the nobility in the eastern part of the Netherlands until the first half of the seventeenth century (Gietman 2004).

---

3   City Archives Mechelen, Old Archives, part K, n° 1.

Contemporary studies show that, today, those lower down on the social ladder are more inclined to use violence. Some authors even claim that high levels of inequality are directly proportional to high homicide rates (Fajnzylber, Lederman & Loayza 2002; Wilkinson & Pickett 2009). Historical research shows that this relationship between interpersonal violence and inequality is more complex than contemporary social science studies indicate. In their long-term study on violence based on archaeological bone evidence Baten and Steckel conclude that a lot of questions are still unanswered and that a direct one-to-one relationship between violence and inequality is missing (Baten & Steckel 2018, 318). Their conclusions are in line with the available evidence for early modern Mechelen, a city in the Low Countries: homicide rates in Mechelen declined between 1350 and 1800, but growing inequality cannot account for this development. On the contrary, a fairly constant economic inequality can be inferred from a stable house rental tax Gini coefficient in the early modern period (Ryckbosch 2016, appendix B; Van Dijck 2007, 193).

In this chapter we will make the case that the use of interpersonal violence evolved into a cultural repertoire typical of the lower social groups. While the elite and the middle groups in less than a century stopped relying on violence to resolve day-to-day conflicts, lower income categories still used physical force to solve conflicts (Van Dijck 2009). A close examination of taxation and crime records in late medieval and early modern Mechelen is the central focus of this chapter. This will help us to get a better understanding of the relationship between social status and interpersonal violence in an urban context.

The decline of interpersonal violence in Mechelen

Mechelen is located in the centre of the southern part of the Low Countries. Its cloth industry flourished during the late medieval period and it became an important administrative centre in the Low Countries after the Burgundian rulers established the highest court of Burgundy in the city in 1473. The urban population doubled from 15,000 to 30,000 during the fifteenth and the first half of the sixteenth centuries, but the political unrest and economic decline of the second half of the sixteenth century resulted in a downturn in the urban population. Thereafter, Mechelen developed into a centre of Catholic life in the Spanish Netherlands as the city became the seat of the archbishop of the Spanish Netherlands, but this could not save it from economic decline. The urban economy recovered only slowly during the seventeenth and eighteenth centuries, a fact which was reflected in the city's demographic stability after 1630. In many respects, the social and economic history of Mechelen was quite exemplary of the developments in the Southern Low Countries (Van Dijck 2017, 61). Once a major industrial centre, eighteenth-century Mechelen was first and foremost a grounded central place, albeit an important one (Blondé 1998).

The existence of a long series of criminal records enables us to map the evolution of interpersonal violence in late medieval and early modern Mechelen. The accounts of the royal sheriff provide information on the prosecution of serious crimes from the second half of the fourteenth century until the end of the sixteenth. These sources are also available for the seventeenth and eighteenth centuries, but research has shown that the information in the sheriff's accounts should be compared with the offences mentioned in the urban correction books for the period after 1600, because both sources sometimes overlap but they also complement each other. Luckily enough, these urban sources are also well preserved in Mechelen with the exception of those relating to the period between 1712 and 1773 (Van Dijck 2006, 9). The availability of a couple of registers containing urban ordinances makes it possible to obtain a more comprehensive picture of the prosecution policy of the urban authorities during the late medieval and early modern periods.

These legal documents show how interpersonal violence became criminalised during the late medieval period. Murder has always been punished by the death penalty, but manslaughter and other forms of physical violence were most often punished with a fine, while property crimes were penalised by corporal or capital punishment (Maes 1947, 258-296). Aggressors could still buy off their offences with a simple fine or a financial arrangement until the end of the eighteenth century, but the authorities redefined the boundaries between legal and illegal violence after the late medieval period. Violence was transformed from a socially and legally accepted tactic for solving conflicts into a crime prosecuted and punished by the urban authorities.

The Mechelen registers containing local ordinances have been preserved only since 1439, but this is early enough for us to get an insight into the changing attitudes to violence. The first ordinance relevant to our research dates from 2 January 1443. The text makes clear that foreigners were no longer allowed to wear arms inside the city. The wording of the regulation makes clear that this prohibition applied only to people from outside the city. City dwellers could still walk around with their daggers, knives and swords.[4] This interpretation is supported by the registers of the local sheriff which contain a lot of punishments for assaults with all kinds of weapons. Urban aggressors were penalised only for attacking other people, not for wearing weapons on the streets.[5] Another ordinance dating from 12 June 1448 also targeted physical violence committed or initiated by strangers. This was probably a consequence of the conflicts between the duchy of Brabant, the county of Flanders and the principality of Liège.[6] Violence amongst citizens was still not forbidden, only regulated.

In 1452 the urban authorities decided to introduce stricter rules for urban dwellers to contain physical violence in the city. A new regulation prohibited all people in the city from leaving their houses armed at night. This ordinance no longer discriminated between people living inside and outside the city. Yet, the frequent reissuing of this ordinance made clear that non-compliance posed a real challenge for the urban community. The city magistrate re-issued the same ordinance in 1462, 1469, 1475, 1477, 1479 and 1483, which indicates that people continued to go out at night wearing arms.[7] The magistrate also took other initiatives to control the level of violence within the city. An ordinance of 1469 prohibited people from wearing clothes in the colours of their family or clan.[8] This was a typical regulation to avoid blood feuds; distinctive costumes made it easy to recognise members of a friendly or hostile family in the streets. It strengthened group identity, but it also made it easy to continue feuds. Mechelen was quite late in banning such markers of

---

4   City Archives Mechelen, Old Archives, part C-S-II, n° 1, f. 78r°.
5   National State Archives Brussels, Audit-Office, Registers, n° 15,663.
6   City Archives Mechelen, Old Archives, part C-S-II, n° 1, f. 82r°.
7   City Archives Mechelen, Old Archives, part C-S-II, n° 2, f. 28r°, 81r°, 122v°, 131r°, 131v°, 133r°.
8   City Archives Mechelen, Old Archives, part C-S-II, n° 2, f. 122r°.

familial identity compared to nearby Antwerp, where the urban authorities issued a similar ordinance as early as in 1395 (Van Gerven 1999, 199). It was not just cities that took the initiative to control feuds. To this end Philip the Good issued a prohibition against wearing liveries in the whole of the duchies of Brabant and Limburg in 1441 (Godding 2005, 190).

All these ordinances were aimed at containing urban violence, but the urban authorities did not prohibit all kinds of violence. They started to distinguish between legitimate and illegitimate forms of physical assaults. Violent revenge or aggressive reactions to being insulted were still considered appropriate reactions although the perpetrators had to pay financial compensation when this resulted in manslaughter. The regulations became stricter in 1480 when the city magistrate issued two ordinances that prohibited the carrying of all weapons inside the city at night ánd during the day.[9] This was probably related to the civil unrest in Flanders and Brabant following the revolt against Maximilian of Austria in 1482. These regulations were the first steps to criminalising all forms of violent behaviour inside the city.

An ordinance of 17 November 1529 heralded the next phase in the process. The urban authorities proclaimed a new, far-ranging decree aiming 'to prevent all unrest, lawsuits, force, and violence ... and to avoid manslaughter'.[10] This new decree was not limited to combating physical violence, but it combined a set of several new regulations against all kinds of immoral behaviour. The text not only forbade violence, but it also attempted to ban prostitution, adultery, dice games, bowling games, swearing, idleness and vagrancy. The inclusion of violence in an ordinance against immoral behaviour shows that all kinds of violence were criminalised from then on. Two years later, Emperor Charles V published a general ordinance which perfectly suited this new attitude to violence. This ordinance contained all kinds of rules to tackle 'immoral' behaviour and it stipulated that drunkenness could no longer be used as a mitigating circumstance to excuse violent behaviour. Another central regulation issued in 1562 portrayed taverns as sinks of crime and places of violent and immoral behaviour (Van Dijck & Vrints 2011, 184). This analysis of the Mechelen ordinances shows that the attitude towards violence changed dramatically in less than a century and that all types of physical violence became criminalised and associated with immorality.

An examination of the criminal records allows us to evaluate the effects of this policy on actual behaviour in Mechelen. The accounts of the sheriff and the urban correction books contain information about a wide range of violent offences, but only the number of registered manslaughters will be used to enable us to understand the long-term evolution of violent behaviour. Homicide rates have become accepted as the best indicator of interpersonal violence because these crimes were more systematically reported than any other type of violent behaviour (Monkkonen 2001). Figure 1 provides an overview of the homicide rates in Mechelen between 1300 and 1800. The evolution of interpersonal violence in Mechelen fits well into the general European pattern discussed by Manual Eisner. The data set starts in 1370 with an average of 39 manslaughters per 100,000 inhabitants but drops very quickly during the next two centuries. This number declined further to an

9   City Archives Mechelen, Old Archives, part C-S-II, n° 2, f. 133r°, 134v°.
10 City Archives Mechelen, Old Archives, part C-S-V, n° 1, f. 60r°.

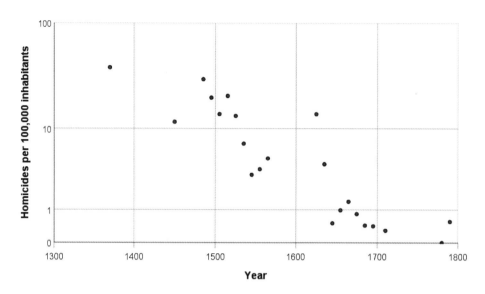

Figure 1. The long-term trend of homicide rates in Mechelen (1300-1800)

Sources: National State Archives Brussels, Audit-Office, Account Rolls, n° 2.147-2.157; National State Archives Brussels, Audit-Office, Registers, n° 15.660-15.694; City Archives Mechelen, Old Archives, part J, II, n° 1-5; Kocken 1990, part II; 1973, 175-177; Maes 1947, 546-698; Mertens 1991, 83; Van Uytven and De Laet 1991, 41.

annual average of less than one manslaughter per 100,000 inhabitants in the eighteenth century. A temporary rise was visible during periods of civil disturbance and war such as the end of the fifteenth, the end of the sixteenth and the end of the eighteenth centuries, comparable to what was observed for other European cities (Eisner 2003, 98-107).

It is tempting to link the decline in homicides in Mechelen to the criminalisation of physical violence during the late medieval period. However, a close examination of the quantitative data shows that the first dramatic drop in the homicide rates occurred between 1370 and 1450, before the first ordinances were issued on the subject. In fact, the number of manslaughters dropped from 39 to 12 per 100,000 inhabitants between 1370 and 1450 (figure 1). The homicide rate increased again at the end of the fifteenth century after the first attempts to criminalise physical violence in Mechelen, but this growth was probably caused by the civil unrest in those years. This means that the new urban policy, rather than being an important independent variable, dialectically interacted with declining homicide rates. The absence of a register of urban ordinances for the period before 1439 makes it difficult to draw firm conclusions, but it seems difficult to maintain that the changing urban policy can entirely explain the declining homicide rates.

A social history of interpersonal violence

A combination of judicial sources and tax records can now offer new insights into long-term trends in interpersonal violence. Most historical crime studies limit themselves to a particular time-frame or take into account only one social group, especially the nobility

(Eisner 2003, 117). The existence of the two long series of judicial sources and taxation records makes it possible to discover the social positions of convicted perpetrators of violent offences in Mechelen. This is very valuable since it remains unclear whether the decline in noble feuds went hand-in-glove with changes in the behaviour of other elite groups. The nobility was only a small class in the highly urbanised Low Countries and the effect of the pacification of that group should not be overestimated. Therefore, it is necessary to investigate whether other elite groups – like the rich merchant elites and the urban patriciate – followed the example of the noble class in urban contexts. This is especially important since this is a central point in Elias' theory of civilisation which is currently the dominant model for explaining the decreasing levels of interpersonal violence in Europe (Eisner 2014, 91-98).

Manual comparison of the names of perpetrators in judicial sources and taxation records enables us to find out which social groups were prosecuted for violent behaviour in Mechelen between the late medieval period and the middle of the seventeenth century.[11] Taxation lists are available for only the sixteenth, seventeenth and eighteenth centuries. However, the social profile of violent offenders in Mechelen during the late medieval period can be traced by using a list of people who contributed to a new shrine for Saint Rumbold, the patron saint of the city, in 1370 (De Munck 1777). This source is not a fiscal source but a list of voluntary contributions, which means that not all inhabitants were included. Some historians believe that all urban dwellers tried to contribute as much as they could because Saint Rumbold was the city's patron saint and his cult was essential to the identity of the urban community (Van Uytven 1962, 387-388). However, other researchers have shown that not all parishes are equally represented in the list of 1370. The rich, central parish of Saint Rumbold is over-represented in that document because Rumbold was the patron saint not only of the city but also of this central urban parish. An in-depth analysis of the list shows that the name Rumbold appeared far more often in this parish, which indicates that he was also more popular in this central, urban district. This means that contributors from the Saint Rumbold parish are probably over-represented in the list of 1370. Other research has shown that several (rich) aldermen were not included in that document, implying that the list is far from complete (Depuydt, Van de Vijver & Kinnaer 2013, 302-305).

This means that the list of 1370 is not unproblematic and it can only be used with some reservations. However, a comparison of the population figures of 1370 and the accepted population numbers for Mechelen shows that the list still contains 15 per cent of urban residents. This is a lower ratio compared to the 19 per cent included in a taxation list of 1544, but comparable to the 15 per cent of heads of households mentioned in a similar fiscal list of 1643 (Depuydt, Van de Vijver & Kinnaer 2013, 302-313; Muylle 1983, 170-182). This implies that all available late medieval and early modern taxation records contain only a part of the urban population. The list of 1370 is no exception to this rule. Voluntary contributions to the shrine of Saint Rumbold were of course not a fixed proportion of the

---

11 The names of the heads of households in the taxation lists were compared with the names of the people convicted of violent offences in the urban judicial records from five years before until five years after the available taxation list. When more people with the same name (homonyms) popped up in the taxation records, these data were not taken into account.

wealth of the inhabitants, but we believe that they still might be used as a crude indicator of social status. However, we assume that the poorest people in the contribution list of 1370 were still wealthier than the households with the lowest taxation payments in the fiscal lists of 1544 and 1643. The taxation of the rental values of houses, which will be used for the sixteenth and seventeenth centuries, is a more systematic and consistent expression of someone's wealth. For this reason, social and economic historians often make use of these sources. The money spent on house rent reflects the total income of a household, and so can be considered as a proxy for economic inequality (Ryckbosch 2016).

However, the rental value of a house is not a perfect reflection of the income of a household. Taxation based on rental value offers the advantage that it also included (a part of) the poor (Soltow & van Zanden 1998, 25-26), but these lower social groups usually spent a higher proportion of their income on housing than the rich social elite (Van Zanden 1994, 442; Deneweth Ch. 14). In sum, these taxation records tend to underestimate underlying social differences. However, all sources offer us the opportunity to estimate the relative positions of people in relation to one another. For this purpose, the urban population is divided into four quartiles – which contain an equal number of persons – in order to make the results for the fourteenth, sixteenth and seventeenth centuries as comparable as possible. Again, it needs to be stressed that the lowest quartile in 1370 contains slightly richer people than the lowest quartile of the taxation lists of 1544 and 1643. The contribution list of 1370 contains people who contributed only half a groat, but the taxation list of 1544 also included people who were too poor to pay any contribution. However, the latter applies to only 4 per cent of the households in the fiscal list of 1544. The lowest tax band just above this poor class with no means paid a tariff of two pennies which was already slightly higher than the smallest contribution in the list of 1370.[12]

Although manslaughter figures are considered the best proxy for measuring the evolution of violent behaviour in criminal records, it is not possible to limit ourselves to these offences for a comparison of the social profiles of aggressors through time. The decline in manslaughters, in the long run, implies that the numbers are too low for one to be able to construct a social profile of the perpetrators in the later centuries. This would be possible only for the period between 1365 and 1375 because the criminal records contain 13 cases of manslaughter which could be traced in the social list of 1370. This number drops to only one person for the data between 1539 and 1549. For this reason, all violent offences are taken into account to reconstruct the social background of the offenders.

The sheriff's accounts list 490 prosecuted offences for the 1365-1375 period.[13] It was possible to trace the social background of 93 perpetrators (19 per cent). Violent offences dominated the accounts with a share of 83 per cent of all infringements. Property crimes were also a relevant category with 12 per cent of all crimes. Crimes against public order, sexual misconduct, religious offences and crimes against the authorities were also mentioned in the sheriff's accounts, but their share was marginal in this period. The sample of offenders found in the contribution list of 1370 reflects this distribution over the different categories.

---

12   The daily wage of a master carpenter or mason was used to index the tariffs in the different lists. Van Uytven mentions a daily wage of 10.5 groats in 1370. The urban accounts reveal that this corresponds to a wage of 16.5 groats in 1544 (Scholliers 1965; Van Uytven 1962, 387).

13   National State Archives Brussels, Audit-Office, Account Rolls, n° 2,147-2,157.

Table 1. The social positions of perpetrators of violence in Mechelen (1365-1374).

Quartile	1365-1374
Q1	23 (28%)
Q2	16 (20%)
Q3	16 (20%)
Q4	26 (32%)
Total	81 (100%)

Sources: National State Archives Brussels, Audit-Office, Account Rolls, n° 2,147-2,157; De Munck 1777, Oo; Maes 1947, 546-698.

Violent offences are the largest group in this selective sample (87 per cent). Property crimes are, with 10 per cent of the offences, the only other relevant group.

Table 1 shows that in the late fourteenth century the prosecuted aggressors in our sample came from all social layers of urban society, but the 'poorest group' and the top segment of society were over-represented. This dominance of the elite is in line with the findings of other studies. Ruggiero reconstructed the social profile of violent offenders in late medieval Venice (1324-1406). He could not rely on social or economic data, but he was able to make a distinction between nobility, clergy, important people, workers and marginal people for a sample of 301 offences. His analysis pointed out that the nobility was considerably over-represented in the categories of speech crimes, assaults and rapes. The group of speech crimes includes not only insults, but also offences against the urban authorities. The dominance of the elite in the assault and rape categories amply demonstrates that the Venetian nobility was more often prosecuted for violent behaviour than other social groups (Ruggiero 1980, 67). The Mechelen data seem to confirm this picture, although the highest quartile in the contribution list of 1370 did not overlap with the nobility. The latter was only a small group in most urban centres in the highly urbanised Low Countries.

A fiscal source from 1544 allows us to reconstruct the social backgrounds of aggressors in sixteenth-century Mechelen. This list was compiled to assess the population for tax on the basis of the value of their houses. Both owners and tenants had to pay a tax that corresponded to 5 per cent of the value of their houses.[14] Although this list is more inclusive compared to the contribution list of 1370, it was possible to trace only 8 per cent of all offenders mentioned in the urban judicial sources and the sheriff's accounts. Alongside the 'traditional identification problems', this low rate suggests that the number of prosecuted foreigners, people who rented a single room in a larger house and marginal people without an address in the city dramatically increased in the sixteenth century. The records for Mechelen only rarely inform us about the origin of delinquents, but the data for 's-Hertogenbosch and Antwerp support this view (Van Dijck 2006, 23; 2007, 442).

In the end, it was possible to find 35 names in the taxation list of 1544 which also appeared in the list of all 447 offenders who received a punishment between 1538 and 1548. Violent offences still dominated in the sixteenth century with a share of 67 per cent

---

14   City Archives Mechelen, Old Archives, part K, n° 1.

Table 2. The social positions of perpetrators of violence in Mechelen (1539-1649).

Quartile	1539-1549	1637-1649
Q1	1 (4%)	20 (45%)
Q2	9 (32%)	12 (27%)
Q3	7 (25%)	10 (23%)
Q4	11 (39%)	2 (5%)
Total	28 (100%)	44 (100%)

Sources: National State Archives Brussels, Audit-Office, Registers, n° 15,660-15,676; City Archives Mechelen, Old Archives, part K, n° 1 and 6; Kocken 1990, part II; 1973, 175-177; Maes 1947, 546-698.

of all crimes. However, this smaller proportion is also the result of the high number of unknown crimes. If we remove the 71 people who were penalised by the urban authorities without any mention of their offences, the proportion of violence rises to 80 per cent. The proportion of crimes against public order was 7 per cent. The rise in these crimes was due to the growing repression of vagrancy and idleness.[15] Significantly, the proportion of manslaughters and murders decreased between the fourteenth and the sixteenth centuries from 14 to 3 per cent of all violent offences. On the other hand, the number of aggressive threats without physical violence increased from 4 to 31 per cent, which points to a growing control of emotional impulses and fewer violent outbursts.

A comparison of the social backgrounds of the perpetrators of violent infraction between the fourteenth and the sixteenth centuries shows that the economic elite was still the most prominent group in our sample of 28 prosecuted aggressors. Even when we account for the identification problems which are often more pronounced at the bottom of the social ladder, the poorest quartile was remarkably enough very small in this period (table 2).[16] This does not change if we also consider all other types of crimes, and not just violence. Although the poorest social strata were targeted in the central and urban ordinances as an immoral social group, this is not visible in the actual prosecution rates in Mechelen. The situation was totally different in Antwerp where the group of prosecuted poor people rose dramatically during the sixteenth century (Van Dijck 2006, 21).

An analysis of the weapons used during violent attacks points out that the most frequently used weapon in Mechelen was the rapier. This weapon was typical for more ritualised aristocratic duels, and so characteristic of elite violence (Spierenburg 2008, 74). The figures are striking: the rapier was used in only 3 per cent of all violent offences committed using arms in Antwerp, while its proportion was 31 per cent in Mechelen. It is also telling that two Antwerp citizens mentioned in 1519 that they both went to Mechelen for

---

15   National State Archives Brussels, Audit-Office, Registers, n° 15,667; Maes 1947, 546-698.

16   The use of family names was not a prerogative of the elite in Mechelen. We counted 365 different family names in the lowest quartile in the contribution list of 1370. The top quartile consisted of 335 distinct family names. In 1544, we were able to identify 630 family names in the lower quarter and 606 in the highest quartile. Specific family names were still not dominant in the elite in 1643. We distinguished 400 different family names in the lowest quartile versus 341 in the richest quarter for the purposes of taxation. This means that the lowest social strata in Mechelen had distinctive family names just as the elite, and that it is not more difficult to trace them in the late medieval and early modern records as was the case in some other cities.

fencing lessons.[17] This was probably the result of a noble culture in Mechelen pointing to the influence there of the court of Margaret of Austria (1507-1530) in this period. The popularity of the rapier in Mechelen was a recent phenomenon. In fact, the rapier was more often used in Antwerp at the end of the fifteenth century, but this evolution was reversed in the course of the sixteenth. While the rapier was replaced by common knives in Antwerp, it gained popularity in Mechelen after the court's arrival in the city (Van Dijck 2007, 446-447).

The availability of a taxation list based on rental values for the year 1643 allows a comparison of the social profiles of the perpetrators of violent offences in Mechelen in the sixteenth and seventeenth centuries. The figures for the seventeenth century are based on a sample of 391 offences recorded between 1637 and 1649. The proportion of violent transgressions further decreased to 60 per cent of the sample, while the proportion of property crimes rose to 29 per cent.[18] Crimes against the authorities were also a relevant category of 8 per cent, but the other groups were negligible.[19] The proportion of violence leading to death slightly declined to 2 per cent of all violent acts, while the percentage of threats and insults stayed at the same level as that in the sixteenth century. Although the sample for the seventeenth century is a little smaller, the number of identified perpetrators is higher for the 1637-1649 period (table 2). The profile of the perpetrators of violent offences changed dramatically over a period of 100 years. The proportion of the elite shrank to 5 per cent, while the poorest quartile committed almost half of all violent crimes prosecuted.

This means that the elite almost totally renounced violent conflicts. Although the initial decline in violence in Mechelen in the fifteenth and sixteenth centuries cannot be attributed to the pacification of the elite, the evolution in the seventeenth century confirms earlier claims that the elite became less violent in the long term. This conclusion still stands if we calculate the share of elite violence as a proportion of the total number of violent offences in our sample periods. This means that we must also include the non-identified criminals in our calculations and divide the number of identified elite offenders by the total number of all prosecuted violent crimes. This computation shows that the proportion of the elite changed from 6 per cent in 1365-1374 to 4 per cent in the years between 1539 and 1549. In the end, the elite was responsible for only 1 per cent of the violent offences in the period from 1637 to 1649.[20]

Conclusion

This chapter has traced the changes in the social backgrounds of violent offenders over more than three centuries in a single city. The combination of criminal and taxation records resulted in a more refined method than that used in existing studies that rely on

---

17 National State Archives Brussels, Audit-Office, Registers, n° 12,904, f. 480r°.

18 Chi-square (3) = 21.905; p < 0.01, Cramer's V 0,52.

19 National State Archives Brussels, Audit-Office, Registers, n° 15,674-15,676; City Archives Mechelen, Old Archives, part J, II, n° 3.

20 In absolute terms the number of violent offences committed by the elite was 26 in 1365-1374, 11 during the years 1539-1549 and only two in the final sample period from 1637 to 1649.

the occupations or titles of perpetrators to examine the social backgrounds of offenders. The analysis in this chapter shows that the urban elite was still a relatively violent social group in the city until the middle of the sixteenth century, when the homicide rates had already been declining for more than a century. However, the situation changed radically between 1544 and 1643. The social elite withdrew from violent behaviour while the poorest quartile of the population became responsible for almost half of all violent offences.

This means that followers of Norbert Elias' civilisation theory are correct in that the pacification of the elite was a crucial element in the decline in homicide ratios in Europe, but the timing of this decline requires further research. The Mechelen case suggests that the presence of a princely court was not a trigger reducing violent behaviour in the city. On the contrary, elite violence was rife in the city and other classes adopted the use of noblemen's arms such as the rapier. The pacification of the elite was achieved only in the seventeenth century when manslaughter ratios were already quite low. The poorest section of the population experienced a different evolution. This deprived class still used violence to resolve everyday conflicts. However, this violent repertoire was criminalised by the urban and central authorities, and it was associated with immoral behaviour from the first half of the sixteenth century.

The publication of several studies on interpersonal violence has made clear that the decline in violence in late medieval Europe is no longer debatable. However, it is still unclear why homicide rates dropped dramatically all over Europe. Studies of the social backgrounds of offenders can offer new insights into the main agents of change, but such studies also make clear that inequality is relevant not just from an economic perspective. Long-term evolutions created important cultural divides in Europe. The contrasting levels of interpersonal violence in different social groups are a good example of such a development. They suggest that behaviour repertoires contributed to persistent forms of social inequality that have their origin in late medieval and early modern changes.

References

Baten, Joerg, and Richard H. Steckel. 2018. "The History of Violence in Europe." In *The Backbone of Europe: Health, Diet, Work and Violence over Two Millennia*, ed. Richard H. Steckel, Clark Spencer Larsen, Charlotte A. Roberts and Joerg Baten. 300-324. Cambridge: Cambridge University Press, available at https://doi.org/10.1017/9781108379830.012.

Blondé, Bruno. 1998. "Disparities in the development of the Brabantine urban network: urban centrality, town-countryside relationships, and transportation development." In *Recent Doctoral Research in Economic History*, ed. Clara Eugenia Núñez. 41-52. Madrid: Universidad nacional de educacion a distancia.

Blondé, Bruno. 2002. "Tableware and Changing Consumer Patterns: Dynamics of Material Culture in Antwerp, 17th-18th Centuries." In *Majolica and Glass from Italy to Antwerp and beyond. The Transfer of Technology in the 16th-Early 17th Century*, ed. Johan Veeckman. 295-311. Antwerp: Stad Antwerpen.

Cooney, Mark. 1997. "The Decline of Elite Homicide." *Criminology* 35 (3): 381-407.

De Munck, Jozef Jacob. 1777. *Gedenck-Schriften Dienende Tot Ophelderinge van Het Leven, Lyden, Wonderheden, Ende Duysent-Jaerige Eer-Bewysinge van Den Heyligen Bisschop Ende Martelaer Rumoldus.* Mechelen: Joannes-Franciscus Van der Elst.

Depuydt, Silvia, Katrien Van de Vijver and Frank Kinnaer. 2013. "In de Schaduw van de Toren. Resultaten van Het Archeologisch Onderzoek van Het Sint-Romboutskerkhof in Mechelen." Archaeological excavation report. Mechelen: City of Mechelen, Archeology Department.

Eisner, Manuel. 2003. "Long-Term Historical Trends in Violent Crime." *Crime and Justice. A Review of Research* 30: 83-142.

Eisner, Manuel. 2011. "Killing Kings: Patterns of Regicide in Europe, AD 600-1800." *The British Journal of Criminology* 51 (3): 556-77, available at https://doi.org/10.1093/bjc/azr004.

Eisner, Manuel. 2014. "From Swords to Words: Does Macro-Level Change in Self-Control Predict Long-Term Variation in Levels of Homicide?." *Crime and Justice. A Review of Research* 43: 65-134.

Fajnzylber, Pablo, Daniel Lederman and Norman Loayza. 2002. "Inequality and Violent Crime." *The Journal of Law and Economics* 45 (1): 1-39, available at https://doi.org/10.1086/338347.

Gauvard, Claude. 1991. *"De Grace Espaciale". Crime, État et Société En France à La Fin Du Moyen Âge.* Paris: Publications de la Sorbonne.

Gietman, Conrad. 2004. "Eer en geweld in de Oost-Nederlandse adelcultuur (1550-1700)." In *Adel en macht. Politiek, cultuur, economie*, ed. Guido Marnef and René Vermeir. 75-93. Maastricht: Shaker.

Godding, Philippe. 2005. *Verordeningen van Filips de Goede Voor de Hertogdommen Brabant En Limburg En de Landen van Overmaas 1430-1467.* Brussels: Royal Academy of Belgium.

Kocken, Marcel. 1990. "Van Bedelaars, Vagebonden En Andere 'Schuinmarsjeerders'. Kleine En Grote Criminaliteit Te Mechelen in de 17de Eeuw." Brussels: unpublished Master's dissertation, Vrije Universiteit Brussel.

Maes, Louis T. 1947. *Vijf Eeuwen Stedelijk Strafrecht. Bijdrage Tot de Rechts- En Cultuurgeschiedenis Der Nederlanden.* Antwerp: De Sikkel.

Mertens, Wenceslas. 1991. "Toenemende Economische Welvaart." In *De Geschiedenis van Mechelen. Van Heerlijkheid Tot Stadsgewest*, ed. Raymond Van Uytven. 82-94. Tielt: Lannoo.

Monkkonen, Eric H. 2001. "New Standards for Historical Research." *Crime, History and Societies* 5: 5-26.

Muylle, Eric. 1983. "Een Stedelijk Sociaal Patroon: Mechelen circa 1643." *Bijdragen Tot de Geschiedenis* 66: 169-187.

Ruggiero, Guido. 1980. *Violence in Early Renaissance Venice.* New Brunswick, NJ: Rutgers University Press.

Ryckbosch, Wouter. 2016. "Economic Inequality and Growth before the Industrial Revolution: The Case of the Low Countries (Fourteenth to Nineteenth Centuries)." *European Review of Economic History* 20 (1): 1-22, available at https://doi.org/10.1093/ereh/hev018.

Scholliers, Etienne. 1965. "Lonen te Mechelen in de XVde en XVIde eeuw." In *Dokumenten voor de geschiedenis van prijzen en lonen in Vlaanderen en Brabant*, ed. Charles Verlinden. Volume 2, 1244-1299. Bruges: De Tempel.

Soltow, Lee, and Jan Luiten van Zanden. 1998. *Income and Wealth Inequality in the Netherlands, 16th-20th Century.* Apeldoorn: Het Spinhuis.

Spierenburg, Petrus Cornelis. 2008. *A History of Murder: Personal Violence in Europe from the Middle Ages to the Present.* Cambridge: Polity.

Van Dijck, Maarten F. 2006. "De Stad Als Onafhankelijke Variabele En Centrum van Moderniteit. Langetermijntrends in Stedelijke En Rurale Criminaliteitspatronen in de Nederlanden (1300-1800)." *Stadsgeschiedenis* 1: 7-26.

Van Dijck, Maarten F. 2007. "De Pacificering van de Europese Samenleving. Repressie, Gedragspatronen En Verstedelijking in Brabant Tijdens de Lange Zestiende Eeuw." Antwerp: unpublished PhD thesis, University of Antwerp.

Van Dijck, Maarten F. 2009. "Towards an Economic Interpretation of Justice? Conflict Settlement, Social Control and Civil Society in Urban Brabant and Mechelen during the Late Middle Ages and the Early Modern Period." In *Serving the Community. The Rise of Public Services*, ed. Manon P. C. van der Heijden, Martijn van der Burg, Elise van Nederveen Meerkerk and Griet Vermeesch. 62-88. Amsterdam: Aksant.

Van Dijck, Maarten F. 2017. "Democracy and Civil Society in the Early Modern Period: The Rise of Three Types of Civil Societies in the Spanish Netherlands and the Dutch Republic." *Social Science History* 41 (1): 59-81, available at https://doi.org/10.1017/ssh.2016.38.

Van Dijck, Maarten F., and Antoon Vrints. 2011. "De Kroeg Als Bron van Alle Kwaad? Percepties van Het Openbaar Lokaal in Antwerpen, 1350-1950." In *Antwerpen Bierstad: Acht Eeuwen Biercultuur*, ed. Ivan Derycke. 180-194. Antwerp: Pandora.

Van Gerven, Jan. 1999. "War, Violence and an Urban Society: The Brabantine Towns in the Later Middle Ages." In *Secretum Scriptorum. Liber Alumnorum Walter Prevenier*, ed. W. P. Blockmans, Marc Boone and Thérèse De Hemptinne. 183-211. Leuven/Apeldoorn: Garant.

Van Uytven, Raymond. 1962. "Plutokratie in de 'Oude Demokratieën Der Nederlanden'. Cijfers En Beschouwingen Omtrent de Korporatieve Organisatie En de Sociale Struktuur Der Gemeenten in de Late Middeleeuwen." *Handelingen van de Koninklijke Zuidnederlandse Maatschappij Voor Taal- En Letterkunde En Geschiedenis* 16: 373-409.

Van Uytven, Raymond, and M. De Laet. 1991. "Het Sociaal-Economische Leven." In *De Geschiedenis van Mechelen. Van Heerlijkheid Tot Stadsgewest*, ed. Raymond Van Uytven. 41-56. Tielt: Lannoo.

Van Zanden, Jan Luiten. 1994. "Industrialisatie En Inkomensverdeling in Overijssel, 1750-1875." *Bijdragen En Mededelingen Betreffende de Geschiedenis Der Nederlanden* 109 (3): 434-449.

Wilkinson, Richard, and Kate Pickett. 2009. *The Spirit Level. Why Equality Is Better for Everyone*. London: Penguin.

The New Police as Agents of Class Control?

Urban Policing and its Socio-Geographical Focus
in Nineteenth-Century Antwerp

Introduction

In the 1970s left-wing historians and social scientists profoundly renewed the study of social control and policing. This – welcome – paradigm shift came with the powerful and enduring narrative that the modern police, ever since their creation in the nineteenth century, simply served as a lever of urban discipline and to protect the interests of the ruling classes (Chambliss 1975, 165-168; Crowther 2000, 39-40). The police were thus portrayed as an elite device to preserve the social status quo; to justify and reproduce socio-economic inequality. According to this narrative, in the course of the nineteenth century the police forces of large European cities acquired unprecedented powers to intervene in the heart of working-class communities and to identify, discipline and exclude the 'dangerous classes' (Harring 1983, 198). Marxist police histories portrayed the 'new' police as 'blue locusts' (Storch & Engels 1975, 84), rapidly invading urban territory, and as 'domestic missionaries' (Storch 1976, 481), successfully imposing bourgeois values upon the working class. According to this view, the modern police were also a fundamentally 'new' device that addressed new needs for law enforcement and introduced new forms of social control. This has led many scholars to conclude that the second half of the nineteenth century marked a watershed in social control and policing, the start of the 'policed society' (Silver 1967, 8) and the 'policeman-state' (Gatrell 1992, 257-260), characterised by ever widening nets of formal social control (Cohen 1985) and a focus on the policing of class (Garland 2002).

In the rapidly expanding urban centres in Europe, important investments in public police personnel and resources indeed resulted in highly increased police presence and activity towards the end of the nineteenth century (Emsley 2004, 194). Furthermore, in the context of explosive urban growth and a growing need for order on the part of local elites, a new discourse emerged about the so-called 'dangerous classes', which would become the main targets of the bourgeois civilising offensive of the late nineteenth century. Urban authorities and the bourgeoisie began to strive for a more orderly, hygienic and safe urban environment. In addition to urban embellishment through the creation of public parks and squares, 'respectable' neighbourhoods with lawful entertainments were delineated and separated from the densely populated working-class neighbourhoods, which were designated as breeding grounds for vice and crime. Moreover, urban middle groups increasingly contrasted their 'refined' manners and frugal and orderly life with what they considered the uncivilised and 'immoral' behaviour and lifestyle of the working class.

Margo De Koster and Antoon Vrints • Universiteit Gent

Inequality and the City in the Low Countries (1200-2020), ed. by Bruno BLONDÉ, Sam GEENS, Hilde GREEFS, Wouter RYCKBOSCH, Tim SOENS & Peter STABEL, SEUH 50 (Turnhout, 2020), pp. 343-356.

 DOI 10.1484/M.SEUH-EB.5.120454

In the 1840s, a new word appeared in the Brockhaus Real-Enzyklopädie that expressed these official fears for the 'problematic' lifestyle of the ever-growing army of impoverished social groups: Pauperismus (Emsley 2007, 140-141). The 'pauper' was identified primarily with those groups that flocked into the cities and came to constitute the new industrial working class.

The term 'dangerous classes' came into vogue with the work by Parisian police officer Honoré Frégier, 'Des classes dangereuses dans la population dans les grandes villes et des moyens de les rendre meilleures', published in 1840, and was inextricably linked with the urban context (Frégier 1840, 7). These lower strata of morally depraved, idle, lazy, licentious, violent and criminal tramps and paupers would henceforth constitute the core of definitions of social problems in Europe, and the alarmed bourgeoisie increasingly associated them with the danger of social and political unrest (Philips 2003, 79-107). This problematising perception of the city and its 'dangerous classes' was also present in the work of nineteenth-century criminologists. The urban condition and the effects of urbanisation soon appeared as important criminogenic factors in early studies on the causes of crime (Becker 2002; Musumeci 2018). Against this background, a sociological school developed in the last two decades of the nineteenth century, under the influence of Durkheim and Tarde in particular. These studies tried to reveal the interrelationships between urbanisation, class and criminal behaviour through extensive observation and description of the urban 'underclass', as the journalist Henry Mayhew did in 1862 for the London "dangerous classes, the idle, the profligate, and the criminal" (Mayhew & Binny 1862, iii).

Although official fears and discourses about the 'dangerous classes' undeniably soared and the capacity of urban police forces greatly expanded towards the end of the nineteenth century, several scholars have recently called for closer scrutiny to add nuance to and challenge the traditional narrative about the modern police as a bourgeois instrument of class control. First, early modern police historians began to question the chronology and the supposed novelty of the coming of the modern police. They have demonstrated that in Paris, London, Geneva, Berlin, Saint Petersburg and many other European cities – especially in the German regions where 'Polizeiwissenschaft' developed – significant police growth and modernisation had already occurred in the final decades of the eighteenth century (Denys 2010; Vidoni 2011; Milliot 2006; Cicchini 2012; Beattie 2012; Barrie 2008). Moreover, these studies suggest that there was no clear or distinct break between early modern and modern policing concerns and strategies. Eighteenth-century urban authorities and the upper classes in general were also apprehensive of the movements of the lower orders and charged their powerful police forces not only with tasks of political policing, but also with order maintenance in 'rookeries' and surveillance of 'dangerous groups'. In Naples during the 1780s the official categories of dangerous individuals began with 'the idle, vagabonds, and adventurers' (*oziosi, vagabondi, avventurieri*) (Alessi 1992, 7). In his work on crime, police and penal policy in Europe, Clive Emsley confirms that next to the Gauner inhabiting the urban underworld, early modern perceptions of the crime problem focused on the lower orders of society and the mobile groups of 'wandering poor' in particular (Emsley 2007, 42-43).

Second, new research has demonstrated that class was only one of many interrelated factors shaping police attention and strategies on the ground. As a result of organisational, legal and political mechanisms, the police's need for public support and the complex reality of everyday police work, European police forces all operated under similar crucial constraints. These constraints were at least as important in shaping their practice – and their authority – as were the unprecedented powers they acquired during this same time (Emsley 2000). Consequently, a high level of selectivity entered the everyday operations of the police, a blind eye being turned to certain types of criminal behaviour deemed not to challenge the social order. Overall, practical policing concerned crime management, not elimination, for the police required minimum compliance even from lower classes in order to operate, and in certain areas they faced a hostile public until well into the twentieth century (Deluermoz 2012; De Koster, Deruytter & Vrints 2018; Vrints 2019). As has been demonstrated for nineteenth-century London, Paris, Antwerp and Milan, for example, the police pursued a policy of 'containment', keeping crime and disorder within bounds in a well-policed area. They did not simply target the lower classes but literally patrolled the boundary between respectability and disreputability; for most arrests were not made in the 'rookeries' that cradled the 'dangerous classes', but at the margins between those areas and their more respectable neighbours (Davis 1991, 16-17; De Koster 2008, 360-362; Mori 2016, 282).

Third, recent work has shown that the 'new' police were not simply an instrument of the ruling classes but were also used by the populations under their control to serve their own ends and interests. This has served as a useful corrective to images of the police as a 'monolithic' instrument of coercion, which was external to local society. Yet the analytical pendulum has now swung to the other extreme. Some recent accounts are inclined to overstate the weaknesses of urban police forces and, in highlighting processes of mutual accommodation and reciprocity, to play down the conflictual logic that governed the relationship between the police and the urban working classes. Yet, as Churchill and De Koster, Deruytter and Vrints, for example, have demonstrated for nineteenth- century British and Belgian cities, everyday relations between the police and the poor were marked by persistent antagonism and friction (Churchill 2017; De Koster, Deruytter & Vrints 2018, 158-159).

In sum, on the one hand, recent work on nineteenth- century urban policing challenges the narrative of the police as agents of class control while, on the other, it suggests that class remains an important category for the analysis of day-to-day police practices. Unfortunately, except for Paris, London and several port cities (Davis 1991; Slater 2012; Churchill 2017; De Koster 2008; Conchon, Montel & Regnard 2018), studies that attempt to reconstruct daily activities and police-public interactions drawing on research of archival police records are still relatively scarce. This chapter hopes to bring new insights to this field and discussion by examining the socio-geographical focus and the social interactions that characterised day-to-day police operations in the city of Antwerp. We aim to demonstrate that police activity was undeniably shaped by class dynamics, and thereby helped to reproduce unequal power relations, yet this was done in more complex ways and by more diverse agents and interests than is often suggested.

Antwerp as test case: central approaches, questions and sources

In order to deepen our understanding of class dynamics in the policing of nineteenth-century cities, this article focuses on the Belgian city of Antwerp. Antwerp is a particularly good test case in this respect, since it was a very rapidly expanding port city – whose population more than tripled between 1847 and 1900 (86,000 to 300,000) – that evolved from being lightly to rather heavily policed during this period. The Antwerp police force grew exponentially from only 24 policemen in 1847 to 634 men in 1900. As a result, police density intensified from only one police officer for every 3,500 inhabitants in 1847 to one per 473 inhabitants in 1900, turning it into one of the most strongly policed European cities at the time. The number of offences registered by the Antwerp police (per 1,000 inhabitants) increased fivefold in the same period, suggesting that the police's role developed significantly in the second half of the nineteenth century. As a port city, Antwerp was confronted with distinct challenges and problems of crime and disorder such as concentrations of a rather 'rough' clientele in vice districts (brothels and bars), large flows of people and goods to be monitored and secured, and numerous incidences of dockside theft or destruction of merchandise. This of course shaped specific police concerns, forms of control and police-public relations, yet these were mainly concentrated in the harbour area and its immediate surroundings. In the rest of the city, police activities mainly concerned the usual street and neighbourhood policing, with mediation in fights and conflicts, arrests of drunks, prostitutes, vagrants and 'disorderly' persons, and a broad range of tasks of administrative control. Overall, everyday policing in the city of Antwerp was characterised by similar patterns of urban policing to those observed in other nineteenth-century European cities (De Koster, Deruytter & Vrints 2017).

We adopt a layered approach to reconstructing the class dynamics of police activity. To begin with, we use the spatial dimensions of police-public interactions as an indicator for social class. After all, there was socio-geographic segregation in Antwerp just like in many other nineteenth-century cities. The Antwerp police districts had different social profiles, and also within the districts' borders there were differences between the inhabitants of broader avenues, who were generally more well-to-do, and those living in smaller alleys and slums. When certain social groups in specific neighbourhoods became the subject of intensified police control, this can be observed in terms of space. To what extent were (shifting) police priorities in terms of law enforcement, crime fighting and municipal regulations enforcement translated into geographically differentiated practices on the ground? Were certain neighbourhoods or streets targeted or avoided altogether because of their social profile (hotspots versus no-go areas)? Conversely, did residents of certain streets or neighbourhoods call upon the police more frequently than others? We examine the professional backgrounds of those who came into contact with the police. Which social groups were possibly targeted by the police? Did all social groups resort to the police with comparable frequency? Examining these issues from a historical perspective, we ask whether the socio-spatial pattern of everyday police activity shifted as the Antwerp police apparatus expanded towards the end of the nineteenth century.

Such an inquiry is possible because the city police archives in Antwerp have been better preserved than elsewhere in the Low Countries and Europe. For this contribution we use published police statistics as well as archival records at the level of the district police station. The police statistics are published in the annual report of the City of Antwerp and allow for drawing the main contours and evolutions of police activity in the city as a whole. In order also to cast a glance at the grassroots level, we analysed the police reports (registers of *procès-verbaux*) of the second police district for the years 1825 (n=130, all) and 1890 (n=126, randomised sample of one in 20). The police reports or *procès-verbaux* result from various types of interaction between the police and the public. For one, they attest to the wish of the governmental authorities to control urban space by means of law enforcement, crime fighting and the enforcement of municipal regulations. They are also very informative about how the population uses the police. They comprise many reports on offences (violence, defamation and theft) which are most often reported by the population.

We opted for the second police district because its social heterogeneity can be seen as a sort of microcosm for the entire city. In the nineteenth century this district comprised the north-easterly part of the old town between the Oude Leeuwenrui in the north and the Lange Nieuwstraat in the south and expanded to the east in the course of the century as the city grew to incorporate the neighbourhood between the Sint-Jansplein and the De Coninckplein. As a result, the district's area increased by one third after the demolition of the city walls in 1860. There were streets with a pronounced bourgeois profile such as those in the vicinity of the Keizerstraat. A number of streets and corridors in the northern half of the district had a predominantly working-class population, while in the southern half the workers were concentrated in the so-called Kattenkwartier (Cat Quarter), one of the city's biggest slums. There was a nightlife area round the De Coninckplein with many cafes and dance halls. We analysed the places of residence and the occupations of the offenders and the complainants (using the HISCLASS classification: see Mandemakers et al. 2018) who appeared in the registers of the police of the second district in order to determine the social profile of the 'targets' and the 'clients' of the police.

Police activity in the entire city

The published police statistics make it possible to gauge certain trends across time for the city of Antwerp as a whole. One glance at the officially registered offences is enough to add nuance to the image of the police imposing top-down repression upon the population. Police prosecution of all sorts of violations (ranging from public drunkenness to stray dogs) increased greatly towards the end of the nineteenth century yet shifted rapidly from one category of offences to another. This mirrors the extent to which policy makers managed to impose their rapidly changing priorities on the police and the population. The more gradual but sustainable increase in the number of registered cases of theft and violence, however, points to an equally important phenomenon, namely that large sections of the population started to call on the police as part of their own strategies of conflict settlement. Indeed, no less than 90 per cent of police reports on theft or violence resulted from a complaint lodged by citizens. A double reality therefore lurks behind the development of police statistics. Greater control was indeed exerted over the population, but that same population also turned to the police much more frequently to serve its own purposes (De Koster, Deruytter & Vrints 2017). Reducing the coming of the new police entirely to a top-down regulating offensive is therefore an oversimplification.

We have only the number of prosecutions by the police court per police district to help us to differentiate spatially at city level. These police courts were the lowest courts and were responsible for dealing with the majority of *procès-verbaux* produced by the police. The close connection between the police and the police court is illustrated by the fact that

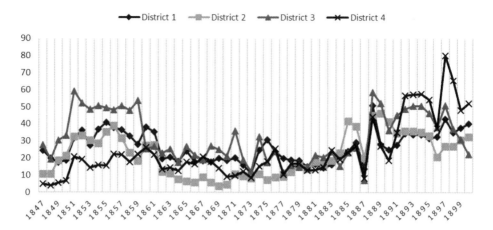

Figure 1. Prosecutions before the police court per 1,000 inhabitants in four inner districts of the city of Antwerp, 1847-1900

Source: Verslag over het bestuur en den zakentoestand der Stad Antwerpen (annual report of the city of Antwerp). Antwerp, years 1847-1900.

the police commissioner of the district acted as the crown prosecution service. Was the intensity of prosecution by the police court the same throughout the entire city? To keep the scale of the analysis constant, we focus on the four districts in the old city centre. The boundaries of these districts have remained relatively constant (unlike the districts extra muros) and their social profile is relatively well-known. Districts 3 and 4 can be considered as rather homogeneous. District 3 comprised the key points of bourgeois sociability in the Antwerp city centre and was inhabited by the higher social groups. District 4, on the other hand, had a predominantly poor working-class population. Districts 1 and 2 were more heterogeneous: they comprised both richer and poorer neighbourhoods.

If we now look at the intensity per district and per 1,000 inhabitants of prosecutions before the Antwerp police court (Figure 1), a striking counter-intuitive pattern comes to the fore. The spatial focus of the activities of the Antwerp police court shifts over time. On the one hand, police prosecutions up to 1870 were roughly the most common in the richest, third district. On the other hand, police prosecutions were much lower in the poorest fourth district up to 1860. After a period of convergence between the districts, at the end of the century prosecutions before the Antwerp police court turned out to be the most intense precisely in the fourth and predominantly working-class district (although it started to attract more bourgeois households after the construction of a new avenue to the posh South district). In other words, whereas the prosecution activity was more intense in the bourgeois neighbourhoods than in the neighbourhoods of the alleged 'dangerous classes' during the darkest days of proletarianisation, this ratio was reversed during the expansion phase of the Antwerp police in the late nineteenth century.

Given that the activity of the police court is closely connected with the action of the district police on the beat, a two-fold hypothesis emerges. First, it seems that in expanding, the police focused primarily on controlling the better neighbourhoods, and that they developed more comprehensive regulating ambitions in the poor neighbourhoods only in a second stage. It very much looks as if the police would 'sweep' the bourgeois neighbourhoods first, while leaving the poorer neighbourhoods relatively untouched at the outset. The ambition to regulate the behaviours of broader layers of the Antwerp population apparently arose only late in the nineteenth century. The more comprehensive regulatory ambitions during this period may be linked to the gradual democratisation of voting rights. If the entire population was to have some say in government, then the people had to behave as the bourgeoisie did. Secondly, it seems that far into the nineteenth century, the people living in the better-off neighbourhoods were more inclined to call on the police in order to resolve their own conflicts than their counterparts in the poorer neighbourhoods. They acted far earlier as complainants or as informers about incidents in the neighbourhood, because the police had already been present in their well-to-do neighbourhoods for quite some time. The socially heterogenous second district of the city of Antwerp therefore constitutes an ideal testing ground for the tenability of our two-fold hypothesis.

Into the district

A glance at district level proves most insightful. As will be discussed below, the nature of police activities changed radically between 1825 and 1890. This significant shift in type of activities in the course of the nineteenth century seems to be reflected in spatial terms as well. In other words, not only did the police turn to doing other things over the years, they also focused their activities on neighbourhoods and social groups with another socio-economic profile. An exploratory analysis of the police reports of the second district evidently seems to confirm the hypotheses which we formulated at city level.

In order to detect long-term trends, we categorised the huge number of denominations of offences registered by the second district police, grouping them into types of offences (see Table 1). These types fall into three major categories: administrative control (administrative duties and economic life); crimes (theft and violence); and public hygiene and public order offences (public hygiene, traffic, bars, prostitution, etc.).

Table 1 on the nature of police activities in Antwerp's second district clearly shows that police tasks of predominantly economic and administrative regulation in 1825 shifted to various forms of public order maintenance and behaviour regulation in 1890. In 1825 the police were primarily concerned with supervising economic activity (issuing licences of all kinds, checking hygiene regulations for trade and compliance with market regulations) and the addresses of the population (verification of registration in the population register), just as had been the case during the Ancien Régime. By 1890, the Antwerp police had a far broader task package with clearly more comprehensive behaviour regulating ambitions; they went after alcoholism and unlawful frequenting of bars and prostitution. The categories of public order and hygiene offences were 'inflated' considerably as new sorts of public order offences and forms of 'unruly behaviour' were added to the Antwerp police ordinances (local by-laws).

This substantive shift ran parallel to equally sweeping socio-geographic changes. As Figure 2 indicates, the spatial focus of police attention, measured on the streets to which the police report belonged, shifted significantly. In 1825, police activity was concentrated

Table 1. Police activity in Antwerp 2nd district: categories of offences registered in 1825 and 1890

	1825		1890	
administrative duties	30	23%	6	4%
economic life	21	16%	14	10%
theft and damage	14	11%	19	14%
physical violence	11	8%	7	5%
verbal violence	2	2%	7	5%
public hygiene	9	7%	2	1%
traffic	7	5%	3	2%
public drunkenness	0	0%	16	11%
pubs	3	2%	13	9%
prostitution	1	1%	9	6%
diverse public order offences	11	8%	12	9%
other offences	24	18%	32	23%
total offences registered	133	100%	140	100%

Source: Antwerp City Archives (Felixarchief), Police Fund, 2nd district, police reports (processen-verbaal), year 1825, 450#62; year 1890, MA#24557-24561

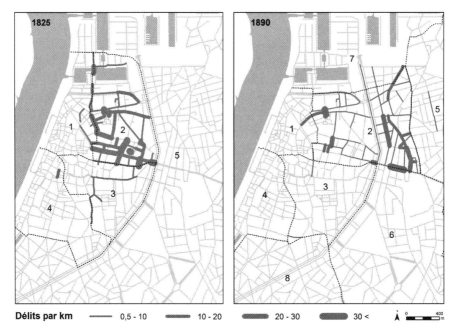

Délits par km ——— 0,5 - 10   ▬▬ 10 - 20   ▰▰ 20 - 30   ◼ 30 <   Å 0 ▬▬ 400 m

Figure 2. Offences registered by Antwerp 2nd district police per km (per street) in 1825 and 1890

Source: Antwerp City Archives (Felixarchief), Police Fund, 2nd district, police reports (processen-verbaal), year 1825, 450#62; year 1890, MA#24557-24561

Table 2. Accused (arrested by or reported to the police): professions (HISCLASS)

	1825	1890		1825	1890
non-manual	52%	24%	*higher skilled*	29%	1%
			medium skilled	13%	20%
			lower skilled	11%	2%
manual	48%	76%	*medium & higher skilled*	26%	8%
			lower skilled	12%	9%
			unskilled	10%	60%
professions known	119	89			

Source: Antwerp City Archives (Felixarchief), Police Fund, 2nd district, police reports (processen-verbaal), year 1825, 450#62; year 1890, MA#24557-24561

primarily on the better neighbourhood round the Keizerstraat. In 1890, the focus was clearly round the Sint-Jans and De Coninckplein, a (new) neighbourhood outside the old city walls characterised by the presence of poorer social groups, including many newcomers, but above all by a very busy nightlife and prostitution. Consistent with this shift from richer to poorer districts, there was also a proletarianisation of the public against whom the police acted. In 1825, those who came into negative contact with the police in the port city generally belonged to the middle and even top layers of Antwerp society (see Table 2). No fewer than 30 per cent of the accused and arrested stemmed from the highly skilled commercial and wealthy elites of Antwerp (merchants, entrepreneurs, people of independent means, brokers, army officers, pharmacists, members of the nobility, etc.). The preponderance of the better-off segments of the population was to be seen even among occupations that entailed manual labour. Most people accused or arrested by the police in 1825 were skilled craftsmen who, unlike those in the lower manual occupations, were often self-employed, had certain assets and managed their own workforce. The image of merchants and craftsmen squares with that of the trade-oriented port city which had retained many characteristics of the Ancien Régime as industrialisation had been delayed until the last decades of the nineteenth century.

Remarkably, at the beginning of the nineteenth century the police thus concentrated not on the lower classes but on the middle classes and even the elites. This observation is consistent with the fact that the police focused primarily on regulating economic life. Furthermore, when it came to the enforcement of administrative obligations, the focus was clearly on the property-owning class. The police kept watch on whether employers and homeowners registered their (domestic) staff or tenants correctly in the population registers. The impoverished inhabitants of the city, many of whom were concentrated in the slums of the socially heterogeneous second district, were left completely out of the picture of this early nineteenth-century police. During this period, the police acted as inspector, standard compliance officer and mediator on behalf of the city council, geared to and for the well-to-do classes, while the lower and certainly lowest classes lay largely beyond their focus. In the early nineteenth century, the Antwerp police was there first and foremost to facilitate economic life in the trading city: the regulation of broader behaviours was clearly not part of their remit.

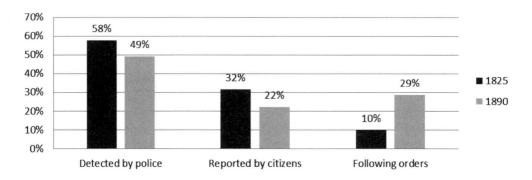

Figure 3. Origin of the police reports (*procès-verbaux*) in 1825 and 1890

Source: Antwerp City Archives (Felixarchief), Police Fund, 2nd district, police reports (processen-verbaal), year 1825, 450#62; year 1890, MA#24557-24561

By the end of the nineteenth century, however, the focus of the Antwerp police appears to have shifted markedly to other social groups in urban society (see Table 2). The public targeted by the police underwent a striking proletarianisation, which was initially reflected in a far greater number of accused who earned their daily bread through manual labour. Secondly, an important shift from highly skilled to less skilled workers took place in various sectors. The elites in the early nineteenth century trading city disappeared off the police radar (from 29 to 1 per cent) and the focus was clearly placed on the working class and unskilled labourers in particular (from 10 to as much as 60 per cent). The above-discussed shift of police tasks to the maintenance of public order and the regulation of popular leisure activities went hand in hand with increased control over and criminalisation of the lower classes. The social shift was also reflected spatially. Whereas at the beginning of the century the accused registered by the Antwerp police of the second district lived predominantly in the richer streets in the heart of the district, in 1890 they were to be found in the more recent and more working-class areas outside the old city centre.

When we look at the origin of the police reports in Figure 3, the picture of the police as an unequivocal, top-down control mechanism of the ruling classes is not confirmed at district level either. A substantial number of the police reports were drawn up as a result of complaints. In such cases, the initiative for intervention did not stem from the police themselves, but from the population. This observation is in line with recent historical research where it is stressed that a significant part of police work is reactive. However, contrary to what might be expected, the proportion of cases reported by citizens in police reports did not increase. This can be attributed to the increase in so-called 'duties fulfilled following orders', reports on actions (such as collecting witness statements or conducting an extra investigation) that the police carried out by order of higher authorities (usually the public prosecutor's office). However, the absolute numbers of complaints by citizens did increase, and did so at a much faster pace than the population during the second half of the nineteenth century.

Can we now also say something about the social background of the users of the police (Table 3)? Although the number of complainants with a known occupation is relatively limited, a clear pattern emerges. In 1825, it was predominantly the better-off who called

Table 3. Complainants: professions (HISCLASS)

	1825	1890		1825	1890
non-manual	45%	45%	*higher skilled*	25%	21%
			medium skilled	20%	21%
			lower skilled	0	3%
manual	55%	55%	*medium & higher skilled*	35%	10%
			lower skilled	5%	10%
			unskilled	15%	34%
professions known	20	29			

Source: Antwerp City Archives (Felixarchief), Police Fund, 2nd district, police reports (processen-verbaal), year 1825, 450#62; year 1890, MA#24557-24561

upon the police. They were first and foremost wholesalers and retailers and self-employed craftsmen, as had been the case in the Ancien Régime. The fact that it was primarily the property-owning class that made use of the police strengthens the impression that the police's primary role was in regulating economic life. In 1890, the proportion of the elites and middle groups among the non-manual professions continued to be high, but the profile of the complainants with a background of manual work shifted significantly. The proportion of unskilled workers increased substantially, and that of skilled craftsmen decreased correspondingly. Is this phenomenon a reflection of the contraction of the group of self-employed craftsmen as a result of the Industrial Revolution? Is this an indication that the bottom social groups also proceeded cautiously to involve the police in their strategies of conflict settlement?

Overall, this process of instrumentalisation and appropriation of the police by the lower classes appears to have started after something of a delay. The proportion of the higher and middle classes among complainants remained high towards the end of the nineteenth century. The proletarianisation of the profiles of the complainants did not proceed apace with the rate of those accused and arrested by the police. The increasing intervention by the police in the lives of the lower classes and the poorer streets was not immediately reflected in a generalised popularised use of the police, as would be the case in Antwerp some 30 years later (Vrints 2019). The focus of police control over the poorer segments of the Antwerp population, combined with the relatively slow appropriation of the police by the lower social groups, suggests that in the latter decades of the nineteenth century, the police remained first and foremost a regulating body at the service of the better-off layers of the population.

Conclusion

The Antwerp police took on the role of 'domestic missionary' towards the end of the nineteenth century by executing many more tasks pertaining to public order maintenance and the regulation of vice (public drunkenness, pubs, prostitution) that directly impinged upon the lives and sociability of the working class, and by intervening more often in the heart of working-class neighbourhoods. Police activity in Antwerp was thus undeniably shaped by class dynamics, yet in much more complex ways than is often suggested. In terms of geographical focus, the police did not solely, nor continuously, concentrate their attention on the poorer city areas and their working-class inhabitants, but rather developed different strategies for regulating the urban territory and its myriad of social groups. In the beginning of the nineteenth century the Antwerp force still functioned like an Ancien Régime police body, regulating economic life and mediating conflicts between the better-off. By the end of the century their enforcement strategies reflected much broader regulatory ambitions. A common feature of these strategies was that they distinguished the 'respectable' from the 'rough'. Within working-class communities, discretionary law enforcement specifically targeted the lower orders of the working class – the 'dangerous classes' of the most disadvantaged and deprived. Our evidence for Antwerp suggests that towards the end of the nineteenth century police targets were not to be found among the respectable middle and working classes but among the disreputable sections of the so-called 'Lumpenproletariat' of unskilled casual labourers and the unemployed. When dealing with the more respectable sections of the working class, on the other hand, the police were willing to turn a blind eye to minor offences in exchange for cooperation with witness statements and criminal investigations. Or, as Cohen pointed out in 1979, 'in the new heartlands of the working class city [the statutory norms] were increasingly used only as an emergency measure … a system of informal, tacitly negotiated and particularist definitions of public order were evolved which accommodated certain working-class usages of social space and time and outlawed others' (Cohen 1979, 31).

Yet everyday urban policing involved much more than surveillance and disciplining of the 'dangerous' lower strata only. Middle classes and the bourgeoisie equally came into contact with the Antwerp police on a regular basis: both in 1825 and in 1890, the police of the Antwerp second district remained an instrument for conflict settlement between the more well-to-do citizens. Further, our evidence suggests that the poorer layers of the population in Antwerp – even the most disadvantaged ones – were not just 'targets' of police operations, but increasingly used the police for their own ends, thereby mobilising these 'domestic missionaries' in significantly different ways from those the authorities had initially planned.

References

Alessi, Giorgia. 1992. *Giustizia e Polizia: Il controllo di una capitale, Napoli 1779– 1803*. Naples: Jovene.

Barrie, David G. 2008. *Police in the Age of Improvement: Police development and the civic tradition in Scotland, 1775-1865*. Cullompton: Willan.

Beattie, J. M. 2012. *The First English Detectives: The Bow Street Runners and the Policing of London, 1750-1840*. Oxford: Oxford University Press.

Becker, Peter. 2002. *Verderbnis und Entartung: eine Geschichte der Kriminologie des 19. Jahrhunderts als Diskurs und Praxis*. Göttingen: Vandenhoeck und Ruprecht.

Chambliss, William. 1975. "Toward a political economy of crime." *Theory and Society* 2 (1): 149-170.

Churchill, David. 2017. *Crime Control and Everyday Life in the Victorian City: The Police and the Public.* Oxford: Oxford University Press.

Cicchini, Marco. 2012. *La police de la République. L'ordre public à Genève au XVIIIe siècle.* Rennes, Presses Universitaires de Rennes.

Cohen, Stanley. 1985. *Visions of Social Control.* Oxford: Polity.

Cohen, Phil. 1979. "Policing the working-class city." In *Capitalism and the rule of law: from deviancy theory to Marxism,* ed. Bob Fine et al., 118-136. London: Hutchinson.

Conchon, Anne, Laurence Montel and Céline Regnard, eds. 2018. *Policer les mobilités.* Paris: Presses universitaires de la Sorbonne.

Crowther, Chris. 2000. *Policing Urban Poverty.* London: Palgrave Macmillan.

Davis, Jennifer. 1991. "Urban policing and its objects: comparative themes in England and France in the second half of the nineteenth century." In *Policing Western Europe: politics, professionalism, and public order, 1850-1940,* ed. Clive Emsley and Barbara Weinberger, 1-17. Westport, CT: Greenwood Press.

De Koster, Margo. 2008. "Routines et contraintes de la police urbaine à Anvers, 1890– 1914." In *Etre policier: Les métiers de police en Europe, XVIIIe-XXe siècle,* ed. Jean- Marc Berlière, Catherine Denys, Dominique Kalifa and Vincent Milliot, 345-362. Rennes: Presses Universitaires de Rennes.

De Koster, Margo, Barbara Deruytter and Antoon Vrints. 2018. "Police–public relations in transition in Antwerp, 1840s–1914." *European Review of History: Revue européenne d'histoire* 25 (1): 147-165.

Deluermoz, Quentin. 2012. *Policiers dans la ville. La construction d'un ordre public à Paris (1854-1914).* Paris: Publications de la Sorbonne.

Denys, Catherine. 2010. "The Development of Police Forces in Urban Europe in the Eighteenth Century." *Journal of Urban History* 36, no. 3: 332-344.

Emsley, Clive. 2004. "Control and Legitimacy: the police in comparative perspective since circa. 1800." In *Social Control in Europe: 1800-2000,* ed. Clive Emsley, Pieter Spierenburg and Eric Johnson, 193-209. Columbus OH: The Ohio State University Press.

Emsley, Clive. 2007. *Crime, Police, and Penal Policy: European Experiences 1750-1940.* Oxford: Oxford University Press.

Frégier, Honoré. 1840. *Des classes dangereuses de la population dans les grandes villes et des moyens de les rendre meilleures.* 2 vols. Paris: Paul Renouard.

Garland, David. 2002. *The Culture of Control: Crime and Social Order in Contemporary Society.* Chicago, IL: Chicago University Press.

Harring, Sidney. 1983. *Policing a Class Society.* New Brunswick, NJ: Rutgers University Press.

Mandemakers, Kees, et al. 2018. *HSN standardized, HISCO-coded and classified occupational titles.* Amsterdam: IISG.

Mayhew, H., and J. Binny. 1862. *The criminal prisons of London.* London: Griffin, Bohn and Company.

Milliot, Vincent. 2006. "Réformer les polices urbaines au siècle des Lumières: le révélateur de la mobilité." *Crime, Histoire & Sociétés/Crime, History & Societies* 10 (1): 25-50.

Mori, Simona. 2016. "The police and the urban 'dangerous classes': the culture and practice of public law and order in Milan after national unity." *Urban History* 43 (2): 266-284.

Musumeci, Emilia. 2018. "Against the Rising Tide of Crime: Cesare Lombroso and Control of the 'Dangerous Classes' in Italy, 1861-1940." *Crime, Histoire & Sociétés/Crime, History & Societies* 22 (2): 83-106.

Philips, David. 2003. "Three 'Moral Entrepreneurs' and the Creation of a 'Criminal Class' in England, *c.* 1790-1840." *Crime, Histoire & Sociétés/Crime, History & Societies* 7 (1): 79-107.

Slater, Stefan. 2012. "Street Disorder in the Metropolis." *Law, Crime and History* 1: 59-91.

Storch, Robert D. 1976. "The Policeman as Domestic Missionary: Urban Discipline and Popular Culture in Northern England, 1850-1880." *Journal of Social History* 9 (4): 481-502.

Storch, Robert D., and F. Engels. 1975. "The Plague of the Blue Locusts: Police Reform and Popular Resistance in Northern England, 1840-57." *International Review of Social History* 20 (1): 61-90.

Vidoni, Nicolas. 2011. *La Lieutenance générale de police et l'espace urbain parisien (1667-1789). Expériences, pratiques et savoirs.* Unpublished PhD thesis, Université de Provence, 2 vol.

Vrints, Antoon. 2019. *The Theatre of the Street. Public Violence in Antwerp During the First Half of the Twentieth Century.* Leiden: Brill, Crime and the City in History Series, vol. 2.

PART VI

Methodological, Theoretical and Contemporary Perspectives

How was City Life?

Moving beyond GDP and Real Income to Measure Pre-modern Welfare and Inequality Levels

Introduction

It appears that the main goal of measuring inequality and living standards has been to produce comparable indices and define clear trends. Inequality is expressed in Gini coefficients, and GDP figures and average real wages are the most important measures of welfare. These clear and straightforward indicators allow historians and economists to compare inequality and welfare levels between countries, regions and cities, as well as their evolution over time (Maddison 2006; Vries 2013; Guido Alfani 2015; Humphries & Weisdorf 2017; Broadberry et al. 2015; Van Zanden 1995). A calculation of uniform GDP figures is subsequently used to analyse differences in productivity and welfare on both sides of the Eurasian continent despite entirely different economic systems and archival source material. Not surprisingly, GDP figures and wages are at the heart of the debate on the Great and Little Divergence (Vries 2013). Also, these indicators have been visualised using compelling graphs and images, turning them into powerful narratives. For example, the 'hockey stick curve', popularised by Angus Maddison, summarises the idea that welfare levels remained consistently low, harldy exceeding bare-bones subsistence levels, until modern economic growth started to boost them to the prosperity levels that we know today (Maddison 2006, 44). Thomas Piketty and Guido Alfani have visualised the continually rising trend of wealth inequality throughout history, it having shown only a short-term decline immediately after the Black Death and both World Wars (Piketty 2013; Alfani 2017).[1] For Piketty this continuous rise in inequality is explained by the return on capital, which permanently exceeded the growth rate of the economy. Finally, the U-curve of northwestern European real wages, as told by Bob Allen, suggests that living standards during most of the early modern period were low and declining, before rising significantly from the seventeenth century onwards in the Dutch Republic and England (Allen 2011, 360).

The primary evidence for these indices and trends has been either construction workers' or servants' wages and consumer prices (Allen 2001; Humphries & Weisdorf 2019; Federico, Nuvolari & Vasta 2019; Williamson & Lindert 1980) or wealth indicators based on wealth

---

[1] For graph see: https://voxeu.org/article/europe-s-rich-1300.

Maïka De Keyzer • KU Leuven

Inequality and the City in the Low Countries (1200-2020), ed. by Bruno BLONDÉ, Sam GEENS, Hilde GREEFS, Wouter RYCKBOSCH, Tim SOENS & Peter STABEL, SEUH 50 (Turnhout, 2020), pp. 359-376.

© BREPOLS ☙ PUBLISHERS   DOI 10.1484/M.SEUH-EB.5.120455

taxes (Alfani 2010; Broad & Schuurman 2014; Dombrecht & Ryckbosch 2017).[2] Firstly, notwithstanding the fundamental criticism of the data used to construct the wage and price series, the same long-term series remain the main evidence for debates on income inequality and living standards (for criticisms see Hatcher & Stephenson 2018; O'Brien & Deng 2015). As a result, adjustments and better datasets have been proposed (Allen, Bengtsson & Dribe 2005; van Zanden et al. 2014; Steckel et al. 2018; Vecchi 2017). The problem is more significant than the 'unrealness' of the wage series, however. The reliance on wages is omnipresent, while historians have long accepted that for many households wages were only part of their total income (Muldrew 2011; Hatcher & Stephenson 2018). In order to understand inequality, it is thus vitally important to study the actual composition of the household income, as this income may have relied on wage labour, household labour, subsistence farming, capital investments, the sharing economy, self-employment or, in many cases, a combination of two or more of these potential sources of income.

Despite the added value of aggregate indicators like GDP or Gini coefficients for purposes of clarity and comparison, the exclusive focus on these types of indicators is not beneficial for our understanding of inequality and living standards in the past. Measuring unequal levels of welfare is a challenge, but the endeavour deserves more effort. First of all, the use of average wages and GDP per capita figures hides enormous discrepancies between and within social groups. Similar Gini coefficients and real wages can be found in entirely different economies and societies. The main question thus remains what standards of living could different social strata in society actually obtain? How did long-term trends such as falling real wages, the industrious revolution and economic boom and bust cycles affect the living conditions of the poor, the average craftsmen and the upper social strata in the city? What was their income? Were they able to provide a decent living for their families?

In addition, most research has focused on the macro level: the state or the nation. Cities and their surrounding countryside, market economies and subaltern regions are merged together, creating an average picture of a country that ignores the significant differences that must have existed in the different entities. If we want to know how city life unfolded and what the living standards of urban dwellers were, a macro approach must be abandoned to allow for a detailed perspective on individual cities or a group of urban centres.

As a result, research into unequal living standards in the past must be more ambitious and include more diverse data and information about living standards. This transition will be to the detriment of uniform indices and comparability of data series. Nevertheless, for the sake of historicity, nuance and realism, research should urgently reach this next level. Fortunately, urban societies have the sources and data required to obtain a more nuanced and complete picture of welfare levels and inequality. From the late medieval period onwards, tax registers, city accounts, court records, contracts, probate inventories, wills, parish records as well as archaeological and anthropological data provide us with indispensable traces and information on the prosperity, education, health and longevity of individuals and groups in the past. While all of these sources have been used and analysed

---

2   Another approach includes the use of social tables to estimate income inequality (Lindert & Williamson 1982; Malinowski & van Zanden 2017). Since social tables do not exist for the Low Countries or for most of the surrounding areas and time periods (Dombrecht & Ryckbosch 2017, 70), and since they provide a rather crude indication of income inequality, they are not discussed in this chapter.

in some way before (see, for example, Dyer 1989 and 2000), few scholars embraced such encompassing methodology, combining all of these sources or perspectives to study standards of living in the past.

Therefore, this chapter proposes to embark on the search for a new multidimensional welfare index. Significant advances have already been made, and this quest can build upon the endeavours of, for example, Bob Allen and Giovanni Vecchi (Allen, Bengtsson & Dribe 2005; Vecchi 2017). However, their work also revealed serious methodological issues which will have to be addressed in this contribution. First, instead of looking at the population in general, the index can and must be used per social group within the population. Second, based on new trends in welfare research, the multidimensional index has to move beyond real wages and include at least health and education. These indicators allow us to grasp all vital or indispensable aspects of welfare, next to income. Finally, this chapter will propose an alternative to real wages, by calculating the number of consumption baskets a household could obtain via income pooling, rather than relying on wages alone.

In the first section, an overview of the current state of the art on multidimensional indices will be given. The second section introduces a critique on the reliance of income inequality indices on real wages to assess income. The final section will discuss a new methodology and provide an overview of the available source material to take steps forward in approaching the real levels of inequality and living standards in the past.

Human development indices as an alternative welfare indicator

Most scholars by now agree that welfare is defined by at least three indicators: income, health and education. Nevertheless, in economic history, GDP and real wages still play an important role in measuring welfare levels in the past (Schmelzer 2016; Malinowski & van Zanden 2017). The ground-breaking but much-debated work of Maddison is a good example. According to Maddison, 'from the year 1000 to 1820, the advance in per capita income was a slow crawl – the world average rose about 50 per cent' (Maddison 2006, 29). Only after 1820, when modern economic growth was achieved, did living standards soar from bare-bones subsistence levels towards the prosperity levels experienced today. In this strand of historiography, wages and prices are the protagonists. Bob Allen was one of the first to collect and publish an encompassing database of nominal wages and consumption prices reaching back to the later Middle Ages.[3] In his opinion, '[w]ages and prices have long been central concerns of economic historians, for they bear on such fundamental issues as the pace of economic development, economic leadership and the standard of living' (Allen 2001, 411). In his wake, similar datasets have been generated for a wide range of countries and regions.[4] These series have revealed some general trends in welfare evolutions in north-western Europe. Before the Black Death real wages and therefore total income were low. This situation was reversed after the demographic shock, producing a Golden Age of Labour. The Early Modern period was subsequently characterised by deteriorating real wages and lower living standards, which from the seventeenth century were pushed

---

3   https://www.nuffield.ox.ac.uk/people/sites/allen-research-pages/.
4   See the IISG website for available data: http://www.iisg.nl/hpw/data.php.

up in some regions due to (proto) modern economic growth (Broadberry et al. 2015; Humphries & Weisdorf 2019; Van Zanden 2005).

But how real and useful is such a long-term and aggregate overview of GDP and real wages if we want to know the welfare levels of urban inhabitants in the past? First of all, these total welfare levels nationally provide little information on the actual prosperity achieved at the level of cities or social groups within cities (for a micro level approach, see chapters 13 and 14 in this volume). Second, the unrelenting critique on the numbers and calculations used has made it abundantly clear that aggregate GDP figures and total income figures of entire countries in benchmark years add little to a real understanding of living standards in the past (Clark 2009; O'Brien & Deng 2015). But, most importantly, a focus on income ignores two very fundamental aspects of welfare.

Therefore, debates on wellbeing or standards of living can no longer ignore the urgent call for a more multidimensional approach to human welfare. In order to prevent a one-sided interpretation of welfare, income-focused parameters like GDP and real wages are increasingly merged with other indicators, notably related to health and education, into broader indices like the Human Development Index (HDI), which is gaining in popularity among economic historians (van Zanden et al. 2014; Allen, Bengtsson & Dribe 2005; Jordan 2010; Steckel et al. 2018). According to the HDI, extra income, without any progress in health or longevity and educational standards, would provide only meagre growth in welfare. A second strand of research explores the so-called capabilities or opportunities of individuals or groups. This capabilities approach as defined by Amartya Sen and Martha Nussbaum acknowledges that welfare is reliant on materiality and income, but stresses that it is not defined by it, because welfare is strongly contextual and to a certain extent dependent on individual preferences. To reach a threshold level of quality of life humans or households require a 'capability set' – 'a minimum set of what respect for human dignity requires' in a given context (Nussbaum 2011; Robeyns 2016; Sen 1999).

Both HDI and capability inspired research produced important results, challenging the common wisdom received from previous research limited to real wages and GDP data. For instance, advances in income and material wealth did not necessarily lead to better health and longer life spans. During the industrial revolution real wages and productivity figures may have soared, but human health was negatively affected. The average human lifespan dropped significantly, showing that the income gains were countered by increased disease and strain on the body due to changing living and working conditions (Steckel & Floud 1997). Counterintuitively, the Middle Ages appear as a period with remarkably tall people, suggesting that despite a lack of economic growth and low productivity the biological standards of living – combining nutrition and exposure to disease and bodily strain – were relatively high. In addition, an analysis of Italian living standards showed that education, health and income could follow diverging trends. While some Italian regions might have been front-runners in economic development and growth, they did not necessarily outperform other regions with regard to education standards or health indicators, and vice versa (Vecchi 2017).

Promising as this encompassing approach is, some methodological issues remain. First of all, even though the consensus is growing that these different dimensions of welfare should be included in the research, opinions on the way to do so have varied widely.

Table 1 Welfare indicators used in *How Was Life* (van Zanden et al. 2014, 27-30).

Income	GDP Income inequality Real wages
Health	Life expectancy Height
Education	Schooling rate
Personal security	Homicide rate and incidence of warfare
Institutions	Participation rate in decision-making
Environmental quality	Sustainability
Gender inequality	Gender relations

Some scholars have used the modern HDI and altered it only slightly to include historical parameters (Crafts 2002; Crafts 1997; Prados de la Escosura 2010). Thus, human welfare levels in the past have been expressed in a single index that can be compared through time and space. This approach has been severely criticised, however. In these versions of the HDI, paradoxically, low life expectancy can be entirely 'compensated' for by sufficiently high education and income levels. As Giovanni Vecchi has stressed, perfect substitutability is incompatible with the idea that the components of the index are essential dimensions of welfare (Vecchi 2017). As a result, multidimensional indices which do not aggregate results into one 'overall' figure are mostly preferred. Allen and Vecchi, for example, have pleaded to avoid a rigid index and study all the different aspects of welfare separately to prevent the loss of information by combining them into one index (Allen, Bengtsson & Dribe 2005, 8; Vecchi 2017).

Second, there is no agreement on the number and type of welfare indicators to be included in the analysis. All studies include income, health and education, but most add additional categories or define indicators differently. In their book on living standards in the past, Allen et al. have brought together studies concerning real wages and income, length and longevity, as well as analyses of schooling and human capital formation. As an addition to this list, they have proposed including resilience as a vital component of welfare, to test whether societies could cope with shocks and crises. Vecchi has combined nutrition with height, health, child labour, education, migration, income, inequality, poverty, wealth, vulnerability, human development, household budgets and the cost of living. Van Zanden et al. have calculated an overall indicator of welfare based on different individual components. They started from the *How's Life* report of the OECD and the capabilities approach of Amartya Sen and proposed a multidimensional index including a wide range of parameters (see Table 1) (van Zanden et al. 2014).

While posing a nightmare for comparative history, every approach has tried to create the best overview of living standards in the past, given the available source material and context. In this respect it is better to be nuanced and detailed, rather than to limit the indicators to a restricted common denominator that can be studied all over the world and for every period. Downsizing the number of parameters or merging some categories afterwards is always easier than expanding the analysis.

Lastly, and most importantly, all indices still rely on real wages and productivity figures. While the importance of income has diminished in a multidimensional index or in the capabilities approach, real wages and estimates of total income or productivity are still an essential and important part of the analysis, notwithstanding the severe methodological criticisms raised with regard to the use of real wages as indicators of income. In the next section, the problems regarding the use of real wages in welfare studies are discussed.

Average wages as the cornerstone of living standards

The underlying assumption of welfare research is that real wages provide the best indicator for studying living standards, purchasing power and welfare in the past. To secure comparability, most scholars rely on construction workers' or rural labourers' annual or casual day wages. These are the building blocks of almost all research into living standards in the past. Nevertheless, these series rely on certain questionable assumptions that must be discussed.

First of all, wage-earning construction workers or servants are considered representative of the entire wage-earning population. The reason for the selection of construction workers is the lucky coincidence that big building projects and general maintenance works ordered by cities and elites are over-represented in our surviving archival material. However, construction workers are not necessarily the most common workers or average earners in the past. Similarly, wages earned by servants and casual rural labourers are omnipresent in manorial accounts generated by large ecclesiastical and lay landowners. Here, the problem of representativity is more nuanced: servants and rural day labourers were indeed the dominant wage-earning categories in rural communities (Shaw-Taylor 2012; Whittle 2000).

Nevertheless, the information on these two types of labour and labourers is considered representative for the entire population. In their latest article, Jane Humphries and Jacob Weisdorf use rural servants' wages to paint a general picture of English society, stating that rural wages were even representative for urban communities, since the additional living costs faced by urban labourers would eliminate the wage differential between town and countryside (Humphries & Weisdorf 2019, 6). Such series then suggests that there was a uniform trend for an entire nation irrespective of differences in class, region or gender, which is debatable.

A first alternative is to move beyond the national level and create different real wage series per city. By now, almost all the major European cities are represented in one series or another (Rota & Weisdorf 2019; Allen 2001; Özmucur & Pamuk 2002).[5] But then other assumptions pop up. First of all, for urban dwellers skilled and unskilled construction workers are selected as representative of the entire population, which was not the case. Even more problematic is the fact that the valuation of construction work might have changed over time. Jord Hanus has shown for the city of 's-Hertogenbosch in the northern Low Countries that, in the course of the sixteenth century, carpenters and masons employed by

---

5   See the IISG website for available data: http://www.iisg.nl/hpw/data.php.

the city witnessed a relative decline in social position compared to other groups in society. Whereas in 1500 they still belonged to the 'middling groups' of urban society, their position on the social scale of the city gradually deteriorated. By 1560, their tax rates were lower than the urban average, reaching a nadir in 1580 (Hanus 2014, 113-123; Blondé & Hanus 2010). Because of price inflation and monetary depreciation, these full-time labourers saw their relative social position change fundamentally, which indicates that a real wage series based exclusively on construction wages cannot be deemed representative for the entire population of a city. Second, it is believed that the wages that are registered in the accounts reflect remuneration equal to our current money wage. Judy Stephenson, however, has convincingly shown that many of the wages used in wage indices constitute above-average wages, as they are often related to exceptional or prestigious building projects that paid substantially higher wages than construction workers would usually receive (Stephenson 2017). Also, not all workers listed as labourers earning a money wage were actual wage earners, but instead self-employed artisans who had to buy tools and building material, pay assistants and cover additional costs (Hatcher 2018). The actual income enjoyed by such 'contractors' might have been significantly different from the earnings of a full-time wage-labourer. Moreover, the relationship between wages and additional benefits such as food, drink, textiles and fuel for labourers is still unclear for most European wage labourers in the pre-modern period. As a result, wage series must be assessed thoroughly and critically.

Second, our modern idea about full-time labour is held as a standard for past societies. Usually day-wages are used. The annual wage is then extrapolated by assuming 250 working days per year (Allen 2001). Nevertheless, it has been proven multiple times that only a small proportion of labourers worked full-time for a wage (Gary 2017). Sam Geens and Tim Soens, for example, have used exceptionally detailed accounts on construction work in drainage and flood protection in Coastal Flanders to calculate the actual days worked by skilled wage labourers (mostly carpenters) in the late medieval period. Depending on the real wage the labourers could obtain and the demand for labour from employers, the actual number of days worked by these carpenters fluctuated wildly; in some decades the average was as low as 147 working days, whereas in others it was as high as 278 working days per year (Geens & Soens, forthcoming). The uncertainty about supply and demand for labour caused Humphries and Weisdorf to use the annual wages of full-time employed servants to circumvent this problem. In this way, they calculated an aggregate real wage and total income series for England (Humphries & Weisdorf 2019). Nevertheless, the dominance of servants in the labouring rural population was not constant. It has been stated that throughout the early modern period the ratio between casual and annual labourers changed significantly, due to wage and boarding costs (Whittle 2000, 252-256). As a result, day or annual wages by themselves are poor indicators of income and standards of living. John Hatcher has articulated it as follows: 'Our understanding of wages and living standards from the thirteenth century to the late nineteenth is grossly inaccurate. The original statistical series on which it rests – the day wages assumed to have been paid to builders and casual agricultural labourers – are riddled with debilitating errors and limitations and undermined by a plethora of unfounded assumptions' (Hatcher 2018, 15).

Even though suggestions for better wage and price series are continuously proposed, the fundamental issues of reliance on wages to reconstruct living standards are addressed less frequently. In order to study material welfare in the past, we do not need wage information, but rather an overview of the total income enjoyed by a person or a household (see chapter 9 for a discussion on household incomes versus labour wages).

And in this respect gender also comes into play. Time and again, research has revealed the substantial gap between household income on the one hand and male wages on the other. Male wages were not the sole component of income enjoyed by a household. Gender studies have fundamentally altered our understanding of household income by showing the importance of women's work in the past. Women and children contributed to the household budget by income pooling. Despite the more limited options for women to work in formal sectors and the lower wages women often earned for their labour, women were very active participants in the economy and therefore contributed significantly to the family income (Humphries & Sarasúa 2012; van der Heijden & Schmidt 2009; Devos, De Groot & Schmidt 2015). Married women spun, produced dairy products, cured meat and sold these products on the local markets. Single women and widows were even more active and made a living as labourers and craftswomen, were self-employed as market vendors, earned an income by money lending or leasing out rooms (Whittle 2014; 2005). Wages were not the main component of their income, but women did enter the labour market even in male-dominated sectors such as construction work (Gary 2017). Nevertheless, the male breadwinner's wage is still dominant in debates on living standards.

Moreover, income was derived not only from wages but also from outside the market, even in cities that were highly market- and wage-orientated. Ample research has shown that urban agriculture was omnipresent and that the required consumption baskets were in part obtained via additional channels outside the formal market system (for urban landownership in the countryside see chapter 12). This was even the case for the largest urban centres, but during the pre-industrial era most cities had important rural characteristics and were semi-rural at best (Stouff 1970; Thirsk 1997; Leguay 2009; Gurvil 2010). In German, such hybrid agro-towns are called *Ackerbürgerstädte*, which have been considered a vital component of the urban network in Germany, but small towns with rural characteristics existed in large parts of northwestern Europe (Jäschke, Andermann & Friess 2003; Björklund 2010; Van De Walle 2019). In Colchester, for example, two thirds of all taxpayers were involved in food production during the fourteenth century (Britnell 1986). Food, being one of the most crucial household expenditures, was produced rather than bought, while wage-earning could complement the household income. Going beyond the market for food security profoundly influences the correctness of real wages as a measure of living standards.

Finally, earnings are not derived just from labour. From the late medieval periods onwards there were vibrant markets in most of Europe for labour, land and capital (Van Bavel et al. 2012). For modern economists, wealth inequality and the income derived from wealth have become a vital part of living standards studies, and the constant interplay between wealth and income inequalities has been stressed (Ranaldi 2018; Milanovic 2017). In economic history this is not yet the case, although rural historians have often turned to access to land and hence immovable property to model differences in living standards and income (Alfani 2015; Ryckbosch 2015; Schofield 1965) (see chapter 8 for a discussion on rural wealth inequality). In an urban context as well, the importance of immovable property within and outside the city walls was of equal importance (see chapters 12, 13 and 14 for a discussion on the importance of real estate). For the upper-middle classes and the rich, rents and leases were often vital components of their income (van Bochove, Deneweth & Zuijderduijn 2013). In addition, investment in land, often in the surrounding countryside, provided food which could be consumed or sold. For Italy, the link between the countryside and cities has been studied most intensively. In Siena in the fourteenth century, urban households, ranging from the middling classes to the richest segment of society, owned swathes of land in their contado (Cherubini 1974). As a result, they had a steady stream of income thanks to the produce and rent that they received from their tenants.

Furthermore, urban dwellers were active in the capital markets that started to develop since the fourteenth century. The most important financial products were long-term loans that earned interest of between 6 and 10 per cent, depending on the risk and flexibility of the loan (Zuijderduijn & Moor 2013, 43). State authorities and municipalities were increasingly reliant on annuities that were sold to their inhabitants and investors to finance their activities. But also private individuals found their way to the capital markets to invest (Blockmans 1987; Van Bavel et al. 2012; Van Onacker 2018). Credit was increasingly needed to invest in the family business, and there were creditors with capital waiting for an opportunity to invest (see chapter 9). Older couples who wanted to secure a steady income after retirement, orphans who had received a monetary inheritance, women or younger siblings who were bought out of the family business by the eldest heir and rentiers who wanted to live off their wealth: they were all active on the financial markets, albeit with different interests and strategies (Zuijderduijn 2018; Dermineur 2018). For the urban centre of Edam in Holland, Zuijderduijn et al. observed that between 25 and 56 per cent of all households possessed at least one (life or redeemable) annuity (Zuijderduijn & Moor 2013, 50). An increasing number of studies have shown the importance of capital as a source of income for urban and rural households alike. Especially in gender studies, it has been shown that women, single, widowed and even married, were keen investors because moneylending was an ideal profession for women who had difficulty entering the formal labour market. In the Low Countries almost 20 per cent of all urban households were headed by women (Schmidt & van Der Heijden 2016, 24-25; Devos, De Groot & Schmidt 2015) and those women with some capital at hand were ready to invest it as an alternative source of income, next to letting out rooms and self-employment as market vendors for instance (Spicksley 2018; Dermineur 2018; Spicksley 2007; 2008; 2015; Bardyn 2018; Fynn-Paul 2018; Zuijderduijn 2018; Van Zanden, Zuijderduijn & De Moor 2012). The same goes for elderly people, orphans and people belonging to minority groups, which disqualified them from the regular labour market. Even though evidence of these capital products is to be found in wills, probate inventories and some tax lists, this type of income is yet again ignored in debates on living standards.

To sum up, a reconstruction of welfare in the past should move beyond real wages and look at total income, preferably on a household level. In the past (as well as today for that matter), regular household income consisted only partly of wages. In his reconstruction of the total urban income of 's Hertogenbosch, Jord Hanus demonstrated the minor importance of wages (see chapter 9; Hanus 2014, 97-131). The household budget was fuelled by a combination of wages, subsistence farming, household labour, rent and goods derived from an informal sharing economy (Figure 1).

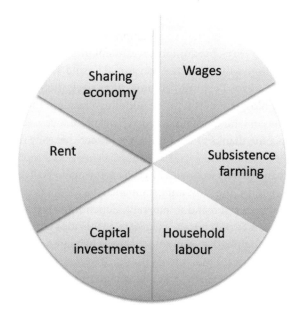

Figure 1 Theoretical income structure of an urban household in the early modern period.

Welfare index beyond real wages

A welfare index for historical cities should not focus on comparability, but on estimating the welfare levels of the inhabitants as closely as possible. This chapter proposes to follow Allen et al. and Vecchi in constructing a multidimensional welfare index studying at least three components: income, health and education (Allen, Bengtsson & Dribe 2005; Vecchi 2017). These three aspects can be analysed for most urban centres, stretching back at least until the later Middle Ages.

Health can be studied via several proxies. First, life expectancy has been an important variable. Life expectancy at birth calculates the average life span an individual can expect to achieve at any given moment in time. Thanks to parish records and later municipal documents that have become readily available since at least the sixteenth century, life expectancy can be calculated quite easily for different groups in society (Devos 2010). Child mortality is a variation on this parameter that is more difficult to reconstruct for earlier periods, but that can add to our understanding of health and longevity in the past. Recently, human height has also been rediscovered as an indicator of human welfare. Height is strongly correlated with life expectancy indicators but has several advantages. The average height, registered in medical and military registers from the eighteenth century onwards or measured via the femur or long bone of a human skeleton, provides information on the human diet minus 'claims' on that diet (Steckel 2005). The most important claims were disease and strain on the body because of working conditions. Thus, height can reveal more information regarding welfare than life expectancy or mortality rates (Floud 2002; Heyberger 2012; Stolz, Baten & Reis 2013; Floud & Wachter 1982; Steckel 1995). Skeleton information is particularly promising. Steckel convincingly argues that 'skeletal evidence greatly extends backwards in time, broadens it to include women and children, and unlike stature alone, includes information on degenerative health processes associated with hard work and ageing' (Steckel 2005, 229). Recently an extensive database on skeleton information was produced, including large stretches of northwestern Europe (Steckel et al. 2018). Unfortunately, because of a lack of sufficient evidence and the requirement of statical significance, data on human height are mostly aggregated at the level of states or Europe as a whole. It will be essential in the coming years to add extra skeleton information for different cities (and rural regions for that matter), so that enough data become available to allow one to de-aggregate health indicies and compare different cities in different types of societies. Height differences between cities and their rural surroundings should also be reconsidered, as living standards between town and countryside may have been profoundly different (Devos 2010, 57; Scheidel 2001; Van der Woude 1982). Of course, rural-to-urban as well as intra-regional migration significantly complicates the analysis of skeleton information, looking for regional divergences. Contextual information on skeleton assemblages is often lacking, but should be maximally exploited. Careful contextualisation of skeleton data might also allow one to reveal health inequalities within urban and rural communities, allowing us to analyse the impact of specific living conditions on health. This would be an important addition to the current standard of living debate.

Education is a complicated matter and few indicators allow a quantifiable and detailed index. Currently, education is considered a human right, but even for societies in the past the importance of training and education is increasingly pointed out (De Munck 2007). Van Zanden et al. claimed that having some basic level of literacy or education improved welfare levels because of the higher level of control an individual obtained over his or her life. Literacy is required for everyday transactions and even household economics. Indirectly, literacy or human capital can lead to higher skills or technological advances, which can lead to higher productivity and better living standards (van Zanden et al. 2014). Assessing a schooling rate is difficult for the pre-modern period, but attempts are made to look at training and the transference of skills. Due to a lack of suitable data for pre-modern societies, literacy rates are widely used, with signatures as the dominant proxy. Even though this approach has been criticised, it is widely endorsed and can be justified because of its homogeneous character and the ability to quantify and compare literacy levels through time and space (Reis 2005; Hoyler 1998; Schofield 1973). Currently, scholars use contracts and, more specifically, marriage contracts, available from the later Middle Ages onwards, to analyse the proportion of people who could sign their names. Contracts of all sorts can be found in the parish archives and can be browsed systematically via sample cases to quantify the literacy rate.

Income is the most challenging indicator to calculate. As mentioned before, we have to move beyond real wages and productivity figures such as GDP and assess the income of households. The average income on a city level hides inequality and the changing social positions of different social strata in society. As Allen et al. and Jord Hanus have stated, it is vital to break down these averages and look at different social groups (Hanus 2013, 743; Allen, Bengtsson & Dribe 2005, 8). A reconstruction of the income of poor households, labourers, lower-middle classes, upper-middle classes and the wealthiest segment – the top 10 per cent – should be made. The critical factor is to assess income profiles per social group. Research by Jane Whittle and Judith Spicksley has shown that it is possible to derive the detailed social profile of a household from information in wills and probate inventories, for instance relating to the possession of tools, references to debts, a shop, immovable property, financial products, etc. Then, the potential contribution of each of these assets to household income can be modelled. Wills and probate inventories are widely available, particularly for urban communities. Although a social bias is always present, because the middle classes and elderly are over-represented (Lindert 1986, 1133), Jane Whittle has convincingly shown that 'in terms of sheer numbers and their stretch down the social structure, no other type of document from this period can equal the reach of wills and inventories' (Whittle, 2005, 53). After all, taxes and wage series similarly exclude the poorest segments of society, apart from some very exceptional sources (Alfani 2015; Ryckbosch 2015). Research into female-headed households has also provided promising results that show that this social profiling is possible (Spicksley 2018; 2007; Zuijderduijn 2018; Whittle 2014).

Once such general framework has been set up per city, additional research is needed to push these findings even further, by investigating the income or return of different types of assets. Using a tax called the *verpachtingscohieren*, Jaco Zuijderduijn and Tine De Moor could calculate for Edam that immovable property secured an average return of 4 per cent as against 5 per cent for cows and between 6 and 10 per cent for financial assets, depending on the rate of risk (Zuijderduijn & Moor 2013, 44-45). Combining these data on returns with the actual distribution of these assets among different households, we can calculate their contribution to household income. While this is certainly a labour-intensive process that can only be done for limited samples, it is worthwhile to get this detailed understanding of income from wealth. The same can be done for the agricultural produce that was obtained from urban gardening and plots of land outside the city. Finally, an estimate of household labour should be calculated. Even though such an estimate will always remain a hypothetical calculation, a proxy should be included for those social groups that are shown to possess the tools and means of production to engage in commercially oriented household labour. Jane Whittle has indicated that several activities that are typically referred to as housewifery were in reality commercial activities, oriented at commodity markets and making a vital and significant contribution to total household income (Whittle 2014).

A final step is the conversion of income into consumption baskets, expressing the material living standards of an individual or a household in the number of baskets each of them can afford. For this purpose, several consumer price indices and consumption basket compositions have been developed, also for premodern societies (Phelps Brown & Hopkins 1956; Allen 2009). Bob Allen has pointed out the difference between a bare bones and respectable consumption basket indication. Nevertheless, these different types of consumer baskets still do not reflect changing consumption patterns when economic conditions of families and the economy change, nor do they account for demographic differences between poorer and richer households (Hanus 2013; Hoffman et al. 2002). As a consequence, we need more diversified consumer baskets for different social groups and evolving over time.

Conclusion

The holy grail of economic historians has been the reconstruction of the perfect real wage series to reconstruct the welfare trends in the past. This endeavour to construct a comparative and long-term series, however, has prevented one from digging deeper and revealing all aspects of welfare in the past. Advances in socio-economic history, revealing the importance of income from capital and land, the unrepresentativeness of construction workers' wages as well as the importance of taking into account additional welfare indicators such as health and literacy have only barely trickled down into welfare research. Nevertheless, a more realistic welfare index, even to the detriment of comparability, must be the main goal of future research. Even though the construction of such alternative welfare indices will require a wide range of preparatory enquiries into the different kinds of income available to households with different profiles and living and working in very different contexts, socio-economic historians should be ambitious when it comes to calculating welfare levels and inequality in the past. Therefore the quest for the perfect real wage series should be replaced by detailed research into probate inventories, wills, tax registers and household accounts, until we know as much about income from land, capital and household labour as we do today about wage labour.

References

Alfani, G. 2010. "Wealth Inequalities and Population Dynamics in Early Modern Northern Italy." *Journal of Interdisciplinary History* 40: 513-549.

Alfani, Guido. 2015. "Economic Inequality in Northwestern Italy: A Long-Term View (Fourteenth to Eighteenth Centuries)." *The Journal of Economic History* 75 (4): 1058-1096.

Alfani, Guido. 2017. "The Rich in Historical Perspective: Evidence for Preindustrial Europe (ca. 1300-1800)." *Cliometrica* 11 (3): 321-348.

Allen, Robert C. 2001. "The Great Divergence in European Wages and Prices from the Middle Ages to the First World War." *Explorations in Economic History* 38 (4): 411-447.

Allen, Robert C. 2009. *The British Industrial Revolution in Global Perspective*. Cambridge: Cambridge University Press.

Allen, Robert C. 2011. "Why the Industrial Revolution Was British: Commerce, Induced Invention and the Scientific Revolution." *Economic History Review* 64: 357-384.

Allen, Robert C., Tommy Bengtsson and Martin Dribe. 2005. *Living Standards in the Past. New Perspectives on Well-Being in Asia and Europe*. Oxford: Oxford University Press.

Bardyn, Andrea. 2018. "Women's Fortunes. Female Agency, Property and Investment in Late Medieval Brabant." Unpublished PhD thesis, Leuven: KULeuven.

Björklund, Annika. 2010. *Historical Urban Agriculture. Food Production and Access to Land in Swedish Towns before 1900*. Stockholm: Stockholm Studies in Human Geography.

Blockmans, Wim. 1987. "Finances Publiques et Inégalité Sociale Dans Le Pays-Bas Aux XIVe-XVIe Siècles." In *Genèse de l'état Moderne: Prélèvement et Redistribution: Actes Du Colloque de Frontrevaud 1984*, ed. Jean-Philip Genet. Paris: Editions du centre national de la recherche scientifique.

Blondé, Bruno, and Jord Hanus. 2010. "Beyond Building Craftsmen. Economic Growth and Living Standards in the Sixteenth-Century Low Countries: The Case of 's-Hertogenbosch (1500-1560)." *European Review of Economic History* 14 (2): 179-207.

Bochove, Christiaan van, Heidi Deneweth and Jaco Zuijderduijn. 2013. "Real Estate and Financial Markets in England and the Low Countries, 1300-1800." No 0042, Working Papers, Utrecht University, Centre for Global Economic History.

Britnell, R. H. 1986. *Growth and Decline in Colchester 1300-1525*. Cambridge : Cambridge University Press.

Broad, John, and Anton Schuurman, eds. 2014. *Wealth and Poverty in European Rural Societies from the Sixteenth to Nineteenth Century*. Turnhout: Brepols.

Broadberry, Stephen, Bruce M. S. Campbell, Alexander Klein, Mark Overton and Bas van Leeuwen. 2015. *British Economic Growth, 1270-1870*. Cambridge: Cambridge University Press.

Cherubini, Giovanni. 1974. "La Tavola Delle Possessioni Del Comune Di Siena." In *La Proprietà Fondiaria in Alcune Zone Del Territorio Senese All'inizio Del Trecento*, 5-14. Firenze: Accademia dei Georgofili.

Clark, Gregory. 2009. "Contours of the World Economy, 1-2030 AD: Essays in Macro-Economic History. By Angus Maddison. Oxford: Oxford University Press, 2007. Pp. Xii, 418." *The Journal of Economic History* 69 (4): 1156-1161.

Crafts, Nicholas. 1997. "Some Dimensions of the 'Quality of Life' during the British Industrial Revolution." *The Economic History Review* 50 (4): 617-639.

Crafts, Nicholas. 2002. "The Human Development Index, 1870-1999: Some Revised Estimates." *European Review of Economic History* 6 (3): 395-405.

De Munck, Bert. 2007. *Technologies of Learning: Apprenticeship in Antwerp Guilds from the 15th Century to the End of the Ancient Régime*. Studies in European Urban History (1100-1800) 11. Turnhout: Brepols.

Dermineur, Elise M. 2018. "Women and Credit in Pre-Industrial Europe: An Overview." In *Women and Credit in Pre-Industrial Europe*, 12:1-18. Early European Research 12. Turnhout: Brepols Publishers.

Devos, Isabelle. 2010. "Introduction to Special Section on the Biological Standard of Living." *The History of the Family* 15 (1): 55-59.

Devos, Isabelle, Julie De Groot and Ariadne Schmidt, eds. 2015. *Single Life and the City 1200-1900*. Basingstoke: Palgrave Macmillan.

Dombrecht, Kristof, and Wouter Ryckbosch. 2017. "Wealth Inequality in a Time of Transition: Coastal Flanders in the Sixteenth Century." *TSEG* 14 (2): 63-84.

Dyer, Christopher. 1989. *Standards of Living in the Later Middle Ages. Social Change in England c. 1200-1520*. Cambridge: Cambridge University Press.

Dyer, Christopher. 2000. *Everyday Life in Medieval England*. London: Hambledonand London.

Federico, Giovanni, Alessandro Nuvolari and Michelangelo Vasta. 2019. "The Origins of the Italian Regional Divide: Evidence from Real Wages, 1861-1913." *The Journal of Economic History* 79 (1): 63-98.

Floud, Roderick. 2002. "The Dimensions of Inequality: Height and Weight Variation in Britain, 1700-2000." *Contemporary British History* 16 (3): 13-26.

Floud, Roderick, and Kenneth W. Wachter. 1982. "Poverty and Physical Stature: Evidence on the Standard of Living of London Boys 1770-1870." *Social Science History* 6 (4): 422-452.

Fynn-Paul, Jeff. 2018. *Family, Work and Household in Late Medieval Iberia: A Social History of Manresa at the Time of the Black Death*. Routledge Research in Medieval Studies 13. New York: Taylor & Francis Ltd.

Gary, Kathryn E. 2017. "Constructing Equality? Women's Wages for Physical Labor, 1550-1759." *Lund Papers in Economic History*, no. 158.

Geens, Sam, and Tim Soens. n.d. "From Lazy Peasants Tot Industrious Workers? The Evolution of the Pre-Modern Working Year in the Low Countries." [are there no further publication dtails for this?

Gurvil, Clément. 2010. *Les Paysans de Paris Du Milieu Du XVe Au Début Du XVIIe Siècle*. Paris: Honoré Champion.

Hanus, Jord. 2013. "Real Inequality in the Early Modern Low Countries: The City of 's-Hertogenbosch, 1500-1660." *The Economic History Review* 66 (3): 733-756.

Hanus, Jord. 2014. *Affluence and Inequality in the Low Countries. The City of 's-Hertogenbosch in the Long Sixteenth Century, 1500-1650*. Verhandelingen van de Koninklijke Vlaamse Academie van België Voor Wetenschappen En Kunsten. Nieuwe Reeks,. Leuven: Peeters Publishers.

Hatcher, John. 2018. "Seven Centuries of Unreal Wages." In *Seven Centuries of Unreal Wages The Unreliable Data, Sources and Methods That Have Been Used for Measuring Standards of Living in the Past*, ed. John Hatcher and Judy Z. Stephenson, 15-70. Cham: Palgrave Macmillan.

Hatcher, John, and Judy Z. Stephenson, eds. 2018. *Seven Centuries of Unreal Wages. The Unreliable Data, Sources and Methods That Have Been Used for Measuring Standards of Living in the Past*. Cambridge: Palgrave Macmillan. [why has this book got 2 different places of publication?]

Heijden, Manon van der, and Ariadne Schmidt. 2009. "Terugkeer van Het Patriarchaat? Vrije Vrouwen in de Republiek." *TSEG* 6 (3): 26-52.

Heyberger, Laurent. 2012. "New Anthropometric History: An Analysis of the Secular Trend in Height." In *Handbook of Anthropometry: Physical Measures of Human Form in Health and Disease*, ed. Victor R. Preedy, 253-270. New York: Springer New York.

Hoffman, Philip T., David S. Jacks, Patricia A. Levin and Peter H. Lindert. 2002. "Real Inequality in Europe Since 1500." *The Journal of Economic History* 62 (2): 322-355.

Hoyler, M. 1998. "Small Town Development and Urban Literacy: Comparative Evidence from Leicester Marriage Registers 1754-1890." *Historical Social Research* 23: 202-230.

Humphries, Jane, and Carmen Sarasúa. 2012. "Off the Record: Reconstructing Women's Labor Force Participation in the European Past." *Feminist Economics* 18 (4): 39-67.

Humphries, Jane, and Jacob Weisdorf. 2017. "Unreal Wages? Real Income and Economic Growth in England, 1260-1850." *IDEAS Working Paper Series from RePEc*.

Humphries, Jane. 2019. "Unreal Wages? Real Income and Economic Growth In England, 1260-1850." *The Economic Journal* 129 (10): 2867-2887.

Jäschke, Kurt-Ulrich, Kurt Andermann and Peer Friess, eds. 2003. *Ackerbürgertum Und Stadtwirtschaft : Zu Regionen Und Perioden Landwirtschaftlich Bestimmten Städtewesens Im Mittelalter*. Heilbronn: Stadtarchiv Hailbronn.

Jordan, Thomas E. 2010. "Quality of Family Life and Mortality in Seventeenth Century Dublin." *Social Indicators Research* 98 (2): 251-263.

Leguay, Jean-Pierre. 2009. *Terres Urbaines. Places, Jardins et Terres Incultes Dans La Ville Au Moyen Âge*. Rennes: Presses universitaires de Rennes.

Lindert, Peter H. 1986. "Unequal English Wealth since 1670." *Journal of Political Economy* 94 (6): 1127-1162.

Lindert, Peter H., and Jeffrey G. Williamson. 1982. "Revising England's Social Tables 1688-1812." *Explorations in Economic History* 19: 385-408.

Maddison, Angus. 2006. *The World Economy: A Millennial Perspective ; Historical Statistics*. Paris: OECD Publishing.

Malinowski, Mikołaj, and Jan Luiten van Zanden. 2017. "Income and Its Distribution in Preindustrial Poland." *Cliometrica* 11 (3): 375-404.

Milanovic, Branko. 2016. "Increasing Capital Income Share and Its Effect on Personal Income Inequality." *LIS Working Paper Series* 663.

Milanovic, Branko. 2017. "Increasing Capital Income Share and Its Effect on Personal Income Inequality." In *After Piketty. The Agenda for Economics and Inequality*, ed. Heather Boushey, Bradford J. DeLong and Marshall Steinbaum. London: Harvard University Press.

Muldrew, Craig. 2011. *Food, Energy and the Industrious Revolution: Work and Material Culture in Agrarian England, 1550-1780*. Cambridge: Cambridge University Press.

Nussbaum, Martha C. 2011. *Creating Capabilities: The Human Development Approach*. Cambridge, MA: The Belknap Press of Harvard University Press.

O'Brien, Patrick, and Kent Deng. 2015. "Can the Debate on the Great Divergence Be Located within the Kuznetsian Paradigm for an Empirical Form of Global Economic History?" *TSEG* 12 (2).

Özmucur, Süleyman, and Şevket Pamuk. 2002. "Real Wages and Standards of Living in the Ottoman Empire, 1489-1914." *The Journal of Economic History* 62 (2): 293-321.

Phelps Brown, E. H., and Sheila V. Hopkins. 1956. "Seven Centuries of the Prices of Consumables, Compared with Builders' Wage- Rates." *Economica* 23 (92): 296-314.

Piketty, Thomas. 2013. *Le Capital Au XXIe Siècle*. Paris: Seuil.

Prados de la Escosura, L. 2010. "Improving Human Development: A Long-Run View." *Journal of Economic Surveys* 24 (5): 841-894.

Ranaldi, Marco. 2018. "On the Measurement of Functional Income Distribution." *Halshs-01379229v4*.

Reis, Jaime. 2005. "Economic Growth, Human Capital Formation and Consumption in Western Europe Before 1800." In *Living Standards in the Past. New Perspectives on Well-Being in Asia and Europe.*, ed. Robert C. Allen, Tommy Bengtsson and Martin Dribe Oxford: Oxford University Press.

Robeyns, Ingrid. 2016. "The Capability Approach." In *Oxford Handbook of Distributive Justice*, ed. Serena Olsaretti. Oxford: Oxford University Press.

Rota, Mauro, and Jacob Weisdorf. 2019. "Why Was the First Industrial Revolution English? Roman Real Wages and the Little Divergence within Europe Reconsidered." Conference paper at WEHC, Boston, MA.

Ryckbosch, Wouter. 2015. "Economic Inequality and Growth before the Industrial Revolution: The Case of the Low Countries (Fourteenth to Nineteenth Centuries)." *European Review of Economic History* 20 (1): 1-22.

Scheidel, Walter. 2001. *Death on the Nile: Disease and the Demography of Roman Egypt*. Leiden: Brill.

Schmelzer, Matthias. 2016. *The Hegemony of Growth: The OECD and the Making of the Economic Growth Paradigm*. Cambridge: Cambridge University Press.

Schmidt, Ariadne, and Manon van Der Heijden. 2016. "Women Alone in Early Modern Dutch Towns: Opportunities and Strategies to Survive." *Journal of Urban History* 42 (1): 21-38.

Schofield, R. S. 1965. "The Geographical Distribution of Wealth in England, 1334-1649." *The Economic History Review* 18 (3): 483-510.

Schofield, Roger. 1973. "Dimensions of Illiteracy, 1750-1850." *Explorations in Economic History* 10: 437-454.

Sen, Amartya. 1999. *Commodities and Capabilities*. 4th impression. New Delhi: Oxford University Press.

Shaw-Taylor, Leigh. 2012. "The Rise of Agrarian Capitalism and the Decline of Family Farming in England1." *The Economic History Review* 65 (1): 26-60.

Spicksley, Judith M. 2007. "'Fly with a Duck in Thy Mouth': Single Women as Sources of Credit in Seventeenth-Century England." *Social History* 32 (2): 187-207.

Spicksley, Judith M. 2008. "Usury Legislation, Cash, and Credit: The Development of the Female Investor in the Late." *The Economic History Review* 61 (2): 277-301.

Spicksley, Judith M. 2015. "Women, 'Usury' and Credit in Early Modern England: The Case of the Maiden Investor." *Gender and History* 27 (2): 263-292.

Spicksley, Judith M. 2018. "Never-Married Women and Credit in Early Modern England." In *Women and Credit in Pre-Industrial Europe*, ed. Elise Dermineur, Turnhout: Brepols Publishers : 227-252.

Steckel, Richard H. 1995. "Stature and the Standard of Living." *Journal of Economic Literature* 33 (4): 1903-1940.

Steckel, Richard H. 2005. "Health and Nutrition in the Pre-Industrial Era: Insights from a Millennium of Average Heights in Northern Europe." In *Living Standards in the Past. New Perspectives on Well-Being in Asia and Europe*, ed. Robert C. Allen, Tommy Bengtsson and Martin Dribe. Oxford: Oxford University Press.

Steckel, Richard H., and Roderick Floud, eds. 1997. *Health and Welfare during Industrialization*. Chicago, IL: University of Chicago Press.

Steckel, Richard H., Clark Spencer Larsen, Charlotte A. Roberts and Joerg Baten. 2018. *The Backbone of Europe: Health, Diet, Work and Violence over Two Millennia*. Cambridge Studies in Biological and Evolutionary Anthropology. Cambridge: Cambridge University Press.

Stephenson, Judy Z. 2017. "'Real' Wages? Contractors, Workers, and Pay in London Building Trades, 1650-1800." *The Economic History Review* 71 (1): 106-132.

Stolz, Yvonne, Joerg Baten and Jaime Reis. 2013. "Portuguese Living Standards, 1720-1980, in European Comparison: Heights, Income, and Human Capital1." *The Economic History Review* 66 (2): 545-578.

Stouff, Louis. 1970. *Ravitaillement et Alimentation En Provence Aux 14e et 15e Siècles*. Paris: Mouton.

Thirsk, Joan. 1997. *Alternative Agriculture. A History from the Black Death to the Present Day*. Oxford: Oxford University Press.

Van Bavel, Bas, Jessica Dijkman, Erika Kuijpers and Jaco Zuijderduijn. 2012. "The Organisation of Markets as a Key Factor in the Rise of Holland from the Fourteenth to the Sixteenth Century: A Test Case for an Institutional Approach." *Continuity and Change* 27 (3): 347-378.

Van De Walle, Tineke. 2019. "Van twee wallen eten? De stadsrand als overgangszone tussen stad en platteland in de late 15de en 16de eeuw : Casus Oudenaarde." Unpublished PhD thesis, Antwerp: University of Antwerp.

Van der Woude, A. M. 1982. "Population Developments in the Northern Netherlands (1500-1800) and the Validity of the 'urban Graveyard' Effect." *Annales de Demographie Historique*, 55-75.

Van Onacker, Eline. 2018. "Proactive Peasants? The Role of Annuities in a Late Medieval Communal Society: The Campine Area, Low Countries." In *Land and Credit: Mortgages in the Medieval and Early Modern European Countryside*, ed. Chris Briggs and Jaco Zuijderduijn, 253-280. Cham: Springer International Publishing.

Van Zanden, Jan Luiten. 1995. "Tracing the Beginning of the Kuznets Curve: Western Europe during the Early Modern Period." *Economic History Review* 48: 645-647.

Van Zanden, Jan Luiten. 2005. "What Happened to the Standard of Living Before the Industrial Revolution? New Evidence from the Western Part of the Netherlands." In *Living Standards in the Past: New Perspectives on Well-Being in Asia and Europe,* ed. Robert C. Allen, Tommy Bengtsson and Martin Dribe. Oxford: Oxford University Press.

Van Zanden, Jan Luiten, Jaco Zuijderduijn and Tine De Moor. 2012. "Small Is Beautiful: The Efficiency of Credit Markets in the Late Medieval Holland." *European Review of Economic History* 16 (3): 3-22.

Vecchi, Giovanni. 2017. *Measuring Wellbeing: A History of Italian Living Standards.* Oxford: Oxford University Press.

Vries, Peer. 2013. *Escaping Poverty. The Origins of Modern Economic Growth.* Goettingen: V&R Unipress GmbH.

Whittle, Jane. 2000. *The Development of Agrarian Capitalism: Land and Labour in Norfolk 1440-1580.* Oxford: Clarendon Press.

Whittle, Jane. 2005. "Housewives and Servants in Rural England, 1440-1650: Evidence of Women's Work from Probate Documents." *Transactions of the Royal Historical Society* 15: 51-74.

Whittle, Jane. 2014. "Enterprising Widows and Active Wives: Women's Unpaid Work in the Household Economy of Early Modern England." *The History of the Family* 19 (3): 283-300.

Williamson, Jeffrey G., and Peter H. Lindert. 1980. *American Inequality. A Macroeconomic History.* New York: Academic Press.

Zanden, Jan Luiten van, Joerg Baten, Marco Mira d'Ercole, Auke Rijpma, Conal Smith and Marcel Timmer. 2014. *How Was Life? Global Well-Being since 1820.* Paris: OECD Publishing.

Zuijderduijn, Jaco. 2018. "The Ages of Women and Men: Life Cycles, Family, and Investment in the Fifteenth-Century Low Countries." In *Women and Credit in Pre-Industrial Europe,* 12: 95-120. Early European Research 12. Brepols Publishers. [why does this appear to be both a journal article and a book?]

Zuijderduijn, Jaco, and Tine De Moor. 2013. "Spending, Saving, or Investing? Risk Management in Sixteenth-century Dutch Households1." *The Economic History Review* 66 (1): 38-56.

BERT DE MUNCK

Diachrony, Synchrony and Modernity

How to Contribute to the Debate on Economic Inequality from an Historical Perspective?

Introduction

How can historians contribute to the debate on economic inequality? This question seems simple on the surface, but is more difficult to answer than might appear at first sight. In a paradoxical way, this is all the more the case as recent developments have called for a long-term view. While the usefulness thereof seems to follow naturally from the impact of Thomas Piketty's *Capital in the Twenty-First Century* (2014), a strong call for a long-term perspective was also voiced in the famous *History Manifesto* of Jo Guldi and David Armitage (2014). Both books have given new impetus and credibility to the work of historians studying economic inequality – including those who study the pre-modern period. Yet they also invite one to gloss over the epistemological issues one inevitably encounters. Most historians would probably agree that measuring inequality over the long term inevitably brings with it the risk of anachronism, as it necessitates the use of a stable analytical lens for a period of several centuries. This is defendable as long as one wants to simply *measure* long-term trends in inequality, but the issue becomes more complicated as soon as the historian in question also wants to *explain* changing levels of economic inequality – as the economist Piketty has experienced.

Piketty (Piketty 2014) sees the growth of inequality as resulting from the return on capital being higher than economic growth (and from the fact that the share of capital in national income increases). His famous notation r > g has given the impression that this evolution (at least in a market economy) follows a mathematical law and is therefore an ahistorical phenomenon, although his book has actually shown that the long-term evolutions with respect to economic inequality result more from politics than from the economy (for a discussion see Boushey, Delong & Steinbaum 2017; Piketty 2019). The subsequent debate has moreover revealed that it is extremely difficult, if not impossible, to distinguish technical issues about how to measure (the growth of) inequality from normative and epistemological positions about how to explain it. Piketty is, for instance, criticised for his very definition of capital, which he sees as the total of all assets of private individuals, corporations and governments (from cash, bonds and shares to assets such as equipment and machinery, real property and also intellectual property) the value of which is contingent on the market, where it receives a monetary value by virtue of its saleable nature. This was addressed by economist Stefan Homburg (Homburg 2015), who noted that Piketty's definition equates capital with wealth, and criticised by Joseph Stiglitz

Bert De Munck • University of Antwerp

Inequality and the City in the Low Countries (1200-2020), ed. by Bruno BLONDÉ, Sam GEENS, Hilde GREEFS, Wouter RYCKBOSCH, Tim SOENS & Peter STABEL, SEUH 50 (Turnhout, 2020), pp. 377-396.

  DOI 10.1484/M.SEUH-EB.5.120456

(Stiglitz 2014) because most of the increase in wealth would be due to the increasing value of (especially urban) land (rather than the amount of capital goods). Critical geographer David Harvey (Harvey 2014) has moreover expressed an ideological critique, arguing that Piketty's definition of capital builds on neo-classical economic thinking and fails to appreciate that, from his perspective, determining the value of capital already implies market mechanisms and the accumulation of capital the exploitation of labour.

In other words, while the discussion very much revolves around the question whether growing inequality is to be attributed to accumulation, or rather appropriation, Piketty is criticised for adopting an analytical lens borrowed from neo-classical economics, his leftist image notwithstanding. Such discussions reveal the normative and anachronistic dimension of historical research on economic inequality and they present fundamental challenges to historians who want to contribute to the debate. Should historians help to chart long-term trends in a descriptive way, thus adding to the amount of data while disregarding the increasingly anachronistic nature of their work as they move further back in time? Or should they rather focus on the changing definitions of capital, wealth and inequality itself at the expense of nicely benchmarked long-term trends in the level of economic inequality? Some of the best recent studies try to do both, as they identify changes in factor markets as causes of changing levels of economic inequality, but these studies may then run the risk of creating teleological views – as they also proceed from a present-day definition of what inequality is exactly and what the determining factors are.

My chapter will develop a critique on the present trend in historical research to see history as a laboratory which simultaneously delivers extra data to the broader social sciences and helps to identify the causal factors at play (cf. Van Bavel 2015). In the first part of this chapter, I will argue that measuring inequality over the (very) long term (i.e., including the early modern period) while at the same time explaining these trends is not self-evident. On the one hand, addressing the issue of inequality in the long run seems to necessitate addressing old debates like proletarianisation, commodification and the development of factor markets. This has already been suggested recently by historians dealing with inequality like Wouter Ryckbosch (Ryckbosch 2015) and Bas Van Bavel (Van Bavel 2016). On the other hand, however, identifying such processes as causes inevitably amounts to projecting a specific definition of inequality in the distant past with the causal factors already implied at least to a degree. While debates following Piketty's famous study have revealed a correspondence between his conception of economic equality and the causes and solutions he identifies (r > g and taxing capital), there is no reason to believe that it would be easier to prevent this with a focus on the early modern period – rather the contrary.

Among other things, the role and impact of both real property and human capital on economic inequality very much depend on how saleable they are and on the extent to which they are withdrawn from the market. This is still the case in a capitalist context, but the early modern context is very different in that regard. Not only were factor markets less well developed, the values of real property and human capital were also connected to political privileges and status. In the second part of the chapter, I will therefore turn to the attitudes to inequality of early modern middling groups – proxied by guild-based artisans – which will be presented as a challenge to the conceptual and analytical approaches currently dominating in historical research. The ideas about inequality of guild-based artisans clearly differed from those currently identified in most research, and their remedies are almost invariably seen as problematic from our present-day political and epistemological point of view. Nevertheless, they might be a necessary complement for understanding the causes of economic inequality in the early modern period. As I will argue, transformations with regard to how middling groups are connected to the local community must be taken into account.

In the third part I will then reflect about other ways of adding to the debates from a historical perspective, proceeding from the observation that the context confronted by early modern artisans resembles the context of cities today. In both cases cities are competing for capital and skills in a competitive environment, while the capacity of both cities and overarching territorial states to control the circulation of capital is limited. Nevertheless, the solutions adopted by urban actors are entirely different, due to the different cultural and political context. As I will try to show, the main difference is to be found in how the body politic and the relationship between political subjects and a political territory are imagined, and how this transformed in the long run. Although this has consequences for how to measure and address economic inequality, it should not discourage us from tackling the issue. While we can still address the history of the perception and conception of (economic) inequality, my ultimate argument will be that we should re-engage with the debate on 'modernity', not to invoke parts of it as explanatory variables, but rather to reveal our own blind spots when addressing the issue of inequality. Doing so opens the possibility of contributing to the debate in an entirely different way, including a way in which history serves as a challenge to the other disciplines in which the issue of inequality (at the urban level) is tackled.

The impossibility of measuring long-term trends of inequality?

Present-day measurements of inequality across the late medieval and early modern period are typically based on measurements of income and wealth, whether the proxies used are fiscal data or the (rental) value of houses. The problems with these sources are mostly raised by social and economic historians who try to reveal long-term trends as purely methodological. The problem with the first type of source would be that it reflects changing perceptions rather than changing levels of poverty and inequality. The problem with the latter type of source would be that it is affected by demographic transformations and related changes on the property market partly independent of changes in income and wealth distribution. These caveats are entirely justified in both cases, but they are mostly glossed over in the end. This is often the case with fiscal sources, the methodological critique of which makes it impossible, in principle, to reveal any long-term trend whatsoever. It might be less the case with data on the (rental) value of houses, as Ryckbosch (Ryckbosch 2015, 5-9) argues, but here other issues arise – issues related to the changing nature of factor markets and the way in which markets determine the value of physical assets.

Such issues have surfaced in discussions on Piketty's landmark book (Piketty 2014). One of the most interesting dimensions of it is the discussion about the definition of capital, which entailed the idea that this changes over time. Economist Geoffrey M. Hodgson (Hodgson 2014a; 2014b) was among those who argued that Piketty's definition is by and large the every-day and commonplace notion of capital of present-day business circles, but he added that this definition can be traced back to medieval and early modern notions in which the term 'capital' referred to the saleable assets of a merchant or the money invested (or investable) in a firm or a business. Hodgson's point is, however, that this definition changed during the early modern period, a fact which poses a crucial challenge to historians studying economic inequality in this period. Following Hodgson, Adam Smith would have stressed the physical assets that were used in production rather than ownership rights or the money-value of an investment. For Smith capital was fixed capital 'of which the characteristics is, that it affords a revenue or profit without circulating or changing masters' (Smith 1976, 282; quoted in Hodgson 2014, 1065). Following Smith, this included what we now call 'human capital', i.e. 'the improved dexterity of a workman [which] may be considered in the same light as a machine or instrument of trade' (Smith 1976, 281; quoted in Hodgson 2014, 1065).

The challenges which result from this for early modern historians are manifold. Hodgson argues in favour of a return to pre-Smithian notions of capital because this limits capital to assets which can be collateralised. This is needed, he argues, to exclude human capital (which can be used as collateral only if it is related to slaves) and social capital (which is relational rather than privately owned). Excluding these factors up to a point seems defendable from a methodological point of view, but it nevertheless jeopardises attempts to even describe long-term trends in economic inequality because the weight of human capital relative to other forms of wealth might change over time. One way of dealing with this would be to try to integrate the changing importance of human capital relative to physical capital in the analysis and to model the changing ratio of both in the long run (for example, Galor & Moav 2004). A more straightforward way would be to focus on outcomes in terms of income and wealth and hypothesise about the impact of social and human capital on them, which is what most social historians would be tempted to do. In either way, however, we would be forced to delve deeply into the very development of economic mechanisms and how they transformed in the long run. In short, we would have to deal with the history of capitalism.

A similar challenge results from the changed role of 'physical stuff' in the definition of capital. As Van Bavel argues in his book *The Invisible Hand* (2016, 260-265), the development of factor markets (markets for land, labour and capital) is related to the evolution of inequality. Specifically, the rise of factor markets would in the long run lead to rising levels of inequality, not because of a mathematical law such as could be derived from Piketty's r > g, but because market mechanisms are in the end distorted by an economic elite which succeeds in bending them in its favour. Such views re-connect present-day research on inequality to old debates about the rise of capitalism and the changing power relations inherent in it. This is also the case in recent research by Ryckbosch (Ryckbosch 2015, 17), who attributes rising levels of inequality in the early modern period to the 'decline of the wage rate relative to overall average incomes and the growth in the concentration of capital ownership'. Not unlike Van Bavel, Ryckbosch moreover adds an institutional dimension, referring to the guilds' measures to protect the bargaining position of hand workers after the late medieval urban revolts and the subsequent rising predominance of central state institutions protecting private property rights (references and recent views are in Blondé, Hanus & Ryckbosch 2018).

This bring us full circle to classic debates about proletarianisation, state formation and the related dismantling of communities and communal privileges, both in cities and in the countryside. Both Van Bavel and Ryckbosch invoke the development of capitalist market mechanisms as causal factors in rising levels of inequality, but they do so without reflecting on how the related changing definition of inequality would affect their measurements. I am not implying here that it would at all be possible simultaneously to present long-term trends and take into account changing definitions of economic inequality. Instead, my intention is to show that their work leads to the paradox that revealing long-term trends in the level of (economic) inequality is difficult to reconcile with revealing causal mechanisms without adopting a teleological view. This is exactly what William Sewell has argued in *Logics of History* (2005, especially ch. 3): historians are in such cases tempted, if not forced, to invoke known outcomes as explanations. In the case of explaining economic inequality in the early modern period, the causal factors invoked are typically related to capitalistic market forces as they gradually unfolded in history, the problem being that these mechanisms are also translated in the very analytical framework with which economic inequality is measured over the long term.

In concrete terms, the point is that a stable definition of capital or wealth is needed to measure long-term trends in levels of (economic) inequality, while explaining them implies long-term transformations in the saleability of physical assets and assets related to knowledge and skills such as intellectual property and human capital. But how does one distinguish cause and effect in the absence of a preconceived economic model? Recent research shows that not only the extent to which both human (and social) capital and physical assets such as houses were conceived as capital or wealth, but also the extent to which they could contribute to (inequalities in) capital and wealth, changed during the early modern period. Guido Alfani (Alfani 2010, 67-68) has for instance referred to the impact of new inheritance practices intended to secure the patrimony for the eldest son in Northern Italy, which implied that real property, which could previously be traded and divided up, became less accessible. Based on her research into the real property market in early modern Milan, Michela Barbot (Barbot 2015; 2008) has argued that the perception of the value of a house as an asset changed even beyond such measures around the dawn of the eighteenth century. While engineers of the college of Milan – which held the exclusive privilege of assessing house value – had based their assessments on certain 'objective' characteristics of the property like its function, location and architectural characteristics, this was abandoned when the college lost its privilege in the early eighteenth century (when the Austrian Habsburgs seized power over the city). Thereafter the value of a house was based rather on its ability to yield revenue, which suggests that houses had transformed into a more modern type of asset. Current research does not enable us to understand exactly how such transformations impacted upon either the measured levels of economic inequality or the causes thereof, but it is clear that taking this into account is inescapable in any explanation.

Something similar applies to the transformations related to human capital formation and the saleability of skills and knowhow. Research on apprenticeship and the relationship between master and apprentice and between master and journeyman has suggested that this, too, transformed during the early modern period. In apprenticeship contracts, apprentices or their guardians appear to have gradually made a distinction between learning and performing household chores, which suggests that learning and acquiring skills become more sharply distinguished from socialisation and education in a broader sense. This suggests, in turn, that skills actually commodified during the early modern period and, thus, that their nature as an 'asset' transformed (De Munck 2010a; De Munck & De Kerf 2018). While proletarianisation certainly had an impact on this (see, for example, Grießinger & Reith 1986; Reith 2007), there are reasons to believe that long-term transformations in this relationship cannot be reduced simply to proletarianisation and that cultural and institutional factors were involved. Recent research has for instance shown that the practices of boarding declined, including in sectors which were not subject to proletarianisation, like gold- and silversmithing. All this was moreover related to transformations in the role of the guilds, on the one hand, and private contracting, on the other. While the apprenticeship system of late medieval guilds had functioned as a mechanism for obtaining skills and access to a community simultaneously, these two functions had been separated by the eighteenth century. By then, the guilds' regulations related to apprenticeship were intended to guard access to their collective privilege, while private contracts were simply used to agree on the transfer (price, duration etc.) of a specified range of skills and technical knowledge (see, for example, Haupt 2002; De Munck 2008; De Kerf 2014b; De Munck & De Kerf 2018; a recent synthesis in Ogilvie 2019).

These transformations urge us to re-address the issue of community, including the relationship of physical assets to it. In her abovementioned research on the Milan property market, Barbot (2008, 230-240; 2015) has shown that the conventions for assessing the price of a house depended not only on its function (whether it was a residence or a workshop) and its physical location (the importance of centrality) but also on the social status of its residents. This raises questions about the relationship between owner and house, as well as about the extent to which houses were saleable at all. In the late medieval and early modern period, at least the palaces of nobles were connected to status and titles, as a result of which their saleability might have been limited. There are reasons to believe that this was also the case with the houses of middling groups, as for them owning a house was connected to their status as citizen. In late medieval Frankfurt am Main, among other cities, burghership rights were conditional upon residence and the possession of real property in the city, while citizenship rights restricted the right to move away from the city. Such mechanisms were eventually replaced with the more businesslike and monetary mechanism of paying dues, but this happened only gradually and passed through stages such as proving a certain rental income from local realty or lending a sum of money to the city in return for a rent, which suggests that the relationship between owner and house and between house and the privilege of local citizenship changed (Dilcher 1996, 139-140, 147; Isenmann 2002, 220-221; recent views on early modern urban citizenship are in Prak 2018). While attachment to real property might be even more critical in the countryside, changing sensitivities with regard to the saleability of goods and realty also surface in research done on wills (for example, Cohn, 2012).

The importance of community, and its correlate, geography, is even clearer in the case of human capital. The capital of early modern middling groups to a large extent consisted of human capital, i.e., technical knowhow and skills. As with real property, the value of this 'capital' was connected to a place and, even more so, a political community. In concrete terms, the value of one's technical knowhow and skills largely depended on the right to use them in a certain locality. In the late medieval and early modern period, this was typically regulated by guilds (see recent views in Prak et al. 2020). Exercising a trade as a master (freeman) in a certain city was conditional upon finishing an apprenticeship term and a mastership test, which gave access to the group which held the local monopoly. Journeymen could sometimes work freely for a regular master, but often could obtain a privileged position as well by finishing an apprenticeship term (and journeyman's test). Thus, the extent to which skills and knowledge could be transferred to another location was limited – or at least contingent on regulations related to obtaining access to a local community (cf. De Munck 2018; Prak 2018). In other words, the extent to which skills and knowledge can at all be seen as 'human capital' very much depends on the institutional and political context.

With an eye to revealing long term-trends in economic inequality, one might deduce from this that we need to establish the changing value of local privileges, but this would still be anachronistic in that it would imply that privileges can be treated simply as investments or assets, which just yield a return, as Maarten Prak and Jan Luiten van Zanden (Prak & van Zanden 2006) are tempted to do in a much-cited article. It would come down to reducing the commitment to a community and the importance of communal attachments to a calculation, and it would preclude addressing transformations in the nature of that commitment. What is basically at issue here, rather, is the connection of people and their assets to both a political community and a territory. These are exactly the issues which the early modern policy makers addressed, and therefore also the issue to which we turn now.

Guilds, *Nahrung* and incorporation

An important but somewhat forgotten discussion about the role and rationale of early modern guilds started with an article by Robert Duplessis and Martha Howell in 1982, in which they argued that small commodity production in the context of guilds was not necessarily at odds with a dynamic and competitive economic environment. Duplessis and Howell argued that urban policy making in Leiden and Lille succeeded in reconciling economic competitiveness with the common good of the city by favouring small commodity producers. Catharina Lis and Hugo Soly (Lis & Soly 1994, 366-367; 1997a; 1997b, 17-19; 2006a, 14-17; 2006b) considered this too optimistic a view, and responded that workshop size in early modern cities was kept small for the sake of merchants rather than the common good of the city. In their view, mercantile elites in particular had a lot to gain from regulations which limited workshop size, because they prevented manufacturing masters from becoming larger and acting as competitors to the merchants, while making sure that the masters were available to be enlisted in the merchants' productive networks. What both perspectives have in common, however, is that limiting workshop size was intricately entangled with a regional and interregional economic reality in which cities had to compete with other cities and regions for markets on the one hand, and knowhow and capital on the other.

Nor was keeping workshop size small the only measure which can be looked at from this perspective. Another, more recent debate about the guilds concentrates on their accessibility. Given that guilds had a monopoly on the production of a specific range of products within the confines of the city, they could decide who was entitled to be economically active within the city. Here as well, optimists have clashed with pessimists. While Stephan R. Epstein (Epstein 1998; 2008) argued that the guilds' barriers to entry (among which the obligatory apprenticeship term figures prominently) lowered transaction costs on the learning market and thus increased the likelihood of economic innovation, Sheilagh Ogilvie (Ogilvie 2007; 2008) responded that guilds acted as cartels and that their barriers to entry served rent-seeking purposes (see recent views in Minns et al. 2019; Prak et al. 2020). Yet here, too, the crux of the matter is that the guilds' regulations tried to reconcile economic competitiveness with a political logic. From both perspectives, the guilds were instrumental in ensuring economic persistence (for a group of economic actors) while at the same time giving shape to a political community. This is why access to the guilds often coincided with obtaining urban citizenship rights. Being granted an economic privilege implied assuming a political role and becoming a committed member of a political community (De Munck 2018, 47-50; Prak 2018, 30, 85). In concrete terms, membership of the guilds implied taking part in collective activities like masses, urban processions, funerals of co-members, meals on the occasion of the patron saint's feast day, etc. Simultaneously, urban citizenship not only granted juridical and political privileges but also entailed duties like night watch, the willingness to defend the city, and the obligation to reside and have one's economic activities in the city (De Munck 2018, 47-50; Prak 2018, 31-32).

So, early modern policy makers dealt with problems which are very similar to those faced by cities today and which revolve around the mobility of capital and skills and the capacity of local actors and governments to produce and distribute a surplus at the local level. Yet the types of regulations used to deal with them are obviously very different from those available to present-day urban policy makers. The challenge is to interpret them in a non-anachronistic way. The conceptual frames of reference used by both Epstein (efficiency) and Ogilvie (a rational actor looking for rents) are arguably at variance with both the early modern political and cultural reality. We need to try to understand the frames of references of the historical actors themselves and unpack their view on the economy and the body politic, and on such notions as equality and circulation. One concept which comes to mind in this respect is *Nahrung*, which refers to a state of mind – originating, according to Werner Sombart's classic, *Der Moderne Kapitalismus,* in the self-sufficiency of farmers – in which competition is subordinate to the ability to sustain individuals in a community (Sombart 1921, 29-39; see also Brandt & Buchner 2004). On the surface, this concept refers to a communal and protectionist tradition reminiscent of the guilds as we know them from the old literature, but in concrete terms it is very much defined in terms of what it is not. Sombart (1921, vol. 1, 36) situates it in the context of a 'pre-capitalist system' ('*vorkapitalistische Wirtschaftsgesinnung*') characterised by the absence of a calculatory sense ('*Mangel an kalkulatorischem sinn*') and by a poorly developed aptitude for dealing with precise sizes and numbers ('*Der gering entwickelte Sinn für das Rechnungsmäßige, für das exakte Abmessen von Größen, für die richtige Handhabung von Ziffern*') (also quoted in Reith 1999, 44). Is this yet another anachronistic point of view, or does it come closer to the mind-set of early modern (guild-based) actors?

What is clear is that guilds were not only preoccupied with raising barriers for newcomers. While apprenticeship terms, master pieces, entry fees and a range of ceremonial obligations were mandatory for most prospective new members, guilds often also capped workshop size and severely restricted the number of workshops one master could control. The former goal was achieved by limiting the number of journeymen (and apprentices) or workbenches a master could put to work, or by limiting output or working hours. Examples abound of regulations stipulating that a master could employ a maximum of only one or two apprentices or two, three or four journeymen (see, for example, Mackenney 1987, 16-21; Kluge 2009, 303-305; De Munck 2018: 233-238). At least in the eyes of the guild members themselves, this was done 'to maintain a certain equality among the masters', as the Antwerp shoemakers and tanners argued in the early seventeenth century (De Munck 2011, 238). Moreover, and perhaps even more importantly, a master could as a rule not run more than one workshop (see, for example, Mackenney 1987, 16-21; Kluge 2009, 303-305; De Munck 2018, 233-238). This too was enacted to prevent masters of large workshops from outcompeting those with smaller ones and, thus, to make sure that inequality among masters would not escalate. Other measures enacted to hinder inequality included ensuring equal access to raw materials, which for instance materialised in limitations on the amount of raw materials purchased, bans on having their raw materials purchased by third parties (preventing masters from sending out several people) and rules which obliged masters to share parts of what they had purchased with fellow masters at the latters' request (and at the prices at which they had purchased them themselves) (De Munck 2018, 233).

In a somewhat paradoxical way, this does not preclude the existence of a deeply hierarchical system in which guild masters were enlisted in patronage-like networks of merchants or larger masters. The former situation typically applied when merchants were in control of the guilds, as was the case in most large Italian cities and city-states from the late medieval period on (Farr 2000, ch. 4). The latter situation was typical for cities in which guilds not only were more powerful politically, but also were in the hands of manufacturing masters. Lis and Soly (1997a; 2006b; 2008) have rightly pointed out that prohibitions on subcontracting were remarkably non-existent in the guilds' regulations in the Southern Netherlands. Yet on closer scrutiny this is perhaps less remarkable than it may seem at first sight. Early modern societies, including urban societies, were far removed, mentally, from our present-day sense of equality, which is mostly measured in terms of income and wealth and based on juridically equal citizens in the possession of universal rights. This situation was largely non-existent before the late eighteenth century, which explains the difficulty in understanding both the regulatory context and the claims of early modern middling groups.

As I have argued elsewhere, early modern manufacturing masters did not protest at having to work for a merchant and the threat of becoming – in our modern definition – proletarianised. They were often willing to sell all their produce to one and the same merchant and accepted being paid by the piece after having received the raw material from the same merchant (De Munck 2007b; 2010b; 2018, 184). Simultaneously however, they strove for a certain independence and to be recognised as political subjects, i.e. as urban citizens (cf. De Munck 2018, 47-53; see also Farr 2000, 164-169). This is what was at stake in the late medieval urban revolts in which manufacturing masters fought against both their economic exploitation by powerful merchants and their political impotence (Schulz 1992; Dumolyn & Haemers 2005; Cohn 2009). The crux of the matter is that being recognised as a citizen with political and juridical rights did not entail the predominance of horizontal social relationships. The guild masters actually strove to have their corporations recognised as one member, among others, of the larger corporative political body. It was through membership of this collective that they then gained political potency, rather than as individuals. In short, the rationale behind measures relating to equality can be understood properly only when taking into account the deeply corporative and, hence, hierarchical way in which the body politic was conceived in the early modern period.

Something similar applies to the guilds' and the cities' entry barriers. It has been amply shown already that a one-dimensional distinction between insiders and outsiders does not adequately describe late medieval and early modern urban citizenship. In addition to the difference between aristocrats, clerics and others, there was the difference between citizens with full citizenship rights and residents with a more limited set of rights (examples are in De Munck & Winter 2012a). Moreover, while access to citizenship was entirely different for men and women, specific ethnic (for example, Jews) or corporative groups (like nations of foreign merchants) could enjoy specific rights, whether in their favour or not (De Munck & Winter 2012b; Prak 2018, ch. 1). This, too, is related to the underlying political imaginary in which cities were imagined as bodies with members and in which groups (members) took precedence over the abstracted individual. And there is more. Granting special rights to specific groups at the urban level is at odds with the correspondence between territory and sovereignty implied in most approaches. Closer scrutiny reveals that this is yet another modern conceptual framework projected on an early modern reality which is deeply at variance with it. A great deal of the guilds' regulations are not at all in correspondence with such a framework. The most well-known system that does not conform to it is arguably the famous wander system, in which journeymen were obligated to move from city to city for one or two years before they were entitled to master status (see Kluge 2009, 174-198). While historians have typically discussed the economic benefits of the system for either the guilds or the journeymen themselves (see, for example, Elkar 1983; Reith 2008), they have failed to appreciate the governmental implications – which is that membership of a political body was not tied to a territory and sovereignty could in a way also be linked to a network.

This can be illustrated by the existence of a system in the Southern Netherlands, in which one could become entitled to master status (on the condition of performing the master's test and paying the fees due) based on an apprenticeship served in another city. While cities were relatively autonomous in this region and had a strong tradition of defending that autonomy, the guilds in those cities concluded agreements in which they recognised each other's apprenticeship systems. This means that they accepted each other's apprentices as legitimate prospective masters – albeit only on the condition that they had served their apprenticeship with a guild-based master (De Munck 2007a, 176-177; De Kerf 2014a, 258; De Munck 2018, 153-159, 293). This condition suggests that the corporation trumped the territory as the relevant political context.

Towards a politics of place?

We seem to have drifted far away from economic inequality here, but the conditions under which craftsmen moved and could move from one city to another directly touch upon the extent to which both physical assets (houses as well as machinery) and labour (human capital) could be sold and yield a return. However, I am not presenting this as an invitation to include measurements of geographic mobility or to model exclusionary thresholds at the level of guilds or cities. My aim is rather to show that early modern middling groups proceeded from other normative and epistemological frameworks when they addressed issues of inequality. While this may sound like a truism, it entails that looking at the causal mechanisms of changing levels of inequality in these contexts may lead to explanations which are in part different from those invoked in recent research. For one thing, changing conceptions of sovereignty and territory – and the relationship between the two – may have been important.

The above-mentioned mechanisms of wandering and the reciprocal acceptance of apprentices trained in another city suggest that guilds were able to connect sovereignty to a network rather than a territory. This was of course not exceptional in pre-industrial societies, as research on Jewish networks and networks of merchant communities suggests (see, for example, Greif 2006; Trivellato 2009; Ogilvie 2011). Yet over the seventeenth to nineteenth centuries, the ability to do so seems to have declined drastically, due to the development of territorial states and bureaucracies, the declining autonomy and power of corporations and cities, and, finally, the emergence of nation states (see, for example, Farr 2000, chs 6 and 8; Kaplan 2001; Haupt 2002; for forms of continuity in the nineteenth century see, among others, Crossick & Haupt 1984; Kaplan & Minard 2004; Coppens & Debackere 2015). These transformations were related to transformations in the very concept of both a political community and a territory. On the one hand, intellectual and political historians have pointed to transformations in the relationship between state and subject, in which individuals were gradually granted natural rights while they were at the same time reduced to factors in a logic of productivity (see the classic Macpherson 1962). On the other hand, geographer Stuart Elden has argued that the notion of a territory to be governed would have emerged (in Europe) only in the early modern period, due in part to epistemological transformations in the field of geometry, with the emergence of modern notation and measurement techniques as developed by Descartes among others. According to Elden (Elden, 2005; 2009, 279-321), these concepts and techniques helped to transform land from terrain into an autonomous, abstract and metrical territory, which can be governed using quantifiable techniques. Still according to Elden, this was entangled with the emergence of a modern governmentality focused on governing a population indirectly (with the help of experts and proto-statistical data) rather than through the direct relationship between prince and subject, as Michel Foucault suggested in his famous lectures on governmentality and biopolitics (Foucault 2004a; 2004b).

In other words, the abstract individual to be governed through demographic data and data on productivity would have emerged in a context in which the notion of territory transformed, too. Moreover, while traditional scholarship has attributed the emergence of a territorial logic to state formation at the central level, this process would have originated in cities, according to Elden. While this might explain some of the guilds' exclusionary measures employed during the seventeenth and eighteenth centuries – which at least in some cases implied a territorial logic too (for example, because those who had trained locally were distinguished from others: cf. De Kerf 2014a, 100, 121, 179, 181, 195, 232-233; 2014b, 269-271; De Munck 2018, 159) – it implies also an entirely different approach to economic inequality, one based on an abstracted individual the assets of whom are detached from both his identity and his community. This is not something which can be resolved by addressing the definition of equality and deciding whether measures of it should be based on standards of living (proxied by income or wealth) or rather 'functionings' (what people consider important) and 'capabilities' (the freedom and capacity to live the life one wants) (cf. Sen 1979; 1985; 1989; Nussbaum 1988). Nor is it a question of benchmarking and deciding how inequality can be compared across regions (taking into account relative prices, values and standards of living). It actually implies that any measurement of inequality will have to take into account the changing nature of political communities and the related notion of territory involved.

Even so, rather than myself introducing a new normative and epistemological framework for explaining economic inequality, my aim is to present this as an invitation for a more thorough reflection on historical research. As I see it, the challenge posed by the experiences and attitudes of urban artisanal middling groups is to rethink the way in which history – and early modern history in particular – can contribute to the debate at all. Instead of adding more data or additional case studies, we could, for instance, try to write the history of the different conceptions of inequality, as articulated and experienced by different historical actor groups. Related to that, we could see history as a source of inspiration for present-day solutions. As my case study illustrates, this would of course immediately cause discomfort, as the solutions of early modern artisans are fundamentally at odds with present-day notions of equal opportunities and universal rights. However, such early modern (or other) views can nevertheless help to dislodge present-day frameworks, including frameworks from other disciplines. Historical research could pose a challenge to the normativity of other disciplines and kindle fruitful interdisciplinary debates.

Present-day approaches to cities and inequality provide a nice illustration of this. Cities are considered to produce growth but also to breed, or at least accommodate, inequality. Yet the way in which they are considered to do so also very much depends on the analytics lens which the scholar in question adopt. From a neo-classical analytical point of view, urban inequality reflects spatial differences in profit margins and earnings, and from a neo-Marxist approach exploitation, the spatial distribution of capital and the geographic divisions of labour (cf., for example, Glaeser 2009; Massey 1994; Harvey 1973; 1996). Given the different nature of pre-industrial forms of economic exchange and capital accumulation, both perspectives are again difficult to integrate into research concentrating on long-term trends. Like the notion of capital, the notion of geography (and its relationship with such notions as space, place and network: see, for example, Malpas 2012) is a historical construct. Historians can use such constructs in historical research, but historical research into the development of them can also challenge scholars from other disciplines by pointing to the normativity implied in them. For historians this could result in an exciting research agenda, which in a way is far more radical than the one behind most present-day research on economic inequality. Rather than limiting ourselves to the history of capitalism, we would need to address the broader history of modernity – not in order to invoke it as an explanation, but rather better to understand how the 'modern' context affects the way in which we frame and address economic inequality today. This requires a reflective approach, in which our own analytical frames are held up to the light and which opens up the possibility of a dialogue with other political imaginaries, like those of guild-based artisans.

Conclusion

The methodological and epistemological problems identified above are not new. They can rather be seen as the ever-returning stumbling blocks encountered by historians who want to integrate their work into the broader social sciences or who conceive history as a social science by looking for causal mechanisms in the past. As William Sewell has shown in his classic *Logics of history*, these ambitions bring a range of problems which are virtually unsurmountable. Identifying causal mechanisms invites one to freeze history and to treat a specific historical context as one case study among others. It necessitates a comparative approach, but the cases to be compared need to be independent and at the same time sufficiently equivalent, so that the same potential causal factors (internal to each specific case) can be tested while the cases selected do not influence each other. This is difficult enough, but the difficulty only increases if history itself is included as a factor. Referring to the work of Immanuel Wallerstein and Charles Tilly, Sewell showed that the causal factors identified are mostly found in an overarching historical system which is preconceived rather than revealed by the research – think about the world system in the case of Wallerstein or urbanisation in the case of Tilly.

In a similar way, research on the determining factors of growing (economic) inequality is bound to lapse into teleological reasoning as soon as long-term transformations are invoked as explanatory factors. The key problem is that measuring inequality requires an ex ante process of definition and coding, which inevitably proceeds from a specific normative and epistemological framework (Biernacki 2012). Adopting a specific framework enables one to benchmark and measure long-term trends, but explaining these trends is a different matter. How can one identify and distinguish causes and effects if rising levels of inequality coincide with proletarianisation and the accumulation of capital as well as with the commodification of skills, land and houses – with the latter transformations moreover being connected to changing conceptions of privilege, status and the local body politic? Did proletarianisation and the commodification of skills cause the waning of the corporative system or was it the other way around? The problem is all the more important as identifying a specific explanatory framework not only eclipses the possible explanatory power of other factors, but also has consequenses for the measurements – e.g., for the way in which skills and social and political capital (privileges) are brought in (as either causes or effects).

The dominant conceptual frameworks in current research are mostly derived from either Marxist views or neo-institutional economic approaches, or both, as a result of which cultural transformations are mostly seen as secondary – while the latter could perhaps explain the demise of communal and corporative mechanisms (and proletarianisation) in general and the commodification of skills, land and houses specifically. And this is not to mention possible espistemological transformations, which may be at the roots, in turn, of key transformations on the economic as well as the political terrain. Specifically, the changing relationship of political communities (and privileges) to changing conceptions of territory and sovereignty may have had an impact on the development of specific factor markets (like the markets for real estate and technical knowledge). But, again, this is not a plea for modelling these transformations and integrating them into the quantitative analysis. As Bruno Latour and others have tried to argue, distinguishing explananda from explanantia is in itself already adopting a 'modern' lens through which to look at the past (cf. Latour 1988; 1991; 2005, 107-108). A more productive strategy than identifying causal factors up front might therefore be to look at the historical entanglement of different factors and see which factors become dominant in exactly which historical period and why.

All this is not to invalidate recent research, but long-term diachronic perspectives should at least be complemented by synchronic in-depth studies focusing on the changing conceptions of inequality and its determining components. This implies that history can hardly serve as a laboratory for testing causal variables identified in research on present-day societies by, for instance, correlating growth and inequality – at least not with regard to long-term trends which include the pre-industrial period. The conceptions and definitions of all crucial factors involved are simply too different. What is wealth or profit in a community in which cultural or symbolic capital is perhaps more important than monetary assets? What is the value of a wage in a context in which access to work is contingent on social capital and access to privileges? As I have tried to show, measuring long-term trends of inequality would require us to understand long-term changes in the definition of capital as well as in the shifts of the relative importance of different aspects of capital – up to and including human capital and also such notions as social and cultural capital. It would require us first to examine the commodification of realty and the extent to which houses can be bought, sold and collateralised as part of an investment portfolio and detached from social, cultural and ideological values. Similarly, it would require a proper understanding of the commodification of skills, and the extent to which skills and knowhow can be detached from the cultural and political context. Hence the need to delve deeply into a certain historical period so as to understand qualitative transformations.

At the same time, we need to take into account the *outcome* of long-term transformations and the way in which they shape our research questions and methodologies. In my view, we need to address transformations in what one could call 'modernity', not in order to invoke it as a causal factor but rather in order to understand how it determines how we look at the past. Some recently developed notions in the context of Actor-Network Theory (ANT) enable us to do so in a non-normative way. The notions of framing and disentanglements as developed by Michel Callon (Callon 1998) in particular enable us to describe the commodification of physical and non-physical assets while taking into account material as well as cultural and institutional factors. ANT moreover invites us critically to integrate reflections on the normative framework of the present-day researcher and, hence, to add a meta-dimension in which the normative implications of the research are discussed (there is a synthesis in Latour 2005). In concrete terms, such an approach would help us to understand better the coming about of 'modern' forms of capital (in a descriptive way) while at the same time revealing the normativity of the present-day epistemological and methodological approaches to economic inequality. Ultimately, this would then open up the possibility of reflecting about new ideas and new potential solutions to economic inequality – like the ones adopted by early modern artisans.

I am not suggesting here, of course, that these can be simply copied and pasted to present-day cities, but looking at the early modern city through the eyes of those artisans at least points to the fact that addressing economic inequality more effectively might require new political imaginaries for which early modern artisans may provide some inspiration.

To a certain degree, the context in which urban actors and policy makers operate today resembles the late medieval and early modern context in crucial respects. As did early modern guild-based artisans and policy makers, present-day urban policy makers face the fact that cities are to be situated at the nexus of a territorial and a network logic (see the recent views in Scott & Storper 2015; Walker 2016). While cities are in the main subject to the dynamics inherent in advanced capitalism and the global economy, the dynamics of inequalities in cities as produced by flows of capital and people are beyond the reach of the political levers of municipalities. This is why cities try to regain political clout and to reclaim some of the competences now situated at the national and supranational levels (cf. Barber 2013; Oosterlynck et al. 2018). At present, however, this is not likely to provide solutions, perhaps because we fail to escape the territorial logic of present-day political thinking as well as the conception of capital (or wealth) as something entirely contingent on market mechanisms.

References

Alfani, Guido. 2010. "The Effects of Plague on the Distribution of Property: Ivrea, Northern Italy 1630." *Population Studies* 64, no. 1: 61-75.

Barber, Benjamin R. 2013. *If Mayors Ruled the World: Dysfunctional Nations, Rising Cities*. New Haven, CT: Yale University Press.

Barbot, Michela. 2008. *Le architetture della vita quotidiana. Pratiche abitative e scambi immobiliari a Milano in età moderna*. Venice: Marsilio.

Barbot, Michela. 2015. "The Justness of Aestimatio and the Justice of Transactions: Defining Real Estate Values in Early Modern Milan." In *Concepts of Value in European Material Culture, 1500-1900*, ed. Bert De Munck and Lyna Dries, 133-150. Aldershot: Ashgate.

Biernacki, Richard. 2012. *Reinventing Evidence in Social Inquiry. Decoding Facts and Variables*. New York: Palgrave Macmillan.

Blondé, Bruno, Jord Hanus and Wouter Ryckbosch. 2018. "The Predatory State: Urban Finances, Politics and Social Inequality in Sixteenth-Century 's-Hertogenbosch." In *Entrepreneurs, Institutions and Government Intervention in Europe (13th-20th centuries): Essays in Honour of Erik Aerts*, ed. Brecht Dewilde and Johan Poukens, 101-115. Brussels: Academic and Scientific Publishers.

Boushey, Heather, J. Bradford Delong and Marshall Steinbaum, eds. 2017. *After Piketty: The Agenda for Economics and Inequality*. Cambridge, MA: Harvard University Press.

Brandt, Robert, and Thomas Buchner. 2004. *Nahrung, Markt oder Gemeinnutz. Werner Sombart und das vorindustrielle Handwerk*. Bielefeld: Verlag für Regionalgeschichte.

Callon, Michel. 1998. "Introduction: The Embeddedness of Economic Markets in Economics." In *The Laws of the Market*, ed. Michel Callon, 1-57 (*The Sociological Review*, 46 (1_suppl)).

Cohn, Samuel K., Jr. 2009. *Lust for Liberty: The Politics of Social Revolt in Medieval Europe, 1200-1425*. Cambridge, MA: Harvard University Press.

Cohn, Samuel, Jr. 2012. "Renaissance Attachment to Things: Material Culture in Last Wills and Testaments." *Economic History Review* 65, no. 3: 984-1004.

Coppens, Alexander, and Ellen Debackere. 2015. "De toepassing van het Belgische immigratiebeleid in de negentiende eeuw." *Belgisch tijdschrift voor nieuwste geschiedenis* 45, no. 2-3: 12-45.

Crossick, Geoffrey, and Heinz-Gerhard Haupt, eds. 1984. *Shopkeepers and Master Artisans in Nineteenth-Century Europe*. London and New York: Methuen.

De Kerf, Raoul. 2014a. *De circulatie van technische kennis in het vroegmoderne Antwerpse ambachtswezen, 1500-1800 (casus kuipers en edelsmeden)*. Unpublished PhD thesis, Antwerp: University of Antwerp.

De Kerf, Raoul. 2014b. "The Early Modern Antwerp Coopers' Guild: From a Contract-Enforcing Organization to an Empty Box?" In *Innovation and Creativity in Late Medieval and Early Modern European Cities*, ed. Karel Davids and Bert De Munck, 245-267. Aldershot: Ashgate.

De Munck, Bert. 2007a. *Technologies of Learning. Apprenticeship in Antwerp from the 15th Century to the End of the Ancien Régime*. Turnhout: Brepols.

De Munck, Bert. 2007b. "La qualité du corporatisme. Stratégies économiques et symboliques des corporations anversoises du XVe siècle à leur abolition." *Revue d'histoire moderne et contemporaine* 54, no. 1: 116-144.

De Munck, Bert. 2008. "Skills, Trust and Changing Consumer Preferences. The Decline of Antwerp's Craft Guilds from the Perspective of the Product Market, ca. 1500 – ca. 1800." *International Review of Social History* 53, no. 2: 197-233.

De Munck, Bert. 2010a. "From Brotherhood Community to Civil Society? Apprentices Between Guild, Household and the Freedom of Contract in Early Modern Antwerp." *Social History* 35, no. 1: 1-20.

De Munck, Bert. 2010b. "One Counter and Your Own Account. Redefining Illicit Labour in Early Modern Antwerp." *Urban History* 37, no. 1: 26-44.

De Munck, Bert. 2011. "Gilding Golden Ages. Perspectives From Early Modern Antwerp on the Guild-Debate, c. 1450-c. 1650." *European Review of Economic History* 15: 221-253.

De Munck, Bert. 2018. *Guilds, Labour and the Urban Body Politic: Fabricating Community in the Southern Netherlands, 1300-1800*. London and New York: Routledge.

De Munck, Bert, and Anne Winter. 2012a. *Gated communities? Regulating Migration in Early Modern Cities*. Aldershot: Ashgate.

De Munck, Bert, and Anne Winter. 2012b. "Regulating Migration in Early Modern Cities: An Introduction." In *Gated communities? Regulating Migration in Early Modern Cities*, ed. Bert De Munck and Anne Winter, 1-24. Aldershot: Ashgate.

De Munck, Bert, and Raoul De Kerf. 2018. "Wandering About the Learning Market: Early Modern Apprenticeship in Antwerp Gold- and Silversmiths Ateliers." In *Navigating History: Economy, Society, Knowledge and Nature. Essays in Honour of Prof. Dr C. A. Davids*, ed. Pepijn Brandon, Sabine Go and Wybren Verstegen. 36-63. Leiden: Brill.

Dilcher, Gerhard. 1996. *Bürgerrecht und Stadtverfassung im europäischen Mittelalter*. Cologne: Böhlau.

Dumolyn, Jan, and Jelle Haemers. 2005. "Patterns of Urban Rebellion in Medieval Flanders." *Journal of Medieval History* 31: 369-393.

DuPlessis, Robert S., and Martha C. Howell. 1982. "Reconsidering the Early Modern Urban Economy: The Cases of Leiden and Lille." *Past and Present* 94: 49-84.

Elden, Stuart. 2005. "Missing the Point: Globalization, Deterritorialization and the Space of the World." *Transactions of the Institute of British Geographers* 30, no. 1: 8-19.

Elden, Stuart. 2009. *The Birth of Territory*. Chicago, IL, and London: University of Chicago Press.

Elkar, Rainer S. 1983. "Umrisse einer Geschichte der Gesellenwanderungen im Übergang von der Frühen Neuzeit zur Neuzeit." In *Deutsches Handwerk im Spätmittelalter und frühen Neuzeit*, ed. Rainer S. Elkar, 85-116. Göttingen: Göttinger Beiträge zur Wirtschafts- und Sozialgeschichte.

Epstein, Stephan R. 1998. "Craft Guilds, Apprenticeship, and Technological Change in Pre-Industrial Europe." *Journal of Economic History* 58, no. 3: 684-713.

Epstein, Stephan R. 2008. "Craft Guilds in the Pre-Modern Economy: A Discussion." *Economic History Review* 61, no. 1: 155-174.

Farr, James R. 2000. *Artisans in Europe, 1300-1914*. Cambridge: Cambridge University Press.

Foucault, Michel. 2004a. *Sécurité, territoire, populations. Cours au College de France (1977-1978)*, ed. M. Senellart. Paris: Seuil/Gallimard.

Foucault, Michel. 2004b. *Naissance de la biopolitque. Cours au Collége de France (1978-1979)*, ed. M. Senellart. Paris: Seuil/Gallimard.

Galor, Oded, and Omer Moav. 2004. "From Physical to Human Capital Accumulation: Inequality and the Process of Development." *Review of Economic Studies* 71: 1001-1026.

Glaeser, Edward L., Matt Resseger and Kristina Tobio. 2009. "Inequality in Cities." *Journal of Regional Science* 49, no. 4: 617-646.

Greif, Avner. 2006. *Institutions and the Path to the Modern Economy: Lessons from Medieval Trade*. Cambridge: Cambridge University Press.

Grießinger, Andreas, and Reinhold Reith. 1986. "Lehrlinge im deutschen Handwerk des ausgehenden 18. Jahrhunderts. Arbeitsorganisation, Sozialbeziehungen und alltägliche Konflikte." *Zeitschrift für Historische Forschung* 13: 149-199.

Guldi, Jo, and David Armitage, 2014. *The History Manifesto*. Cambridge: Cambridge University Press.

Harvey, David. 1973. *Social Justice and the City*. Baltimore, MD: Johns Hopkins University Press.

Harvey, David. 1996. *Justice, Nature and the Geography of Difference*. Oxford: Wiley-Blackwell.

Harvey, David. 2014. "Afterthoughts on Piketty's Capital." *Reading Marx's Capital with David Harvey* (May, 17). http://davidharvey.org/2014/05/afterthoughts-pikettys-capital/. Accessed 11 November 2019.

Haupt, Heinz-Gerhard, ed. 2002. *Das Ende der Zünfte. Ein europäischer Vergleich*. Göttingen: Vandenhoeck & Ruprecht.

Hodgson, Geoffrey M. 2014a. "What is Capital? Economists and Sociologists Have Changed its Meaning: Should it be Changed Back?" *Cambridge Journal of Economics* 38: 1063-1086.

Hodgson, Geoffrey M. 2014b. "Piketty has Redefined Capital, After 200 Years of Confusion." *The Conversation* (April, 22). https://theconversation.com/piketty-has-redefined-capital-after-200-years-of-confusion-25770. Accessed 11 November 2019.

Homburg, Stefan. 2015. "Critical Remarks on Piketty's Capital in the Twenty-First Century." *Applied Economics* 47, no. 14: 1401-1406.

Isenmann, Eberhard. 2002. "Bürgerrecht und Bürgeraufnahme in der spätmittelalterlichen und frühneuzeitlichen Stadt." In *Neubürger im späten Mittelalter: Migration und Austausch in der Städtelandschaft des alten Reiches (1250-1550)*, ed. Rainer C. Schwinges. 203-249. Berlin: Duncker and Humblot.

Kaplan, Steven L., 2001. *La fin des corporations*. Paris: Fayard.

Kaplan, Steven L., and Philippe Minard, eds. 2004. *La France, malade du corporatisme? XVIIIe-XXe siècles*. Paris: Bélin.

Kluge, Arnd. *Die Zünfte*. Stuttgart: Franz Steiner Verlag.

Latour, Bruno. 1988. "The Politics of Explanation: An Alternative." In: *Knowledge and Reflexivity. New Frontiers in the Sociology of Knowledge*, ed. Steven Woolgar. 155-176. Albany, NY: Sage.

Latour, Bruno. 2005. *Reassembling the Social. An Introduction to Actor-Network-Theory*. Oxford: Oxford University Press.

Lis, Catharina, and Hugo Soly. 1994. "Corporatisme, onderaanneming en loonarbeid. Flexibilisering en deregulering van de arbeidsmarkt in Westeuropese steden (veertiende tot achttiende eeuw)." *Tijdschrift voor sociale geschiedenis* 20: 365-390.

Lis, Catharina, and Hugo Soly. 1997a. "Different Paths of Development. Capitalism in the Northern and Southern Netherlands During the Middle Ages and the Early Modern Period." *Review*: 211-242.

Lis, Catharina, and Hugo Soly. 1997b. "Ambachtsgilden in vergelijkend perspectief: de Noordelijke en de Zuidelijke Nederlanden, 15de-18de eeuw." In *Werelden van verschil. Ambachtsgilden in de lage landen*, ed. Catharina Lis and Hugo Soly. 11-42. Brussels: VUB-Press.

Lis, Catharina, and Hugo Soly. 2006a. "Craft Guilds in Comparative Perspective: The Northern and the Southern Netherlands, a Survey." In *Craft Guilds in the Early Modern Low Countries. Work, Power and Representation*, ed. Maarten Prak, Catharina Lis, Jan Lucassen and Hugo Soly. 1-31. Aldershot: Ashgate.

Lis, Catharina, and Hugo Soly. 2006b. "Export Industries, Craft Guilds and Capitalist Trajectories.' In *Craft Guilds in the Early Modern Low Countries. Work, Power and Representation*, ed. Maarten Prak, Catharina Lis, Jan Lucassen and Hugo Soly. 107-132. Aldershot: Ashgate.

Lis, Catharina, and Hugo Soly. 2008. "Subcontracting in Guild-Based Export Trades, Thirteenth-Eighteenth Centuries." In *Guilds, Innovation, and the European Economy, 1400-1800*, ed. Stephan R. Epstein and Maarten Prak. 81-113. Cambridge: Cambridge University Press.

Mackenney, Richard. 1987. *Tradesmen and Traders: The World of the Guilds in Venice and Europe, c. 1250 – c. 1650*. London and Sydney: Croom Helm.

Macpherson, C. B. 1962. *The Political Theory of Possessive Individualism: From Hobbes to Locke*. Oxford: Oxford University Press.

Malpas, Jeff. 2012. "Putting Space in Place: Philosophical Topography and Relational Geography." *Environment and Planning D: Society and Space* 30: 226-242.

Massey, Doreen. 1994. *Spatial Divisions of Labour*. Basingstoke: Macmillan.

Minns, Chris, Clare H. Crowston, Raoul De Kerf, Bert De Munck, Marcel J. Hoogenboom, Christopher M. Kissane, Maarten Prak and Patrick Wallis. 2019. "The Extent of Citizenship in Pre-Industrial England, Germany, and the Low Countries." *European Review of Economic History*, 1-25, online first, doi:10.1093/ereh/hez005.

Nussbaum, Martha. 1988. "Nature, Function, and Capability: Aristotle on Political Distribution." In *Oxford Studies in Ancient Philosophy*, 145-184. Oxford: Oxford University Press.

Ogilvie, Sheilagh. 2007. "'Whatever is, is right?' Economic Institutions in Pre-Industrial Europe." *Economic History Review* 60, no. 4: 649-684.

Ogilvie, Sheilagh. 2008. "Rehabilitating the Guilds: A Reply." *Economic History Review* 61, no. 1: 175-182.

Ogilvie, Sheilagh. 2011. *Institutions and European Trade: Merchant Guilds, 1000-1800*. Cambridge: Cambridge University Press.

Ogilvie, Sheilagh. 2018. *The European Guilds: An Economic Analysis*. Princeton, NJ, and London: Princeton University Press.

Oosterlynck, Stijn, Luce Beeckmans, David Bassens, Ben Derudder and Barbara Segaert, eds. 2018. *The City as a Global Political Actor*. London: Routledge.

Piketty, Thomas. 2014. *Capital in the Twenty-First Century*. Cambridge, MA: Harvard University Press.

Piketty, Thomas. 2019. *Capital and Ideology*. Cambridge, MA: Harvard University Press.

Prak, Maarten. 2018. *Citizens without Nations: Urban Citizenship in Europe and the World, c. 1000-1789*. Cambridge: Cambridge University Press.

Prak, Maarten, Clare H. Crowston, Bert De Munck, Christopher Kissane, Chris Minns, Ruben Schalk and Patrick Wallis. 2020. "Access to the Trade: Monopoly and Mobility in European Craft Guilds, 17th and 18th Centuries." *Journal of Social History,* first online 2019: doi:10.1093/jsh/shz070: 1-32.

Reith, Reinhold. 1999. *Lohn und Leistung: Lohnformen im Gewerbe, 1450-1900*. Stuttgart: Franz Steiner Verlag.

Reith, Reinhold. 2007. "Apprentices in the German and Austrian Crafts in Early Modern Times – Apprentices as Wage Earners?" In: *Learning on the Shop Floor. Historical Perspectives on Apprenticeship*, ed. Bert De Munck, Steven L. Kaplan and Hugo Soly. 179-202. London and New York: Berghahn Books.

Reith, Reinhold. 2008. "Circulation of Skilled Labour in Late Medieval and Early Modern Central Europe." In *Guilds, Innovation, and the European Economy, 1400-1800*, ed. Stephan R. Epstein and Maarten Prak. 114-142. Cambridge: Cambridge University Press.

Ryckbosch, Wouter. 2015. "Economic Inequality and Growth Before the Industrial Revolution: The Case of the Low Countries (Fourteenth to Nineteenth Centuries)." *European Review of Economic History* 20: 1-22.

Schulz, Knut. 1992. *Denn sie lieben die Freiheit so Sehr… : Kommunale Aufstände und Entstehung des europäischen Bürgertums im Hochmittelalter*. Darmstadt: Wissenschaftliche Buchgesellschaft.

Scott, Allen, and Michael Storper. 2015. "The Nature of Cities: The Scope and Limits of Urban Theory." *International Journal of Urban and Regional Research*, 39, no. 1: 1-15.

Sen, Amartya. 1979. *Equality of What?* Stanford, CA: Stanford University, Tanner Lectures on Human Values.

Sen, Amartya. 1985. *Commodities and Capabilities*. Amsterdam: North-Holland.

Sen, Amartya. 1989. "Development as Capability Expansion." *Journal of Development Planning* 19: 41-58.

Sewell, William H., Jr. 2005. *Logics of History: Social Theory and Social Transformation*. Chicago, IL: University of Chicago Press.

Smith, Adam. 1776. *An Inquiry into the Nature and Causes of the Wealth of Nations*. 2 vols, ed. R. H. Campbell and A. S. Skinner. London: Methuen.

Sombart, Werner. 1921 (4th ed. [1902]). *Der Moderne Kapitalismus, Erster Band, Die Genesis Des Kapitalismus*. Munich and Leipzig: Duncker & Humblot.

Stiglitz, Joseph. 2014. "Thomas Piketty Gets Income Inequality Wrong." Interview by Lynn Stuart Parramore. Salon (3 January). https://www.salon.com/2015/01/02/joseph_stiglitz_thomas_piketty_gets_income_inequality_wrong_partner/. Accessed 11 November 2019.

Trivellato, Francesca. 2009. *The Familiarity of Strangers: The Sephardic Diaspora, Livorno, and Cross-cultural Trade in the Early Modern Period*. New Haven, CT, and London: Yale University Press.

Van Bavel, Bas. 2015. "History as a Laboratory to Better Understand the Formation of Institutions." *Journal of Institutional Economics* 11, no. 1: 69-91.

Van Bavel, Bas. 2016. *The Invisible Hand? How Market Economies Have Emerged and Declined Since AD 500*. Oxford: Oxford University Press.

Van Zanden, Jan Luiten, and Maarten Prak. 2006. "Towards an Economic Interpretation of Citizenship: The Dutch Republic between Medieval Communes and Modern Nation-States." *European Review of Economic History* 10, no. 2: 111-145.

Walker, Richard A. 2016. "Why Cities: A Reponse." *International Journal of Urban and Regional Research* 40, no. 1: 164-180.

NOEL CLYCQ, LORE VAN PRAAG AND FRANÇOIS LEVRAU

Different systems and inequalities?

Comparing education in the Low Countries

Introduction

In this chapter we discuss how educational (in)equalities in the Low Countries persist and relate to structural arrangements of education systems. We first demonstrate the existence of persistent inequalities within educational systems, especially in urban areas, and hence the difficulties in reducing them through education. By comparing these systems, we shed light on how education could function as a 'social elevator' in so-called meritocratic societies (Schneider et al. 2014). The choice of the Low Countries is especially relevant as the education systems within these countries are characterised by a more or less similar structural logic, but nonetheless distinct outcomes and inequalities can be observed (Van Praag et al. 2018).

In the first section we present a brief overview of the design of the education systems in Belgium and the Netherlands. We will focus only on primary and especially on secondary education, basing our descriptions of the structures of these education systems on official documents (Onderwijskiezer 2019; Eurodyce 2019). Then we compare and reflect upon existing studies on social and ethnic inequalities in the Low Countries and contextualise them by looking at the institutional factors that partly explain the observed inequalities. We pay attention to policies aimed to increase equal educational opportunities. These policies are especially applied or designed for urban areas, in which ethnic and social inequalities are higher. However, before we present our arguments a short reflection on the notion of 'urban education' in the Low Countries might be helpful. While much research claims to study 'urban education', a clear and widely shared definition is difficult to find and varies across regions. Nevertheless, as most of the research on education in the Low Countries is conducted in schools in the larger cities, this research often contains an 'urban' element of education. Moreover, though the Low Countries are generally argued to be highly urbanised regions, their cities remain relatively small in size, compared to some other urban areas elsewhere. Therefore, what 'urban' exactly means in this type of research is difficult to identify and is very much context-dependent. Indeed, in this context, what seems to be 'urban' about urban education is the more pronounced presence of inequalities and/or diversity due to migration. Research shows that inequalities related to socio-demographic variables – in particular migration background (ethno-cultural diversity rates) and socio-economic status (poverty rates) – are often perceived as an urban characteristic. This is nicely illustrated by an anecdote from Richard Milner, the editor of the academic journal *Urban Education*, wherein a superintendent in a rural area in the USA wanted to show Milner a struggling 'urban' school but actually showed him a

Noel Clycq, Lore Van Praag and François Levrau • University of Antwerp

Inequality and the City in the Low Countries (1200-2020), ed. by Bruno BLONDÉ, Sam GEENS, Hilde GREEFS, Wouter RYCKBOSCH, Tim SOENS & Peter STABEL, SEUH 50 (Turnhout, 2020), pp. 397-409.

     DOI 10.1484/M.SEUH-EB.5.120457

'rural' school mainly populated by black, Mexican and poor white students with so-called poor motivation, high truancy and unengaged parents (Milner 2012). While in education systems across the world socio-economic status and migration background (and gender too) are often some of the most important variables predicting educational inequalities, it is too much of a stretch to categorise schools as 'urban' based upon the presence of ethnic minority and/or 'poor' children. This nuance is important, especially considering the high rates of segregation in cities (in the Low Countries) and the presence of 'enclave schools' populated by mainly middle- and upper-class white students. Thus, we aim to go beyond the equation of 'urban education' with 'ethnic diversity and poverty', even though the majority of studies focusing on urban contexts often end up studying socio-economic and ethnic inequalities in the Low Countries. Therefore, in this chapter we focus on the broader national/regional education systems in the Low Countries and do not explicitly discuss the urban character of inequalities as these are difficult to unravel if one aims to move beyond a simple 'in an urban school all the problems are more pronounced'.

Education systems in the Low Countries

Before discussing potential explanations of inequalities we first give an overview of the three main education systems we focus on in this chapter.

Education in Belgium

In Belgium, *freedom of education* is a constitutional right. This means that the government organises non-denominational education and that every legal person is free to organise education and establish schools in accordance with his/her own (religious or pedagogical) convictions. The Constitution also stipulates that parents have the right freely to choose a school for their child. Since the state reform of 1988-89, education in Belgium has been assigned to the three communities (Flemish, French and German). However, certain competences, such as the determination of the beginning and end of *compulsory education* (i.e. from six to 18 years old for all children residing in Belgium, but from 2020-21 compulsory education will start at the age of five), remains vested at the federal level. Compulsory education does not imply that students are obliged to go to school, as home education is also an option. Students must attend full-time compulsory education until the age of 16, after which they may opt to combine part-time vocational education in an educational institution with part-time employment or continue in full-time education until the age of 18.

The relatively small German-speaking community (around 77,000 inhabitants) is not part of our analysis. Both in the Flemish and French communities, childcare and non-formal education are organised for children under formal education age. *Day care centres* look after babies and children up to the age of two and a half, after which *kindergartens* provide daycare facilities for children until they reach school age. As the kindergartens are often connected to local primary schools, the transition to formal education is quite smooth.

After pre-school education, Belgian education is organised in three educational networks. Education and training organised by the government is called *official education*. It consists of two networks and respects the philosophical and religious views of all parents. (1) *Community Education* is the official education organised by the Dutch-speaking, French-speaking and German-speaking Communities. (2) *Government-subsidized Public Education* comprises schools run by the municipal or provincial authorities. Education and training organised by a private person or organisation is known as *Free Education* and consists of one network: (3) *Government-subsidised Free Education*. This network consists primarily of Catholic schools, but also includes schools based on the teachings or methods of Freinet, Montessori and Steiner. While the latter schools follow their own curricula, their students are obliged to take exams organised by the Examination Committee of the Community.

Elementary education consists of both pre-school and primary education. *Pre-school education* is accessible to children aged from two and a half to six years. Although it is not obligatory, almost all children participate in pre-primary education which stimulates their cognitive, motor and affective development. *Primary education* thus comprises the next six school years. When children complete primary education successfully, they are granted a certificate that allows them to go on to secondary education.

Secondary education in the Flemish and French communities is organised for young-sters from the ages of 12 to 18 and consists of three stages and various tracks. Each stage consists of two grades, after which students have to refine their choices of direction. In the first stage a common curriculum is offered, divided into two tracks (i.e., academic and professional). Students choose a track only at the start of the second stage where four different tracks are provided. The four tracks are: (1) *General Secondary Education* (GSE), general education that does not prepare students for a specific profession, but rather lays a firm foundation for higher education. (2) In *Technical Secondary Education* (TSE) attention switches to general and technical-theoretical issues. After completing TSE, youngsters may practise a profession or transfer to higher education. (3) *Secondary Education in the Arts* (SEA) combines a broad general education with active practice of the arts. After completing SEA, youngsters may get a job or start higher education. (4) *Vocational Secondary Education* (VSE) is practically oriented education in which the youngsters primarily focus on learning a specific trade. While the Flemish and French education systems in Belgium have similar structures and tools to change tracks ad fields of study students during their educational career, orientation seems to occur earlier and more intensively in the Flemish system, whereas grade repetition rates are higher in the French educational system (Danhier et al. 2014).

In the Flemish community actions have been undertaken by policy makers with the intention of promoting equal opportunities and reducing educational inequalities. These include the *Equal Opportunities Parliamentary Act* of 2002, the *Parliamentary Act on the Operational Budgets of Schools* of 2008, the *Parliamentary Act on the Right to Enrolment* of 2011 and the M-decree of 2015. These policies have all been implemented with the aim (1) of providing all children with the same optimal opportunities to learn and develop, and (2) of combatting exclusion, social separation and discrimination. Concrete measures include, amongst other things, the creation of local structures to increase the fairness of school admission procedures, the safeguarding of the right to enrolment and free school choice for all children and the weighted funding in favour of schools with higher numbers of children with less educated mothers or who do not speak Dutch at home. Given the persistence of educational inequalities in recent decades, in these policies special attention is paid to children from disadvantaged backgrounds, and recently also to children with special educational needs (Ramberg, Lénárt & Watkins 2018).

Similarly, the French community in Belgium takes measures to create equal opportunities. The *DASPA decree* (Reception and Schooling of Newly Arrived Students) of 2012 (further strengthened in 2015), for example, provides a series of measures, such as special reception classes and tailored pedagogical support, to support the integration of newly arrived children and those with a linguistic background other than the language of instruction (French). A *2016 government decree* contains a number of measures strengthening pre-primary education such as closer monitoring of French language acquisition, learning outcomes and the very exceptional permission for children to repeat the third year of pre-primary education. From 2020, a uniform programme will be introduced in all Brussels and Walloon schools, starting from the third kindergarten year up to and including the third year of secondary education. This *Pact of Excellence* entails considerable reform, given that today the universal courses are provided during only the first two years of secondary education.

Education in the Netherlands

As in Belgium, in the Netherlands people have a constitutional right to set up schools and to provide teaching based on religious, ideological or educational beliefs. Consequently, there are both publicly-run and privately-run schools. The overall responsibility for the education system lies with the state, specifically the *Minister of Education, Culture and Science* and the State Secretary for Education, Culture and Science. The Ministry lays down statutory requirements for education in early childhood, primary and secondary education and secondary vocational education, and has overall control of general secondary education for adults. It sets the framework (in law and other rules) within which individual schools have to perform. There is no national curriculum, but there are attainment targets in general education. In the Netherlands the *Compulsory Education Act* applies to students age between five and 16.

The Dutch education system consists of different educational levels. *Prior to primary school*, children from six/eight weeks to four years old can go to a kindergarten. Children from two to four years old can also go to play schools. The municipalities are responsible for maintaining their quality. In addition, there is non-obligatory early childhood education for children from two and a half to five years old who are likely to be educationally disadvantaged.

Primary education lasts for eight years, has eight grades (known as Groups) and is organised for all children aged four/five to 12. While it is not compulsory to attend primary school before Group 2 (the age of five), most children begin in Group 1 and thus at the age of four. All children must take an attainment test in Group 8, on the basis of which advice is given on the level the child has reached and the appropriate secondary school level. The secondary school has to place the child at least at the level the primary school advises, but can raise the level.

Secondary education comprises schools providing education for children at the age of 12. Based on their academic level and interests, children enter one of three different tracks that represent different educational paths. (1) The *University Preparatory Education* (VWO) is a six-year education track focussing on theoretical knowledge, preparing students to study at a research university, which are universities that mainly have research as their main mission. Students study at schools known as Athenaeums and Gymnasiums and complete the track at around the age of 18. (2) *Senior General Secondary Education* (HAVO) is a five-year middle track that prepares students for higher professional education at https://www.iamexpat.nl/education/studying-netherlands/dutch-higher-education/hogescholen. Students complete the HAVO around the age of 17. (3) *Preparatory Secondary Vocational Education* (VMBO) is a four-year vocationally-orientated track that focuses on practical knowledge, which leads to vocational training. It has two qualification levels and students complete the curriculum at the age of 16.

Next to maintrack primary and secondary education, there are *schools* for students who need ortho-pedagogical and ortho-didactical support. For students who have not obtained their diplomas in VMBO there are practical training schools. These schools prepare students for more direct enrolment in the labour market after secondary education. Additionally, the national government's *Municipal educational disadvantage policy* provides care for students (aged four to 12) who have an educational disadvantage or for children who are likely to fall behind in education if they do not receive special attention (e.g., children who belong to an at-risk group). This policy aims to improve the learning performance and school careers of children in disadvantaged situations, so that they can develop their talents best. The schools in the municipality which are eligible for money or resources from this policy are determined by the municipality and the school boards. The *Development Opportunities through Quality and Education Act* has supported the municipalities' educational disadvantage policy since August 2010 and municipalities have therefore received specific payments for this since January 2011. The aim of this Act is, among other things, to create a safe, stimulating environment for young children in daycare centres and playgroups. As part of the 2013 National Reform Programme, the Dutch Government has introduced several key initiatives (e.g. *Drive to Reduce Dropout Rates & Multi-annual voluntary agreements*) to reduce the number of early school leavers.

Inequalities across education systems

Are the education systems in Belgium and the Netherlands facing the same type of inequalities or are there significant differences? Studying international comparative data is an important – albeit not the only – way to get a sense of inequalities in education. Various indicators and data can be used to compare the results of different education systems. A quick glance at the many 'international agencies' working on education and learning shows that there is increasing globalisation (e.g., via UNESCO and OECD) and Europeanisation (in particular via the European Union) of education policy. As an in-depth comparison is not possible in this chapter, we will mainly focus on the PISA (Programme for International Student Assessment) data from the OECD to present a brief comparison of the unequal results (of vulnerable groups) across educational systems in the Low Countries. These triennial PISA surveys on students' performance in science, reading and mathematics cover more than 500,000 15-year-old students across the world. However, we mainly choose the PISA data as they have become one of the most important education policy influencers in the world. Every three years an international comparative ranking shows whether an education system has changed in the ranking of schools over the past years.

General findings from international comparative research

If we look at the situation in Belgium, it becomes clear that there is a huge difference between the students' performance in the Flemish education system vs. that in the French-speaking one. Flanders is generally ranked in the top five or top ten of the participating educational systems in the PISA data, while the French-speaking system generally performs at the average OECD level. Moreover, across all three main subject areas (i.e. mathematics, sciences, reading), the former strongly outperforms the latter. For example, in the PISA 2015 data, students in the Flemish education system score on average 522 in mathematics, while students in the French-speaking system score on average 489 (Singapore is the top scoring country with 564 points in this subject area). According to the OECD, a difference of around 30 points equals a difference of around one full school year. This means that while students are supposed to be around the same stage with respect to (applied) knowledge and skills (considering that they are all around 15 years old and supposedly at the same 'point' in their education), students in the French education system in Belgium are a whole year behind their peers in the Flemish system. In comparison, students' PISA performances in the Dutch education system occupy an intermediate position between the two Belgian systems.

The PIRLS (Progress in International Reading Literacy Study) studies the literacy level of grade 4 students (around nine to ten years old). When comparing these data with the PISA data from the OECD on the literacy of 15-year-olds a longitudinal perspective on educational trajectories can be constructed. The PIRLS data show that with regard to reading comprehension, the performance gaps between the 10 per cent best-scoring and 10 per cent worst-scoring students are (relatively) the smallest in the Netherlands and the Flemish system. The French education system in Belgium is positioned in the middle. However, when comparing these findings with the literacy and reading tests in the PISA data, the performance gap has widened dramatically and both the Netherlands and Belgium end up in the group of countries with the widest performance gaps. Thus, between the ages of nine to ten and 15, equalities seem to emerge that still have not been grasped adequately.

What is the impact of socio-economic status and migration status on educational performance?

From an (in)equality perspective, it is interesting to study whether there are specific categories of students who perform differently. (Social) class has long been one of the most important socio-demographic factors influencing educational performances and outcomes. The PISA data indeed show that there is no education system in the world that does not experience some impact of 'class' – or the socio-economic status (SES) of the student's family of origin – on educational performance. However, what is clear is that 'class' has more impact on educational performance in some systems than in others. Indeed, the data on the Dutch education system reveals that 11 per cent of the variation in students' performance on the PISA assessment is explained by their SES. While this is already considerable, the data on the Flemish and French-speaking systems show an even higher impact: respectively 16 per cent and 19 per cent of students' performance is explained or predicted by SES. We discuss this further in the final section.

Another important socio-demographic variable is students' migration background. In public and political discourse educational difficulties are often framed as related to migration and the ethno-cultural diversification of Western-European societies (Van Praag et al. 2019). However, the PISA data show that the impact of SES on explaining educational performance is much greater than the impact of migration background. In the Netherlands, migration background explains only around 1 per cent and in the French system in Belgium around 0.5 per cent of the variation. In the Flemish system the effect of a migration background is greater and reaches up to 3 per cent, but it is still much lower than the impact of SES. This is important to acknowledge as an analysis of the PISA data shows that students with a migrant background perform much worse in all three systems. These differences are thus more related to their socio-economic status than to their migration background. Nevertheless, this does not devalue the finding that students with a migrant background experience highly problematic educational trajectories, in particular in the Flemish education system.

Explaining inequalities: the role of the institutional level

Explanations for this persistence of inequalities are complex, and are situated on several levels: (1) the systemic macro level (e.g., nation-based factors, institutional contexts), the meso level (e.g., schools and classrooms, family context) and (3) the micro level (e.g., interpersonal student-teacher relations, intrapersonal processes). While this chapter does not aim to make an exhaustive list of the various explanations of the differences and inequalities in the three aforementioned education systems, it does provide some insights into what mechanisms lead to the current situation. Given the scope of this chapter we will mainly focus on the impact of the institutional level. In order to understand how inequalities are shaped, transformed and reproduced through education within the Low Countries one has to understand how the education systems function, as well as which educational practices are prevalent in these institutional systems. After all, the ways in which education systems are formally presented often do not fully reflect the ways in which they are used in daily practice.

Early selection and the tracking of students in secondary education

If one wants to understand the existence of educational inequality, a reflection on how the education structures function is important. After all, the education systems have created specific educational structures which students need to navigate. The systematic literature review by Mijs and van de Werfhorst (2016) shows that the more rigid education structures are, the less room they leave for individual agency, and the more negative (or unequal) the educational trajectory of children from a lower SES background and with a migrant background becomes. Some of the most important systemic features of the education systems under discussion are the *early selection and tracking of students in secondary education*. This is the case in all three systems, which are strongly differentiated. Because the selection of a particular school type and/or specific track needs to be made at an early age (from 12 to 14 years on) and is very determinative of one's future educational and labour market opportunities, children coming from socially vulnerable families are disadvantaged. In this respect, the two Belgian education systems are quite comparable, due to their shared history, similar educational structure, and similar trends within their efforts at reform in secondary education. Both systems are very hierarchically structured in their reliance on tracks and fields of study within those tracks. Each track and field of study is accorded a particular status by parents, teachers and students. In general, the academic track is regarded as of relatively 'higher' status than the technical and vocational track (Verhoeven 2011; Van Praag et al. 2017).

Although all students are able to change tracks and fields of study, this is not commonly done and not recommended, either. Due to the differences in curricula and ways in which the tracks and fields of study within those tracks are seen as a complete fixed set of courses, it is often hard to change from more vocational or technical tracks to more academic ones (Van Praag et al. 2015). Consequently, students tend to change tracks and fields of study, not necessarily because their interest in certain subjects has changed, but mainly when they are not succeeding in their current track/field of study. This had led to the creation of a cascade-like education system, in which students change only from more highly regarded tracks to those less highly so, and not vice versa (Van Praag et al. 2015; 2019; Delvaux & Joseph 2006). These track choices are important, as they not only determine the curricula students learn and structure the ways in which society evaluates particular jobs, but also determine students' future opportunities. The track chosen determines whether students can go on to higher education, unlike in other education systems where entrance exams for higher education institutions or standardised tests at the end of secondary education are organised. While students in academic, art and technical tracks can directly enter higher education, students in vocational tracks must first undertake a specialisation year before they can o so (Van Praag et al. 2015; 2017).

It is exactly in the enrolment for and changing of tracks and fields of study in secondary education that educational inequalities occur. Furthermore, these inequalities are reproduced as a result of the different advice students receive from education professionals when making educational choices in education and the different understandings of widespread educational practices. As shown by the PISA results (Danhier et al. 2014), the distribution of students across tracks and fields of study remains unequal in terms of ethnicity and social background. A relatively higher proportion of students from lower social and immigrant backgrounds is over-represented in the technical and vocational tracks and under-represented in academic education tracks and in higher education. The unequal distribution of students across tracks and fields of study even increases over the course of secondary education (Monseur & Lafontaine 2012; Boone, Seghers & Van Houtte 2018; Fédération Wallonie-Bruxelles 2015). Given the differing societal appreciation and opportunities associated with each track, this unequal distribution seems to jeopardise the equalising potential of education. In this respect, the early choices that need to be made right at the start of secondary education are found to strengthen or reinforce existing ethnic and socio-economic inequalities (De Witte et al. 2013). Although these processes are comparable across the Flemish and French education systems in Belgium, some differences should be noted as well, such as the ways in which tracking choices are made at the beginning of secondary education (centralised/individualised) and the organisation of the curricula at the first stage of secondary education (see above). These findings suggest the importance of the institutional arrangements across systems and their differing impact on outcomes and inequalities in education.

Rigid or flexible trajectories

The age of selection is not the only feature that matters; the lower inequality rates observed in the Netherlands are assumed to be (partly) explained by a second systemic feature, namely the flexibility of the trajectories of students in secondary education. Indeed, systems can compensate for this early tracking for example by offering more flexibility for students to change direction later on in their educational careers, a practice that is applied much more often in the Netherlands than in the Flemish and French communities in Belgium. Thus, next to the differentiation that seems to increase inequality, *flexibility* is a crucial systemic feature that might compensate for the rigidity of differentiation. What all three of these education systems have in common is their relatively early divergence and the rigid organisation of students into tracks. Grouping students together in vocational tracks can support students less interested in a more 'theoretical degree' to obtain an educational qualification at the end of their educational careers (Mijs & van de Werfhorst 2016). However, offering vocational tracks alone is not sufficient. For instance, while the Flemish education system has invested in the establishment of vocational education, in recent decades this track has become the symbol of what is going wrong in education and is often seen as the track for students who are not willing and/or able to stay enrolled in the more academic tracks. This suggests that the specific institutional features matter for the ways in which students navigate through the education systems and how this impacts on the results of their education (Van Praag et al. 2015; 2017; 2018).

Standardisation

A third systemic feature that might explain the persistence of inequalities across the three systems is the level of standardisation. This feature is much more pronounced in the Netherlands, in particular in comparison to the Flemish education system, while the French-speaking system has limited standardisation. In the Netherlands a great deal of standardisation is aimed for, primarily based upon standardised testing at the end of primary education and in secondary education (Mijs & van de Werfhorst 2016). Yet, in the Flemish education system schools – and their governing bodies – have much more autonomy to set their own standards. The absence of standardisation could give more room to the impact of social bias, for instance, with respect to grading or the 'track advice' students receive at the end of the academic year (Boone, Seghers & Van Houtte 2018). The French-speaking education system in Belgium occupies an intermediate position as it organises 'standardised testing' but these results remain confidential and do not lead to a specific certificate. Moreover, when standardisation is not combined with other important features, such as flexibility, its 'bias correcting' role may diminish.

Conclusion

In this chapter on educational (in)equalities in the Low Countries we have elaborated on the structural features of the education systems and their (potential) impact on (in) equality. There are many potential reasons why inequalities might emerge, but the role of the social and institutional structures individuals have to navigate is paramount. Students, in particular those coming from socially disadvantaged families, are confronted with certain pre-defined educational routes that have a massive impact on their future educational directions and their position in the labour market. As individuals with a university or higher educational college's degree on average live longer and in better health, have a better position in the labour market and are accorded higher levels of social trust and show more social behaviour (King & Ritchie 2013), it is safe to say that creating an education system that provides the greatest opportunity for all is crucial. Yet, as we have argued in this chapter, certain socio-demographic background characteristics, such as the socio-economic status of one's family and migration background, seem to have an important impact on educational outcomes. More specifically, working class and/or migrant students have a smaller chance of performing well and are dramatically underrepresented in higher education, in particular in the two education systems in Belgium. The serious impact of class or migration status on performance can be viewed as unjust, as it implies that certain categories of individuals have a smaller chance of being 'successful' due to their 'background'. This seriously nuances the argument that education is meritocratic and solely (or mainly) based upon personal merit, intellectual capacity and effort (Schneider et al. 2014; Clycq et al. 2014).

As argued, part of the explanation seems to lie in the structural features of the education system. Research has shown that the impact of, for example, class and migration status is much less in the Dutch education system, compared to the two Belgian systems. Even though the Dutch system has students with comparable class and migration backgrounds, the performance gap between these categories of vulnerable students and middle/upper class and 'native' students is much smaller. On the structural level, the Dutch education system seems to have certain features, such as a higher level of flexibility, that could reduce the negative impact of background features (for example, to compensate for early tracking and to enable students to change direction at a later time) and a higher level of standardisation (for example, to compensate for social bias in teachers' evaluations and in advice given on tracking).

While institutional structures limit, enable and steer individuals in the choices they (can) make in everyday life, they do not fully determine what individuals can do. Thus, the full explanation of existing inequalities is not to be found just at the structural level. Education, as a social endeavour, is a relational process between humans. It is therefore important to study how individuals interact in these settings. The relationship between teachers and students in particular is crucial, as research commonly shows that supportive teacher relations have the most positive social influence on students' school belonging and even performance (Nouwen & Clycq 2019). This might imply that even in more 'restrictive' institutional structures supportive social relations can enable vulnerable students to perform better.

Thus, research also needs to go beyond the institutional focus to study also interpersonal and intrapersonal processes, such as perceptions and interpretations, as well as to steer educational practices more than it currently does. For example, studying educational inequalities has made clear that it is not necessarily the particular make-up of students in a school as such that is responsible for differences in achievement among students. Rather, the perceived impact of the make-up of particular ethnic or social school compositions by school personnel and school management practices is found to matter (Agirdag et al. 2012). These distinct perceptions concerning schools according to their school population are found to result in lower educational expectations by school personnel, less trust in their students, less input and also a greater sense of futility among the students themselves (Opdenakker & Hermans 2006; Agirdag et al. 2012; Danhier et al. 2014).

Others have argued that families' financial resources are a very important factor influencing students' performance, as this allows families to enrol their children to participate in extra-curricular activities or to seek professional support with respect to school choices (Poesen-Vandeputte & Nicaise 2015). Next to their financial resources, the cultural capital of families, including language proficiency and knowledge about the education system or social networks that can help with choices in education and schoolwork, is found to explain these achievement gaps across social and ethnic groups (Stevens & Dworkin 2019; Van Praag et al. 2019).

To conclude, while structural and institutional features provide the playing field for individuals, they offer only part of the explanation for the inequalities that persist in education systems in the Low Countries. Research into how individuals navigate these problems, what resources they can apply, and how these resources are valued in education offers crucial complementary information for developing policies to tackle the inequalities.

References

Agirdag, O., W. Nouwen, P. Mahieu, P. Van Avermaet, A. Vandenbroucke and M. Van Houtte. 2012. *Segregatie in het basisonderwijs: Geen zwart-witverhaal.* Antwerp: Garant.

Boone, S., M. Seghers and M. Van Houtte. 2018. "Transition from primary to secondary education in a rigidly tracked system – the case of Flanders." In *Educational choices, aspirations and transitions in Europe: systemic, institutional and subjective challenges,* ed. A. Tarabini and N. Ingram. [p. 53-70] London: Routledge.

Clycq, N., W. Nouwen and A. Vandenbroucke. 2014. "Meritocracy, deficit thinking and the invisibility of the system: Discourses on educational success and failure." *British Educational Research Journal,* 40(5): 796-819.

Danhier, J., D. Jacobs, P. Devleeshouwer, E. Martin and A. Alarcon. 2014. *Vers des écoles de qualité pour tous? Analyse des résultats à l'enquête PISA 2012 en Flandre et en Fédération Wallonie-Bruxelles.* Brussels: Fondation Roi Baudoin.

Delvaux, B. and M. Joseph. 2006. "Hiérarchie scolaire et compétition entre écoles: le cas d'un espace local belge." *Revue française de pédagogie,* 156 : 19-27.

De Witte, K., I. Nicaise, J. Lavrijsen, G. Van Landeghem, C. Lamote and J. Van Damme. 2013. "The impact of institutional context, education and labour market policies on early school leaving: A comparative analysis of EU countries." *European Journal of Education*, 48(3): 331-345.

Eurodyce. 2019. https://eacea.ec.europa.eu/national-policies/eurydice/national-description_en. Accessed 22 July 2019.

King, A., and C. Ritchie. 2013. *The benefits of higher education participation for individuals and society: Key findings and reports The Quadrants*. Bis Research Paper, nr. 146. London: Department for Business, Innovation and Skills.

Mijs, J. and H. Van de Werfhorst. 2016. "Het onderwijsstelsel en kansengelijkheid: op zoek naar een meritocratie." In Eidhof, Bram, Van Houtte, Mieke, and Vermeulen, Marc (eds.). *Sociologen over onderwijs. Inzichten, praktijken en kritieken*, ed. Bram Eidhof, Mieke Van Houtte and Marc Vermeulen. 199-217. Antwerp/Apeldoorn: Garant.

Monseur, C., and D. Lafontaine. 2012. "Structure des systèmes éducatifs et équité: un éclairage international." In *Pour une école juste et efficace*, ed. M. Crahay. 185-219. Brussels: De Boeck.

Milner, R. 2012. "What is urban education?" *Urban Education*, 47(3): 556-561.

Nouwen, W., and N. Clycq. 2019. "The role of social support in fostering school engagement in urban schools characterised by high risk of early leaving from education and training." *Social Psychology of Education*, DOI: 10.1007/s11218-019-09521-6.

Onderwijskiezer. 2019. https://www.onderwijskiezer.be/v2/index.php. Accessed 22 July 2019.

OECD. 2019. http://www.oecd.org/education/Education-Policy-Outlook-Country-Profile-Belgium.pdf. Accessed 22 July 2019.

Opdenakker, M.-C., and D. Hermans. 2006. "Allochtonen in en doorheen het onderwijs: cijfers, oorzaken en verklaringen." In *Onderwijs onderweg in de immigratiesamenleving*, ed. S. Sierens, M. Van Houtte, P. Loobuyck, K. Delrue and K. Pelleriaux. 33-66. Ghent: Academia Press.

Ramberg, J., A. Lénárt and A. Watkins. 2018. *European Agency Statistics on Inclusive Education: 2016: Dataset Cross-Country Report*. Odense: European Agency for Special Needs and Inclusive Education.

Schneider, J., M. Crul and L. Van Praag. 2014. "Upward Mobility and Questions of Belonging in Migrant Families." *New Diversities*, 16(1): 1-6.

Stevens, P. A. J., and G. A. Dworkin. 2019. *The Palgrave Handbook of Race and Ethnic Inequalities in Education*. London: Palgrave.

Poesen-Vandeputte, M., and I. Nicaise. 2015. "Rich schools, poor schools. Hidden resource inequalities between primary schools." *Educational Research*, 57(1): 91-109.

Van Praag, L., S. Boone, P. A. J. Stevens and M. Van Houtte. 2015. "De paradox van het watervalsysteem: wanneer het groeperen van studenten in homogene groepen tot meer heterogeniteit leidt in het beroepsonderwijs." *Sociologos. Tijdschrift voor Sociologie*, 36(2): 82-101.

Van Praag, L., J. Demanet, P. A. J. Stevens and M. Van Houtte. 2017. "'Everyone has their own qualities': Tracking and academic self-appraisal in Flemish secondary education." *Social Psychology of Education*, 20(3); 601-618.

Van Praag, L., M. Verhoeven, P. A. J. Stevens and M. Van Houtte. 2019. "Belgium. Cultural versus Class explanations for ethnic inequalities in education in the Flemish and French Communities." In *The Palgrave Handbook of Race and Ethnic Inequalities in Education* ed. P. A. J. Stevens and G. A. Dworkin. 159-214. London: Palgrave.

Van Praag, L., E. Keskiner, W. Nouwen, T. Stam, R. Van Caudenberg, N. Clycq, M. Orozco, M. Crul and C. Timmerman. 2018. "Switching practices in vocational education: A comparative case study in Flanders (Belgium) and the Netherlands." In *Comparative Perspectives on Early School Leaving in the European Union,* ed. L. Van Praag, W. Nouwen, R. Van Caudenberg, N. Clycq and C. Timmerman. 135-148. Oxford: Routledge.

Verhoeven, M. 2011. "Multiple Embedded Inequalities and Cultural Diversity in Educational Systems. A theoretical and empirical exploration." *European Educational Research Journal,* 10(2): 189-203.

Wouters, T., and S. Groenez. 2013. *De evolutie van schoolse segregatie in Vlaanderen. Een analyse voor de schooljaren 2001-2002 tot 2011-2012.* Leuven: Steunpunt Beleidsrelevant Onderzoek, Studie- en Schoolloopbanen.

Aipril

The mission of the Antwerp Interdisciplinary Platform for Research into Inequality (AIPRIL) is to advance our understanding of what drives the fortunes of the rich, the poor and those in between, especially in the long run. To that end, the Herman Deleek Centre for Social Policy, the Centre for Urban History and the Institute for Development Studies of the University of Antwerp have joined forces. Current research on inequality often focuses on a limited set of 'universal' drivers of inequality, such as globalisation and technological change. We aim to go beyond this approach by focusing instead on the diversity of trajectories and modalities of inequality. Particular attention is paid to those exceptional cases in which the seemingly universal drive towards rising inequality is, or was, successfully 'resisted'. In search of equality, we aim to develop multi-dimensional data sets and methodologies and to reflect on the relationship between institutional dynamics and (in)equality. In our work we bring to bear our complementary insights gained from case studies in pre-industrial Europe, contemporary Europe and the developing world.

AIPRIL
Antwerp Interdisciplinary Platform for Research into Inequality
University of Antwerp